The Dictionary of
STAMPS
IN COLOUR

The Dictionary of
STAMPS
IN COLOUR

James A. Mackay

Michael Joseph

First published in Great Britain by
MICHAEL JOSEPH LTD
52 Bedford Square, London, W.C.1.
1973

ISBN 0 7181 1124 9

This book was designed and produced by
Rainbird Reference Books Ltd,
Marble Arch House, 44 Edgware Road, London, W.2.

House Editor: Peter Coxhead
Designer: George Sharp
Photographer: Bill Grout

The text was photoset by
Jolly & Barber Ltd, Rugby, Warwickshire.
The colour plates were originated,
and the book was printed by
The Westerham Press Ltd, Kent
and bound by Webb, Son & Co. Ltd, London.

Printed in England

CONTENTS

ACKNOWLEDGMENTS

The author and publisher wish to thank the following for supplying material illustrated in this book: the Crown Agents for Overseas Territories and Administrations, the Philatelic Bureaus of Australia, Austria, Bhutan, Bulgaria, Burundi, the Cook Islands, China (Taiwan), Czechoslovakia, the German Democratic Republic, the German Federal Republic, Guinea, Greece, Ireland, Israel, Mexico, Mongolia, the Netherlands, New Zealand, Nicaragua, Papua, New Guinea, Rhodesia, Rwanda, Samoa, Sudan, Sweden, Switzerland, the United Nations, the United States of America, the Republic of Vietnam, the People's Republic of Vietnam. The author is also indebted to the National Postal Museum, G. Vincent Base of the Camberley Stamp Centre, A. Constantine, Dr. O. Bacher, of the Westminster Stamp Company, M. A. Bojanowicz of Arthur Boyle Ltd, Campbell Paterson Ltd, Peter Rickenback of the Waltham Stamp Company, the Harrow Coin and Stamp Company, the Lindsay Stamp Company and Stanley Gibbons Ltd who helped to supply many of the more elusive items.

To Sydney Rutter

INTRODUCTION

Postage stamps are one of the commonest and most familiar objects in everyday life all over the world. Many people take them for granted, sparing neither a glance at the design printed on them, nor wondering at the marvels of modern communications which enable us to send letters to the farthest corner of the globe in a matter of days. Some people, however, do pause to examine the stamps on their mail, or subconsciously study the postmark before opening the envelope. And then there is the minority – but a rapidly growing one – which is devoted to the study and collecting of stamps. Their ranks include schoolboys and housewives, manual labourers and clerical workers, and even millionaires and heads of state. In their eagerness to possess the rarest stamps the world's wealthiest men have competed in the auction rooms and paid such vast sums that the humble postage stamp, bearing in mind its size, now ranks as the most expensive man-made object. In 1970 $280,000 was paid for the unique One Cent Black on Magenta of British Guiana, 1856 – a square inch of paper, with dog-eared corners, a smudgy postmark and a badly rubbed surface.

Philately, the name coined by Georges Herpin in the 1860s to describe the hobby, appeals to people of every race, colour and creed and in every walk of life. It is a hobby which knows no frontiers and, in fact, is now being astutely employed as a means towards world peace and a greater understanding between peoples. Since the first adhesive stamps appeared in 1840 more than 150,000 different stamps have been issued by over 800 countries and postal administrations. At the present day there are about 240 stamp-issuing entities ranging in size and population from the Chinese People's Republic to diminutive Pitcairn Island (population 80). At one time cynics would have said, with some justification, that a country's output of stamps was in inverse proportion to its size, population and commercial importance and pocket states, such as Liechtenstein, Monaco and San Marino, were heavily criticized for deriving revenue so blatantly from sales of stamps to collectors. Ever since postal administrations woke up to the fact that postage stamps could be a source of income *per se* there have been abuses and excesses, but generally the good sense of philatelists has kept this in check and the country which tried to mulct the collector soon found to its cost that philatelic sales dwindled rapidly. Strictly, an adhesive postage stamp is merely an indication that postage on a letter, parcel or postcard has been prepaid and until recently the British Post Office, for example, regarded stamps in this light. But nowadays stamps can be used to raise money for government projects and charities, to promote the image of the country, both to its own inhabitants and the the world at large, and to publicize all manner of persons, places, events and even commercial products. The postage stamp, in the Arabian Gulf sheikdoms and certain African states at least, has become the latest weapon in the arsenal of the advertising executive.

All this is a far cry from the original purpose for which the postage stamp was devised. Adhesive postage stamps were adopted by Great Britain in May 1840 as part of the reforms introduced by Rowland Hill, who is generally accepted as the 'Father of the Stamp'. Until the adoption of Uniform Penny Postage in January of that year the use of adhesive labels to denote prepayment would have been difficult, though not impossible. Conversely the drastic revision of the complicated system of computing the postage on letters, according to their weight and distance carried, and the substitution of a flat rate of one penny per half ounce regardless of distance, made the adhesive postage stamp possible, and these handy little pieces of paper rapidly won favour with the letter-writing public.

Like all simple devices that have revolutionized the human condition, the postage stamp was not the brainchild of any one person. Neither the prepayment of postage nor the use of adhesive labels for prepayment of charges was new in 1840. Since the late seventeenth century it had been possible, in Britain, to prepay the postage on letters, though it was regarded as impolite to do so except in business correspondence, and a highly efficient penny post operated in the London area from 1680 onwards, with triangular and heart-shaped 'stamps' struck directly on to the letter to indicate prepayment. Postmarks struck in red and including the word 'Paid', or its equivalents in other languages, were used in many European countries as well as Britain on prepaid correspondence in the eighteenth and early nineteenth centuries. In every case, however, the sender had first of all to take the letter to a post office or receiving house, so that the postage could be computed and the amount paid in cash. The adhesive labels introduced by Hill in 1840 did away with this necessity and enabled the sender to drop the letter into the nearest pillar box – though posting boxes of this nature were not adopted till 1852. Even after the introduction of adhesive stamps handstruck postage stamps continued to be used for many years and the use of adhesive stamps did not become compulsory in the British Isles for more than a decade after their inception. Ironically, ever since the adhesive stamp became widespread men have been devising ways and means of dispensing with it, especially for business correspondence. Meter franking, first used in Norway and New Zealand in the early 1900s, is now universal as an aid to business efficiency. In certain countries, like Canada and the United States, slot machines known as mailomats dispense gummed slips bearing a meter frank of the desired amount. In Britain bulk posting and rebate posting schemes introduced in the 1960s have not only cut down the postal costs of large companies but have speeded up the processing of mail by doing away with adhesive stamps. Business reply envelopes and cards, permit mailing and the freepost system have further eroded the necessity for adhesive stamps. Stamps in the traditional sense are now confined to the private sector and until such times as every post office is equipped with mailomat facilities it is assumed that adhesive stamps will continue to exist. Were stamps used merely to indicate prepayment they would have a bleak future, but as their function in the strict sense has diminished the other purposes already mentioned have become increasingly important and stamps are now regarded as an art form in their own right.

Adhesive labels to indicate the payment of a charge were first used in Britain in 1802, when they were adopted by the Board of Customs and Excise to denote the payment of the taxes on patent medicines and other dutiable articles. Long before that, of course, stamps were impressed directly on to various articles on which there was a tax. Legal documents bore a large embossed stamp denoting the government tax on legal transactions. These embossed stamps were affixed to vellum or parchment documents by means of a small lead staple which pierced the document and was held securely in place at the back by means of a small rectangular adhesive label bearing the royal monogram. These small labels did not, themselves, indicate the payment of the tax, but their small upright format, slightly less than a square inch in area, dictated the shape and size of the postage stamps of 1840, and the vast majority of definitive stamps used throughout the world ever since.

Recent research has revealed that there were several forerunners of adhesive postage stamps. A Scottish shipping company used adhesive labels on packets carried by its ships in 1811, and at least one light railway, established in the late 1820s to serve a coal-mine in the north of England, was using adhesive labels on correspondence carried by its locomotives. These expedients were unofficial and purely local in their application and it is probable that Hill and his rivals thought of adhesive labels quite independently of these railway and shipping stamps. Neither Hill nor his competitors, however, knew that adhesive stamps had been used in Paris almost two centuries earlier. Some time after the adoption of stamps in Britain, while France was still toying with the idea, M. Piron, deputy director of Posts, unearthed records in the archives of the French Post Office relating to the Paris Petit Poste which functioned between 1653 and 1665 under the direction of Renouard de Velayer. This post relied for its success on a network of posting boxes at street intersections where the citizens of Paris could despatch local correspondence. The letters bore printed 'receipts' inscribed *Billet Port Payé* (post paid ticket), which were affixed to the wrapper of the letter by means of isinglass wafers.

It is now believed that the *billets* were the idea of the Duchess of Longueville, who suggested small pieces of paper bearing the royal coat of arms and priced at two sous (ten centimes). Curiously enough this system of prepayment was designed not so much to simplify accountancy but to enable Parisians to post their letters in privacy rather than declare them openly to officers of the secret police who examined all mail at the post office, as was formerly the case. This scheme had the enthusiastic support of the young King Louis XIV, who saw in it a way of defeating the intrigues of his mother Anne of Austria and her chancellor, Cardinal Mazarin. Though the Petit Poste was presumably successful it had vanished without trace by 1665 and no examples of its stamps have ever been found, though contemporary reference to it – and even popular ballads mentioning it – have come to light.

Rather plain type-set labels inscribed 'tesserakonta lepta' (40 lepta) were produced in Greece in 1831, shortly after independence had been won from the Turks. These labels were intended to raise funds for victims of the Cretan uprising which took place earlier that year. In recent years, however, a number of letters dating from the 1830s have been discovered bearing these labels in circumstances which seem to suggest that long after the original fund-raising purpose of the labels had ceased they were used to denote the payment of postage. About a dozen of these letters have now been found, with dates between 1832 and 1838 and the postmarks of Athens and Piraeus. Greek philatelists, not unnaturally, are now advancing the tesserakonta lepta label as the true ancestor of stamps,

but the concensus of world opinion still favours the British Penny Black.

As well as adhesive stamps Rowland Hill introduced letter sheets and wrappers sold for one penny (black) or twopence (blue). These sheets bore a somewhat pompous design symbolizing Britannia and her far-flung empire, devised by the Irish-born artist William Mulready. Hill placed greater reliance on the 'Mulreadies' than the adhesive stamps and was pained that the public ignored and derided the sheets though readily accepting the stamps themselves. At that time adhesive labels were such a revolutionary idea that stamped letter sheets seemed a more acceptable system, and, in fact, there were several precedents for them. From 1819 onwards the kingdom of Sardinia had stamped letter sheets, sold for 15, 25 or 50 centisimi according to the distance carried. These stamps, known as *Cavallini* (little horsemen) since they depicted a mounted postal messenger, denoted the payment of a government tax on correspondence and postage had still to be charged in the normal way. Thus the *Cavallini* cannot be regarded as postal stationery in the strict sense. James Raymond, postmaster of Sydney, New South Wales, introduced embossed letter sheets and wrappers in January 1838 – fully two years before the Mulreadies were adopted in Britain. Raymond picked up the idea in Britain, where the subject of postal reform was then topical, and anticipated the mother country with his Sydney letter sheets. They were unpopular, however, and used examples are quite scarce. Significantly New South Wales did not adopt adhesive stamps until 1850. Stamped stationery was proposed in Sweden as early as 1823 by Lieutenant Gabriel Curry Treffenberg. Though the proposal was rejected it was used as the basis of the newspaper stamps adopted the following year and, in fact, the three crowns emblem and layout of the *tidningstamplarna* closely resembled that of the *Charta Sigillata* (stamped sheets) of 1823. Taxes on newspapers were universal in the early nineteenth century, not only as a source of revenue but as a means of exercising government control over the press. Stamps were struck directly on to newspapers and though designed for fiscal purposes usually permitted the carriage of newspapers free through the post.

Though credit for the invention of adhesive postage stamps is usually given to Rowland Hill there are several other claimants to the title of Father of the Stamp. In Britain the strongest contender was James Chalmers, a Dundee publisher and bookseller, who took a close interest in postal reform from the late 1820s and in later years claimed to have thought of adhesive stamps as early as 1834. He even produced typeset essays for postage stamps, but these did not appear until 1837 at the earliest, by which time Hill's proposals were well-known, Chalmers acknowledged, during his own lifetime, that Hill had the prior claim, but after his death there was an unseemly wrangle between his son Patrick, and Hill's son Pearson, and this feud has been continued by successive generations of the Hill and Chalmers families down to the present day. Among the other British contenders for the title are Dr John Gray of the British Museum who took a close interest in postal reform and later claimed to have first thought of adhesive stamps. Even if he were not the inventor of these labels he could claim with some justification to have been the earliest philatelist since he purchased blocks of the stamps on the day of issue and retained them as mementoes of the occasion. Subsequently he attained eminence as a collector and also as the publisher of one of the earliest stamp catalogues which ran to several editions in the 1860s. Samuel Roberts of Llanbrymair claimed to have been engaged in postal problems since 1827 and to have thought of adhesive stamps, but this claim has never been substantiated. Francis Worrell Stevens, a schoolmaster employed at the same school as Rowland Hill, claims to have submitted proposals for adhesive stamps in 1833 and went so far as to allege that Hill had stolen the idea from him. Again this claim does not stand up to close investigation.

Laurenc Kosir or Koschier of Laibach (Ljubliana) suggested various postal reforms to the Austrian authorities in 1836 and these included provision for adhesive stamps. The proposals were rejected, but in hindsight Yugoslavia now claims for Kosir the title of 'ideological creator of the postage stamp' and issued a series of stamps in 1948 in his honour. Kosir claimed that he communicated his plan to an English businessman named Galloway and that Galloway subsequently passed on his ideas to Hill.

Rowland Hill had been actively involved in the campaign for postal reform since 1834, and in February 1837 published a pamphlet containing an alternative suggestion to the use of stamped stationery – 'a bit of paper just large enough to bear the stamp and covered at the back with a glutinous wash, which the bringer might, by the application of a little moisture, attach to the back of the letter, so as to avoid the necessity of re-directing it'. The following year Hill produced sketches for his proposed stamps, as did Chalmers, Sir Henry Cole and several others. The government reluctantly accepted postal reform in principle, and in 1839 the Treasury held a competition to find suitable designs for the stamps. More than 2,000 entries were received but none of them was felt to be suitable and in the end it was the simple device featuring the queen's head, which Hill himself had advocated, which was adopted.

The cumbersome system of estimating postage by distance and the number of sheets comprising the letter was swept away in December 1839 and a uniform rate of fourpence for a half-ounce letter was introduced. The rate was reduced to one penny on 10 January 1840, but a further four months elapsed before the adhesive stamps and Mulready sheets were on sale. The stamps, in denominations of 1d. black and 2d. blue, were recess-printed by Perkins Bacon and Petch in sheets of 240 and released on 1 May 1840, though they were not valid for postage until 6 May. A few examples are known on cover with postmarks from 2 May onwards, and these are very highly regarded.

The profile of Queen Victoria was taken from the Guildhall Medal of 1837 engraved by William Wyon. Henry Corbould made several sketches of this profile, from which the engravers, Charles and Frederick Heath produced the master die for the stamps. The queen's portrait was chosen not so much out of loyalty to Her Majesty but as a security precaution. The authorities were concerned lest the new stamps be forged and therefore chose a motif which was instantly recognizable and difficult to imitate accurately. For good measure Perkins Bacon applied a complicated background engraving of entwined lines to the stamps, and a sequence of letters was added to the lower corners of the design to make forgery even more difficult. This curious system, used by Britain for more than forty years, never caught on anywhere except briefly in the Australian state of Victoria (1852). For much of that period British stamps also incorporated the number of the printing plate in their design, and this encouraged later generations of collectors to reconstruct entire sheets of stamps, according to plate number and corner letters.

The earliest stamps were released imperforate and had to be cut apart with a knife or scissors. Blocks and large multiples of these early stamps are rare, since the post office clerks invariably kept them partially cut into strips from which they could quickly detach the stamps required by each customer. Experiments by Henry Archer and David Napier with perforation, rouletting and other mechanical methods of separation began in the early 1840s but were not officially adopted until 1854. The early stamps of most countries were released imperforate, but from the early 1860s onwards perforation became the general rule. No country name appeared on these early British stamps. Since the stamps were restricted to the country of issue such an inscription would have been superfluous. When stamps were first adopted by many other countries they likewise did not bear a country name, but when the network of postal treaties was developed in the 1850s it became increasingly necessary for some form of identification to appear on stamps. One of the first acts of the Universal Postal Union (UPU), founded in 1874, was to make the identification of stamps by the country of issue compulsory. In deference to Britain, as instigator of the postage stamp, the rule was relaxed in the case of that country and to this day the portrait of the reigning monarch is regarded as sufficient identification for British stamps.

During the six-month period in which they were current more than 72 million Penny Blacks were sold to the public. Thereafter the colour of the penny stamp was changed to red. Bearing in mind the low level of literacy, the development of commercial correspondence and the relatively high cost of postage, the new system of prepayment seems to have been eagerly embraced by the public, though several years passed before Hill's reforms actually made a profit for the Post Office. His reforms were so radical that other countries let several years elapse before emulating Britain. In several instances it was left to enterprising businessmen, like Henry Thomas Windsor in New York and David Bryce in Trinidad, to adopt adhesive stamps for private mail services long before their respective governments did so.

The first adhesive postage stamps to appear anywhere in the world outside the United Kingdom were released in February 1842 by a private company called the New York City Despatch Post. Windsor, an Englishman residing in New York City, founded the post and introduced the stamps which he had seen working so admirably in his home country. The 3c. stamps portrayed George Washington, thereby setting a precedent; Washington was also portrayed on the first quasi-governmental postage stamp of the United States – the New York Postmaster's issue of 1845 – the 5c. stamp of the first general issue of 1847 and on at least one stamp in every American definitive series from that date to the present time. Local posts sprang up in many of the larger cities of the United States, encouraged by the fact that, until 1863, the United States Post Office did not undertake to deliver letters from the post office to the addressee. In addition to those issued by the numerous private letter companies, stamps were issued by carriers who held government contracts, and by several postmasters, in the period from 1845 to 1847, before a general issue was made for use throughout the entire country.

While the United States government delayed the introduction of stamps till 1847 the Brazilian government was more enterprising. In August 1843 Brazil became the second country to adopt stamps and the first in the Western Hemisphere. The idea was borrowed from Britain, but the Brazilian authorities objected to placing the youthful profile of Dom Pedro on the stamps as it was felt that a postmark would constitute an insult to the Emperor. Instead the stamps took the numerals of value as their motif, in a circular frame which earned for these stamps the nickname of 'Bull's-eyes'. Numeral designs were used for subsequent Brazilian issues, known to collectors as the 'Goat's-eyes' and the Inclinados, and Dom Pedro was a relatively old man before his features graced his country's stamps for the first time (1866).

The Swiss canton of Zürich adopted postage stamps in March 1843, and again a plain numeral design was employed, though for the first time the name of the place of issue was inscribed on the stamps. Geneva introduced stamps later the same year in an unusual double format. Each part could be used as a 5c. stamp for local postage while the complete stamp (10c.) prepaid the postage to letters in other parts of Switzerland. The so-called 'Double-Geneva' was sold at a discount of 2c. for the complete unit – an incentive to the public to make use of the stamps. Basle adopted stamps in July 1845 and issued a handsome stamp, known to collectors as the 'Basle Dove', printed in three colours – the world's first multicoloured stamp. The eagle of Geneva and the dove of Basle set the precedent for heraldic symbols as a popular motif on postage stamps. These cantonal issues were superseded by a Swiss federal series in 1850.

In April 1847 David Bryce introduced a 5c. stamp for use on mail transported between San Fernando and Port of Spain, Trinidad, by his steamship, the *Lady McLeod*. The stamp bore the initials of the ship and a tiny picture of it. This was the first pictorial postage stamp and completed the four major elements in stamp design – portraiture, numerals, heraldry and pictorialism – which have dominated philately to the present day. This stamp was a private issue, so credit for the first British colony to issue stamps must be given to Mauritius, which adopted stamps in September 1847. The stamps of Mauritius were engraved and printed in the island and were crude parodies of the contemporary British 1d. red and 2d. blue stamps with the inscriptions suitably altered. They set the trend for the early stamps of several other British overseas territories, imitating the stamps of the mother country as best they could.

In 1849 Bavaria, Belgium and France adopted adhesive postage stamps, with numeral, portrait and heraldic designs respectively. France borrowed a profile of Ceres, goddess of agriculture and allegory of the republic, from the profiles found on ancient coins, but Belgium produced a refreshingly realistic full-face portrait of King Leopold for its first stamps. Bavaria was content with a numeral motif – and this was the pattern followed by most of the German states which issued their own stamps prior to the establishment of the German Empire in 1871.

Elsewhere in the 1840s there was a crude penny stamp from the postmaster of Hamilton in the island of Bermuda (1848), and stamped stationery in Finland and Russia (1846), though adhesive stamps were not adopted till 1856 and 1858 respectively. The Thurn and Taxis postal administration issued franked envelopes for use in Württemberg in 1846, though a further six years elapsed before that organization issued adhesive stamps.

By the end of the first decade, therefore, postage stamps were in use in nine countries, and stamped stationery in a few others. Wherever stamps were adopted they were regarded as a great boon, and it often seems puzzling that they were so slow to catch on universally. A century ago, however, communications were poor and the standards of literacy were low. Letter-writing was a pursuit confined to the upper classes and even the new low postal rates represented a sizeable sum of money, when related to the average earnings of the working classes in the 1840s. In an age when skilled workmen earned between 18 and 30 shillings a week a penny for a letter would be the equivalent of 10p. (23c.) in present day currency – or more than three times the current inland letter rate in Britain!

During the 1850s the postage stamp made steady, if unspectacular progress, extending its use to eighty countries in all and finding its way into every continent of the globe. The most significant development of that decade, however, was the first attempts at international postal agreements. In 1850 the German-Austrian Postal Union was established and embraced the German states, the dominions of the Habsburg Empire and several principalities and duchies in Italy which were more or less dependencies of Austria at that time. This Union not only regulated the postal rates between its member states but laid the foundations of standard designs and uniform colours according to the various postal rates, features which were subsequently expanded under the Universal Postal Union. Reciprocal postal treaties were negotiated between most of the leading European countries, between the United States and the colonies of British North America and between Britain and many countries in Latin America whose external postal traffic was largely in British hands. These international developments paved the way for the Paris Postal Conference of 1863, when representatives of fifteen countries met to discuss a world-wide postal union. The American Civil War and the three Prussian campaigns which culminated in the emergence of a united Germany intervened and it was not until 1874 that the Universal Postal Union was founded.

Postage stamps came to Australia in 1850, when both New South Wales and Victoria began issuing stamps produced in the respective colonies. The early primitives of the Australian colonies showed great ingenuity in their designs: the great seal of New South Wales and a half-length seated portrait of Queen Victoria respectively. Because of the great distance involved (ships took six months to voyage from England to Australia in the days of sail) the Australian colonies were forced to print their own stamps, but even after communications were speeded up they preferred this and seldom granted contracts to Perkins Bacon or De La Rue, the two great firms of security printers which developed in Britain in the 1850s. New Zealand, on the other hand, began in 1855 with London-printed stamps, had a period of local productions up to World War I and has since then preferred to rely on the British printers.

Among the other primitive issues of the 1850s were the aptly named 'Cottonreels' of British Guiana, produced by the postmaster striking his date-stamp on paper of various colours and inserting the value. From the remote Pacific island kingdom of Hawaii came the famous 'Missionaries' of 1851, thus named because they were often found on correspondence sent by missionaries to their friends and relations in the United States. Several of these crudely typeset stamps were inscribed in Polynesian as well as English and thus constitute the first bilingual stamps, though some philatelists might argue that this title should go to the stamps of New South Wales, 1850, which bore the Latin motto of the colony *Sic fortis Etruria crevit* (thus did Etruria grow in strength).

Asia's first stamps appeared in 1852 when the district of Scinde in the presidency of Bombay (now part of Pakistan) issued curious circular stamps embossed on red paper. The Scinde 'Dawks' are surrounded by mystery. According to the governor of the district, Sir Bartle Frere, they were printed by De La Rue in London, but they are quite unlike anything else ever printed by this company. Their circular format and method of printing seem to point to local manufacture, in which case they should be regarded as the first stamps printed in Asia, a title usually reserved for the primitives of the Philippines portraying Isabella II of Spain, released in 1854. The Philippine stamps, like the contemporary issues of Mauritius, were crude imitations of those of the mother country.

The Scinde 'Dawks' were suppressed in 1854, when stamps were lithographed at Calcutta for use throughout British India. The $\frac{1}{2}$, 1 and 2 annas denominations were monochrome, but the 4 annas was printed in indigo and red. A few examples are known with the queen's head upside down – one of the earliest examples of an error in stamp production. In 1855 De La Rue won the contract to print Indian stamps, a monopoly which they enjoyed until 1926. Elsewhere in Asia stamps were slow to catch on. Of the Indian princely states Soruth adopted stamps in 1864 and Kashmir two years later. Persia and Afghanistan adopted stamps in 1868 and 1870 respectively, Japan in 1871 and China in 1878.

The first stamps of Africa appeared in 1853, when the celebrated triangular 1*d.* and 4*d.* stamps of the Cape of Good Hope were released. The unusual format was adopted to help native sorting clerks identify correspondence emanating locally. The seated figure of Hope, exquisitely engraved by Perkins Bacon, ranks as one of the most beautiful and most popular stamp designs of the classic period. The Orange Free State did not issue stamps till 1868 and neighbouring Transvaal followed a year later. Elsewhere in the Dark Continent stamps were first issued by Liberia in 1860 and by Egypt in 1866. Gambia and Sierra Leone also adopted stamps in the 1860s but it was not until the end of the century that the postage stamp was employed generally throughout the continent.

In 1851 Perkins Bacon produced a handsome design showing a full-scale Britannia seated on sugar bags, symbolising the wealth of the British Empire. This design was used for stamps of Barbados, Mauritius and Trinidad, employing the same master die and merely adding the name of the colony concerned. Perkins Bacon also effected economies by

omitting the value from the design and relying on the colour of the stamp to determine its denomination. This expedient was subsequently adopted for the early stamps of St Lucia (1860–82) and St Helena (1856–94), often with the addition of a surcharge to indicate the value. As the second half of the nineteenth century wore on economy became the over-riding factor in awarding stamp contracts. The 1850s were the heyday of Perkins Bacon, who not only printed the stamps for most of the British colonies but also produced stamps for many foreign countries as well, and held the lucrative contracts to print the low value British stamps. Their only serious rival was the American Bank Note Co of New York, which enjoyed a virtual monopoly of stamp production in Latin America, British North America and the United States, with attractive pictorial designs (New Brunswick, Canada and Newfoundland), fine portraiture (Canada and the United States) and heraldic and allegorical subjects in great profusion.

Perkins Bacon's supremacy took a severe knock in 1854 when De La Rue were awarded a contract to print British stamps of denominations above 2*d.* Though Perkins Bacon held on to the low-value contracts till 1880 they were routed on every other front by their rival. In 1863 they were forced to surrender their colonial contracts and hand over the plates and printing equipment to De La Rue. Though they continued to print the stamps of a few independent countries, and the more independent colonies, until the 1930s, Perkins Bacon never recovered from their defeat in 1863. De La Rue's surface-printing process was less versatile, less pleasing aesthetically and much coarser than the recess-printing favoured by Perkins Bacon, but aesthetics in mid-Victorian times were everywhere sacrificed to expedience and economy. Fears of forgery, which had given Perkins Bacon a decided advantage over their competitors, receded as the century wore on, and De La Rue compensated for their utilitarian designs by using chalk-surfaced papers and fugitive inks, which foiled attempts to re-use the stamps by washing off the postmark.

De La Rue were content at first to continue using the recess plates of Perkins Bacon but gradually substituted their own cheaper process. By the early 1870s De La Rue had erected a monopoly of colonial stamp production and were able to offer further economies by standardizing stamp design and production in ways which had never been considered hitherto. In 1870 De La Rue began printing stamps for the West Indian island of St Christopher and adopted a simple design with a profile of Queen Victoria. Not only was the same design used for all stamps of the series, but the same design, with modified inscriptions, was subsequently used for the stamps of Lagos (1874) and Tobago (1879). This paved the way for the long range of interchangeable head and duty keyplates by which De La Rue were able to print colonial stamps at a fraction of the former cost. Eventually the stamps of the British colonies were standardized – a profile of the reigning sovereign, a choice of three different frames, and identical lettering, colours and inscriptions. The De La Rue keyplates of the British colonies dominated the philatelic scene in the Middle Period (1870–1920) and survived in certain areas until 1956 (Leeward Islands).

The relative monotony of stamps in the late Victorian, Edwardian and

Georgian periods, caused by the De La Rue monopoly, had its counterparts all over the world. All of the major European powers developed their colonial empires in the latter part of the nineteenth century and eventually produced sets of stamps for every territory. Keyplates were used enthusiastically by France ('Tablet', 'Peace and Commerce'), Germany ('Yacht' types), Portugal ('Carlos', 'Manoel' and 'Ceres' designs) and Spain ('Baby', 'Curly Head' and other designs portraying King Alfonso XIII). Everywhere recess-printing was abandoned in favour of the less expensive surface process and the standard of design and production dropped lamentably.

Here and there, however, there were oases of fine design and printing in the wilderness. The American Bank Note Co continued to produce excellent pictorials for certain Latin American countries. While Perkins Bacon's star was waning, other companies, notably Bradbury Wilkinson and Waterlow & Sons, were securing contracts to print attractive portrait and pictorial stamps for some colonies and the emergent nations of the late nineteenth century. Countries were beginning to appreciate the revenue which could be raised from the sale of stamps to collectors and a few of the more indigent administrations exploited the situation by issuing handsome stamps featuring animals and birds, ships and locomotives. In the closing decade of the century, Tonga, North Borneo, New Zealand and Newfoundland produced excellent series featuring scenery.

The Middle Period, as it is known, threw up several other phenomena which demonstrated the growing awareness of the philatelic market. The first stamps of Baden, Thurn and Taxis and Württemberg bore in their designs a date and a reference to the German-Austrian Postal Union, and for this reason it has sometimes been stated that these were the first commemorative stamps. But these stamps were not intended for such a narrow role and remained in use for some years as ordinary definitive issues. The earliest philatelic items of a commemorative nature were the envelopes issued by the United States in 1876 to celebrate the Philadelphia Centennial Exposition and to commemorate the hundredth anniversary of the Declaration of Independence. The earliest adhesive stamps designed to commemorate an event were produced by a German local delivery company, the *Privat Brief Verkehr* of Frankfurt-am-Main in July 1887 to mark the ninth German Federal and Jubilee Shooting Competition. The following year New South Wales issued a lengthy series of stamps inscribed ONE HUNDRED YEARS, to commemorate the centenary of the British settlement at Sydney Cove. Few of the stamps were directly relevant to the subject commemorated. The 4d. stamp portrayed Captain James Cook who first discovered and named New South Wales, while the 20s. stamp portrayed Captain Arthur Phillip and Lord Carrington, governors of the colony in 1788 and 1888 respectively, but the remaining stamps featured wildlife, scenery or portrayed Queen Victoria. This series was retained in use until 1913, when New South Wales ceased to have its own stamps, and in that period the series underwent numerous changes in perforation, shade and watermark. There was a tendency for early commemorative issues to be kept in circulation for a relatively long time, so that they fulfilled the purpose of definitive issues. Moreover they tended to be lengthy, with denominations covering the full range of values. Glaring examples of this, which upset stamp collectors enormously, included the United States Columbus series (1893), the Greek Olympic Games set (1896) and the Canadian Jubilee series (1897).

Gradually, however, commemorative stamps changed in character. Sets became shorter and less expensive for the collector and souvenir hunter, and they were valid for the comparatively short periods of a month or two. At the same time they became more frequent in appearance. When, in 1909, the United States issued three 2c stamps in eight months, collectors rose in protest at this blatant exploitation. Nowadays the United States releases about 30 commemorative stamps annually and is regarded as one of the more moderate countries in this respect.

Commemorative stamps were surprisingly slow to be adopted in many countries. Germany's first commemorative appeared in 1919 (though both Bavaria and Württemberg had issued them before World War 1). Denmark's first commemoratives appeared in 1920, France's in 1923 and Britain's in 1924. While most countries made up for lost time once they had embarked on a policy of commemorative stamps, Britain continued to be ultra-conservative in this matter. Between 1924 and 1953 there were 34 stamps altogether, marking nine events. In the early years of the present reign this policy was maintained: between 1953 and the end of 1960 only 15 stamps were issued, for six events. Moreover commemorative stamps were confined to current events of national, royal or postal significance. Thus anniversaries of historic events and personalities were completely ignored. The first sign of a break with this tradition was the appearance, in 1964, of five stamps honouring the Shakespeare Quatercentenary Festival. For the first time the portrait of a historic person was shown on British stamps, and since then the criteria for issues has been greatly relaxed. Nowadays the British Post Office plans to release an average of six new sets each year.

In 1890, in connection with the jubilee of Penny Postage, Britain issued stamped stationery priced at a shilling but doing postal service of only one penny. The remaining elevenpence was credited to a Post Office charity. Seven years later both New South Wales and Victoria released adhesive stamps on a similar basis and awarded the substantial premiums to hospital funds. In this way the charity or semi-postal stamp was born. Russia issued charity stamps during the Japanese War of 1905 and from then onwards countries all over the world have induced the stamp collector to support all manner of good causes ranging from postmen's TB sanatoria (Bulgaria) and the restoration of churches (Belgium and the Netherlands) to Hitler's Culture Fund (Germany). Though charity stamps, in general, are unpopular with collectors, certain issues, such as the Pro Juventute series of Switzerland (since 1913) and the Health stamps of New Zealand (since 1929), are perennial favourites.

Traditional printing processes continue up to the present time, but on the eve of World War I Bavaria introduced photogravure for a series portraying the Prince Regent Luitpold. Little notice was taken of this process at the time. The French firm of Vaugirard and the British company, Harrison & Sons, adopted it in the 1920s and stamps were printed for Egypt, Syria and the Gold Coast by this method. Germany began using photogravure in 1933 and Britain the following year and since that date this relatively cheap, but highly effective process, has gradually become universal. Its increasing use coincided with a movement away from the monotony of the keyplates towards greater pictorialism and it was ideally suited to this type of stamp design. Since the middle 1950s multicolour photogravure and offset-lithography have made possible the reproduction of photographic designs in full colour, and in recent years there has been a considerable vogue all over the world for stamps reproducing works of art in miniature.

Although a label purporting to prepay the postage on letters carried by the balloon *Buffalo* was produced privately in the United States as long ago as 1877 the first airmail stamps appeared forty years later, when Italy overprinted the 25c. stamp to mark an experimental air post between Rome and Turin. The period between the world wars was the heyday of the airmail stamp, with special (and usually very expensive) issues to mark the great pioneer flights of that period. Many countries issued special stamps whose use was compulsory on letters carried by air, but now that most letters are flown at some stage or other in their travels the use of special airmail stamps has gone into decline. Nevertheless airmails constitute an important and very popular facet of philately. The use of air letter sheets, or aerogrammes, over the past thirty years has, to a great extent, obviated the necessity for adhesive stamps.

World War I resulted in a vast number of provisional issues, occupation stamps, refugee charity issues and war-tax stamps. World War II, though far more extensive in its scope and effect, did not produce the same flood of philatelic material though most of the belligerents issued stamps with a propaganda theme, or celebrated victory at the end of the war. Between the wars, however, the Successor States of Europe, which emerged from the ruins of the Habsburg and Romanov empires, gave philatelists plenty of scope and the opportunity to get in on the ground floor with countries which did not have a long or costly stamp-issuing tradition behind them. Each of the ephemeral plebiscite districts had its own stamps and these are to be found in schoolboy collections to this day. The dramatic events of the inter-war years, the invasions of Manchuria, Abyssinia and Albania, and the rape of Austria, Czechoslovakia and Poland, all left their mark in the stamp album. The stamps of Nazi satellites such as Slovakia and Croatia, the occupation issues of the Ukraine and the Baltic, and the welter of local issues which appeared as the Third Reich crumbled into oblivion, are the philatelic mementoes of 1939–45.

To some extent the conflict of ideologies known as the Cold War has also been reflected in the postage stamps of the postwar era. From about 1948 to 1960 the stamps of the Communist bloc, for example, tended to be didactic and preach a political message to the world at large. Since then, however, the importance of stamps as hard currency earners has led to a diminution of the political message and emphasis is now laid on scenery, birds, animals, flowers and the thousand and one subjects which delight the heart of the collector. Stamps have become increasingly pictorial and there is scarcely a subject that has not found its way on to the postage stamp.

Fashions in philately have changed radically since the end of World War II. Formerly collectors would study their stamps according to the country of issue. Nowadays thematic or topical collecting is all the rage and collections are formed according to the subject of the designs or the purpose of the issue. For this reason religion, art, sport, folklore, zoology and space travel figure high among the subjects depicted on stamps. Countries in equatorial Africa or the South Pacific, which have never seen a snowflake, will quite blithely commemorate the Winter Olympic Games with lengthy sets of stamps. The same countries will issue stamps honouring the astronauts of both Russia and America with praiseworthy impartiality. The countries of the Communist bloc portray American astronauts on their stamps – though no country of the Western camp has returned the compliment as yet.

Philately is said to have begun on the continent of Europe in the early 1850s when a Brussels schoolmaster encouraged his pupils to adorn the pages of their atlases with such stamps as were then available. In this humble way the theory that stamp-collecting could teach history and geography was born, though bearing in mind the relative monotony of nineteenth century stamps and the restricted range of subjects featured on them, it is doubtful whether stamps could have taught much. Nowadays, however, stamps are recognized as a valuable teaching aid and they are being used increasingly in schools and colleges for this purpose. Apart from a few gimmicks, such as free-form, self-adhesive stamps from Sierra Leone (since 1963), circular, metal foil embossed stamps which simulate coins and medals, and stamps shaped like the outline of the Rock of Gibraltar, traditional shapes and processes continue and greater thought is given than ever before to the development of the stamp as a work of art in its own right. We began with a phase in which stamps were regarded as receipts for the payment of postage; we have since passed through a phase where stamps were treated as miniature posters on which as much as possible was crammed by means of photographic reduction; and now there are a few hopeful signs that stamp design should be regarded as a distinct branch of minuscule art. If this can be fostered, and good stamp design becomes the rule rather than the exception, the future of philately will be assured.

THE PLATES

The reproduction of the postage stamps on the following plates are increased by fifteen per cent, and are therefore slightly more than one seventh larger than life size. The unused stamps have been cancelled, either with an oblique line or an arc, to comply with the official regulations, which forbid the reproduction of stamps in colour unless the reproduced size is much greater or smaller than the original. The plates have been printed by four-colour offset-lithography. The reader should realize that the original stamps were printed by various processes and that some – especially the modern issues – were printed in more than four colours. It may therefore be difficult to guarantee, in all cases, that these reproductions constitute a completely accurate rendition of the colour values of the originals.

1

2

SHQIPENIA E LIRE
10 PARA
5 QINT 5

3

QEVERRIA E SHQIPNIS
MESME
ALBANIE CENTRALE
TARABOSH 1913
40 PARA

4

KORCË
REPUBLIKA SHQIPETARE
5 CTS

5

15 QIND 15
ADMINISTRAT E FINAN
FINANZVERWALTUNG
ALBANIENS
8 HELER

6

SHQIPÈNIE
25 QINTAR 25

7

Republika Shqiptare
21 Kallnduer 1925
5 QIND
POSTA SHQIPTARE

8

POSTA AERORE
5 QIND SHQIPTARE 5

9

REP. SHQIPTARE
1 QINDAR

10

REP. SHQIPTARE
2 QINDAR 2

11

POSTAT AJRORE
5 QIND MBRETNIJA SHQIPTARE 5 QIND

12

MBRETNIJA SHQIPTARE
14 Shtator 1943
POSTAT EKSPRES
QIND. 25

13

3 Fr.Sh. QEVERIA DEMOKRATIKE E SHQIPNIS

14

REPUBLIKA POPULLORE E SHQIPËRISË
0.20 QEVERIA DEMOKRATIKE E SHQIPNIS

15

R.P. E SHQIPERISE
28 NËNDOR
1912 1957

16

SHQIPERIA 1 Lek

17

SHQIPERIA 15

18

POSTE ITALIANE
ALBANIA
10 Para 10

19

POSTE ITALIANE
5 Durazzo 5
10 Para 10

20

POSTE ITALIANE
Janina
20 Para 20

21

POSTE ITALIANE
Scutari di Albania
4 Para 4

22

POSTE ITALIANE
Valona
1 Piastra 1

23

HPEIROΣ
25 ΛΕΠΤΑ 25

24

ΕΛΛΑΣ
2 ΛΕΠΤΑ 2

25

ΕΛΛΑΣ
ΕΛΛΗΝΙΚΗ ΔΙΟΙΚΗΣΙΣ
ΚΟΙΝΩΝΙΚΗ ΠΡΟΝΟΙΑ

26

1

1

2

3

4

5

6

7

8

9

10

11

12

13

14

15

16

17

18

19

20

21

22

1

2

3

4

5

6

7

8

9

10

11

12

13

14

15

16

17

18

19

20

21

22

23

24

25

1

2

3

4

5

6

7

8

9

10

11

12

13

14

15

16

17

18

19

20

21

22

23

24

25

26

27

1

2

3

4

5

7

8

9

11

12

13

14

16

17

18

19

21

22

23

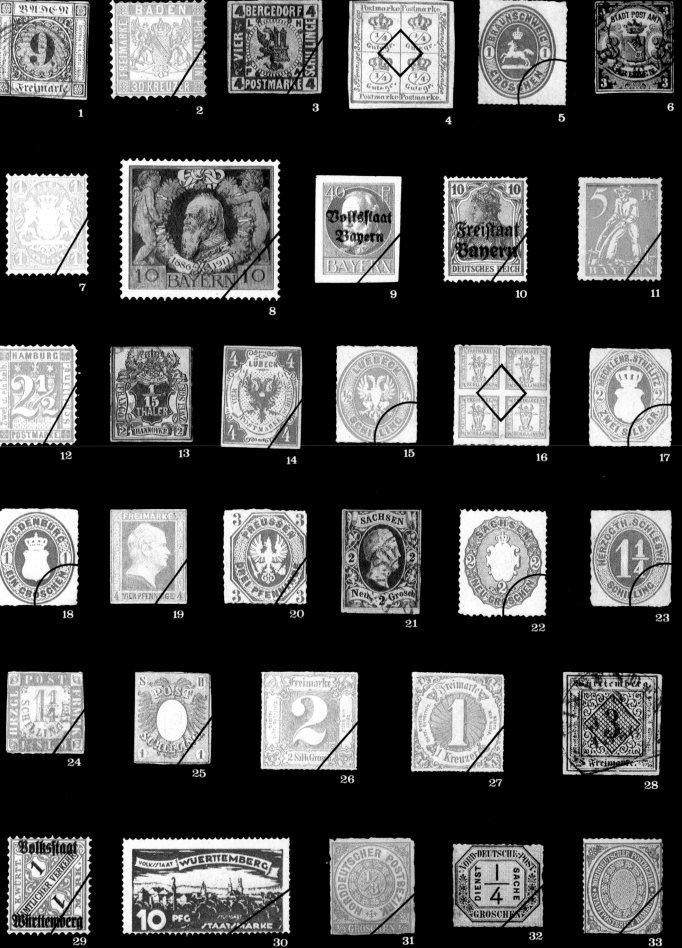

5 DEUTSCHES REICH 5

1

DEUTSCHE 3 PFENNIG POST

2

2 MARK Deutſche Poſt

3

LEIPZIGER MESSE 1948
DEUTSCHE POST
DEUTSCHE POST
1433: Errichtung von Stapellagern
84

4

DEUTSCHE 45 PFENNIG BERLIN POST

5

Gebühr bezahlt
Wiederaufbau
12 Pfg.
1 Mark
Spremberg N.L.

6

Cottbus 10 +5 Aufbau-Marke

7

60 PFENNIG DEUTSCHE POST

8

40 PFENNIG Sowjetische Besatzungs Zone DEUTSCHE POST

9

30 FRIED ENGELS DEUTSCHE POST

10

6 Pfg STADT BERLIN

11

3 Pf MECKLENBURG VORPOMMERN

12

12+8 WIEDERAUFBAU PROVINZ SACHSEN

13

DEUTSCHE POST 12 PFENNIG DEUTSCHE POST

14

POST 20

15

12 12 THÜRINGEN

16

3 AM POST 3 PFENNIG PFENNIG DEUTSCHLAND

17

2

18

Dom zu Köln 1948 1948 24 +16 Pf DEUTSCHE POST

19

NOTOPFER 2 BERLIN STEUERMARKE

20

50 DEUTSCHE POST

21

ZONE FRANCAISE 5 F BRIEFPOST 5 F

22

BADEN INGENIEUR-KONGRESS KONSTANZ 1949 30

23

RHEINLAND-PFALZ 30 +50 HILFSWERK LUDWIGSHAFEN

1749 GOETHE 1949 10 WÜRTTEMBERG

25

 1

 2

 3

 4

 5

 6

 7

 8

 9

 10

 11

 12

 13

 14

 15

 16

 17

 18

 19

 20

 21

 22

 23

1

2

3

4

5

7

8

9

10

11

12

13

14

15

16

17

18

19

20

21

22

23

24

25

1

2

3

4

5

6

7

8

9

10

11

12

13

14

15

16

17

18

19

20

21

22

23

17

1

2

3

4

5

6

7

8

10

11

12

13

14

15

16

17

18

20

21

22

19

23

24

25

1

3

4

6

7

8

10

11

12

13

14

15

16

17

18

19

20

1

2

3

4

5

6

7

8

9

10

11

12

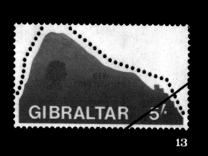
13

14

15

16

17

18

19

20

21

22

23

24

25

26

27

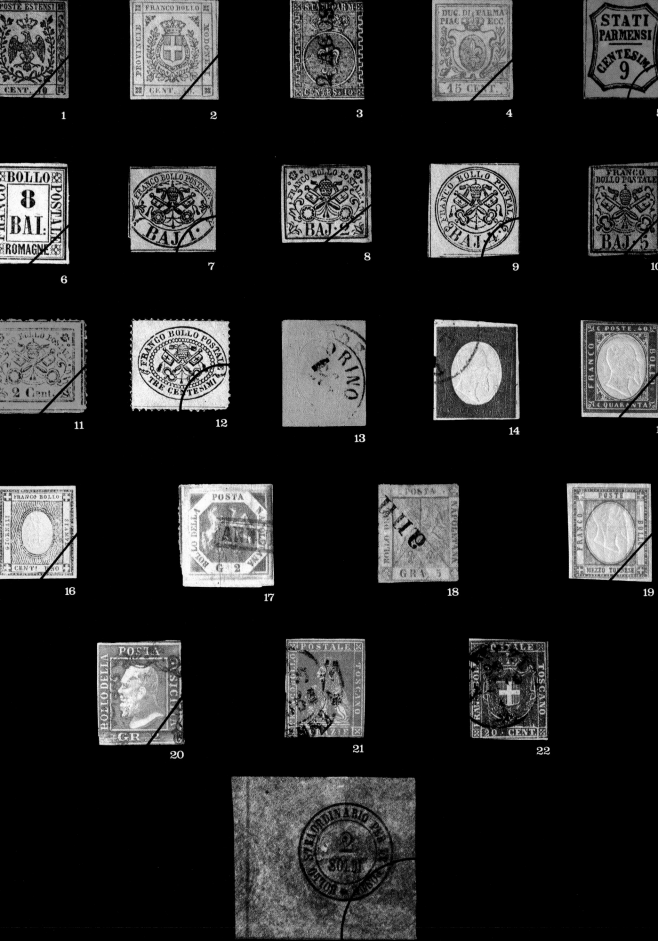

1

2

3

4

5

6

7

8

9

10

11

12

13

14

15

16

17

18

19

20

21

22

23

24

1

2

3

4

5

6

7

8

9

10

11

12

13

14

15

16

17

18

19

20

21

22

23

24

25

 1

 2

 3

 4

 5

 6

 7

 8

 9

 10

 11

 12

 13

 14

 15

 16

 17

 18

 19

 20

 21

 22

1

2

3

4

5

6

7

8

9

10

11

12

13

14

15

16

17

18

19

20

21

22

23

24

25

26

26

1

3

4

5

6

7

8

9

10

11

12

13

14

15

16

17

18

19

20

21

22

23

24

25

27

1

2

3

4

5

6

7

8

9

10

11

12

13

14

15

16

17

18

19

20

21

22

23

24

25

1

2

3

6

7

8

9

10

11

12

13

14

15

16

17

18

19

20

21

22

24

25

34

1

2

3

4

5

7

8

9

10

11

12

13

14

15

16

17

18

19

20

21

22

23

24

25

1

2

3

4

5

6

7

8

9

10

11

12

13

14

15

16

17

18

19

20

21

 1

 2

 3

 4

 5

 6

 7

 8

 9

 10

 11

 12

 13

 14

 15

 16

 17

 18

 19

 20

 21

 22

 23

 24

25

 26

 27

 28

1

2

3

4

5

6

7

8

9

10

11

12

13

14

15

16

17

18

19

20

1

2

3

4

5

6

7

8

9

10

11

12

13

14

15

16

17

18

19

1 — PAKISTAN / INDIA POSTAGE / SERVICE / 10 Rs

2 — POSTAGE / پاکستان / 1 R / PAKISTAN

3 — 12 ANNAS PAKISTAN

4 — پاکستان ڈاک / 1852-1952 / 12 As CENTENARY 1st POSTAGE STAMP

5 — پاکستان ڈاک / SERVICE / PAKISTAN POSTAGE

6 — پاکستان ڈاک / ANNAS 12 / TENTH ANNIVERSARY UNITED NATIONS / 24.10.55. / SUI GAS / PAKISTAN POSTAGE

7 — ISLAMIC REPUBLIC OF PAKISTAN / 23RD MARCH 1956 / REPUBLIC DAY / 2 As.

8 — পাকিস্তান / POSTAGE / 10 RUPEES / ORANGE TREE / PAKISTAN

9 — PAKISTAN / 2 As / ARMED FORCES DAY / JAN: 1960

10 — PAKISTAN / پاکستان / SERVICE / 2 As POSTAGE / 13 PAISA / POSTAGE

11 — 25 PAISA POSTAGE / PAKISTAN پاکستان

12 — HELP THE BLIND / POSTAGE PAISA 15 / PAKISTAN

13 — W. P. ENGINEERING UNIVERSITY LAHORE / 15 PAISA / پاکستان PAKISTAN / FIRST CONVOCATION DECEMBER 1964

14 — PAISA 15 / POSTAGE / PAKISTAN / HAKIM IBN-E-SINA (980-1037) / HEALTH FROM HERBS

15 — th ANNIVERSARY OF INDEPENDENCE / POSTAGE / 15 PAISA / پاکستان PAKISTAN

16

17 — LAS BELA / HALF ANNA / STATE

18 — VICTORY / SERVICE / BAHAWALPUR

19 — SILVER-JUBILEE / 1924-1949 / COTTON / BAHAWALPUR / PIES 9

20 — U.P.U. / BAHAWALPUR / 9 PIES

21 — Bangladesh / 1 PAISA POSTAGE

22 — শহীদ স্মরণে / বাংলাদেশ / 20 P.

1

2

3

4

5

6

7

8

9

10

11

12

13

14

15

16

17

18

19

20

21

22

23

24

25

1

2

3

4

5

6

7

8

9

10

11

12

13

14

15

16

17

18

19

20

21

22

23

24

25

1

2

3

4

5

6

7

8

9

10

11

12

13

14

15

16

17

18

19

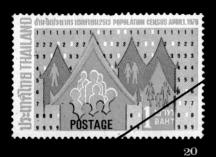

20

21

22

23

24

49

1

2

3

4

5

6

7

8

9

10

11

12

13

14

15

16

17

18

19

20

21

23

24

25

22

1

2

3

4

5

6

7

8

9

10

11

12

13

14

15

16

17

18

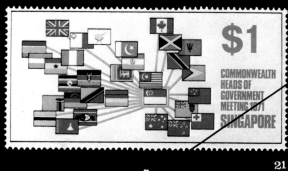
19

20

21

22

23

24

25

51

1

2

3

4

5

6

7

8

9

10

11

12

13

14

15

16

17

18

19

20

1

2

3

4

5

6

7

8

9

10

11

12

13

14

15

16

17

18

19

21

22

23

20

1

4

5

10

11

12

13

14

16

17

18

19

20

21

22

56

1 2 3 4 5

6 7 8 9 10

11 12 13 14 15

16 17 18 19 20

21 22 23 24 25

26 27 28 29 30

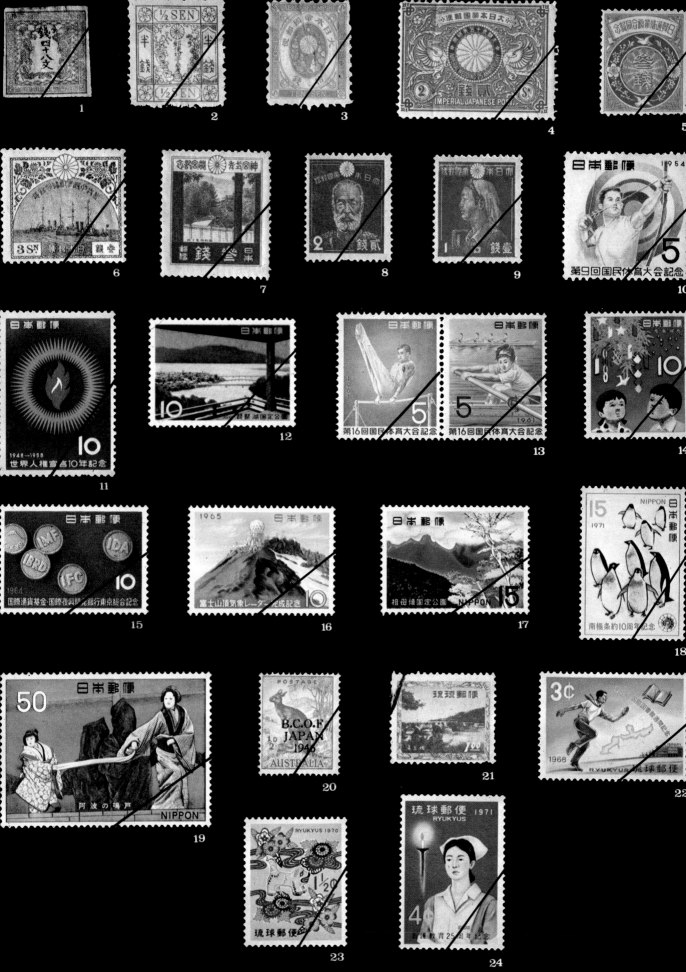

1

2

3

4

5

6

7

8

9

10

11

12

13

14

15

16

17

18

19

20

21

22

23

24

1

2

3

4

5

6

7

8

9

10

11

12

13

14

15

16

17

18

19

20

21

22

23

24

25

26

27

1

2

3

4

5

6

7

8

9

10

11

12

13

14

15

16

17

18

19

20

21

22

1

2

3

4

5

6

7

8

9

10

11

12

13

14

15

16

17

18

19

20

21

22

23

24

25

1

2

3

4

5

6

7

8

9

10

11

12

13

14

15

16

17

18

19

20

21

1

2

3

4

5

6

7

8

9

10

11

12

13

14

15

16

17

18

19

20

21

22

23

24

25

26

1

2

3

4

5

6

7

8

9

10

11

12

13

14

15

16

17

18

19

20

21

22

23

24

25

26

27

1

2

3

4

5

6

7

8

9

10

11

12

13

14

15

16

17

18

19

20

21

22

23

24

25

26

SIERRA LEONE · POSTAGE · FOUR PENCE

1

GOLD COAST · POSTAGE · 2½ PENNY

2

GAMBIA · HALFPENNY

3

GOLD COAST · POSTAGE & REVENUE · 1d · 1d

4

GOLD COAST · 2/- · POSTAGE & REVENUE · 2/-

5

GAMBIA · 1½d · THREE HALF PENCE

6

SIERRA LEONE · 2/- · POSTAGE & REVENUE · 2/-

7

SIERRA LEONE · 4d · FREETOWN FROM THE HARBOUR · FOUR PENCE

8

GOLD COAST · 5/- · SURFBOATS

9

INDEPENDENCE 1961 · ½d · SIERRA LEONE · PALM FRUIT GATHERING

10

Fireball Lily · ½d · SIERRA LEONE

11

SIERRA LEONE · Land of Iron & Diamonds · 1967 · Specimen · 1963 · JOHN F. KENNEDY · Friend of The African People · AIR MAIL · 9d

12

SELF GOVERNMENT 1963 · Red-eyed Turtle Dove · Gambia · 1/3

13

THE GAMBIA · 6d · GAMBIA · SIX PENCE · CENTENARY OF FIRST POSTAGE STAMP 1869-1969

14

THE GAMBIA · REPUBLIC DAY 24th APRIL 1970 · 2d

15

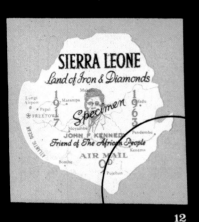

PRIME MINISTER'S VISIT, U.S.A. AND CANADA · GHANA · 2½d · GHANA INDEPENDENCE COMMEMORATION 6th MARCH 1957

16

GHANA · 8½d · "AFRICA FREEDOM DAY" · 15TH. APRIL 1959

17

THIRD ANNIVERSARY OF THE REVOLUTION 1966-1969 · CONSTITUENT ASSEMBLY · 20np · GHANA

18

FIRST MAN ON THE MOON · GHANA · 12½NP

19

LIBERIA · REGISTERED · MONROVIA · 10 CENTS · 10

20

LIBERIA POSTAGE · 10 · TEN CENTS · 10

21

POSTAGE · LIBERIA · ONE CENT · 1

22

LIBERIA · POSTAGE · 1936 · 2 CENTS

23

JOHN F. KENNEDY ANNIVERSARY MEMORIAL · Liberia · 15¢

24

LIBERIA · L.F.F. · 1¢ · ONE CENT · 1

25

1

2

3

4

5

7

8

9

10

12

13

14

16

17

18

20

21

22

23

1

2

3

4

5

6

7

8

9

10

11

12

13

14

15

16

17

18

19

20

21

1

2

3

4

5

6

7

8

9

10

11

12

13

14

15

16

17

18

19

20

21

22

23

24

25

1 — REPUBLIQUE FRANÇAISE / 10 / POSTE / CONGO FRANÇAIS

2 — POSTES / RF / AFRIQUE EQUATORIALE / GABON / 25 / L.COURET-RAME

3 — RF / GABON / AEF / 1 / 1 / C.H.DEL / SUR L'OGOOUÉ / H.V.PARIS / POSTES

4 — REPUBLIQUE GABONAISE / 0.50 / COMBRETUM / POSTES

5 — RF / 4c / AFRIQUE EQUATORIALE FRANÇAISE / POSTES / AFRIQUE EQUATORIALE GABON

6 — 0F50 / TIMBRE TAXE / ANANAS / REPUBLIQUE GABONAISE / MANGUE / REPUBLIQUE GABONAISE / TIMBRE TAXE / 0F50

7 — EUROPAFRIQUE / POSTE AERIENNE / EUROPAFRIQUE / 50F / REPUBLIQUE GABONAISE / BEQUET / DELRIEU

8 — REPUBLIQUE GABONAISE / POSTES / 25F / Premier Ministre LÉON MBA

9 — REPUBLIQUE · FRANÇAISE / 20 / POSTE / MOYEN CONGO / c

10 — REPUBLIQUE DU CONGO / POSTES / 15F / PRESIDENT FULBERT YOULOU

11 — ELAGATIS BIPINNULATUS / 0,50 / POSTES / REPUBLIQUE DU CONGO

12 — REPUBLIQUE DU CONGO / 80F / POSTE AERIENNE / PRÉSIDENT BARTHÉLÉMY BOGANDA 1910-1959 / DELRIEU

13 — REPUBLIQUE DU CONGO / TIMBRE TAXE / 0F50

14 — REPUBLIQUE · FRANÇAISE / 10 / POSTE / OUBANGUI-CHARI-TCHAD / MOYEN CONGO / c

15 — REPUBLIQUE · FRANÇAISE / 1 / POSTE / AFRIQUE EQUATORIALE FRANÇAISE / OUBANGUI-CHARI / c

16 — AEROPORT DE BANGUI M'POKO / 100F / POSTE AERIENNE / REPUBLIQUE CENTRAFRICAINE

17 — TIMBRE TAXE / 0F50 / REPUBLIQUE CENTRAFRICAINE

18 — REPUBLIQUE · FRANÇAISE / AFRIQUE EQUATORIALE FRANÇAISE / 1 / TCHAD / c

19 — REPUBLIQUE DU / TCHAD / 100F / POSTE AERIENNE / Président / John F. KENNEDY / 1917-1963 / Discours sur les droits civiques - 11 Juin 1963 / R.AUBRY / DELRIEU

20 — REPUBLIQUE DU TCHAD / POSTES / 25F / GENDARMERIE NATIONALE / P.LAMBERT / DELRIEU

21 — FRANCE LIBRE / POSTES / RF / 5c / 5c / AFRIQUE EQUATORIALE FRANÇAISE

— POSTES / RF / 10c / AFRIQUE EQUATORIALE FRANÇAISE

1

2

3

4

5

6

7

8

9

10

11

12

13

14

15

16

17

18

19

20

23

21

22

25

24

1

2

3

4

5

6

7

8

9

10

11

12

13

14

15

16

17

18

19

20

21

1   2   3   4   5

6   7   8   9   10

11   12   13   14

15   16   17   18   19

20   21   22   23

24   25   26

78

1

2

3

4

5

6

7

8

9

10

11

12

13

14

15

16

17

18

19

20

22

23

24

25

1

2

3

4

5

6

7

8

9

10

11

12

13

14

15

16

17

18

19

20

21

22

23

24

25

26

1

2

3

4

5

6

7

8

9

10

11

12

13

14

15

16

17

18

19

20

21

22

23

1

2

3

4

5

6

7

8

9

10

11

12

13

14

15

16

17

18

19

20

21

22

23

1

2

3

4

5

6

7

8

9

10

11

12

13

14

15

16

17

18

19

20

21

22

23

24

25

1

2

3

4

5

6

7

8

9

10

11

12

13

14

15

16

17

18

19

20

21

22

23

24

25

1

2

3

4

5

6

7

8

9

10

11

12

13

14

15

16

17

18

19

20

21

22

23

24

25

26

27

28

29

1

2

3

4

5

6

7

8

9

10

11

12

13

14

15

16

17

18

19

20

21

22

1

2

3

4

5

6

7

8

9

10

11

12

13

14

15

16

17

18

19

20

21

22

23

24

25

26

BRITISH HONDURAS
6
10 CENTS

1

5c 5c
POSTAGE REVENUE
BRITISH HONDURAS

2

2 CENTS
BRITISH HONDURAS

3

BRITISH HONDURAS
ARMADILLO
$1 POSTAGE & REVENUE $1

4

BRITISH HONDURAS
VR EⅡR
1860 POST OFFICE CENTENARY 1960
15c TAMARIND TREE, NEWTOWN BARRACKS

5

BRITISH HONDURAS
MONTEZUMA OROPENDOLA (Gymnostinops montezuma)
POSTAGE REVENUE
$5

6

British Honduras
EⅡR
50 CENTS
NEW GENERAL POST OFFICE
ESTABLISHMENT OF THE NEW CAPITAL CITY AT BELMOPAN

7

MOUNTAIN LION Puma concolor
EⅡR
$5
BRITISH HONDURAS

8

NATIONAL TREE (Swietenia macrophylla)

9

British Honduras
EⅡR
15c
ORCHIDS OF BELIZE

10

ANTILLAS
PANAMA
1 CENTAVO

11

CORREOS
REPUBLICA DE PANAMA
AR
5 CINCO CENTAVOS

12

REPUBLICA DE PANAMA
CORREOS
1 UN CENTESIMO DE BALBOA 1

13

REPUBLICA DE
HOMENAJE A
LINDBERGH
2 CENTESIMO DE BALBOA 2

14

REPUBLICA DE PANAMA
CORREOS
½ MEDIO CENTESIMO DE BALBOA ½

15

CORREO AEREO PANAMA
B/.1.00
EXPOSICION MUNDIAL DE BELGICA 1958

16

PANAMA 3¢
CORREOS
HOSPITAL DEL SEGURO SOCIAL — JUNIO 1° DE 1962
EDITORA PANAMA AMERICA, S.A.

17

GIAMBATTISTA
PANAMA B/.0.005
DE LA RUE DE COLOMBIA

18

PANAMA
½c.
X JUEGOS OLIMPICOS DE INVIERNO
GRENOBLE 1968
DE LA RUE DE COLOMBIA

19

PANAMA CORREOS
B/.0.01
PESCA SUBMARINA
DE LA RUE DE COLOMBIA

20

CORREOS
REPUBLICA DE PANAMA
2 DOS CENTESIMOS DE BALBOA 2

21

GOETHALS
3 CENTS POSTAGE
CANAL ZONE

22

Theodore Roosevelt 1858 1958
1904 1914
CANAL ZONE POSTAGE
4¢

23

CANAL ZONE
AIR MAIL POSTAGE
6c

24

CANAL ZONE
8c

25

1

2

3

4

5

6

7

8

9

10

11

12

13

14

15

16

17

18

19

20

21

22

23

24

25

1

2

3

4

5

6

7

8

9

10

11

12

13

14

15

16

17

18

19

20

21

23

1

2

3

4

5

6

7

8

9

10

11

12

13

14

15

16

17

18

19

20

21

22

23

24

25

1

2

3

4

5

6

7

8

9

11

12

13

14

15

16

17

18

19

20

21

22

23

1

2

3

4

5

6

7

8

9

11

12

13

14

10

15

16

17

18

19

20

21

22

23

1   2   3   4   5   6

7   8   9   10   11

12   13   14   15

16   17   18   19

20   21   22   23

24   25   26

JAMAICA POSTAGE
FOUR PENCE

1

JAMAICA — REVENUE
LLANDOVERY FALLS
ONE PENNY
1d

2

6d JAMAICA 6d
SIX PENCE

3

2d JAMAICA 2d
KING'S HOUSE SPANISH TOWN 1762–187
POSTAGE × REVENUE

4

2½ JAMAICA 2½
POSTAGE CHILD WELFARE REVENUE

5

GEORGE VI
POSTAGE · REVENUE
10s JAMAICA 10s
SUPREME LORD

6

JAMAICA
5/- NEW CONSTITUTION 1944

7

1655 JAMAICA 1955
ABOLITION OF SLAVERY PROCLAIMED 1655
6d

8

JAMAICA
INDEPENDENCE
ACKEE
5d

9

INTERNATIONAL HUMAN RIGHTS YEAR 1968
3/- JAMAICA

10

SPORT FISHING
30c C-DAY 8th SEPTEMBER 1969
BLUE MARLIN
JAMAICA
3/-

11

JAMAICA
THE MAIN CABLE
THE "SHORE-END"
Centenary of the Introduction of the Telegraph Service 1870–1970
10c

12

TURKS ISLANDS
ONE PENNY

13

TURKS AND CAICOS ISLANDS
1848 1900
HALFPENNY

14

1848 TURKS & CAICOS ISLANDS 1948
10/-

15

E II R
35 CENTS
NEW CONSTITUTION 1969
TURKS AND CAICOS ISLANDS

16

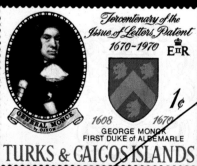

Tercentenary of the Issue of Letters Patent
1670–1970
E II R
1608 1670
GEORGE MONCK
FIRST DUKE of ALBEMARLE
1c
TURKS & CAICOS ISLANDS

17

CAYMAN ISLANDS POSTAGE
¼d

18

CAYMAN ISLANDS
CAYMAN SCHOONER
5/-

19

5/-
FORT GEORGE
CAYMAN ISLANDS

20

CAYMAN ISLANDS
4/= 40c
C-DAY 8th September 1969
GOVERNMENT HOUSE

21

CAYMAN ISLANDS
2/-
OLYMPIC GAMES MEXICO 1968
pole vault

22

CAYMAN ISLANDS
$2

23

1

2

3

4

5

6

7

8

9

10

11

12

13

14

15

16

17

18

19

20

21

22

24

1 — NEVIS / ONE PENNY

2 — NEVIS / SIX PENCE

3 — ONE PENNY

4 — St KITTS-NEVIS / POSTAGE / REVENUE / TWO PENCE

5 — St KITTS-NEVIS / POSTAGE / ONE PENNY

6 — POSTAGE / REVENUE / 1½d / St KITTS-NEVIS / 1½d

7 — St KITTS-NEVIS 1623 / POSTAGE / REVENUE / 1d / THE FOUNDING OF THE COLONY OF St KITTS 1623 / 1d

8 — St KITTS NEVIS / ANGUILLA / 10/- / 10/-

9 — ANGUILLA / TERCENTENARY / 1650-1950 / St KITTS-NEVIS / 1/- / 1/-

10 — SAINT CHRISTOPHER / NEVIS / ANGUILLA / SUGAR FACTORY, St KITTS / POSTAGE / REVENUE / $4.80

11 — SAINT CHRISTOPHER-NEVIS-ANGUILLA / Alexander Hamilton Bicentenary / Born in Nevis 11th January 1757 / 24 CENTS

12 — St. CHRISTOPHER - NEVIS - ANGUILLA / NEVIS / SIX PENCE / 12c / 1861 NEVIS STAMP CENTENARY 1961

13 — St.Christopher / Nevis Anguilla / St.Christopher Nevis Anguilla / ARTS FESTIVAL / 1966 / 3 CENTS

14 — STATEHOOD 27th. Feb. 1967 / NATIONAL FLAG / ANGUILLA / St. CHRISTOPHER / NEVIS / 10 CENTS / St. CHRISTOPHER-NEVIS ANGUILLA

15 — St. Christopher / Nevis Anguilla / ALEXANDER HAMILTON / Born in Nevis, / JANUARY 11th, 1757 / 60 CENTS

16 — 25 CENTS / ST KITTS NEVIS ANGUILLA

17 — 50 CENTS / 1929 1968 / Dr. MARTIN LUTHER KING / St. KITTS NEVIS ANGUILLA

18 — St CHRISTOPHER / NEVIS / ANGUILLA / 40 CENTS / 40 CENTS / GEERTGEN TOT St. JANS / THE ADORATION OF THE KINGS / CHRISTMAS 1969

19 — St Kitts Nevis Anguilla / 40c

20 — EASTER 1969 / THE CRUCIFIXION - STUDIO OF MASSYS / ANGUILLA 25c

21 — CHRISTMAS 1970 / THE ADORATION OF THE SHEPHERDS-RENI / ANGUILLA / c

22 — COTTAGE HOSPITAL EXTENSION / 5c / ANGUILLA

— ANGUILLA / THE VALLEY / MAP OF ANGUILLA / 40 CENTS

24 — ANGUILLA / INDEPENDENCE / VALLEY POST OFFICE / 6 CENTS

25 — ANGUILLA / 1933 G G 1968 / 10c / 10c

1

2

3

5

6

7

8

9

10

11

13

14

15

16

17

18

19

20

21

22

23

24

25

1

2

3

4

5

6

7

8

9

10

11

12

13

14

15

16

17

18

19

20

21

22

23

24

25

1

2

3

4

5

6

7

8

9

10

11

12

13

14

15

16

17

18

19

20

21

22

23

24

FALKLAND ISLANDS

2½ PENNY

1

FALKLAND ISLANDS

ONE PENNY

2

FALKLAND ISLANDS

6d 6d

POSTAGE & REVENUE

3

FALKLAND ISLANDS

1633 1933

POSTAGE REVENUE

ONE POUND

4

THREE PENCE

3d 3d

FLOCK OF SHEEP

FALKLAND ISLANDS

5

FALKLAND ISLANDS

2d 2d

UPLAND GOOSE

POSTAGE AND REVENUE

6

OF RADIO COMMUNICATIONS

2'-

50th ANNIVERSARY OF THE ESTABLISHMENT

FALKLAND ISLANDS

FALKLAND

7

FALKLAND ISLANDS

STEAMER DUCKS

4d

8

FALKLAND ISLANDS

2'-

50th ANNIVERSARY

FALKLAND ISLANDS

BATTLE MEMORIAL

OF THE BATTLE OF THE

9

FALKLAND ISLANDS

NORSEMAN 1950-1953

6d

21ST ANNIVERSARY of the GOVERNMENT AIR SERVICE 1969

10

FALKLAND ISLANDS

2'-

Dieu et Mon Droit

FALKLAND ISLANDS AND DEFENCE FORCE

GOLDEN JUBILEE 1920 — 1970

11

Falkland

Islands

£1

Yellow Orchid

12

ONE PENNY

GRAHAM LAND

DEPENDENCY OF

BATTLE MEMORIAL

1d 1d

FALKLAND ISLANDS

13

TWO PENCE

SOUTH ORKNEYS

DEPENDENCY OF

2d 2d

(BLACK NECKED SWAN)

FALKLAND ISLANDS

14

THREE PENCE

SOUTH SHETLANDS

DEPENDENCY OF

3d 3d

FLOCK OF SHEEP

FALKLAND ISLANDS

15

FALKLAND ISLANDS DEPENDENCIES

SOUTH POLE

3d

POSTAGE & REVENUE

16

FALKLAND ISLANDS

DEPENDENCIES

½D

JOHN BISCOE 1947-52

17

FALKLAND ISLANDS DEPENDENCIES

TRANS-ANTARCTIC EXPEDITION 1955-1958

2½D

PENOLA 1934-37

18

SHACKLETONS CROSS

2'-

South Georgia

19

1922 · SIR ERNEST SHACKLETON · 1972

20P

QUEST

SOUTH GEORGIA

20

£1

BRITISH ANTARCTIC TERRITORY

21

BRITISH ANTARCTIC TERRITORY

2'-

22

SNOCAT

25P

BRITISH ANTARCTIC TERRITORY

2

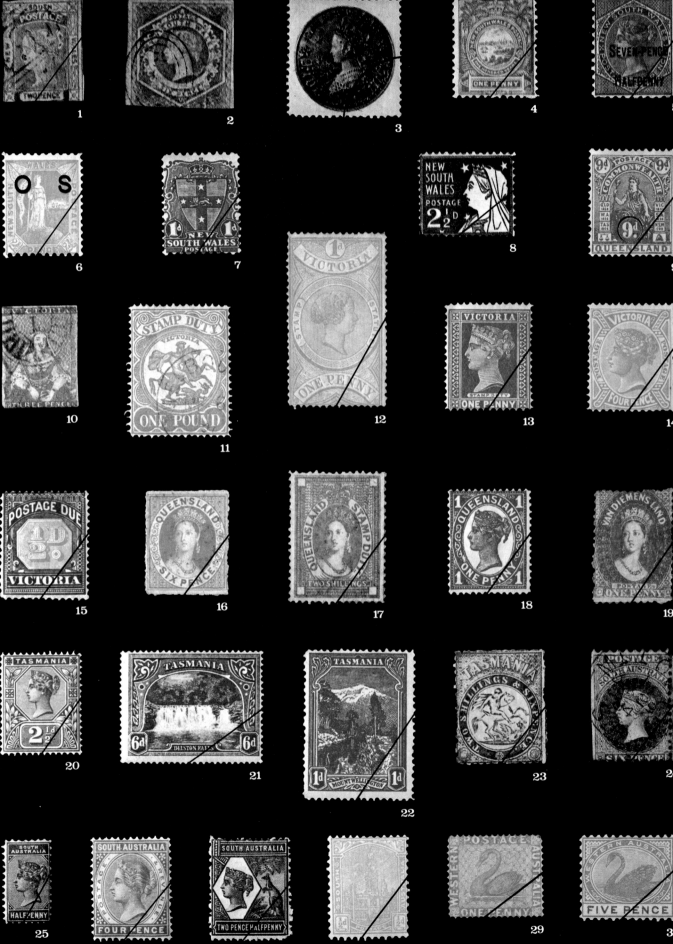

AUSTRALIA
POSTAGE
TWO PENCE HALFPENNY
2½d

1

AUSTRALIA
2 POSTAGE 2
TWO PENCE

2

CANBERRA 1927
AUSTRALIA
POSTAGE
THREE HALFPENCE
1½d

3

AUSTRALIA
POSTAGE
STURT EXPLORER
1830 3d 1930

4

1788 AUSTRALIA 1938
POSTAGE
2d
150TH ANNIVERSARY

5

2/-
SILVER JUBILEE
KING GEORGE 1910 35
2/-
AUSTRALIA
POSTAGE

6

POSTAGE AUSTRALIA POSTAGE
10 10

7

AUSTRALIA
2d
POSTAGE

8

AUSTRALIA
3½d POSTAGE 3½d
1945

9

AUSTRALIA
3½d
STEEL
1797 NEWCASTLE 1947

10

AUSTRALIA AUSTRALIA
2d 2d
ONE HUNDRED YEARS ONE HUNDRED YEARS

11

ROYAL FLYING DOCTOR SERVICE OF AUSTRALIA
AUSTRALIA 7d

12

5½d 5½d
AUSTRALIA AUSTRALIA
AUSTRALIAN WAR MEMORIAL · CANBERRA AUSTRALIAN WAR MEMORIAL · CANBERRA

13

BIRTH OF THE POST OFFICE 1809
4d AUSTRALIA

14

5d
AUSTRALIA
NORTHERN TERRITORY CENTENARY OF EXPLORATION 1960

15

3/- WARATAH
AUSTRALIA

16

AUSTRALIA
$4
KING

17

25c
COOKTOWN ORCHID
AUSTRALIA
R WARNER RBA

18

AUSTRALIA
25c
OLYMPIC GAMES MEXICO 1968

19

CHRISTMAS 1969 AUSTRALIA
25c
J COBURN RBA

20

5c International Ports & Harbors Conference AUSTRALIA
J MASON RBA

21

5c MACQUARIE LIGHTHOUSE 1818
AUSTRALIA

22

Australia Cook Bicentenary 1970
30c

23

AUSTRALIAN
MELBOURNE
2/-
ANTARCTIC TERRITORY

24

$1
AUSTRALIAN ANTARCTIC TERRITORY

25

1

2

3

4

5

6

7

8

9

10

11

12

13

14

15

16

17

18

19

20

21

22

23

24

25

26

1

2

3

4

5

6

7

8

9

10

11

12

13

14

15

16

17

18

19

20

21

22

23

24

25

TAHITI
10
CENTIMES

1

2

FRANCE LIBRE
POSTES
5c
OCEANIE

3

RF POSTES
10c
Ets FRANÇAIS DE L'OCEANIE

4

POLYNESIE FRANÇAISE
0F10

5

CAMBIER
20F
POLYNESIE FRANÇAISE POSTES

6

POLYNESIE FRANÇAISE
10f RF
IIes JEUX DU PACIFIQUE SUD

7

REPVBLIQVE FRANÇAISE
COLONIES POSTES
1
Nlle CALEDONIE et DEPENDANCE

8

RF. NOUVELLE CALEDONIE et DEPENDANCES
POSTES 2c

9

FRANCE LIBRE
POSTES
RF
40c
NOUVELLE CALEDONIE

10

NOUVELLE CALEDONIE ET DEPENDANCES
CENTENAIRE DE LA CROIX-ROUGE
37f
RF POSTES

11

NOUVELLE-CALEDONIE ET DEPENDANCES RF
POSTE AERIENNE
JEUX OLYMPIQUES DE TOKYO 1964
10F

12

NOUVELLE CALEDONIE et DEPENDANCES
RF.
ILES WALLIS et FUTUNA
POSTES 15

13

0.02
ILES WALLIS et FUTUNA

14

POSTES FRANCE LIBRE RF
25c 25c
ILES WALLIS & FUTUNA

15

WALLIS et FUTUNA
1F
POSTES RF
MITRA EPISCOPALIS

16

CONDOMINIUM POSTES 15 CENTIMES OR
1865 1965
NOUVELLES HEBRIDES
EIIR RF

17

Condominium des Nouvelles Hebrides
EIIR RF
POSTES CENTIMES OR
H.M.A.S. CANBERRA EN TETE D'UN CONVOI
1942 FRONT DU PACIFIQUE SUD 60

18

CONDOMINIUM DES NOUVELLES HEBRIDES RF EIIR
1.10 FRANC OR
30eme ANNIVERSAIRE
du RALLIEMENT à la FRANCE LIBRE

19

65 CENTIMES OR RF
CONDOMINIUM DES
NOUVELLES HEBRIDES
MISSION DE LA SOCIÉTÉ ROYALE
AGATHIS DE LONDRES AUX
NOUVELLES-HEBRIDES 1971

20

THE DICTIONARY

EUROPE

PLATE 1

Albania

---

1. 2 paras, 1913

During the First Balkan War Albania declared its independence of Turkey and this was recognized by the Treaty of London on 30 May 1913. The first stamps of the new state appeared on 16 June and consisted of contemporary Turkish stamps overprinted 'Shqipenia' (Albania) and the double-headed eagle, emblem of the medieval Albanian kingdom. The 10*pa.* of the 1908 series and the 1909–11 set from 2*pa.* to 10*pi.* were overprinted in this way. The example illustrated has the overprint upside down. The 25 and 50*pi.* denominations were also overprinted for presentation to government officials.

2. 5 grosch, 1913

The first distinctive stamps of Albania were released in October 1913 and consisted of stamps in denominations of 10 and 20*pa.* and 1, 2, 5 and 10*g.* (piastres). The stamps were produced in an ingenious manner. Two handstamps were struck to show the circular frame and the eagle, and then the value was inserted by typewriting. In the example illustrated the eagle has been struck upside down. Numerous typing errors are recorded in this series.

3. 10 paras, 1914

The provisional government offered the crown of Albania to Prince William of Wied on 21 February 1914. Stamps issued in December 1913 and portraying the fifteenth-century hero Kastriota Skanderbeg were overprinted on 7 March to celebrate the arrival of the prince at Valona. The stamps were valued in a new currency, based on the frank of 100*q.*, but in April 1914 were issued with surcharges in the old currency since the new money was not yet available. Following the outbreak of World War I Prince William returned to Austria.

4. 40 paras, 1915

Albania was a battlefield of opposing forces in World War I. The north was occupied by Serbs and Montenegrins, later driven out by the Austrians, while the Greeks and the Italians wrestled for control of the south and east. Essad Pasha ruled Central Albania until February 1916, when he was ousted by the Austrians. The Skanderbeg stamps of 1913 were overprinted with a circular mark inscribed in Arabic. Subsequently fiscal stamps inscribed in French were overprinted in Arabic for use in Central Albania.

5. 5 centimes, 1917

On 11 December 1916 General Sarrail, commanding the French forces at Salonika, dispatched troops across the mountains to Korce (Koritza), which they occupied to prevent the Italians and Greeks from dividing the country between them. A series of stamps, with a lithographed background and typographed inscriptions, was produced by A. A. Vanghali and released in 1917. The stamps bore values in French currency and the Albanian inscriptions signified 'Koritza Independent Albania', or 'Koritza Albanian Republic'.

6. 15 qindar, 1919

A provisional government under Turkhan Bey was set up in December 1918 to restore independence and secure the withdrawal of all foreign troops from Albania. Scutari (Shkoder) was ruled by an International Commission as a protection against Serbia, from the end of 1918 till March 1920 and various fiscal stamps overprinted 'Shkodre' or 'Shkoder' were used there.

7. 25 qintar, 1920

Albania was officially reunited in February 1920 and became a regency pending a decision on the restoration of Prince William. Ironically the first stamps issued under the regency consisted of a series, typographed at the Austrian State Printing Works in 1914, portraying Prince William. Because of his precipitate flight in 1914 the stamps were never issued. In 1920 they were released, but overprinted with the Albanian eagle to blot out his features. Examples without the overprint come from stocks looted in the civil disturbances.

8. 5 qindar, 1925

A National Assembly was not convened at Tirana until January 1924 and exactly a year later it voted for the establishment of a republic. The definitive series was overprinted to signify 'Albanian Republic', with the date 21 January 1925 below. An error '1921' instead of '1925' occurs once in every sheet of 50 stamps. The basic stamps were typographed in Vienna and featured views of Albania. Note the chaotic state of Albanian spelling at this time: the currency may be found as 'qintar' or 'qindar' and the word for Albanian may be found as 'Shqiptare' or 'Shqyptare' simultaneously.

9. 5 qindar, 1925

Albania's first airmail service was inaugurated in May 1925, though a military service had operated between Brindisi and the Italian garrisons during World War I. A series of seven air stamps was typographed in Vienna and released in May 1925. The common design showed a monoplane over the mountains in the neighbourhood of Tirana.

10. 1 qindar, 1925

Achmed Zogu Bey, scion of one of Albania's oldest families, welded the country together first as a republic and later as a kingdom. Stamps bearing his portrait were typographed by Aspiotis Brothers (formerly of Corfu and now of Athens), in denominations from 1*q.* to 5*f.* A portrait of the president in civilian clothes was used for the qindar values and a profile in military uniform for the franka denominations. Two years later the series was overprinted with a laurel wreath and the president's initials as a mark of approbation.

11. 2 qindar, 1928

The series of 1928 was not released without an overprint. At first a four-line overprint, occupying the sides of the stamps, was used to signify 'Dedicated to the memory of the Parliament of 25.8.28'. This session of parliament voted for a restoration of a hereditary monarchy and elected the president as King Zog I. On 1 September 1928 the series was issued with the overprint 'Mbretnia Shqiptare' (Albanian Kingdom), with or without accession date.

12. 5 qindar, 1940

On 7 April 1939 Italian troops invaded Albania and ousted King Zog. Five days later the contemporary definitive series was overprinted to signify 'provisional government' and shortly afterward Victor Emmanuel III was declared king of Albania. A definitive series, printed in photogravure at the Italian Government Printing Works in Rome, was released between August 1939 and January 1940. Native costumes, scenery, Roman ruins and various portraits of Victor Emmanuel were depicted. An airmail series followed in March 1940 and a series portraying the king commemorated the third anniversary of the Italian occupation in April 1942. The last series under Italian rule was a semi-postal set with premiums in aid of the anti-tuberculosis fund, issued in April 1943.

13. 25 qindar, 1944

The surrender of Italy to the Allies in 1943 created a

PLATE 1 ALBANIA · PLATE 2 AUSTRIA

vacuum in the Balkans, rapidly filled by the Germans who occupied Albania in September. Contemporary stamps of the Italian regime were overprinted '14 Shtator 1943' (14 September) to mark the change of government. In September 1944 a set of seven stamps inscribed 'Shqipnija' (Albania) was issued to raise funds for war refugees.

14. 3 franka, 1945
Albanian partisans led by the Communist Enver Hoxha drove out the Germans and declared the Democratic State of Albania on 22 October 1944. Various stamps of the Italian regime were overprinted to denote this. Subsequent overprints marked the second anniversary of the people's army and a Red Cross fund-raising campaign. A definitive series featuring Albanian scenery was issued in November 1945 and this, in turn, was overprinted in January 1946 to mark the constitutional assembly. The original stamps were typographed but lithographed forgeries are known.

15. 20 qindar, 1946
The Constitutional Assembly declared Albania a people's republic on 11 January 1946 – the country's twelfth change of status in thirty-five years. Stamps of the Democratic State were overprinted to signify People's Republic and were followed by distinctive stamps bearing the inscription 'Republika Popullore e Shqiperise', either in full or in an abbreviated form. Up to 1957 the stamps of Albania were printed in Prague, Budapest or Belgrade.

16. 8 lek, 1957
The 45th anniversary of the declaration of independence was celebrated by a set of four stamps showing the flag of Skanderbeg being raised. A new currency, based on the lek of 100 qindar, replaced the frank in 1947. This series was lithographed by Mihal Duri, who was responsible for the production of all Albanian stamps between 1957 and 1961. Since that date the Government Printing Works in Tirana has produced the stamps.

17. 1 lek, 1967
Apart from stamps of 1963 portraying Josef Stalin and recent issues portraying Mao Tse-tung, there is little indication of Albania's political alignment in its stamps. Since 1960 the propaganda issues have given way to thematic sets covering every conceivable aspect of Albanian fauna and flora, space exploration, sporting events and, more recently Albanian art. The first series of stamps devoted to Albanian paintings appeared in October 1967 and was lithographed in multicolour. Kole Idromeno's paintings of The Marriage Ceremony and Our Sister were reproduced on the 15q. and 1l. respectively.

18. 15 qindar, 1969
After issuing several sets devoted to modern Albanian paintings Albania turned to classical mosaics for inspiration. The first of these sets appeared in 1969 and reproduced geometric patterns, animal and bird motifs and human portraits from the Roman ruins at Apolloni. A second series, issued in 1970, concentrated on animal and bird mosaics, no doubt hoping to catch the thematic market in both art and zoological stamps.

19. Italian Post Offices in Albania, 10 paras, 1902
Italian post offices functioned in the main towns of Albania during the nineteenth century and used ordinary Italian stamps. These offices were suppressed by the Turkish authorities in December 1883 but were allowed to re-open in August 1902. Contemporary Italian stamps overprinted 'Albania' and surcharged in Turkish currency were introduced in September 1902 and used at Durazzo, Janina, Valona and Scutari until 1909, when separate issues were made for each office.

20. Durazzo, 10 paras, 1909
Italian stamps overprinted 'Durazzo' and surcharged in Turkish currency were introduced in February 1909. The Italian post office was closed in 1911 during the Italo-Turkish War but reopened during World War I when the seaport was under Italian occupation.

21. Janina, 20 paras, 1909
A similar series overprinted 'Janina' was issued in this inland town in February 1909 with values from 10pa. to 20pi. A 40pi. surcharge on the 1l. stamp appeared in 1911. The Italian post office was closed in 1911, reopened briefly at the end of 1913 and closed again on the eve of World War I. Between June and September 1917 an Italian military post functioned in Janina but ordinary Italian stamps without overprint were used. Greek troops occupied Janina in 1913 and since then Greek stamps have been used.

22. Scutari, 4 paras, 1915
Stamps overprinted 'Scutari di Albania' and surcharged in paras or piastres were introduced in 1909. A 40pi. denomination was added in 1911 and a 4pa. stamp in 1915. The Italian post office in this seaport was closed by order of the Allied Commission in 1918.

23. Valona, 1 piastre, 1909
The stamps used in the seaport of Valona follow the same pattern as the other Italian post offices in Albania. 30pa. stamps surcharged on the 15c. of 1911 were issued in September 1915 and the same stamp additionally surcharged 20c. was released in 1916. The Italian post office in Valona closed at the end of 1918.

24. Epirus, 25 lepta, 1914
At the end of 1913, after the Great Powers had allocated Epirus to Albania, the predominantly Greek population set up an independent government and issued their own stamps between February and August 1914. Greek stamps suitably overprinted were issued at Koritza and Chimara, while general issues were lithographed by Aspiotis Brothers of Corfu (later to become the firm of Aspioti-Elka, who now print the stamps of Greece and Cyprus). A series of March 1914 showed an Epirote rifleman, while the series of August depicted the double-headed eagle of Epirus on the Greek flag.

25. Northern Epirus, 2 lepta, 1916
In December 1914 Greek troops occupied Epirus. The area formerly under Albanian control was renamed Northern Epirus (though its boundaries were identical with the territory of Epirus which had previously seceded from Albania). Greek stamps overprinted in Greek to signify 'N. Epirus' were used between December 1914 and June 1916, when Italian troops overran the district. After World War I it was incorporated in Albania.

26. Greek Occupation of Albania, 10 lepta, 1940
Italian troops based in Albania invaded Greece in the summer of 1940. The Greek army repulsed them and drove them back into Albania. By the end of 1940 the Greek forces had occupied the greater part of Albania and remained there till April 1941, when German troops began their Balkan campaign. Between December 1940 and March 1941 various Greek definitive, commemorative and charity tax stamps were overprinted in Greek to signify 'Greek Administration'.

PLATE 2
Austria

1. 9 kreuzer, 1850
Following the establishment of the German-Austrian Postal Union in 1850 Austria introduced stamps in denominations of 1, 2, 3, 6 and 9k. for use throughout the Habsburg dominions. They were engraved by H. Tautenhayn and typographed at the State Printing Works, Vienna, where most Austrian stamps since that date have been printed.

2. Newspaper stamp, 1867
This undenominated stamp, bereft of inscription, was sold for 1 kreuzer in Austria and 1 krajczar in Hungary. Distinctive newspaper stamps for use in Hungary appeared the following year, and postage stamps in 1871 (see plate 21), and the 'lilac Mercury' was designed to avoid offending national sentiment.

3. 1 gulden, 1896
Anaglyptography, a form of machine engraving giving the appearance of relief by means of close parallel lines, was used for the profile of Kaiser Franz Josef.

4. 50 heller, 1908
One of a lengthy series issued to celebrate the 60th anniversary of the Emperor's accession, it was designed by Koloman Moser, an apostle of the Art Nouveau movement, and engraved by Ferdinand Schirnböck, the leading stamp portrait engraver of that period.

5. 15 heller, 1917
One of a set of four stamps, designed by A. Cossmann, marking the brief reign of Kaiser Karl I, last of the Habsburg rulers (1916–18).

6. 5 heller newspaper express stamp, 1919
By the Treaties of St Germain and Trianon Austria was shorn of its non-German dominions and formed into a republic. The stamps of the erstwhile empire were overprinted 'Deutschösterreich' (German Austria), reflecting the desire at that time for political union with the new German republic. The first of these overprints began appearing in December 1918.

7. 40 heller, 1919
The overprinted issues were superseded in 1919–20 by a definitive series for use in 'German Austria'. This design, by J. F. Renner, reflects the strong influence of the Sezessionists in Austrian stamp design from the end of World War I. It symbolizes the dawn of the new republic. Because of postwar shortages many of these stamps were released imperforate.

8. 7½ kronen, postage due stamp, 1921
The basic stamp, valued at 15 heller, was printed on thick greyish paper to facilitate its use as small change during a shortage of coined money. Mounting inflation is reflected in its surcharge for use as a 7½k. denomination. 'Nachmarke' indicates its conversion for use as a postage due stamp.

9. 7½ kronen, 1921
The basic stamp appeared in February 1920 as part of the higher value definitive series. In March 1921 it was overprinted 'Hochwasser' (flood) and sold with a 15k. premium in aid of victims of the 1920 Danube flood disaster. A few stamps are known with the date omitted or rendered as 1020 instead of 1920.

10. 1000 kronen, 1922
By the Treaty of St Germain the Allies forbade the

PLATE 2 AUSTRIA · PLATE 3 THE BALTIC STATES

proposed union of Austria with Germany and the name of the new republic was finally settled as 'Österreich' (Austria). Professor Willi Dachauer designed the series of 1922–24 with its strong elements of Art Deco. On account of inflation the series ranged from $\frac{1}{2}$ to 10,000k.

11. 5 + 2 groschen, Winter Relief, 1933
The currency of Austria was reformed in 1925, when the schilling of 100 groschen was introduced. A new definitive series inscribed in that currency appeared in 1925–27. The 5gr. denomination was reissued in green instead of ochre and overprinted, with a 2gr. premium in aid of winter charity, in December 1933.

12. 1 groschen, 1934
The last definitive series before the *Anschluss* took the varied costumes of the Austrian provinces for its subject. Each pair of stamps depicted a man and a woman from each province, with appropriate background scenery. Note the stylized treatment of the subject by G. Jung.

13. 24 groschen, 1937
One of a set of three stamps marking the centenary of the Danube Steam Navigation Company, it features a river steamer of the Franz Schubert class. The series was produced by photogravure, a process adopted by Austria in 1933.

14. 12 groschen, 1937
One of a pair of stamps released in December 1937 for use on Christmas greetings cards. The stamps, designed by Dachauer, were the last issued by the Austrian republic prior to its absorption into the Third Reich in March 1938. Considerable furor was caused at the time since the central flower in the nosegay was popularly regarded as portraying Adolf Hitler, the German *Führer*.

15. 6 pfennigs, 1945
In May 1945 Austria was occupied by Russian, American, British and French troops and subsequently divided into four zones. In the Soviet Zone stocks of German (Hitler Head) stamps were seized and overprinted 'Österreich' with bars obliterating the dictator's profile. Apart from the authorized overprints, made in Vienna and Graz, there were numerous local overprints, the status of which is doubtful in many cases.

16. 5 marks, 1945
One of a series provided for use in the Soviet Zone. The Austrian arms (prewar version) were revived with the addition of broken chains on the eagle's legs, symbolizing liberation from Nazi tyranny.

17. 20 groschen, 1945
One of a series lithographed by the U.S. Bureau of Engraving and Printing, Washington, for use in Austria after liberation. The stamps were used in the American, British and French zones between June and November 1945.

18. 10 groschen, 1945
The Austrian republic, recognized by the four powers, was established on 14 May 1945. Stamps for use throughout the entire country were designed by A. Chmielowski and produced by photogravure in Vienna. The stamps, featuring Austrian landscapes, were gradually released between November 1945 and January 1947.

19. 2.40 schillings, 1951
The scenery definitive series was gradually replaced from June 1948 onwards by a photogravure series featuring girls in native costume. It remained in use till the early 1960s and during that period underwent numerous changes in colour, gum and paper.

20. 1.50 schillings, 1955
One of a set of five stamps marking the tenth anniversary of the Austrian republic. The theme of this series was reconstruction and featured modern flats, the parliament building, the Western Terminus and the Limburg Dam.

21. 1.50 schillings, 1963
Many Austrian stamps in the postwar period have been designed by Adalbert Pilch and engraved by R. Toth. This stamp, issued in August 1963, commemorated the centenary of the Voluntary Fire Brigades and featured the statue of St Florian, patron saint of firemen. The stamp was recessprinted in black, with a lithographed background.

22. 3 schillings, 1966
One of a series publicizing treasures of the Austrian National Library. The stamps, produced in combined recess and lithography, reflect the modern tendency toward more colourful designs. Austria is one of the few countries which still uses the traditional recess method for many of her stamps.

23. Austrian Italy, 10 centesimi, 1850
The stamps issued in the Austrian provinces in northern Italy (Lombardy and Venezia) were similar to those used in Austria itself, but had values in Italian currency, from 5 to 45c. Like the Austrian series the stamps were engraved by H. Tautenhayn and typographed in Vienna on rough hand-made paper. Medium smooth machine-made paper was introduced in 1854.

24. Austrian Italy, 10 soldi, 1863
The Austrian administered districts of Lombardy and Venezia used stamps identical in design with contemporary Austrian issues, but with values expressed in Italian currency (1850: 100 centesimi = 1 lira, 1858: 100 soldi = 1 florin or gulden). Note the postmark of Venezia (Venice) on this stamp bearing the imperial Austrian coat of arms. After the loss of Lombardy and Venezia to the kingdom of Italy in 1866 these stamps were used in the Austrian post offices in the Turkish Empire, pending the introduction of distinctive stamps in 1867 (see plate 34).

25. Austro-Hungarian Military Post, 80 heller, 1917
Stamps inscribed K.U.K. FELDPOST were provided for the use of Austro-Hungarian troops in occupied territories from 1915 to 1918. Distinctive issues were also produced for the occupying forces in Italy (see plate 23), Rumania (plate 29), Montenegro and Serbia (plate 35).

26. Carinthia, 2 kronen, 1920
One of a series of Austrian stamps overprinted for use in Carinthia during the period (16 September to 10 October 1920) prior to the plebiscite. The stamps were also valid for postal use in Austria itself. A similar issue was made by Yugloslavia (see plate 35).

PLATE 3
The Baltic States

The east coast of the Baltic, meeting place and battleground of Slav and Teuton for a thousand years, was the location of three short-lived republics, Estonia, Latvia and Lithuania which won for themselves an uneasy independence in the period between the world wars. During the 'phoney war' of 1939–40 they were quietly absorbed by the Soviet Union and though they subsequently came under German occupation they were mutely returned to Russia at the end of the war. Also associated with this group are the stamps of Wenden, a feudal anachronism ruled by a subsidiary of the Teutonic Knights into the present century, the stamps of the German occupations of the Baltic coast in two world wars and the stamps of the Lithuanian seizure of Memel.

1. Estonia, 15 kopeks, 1918
One of a series designed by R. Zero and lithographed by M. Pelau at Nömme after Estonia declared its independence of Russia at the end of World War I. The stamps were in denominations of 5, 15, 35 and 70k. and were normally released imperforate, though about twenty sheets of the 15k. were issued at Tallinn perforated $11\frac{1}{2}$.

2. Estonia, 1 marka, 1919
P. Aren designed this stamp, alluding to the ancient Vikings who colonized this part of the Baltic and added the Scandinavian element to the mixture of Slav and Teutonic, which makes the ethnics of this area so complex. The currency, the marka of 100 penni, was based on the contemporary German system of marks and pfennigs. The marka denominations were lithographed by E. Bergmann. These stamps were issued imperforate but some values are known rouletted locally at Port Baltic.

3. Estonia, 35 penni, 1920
One of a series of eight definitive stamps introduced between 1920 and 1924. The design, by E. Poland and K. Triumph, is a stylized view of Tallinn, the framework and lettering deriving from the late flowering of Art Nouveau which characterized many of the stamps of the 'New Europe'. The stamps were typographed by the Government Printing Works, Tallinn.

4. Estonia, 10 marka, 1925
K. Triumph designed a set of five airmail stamps released imperforate in February 1924. In July of the following year they were reissued with perforations. Different aircraft were featured in each vignette. The stamps were intended for an airmail service between Tallinn and Helsinki in Finland. Note the faint grey-blue network applied as a security device to the background of this stamp.

5. Estonia, 2 marka, 1922
T. Björnström designed the definitive series of 1922–25, which was typographed at the Government Printing Works. Two designs were used, a weaver on the values up to 3m. and a blacksmith on the higher denominations up to 20m. The earliest printings of the low values were imperforate.

6. Estonia, 15 senti, 1940
One of a set of four stamps, designed by K. Doll, issued in July 1940 to celebrate the centenary of the first adhesive stamps. The dove, symbol of peace, seems faintly ironic in view of the fact that Estonia was shortly afterward invaded by Russian troops and incorporated into the Soviet Union. With the exception of the period from 1941 to 1944, Russian stamps have been used there ever since.

7. Estonia, 50 + 50 kopeks, 1941
One of a set of six stamps issued in September 1941 to raise money for the Reconstruction Fund. The stamps were designed by H. Sarap and printed in photogravure by Ilutrukk of Tartu. Note the use of the German form 'Estland' and the German name 'Reval' for Tallinn. The stamps were printed on thick brownish paper with a background network of brown lines. Similar stamps without perforations were not issued for postal use. These stamps were superseded by German (Hitler Head) stamps overprinted 'Ostland' for use in occupied Russian territory.

PLATE 3 THE BALTIC STATES · PLATE 4 THE BENELUX COUNTRIES

8. Latvia, 5 kapeikas, 1918

The wheat-ears and sunrise emblem for this series was designed by Ansis Zihrul and lithographed by A. Schnackenburg of Riga. Shortage of paper led to some surprising materials being used. At first the stamps were printed on the back of German military maps in sheets of 228 subjects. Subsequently school exercise-books were used and stamps exhibit a pattern of thin horizontal blue lines and latterly thin transparent (cigarette) paper or medium wove paper was used. Stamps overprinted z.a. were used by the northwestern Army fighting the Bolsheviks during the Russian Civil War.

9. Latvia, 5 kapeikas, 1919

One of a set of three stamps, designed by J. Viebig and lithographed by Gottlieb Meyer of Libau, to celebrate the liberation of Riga, which had been temporarily seized by a force of German *freikorps* waging their own private war on the Bolsheviks. Various types of paper were used for this set.

10. Latvia, 10 kapeikas, 1919

One of a set released in November 1919 to mark the first anniversary of independence. The earliest printings were in a large size, 33 × 45 mm, but subsequently this was reduced to 28 × 38 mm. Again a wide variety of different papers was used, the 1 rouble denomination being printed on the backs of unfinished 5 rouble banknotes prepared by the Workers' and Soldiers' Council in Riga.

11. Latvia, 1 rubli, 1920

A set of four stamps was issued in December 1919 to celebrate the liberation of Courland. Between November 1920 and February 1921 these stamps were re-issued with a premium surcharged in aid of charity. On this, and other surcharged stamps of this period, the surcharge represents the actual selling price of the stamp, while the basic value (35k.) represents the postal value. Thus the amount given to charity was the difference between the two figures.

12. Latvia, 40 santimi, 1939

This stamp, showing the war museum and powder magazine in Riga, was one of a set of eight released to mark the fifth anniversary of the dictatorship established by President Ulmanis. Like many other countries in Europe at the time Latvia adopted a fascist regime in face of the menace from Soviet Russia. The series, printed in photogravure at the State Printing Works, Riga, featured castles, public buildings and historic landmarks of Latvia.

13. Latvia, 35 santimi, 1940

Latvia was forced to sign a defence treaty with the Soviet Union in October 1939, leading to the establishment of Russian bases in the country in June 1940. The following month Latvia elected a strongly communist government which voted almost immediately for inclusion in the Soviet Union. The last distinctive stamps of Latvia appeared in July 1940 showing the hammer and sickle emblem of the Latvian Soviet Socialist Republic.

14. Latvia, 30 kopeks, 1941

As part of Operation Barbarossa Latvia was invaded by the Germans in June 1941. The following month stocks of contemporary Russian stamps then in use were seized by the Nazis and overprinted with the date of the German occupation. Subsequently the German 'Ostland' series was introduced until the Russian reoccupation of Latvia in 1944. Since then ordinary Russian stamps have been used.

15. Lithuania, 40 skatiku, 1919

The first Lithuanian stamps were typeset at Kovno

(Kaunas) in December 1918, but were followed by a series in February 1919 showing the national arms. The stamps were designed by T. Daugirdas and K. Simonis and were lithographed by S. S. Hermann of Berlin. Philatelists distinguish four different Berlin printings of these stamps, varying in perforation, paper, watermark, colour and minute varieties of the designs. The second and subsequent Berlin printings were produced at the State Printing Works.

16. Lithuania, 4 auksinai, 1922

Inflation overtook the new republic in 1922 and led to a spate of provisional surcharges in auksinai (1 auksina = 100 skatiku). This stamp is known with or without bars obliterating the original value, and with double or inverted surcharge.

17. Lithuania, 15 centu, 1928

In 1922 the currency was reformed and a new system based on the litas of 100 centu was introduced. This stamp is one of a series of seven issued in February 1928 to celebrate the tenth anniversary of independence and portrays President Antonas Smetona. The stamps were designed by Bučas and Binderis and lithographed at the Government Printing Works, Kaunas.

18. Lithuania, 5 centai, 1930

In February 1930 Lithuania released a long series of stamps to mark the quincentenary of the death of Grand Duke Vytautas, whose reign marked the golden age of Lithuanian independence. The Grand Duke was portrayed on the fourteen ordinary stamps but modern heroes and patriots were portrayed on the seven airmail denominations. The series was designed by A. Varnas and lithographed at the Government Printing Works. The somewhat crude two or three colour lithography was a hallmark of Lithuanian stamps in the 1920s. Note the variable spellings 'centu' or 'centai' used on these stamps.

19. Lithuania, 40 centu, 1934

In 1933 the Lithuanian aviators Captain Darius and Stanislas Girenas attempted to fly from New York to Kaunas, but were lost without trace somewhere over the Atlantic. In May 1934 a set of six stamps, recess-printed by Bradbury Wilkinson, was issued in mourning. Among the other designs was a 1*l*. stamp showing the female allegory of Flight mourning over the wreckage of the aircraft – the first time that an air crash was depicted on a stamp. Bradbury Wilkinson went on to engrave stamps marking the president's 60th birthday (1934) and the 20th anniversary of independence (1939), which contrast with the crudely lithographed local products.

20. Lithuania, 60 centu, 1939

Lithuania participated in the rape of Poland, receiving Vilna (Vilnius, Wilno) and the surrounding district as her share of the loot. The stamps celebrating the 20th anniversary of independence were overprinted in November 1939 to mark the annexation of Vilna. Ironically, the last stamps issued by an independent Lithuania consisted of a set of four depicting views of Vilna, issued in May 1940 to celebrate the recovery of that district.

21. Lithuania, 50 centu, 1940

A pro-Russian government was formed in June 1940 and shortly afterward asked for admittance to the Soviet Union. The last stamps of Lithuania appeared in August 1940 and consisted of various issues overprinted ltsr (Lithuanian Soviet Socialist Republic) with the date 1940 VII 21 marking its incorporation in the Soviet Union. Ordinary Russian stamps were introduced soon afterward.

22. Lithuania, 5 kopeks, 1941

Following the Nazi invasion of Russia in 1941 stocks of Russian stamps seized in Lithuania were overprinted by the Spindulys Co. of Kaunas to mark the liberation by Nazi troops. Subsequently similar stamps were overprinted 'Vilnius' to mark the liberation of that district. These stamps were superseded in November 1941 by the Ostland series. Ordinary Russian stamps were re-introduced in 1944.

23. Dorpat, 40 pfennigs, 1918

German troops occupied Estonia in the spring of 1918 and drove out the Bolsheviks. Captured stamps of the former Tsarist regime were issued at Dorpat with values surcharged in German currency.

24. German Eastern Command, 20 pfennigs, 1916

Contemporary German stamps, of the Germania series, were issued in 1916–18 with the overprint 'Postgebiet Ob. Ost' to denote their use in the postal district of the Eastern Command, covering Estonia, Latvia and Lithuania.

25. Ostland, 40 pfennigs, 1941

The areas under German occupation were divided for administrative purposes into Ostland (the Baltic states, White Russia and areas to the east) and Ukraine (comprising the Ukraine proper, the Crimea and districts as far east as the Caucasus Mountains). All denominations of the Hitler Head series, from 1 to 80*pf.*, were thus overprinted.

26. Wenden, 2 kopeks, 1893

The Wenden district in Livonia, latterly part of Latvia, was governed by the Military Knights of the Sword, a subsidiary of the Teutonic Order, and issued their own stamps from 1863 till 1903 when they were suppressed by the Tsarist government. The stamps were all of 2 or 4*k*. denomination and had no more than local validity. All but the last issue were inscribed in German, the last being in Russian, reflecting the multi-national nature of Livonia at that period.

27. Memel, 400 markiu, 1923

On 11 January 1923 Lithuanian troops seized the port of Memel and expelled the French garrison which had occupied it since 1918 pending a plebiscite to determine its future. Lithuanian stamps overprinted Klaipeda (Memel) were introduced in February 1923. In May 1924 the town was formally annexed to Lithuania as an autonomous region, but used ordinary Lithuanian stamps. German troops invaded Memel in March 1939 but since 1945 it has formed part of the Soviet Union.

PLATE 4

The Benelux Countries

The kingdoms of Belgium and the Netherlands and the Grand Duchy of Luxembourg have long had close economic and political ties. From 1815 till 1839 Belgium and the Netherlands formed a single kingdom, while the King of Holland was also Grand Duke of Luxembourg. Since World War II the Benelux countries have formed the nucleus of the European Common Market. Stamps were issued first in Belgium (1849) and in the Netherlands and Luxembourg in 1852.

1. Netherlands, 10 cents, 1852

A pair of stamps showing the curious semicircular date-stamp of Rotterdam. The first Dutch stamps consisted of 5, 10 and 15c. values and were engraved

141

PLATE 4 THE BENELUX COUNTRIES

by J. W. Kaiser with a profile of King Willem III as their subject. The inscription POSTZEGEL (postage stamp) was regarded as sufficient identification and it was not until 1867 that the country's name appeared on its stamps. The earliest stamps were recess-printed at the Mint, Utrecht. The majority of stamps, from 1866 onward, have been printed by Johann Enschedé en Zonen, Haarlem.

2. Luxembourg, 25 centimes, 1891, official stamp

Following the death of Grand Duke William (Willem III of the Netherlands) in 1890 the succession passed to Grand Duke Adolf of Nassau, Salic Law forbidding Queen Wilhelmina from succeeding to the throne of Luxembourg. Stamps portraying Grand Duke Adolf appeared in 1891. Those overprinted S.P. (*Service Publique*) were intended for use on government correspondence.

3. German occupation of Belgium, 2 pfennigs, 1916

German stamps, of the 1902 Germania series, were introduced in the occupied districts of Belgium in October 1914. At first the surcharge in Belgian currency was rendered in full, but from 1916 to 1918 the value was abbreviated. The 'Belgien' overprints were the first of several sets produced by the German authorities for use in the territories administered by them during World War I.

4. Belgian occupation of Germany, 1 centime, 1919

Contemporary Belgian stamps, overprinted in French and Flemish, were provided for the use of Belgian forces serving in the Rhineland. Similar stamps overprinted with the names of Eupen and Malmedy were used in 1920, pending their transfer from Germany to Belgium.

5. Belgium, 1 centime, 1919

One of a series known to philatelists as the 'Tin Helmets', from the portrait of King Albert in military uniform and steel helmet. The stamps were designed by Henri Cheffer and recess-printed by Enschedé. Though quasi-commemorative (the dates refer to the First World War) this series remained in use until 1922.

6. Belgium, 10 centimes, 1896

One of a pair of stamps released as advance publicity for the Brussels Exhibition of 1897. These stamps, among the earliest commemoratives in the world, were also the first to exhibit the influence of Art Nouveau. They were provided with a small perforated label signifying in French and Flemish 'Do not deliver on Sunday'. To avoid offending people with strong Sabbatarian principles Belgian stamps, from 1893 till 1914, had these labels for optional use. They are known to collectors as bandalettes or dominical labels.

7. Belgium, 5 + 5 francs, 1938

A notorious feature of Belgian stamps in the period between the two world wars was the prevalence of sets bearing premiums for the restoration of various churches. This 5 francs stamp of 1938 was part of a series of seven stamps and a miniature sheet with a surcharge in aid of the completion of the Koekelberg Basilica of the Sacred Heart. This stamp, featuring an interior view of the proposed basilica, was designed and engraved by J. Debast and recess-printed by the Belgian State Printing Works at Malines.

8. Belgium, 35 + 5 centimes, 1935

Following the death of Queen Astrid in a motoring accident a 70 + 5c. black stamp was issued in mourning. Subsequently the same design, from a photograph of the queen by Marchand, was used for a series of stamps in aid of Anti-Tuberculosis funds. The black border was a feature of mourning stamps issued by several countries in the 1930s, notably Germany (1934) for President Hindenburg and Yugoslavia (1934) for King Alexander.

9. Belgium, 1 franc + 50 centimes, 1962

A series of six stamps was released with premiums in aid of handicapped children and featured various aspects of the work being done to rehabilitate them. This stamp shows a deaf-mute girl who is also partially blind, learning to spell by means of brightly coloured bricks.

10. Belgium, 3 + 1.50 francs, 1964

One of a set of three stamps issued on 1 August 1964 to commemorate the 50th anniversary of the German invasion at the outset of World War I. The stamp, in multicolour photogravure, features a trumpeter of the Grenadiers and drummers of the Infantry and Carabiniers in the uniforms of 1914.

11. Belgium, 1 franc, 1964

One of three stamps released in January 1964 in honour of World Leprosy Day, it portrays Dr G. Armauer Hansen and his laboratory. Other stamps portrayed Father Damien and a leper hospital and publicized the work of FOPERDA (*Fondation Père Damien*). The stamps were also issued in a miniature sheet with a 6fr. premium.

12. Belgium, 9 + 4 francs, 1969

One of a series of four stamps, with premiums in aid of the Belgian Solidarity Fund, featuring musicians in stained glass windows. This stamp features a bag-piper, from a window in the Royal Museum of Art and History, Brussels.

13. Belgium, 3.50 francs, 1969

This stamp, marking the golden jubilee of the National Credit Society, is typical of the work of the modern designer Jean van Noten, combining the emblem of the society and a coin used as a cog-wheel to symbolize the role of money in industry. The background colour and the silver of the coin are photogravure, while the lettering and design are recess-printed, an example of the way in which these techniques are now combined in stamp production.

14. United Nations Post Office, 20 francs, 1958

In connection with the Brussels Exhibition a set of ten ordinary and six airmail stamps was produced for use at the United Nations pavilion. The stamps were inscribed in French, Flemish and English and featured the emblems and symbolism of the various UN agencies. Since these stamps were not valid for postage except at the United Nations Post Office at the Exhibition they have a status similar to those UN stamps issued in New York, Geneva and elsewhere at various times. A similar practice was followed at the Expo '67 in Montreal (see Plate 89).

15. Luxembourg, 1 franc, 1936

The eleventh congress of FIP (Fédération Internationale de Philatelie) had its venue in Luxembourg-Ville in August 1936 and, for the first time, the host country issued a special series of stamps to mark the occasion. The six stamps, printed in photogravure by Courvoisier of Switzerland, featured the Town Hall.

16. Luxembourg, 2 francs + 50 centimes, 1940

In September 1939 a 2f. stamp was produced to publicize the hot springs at Mondorf-les-Bains. The following March it was reissued in a new colour, with a 50c. premium in aid of the anti-tuberculosis fund. This stamp, a fine example of the Art Moderne predilection for fountains and flowing hair, was the last stamp issued by an independent Luxembourg. The basic stamp was printed in photogravure, but the premium and the Cross of Lorraine were added typographically by P. Linden.

17. Luxembourg, 3 pfennigs, 1940

Luxembourg was overrun by German troops in May 1940 and German stamps suitably overprinted were introduced in October of that year. Luxembourg stamps surcharged in German currency were issued in December 1940. From January 1942 to November 1944 ordinary German stamps, without overprint, were used in Luxembourg.

18. Luxembourg, 1.50 francs, 1948

The first postwar definitive series, issued when the grand-duchy was liberated in November 1944, was recess-printed by the American Bank Note Co. and bore a profile of the Grand Duchess Charlotte. It was replaced in 1948 by a series recess-printed by Courvoisier with a more mature profile of the Grand Duchess. The series was designed and engraved by Karl Bickel in denominations from 5c. to 8f. Various denominations were added to the set between 1948 and 1958.

19. Netherlands, 8 + 6 cents, 1965

Since 1924 the Netherlands has issued stamps with a premium in aid of child welfare. The series of 1965 reproduced prize-winning drawings and paintings from a children's art competition.

20. Netherlands, 30 cents, 1944

One of a series portraying Queen Wilhelmina, engraved by E. Dawson and recess-printed by Bradbury, Wilkinson of New Malden, England – one of the few stamps of the Netherlands not produced by Enschedé. These stamps were used on board Dutch warships serving with the Allies during World War II. After the liberation of the Netherlands these stamps were put on sale there.

21. Netherlands, 4 cents, 1951

Special stamps for use at the headquarters of the Permanent Court of International Justice have been issued since 1934. They are not available to the public in unused condition. The stamps feature the Peace Palace at The Hague.

22. Luxembourg, 8.50 francs, 1961

One of a series of four stamps issued to publicize the campaign for animal protection. The stamps featured a Great Spotted Woodpecker, a cat, a horse and a dachshund, and were an early example of multicolour photogravure which is now a speciality of Courvoisier.

23. Luxembourg, 1 franc, 1963

One of a series of stamps released to celebrate the millenium of Luxembourg, it shows the Three Towers Gate dating from the eleventh century. Six stamps were recess-printed by Enschedé and the others were printed in photogravure by Courvoisier, each denomination representing a different century in Luxembourg's history. The complete set could only be bought at face value plus 25f. entrance fee to the Melusina International Stamp Exhibition and was restricted to one set per ticket.

24. Netherlands, 25 cents, 1969

A good example of the poster approach to stamp design in recent years, it marks the 15th anniversary of the Statute for the Kingdom which revised the constitutional relationship of the overseas territories with the mother country.

25. Netherlands, 25 + 10 cents, 1966

Sommerzegels (summer stamps) have been released annually by the Netherlands since 1935 with premiums in aid of various cultural and social welfare funds, often with a unified theme or commemorating some outstanding event. The 1966 series commemorated the Friesian poet Gysbert Japicx and marked the bicentenary of the Netherlands Literary Society. This stamp features the initial D and part

PLATE 4 THE BENELUX COUNTRIES · PLATE 5 BULGARIA

of the illuminated manuscript of the romance *Ferguut*, illustrating how well the restricted confines of the postage stamp can promote other forms of minuscule art.

26. Netherlands, 20 + 10 cents, 1970
One of a set of five stamps in the annual Cultural, Health and Social Welfare Funds issue, featuring overlapping scales. The stamps, printed in combined recess and lithography, were the first in the world to be designed by a computer.

PLATE 5
Bulgaria

---

1. 5 centimes, 1879
The principality of Bulgaria, established by the Congress of Berlin, was nominally still under Turkish suzerainty, though politically and economically dependent on Russia and France. The French influence is reflected in the currency expressed on the first lion definitive stamps, though the stamps themselves were typographed at the Russian Government Printing Office, St Petersburg. French currency was replaced in 1881 by the leva of 100 stotinki, in use to this day.

2. 15 stotinki, 1902
One of a set of three stamps released to commemorate the 25th anniversary of the Battle of Shipka Pass in which Russian troops and Bulgarian volunteers held up the main Turkish advance during the Russo-Turkish War of 1877. The stamp depicts a spirited, if somewhat naïve, impression of the defence of the pass. The stamps were lithographed in Budapest.

3. 15 stotinki, 1901
One of a series typographed for Bulgaria at the Cartographic Bureau of the Russian War Department between 1901 and 1905, it portrays Prince Ferdinand of Saxe-Coburg, who assumed the title of Tsar (emperor) in 1909.

4. 10 stotinki, 1915
The basic stamp, 25s., was part of a series designed in Bulgaria, by A. Mitov and G. Estavien, engraved by Bradbury, Wilkinson & Co. of England and recess-printed at the Government Printing Works in Rome – an early and unusual example of international co-operation. The stamps, portraying Tsar Ferdinand in various uniforms, or featuring famous historic landmarks, formed part of the campaign to promote the image of the new Bulgarian 'empire' in the period of the Balkan wars.

5. 10 stotinki, 1921
One of a series of five stamps prepared for use in 1915 to commemorate the liberation of Macedonia. The 10s. portrays Ferdinand over a map of the Dobrudja and Macedonia, conquered by Bulgaria from Rumania and Serbia. The stamps were not released till June 1921. Owing to protests from Yugoslavia (to whom Macedonia was assigned after World War I) the stamps were on sale for only three days and were then withdrawn. The stamps were typographed in Berlin, reflecting the alliance of Bulgaria with Germany in the war.

6. 3 stotinki, 1918
One of four stamps celebrating the 30th anniversary of the accession of Tsar Ferdinand. Within three months, however, his country had sued for peace and Ferdinand had been forced to abdicate at the behest of the Allies. The stamps were typographed in Vienna.

7. 30 stotinki, 1921
One of the nine stamps which paid tribute to the memory of James D. Bourchier, the Balkan correspondent of *The Times*, whose despatches during the Russo-Turkish War of 1877 and reports on Turkish atrocities helped to mould British public opinion in favour of the Bulgars. Other stamps in this series, recess-printed by Bradbury Wilkinson, show Bourchier in Bulgarian costume and his grave at Rila Monastery.

8. 50 stotinki, 1920
Part of a set released in honour of the 70th birthday of Bulgaria's national poet, Ivan Vazov, this stamp depicts the bear-fighter, a character from his poem *Under the Yoke*. The stamps were produced at the State Printing Works, Sofia and were printed by photogravure. Bulgaria thus became the third country after Bavaria and Czechoslovakia to adopt this method of printing.

9. 15 stotinki, 1917
One of a set of seven stamps released between 1917 and 1919 to mark the liberation of Macedonia. The stamp shows a Bulgarian peasant leading a bullock cart through a blizzard – hardly a heroic subject.

10. 1 lev, 1930
Between 1925 and 1933 Bulgaria issued 1*l*. stamps for use in addition to normal postage to insure delivery on Sundays and public holidays. The money raised from the sale of these stamps was used to maintain a sanatorium for the benefit of postal employees.

11. 15 stotinki, 1929
K. Miladinov, one of the patriots of the war of independence, was featured on this stamp, in a series which partly commemorated the 50th anniversary of liberation and the millennary of Tsar Simeon. The coarse lines of the portrait, against an unshaded background, were characteristic features of Bulgarian typographed stamps in the inter-war period.

12. 15 stotinki, 1938
One of a lengthy series designed to promote Bulgarian agricultural exports, this stamp features a sunflower. Other stamps depicted tobacco, roses, grapes, wheat and chickens. For the first time the name of the country was rendered in French, as well as in the Cyrillic alphabet.

13. 10 stotinki, 1941
Agricultural produce formed the subject of the wartime definitive series. Apart from viticulture, depicted on this stamp, bee-keeping, ploughing and shepherding were featured on other denominations.

14. 150 stotinki, 1945
One of a set of four stamps publicizing the Liberty Loan, at the end of World War II. At this stage Bulgaria was still a kingdom, though occupied by the Red Army. Shortage of machinery and essential materials explains the lack of perforations in this series.

15. 12 stotinki, 1960
Bulgaria was one of the countries which issued stamps in honour of the Rome Olympic Games, with subjects such as wrestling, boxing, football and gymnastics. The Cyrillic inscription on this stamp reads 'N R Bulgariya' (People's Republic of Bulgaria), found on most of the stamps issued between 1947 and 1967.

16. 13 stotinki, 1965
One of a pair of stamps celebrating the 20th anniversary of the 'Victory of 9 May 1945' – the referendum which established the republic. The stylized globes superimposed on a dove typify the trend in modern Bulgarian stamps towards symbolism. Note also the use of the Roman alphabet for the name of the country, though Cyrillic is still used exclusively for the other inscriptions.

17. 80 stotinki, 1969
The earlier issues of the People's Republic of Bulgaria were predominantly political in concept, but in common with other countries of the Communist bloc Bulgaria has been exploring themes more likely to appeal to philatelists all over the world. The rich monastic heritage of Bulgaria, which preserved its cultural independence during the centuries of Turkish rule, is expressed on many modern stamps such as this one which forms part of a series of nine featuring frescoes from Rila. These stamps also commemorated the International Philatelic Exhibition held in Sofia in 1969.

18. Eastern Roumelia, 10 paras, 1880
The Congress of Berlin decided that Eastern Roumelia should remain separate from the principality of Bulgaria, and form a semi-autonomous province in the Turkish Empire. Turkish stamps overprinted R.O. and/or ROUMELIE ORIENTALE were introduced in 1880, pending the production of distinctive stamps for the province.

19. Eastern Roumelia, 20 paras, 1881
The stamps of the province illustrate graphically the anomalous position of this Slav, Christian district nominally under Turkish control. The inscription 'Roumelie Orientale' was rendered in four different languages and scripts – Turkish, French, Greek and Russian, while the crescent and the inscription 'Emp. Ottoman' (Ottoman Empire) emphasized its political subservience. The stamps were typographed in Constantinople.

20. South Bulgaria, 5 paras, 1885
An uprising in Philippopolis (Plovdiv), the capital of Eastern Roumelia, in 1885 led to the unification of the province with Bulgaria. Stocks of stamps were overprinted with the Bulgarian lion and the Cyrillic inscription 'Yuzhna Bulgariya' (South Bulgaria) during the last week of September 1885. Ordinary Bulgarian stamps were introduced in the province on 1 October 1885.

21. Dobrudja, 1 stotinka, 1916
Four denominations of the Bulgarian definitive series of 1915 were overprinted in Cyrillic 'Pochta vi Romaniya' (Posts in Rumania) for use in the Dobrudja district occupied by Bulgarian troops from 1916 till 1918. Many errors of lettering are known in the overprint, as well as double and inverted overprints.

22. Western Thrace, 5 stotinki, 1919
The district of Thrace, on the northern coast of the Aegean, was occupied by Bulgaria at the end of the Balkan Wars but came under Allied control after World War I and eventually passed to Greece. Bulgarian stamps overprinted THRACE INTER-ALLIEE or THRACE OCCIDENTALE were used in 1919–20. The basic stamp was one of a series released in October 1919 to mark the first anniversary of the accession of Tsar Boris III. For stamps issued in Thrace under Greek administration see Plate 15.

143

PLATE 6 CZECHOSLOVAKIA

PLATE 6
Czechoslovakia

1. 20 haleru, 1919

The first stamps of Czechoslovakia were issued in October by the Revolutionary Committee in Prague and were used on mail carried by the Boy Scouts. Professor Alfons Mucha, one of the greatest exponents of Art Nouveau, designed the definitive series of 1918–19 depicting the Hradcany in Prague. In the first printings the sun was depicted behind the castle, but as this position indicates a sunset it was felt to be a bad omen for the new republic, and was therefore omitted from the redrawn designs of 1919. Both versions may be found imperforate, or perforated in various gauges.

2. 120 haleru, 1919

The first anniversary of independence was celebrated in October 1919 with a set of stamps using two designs. The low values depicted the Lion of Bohemia and were typographed from a design by J. Obrovsky. The three higher denominations, 75 to 120h., showed two women embracing, symbolizing the return to the motherland of the Czech legions from Siberia. These stamps, also designed by Obrovsky, were printed in photogravure at the Cartographic Section of the Czechoslovak Army. Czechoslovakia was the first country after Bavaria to use this process for postage stamps.

3. 15 heller, 1919

A vast number of Austrian stamps seized in Bohemia at the time of independence were overprinted 'Posta Ceskoslovenska 1919' and released in December 1919 at a premium of 50 per cent over face value for the benefit of various charities. Austrian definitives, war charities, newspaper, express letter and postage due stamps were treated in this manner and used for ordinary postal purposes regardless of their original function.

4. 2 filler, 1919

In the same way the Hungarian stamps impounded in Slovakia and Ruthenia were overprinted and used to raise funds for charity. Altogether about 120 different stamps were issued in December 1919, the postage due stamps of the 1908–13 series being the rarest.

5. 1.20 koruny, 1927

A definitive series featuring castles and scenery of Czechoslovakia was introduced in 1926–27. The stamps ranged from 20h. to 5k. and were recess-printed by the Czechoslovak Graphic Union, Prague. Paper with a linden leaf watermark was used at first, but later printings (1927–31) were on unwatermarked paper.

6. 2 koruny, 1934

The 20th anniversary of the Czech Legions was marked by a set of four stamps issued in August 1934. The 50h. stamp showed the consecration of the colours at Kiev, while the 1k. depicted the French battalion enlisting at Bayonne. The 2k. featured the standard-bearer of the Russian Legion and the 3k. showed French, Russian and Serbian legionaries side by side.

7. 50 haleru, 1938

Individual battles and campaigns of the Czech Legions were commemorated in several sets from 1935 to 1938, coinciding with the 20th anniversaries of Arras (1935) and Zborov on the Russian front (1937). J. Vlaček designed a set of three 50h. stamps issued in March and May 1938 to mark the anniversaries of the battle of Bachmac (Russian front),

Vouziers (Western front) and Doss Alto (Piave campaign) in which Czech Legions took part. An interesting feature of this series was the coupons printed *se-tenant* throughout the sheet. The coupons were embellished with symbols of each campaign and the battle honours of the Legions. Coupons of this sort have appeared on various Czechoslovak stamps in recent years.

8. 2 korun, 1938

The last stamps issued by the independent republic of Czechoslovakia appeared in December 1938 and ironically celebrated the twentieth anniversary of independence. Max Svabinsky designed and engraved 2 and 3k. stamps depicting a female allegory of peace. Following the seizure of the Sudetenland in September 1938 Germany insisted that the rest of Czechoslovakia be broken up into its components, and this was the prelude to the Nazi invasion in March 1939.

9. 50 haleru, 1937

In March 1937 Czechoslovakia instituted a personal delivery service and issued two triangular stamps in connection with it. The 50h. in blue, with the letter 'v' in each corner prepaid a special fee which insured personal delivery to the addressee and was affixed to the letter by the sender. The 50h. in carmine, with 'D' in each corner represented a special fee payable by an addressee who required all his mail to be delivered to him personally. It was affixed to correspondence by the Post Office delivering the mail.

10. 10 haleru, 1945

At the liberation of Czechoslovakia in 1945 sets of stamps were prepared in three different places and released more or less simultaneously. A series emphasizing the Soviet rôle in the liberation of the country was lithographed at Bratislava and released at Kosice in March 1945. A photogravure series depicting linden leaves was prepared in Prague and put on sale in May 1945. The third series, released in August, was designed and engraved by Vlaček and recess-printed by De La Rue in London. The sixteen denominations from 5h. to 10k. portrayed Czechoslovak war heroes.

11. 50 haleru, 1945

Subsequent definitive issues were produced at Bratislava and in Moscow and showed the coats of arms of Bohemia and Slovakia, and the portrait of Dr Masaryk respectively. The seventh series to appear in the course of one year was designed by Jindra Schmidt and issued in October 1945. The series portrayed Dr Masaryk, General Stefanik and President Benes and various denominations were added to the series up to April 1947.

12. 30 haleru, 1954

After the Communist takeover in 1948 the stamps of Czechoslovakia became progressively more Communist in character, with portraits of Soviet leaders and designs emphasizing the close ties between Czechoslovakia and Russia. Stalin's birthday and the anniversary of Lenin's death provided regular opportunities for stamps of this type. This stamp, designed by Karel Svolinsky and engraved by Jindra Schmidt, was issued in January 1954 to mark the 30th anniversary of Lenin's death. It reproduces the portrait by J. Lauda. Since World War II the Czechs have developed the art of fine stamp engraving and a marked preference for recess-printing.

13. 2 korun, 1964

From the mid-fifties onward the political aspects of Czech stamps became less prominent, and greater attention was paid to producing attractive pictorials devoted to themes calculated to win the interest of

collectors all over the world. Sport, space exploration and the fauna and flora of Czechoslovakia were the most popular subjects. This stamp was one of three issued in January 1964 to mark the Winter Olympic Games at Innsbruck. While most countries were content to reproduce actual photographs, by the photogravure process, Czechoslovakia, which had pioneered photogravure, turned her back on it and concentrated on miniature works of art in which both designer and engraver were allowed to impose their personality on the interpretation of the subject.

14. 1 koruna, 1968

The infamous Munich Agreement of 1938, by which Britain and France consented to the Nazi rape of Czechoslovakia, was commemorated by a set of three stamps issued in September 1968. The stamps reproduced pictures painted by children who had been incarcerated in Terezin concentration camp. This design shows The Window, painted by ten-year-old Jiri Schlessinger.

15. 60 haleru, 1972

In 1942 the Nazis massacred the inhabitants of Lidice and razed the village to the ground, as a reprisal for the murder of Reinhard Heydrich, *Reichsprotektor* of Bohemia. The fifth anniversary of this atrocity was commemorated in 1947 by three stamps symbolizing grief and the flame of remembrance. Pairs of stamps marked the tenth, fifteenth and twentieth anniversaries, while a single stamp appeared in 1967 for the 25th anniversary. A set of three stamps released in 1972 marked the thirtieth anniversaries of the destruction of Lidice and Lezaky and the establishment of Terezin concentration camp. Stamps in memory of Lidice have also been issued by East Germany.

16. Czech Legion in Siberia, 25 kopeks, 1919

A series of stamps, in denominations of 25 and 50k. and 1 rouble, were lithographed by Makusin and Poschin of Irkutsk and issued in 1919. Subsequent printings were made at Prague and may be distinguished by their perforations and gum. The stamps featured the church in Irkutsk (25k.), the Czech armoured train Orlik (50k.) and a sentry (1r.). An undenominated 25k. stamp, featuring the Lion of Bohemia, was released later in 1919 and re-issued in 1920 surcharged from 2k. to 1r. These stamps were used by Czech troops fighting the Bolsheviks in Siberia.

17. Sudetenland, 2 haleru, 1938

Following a propaganda campaign waged against the Czechoslovak government alleging maltreatment of the Sudeten German minority Nazi Germany demanded that the Sudetenland should be handed over to the Third Reich. Following the Munich Agreement of 21 September 1938, local Nazis seized control pending the transfer of the district to Germany on 1 October. Czechoslovak stamps overprinted 'Wir sind frei' (we are free) or surcharged with new values were issued at Asch, Karlsbad, Konstantinsbad, Niklasdorf, Reichenberg-Maffersdorf, Mährisch-Ostrau and Rumburg between 21 September and 17 October when ordinary German stamps were introduced.

18. Carpatho-Ukraine, 3 koruny, 1939

In January 1939 Czechoslovakia was divided into its components and distinctive stamps were issued in Slovakia. Ordinary stamps continued to be used in other parts of the country but were gradually replaced by similar issues with the name hyphenated 'Cesko-slovensko' to indicate the partition. Ruthenia or Carpatho-Ukraine was granted autonomy and a 3k. stamp, inscribed in Cyrillic, was released on 15 March to celebrate the inauguration of the local parliament at Jasina. The stamp was put on

PLATE 6 CZECHOSLOVAKIA · PLATE 7 DENMARK, ICELAND, GREENLAND

sale in Prague and Chust, but was withdrawn the following day when Prague was occupied by the Germans. Subsequently parts of Carpatho-Ukraine were given to Hungary and others to Poland, and now this area forms part of Russia. It is remembered solely by this stamp.

19. Slovakia, 300 haleru, 1939
The first distinctive stamp of Slovakia consisted of the 10 koruny definitive, depicting the Slovak capital, Bratislava, overprinted to mark the inauguration of the Slovak parliament in January 1939. Subsequently Czech stamps were overprinted 'Slovensky Stat' (Slovak State), pending the issue of distinctive stamps.

20. Slovakia, 80 haleru, 1943
Stamps inscribed 'Slovensko' were used in Slovakia from 1939 till 1945, the country being nominally independent though under German tutelage. With the exception of the overprinted Czechoslovak stamps of 1939 all stamps of Slovakia were printed in photogravure at the Slovenska Grafia printing works in Bratislava. This stamp was one of a set of four issued in October 1943 to raise money for cultural activities. It had a postal value of 80h, but a fund-raising premium of 2k. – excessive by current standards but apparently normal in Germany and the Nazi satellites in World War II.

21. Slovakia, 80 haleru, 1943
A set of four stamps was issued in September 1943 to mark the opening of the Strazke-Pressov railway. The stamps featured Pressov Church (70h.), a locomotive (80h.), a railway tunnel (1.30k.) and a railway viaduct (2k.), with a map of the route inset.

22. Bohemia and Moravia, 50 haleru, 1939
The German protectorate of Bohemia and Moravia was established on 15 March 1939, and Czechoslovak stamps overprinted with the names of the protectorate in German and Czech were released in July of that year. Subsequently similar stamps, with the inscriptions re-engraved, were issued between August 1939 and November 1940.

23. Bohemia and Moravia, 2 korun, 1939
A. Erhardt designed a series of postage due stamps, typographed in Prague and issued in 1939–40. The haleru denominations were printed in lake, while the koruny values were printed in blue.

24. Bohemia and Moravia, 10 haleru, 1942
The rump of Czechoslovakia was absorbed into the Third Reich as the protectorate of Bohemia and Moravia (*Böhmen und Mähren*). At first Czechoslovak stamps suitably overprinted in Czech and German were used, and then similar landscape designs with the new inscription were introduced in 1939–40. The growing Nazification of the protectorate is reflected in the release of a series in 1942 portraying Adolf Hitler. The haleru denominations were printed in photogravure while the koruny values were recess-printed in various formats. A 4.20k. denomination added in 1944 was inscribed 'Grossdeutsches Reich'.

25. Bohemia and Moravia, 2.50 koruny, 1943
The commemorative issues of the protectorate emphasized the German connection and included sets in honour of Mozart and Wagner. Three stamps were issued in May 1943 to mark the 130th anniversary of the birth of Wagner. His portrait appeared on the 1.20k. stamp while the other denominations featured scenes from *The Mastersingers* and *Siegfried* and gave the dates of their first performances in Prague. The stamps were designed by A. Langenberg and A. Erhardt and printed in photogravure.

PLATE 7
Denmark, Iceland and Greenland

1. Denmark, 4 rigsbankskilling, 1851
Denmark adopted adhesive stamps in April 1851 when this stamp was issued. A *2rbs*. value, for Copenhagen local letters, was issued later the same month. The stamps were engraved on steel by M. W. Ferslew and typographed by H. H. Thiele of Copenhagen. It is thought that the first printing of these stamps may have been produced by Ferslew himself, since the colour of the background wavy lines varies considerably. The majority of Danish stamps (till 1933) and Icelandic stamps (till 1925) were printed by Thiele.

2. Denmark, 8 øre, 1921
A definitive series portraying King Christian X was introduced in 1913. The framework was designed by G. Heilmann and the dies engraved by Christian Danielsen. The øre values were typographed and the kroner denominations were recess-printed at the Imperial Printing Works in Berlin. New values and colours were introduced between 1918 and 1921. Temporary surcharges of 8ø. and 20ø. were made in 1921 and 1926 respectively.

3. Denmark, 20 øre, 1920
Denmark's first commemorative series was issued in October 1920 to celebrate the recovery of Northern Schleswig from Germany. V. Andersen designed the three stamps featuring Kronborg Castle at Elsinore (10ø.), Sönderborg Castle (20ø.) and Roskilde Cathedral (40ø.). The 10 and 40ø. stamps were re-issued the following year in new colours, while the 10 and 20ø. stamps were subsequently overprinted and surcharged in aid of Red Cross funds.

4. Denmark, 5 øre, 1942
The numeral design was adopted for the Danish low value definitives in 1905 when stamps were typographed in denominations of 1 to 15ø. Other denominations were typographed between 1912 and 1930, and then recess-printed versions were produced at various times from 1933 to the present day. Since 1919 various stamps of this and other definitive designs have been overprinted 'Postfaerge' (postal ferry) to prepay the postage on parcels conveyed on the ferry service between Esbjerg and Fanö and between Lögstör and Aggersund. This particular stamp first appeared in July 1942. A similar stamp but with a sans-serif overprint was released in November 1967.

5. Denmark, 60 øre, 1957
The majority of Danish commemorative issues since World War II have consisted of pairs or single stamps and have invariably been recess-printed. This stamp is one of two released in May 1957 to mark the 150th anniversary of the National Museum in Copenhagen. The 30ø. depicted the museum itself, while the 60ø. featured one of its most famous exhibits, the sun-god's chariot. The stamps were designed by Viggo Bang and engraved by B. Jacobsen.

6. Denmark, 30 + 10 øre, 1960
The 25th anniversary of Queen Ingrid's membership of the Girl Guide movement was celebrated by this stamp, issued in October 1960. The stamp, portraying the Queen in guider's uniform, was designed by Viggo Bang and engraved by B. Ekholm. The 10ø. premium went to Guide funds.

7. Denmark, 35 øre, 1964
Denmark regards 10 October each year as Stamp Day, but unlike other countries which issue stamps on that occasion no stamps have been issued by Denmark for that purpose. The 25th anniversary of Stamp Day, however, was marked by this stamp, designed by H. Philipsen and engraved by the Czech expatriate Czeslaw Slania who has been responsible for most Danish stamps since 1962. The motif of this stamp is unusual, in that it depicts the watermarks and perforations of previous Danish stamps, as well as the varieties found in the framework of the definitive series of 1870–1901.

8. Denmark, 30 øre, 1969
The bicentenary of the Danish Royal Agricultural Society was celebrated by this stamp designed by K. Westman and engraved by Slania. The stark outline and economy of line characterizes several Danish stamps issued in recent years, from the Mother and Child stamp of 1960 to the King's 70th birthday pair of 1969.

9. Denmark, 25 øre, 1966
Several issues in recent years have been dedicated to the preservation of rural Denmark, beginning with a 30ø. stamp of 1961 marking the 50th anniversary of the Society for the Preservation of Danish Natural Amenities (*Dansk Fredning*). Since then stamps have been released each year featuring different aspects of the countryside. Allied to this was the 25 øre stamp of February 1966 marking the jubilee of the Heath Society. The stamp, designed by Mads Stage, features a typical Danish moorland scene.

10. Denmark, 30 øre, 1970
The majority of Danish stamps were recess-printed in one colour, though occasionally a second colour would be introduced (e.g. the red cross on Red Cross semi-postal stamps). In 1969 two- and three-colour recess-printing was introduced and since then has been used most effectively. This stamp, released in 1970, marked the tercentenary of the Danish Naval Museum and features a ship's figurehead embellished with the elephant, the Danish royal emblem.

11. Iceland, 3 aurar, 1882
Iceland used ordinary Danish stamps from 1870 till 1873 and examples of these with the numeral obliterators of Reykjavik (236) or Seydisfjordur (237) are highly prized by specialist collectors. The first stamps were in a modified form of the crowned numeral design adopted by Denmark in 1870 and were designed and engraved by Philip Batz. The stamps were put on sale on New Year's Day 1873 in denominations from 3 to 16 skilling. A series in aur (øre) currency was released two years later. New values, including the 3a., were introduced between 1882 and 1895. The design of the 3a. stamp was redrawn in 1901, the numeral '3' being enlarged.

12. Iceland, 7 aurar, 1933
A series bearing a full-face portrait of King Christian X was introduced in February 1920 in denominations from 1a. to 5k. Various provisional surcharges and changes of colour were produced in 1921–30 and then the series was reissued between 1931 and 1937 with the portrait redrawn with finer lines. The 7a. denomination was added to the series in April 1933. This series remained in use until 1939.

13. Iceland, 50 aurar, 1938
The portrait series was augmented by pictorial designs, recess-printed by De La Rue. In 1931 a series of small-format stamps featured the Gullfoss Falls, while two stamps of 1935 featured the Dynjandi Falls and Mount Hekla. Between April 1938 and March 1945 a series featuring the Great Geyser was recess-printed by De La Rue, the vignettes being designed by O. Magnusson and the frames by

145

PLATE 7 DENMARK, ICELAND, GREENLAND · PLATE 8 NORWAY, SWEDEN, FINLAND

A. Sveinbjörnsson. The 60a. and 1k. denominations were released with new perforations in January 1947.

14. Iceland, 10 aurar, 1944
The majority of Icelandic stamps from 1930 to 1960 were produced by De La Rue. During World War II the island was garrisoned by British and American forces, though Denmark itself was under German occupation. In June 1944 Iceland became an independent republic. A set of six stamps was released on independence day and portrayed the nineteenth century Icelandic statesman Jon Sigurdsson who led the independence movement. The stamps, in denominations from 10a. to 10k., were designed by A. Sveinbjörnsson.

15. Iceland, 5 aurar, 1950
A definitive series featuring scenery and occupations was introduced in 1950, various denominations being added between March 1952 and December 1954. The 5a., 90a. and 2k. stamps depicted the harbour on the Vestmann Islands, while other stamps featured a tractor, a flock of sheep, a fishing trawler, and the Parliament Building in Reykjavik. The stamps were designed by S. Jonsson, who was responsible for many Icelandic stamps in the immediate postwar years.

16. Iceland, 50 + 25 aurar, 1949
A set of five stamps was released in June 1949 with premiums in aid of Red Cross funds. The stamps, designed by Jonsson, showed a children's hospital, a nurse and patient, a nurse arranging a patients bed, an aged couple and a ship and lifeboat, highlighting aspects of Red Cross relief work and medical care.

17. Iceland, 5 kronur, 1963
For the United Nations Freedom from Hunger campaign Iceland chose a novel design, getting away from the conventional symbolism favoured by most other countries. The 5 and 7.50k. stamps featured trawlers and a catch of herring. Multicolour photogravure by Courvoisier was adopted by Iceland in 1960 and has been used virtually exclusively ever since.

18. Iceland, 3.50 kronur, 1965
Many stamps of Iceland have alluded to the thermal and seismic activity of the island, with views of the Great Geyser and Hekla in eruption. Then, in November 1963, a submarine volcano erupted and from the lava and ashes arose the new island of Surtsey. The zoological and botanical development of Surtsey have been observed closely by scientists from all over the world. A set of three stamps was issued in June 1965, each denomination depicting a different phase in the birth and development of the island.

19. Iceland, 20 kronur, 1970
Since 1963 Iceland has issued handsome multicolour pictorials featuring the rugged grandeur of the island. Though released piecemeal these stamps have been kept on sale as definitives and are thus analogous to the 'tourist' pictorials of France, with the same motive of publicizing Iceland's charms as a tourist resort. Four stamps were added to the series in 1970 and depicted Snaefellsjökull (1k.), Laxfoss and Baula (4k.), Hattver (5k.) and Fjaroargil (20k.). The colourful designs, by Courvoisier, serve to dispel the notion of icy wastes implied in the country's name.

20. Iceland, 30 kronur, 1970
Many of the ancient Viking sagas are preserved in the monkish illuminated manuscripts of Iceland and details from these texts have lent themselves admirably to stamp reproduction. The first stamps

in this theme were monochrome and featured the Saga of Burnt Njal (1953). In sharp contrast are the multicoloured stamps of 1970 featuring details from various fourteenth century manuscripts. The 30k. illustrated here shows an illuminated initial from the Flateyjarbók.

21. Faroe Islands, 20 øre, 1940
Following the German invasion of Denmark in April 1940 British troops were landed in the Faroe Islands. During the British occupation ordinary Danish stamps were used, supplies being obtained from Denmark via neutral countries. At various times in 1940 and 1941, however, when stocks were temporarily unobtainable surcharges were made locally to make 20, 50 and 60ø. stamps. As these surcharges are quite distinctive these stamps are classed separately. It is interesting to note, however, that on several previous occasions the Faroe Islands had recourse to local makeshifts. The 4ø. stamp was bisected in January 1919 during a shortage of 2ø. stamps and, at the same time, a local surcharge of 2ø. on 5ø. stamps was made at Thorshavn.

22. Greenland, 1 øre, 1938
Prior to 1938 there was little or no necessity for stamps since mail went to Denmark free of charge. Local stamps were produced at Thule, the cryolite mines of West Greenland, and a linocut air stamp was produced in 1932 by the Universal Film Co. while shooting S.O.S. Iceberg on location. Parcel stamps were issued from 1905 to 1938 and were withdrawn when ordinary postage stamps were introduced. King Christian X in full-dress admiral's uniform was portrayed against a background of icebergs (1 to 20ø.) while a polar bear was shown on the higher values (30ø. to 1k.).

23. Greenland, 10 øre, 1950
A new series, designed by Viggo Bang and engraved by Bengt Jacobsen, was released in August 1950. The values from 1 to 30ø. portrayed King Frederick IX in naval uniform while the four higher denominations featured the Arctic Sea vessel Gustav Holm. The 30ø., introduced in 1953, changed from blue to red in 1959. A 5k. denomination was added to the set in August 1958.

24. Greenland, 60 øre, 1957
This stamp, featuring the Greenland legend of the Mother of the Sea, was released in May 1957 and was the first in an occasional series featuring the folklore of the island. All of these stamps have been designed by J. Rosing. Subsequent issues have featured the Drum dance (1961), the Boy and the Fox (1966), the Great Northern Diver and the Raven (1967), the Girl and the Eagle (1969) and similar folk-tales.

25. Greenland, 5 kroner, 1963
A definitive series in three designs was introduced between 1963 and 1968. The lowest denominations (1 to 15ø.) featured the Northern Lights, while the middle values (20 to 80ø.) portrayed King Frederick IX in an anorak, appropriate dress for the Greenland climate. The four kroner denominations (1 to 10k.) depicted a polar bear. The stamps were designed by Viggo Bang and engraved by Majvor Franzen or Czeslaw Slania.

26. Greenland, 25 kroner, 1969
New 1 and 25k. definitive stamps in pictorial designs were adopted in 1969 and featured a whale and a musk ox respectively. In 1964 a stamp marked the 150th anniversary of the scholar and missionary Samuel Kleinschmidt and in deference to the fact that he was the first to compile a Greenlandish grammar the stamp was inscribed with the Greenlandish name for the island 'Kalatdlit Nunat'. The

definitives of 1969 were the first stamps to be thus inscribed on a permanent basis, reflecting the growing awareness of Greenlandish nationalism.

PLATE 8
Norway, Sweden and Finland

1. Norway, 3 skilling, 1856
Norway's first stamp was a 4s., featuring the lion emblem, introduced in January 1855. The stamp was engraved by N. A. H. Zarbell and typographed by Wulfsberg of Christiania (Oslo). The following year, however, a series portraying King Oscar I was issued. The stamps were designed, engraved and typographed by P. A. Nyman at the Swedish Government Printing Office in Stockholm. The stamps were in denominations of 2, 3, 4 and 8s.

2. Norway, 2 skilling, 1867
C. F. Schwenzen of Christiania lithographed a new lion series between 1863 and 1866, replacing the portrait of King Oscar who had died in 1859. A similar design, but typographed by Petersen of Christiania, was adopted between 1867 and 1868. The main difference in the design lies in the inscription of the value, the latter version repeating the numeral on either side of the abbreviation 'skill'.

3. Norway, 1 øre, 1877
Norway's famous 'posthorn and numeral' stamps have now been in continuous use for over a century – a world record in philately. The design made its debut in January 1872 in a series ranging from 1 to 7s. Five years later the decimal system of øre was adopted and the series reissued in values from 1 to 60ø. The ring of the posthorn was shaded in the version typographed by Petersen, but between 1882 and 1893 a series with unshaded posthorn was typographed by Chr. Johnsen. Trondsen of Christiania typographed the stamps from 1893 to 1908 and rendered the name 'Norge' in serif capitals. Chr. Knudsen's version, between 1895 and 1900, had different inscriptions for the values. A photogravure version, from 1 to 7ø., appeared in 1937 and redrawn types were released between 1940 and 1947, and new values were added in 1950–57. Finally the design was recess-printed between 1962 and 1969.

4. Norway, 5 øre, 1914
Norway's first commemorative series appeared in May 1914 and celebrated the centenary of independence. Prior to 1814 it was a dependency of Denmark but in that year came into union with Sweden under the House of Bernadotte. The common design of the three stamps reproduced Wergeland's painting of the Constitutional Assembly. The dies were engraved by Ferdinand Schirnböck and the stamps recess-printed by the Norges Bank.

5. Norway, 65 øre, 1963
Although the posthorn design was retained for the lower denominations, the higher values of the 1962–69 series featured traditional motifs and subjects. The 65 and 80ø. stamps, for example, depicted a wooden Stave church and the Aurora Borealis. Other stamps featured runic drawings, knots, ears of wheat and fragments of church architecture.

6. Norway, 30 + 5 øre, 1939
Since 1930 Norway has issued a number of charity or semi-postal sets, to raise funds for the Tourist Association, the Nansen Refugee Fund, and various social and medical welfare services. A set of four

PLATE 8 NORWAY, SWEDEN, FINLAND

stamps portraying the late Queen Maud was issued in July 1939 on behalf of the Queen Maud Children's Fund. These stamps, like the majority of other Norwegian stamps from 1937 onward, were printed in photogravure by Emil Moestue & Co. of Oslo.

7. Norway, 20 øre, 1942
Norway continued to issue its own stamps throughout World War II, the only indication of its political alignment being four stamps portraying the fascist leader Vidkun Quisling and a charity stamp on behalf of troops of the Norwegian Legion of the Waffen SS. Two stamps were issued in October 1942 to mark the bicentenary of the birth of the poet J. H. Wessel. The majority of commemoratives in this period consisted of pairs or single stamps.

8. Norway, 40 øre, 1943
A set of eight stamps, designed by J. Bull and recess-printed by De La Rue, was released between January 1943 and June 1945 on behalf of the government-in-exile in London. The stamps were used on Norwegian ships serving with the Allies and from Norwegian camps in Britain. After the liberation of Norway the series was put on general sale. The designs showed aspects of the Free Norwegian war effort.

9. Norway, 20 øre, 1945
A. Arnoldus designed two stamps issued in December 1945 to mark the 50th anniversary of the National Folklore Museum in Oslo. The stamps were the first to be designed after the liberation, so the lion rampant motif was singularly appropriate.

10. Norway, 50 øre, 1968
Pairs of stamps were issued in 1951 and 1968 portraying Arne Garborg and Aasmund Vinje respectively. As both men had advocated the reformation of Norwegian spelling, the country name on these stamps was rendered 'Noreg', which they argued was more correct. Unfortunately this has led many collectors, in all innocence, to suppose that they had acquired stamps showing an error, but in this case the spelling is correct. The Vinje stamps were designed and engraved by K. Løkke-Sörensen and recess-printed by the Norges Bank. In recent years recess-printing has made something of a come-back in Norway, rivalling photogravure in both definitive and commemorative issues.

11. Sweden, 20 øre, 1866
Sweden adopted adhesive stamps in July 1855, using a coat of arms design typographed by Count Sparre in denominations from 3 to 8s. The same designs, expressed in øre, were issued between 1858 and 1872. Higher denominations, up to 20ø., were provided for in a series showing the Swedish lion above the numerals of value. This series was issued between 1862 and 1872.

12. Sweden, 110 øre, 1920
In 1920 the contracts for the production of Swedish stamps passed to the Stamp Printing Office of the Royal Swedish Postal Administration, though the dies continued to be manufactured by outside companies as before. Both Jacob Bagge of Stockholm and the British-American Bank Note Co. of Ottawa supplied dies for the definitive series of 1920–33 featuring the crowned posthorn emblem of the Swedish post office. From 1920 onward Sweden adopted the practice of issuing stamps in coils or booklets instead of sheets, and consequently the majority of stamps from this time onward are imperforate on two sides.

13. Sweden, 25 øre, 1925
Between 1921 and 1936 a series portraying King Gustav V was introduced, to supplement the post-

horn series. The series was designed by E. Österman and the dies engraved by Jacob Bagge and Hasse Tullberg. The stamps were printed on unwatermarked paper but a small quantity of the 15ø. was released on paper with a wavy line watermark. Examples of this rare variety have had a fake watermark to deceive collectors.

14. Sweden, 10 øre, 1941
T. Schönberg designed this stamp, engraved by Sven Ewert, to commemorate the fiftieth anniversary of the open-air museum at Skansen. The stamps, in denominations of 10 and 60ø., featured the Håsjö Belfry, an outstanding feature of the museum. Examples of the 10ø. value, from booklets, may be found perforated $12\frac{1}{2}$ all round.

15. Sweden, 20 øre, 1949
A set of three stamps celebrated the centenary of the birth of the dramatist J. A. Strindberg. The series was designed by A. Kumlien and engraved by Sven Ewert, the latter being responsible for the dies of most Swedish stamps between 1931 and 1958.

16. Sweden, 50 øre, 1962
Stamps in this design were first issued in June 1951 and were designed by M. Sylvan and engraved by Sven Ewert in denominations from 10 to 40ø. In the original version relatively pale backgrounds were used to the portrait and the numerals were in colour. Stamps in this design were released at various times until June 1957 when the design was redrawn, with a cross-hatched background instead of the thin horizontal lines of the original version. In this series the initials of the designer and engraver were given in the margin. Stamps of this series appeared between 1957 and 1965, but a third version, with white numerals on a coloured background, was gradually released between 1961 and 1969, with the initials of D. Tägestrom (designer) and Czeslaw Slania (engraver) in the margin.

17. Sweden, 45 øre, 1969
The close ties among the Scandinavian countries have been manifest in several sets of stamps. Two stamps showing a flight of swans were issued in 1956 to mark Northern Countries' Day and were in an omnibus design common to all the participating countries. Five Viking galleys, symbolizing Denmark, Norway, Sweden, Finland and Iceland, were featured on the stamps of 1969 commemorating the fiftieth anniversary of the Northern Countries' Union. The stamps were designed by Sven Gustaffson and engraved by Czeslaw Slania. Similar designs were used by the other Scandinavian countries.

18. Sweden, 2 kronor, 1970
A pictorial definitive series was adopted in 1967 and various denominations, from 5ø. to 4k., were issued at various times. This 2k. stamp was added to the series in August 1970 and depicts the China Palace at Drottningholm. Since 1967 Sweden has issued several stamps printed in multicolour photogravure, either by the Bank of Finland Printing Works or by Harrison and Sons. This stamp was printed in combined photogravure and lithography.

19. Sweden, 85 øre, 1971
The bicentenary of the Royal Academy of Music was celebrated in August 1971 by 55 and 85ø. stamps with a most unusual theme. The design, by Ingvar Lidholm, had a circular motif with musical notation on it – an original composition produced specially for this purpose. Apparently the music can be played in almost infinite variations by starting at any point in the circle and working round it. The stamps were engraved by H. Gutschmidt.

20. Finland, 5 penni, 1866
Finland had stamped postal stationery from 1845 onward but did not adopt adhesive stamps till 1856. The stamps were imperforate and featured the Finnish arms with an inscription in Russian and Finnish. Four years later a series was typographed at the Senate Printing Office in Helsinki and featured the coat of arms in an upright design. A curious feature of these stamps was the serpentine roulette applied to them at the Stamping Department in Helsinki. The stamps were originally inscribed in Russian kopeks but the Finnish penni currency was adopted in 1866. The majority of Finnish stamps from 1889 onward conformed to contemporary Russian types.

21. Finland, 3 markkaa, 1921
An independent Finnish republic was declared in 1917, following the Russian revolution and the abdication of the monarchy. The outstanding Finnish architect and artist, Eliel Saarinen, designed the first stamps of the republic, featuring the lion rampant. Stamps, from 5p. to 25m., were issued gradually between 1917 and 1929. The stamps were typographed at the State Bank Note Printing Works, from plates made by Lilius and Hertzberg. Note the use of the Finnish and Swedish forms of the name.

22. Finland, 5 markkaa, 1946
The 600th anniversary of the foundation of the city of Porvoo was celebrated in December 1946 by two stamps featuring landmarks in the city. The stamps were designed by Aarne Karjalainen who was responsible for the majority of Finnish stamps in the 1940s.

23. Finland, 30 markkaa, 1961
This stamp was issued in May 1961 to commemorate the 75th anniversary of the Finnish Postal Savings Bank. The design was by Pente Rahikainen, who has produced many Finnish stamps since 1960, while R. Achrén engraved the die.

24. Finland, 40 penni, 1967
The Finnish currency was reformed in 1963, 1 old markkaa being worth one new penni. Finland broke away from the traditional recess process in 1965 by introducing lithography for certain commemorative stamps. To mark the centenary of the birth of Marshal Mannerheim, however, combined recess and lithography was used. The design, featuring the Mannerheim statue in Helsinki, was by Olavi Vepsäläinen, who, with Rahikainen, has designed all the Finnish stamps in recent years.

25. Aunus, 5 penni, 1919
The Russian town of Olonetz was occupied by Finnish troops in June 1919 during the war with Soviet Russia. Contemporary Finnish stamps were overprinted 'Aunus' for use in this town, but shortly afterward the Bolsheviks recaptured it. The stamps were in denominations from 5p. to 10ma.

26. Eastern Karelia, 2.75 markkaa, 1941
During the second Russo-Finnish War the district of Eastern Karelia, extending east to Lake Onega, was occupied by the Finns from October 1941 till mid-1943. During that period various Finnish stamps were overprinted in Finnish to signify 'Eastern Karelia military occupation'. Ordinary Russian stamps have been in use since 1943 when the district was recaptured by the Red Army.

27. Ingermanland, 10 penni, 1920
The Ingermanland district along the Finnish frontier northwest of Leningrad freed itself of Bolshevik rule for several months in 1920, until re-absorbed by Russia as a result of the Treaty of Dorpat. F. Lindstedt designed a series of stamps, modelled

PLATE 9 FRANCE

on the contemporary Finnish series, but featuring the Ingermanland coat of arms. The stamps were lithographed by Kirja ja Kivipaino of Wiipuri (Viborg) in denominations from 5p. to 10ma. A pictorial series designed by G. Niemann appeared in August 1920. Inkeri is the Finnish form of the name. Ordinary Russian stamps have been in use since October 1920.

PLATE 9
France

1. 20 centimes, 1849
The French 'Penny Black' made its début on New Year's Day 1849. Although the French postal administration closely observed the working of Uniform Penny Postage in Britain and the efficacy of adhesive stamps, eight years elapsed before the necessary legislation was passed. The dies were engraved by Jean-Jacques Barre, the profile of Ceres, goddess of Agriculture, being derived from an ancient Greek coin. A 1 franc stamp was released at the same time, and other denominations, from 10 to 40c., were introduced the following year.

2. 1 centime, 1862
Louis Napoleon seized power in 1852 and transformed the Second Republic into the Second Empire the following year. Barre designed the series of 1853–61 bearing the bare-headed profile of the Emperor. The series, ranging from 1c. to 1f., underwent numerous changes in shade. Originally released imperforate, the stamps were perforated from 1862 onward.

3. 2 centimes, 1862
A new design, engraved by Albert Barre, son of Jean-Jacques, was adopted in 1862 to mark the success of Napoleon's campaigns leading to the unification of Italy in 1860. The profile of the Emperor bears a laurel wreath, emblem of victory. The inscription, hitherto abbreviated, is now shown in full.

4. 10 centimes, 1873
The Ceres design was re-introduced during the Franco-Prussian War, after the defeat of the Emperor at Sedan and his abdication had led to the establishment of the Third Republic. Lithographed versions of these stamps appeared first at Bordeaux in November 1870, under the authority of the provisional government. At Paris, however, the plates of 1849–50 were renovated and pressed into service.

5. 20 centimes, 1900
The design showing the female allegory of the republic holding a tablet inscribed 'Droits de l'Homme' (rights of man) is usually known to philatelists as the Mouchon type, after Eugène Mouchon, who designed and engraved the dies. In the earliest printings the figures of value were inserted at a second operation, and consequently they are often misplaced or even missing. New versions of certain denominations were made in 1901 with the entire design printed at one operation.

6. 75 centimes, 1926
La Semeuse (the sower) made her philatelic début in 1903 and stamps with this design remained in use up to World War II. During that period she underwent various changes. At first the sunrise was shown in the background, then she was given a solid background with ground below her feet, and finally the ground was removed. This spirited design, based on the coin obverse by Oscar Roty, was re-introduced in 1960.

7. 2 francs, 1900
This design, with the reclining figure of Marianne, is usually known as the Merson type, after the artist Luc-Olivier Merson. Another relatively long-lived design, it was used for the higher denominations up to World War II.

8. 30 centimes, 1926
A curious departure from the classicism and symbolism of French republican definitives came in 1923, when the effigy of Louis Pasteur was adopted for a series which eventually ran from 10d. to 1.50f.

9. 1.50 francs, 1931
One of a set of five stamps issued in 1930–31 to mark the International Colonial Exhibition in Paris. Four of the stamps portrayed a woman of the Fachi tribe and were, like most other French stamps up to that time, typographed. The double-sized 1.50f. stamp, however, was printed by the photogravure process, the contract being given to the firm of Vaugirard. This remained the only photogravure stamp issued by France until 1966. The design, by J. de la Nézière, symbolizes the French colonies.

10. 1.75 francs, 1938
The only stamp ever issued by France to mark a State Visit, it reflects the political situation in 1938 when Britain and France drew closer together in face of the threat posed by Nazi Germany. A seal symbolising friendship is flanked by the Arc de Triomphe and the Houses of Parliament at Westminster.

11. 50 + 10 centimes, 1937
One of a set of three stamps released to raise funds for postal workers' recreational facilities. The design depicts ramblers approaching the PTT holiday hostel; other subjects were a tug of war and athletes. France made a number of charity or semi-postal issues in the period before World War II in aid of unemployed intellectuals, refugees and soldiers' charities as well as the postal welfare fund.

12. 75 centimes, 1937
A stamp commemorating the tercentenary of the first performance of Le Cid by Pierre Corneille. From 1923 onward, when the Pasteur stamps appeared, France has produced numerous stamps, usually confined to a single value, paying tribute to her famous men and women in all walks of life.

13. 55 centimes, 1937
One of a pair of stamps depicting the Headless Victory of Samothrace in the Louvre. The stamps were sold at certain museums at 70c. over face value in aid of museum funds.

14. 1 franc, 1941
One of four recess-printed stamps issued in 1941 with the portrait of Marshal Pétain head of the French National State. The Third Republic came to an end on 10 July 1940. The inscription 'République Française' (French Republic) or the monogram RF were henceforth omitted from stamp designs and the inscription 'Postes Françaises' (French Posts) adopted instead.

15. 15 francs, 1951
This stamp marked the Popular Pictorial Art Exhibition staged at Épinal and features an illuminated manuscript showing St Nicholas, from the Musée Nationale de l'Imagerie Française. This was the first French stamp recess-printed in multicolour.

16. 10 centimes, 1944
One of a series, released between December 1944 and November 1945 following the liberation of France. The series was recess-printed by De La Rue

in London, one of the few French issues made outside the country. The design portraying Marianne, allegory of the republic, was by Edmund Dulac, the French born artist who later resided in England and designed several British stamps.

17. 10 centimes, 1945
One of a series released in 1945–46 after the resumption of normal postal conditions in France. The design shows the Cross of Lorraine, emblem of the Free French forces, and broken chains symbolizing the liberation of France. The date alludes to the Allied invasion of Normandy in June 1944 and the subsequent liberation.

18. 6 + 4 francs, 1947
Five stamps were issued in January 1947 with premiums in aid of the National Relief Fund. The stamps featured famous cathedrals of France. National Relief Fund stamps first appeared under the Vichy regime in 1940 and since then have been issued annually with premiums in aid of various charities.

19. 5 francs, 1954
Since 1942 France has issued numerous multi-coloured low-value stamps featuring the coats of arms of cities and départements. The first series, in March 1943, bore charity premiums in aid of the National Relief Fund, but those issued in 1943 and subsequent years have augmented the definitive series. This stamp, showing the arms of Saintonge, appeared in a group of seven released in 1954.

20. 15 francs, 1955
Yet another of the many faces of Marianne to grace the stamps of France, this portrait, by Muller, was used for a set of six stamps issued at various times between 1955 and 1959.

21. 1 franc, 1961
One of a set of four stamps featuring famous French paintings in full colour. This stamp features '14th July' by R. de la Fresnaye. Others in the series reproduced works by Braque, Matisse and Cézanne. France repeated the theme in subsequent years and touched off a spectacular boom in art stamps all over the world.

22. 1 franc, 1960
Postwar definitive issues have consisted of coats of arms (low values) and scenery (higher denominations), changed at frequent intervals. The scenery stamps of 1960 took as their theme views in the overseas départements, mainly in Algeria. This stamp, however, featured the Cilaos Church and the Great Bernard Mountains in the Indian Ocean island of Reunion, which now uses French stamps surcharged in local currency (see Plate 78).

23. 50 centimes, 1962
One of two stamps issued to celebrate the first transatlantic telecommunications satellite link. The stamp shows the satellite Telstar, a television screen and a globe with the French station at Pleumeur-Bodou and the American station at Andover, Maine marked. This stamp, designed and engraved by Durrens, is typical of the large-format, multi-colour stamps which France has produced since the early 1960s.

PLATE 10 FRENCH GROUP

PLATE 10
French Group

1. French Colonies, 1 centime, 1862
Albert Barre designed and engraved the series of stamps adopted in 1859 for use throughout the French colonial empire in denominations of 10, 20 and 40c. In 1862, 1 and 5c. values were introduced and an 80c. value was added in 1865. The stamps featured the eagle and imperial crown and were typographed on tinted paper. Subsequently contemporary French stamps were used and may be differentiated from those in metropolitan France by their tinted paper and lack of perforations.

2. French Colonies, 2 centimes, 1881
Prior to the 1890s the various French colonial territories did not issue their own stamps (the exception being Reunion, 1852, and New Caledonia, 1860) but used a general series. This stamp forms part of a distinctive series released between 1881 and 1886 depicting the seated figure of Commerce. The stamps were designed and engraved by Alphée Dubois, and typographed at the Government Printing Works in Paris.

3. Alsace-Lorraine, 2 centimes, 1870
Though these stamps are popularly known as the series of Alsace-Lorraine they were, in fact, designed for use in all the territories of France occupied by German troops in the war of 1870–71. After the German withdrawal from France in 1871 these stamps continued to be used in the provinces of Alsace and Lorraine pending the introduction of the stamps of the German Empire in 1872. The stamps were issued, in denominations from 1 to 25c., shortly after the outbreak of the Franco-Prussian War. Two sets can be made of this series, typographed at the State Printing Works in Berlin – with the points of the net upward or downward, the latter being rather scarcer.

4. German Western Command, 3 centimes, 1916
Stamps of the Germania series of 1905 were overprinted 'Belgien' and surcharged in centimes and francs for use in occupied Belgium at the outset of World War I (see Plate 4). Similar stamps, surcharged in French currency without the word 'Belgien' were issued in 1916 for use in all the territory under the administration of the German Western Command, including parts of northern France as well as Belgium. No stamps were issued in World War I specifically for use in occupied France.

5. Alsace, 100 pfennigs, 1940
After the fall of France in June 1940 Alsace was annexed by the Third Reich, after having been in French hands since 1919. On 15 August 1940 the Hindenburg medallion definitive series, in denominations from 3 to 100pf., was released in the province overprinted 'Elsass', the German version of the name. These stamps were superseded on 1 January 1942 by ordinary German stamps. French stamps were re-introduced in December 1944 following the liberation of the province.

6. Lorraine, 25 pfennigs, 1940
The Hindenburg definitives were overprinted 'Lothringen' for use in Lorraine, and introduced on 21 August 1940. French stamps ceased to be valid on 14 August and ordinary German stamps were thus permitted for one week pending the arrival of the Lorraine overprints. This series was superseded by ordinary German stamps in January 1942 and Lorraine resumed the use of French stamps in December 1944. German stamps overprinted with the Cross of Lorraine were used at Saverne in 1944.

7. Andorra, ½ centime, 1931
France began issuing stamps for the French post office in Andorra three years after Spain (see Plate 28). Pending the supply of a distinctive pictorial series various contemporary French stamps were overprinted 'Andorre' at the Government Printing Works in Paris. As there was a need for a ½c. stamp to cover local printed matter the lowest denominations of the French series had to be surcharged to convert it to this denomination.

8. Andorra, 90 centimes, 1932
A recess-printed definitive series inscribed 'Valles d'Andorre' (Valleys of Andorra) was released on 16 June 1932. Between that date and 1943 increases in postal rates led to numerous changes of colour and the introduction of new denominations so that eventually the series amounted to almost 60 different stamps, while a further 14 small-format stamps, issued in 1937–42, featured the Andorran coat of arms. Five double-sized designs were used for the main series, featuring villages and scenery in the valleys. This design depicts the Gorge of St. Julia.

9. Andorra, 3 francs, 1955
A new pictorial series was introduced between 1955 and 1958 and followed the pattern of earlier issues by featuring scenery and landmarks in the Valleys. In the style of the engraving and the design of the lettering, however, this series reflected contemporary trends in French and colonial stamp design. This design, used for the lowest denominations, features the rock formation known as Les Escaldes.

10. Council of Europe, 35 francs, 1958
The contemporary 35f. stamp of France was released in January 1958 with an overprint to denote its use on official correspondence emanating from the headquarters of the Council of Europe in Strasbourg. Subsequently a series featuring the Council flag was issued. Until March 1960 these stamps could only be used on official Council correspondence but since then they can be used by anyone posting mail from the Council building.

11. UNESCO, 60 centimes, 1966
Stamps for use on correspondence posted within the UNESCO headquarters building in Paris were introduced in January 1961. A set of five featuring portraits of Buddha and Hermes was issued between 1961 and 1965 and was superseded, in December 1966, by a series showing a globe and open book.

12. Monaco, 2 centimes, 1891
Prior to 1885 Monaco used the stamps of Sardinia, Italy and latterly France, but decided to assert its postal independence by releasing distinctive stamps. In a period of less than ninety years the principality has produced almost a thousand different stamps and derives a considerable amount of revenue from philatelic sales. This stamp is one of a series portraying Prince Albert (1889–1922) engraved by E. Mouchon and typographed in Paris. The series was reissued, between 1901 and 1921, in new colours.

13. Monaco, 30 centimes, 1923
A new definitive series was introduced in 1922, but was relatively short-lived on account of the death of Prince Albert a month before its issue. The lower denominations showed him in yachting rig while the higher values featured landmarks of Monaco, including the Oceanographic Museum (shown on this stamp), which was a life-long interest of Prince Albert. The series was designed by Henri Cheffer and the earliest printings were made by Maison Braun of Paris – the only occasion on which Monegasque stamps were produced by a

printer other than the French Government Printing Works. Later printings of this series were made at the Government Printing Works and are indistinguishable from the Braun versions.

14. Monaco, 50 centimes, 1948
One of a series designed by Pierre Gandon to mark the centenary of the death of F. J. Bosio, the sculptor. The stamps featured the Salmacis Nymph and other well-known sculptures. Bosio himself was portrayed on the 4 francs denomination, with his initials reversed by mistake.

15. Monaco, 15 francs, 1952
One of a set of three stamps, featuring the Gallery of Hercules, issued in April 1952 to raise money for the projected Monaco Postal Museum. Compare the design of this stamp, by Henri Cheffer, with the 30c. of 1922 (above) and note how lettering and frame formation had become streamlined over a period of thirty years, while the growing use of two or three colour combinations added greatly to the aesthetic appeal of postwar stamps.

16. Monaco, 10 + 10 centimes, 1939
One of a series with premiums in aid of local charities, released by the principality of Monaco and portraying former rulers. Like the vast majority of Monegasque stamps since 1885 this series was produced at the French Government Printing Works in Paris and closely follows contemporary styles in design and engraving.

17. Monaco, 80 centimes, 1925
Henri Cheffer designed a series with a profile of Prince Louis issued between 1924 and 1933. The dies were engraved by G. Daussy and tinted paper was used for the majority of the stamps typographed in Paris. Frequent changes of colour and additional denominations reflect the fluctuations in postal rates during the late 1920s.

18. Monaco, 1 franc, 1958
One of a series of twelve stamps commemorating the centenary of the Apparition of the Virgin Mary at Lourdes, this stamp shows the Monegasque penchant for diamond-shaped stamps in recent years. The phrase 'I am the Immaculate Conception', said by the Virgin to St Bernadette, appears on these stamps in various languages and on this denomination appears in French and Portuguese. Popes Pius IX and XII are portrayed flanking the statue of the Holy Virgin at Lourdes. Other stamps in the series portrayed St Bernadette and scenes from her life and canonization.

19. Monaco, 10 francs, 1946
Christian Mazelin designed and engraved a new definitive series bearing a profile of Prince Louis II. The higher denominations reproduced the obverse of the Monegasque coins bearing the prince's profile. The series was reissued in new colours, with additional denominations, in 1948.

20. Monaco, 1 franc, 1956
Many of the issues of Monaco in recent years have honoured events which have little direct connection with the principality but which have excited the interest of stamp collectors. In 1956, for example, a set of eight stamps was issued to mark FIPEX (the Fifth International Philatelic Exhibition) in New York. The stamps portrayed famous American presidents, from George Washington to Dwight Eisenhower and similar subjects calculated to appeal to the philatelic market in America. This stamp reproduces a painting by Trumbull and was designed and engraved by J. Piel.

21. Monaco, 4 centimes, 1963
A series of twelve stamps marking the centenary 149

PLATE 10 FRENCH GROUP · PLATE 11 GERMAN STATES

of the British Football Association was issued in December 1963. The diamond-shaped low values featured various football grounds, including Wembley Stadium, London. The 4c. denomination was additionally overprinted in honour of the Association Sportive de Monaco football teams in the French Championships and in the Coupe de France, 1962–63. The higher denominations of the series traced the development of football from the Florentine 'Calcio' of the sixteenth century to the English version of the 1890s, and culminated in a group of four depicting various aspects of the contemporary game.

22. Monaco, 1 centime, 1964

The first – and only – Monte Carlo Air Rally took place in 1914 and was modelled on the car rally, with competitors flying across Europe from various starting points as shown on the map depicted on the 1c. stamp. The finale of the race was a seaplane contest round the bay of Monaco, for which the Schneider Trophy was originally awarded. To mark the 50th anniversary of the rally a series of sixteen stamps was issued in May 1964, depicting the different aircraft which took part in the event and, for good measure, a gallery of airplanes which made historic flights between 1919 and 1961.

23. Monaco, 100 francs, 1956

A 100f. stamp was issued in 1955 to mark the 25th anniversary of the Monte Carlo Rally and featured each of the eight starting points. In subsequent years similar stamps were devoted to each of the starting points in turn. The first of these stamps, designed by B. Minne, depicted the route from Glasgow, Scotland and showed a Scottish piper and Eilean Donan Castle.

24. Monaco, 1 franc, 1953

Monaco is one of the few countries to brighten up the appearance of its postage due labels by using pictorial designs. This stamp is one of a series of triangular designs introduced in 1953–54 featuring various forms of transport. Each denomination was issued in two designs, arranged in *tête-bêche* pairs throughout the sheet. The 1f. stamps featured carrier pigeons and a Sikorsky helicopter and this contrast of old and new was maintained in the other pairs of the series.

25. Monaco, 20 francs, 1957

This stamp was one of a definitive series, portraying Prince Rainier III, issued between 1955 and 1959 in old francs and reissued between 1960 and 1966 in new franc currency. The stamps were designed and engraved by Cheffer, whose work for Monaco has thus spanned a period of more than forty years.

PLATE 11

German States

Prior to the formation of the German Empire in 1871 several kingdoms, grand-duchies, principalities and free cities of Germany issued their own stamps, beginning with Bavaria in 1849. The formation of the German-Austrian Postal Union the following year led to a spate of issues from several states. After the Seven Weeks War of 1866, in which Prussia emerged as head of the North German Confederation, separate issues of stamps in the northern states ceased. Baden surrendered its postal privilege in 1871, but Bavaria and Württemberg continued to exercise the right to issue their own stamps and this survived till after World War I.

1. Baden, 9 kreuzer, 1851

One of a series of four stamps introduced in May 1851, the stamps were typographed in black on various coloured papers by Hasper of Karlsruhe. The inscriptions in the vertical panels allude to the signing of the German-Austrian Postal Convention on 6 April 1850, and for this reason these stamps are sometimes regarded as the world's first commemorative issue. They remained in use, however, for almost ten years, and thus the commemorative aspect became purely incidental.

2. Baden, 30 kreuzer, 1862

The top value of a series engraved by L. Kurz and typographed by W. Hasper of Karlsruhe. In the original versions, of 1860, the coat of arms was placed on a background of coloured dots, but two years later the designs were redrawn without the dotted background. The separate issues of the grand-duchy of Baden ceased at the end of 1871 when the stamps of the German Empire were introduced.

3. Bergedorf, 4 schillings, 1861

The city of Bergedorf was under the joint control of the free cities of Hamburg and Lübeck, a fact alluded to in the initials which appear in the four corners of the design – LHPA (Lübeck Hamburg Post Anstalt) and the coat of arms which conjoins the eagle of Lübeck and the towers of Hamburg. The stamps, lithographed by K. Fuchs of Hamburg, were in use from November 1861 till 1867 when they were superseded by the stamps of the North German Confederation.

4. Brunswick, 1 gutegroschen, 1857

The first stamps of the duchy of Brunswick appeared in 1852 and featured a leaping horse, the ducal emblem. In 1857 an unusual 1gg. stamp was introduced divided into four $\frac{1}{4}$gg. fractions, each of which had the equivalent value of 3 pfennigs. The fractions could be used to pay postage on newspapers and printed matter. The stamps were printed in black on brown paper. The version printed in brown on white paper was prepared for use but never issued.

5. Brunswick, 1 groschen, 1865

Combined embossing and typography was adopted for the series issued in October 1865 in denominations from $\frac{1}{3}$ to 3g. The central motif was the galloping horse emblem of the duchy. Arc-rouletting was used as a means of separation, but most denominations have been recorded imperforate. These stamps were withdrawn from use on 1 January 1868, when the issues of the North German Confederation came into use.

6. Bremen, 3 grote, 1855

The first stamp issued by this free city, it was lithographed by the Hunkel Company in black on bluish paper. All the stamps subsequently produced by Bremen featured the key emblem.

7. Bavaria, 1 kreuzer, 1867

Bavaria's first stamps, from 1849 till 1867, consisted solely of the numeral of value. The series introduced in 1867, with the royal coat of arms embossed on a typographed background, set the pattern for all Bavarian definitives down to World War I. The earliest printings had a vertical silk thread enmeshed in the paper as a security device. From 1870 onwards, however, various watermarks were used.

8. Bavaria, 10 pfennigs, 1911

One of two multicoloured stamps released to celebrate the 25th anniversary of the regency of Prince Luitpold. A lengthy series earlier that year marked the Regent's 90th birthday. Both sets were designed by F. A. von Kaulbach and produced by photolithography by Oskar Consée.

9. Bavaria, 40 pfennigs, 1919

Bavaria's experiments with novel methods of stamp production culminated with the release, in March 1914, of the world's first photogravure series. This process, which has revolutionized modern stamp printing, was slow to catch on. Twenty years elapsed before Britain adopted it and it is only since World War II that it has become widely accepted. The basic stamp was designed by Ferdinand Schirnböck and printed in photogravure by F. A. Bruckmann of Munich. This stamp reflects the troubled condition of Bavaria after World War I. Poor quality ink, rough paper and lack of perforation compared with the earlier printings reflect the economic ruin of the country. The overprint 'Volkstaat Bayern' (People's State) alludes to the communist republic established in November 1918.

10. Bavaria, 10 pfennigs, 1919

After a short-lived revolution Bavaria adopted a constitution and became a Free State (*Freistaat*). German stamps thus overprinted, in denominations of 2$\frac{1}{2}$, 5, 7$\frac{1}{2}$ and 10pf., were first released on 17 May in the Rhineland Palatinate to meet a shortage of stamps. The entire series, ranging in value up to 5 marks, was introduced in Bavaria on 30 September 1919.

11. Bavaria, 5 pfennigs, 1920

One of a series issued shortly before the Bavarian postal administration was absorbed by the German State service on 29 April 1920. The modernist designs embodied the spirit of the new republic in the post-war era.

12. Hamburg, 2$\frac{1}{2}$ schillings, 1864

All the stamps of Hamburg, from 1859 till 1867, featured the numerals of value superimposed on the state coat of arms. The earliest issues were typographed by T. G. Meissner, but the denominations introduced in 1864 were lithographed by C. Adler.

13. Hanover, 1/15 thaler, 1851

A 1 gutegroschen stamp was released in December 1850 and was followed by other values between 1851 and 1855. The complexities of German currency in the mid-nineteenth century are demonstrated in this stamp, inscribed 1/15 thaler in the centre, and 2 silbergroschen in the side panel. One thaler was worth 24 gutegroschen or 30 silbergroschen, the latter currency being used on stamps which circulated on correspondence between the states of the German-Austrian Postal Union. Note also the British coat of arms at the top of the design, an allusion to the close connection between Britain and Hanover, ruled by the same sovereign between 1714 and 1837.

14. Lübeck, 4 schillings, 1859

Stamps in values of $\frac{1}{2}$, 1, 2, 2$\frac{1}{2}$ and 4s. were lithographed by H. G. Rathgens and issued in January 1859. An unusual feature of these stamps was their watermark of myosotis flowers.

15. Lübeck, $\frac{1}{2}$ schilling, 1863

Like many of the other states Lübeck eventually settled for a series of stamps engraved by H. G. Schilling and printed in combined typography and embossing at the Prussian State Printing Works in Berlin. The method of separation used on these stamps, line-rouletting, was popular in the German states as an alternative to perforation.

16. Mecklenburg-Schwerin, 1 schilling, 1864

Unlike the fractional stamps of Brunswick (see

PLATE 11 GERMAN STATES · PLATE 12 GERMANY

no. 4) those of Mecklenburg-Schwerin did not have a border inscription, though rouletting surrounded each block of four $\frac{1}{4}s$. units. The earliest version, released in 1856, had a shaded background and was imperforate. The dies were engraved by Otto of Güstrow who later printed the first stamps of the Transvaal (see plate 66), but on this occasion the actual printing of the stamps was carried out by the Prussian State Printing Works.

17. Mecklenburg-Strelitz, 2 silbergroschen, 1864
One of a series of four stamps issued in 1864 when Mecklenburg-Strelitz adopted adhesive stamps. As with Mecklenburg-Schwerin, the dies were engraved by Otto, but the stamps were embossed and typographed in Berlin.

18. Oldenburg, 1 groschen, 1863
The first stamps of this grand-duchy, issued in 1852–59, closely resembled those of Hanover in design and inscription. The oval design, with the embossed coat of arms, was engraved by Schilling and printed in Berlin.

19. Prussia, 4 pfennings, 1856
One of the series gradually released between November 1850 and 1856; the design by F. E. Eichens portrayed King Frederick William IV. In this version a large profile appeared on a background of crossed lines. In 1857 a smaller head on a solid ground was adopted and in 1858 the crossed lines were re-introduced. Note the curious spelling of pfennige, indicating the transitional nature of German orthography at that time.

20. Prussia, 3 pfennings, 1865
Like the other states Prussia adopted an embossed and typographed series in the 1860s. The set, in denominations from $4pf.$ to $3sg.$, appeared in 1861, but the $3pf.$ value was added four years later.

21. Saxony, 2 neugroschen, 1851
One of a series introduced in 1851 when Saxony subscribed to the German-Austrian Postal Union. The stamps, portraying King Frederick Augustus II, were recess-printed in black on coloured paper. Prussia and Saxony were the only German states to use this process, though it was the most popular method elsewhere at that time.

22. Saxony, 2 neugroschen, 1863
Like most of the other states, Saxony also adopted combined typography and embossing for its stamps in the 1860s, but instead of going to Berlin, relied on the Saxon firm of Giesecke and Devrient of Leipzig. This company subsequently printed stamps for a number of countries and re-emerged after World War II as the state-owned German Banknote Printing Co. of the German Democratic Republic (see plates 12 and 13).

23. Schleswig, 1¼ schillings, 1864
One of a series issued jointly by Austria and Prussia for use in the duchy of Schleswig, after the war between Denmark and the German Confederation in 1863. The stamps were typographed at the Prussian State Printing Works.

24. Holstein, 1¼ schillings, 1864
Though issued under the authority of the German Federal Commissioner, the stamps of Holstein were produced locally, by Köbner and Lehmkuhl of Altona. A subsequent issue was made under Austrian authority, in 1865, but was suppressed by the Prussians when they took over the duchy during the Seven Weeks War.

25. Schleswig-Holstein, 1 schilling, 1850
One of two stamps issued by the local authorities at the time of the abortive rebellion against Danish

rule. The stamps were designed and engraved by M. Claudius and printed in combined typography and embossing by Köbner and Lemkuhl. A joint issue for Schleswig and Holstein was made by Austria and Prussia in 1865, following the occupation of the duchies by German Federal forces.

26. Thurn and Taxis, 2 silbergroschen, 1866
One of a series of stamps produced by the Thurn and Taxis postal network for use in the northern districts of Germany which did not have their own postal service. The stamps were issued originally in 1852 imperforate, but albino rouletting was adopted in 1865 and rouletting in coloured lines the following year.

27. Thurn and Taxis, 1 kreuzer, 1866
A similar series, in kreuzer values for use in southern Germany, was produced at the same time as the preceding issue, and likewise adopted rouletting and coloured lines in 1865–66. The Count of Thurn and Taxis was the Hereditary Postmaster General of the Holy Roman Empire. In the seventeenth century, at the height of its power, the Thurn and Taxis network extended from Belgium to Poland and from Germany to Italy. Prussia purchased the remnants of the services in 1867.

28. Württemberg, 3 kreuzer, 1851
Like Baden, Württemberg featured the date of the establishment of the German–Austrian Postal Union on its first stamps. The stamps were typographed in black on various coloured papers, in denominations from 1 to $9k$.

29. Württemberg, 1 mark official stamp, 1919
Württemberg ceased to issue its own postage stamps in 1902 but retained the privilege to issue distinctive official stamps. The series introduced in 1881 underwent numerous changes in denomination, colours and watermark, and after the collapse of the monarchy in 1918 was overprinted 'Volkstaat' (People's State).

30. Württemberg, 10 pfennigs, 1920
One of a series lithographed by Ebner of Stüttgart for use on government mail. Views of the various leading cities in the republic were featured on the stamps. The series was released on 29 March 1920, and withdrawn from use two days later when the official stamps of the German Republic were introduced.

31. North German Confederation, ⅓ groschen, 1868
Sets of stamps, inscribed in groschen or kreuzer currency, were adopted in 1868 in place of the distinctive stamps of the former north German states. Both issues were engraved by Schilling and typographed at the Prussian State Printing Works.

32. North German Confederation, ¼ groschen, official stamp
One of a series introduced in January 1870. The stamps were typographed in black on a pale red-brown background consisting of the words NORDD. POSTBEZIRK repeated continuously as a security device. The stamps of the North German Confederation were replaced by those of the German Empire on New Year's Day, 1872.

33. North German Confederation, ½ schilling, 1868
Because it had a distinctive coinage Hamburg was given a special stamp for use on mail circulating within the former free city boundaries. Though undenominated it sold for ½ Hamburg schilling. The stamp was designed by C. Schwertler, engraved by J. G. Schilling and typographed at the Prussian State Printing Works. This stamp was superseded by the issues of the German Empire in 1872.

PLATE 12
Germany

1. German Empire, 2 marks, 1875
Like the stamps of the former states the first issues of the Empire were produced in combined embossing and typography. Two versions exist of the coat of arms; the eagle may be found with a small or large shield on its breast. Because there was no single unified currency system two sets had to be issued, in groschen currency for the northern districts, and kreuzer currency for the southern districts. A decimal currency, based on the mark of 100 pfennigs, was adopted in 1875. A typographical series, from $3pf.$ to $2m.$, was issued in January of that year.

2. German Empire, 20 pfennigs, 1902
From 1889 till 1902 German stamps were merely inscribed REICHSPOST (State Post). The expression DEUTSCHES REICH (German State) was adopted in the latter year and remained in use till the end of World War II. The allegory of Germania was based on a portrait of the Wagnerian actress Anna Führing. This popular design survived the German Empire by several years.

3. German Republic, 30 pfennigs, 1920
One of a set of five stamps released in 1919–20 to mark the National Assembly at Weimar which decided on a republican constitution. The modernistic designs symbolized the new order, with emphasis on rebirth and reconstruction. One stamp in each sheet of the $30pf.$ has the error '1019' instead of '1919'.

4. 40 pfennigs, 1919
One of a pair of stamps issued for use on airmail correspondence. Germany was one of the first countries to issue stamps for this purpose. The other design featured a winged posthorn. Both designs were produced by G. A. Mathey.

5. 500 million marks, 1923
Germany was hit by a hyper-inflation in 1922 which rapidly escalated during the latter months of 1923. Between August and December of that year almost a hundred different stamps were issued, the postal rates changing almost daily. The highest denomination, released in November 1923, was 50 milliard marks (1 milliard = 1 thousand million).

6. 5,000 marks, 1923
One of a pair of recess-printed high value stamps released in May–July 1923, which had become virtually worthless by the time of their appearance on account of the inflation. Wartburg Castle, refuge of Martin Luther, appeared on the $5,000m.$ while Cologne Cathedral was shown on the $10,000m.$ stamp.

7. 3 pfennigs, 1928
The lowest denomination of the definitive series released between 1928 and 1932 portraying Friedrich Ebert and Paul von Hindenburg, the first and second presidents of the Weimar Republic.

8. 4 pfennigs, 1932
One of a series issued to celebrate the 85th birthday of Field Marshal von Hindenburg, but subsequently retained as a definitive series. This issue is popularly known as the medallion series, since it reproduces a bronze plaquette by Karl Goetz. In 1933 the colours of the stamps were changed and a multiple swastika watermark was introduced, signifying the establishment of the Nazi state. Six stamps of the series were reissued with black borders in mourning for Hindenburg in 1934.

PLATE 12 GERMANY · PLATE 13 GERMANY UNDER ALLIED OCCUPATION

9. 3 pfennigs, 1935

One of four stamps celebrating the return of the Saar to the fatherland. The design, by E. Glintzer, showing a mother and child, with the caption 'The Saar comes home', typifies the emotionalism of many of the stamps released in the Nazi period. Subsequent issues marked the 'home-coming' of Austria, the Sudetenland and Danzig.

10. 25 pfennigs, 1938

One of a pair of stamps marking the centenary of the birth of Count Ferdinand von Zeppelin, the airship pioneer. The Count is shown in the gondola of an early airship, while the 50*pf.* value depicted a modern airship. Germany developed a fleet of giant airships for global travel in the period before World War II.

11. 12 pfennigs, 1942

The Hindenburg medallion series was gradually replaced, between August 1941 and December 1942, by a set portraying the Führer, Adolf Hitler. The Hitler Heads were subsequently overprinted for use in many of the occupied territories and, conversely, were defaced by local postmasters after the collapse of Nazi Germany (see plate 13).

12. 12 + 38 pfennigs, 1942

One of three stamps issued in honour of the European Postal Congress, held in Vienna. This was an attempt, under Nazi auspices, to create a unified postal system throughout Europe and, as such, it anticipated the Conference of European Posts and Telecommunications by almost twenty years. This series is now in demand as a forerunner of the popular Europa theme.

13. 30 + 20 pfennigs, 1944

The top value of a series marking Armed Forces' and Heroes' Day. The large premium on this, and many other wartime stamps, went to the Hitler Culture Fund. Note the expression GROSSDEUTSCHES REICH (Great German State) formally adopted by the Nazi regime in 1944.

14. German Federal Republic, 4 pfennigs, 1951

The first definitive series of the Federal Republic adopted a simple posthorn and numeral motif. Subsequent issues have portrayed the federal president, German historical celebrities or famous buildings.

15. 2 deutschemarks, 1954

The definitive series of 1954–60 portrayed President Heuss, three sizes and two processes (typography or recess) being employed for the various denominations. Creamy fluorescent paper was adopted in 1960 in connection with electronic sorting of mail.

16. 40 + 10 pfennigs, 1958

One of four stamps issued with premiums in aid of Humanitarian Relief and Welfare Funds. The issue of annual sets for charitable purposes began under the Weimar Republic in 1922 and has continued, in both federal and democratic republics, down to the present day. The theme of the 1958 series was agriculture. In more recent years fairy tales and children's dolls have been featured in these annual sets.

17. 30 pfennigs, 1968

On 19 April 1968 a miniature sheet was issued in memory of Dr Konrad Adenauer, first Chancellor of the Federal Republic. As well as Adenauer, other European statesmen were portrayed on the sheet and included Sir Winston Churchill. A second Adenauer issue, consisting of a single 30*pf.* stamp, was released on 19 July. In the original version the portrait was shown on a scarlet background, but this was never issued and a background of red-

orange was used instead. A few examples of the unissued stamp, stamped 'Muster' (specimen), were circulated to journalists.

18. 60 pfennigs, 1971

A definitive series portraying President Heinemann was adopted by West Germany in 1970 and various denominations have been added to it up to 1972. The series, ranging from 5*pf.* to 2DM., was recess-printed at the Federal Printing Works in Berlin.

19. West Berlin, 5 deutschemarks, 1953

The three western sectors of Berlin constituted a *Land* (province) of the Federal Republic in September 1950, but distinctive stamps have continued to be used in West Berlin to this day. The definitive series released between 1949 and 1954 featured prominent buildings in the city. The 5*m.* showed Tegel Castle.

20. West Berlin, 30 pfennigs, 1971

Many of the stamps issued in West Berlin consist of Federal stamps with the inscription modified to include the word BERLIN. This 30*pf.* stamp celebrated the centenary of the foundation of the German Empire, proclaimed at Versailles in January 1871.

21. German Democratic Republic, 12 pfennigs, 1949

The Soviet zone of Germany was created a Democratic Republic in 1949. At first its stamps continued to be inscribed 'Deutsche Post' (German Post) but from March 1950 onward the full name of the republic has been used. This 12*pf.* stamp marked the Postal Workers' Congress held in East Berlin in October 1949. Note the Brandenburg Gate in the background.

22. 24 pfennigs, 1950

One of a pair of stamps issued to mark the First Winter Sports Meeting at Schierke. The 12*pf.* featured a skier and the 24*pf.* a figure skater. These were the first stamps to bear the inscription 'Deutsche Demokratische Republik' (German Democratic Republic). They were lithographed by Giesecke and Devrient of Leipzig, now renamed the VEB Deutsche Wertpapierdruckerei (German Banknote Printing Company).

23. 20 + 10 pfennigs, 1956

The basic stamp was one of a series printed by photogravure in 1955 and publicizing historic buildings. In December 1956 it was reprinted lithographically and surcharged 10*pf.* in aid of Egyptian victims of the Suez campaign. This stamp also appeared simultaneously with a 10*pf.* premium in aid of 'Socialist Hungary', after the suppression of the Hungarian Uprising.

24. 10 pfennigs, 1965

One of three stamps issued to publicize the Leipzig Autumn Fair of 1965. Special stamps in honour of the Leipzig Fair, one of the oldest in Europe, were first issued in 1940. Since the end of World War II it has been customary to issue stamps in March and September each year in honour of the Spring and Autumn Fairs. The subjects have ranged from historic scenes at previous fairs to examples of modern products displayed at the fairs.

25. 15 pfennigs, 1968

One of a pair of stamps commemorating the 20th anniversary of the Ernst Thalmann Pioneer Organization, a youth movement named in memory of the German Communist leader who died in Buchenwald concentration camp in 1945. Note the abbreviation DDR which is used on many stamps of the Democratic Republic. This abbreviation was first used in 1961.

26. 10 + 5 and 25 + 5 pfennigs, 1970

The gimmick of printing two stamps *se-tenant* to form a composite picture originated in the Communist block in 1957 when Poland issued two stamps showing fencers duelling. Since then the idea has been extended by other countries and multiples have been used to build up a single picture. The Sixth Young Pioneers Meeting at Cottbus in 1970 was marked by two stamps, each of an unusually long horizontal format, printed side by side to make a single motif. An unusual feature of this pair was the fact that each stamp had a different face value. As a general rule *se-tenant* stamps of this sort are usually of similar denomination.

PLATE 13
Germany under Allied Occupation

The four year period, from the defeat of the Nazi regime to the emergence of the Federal and Democratic republics, was marked by alliances and divisions among the four occupying Powers and this is reflected in the stamps. Apart from the differences between the Powers themselves, at one point the Soviet zone was split into five postal administrations and the French into three, each having its own distinctive stamps.

1. 5 pfennigs, 1945

Stocks of Hitler Head definitive stamps seized by the advancing Allies were promptly confiscated. In the east, where the Red Army had made no provision for the civil postal administration at the beginning of the occupation, Hitler stamps were pressed into service, suitably defaced. Various methods of obliteration were used, ranging from a cork or a rubber dipped in black ink to the ornate coats of arms of Wurzen or Gottleuba. Postally used examples of these stamps, on covers of May–June 1945, are of great interest to postal historians.

2. 3 pfennigs, 1946

One of a unified series of stamps, typographed at the State Printing Works in Berlin, for use throughout the American, British and Soviet zones of occupation. The first of these stamps appeared in February 1946 and remained in use for about a year. The French opted out of the scheme, preferring to issue their own stamps for the territory under their control (see below).

3. 2 marks, 1947

One of the Dove of Peace high values in a unified series released between March 1947 and February 1948 for use in the three zones. The lower denominations, from 2 to 84*pf.*, were typographed, while the mark values were recess-printed. The pfennig stamps featured various occupations in industry and agriculture.

4. 84 pfennigs, 1948

Large-format stamps depicting historic events connected with the Leipzig Fair, were recess-printed by Giesecke and Devrient of Leipzig for use in the three-power zones in 1947–48. Similar stamps were subsequently issued by the Soviet-sponsored Democratic Republic. This stamp, designed by E. Gruner, shows merchants arriving at the Fair.

5. West Berlin, 5 pfennigs, 1949

After the currency reform of 1948 stamps then used in the three-power zones had to be distinguished by means of an overprint, since the mark varied in value in the east and the west. In addition, the Russians withdrew from the four-power control of Berlin on 1 July 1948. Inter-zonal stamps overprinted BERLIN were used in 1948–49, pending the introduction of a distinctive definitive series (see plate 12).

6. Spremberg, 1 mark, 1946
Many towns and districts in Germany, mainly in the Soviet zone, issued their own stamps in 1945–46. At first these were intended to fill the gap until the inter-zonal stamps were released, but when it was realized that this was a useful method of raising money the municipal authorites soon began issuing charity stamps. Thus the Spremberg postage stamps of 1945 were reissued with a surcharge in aid of reconstruction.

7. Cottbus, 10 + 5 pfennigs, 1945
Eventually many towns produced attractive charity stamps, theoretically valid for postage within a limited area, but including a premium in aid of social welfare and reconstruction projects. The most ambitious was a series of twenty stamps issued by Cottbus in December 1945 featuring scenery, landmarks and customs of the district.

8. Soviet Zone, 60 pfennigs, 1948
The currency reform took place in the American, British and French zones on 21 June 1948 and the existing postage stamps, hitherto used in the American, British and Russian zones, became invalid. As a temporary measure the Soviet authorities ordered the overprint of stamps with a handstamp giving the number of the postal district and the name of the post office. This stamp bears the number 41 (Chemnitz) and the name of Treiten. These overprints came into use on 24 June and were superseded on 3 July by the overprinted series of the Soviet Zone.

9. Soviet Zone, 40 pfennigs, 1948
The pictorial definitive series, hitherto used in the three zones, was overprinted SOWJETISCHE BESATZUNGS ZONE (Soviet Occupation Zone). The overprint was carried out by Giesecke and Devrient. This series remained valid until 1950.

10. Soviet Zone, 30 pfennigs, 1948
The overprinted series was gradually replaced by a set portraying famous men and women in the fields of art, politics and science. The stamps were printed originally on a quatrefoil-watermarked paper, but were reissued in 1952–53 on paper with the watermark DDR and posthorns.

11. Berlin-Brandenburg, 6 pfennigs, 1945
A set of seven stamps, inscribed 'Stadt Berlin', was lithographed at the State Printing Works, Berlin, and issued in Berlin-Brandenburg under Soviet administration. The stamps depicted the Berlin Bear in various acts of reconstruction. The stamps were normally perforated, but are also known with a zig-zag roulette; only the 5pf. was actually issued for use with this type of separation.

12. Mecklenburg-Vorpommern, 3 pfennigs, 1946
Distinctive stamps were issued in this area between August 1945 and the end of October 1946. This stamp was one of a pictorial series issued in January 1946.

13. Saxony (Halle), 12 + 8 pfennigs, 1946
Stamps inscribed 'Provinz Sachsen' (Saxony Province) were issued between October 1945 and January 1946. Apart from a numeral definitive series three stamps were released, with premiums in aid of reconstruction. The stamps featured rehousing, bridge-building and locomotive repairs.

14. North Western Saxony (Leipzig), 12 pfennigs,
Stamps were issued in this area between September 1945 and May 1946. Incredibly, within five months of the collapse of the Third Reich it was 'business as usual' at the Leipzig Fair and two stamps were issued for the 1945 Autumn Fair, and a set of four the following May for the 1946 Spring Fair.

15. South-Eastern Saxony (Dresden), 20 pfennigs, 1945
Stamps were issued in this district between June 1945 and February 1946. The definitive series of 1945–46 was produced in photogravure by Welzel of Dresden, Hoesch Brothers of Hutten and the *Sächsische Volkszeitung* Dresden, lithographed by J. R. Ulbricht of Limbach and typographed by Giesecke and Devrient. The first stamp of the series was inscribed 'Pochta' in Russian, but was withdrawn on the day of issue following protests from the Allies to the Soviet kommandantura.

16. Thuringia, 12 pfennigs, 1945
Thuringia issued its own stamps between October 1945 and March 1946 and included a miniature sheet in aid of the German National Theatre at Weimar. Goethe,. Schiller, Liszt and Wieland, associated with Thuringia, were featured prominently on its stamps. The definitive series was remarkable for the wide variety of different paper, gum and ink used in its production.

17. Anglo-American Zones, 3 pfennigs, 1945
One of a series prepared by the British and Americans for use in occupied Germany. The inscription AM signifies 'Allied Military'. Three sets can be made of this series–typographed by the Bureau of Engraving and Printing in Washington, photogravure by Harrison and Sons, England, and lithographed by G. Westermann of Brunswick. This series was superseded in February 1946 by the joint issue of the American, British and Soviet Zones.

18. 12 pfennigs, 1948
Separate issues for the Anglo-American Zones were resumed in June 1948, following the currency reform. Existing stamps, of the numeral and pictorial sets, were overprinted with a continuous motif of posthorns, either in a horizontal band or in an all-over pattern. All denominations have been recorded with the overprint inverted or doubled.

19. 24 + 16 pfennigs, 1948
One of a set of four stamps released in the Anglo-American Zones to mark the 700th anniversary of Cologne Cathedral. The premium went to the cathedral restoration fund.

20. 2 pfennigs tax stamp, 1948
As a fund-raiser to combat the Berlin blockade by the Russians a tax of 2pf. was levied on all postal matter in the Anglo-American Zones, and subsequently this was extended to the French zone and later continued by the Federal Republic. The scheme came to an end in March 1956. The tax was denoted by a small label which had no franking validity in its own right but was compulsory on all mail. The earliest issues were imperforate and may be found unofficially perforated by sewing machine.

21. 50 pfennigs, 1948
One of the celebrated Buildings series issued between 1948 and 1951. This series, featuring prominent buildings, was designed by M. Bittrof and lithographed by Bagel of München-Gladbach or Westermann of Brunswick. The series bristles with flaws and minor varieties and has proved to be one of the most philatelically interesting sets ever produced.

22. French Zone, general series, 5 pfennigs, 1945
One of a series of ten stamps, modelled on the French arms stamps (see plate 9), featuring the arms of the Palatinate, Rhineland, Württemberg, Baden and the Saar, administered by France after World War II. The dies were engraved by Cortot or Piel and the stamps were typographed at the French Government Printing Works, Paris.

23. Baden, 30 pfennigs, 1949
Baden issued stamps under French administration from December 1947 till September 1949. This stamp marked the Engineers' Congress at Constance in June 1949 and features the Seehof Hotel, the conference venue.

24. Rhineland-Palatinate, 30 + 50 pfennigs, 1948
One of a pair of charity stamps issued in October 1948 to raise funds for the relief of victims of the Ludwigshafen mine disaster. The stamps depicted St Christopher and St Martin.

25. Württemberg, 10 + 5 pfennigs, 1949
Each of the three French territories of Germany issued a set of three stamps, in uniform designs, to mark the bicentenary of the birth of Goethe. The stamps of the French zone were withdrawn from use on 31 March 1950.

PLATE 14
German Plebiscite Territories

The principle of self-determination for national minorities was rigorously applied by the Allies under the terms of the Treaty of Versailles in 1920. Seven districts, formerly part of the German Empire, held referendums in 1920 to decide their future. For the sake of convenience the stamps of Eupen and Malmedy, ceded to Belgium under the terms of the Treaty without a plebiscite, are also included here. Only one territory, Saar, was the subject of a plebiscite after both world wars. For the stamps of Danzig, a Free City under the terms of the Treaty, see plate 26. For stamps of the Lithuanian occupation of Memel, see plate 3.

1. Allenstein (Olsztyn), 30 pfennigs, 1920
Two sets of stamps were used in Allenstein during the plebiscite period, both consisting of contemporary German stamps suitably overprinted. The first, released in April 1920, was overprinted PLEBISCITE OLSZTYN ALLENSTEIN – in French, Polish and German.

2. Allenstein, 1.25 marks, 1920
The second series, released in May–June 1920, bore a reference to the article of the Treaty of Versailles under which the plebiscite of Allenstein was being conducted. The referendum took place on 11 July 1920, and resulted in a vote of 90% in favour of remaining in Germany.

3. Eastern Silesia, 10 fenigi, 1920
Eastern Silesia (Silesie Orientale) consisted of the district around Teschen. Here the dispute was not between Germany and the Slavs but between the Czechs and the Poles in 1919. Although the Allies decided to hold a plebiscite it never took place because of the disorders and eventually the Congress of Ambassadors arbitrarily divided the area between Poland and Czechoslovakia in July 1920. After the dismemberment of Czechoslovakia in 1938 the Poles seized Teschen as their part of the spoils, little realizing that their time would come a year later.

4. Eastern Silesia, 2 kronen, 1920
Another of the Polish series overprinted for use

153

PLATE 14 GERMAN PLEBISCITE TERRITORIES · PLATE 15 GREECE

in the district in April 1920. The stamps used should have been in the halerzy and kronen denominations of the former Austrian part of Poland but the fenigi (former German) stamps were used because of a shortage of the halerzy (heller) denominations.

5. Eastern Silesia, 5 haleru, 1920
The Czechoslovak definitive series, from 1 to 1000*h.*, was overprinted in February 1920. These stamps may be found imperforate or perforated in several different gauges. The 500 and 1000*h.* stamps portraying President Masaryk were also overprinted but not put on sale, for fear of offending pro-Polish sentiment in the district.

6. Eastern Silesia, 2 haleru, 1920
In addition to ordinary postage stamps the Czechs overprinted various express, newspaper and postage due stamps. This one belongs to the newspaper series depicting a windhover, originally issued in 1918.

7. Marienwerder, 20 pfennigs, 1920
One of a series of fourteen stamps, recess-printed at Officine Grafiche Coen, Milan, for use in the Marienwerder district during the plebiscite period of March–August 1920. The design shows the female allegory of the People's Will surrounded by the flags of the Allies. Various stamps of Germany, overprinted 'Commission Interalliée Marienwerder' were also used. Two versions of the Coen design were used. The first, as illustrated, appeared in March 1920. The second, used between 13 July and 16 August 1920, was inscribed PLEBISCITE at the top and bore the name of the district in German and Polish (Kwidzyn) at the foot. At the conclusion of the plebiscite the district reverted to Germany.

8. Memel, 80 pfennigs, 1922
The German town and district of Memel were in Allied occupation from 1918 till January 1923. In that period no fewer than 125 different stamps were issued under the French administration. German stamps overprinted 'Memelgebiet' and French stamps overprinted 'Memel' were used in that period. Continuing disagreement about the future of the town prevented a plebiscite from taking place and ultimately the Lithuanians took the matter into their own hands by seizing the port in January 1923 (see plate 3).

9. Slesvig, 7½ pfennigs, 1920
Though Denmark had remained neutral throughout World War I the Danish parliament urged that northern Schleswig, or Slesvig, should be surrendered by Germany which had occupied this predominantly Danish-speaking area since 1864. Two sets of stamps were designed by August Carstens and typographed by Thiele & Co. of Copenhagen. The first, released on 25 January 1920, had values expressed in German currency; the second, released on 20 May 1920, had values in Danish øre and kronor. The pfennig and øre denominations in both sets depicted the coat of arms of Slesvig.

10. Slesvig, 1 mark, 1920
The mark and kronor denominations of both sets featured a bleak moorland landscape, typical of the scenery in northern Schleswig. The first series was also overprinted C.I.S. (Commission Interalliée Slesvig) for use on correspondence of plebiscite officials.

11. Saar, 15 pfennigs, 1920
The first stamps used in the Saar consisted of contemporary German stamps overprinted with the French version of the name 'Sarre'. The series was introduced on 30 January 1920.

12. Saar, 5 pfennigs, 1920
The third series used in this territory consisted of German stamps of 1905–20 overprinted 'Saargebiet' (Saar district), and this was the form used on all subsequent issues until distinctive stamps were discontinued in 1935.

13. Saar, 20 pfennigs, 1920
Subsequently obsolete stamps of the kingdom of Bavaria were overprinted with the French version of the name and released on 3 March 1920. The stamps ranged in denomination from 5*pf.* to 10*m.*

14. Saar, 5 pfennigs, 1921
One of a pictorial series, designed by A. Montader from photographs and typographed by Vaugirard of Paris. An unusual feature of these stamps was their ornate frames, a different form of decoration being used with each design. This stamp shows the mill above Mettlach. Other designs showed blast furnaces, steel mills and coal mines. The same designs, inscribed in French currency, were issued in 1922.

15. Saar, 15 francs, 1953
Between 1950 and 1956 the Saar released a stamp each May to mark *Tag der Briefmarke* (Stamp Day). Postmen, postilions and mail coaches old and new were the subjects of these stamps.

16. Saar, 30 pfennigs, 1947
The Saar was occupied by French troops at the end of World War II and at first used the general series of stamps of the French zone. Distinctive stamps were introduced again in 1947. In design and production they followed closely the stamps of the French zone of Germany, being designed by V. K. Jonynas and printed in photogravure by Franz Burda of Offenbach. Miners, steelworkers and farmworkers were featured on the lower values, but it is interesting to note that Marshal Ney, Napoleon's general, was portrayed on the 84*pf.* The series was reissued with surcharges in French currency in November 1947.

17. Saar, 30 francs, 1953
One of a series of pictorial definitive stamps issued between 1952 and 1955. The stamps were recess-printed at the Mint, Paris, and were engraved by French and German artists like Frantzen, Mazelin and Barlangue. This denomination shows the University Library at Saarbrücken.

18. 15 francs, 1954
One of a set of three stamps issued in August 1954 to mark Marian Year. Many stamps issued by the Saar in both plebiscite periods had a strong religious theme. This large-sized series reproduced famous works – The Sistine *Madonna* by Raphael (5*f.*), Holbein's *Madonna and Child* (10*f.*) and Dürer's *Madonna and Child* (15*f.*).

19. Upper Silesia, 10 pfennigs, 1920
The basic series was issued in February 1920 but a temporary shortage of 5 and 10*pf.* denominations led to the provisional surcharge of other values in March. The stamps were typographed at the French Government Printing Works and rendered the name of the district in French, German and Polish.

20. Upper Silesia, 1 mark, 1920
A new series, likewise typographed at the French Government Printing Works, was released in March 1920. The stamps from 2½*pf.* to 40*pf.* were in a small format, and the higher denominations in a large horizontal format. Both used the same design, showing a dove of peace over a Silesian landscape of coal-mine and farmhouse. Many of these stamps were overprinted 'Plébiscite' with the date 20 March on which the referendum was held. As a result of the voting Upper Silesia was divided between Poland and Germany.

21. Upper Silesia, 20 pfennigs, 1920
Various German official stamps (*Dienstmarke*) were overprinted C.G.H.S. (Commission du Gouvernement, Haute Silesie) for use on official correspondence of the Inter-Allied Commission. These stamps have been recorded with double overprints or, as shown here, with the overprint inverted.

22. Eupen, 2 centimes, 1920
The entire contemporary Belgian definitive series, from 1 centime to 10 francs, was overprinted 'Eupen' for use in this border town in 1920–21 after it was surrendered by Germany under the terms of the Peace Treaty. The separate issues were preceded by a series of Belgian stamps surcharged in German currency and overprinted EUPEN & MALMEDY.

23. Malmedy, 1 centime, 1920
Malmedy, like Eupen, had a series of seventeen Belgian stamps overprinted for its own use in 1920–21, pending the absorption of the district into Belgium. The stamps were issued for political reasons, to emphasize the handover of territory, and not for financial reasons, since, by that time, Belgian currency had been brought into circulation in both areas. The sets of 1920–21 provide an interesting example of the way in which postage stamps can be used for national propaganda purposes.

PLATE 15
Greece

1. 1 lepton, 1861
Adhesive stamps were adopted by Greece in October 1861. Albert Barre designed the famous 'Hermes Heads', using a similar frame to the contemporary Ceres and Napoleonic issues of France. The earliest printings were typographed at Paris by Émile Meyer, but subsequently the plates were dispatched to Athens. The Athens printings from November 1861 to 1886 varied considerably in the ink, paper and state of impression. Perforation of various gauges was adopted between 1881 and 1887.

2. 50 lepta, 1902
Perkins Bacon recess-printed a series portraying Hermes, in denominations from 5*l.* to 2*d.*, issued in January 1902. The letters AM in the corners signify 'Axia Metallike' (metal value). These stamps were intended for use on foreign parcels which had to be prepaid in metallic rather than paper currency. The remaining stocks of this short-lived series were used in 1913 in lieu of postage due stamps.

3. Provisional Government, 1 lepton, 1917
In 1917 the Greek politician Eleftherios Venizelos, angry at the vacillation of King Constantine, left Athens and formed a provisional government at Salonika, then headquarters of the Allies in the Balkan campaign. A series of stamps inscribed to signify 'Provisional Government' and depicting the goddess Iris was lithographed by Perkins Bacon and issued by the Venizelists in those areas under their control. The stamps were issued either perforated or imperforate.

4. 3 + 1 lepta, 1917
Since 1914 Greece has issued a number of charity tax stamps, whose use is obligatory on correspondence at certain times. The earliest stamps

PLATE 15 GREECE

raised funds for widows, orphans and refugees from the Balkan Wars of 1912–14. This stamp was one of a series issued in April 1917 to raise money for the relief of victims of the Allied blockade of Greece. The initials K.P. stand for 'Koinonike Pronoia' (social providence) and the surcharge represents the amount of the charity premium.

5. 5 lepta, 1923
The basic stamp was one of a series released in Crete in 1905 when that island was under an independent administration. The stamps were recess-printed by Bradbury Wilkinson and featured ancient Cretan coins. In 1908–09 the stamps were overprinted to signify 'Greece', following the union of the island with the mother country. Greek and Cretan stamps were issued in May 1923 with the overprint 'Epanastasis' (revolution) to celebrate the overthrow of the monarchy in 1922.

6. 3 drachmae, 1935
After thirteen years of a republican regime the Greek monarchy was restored in November 1935. To celebrate the event various postage and postage due stamps were overprinted with a crown or the royal coat of arms and the date of the restoration. The postage due stamps thus treated were then issued for ordinary postal duty. New values were surcharged in each case.

7. 2 drachmae, 1901
Perkins Bacon produced a lengthy definitive series for Greece in 1901. The lower values, from 1l. to 1d., were recess-printed, while the three higher denominations (2, 3 and 5d.) were lithographed, using metallic ink – bronze, silver and gold respectively. The stamps reproduced Giambologna's statue of Hermes or Mercury. The first printing was on thick paper, but the series was reissued in 1902 on thin paper.

8. 2 drachmae, 1924
Many of the commemorative issues of the period before World War II celebrated centenaries of events connected with the struggle for independence from the Turks. The first of these issues consisted of two stamps, recess-printed by Bradbury Wilkinson and released in April 1924. The 80l. stamp portrayed Lord Byron, while the 2d. showed him meeting the Greek insurgents at Missolonghi. Subsequent issues commemorated the Fall of Missolonghi (1926), the Liberation of Athens (1927), the Battle of Navarino (1927–28), the Defence of Arkadi (1930) and the Declaration of Independence (1930).

9. 5 drachmae, 1926
The first Greek airmail stamps were produced in October 1926 to prepay postage on mail carried by the Aeroespresso Company. A set of four stamps was lithographed in multicolour by an unknown printer in Milan and featured aircraft over scenery or a map of the eastern Mediterranean.
espresso Co. operated a network of routes between Italy, Greece and Turkey.

10. 5 drachmae, 1937
A new definitive series was introduced after the return of the monarchy. The stamps, in denominations from 5l. to 100d., were recess-printed by De La Rue or lithographed by Aspioti-Elka of Athens. Prior to this Greece had relied mainly on security printers abroad, in Britain, Italy and even Poland, for most of her stamps. From 1937 onwards, an increasing proportion of Greek stamps were lithographed locally, though recess-printed stamps continued to be produced by De La Rue. The series of 1937–38 harked back to the golden age of Classical Greece and set the precedent for most definitive sets since that time.

11. 5,000 drachmae, 1944
Between April 1941 and October 1944 Greece was under German occupation, though no reference to that regime was made on the stamps of that period. Galloping inflation, however, led to a pictorial definitive series of 1942–44 in denominations from 2 to 200d., and subsequent values up to 5,000,000d. were required. The 75d. value was overprinted in July 1944 and surcharged in aid of the Postal Staff Anti-Tuberculosis fund. Charity tax stamps overprinted for that purpose were issued annually from 1940 to 1951.

12. 1.50 drachmae, 1963
The turbulent Greek monarchy celebrated its centenary in 1963 with a series of five stamps portraying the five kings of the Danish dynasty – George I, Constantine I, Alexander, George II and Paul. No mention was made of the Bavarian king Otto, deposed in 1863, though he appeared in the Royal Family portrait definitive series of 1956–57.

13. 4.50 drachmae, 1968
The first anniversary of the national revolution following the unsuccessful coup of King Constantine II was marked by a set of eight stamps with the theme of the Hellenic fight for civilization. The stamps, lithographed in multicolour, ranged from the defeat of Alkyoneus by Athena (from the frieze on the altar of Zeus at Pergamun) to the reproduction of G. B. Scott's painting entitled 'Evzone' (the Greek soldier). In the background are the dates of more recent conflicts ranging from the Balkan Wars (1912–13) to the Korean War (1950–52) and including the campaign of 1945–50 against the Communists. Several issues in recent years have had a political bias, harking back to the glories of Greece in a chauvinistic manner. Since 1966 Greek stamps have been inscribed HELLAS in the Roman as well as Greek alphabets.

14. Crete, 2 drachmae, 1905
Crete was made an autonomous state under Turkish suzerainty in 1898 and issued its own stamps from 1900 to 1910. In March 1905 Eleftherios Venizelos organized a revolt in favour of *Enosis* (union) with Greece and stamps were issued by the Venizelists at Theriso, the district under their control. A crude hand-struck series was followed, in October 1905, by a series featuring Crete enslaved or portraying King George of Greece. The stamps were lithographed locally. The revolt was suppressed in November 1905.

15. Crete, 5 drachmae, 1905
Two definitive sets were issued during the period of Cretan autonomy. Both were recess-printed by Bradbury Wilkinson and both featured coins and other antiquities of the island. The series of 1905 included a large-sized 5d. depicting a view of Mount Ida flanked by female figures symbolizing sovereignty and victory. The series was overprinted to signify 'Greece' in 1908 after the Cretan Assembly proclaimed union with Greece, though this was not recognized till the Treaty of London ended the Balkan Wars in 1913.

16. Crete, 2 drachmae, 1908
In 1908 the Cretan Assembly proclaimed *Enosis* (union) with Greece, but this was not ratified by the European Powers until 1913. In 1908 the current definitive stamps of Crete were reissued with an overprint in Greek lettering to signify 'Greece'. Apart from double or inverted overprints there are numerous examples of missing or inverted letters. Different styles of lettering were used for the overprints in 1909–10.

17. Cavalla, 10 lepta, 1913
The Turkish town of Cavalla was captured by Bulgaria in the first Balkan War (1912) and then by the Greeks in the second war (1913). Bulgarian stamps were overprinted locally to signify 'Greek Administration' and surcharged in Greek currency. Greek stamps were adopted later in 1913.

18. Dedeagatz, 10 lepta, 1913
The Aegean seaport of Dedeagatz, like Cavalla, was taken from the Bulgars by their former allies in the second Balkan War and Bulgarian stamps were suitably overprinted and surcharged in Greek currency. A makeshift issue, typeset on white paper, appeared in September 1913 pending the introduction of Greek stamps.

19. Icaria, 1 drachma, 1912
The island of Icaria in the Aegean Sea was captured from the Turks in the first Balkan War. A provisional government seized power before the arrival of the Greek troops and issued a set of eight stamps, featuring Hermes, from an ancient coin. The stamps were lithographed for the Icarians by Grundmann & Co. of Athens. Several Greek stamps, suitably overprinted, were also issued in Icaria in 1913.

20. Lemnos, 1 lepton, 1912
Greek stamps of the 1901 and 1911 sets were overprinted 'Lemnos' in Greek capitals and issued on that island in 1912–12 after the Turkish administration had been overthrown. Apart from inverted or double overprints examples are known with capital A or D instead of a Greek L.

21. Mytilene, 5 paras, 1912
Contemporary Turkish stamps were overprinted vertically in three lines 'Elleniki Katochi Mytilenis' (Greek Administration of Mytilene) and issued in November 1912. A number of these stamps were subsequently surcharged in Greek currency.

22. Samos, 50 lepta, 1912
Stamps were issued by the provisional government of Samos between November 1912 and 1915. The first set featured a map of the island and was followed by a series, lithographed by G. Stangel of Athens, featuring the head of Hermes. A set commemorating the evacuation of the Turks appeared in January 1913 and showed the scene of the Turkish repulse in 1824. Subsequent issues were overprinted 'Greece' like the Cretan stamps of 1908. Though united to Greece by the Treaty of London in May 1913 Samos continued to issue its own stamps till 1915, the last series being a charity issue on behalf of a hospital at Vathy.

23. Greek Occupation, 1 lepton, 1912
The Greek definitive series of 1911 was overprinted 'Elleniki Dioikesis' (Greek administration) and issued in those territories acquired as a result of the Balkan Wars. Twelve different types of overprint have been recorded and may be found reading upward or downward, in red or black. The possible combinations are almost infinite.

24. Thrace, 3 lepta, 1920
The Greek occupation of Thrace resulted in several distinct issues of stamps. Turkish stamps overprinted with the Greek coat of arms were used at Goumultsina in August 1913; two months later, the Muslim population of western Thrace drove out the Bulgars and set up an autonomous regime, issuing stamps lithographed in Arabic. After World War I Greek troops reoccupied Thrace (under Bulgarian control since 1913) and issued Greek stamps overprinted to signify 'Greek Administration of Thrace'. Similar overprints for eastern and western Thrace were released in June and July 1920 respectively, while Turkish stamps, overprinted to signify 'High Commission of Thrace',

155

PLATE 15 GREECE · PLATE 16 ITALIAN OCCUPATION OF GREECE

were used following the seizure of Edirne (Adrianople) in August 1920.

25. Dodecanese Islands, 10 drachmae, 1947
Control of the Dodecanese Islands was handed over by the British military authorities in April 1947 and Greek stamps were then introduced. The pictorial series of 1942–44 was surcharged in new values from 10 to 1,000d. and overprinted 's.D.D.' in Greek (Greek Military Administration of the Dodecanese). Ordinary Greek stamps were introduced later in 1947.

PLATE 16
Italian Occupation of Greece

On three occasions in this century the Italians have occupied islands which geographically form part of Greece. The Dodecanese Islands were ceded by Turkey after the Italo–Turkish War and were administered as an Italian colony until the end of World War II. Castelrosso was acquired as a result of World War I and subsequently added to the Dodecanese. In both world wars Italy seized the Ionian Islands and distinctive stamps were issued on both occasions.

1. Calimno, 5 centesimi, 1912
Seven Italian definitive stamps, from 5 to 50c., were overprinted 'Calimno' and released in December 1912. Various denominations, new colours and provisional surcharges were issued between that date and 1921. Subsequently the general series of the Aegean Islands was used, but various Italian stamps overprinted 'Calino' were issued in 1930 and 1932.

2. Carchi, 20 centesimi, 1916
Italian stamps overprinted 'Karki' were adopted in December 1912. This stamp, a 20c. surcharged on 15c., was added to the series in January 1916. The general series of the Aegean Islands was subsequently used, though Italian stamps overprinted 'Calchi' (1930) or 'Carchi' (1932) were also issued.

3. Caso, 40 centesimi, 1912
One of the few islands of the Dodecanese on which the spelling seems to have been agreed. Stamps were issued in December 1912 and subsequently followed the same pattern as in the other Aegean Islands.

4. Cos, 10 centesimi, 1912
The Italian stamps overprinted for use in this island bore the Greek form of the name from 1912 till 1921. In the overprints of 1930–32 the Italian version 'Coo' was adopted.

5. Leros, 5 centesimi, 1912
The stamps used between 1912 and 1922 were overprinted with the Greek form 'Leros', but the later overprints of 1930–32 had the form 'Lero'. Like the stamps of the other islands those of 1930 (Ferrucci) and 1932 (Garibaldi) were issued in colours differing from those used in Italy.

6. Lipso, 50 centesimi, 1912
This stamp was the top value of the 1912 definitive series. As in the case of the other islands the 20c. provisional surcharge appeared in 1916 and the 15 and 20c. stamps in new colours were issued in 1921–22 with the same overprint. The Ferrucci set of 1930 was overprinted 'Lisso', but the Garibaldi series of 1932 reverted to the original spelling. Like the other islands Lipso issued 26 stamps in 20 years.

7. Nisiros, 2 centesimi, 1912
A similar series was used in the island of Nisiros during the same period.

8. Patmos, 5 centesimi, 1912
The earlier stamps, from 1912 to 1922, were overprinted with the Greek name 'Patmos', but in the later overprints the shorter form 'Patmo' was used. These changes, introduced in the Fascist era, reflect the Italian policy of substituting Italian for Greek language on all public documents.

9. Piscopi, 5 centesimi, 1912
In this case the same form of the name was used throughout its philatelic history. Piscopi issued the identical 26 stamps between 1912 and 1932 common to the other Dodecanese Islands under Italian rule.

10. Scarpanto, 10 centesimi, 1912
Probably because the Greek name (Karpathos) was so outlandish to the Italian ear, the form 'Scarpanto' was adopted in the very beginning of the Italian occupation, and retained on all the stamps up to 1932.

11. Simi, 2 centesimi, 1912
The eagle of Savoy was the motif of this Art Nouveau stamp originally issued by Italy in 1901, and retained as the lowest denomination of the series overprinted for use in the Aegean islands. Simi's philatelic history was identical to that of the other islands, without even a change of spelling to relieve the monotony.

12. Stampalia, 5 centesimi, 1912
The Italian form 'Stampalia' was preferred to the Greek 'Astipalaia' from the very outset for the stamps of this, most westerly of the twelve islands.

13. Aegean Islands, 25 centesimi, 1912
Contemporary Italian stamps in denominations of 25 and 50 centesimi were issued throughout the Dodecanese Islands in September 1912 overprinted 'Egeo', the Italian form of Aegean. These were superseded by the separate issues of the twelve component islands and a general issue was not re-introduced until October 1930.

14. Aegean Islands, 50 centesimi, 1930
In addition to the five Ferrucci overprints issued in each of the islands a set of three airmail stamps of the same series was released with the general overprint 'Isole Italiane dell'Egeo' (Italian islands of the Aegean). The 50c., 1 and 5l. stamps were printed in new colours for this purpose. Subsequently numerous Italian commemorative sets were overprinted in this way rather than release separate sets in each of the islands.

15. Aegean Islands, 75 centesimi, 1932
In honour of the Dante Alighieri Society the twelve ordinary and seven airmail stamps were issued in new colours and overprinted for use in the Aegean. Overprinted Italian stamps of this type continued to appear up to 1938.

16. Aegean Islands, 3 lire, 1940
A series of six stamps was issued in 1933 in connection with the Graf Zeppelin world flights. The stamps were designed by G. Rondini and printed in photogravure. The stamps featured landmarks of the Dodecanese with the giant airship overhead.

17. Rhodes, 20 centesimi, 1932
Like the Dodecanese Islands, Rhodes issued Italian stamps with an appropriate overprint in December 1912 and followed the same pattern up to 1929 when a distinctive definitive series was adopted. The series, from 5c. to 10l., was released in May 1929 ostensibly to commemorate the visit

of King Victor Emmanuel to the Aegean, but they were retained afterward for definitive purposes and were reissued in August 1932 with the printer's imprint added to the margin. Though inscribed 'Rodi' these stamps could be used anywhere in the Italian Aegean Islands. The original printings were lithographed by Bestetti and Tuminelli of Milan but the later version was produced at the Government Printing Works in Rome.

18. Rhodes, 50 centesimi, 1934
A set of four airmail stamps, designed by B. Bramanti and typographed in Rome, was released in January 1934. The common design featured the winged emblem from the coat of arms of Francesco Sans. The distinctive designs of Rhodian stamps invariably alluded to the periods when the island had been ruled by the Romans, the Venetians or the medieval Knights of St John, thereby emphasizing Italian claims to the island. The airmail stamps were subsequently surcharged during World War II in aid of the Red Cross and war refugee funds.

19. Rhodes, 1.25 lire, 1935
Express letter stamps in denominations of 1.25 and 2.50l. were designed by Bramanti and printed in photogravure. The basic stamps were released in December 1935 but they were surcharged in aid of war-relief in 1943 and bore a 100 per cent charity premium. The curious design features the leaping stag emblem of Rhodes, flanked by the eight-pointed cross of the Knights of St John and the Fascist emblem of Italy. The unusual lettering was a style favoured by Bramanti on the postage, airmail, parcel post and postage due stamps he designed for Rhodes.

20. Castelrosso, 40 centesimi, 1923
The Turkish island of Castellorizo was occupied by Italian troops at the end of World War I and subsequently annexed to the Aegean Islands. Contemporary Italian stamps overprinted 'Castelrosso' were issued in July 1922 in denominations from 5 to 85c. and two years later a diagonal overprint was adopted. Castelrosso issued the Ferrucci and Garibaldi stamps of 1930–32 with a suitable overprint, but unlike the other islands also had a distinctive series of five stamps depicting a map of the area. The stamps, commemorating the Italian occupation of the island, were released in January 1923.

21. Corfu, 2.40 drachmae, 1923
Italy took advantage of the Greek revolution of 1922 to seize the offshore islands in the Adriatic Sea. Contemporary stamps, from 5c. to 1l. were overprinted 'Corfu'. Subsequently similar stamps, but additionally surcharged with the equivalent value in Greek currency, were issued. Italian troops were forced to evacuate Corfu shortly afterward and ordinary Greek stamps were re-introduced.

22. Saseno, 60 centesimi, 1923
Italian stamps were simultaneously overprinted for use in the island of Saseno. No surcharged series was produced and, like the stamps of Corfu, these were of short duration.

23. Corfu, 2 drachmae, 1941
Following the Italian invasion of Greece in 1941 Greek stamps overprinted 'Corfu' were used in that island, pending its annexation by Italy. In addition to the definitive series of 1937–38 the airmail series, charity tax stamps and postage due series were similarly overprinted.

24. Ionian Islands, 50 centesimi, 1941
Contemporary Italian stamps overprinted 'Isole Jonie' were issued between 1941 and 1943 in the

Ionian Islands, except Corfu, which had been incorporated directly into the Kingdom of Italy. German stamps (1943–45) and British stamps overprinted M.E.F. (1945–46) were used before Greek stamps were re-introduced after World War II.

25. Cerigo, 80 lepta, 1941
Following the Italian occupation of the Ionian island of Cerigo various contemporary Greek stamps were overprinted 'CERIGO Occupazione Militare Italiana', while the Fascist emblem was applied as an underprint. The status of these overprints is doubtful since they were never properly authorized by the occupying forces.

26. Cephalonia and Ithaca, 15 drachmae, 1941
A separate issue of stamps was made by the Italian forces occupying Cephalonia and Ithaca in the Ionian islands. The overprint, signifying 'Italy–Italian military occupation of the islands of Cephalonia and Ithaca', was so lengthy in some cases that it could not be accommodated on one stamp, but had to be overprinted across each pair. These stamps were superseded by the general series of the Ionian Islands.

27. Paxo, 20 lepta, 1941
Like the overprints of Cerigo, those of Paxo are thought to have been purely philatelic in inspiration and are therefore omitted from most stamp catalogues. Various Greek definitive stamps were overprinted 'Isola Italiana di Paxo Anno XIX' (Italian island of Paxo – year 19 in the Fascist era). These local issues were superseded by contemporary Italian stamps overprinted 'Isole Jonie' (see above).

PLATE 17
Foreign Post Offices in Crete and Greece

The stamps illustrated in this plate fall into two main groups, those issued by the European powers for their spheres of administration in Crete at the turn of the century, and those stamps provided for the foreign post offices and postal agencies functioning in areas formerly part of the Turkish Empire but now geographically part of Greece. A third group, however, comprises the oddities thrown up by the turbulent politics of this area – the stamps issued during the Turkish occupation of Thessaly (1898), the British occupation of Salonika (1916) and the German occupation of the Ionian Islands (1943).

1. Crete (Austrian Post Office), 25 centimes, 1903
The stamps of the Austrian post offices in the Levant (see plate 34) were used in Crete prior to 1903 but then Austrian stamps surcharged in French currency were introduced. Austrian definitives of the 1901–02 series were released in March 1903, and were superseded in November 1904 by the 1904 definitives similarly surcharged. In 1907 Austrian stamps surcharged in denominations of 5, 10 and 15c. were issued.

2. Crete (Austrian Post Office), 10 centimes, 1908
Six stamps commemorating the 60th anniversary of Kaiser Franz Josef's accession were printed on tinted paper and valued in French currency for use in Crete. The earliest version of the 10 and 25c. values were printed on chalk-surfaced paper coloured on the face only. In 1914 they were reissued on unsurfaced paper coloured on both sides. Many of the stamps intended for use in Crete were also sold at the Austrian post offices in the Turkish

Empire. The Austrian post offices in Crete closed at the outbreak of World War I.

3. Crete (French Administration), 3 centimes, 1902
Post offices in the French sphere of Crete were established in 1902 and the Blanc, Mouchon and Merson keytypes suitably inscribed were issued in October of that year. The Blanc design was used for five denominations (1, 2, 3, 4 and 5c).

4. Crete (French Administration), 40 centimes, 1902
The five higher denominations, from 40c. to 5f., were in the horizontal design by Olivier Merson. These stamps were used at Heraklion in northern Crete.

5. Crete (French Administration), 1 piastre, 1903
The previous stamps, inscribed in French currency, were intended for inland letters and parcels, but in accordance with international agreements, external letter mail had to be prepaid in Turkish currency. Consequently five values of the series were issued in February–March 1903 surcharged from 1 to 20p. The French post offices in Crete were closed at the end of December 1913.

6. Crete (British Administration), 10 parades, 1898
Before the introduction of distinctive stamps by the Cretan autonomous government in 1900 the British authorities at Heraklion issued on 25 November 1898 a 20 parades stamp handstruck in violet with the inscription 'Prosorinon Tachudrom Herakleiou' (Provisional Posts of Heraklion). This was followed in December by 10 and 20p. stamps lithographed by M. Grundmann of Athens in a square format with the value contained in a circle. Originally the stamps were printed in blue and green but in 1899 the colours were changed to brown and rose respectively. The stamps were normally issued perforated but imperforate varieties of all denominations and colours are known. The stamps were withdrawn in 1900 when the general series of Crete was introduced.

7. Crete (Italian Administration), 1 piastre, 1900
The Italian administration was based in Khania (Canea) in the northwestern part of the island and Italian 25c. stamps overprinted 'La Canea' were introduced in July 1900 surcharged for use as 1p. stamps. The 25c. stamps of both 1893 and 1901 sets were surcharged in this way.

8. Crete (Italian Administration), 1 centesimo, 1906
Italy continued to operate a post office at Canea until the end of 1913, handling mainly external correspondence. In November 1906 the definitive series of 1901–05, from 1c. to 5l., was overprinted 'La Canea', without surcharge. Between 1907 and 1912 stamps of the 1906–09 series were similarly overprinted. The 5c. of 1907 has been recorded with the overprint inverted.

9. Crete (Russian Administration), 1 metalik, 1899
The Russian sphere of Crete was based on Rethymno on the northern coast and stamps inscribed with this name in French or Greek were issued in May 1899. A 1m. stamp inscribed 'Retymno' and the French for 'provisional postage stamp' was handstruck in blue on laid or wove paper. A similar design inscribed entirely in Greek was issued in denominations of 1m. green and 2m. in rose or green, also handstruck on wove or laid paper.

10. Crete (Russian Administration), 2 metaliks, 1899
A series of three denominations, 1 and 2m. and 1 grosion, was lithographed at Athens and introduced in June 1899. The inscription in Greek signified 'Provisional Posts of Rethymno' and featured a trident in an upright oval. Two versions of this design were produced; in one the figures of

value were unshaded, in the other the figures were shaded and stars were added to the oval band bearing the inscription. All three denominations were printed in a wide variety of colours and issued with or without control marks consisting of the Russian eagle in a circle or the word 'Rethymnon' in Greek diagonally overprinted. These stamps were withdrawn from use in 1900.

11. Cavalla, 1 piastre, 1893
A French post office was established in the Aegean seaport of Cavalla in 1893 and contemporary French stamps overprinted 'Cavalle' were introduced. The 5, 10 and 15c. stamps were issued without surcharge, but higher denominations were surcharged in Turkish currency from 1 to 8p. In 1902–03 the Blanc, Mouchon and Merson series was issued with the inscription 'Cavalle'. The colour of the 15c. was changed from red to orange in 1912. This post office closed in 1914 after Greece took over the administration of Cavalla at the end of the Balkan wars.

12. Dedeagatz, 25 centimes, 1893
Prior to 1893 the French post office in Dedeagatz used the stamps of the French Levant series but, like Cavalla, French stamps with a distinctive overprint were then adopted. The stamps were overprinted 'Dédéagh', with or without a surcharge in Turkish currency. The keytype designs were introduced in 1902–03 and the colour of the 15c. was likewise changed in 1913. The French post office closed in 1914.

13. Port Lagos, 10 centimes, 1893
Both France and Austria maintained post offices in this north Aegean seaport, but France alone produced distinctive stamps. Ordinary French stamps, identifiable by the numeral obliterator 5054 (large figures), were used from 1874 to 1893 when contemporary French stamps were overprinted 'Port-Lagos'. The French post office was closed in 1898 and the use of distinctive stamps discontinued. Port Lagos passed from Turkey to Greece during the Balkan wars and ordinary Greek stamps have been used since 1913.

14. Vathy, 15 centimes, 1893
A French post office operated at Vathy, the chief town on the island of Samos, from 1893 to 1914 and during that period contemporary French stamps were issued with a distinctive overprint in the same manner as Cavalla and Dedeagatz. The same series remained in use throughout the entire period. Following the transfer of the administration from Turkey to Greece in 1913 the French post office closed down.

15. Mount Athos, 5 paras, 1909
The Russians maintained a consular post office at Daphne, the seaport at the foot of Mount Athos, the holy mountain of the Orthodox Church, and between 1909 and 1913 issued stamps of the Russian Levant series overprinted 'Mont-Athos' in French. The stamps were additionally surcharged in Turkish currency from 5pa. to 70pi. The values up to 7pi. are known with the overprint inverted, doubled or omitted in pair with a normal stamp and, in addition, various examples of misspelling or missing letters are known.

16. Mount Athos, 5 paras, 1909
The Russians also released the series with the overprint in Russian 'S(veti) Athoes' (Holy Athos). The lettering used for this purpose was the ancient Cyrillic retained for ecclesiastical inscriptions. Oddly enough, this series seems to have been miraculously free of the errors and varieties which distinguish the French version. The Russian post office was suppressed by the Greeks in 1913, when

157

PLATE 17 FOREIGN POST OFFICES IN GREECE · PLATE 18 GREAT BRITAIN

the Chalkidice Peninsula was captured in the Second Balkan War.

17. Mount Athos, 1 shilling, 1916

To forestall German or Bulgarian infiltration of Mount Athos the Allied forces at Salonika planned to occupy the holy mountain in the spring of 1916. In connection with this two sets of stamps were prepared, one consisting of British stamps overprinted 'Levant' for the use of British troops (see Salonika, below) and the other consisting of specially printed stamps for the use of the civil population. The distinctive stamps of Mount Athos were a curiosity in several respects. They were printed in three languages, three scripts and valued in three currencies – British, Russian and Greek. The central motif was the double-headed eagle of Byzantium. The stamps, in denominations from ½d. to 1s., were printed by a photographic process on board H.M.S. *Ark Royal*, and were the only stamps to have been produced aboard a ship in time of war. The Russians ultimately vetoed the proposed occupation of Mount Athos. A few examples of these curious stamps were used 'by favour' on mail from the British field post office at Salonika, but they are generally regarded as having the status of 'prepared for use but never issued'.

18. Mytilene, 5 paras, 1909

A Russian post office functioned at Mytilene, the chief port on the Aegean island of Lesbos, and used stamps of the Russian Levant series. Like the other offices, however, it received its own distinctive overprints in 1909–10, in denominations from 5pa. to 70pi. The 5, 10 and 20pa. stamps are known with the overprint inverted.

19. Salonika, 20 paras, 1909

The important seaport of Salonika at the north-western end of the Aegean Sea handles the bulk of the trade in the Balkans and, as such, attracted the commercial attention of all the major European powers. In the early twentieth century Salonika had, in addition to the Turkish post office, post offices or agencies operated by Britain, France, Germany, Austria, Italy and Russia. Subsequently it had Greek and Bulgarian post offices during the Balkan Wars and a Serbian post office in World War I – not to mention the field post offices operated by the Allies and the postal administration of the Venizelists (see plate 15). The Russian post office briefly issued its own distinctive series in 1909–10, overprinted 'Salonique' in French. The three lowest values are known with inverted overprints.

20. Salonika, 1 piastre, 1909

With the appearance of the Russian series the Italian post office simultaneously introduced stamps overprinted 'Salonicco' and surcharged in Turkish currency, from 10 paras to 20 piastres. A 40pi. on 10l. stamp was added to the series in 1911. The Italian post office was suppressed by the Turks during the Italo–Turkish War of 1911–12 and in the upheavals of the Balkan Wars the office was never reopened.

21. Salonika, 1 shilling, 1916

A British field post office operated at Salonika during World War I and used ordinary British stamps without surcharge or overprint. In the spring of 1916, however, a stock of stamps, from ½d. to 1s., was overprinted at the Army Printing Office 'Levant' in upper and lower case lettering. These stamps were intended for use at the proposed British post office to be established on Mount Athos. When the expedition was cancelled the stamps were used on mail from Salonika, between the end of February and 9 March 1916. Their use was unnecessary and unauthorized, but it seems to have been condoned by the military postal service.

The British stamps used in the Levantine post offices (including Salonika) before World War I were always overprinted in capitals.

22. Thessaly, 5 piastres, 1898

During the Graeco–Turkish War of 1898 the Turks invaded the Greek province of Thessaly. During their brief occupation they produced a series of five stamps, in denominations from 10pa. to 5pi. The stamps were octagonal – the only issue ever produced in that shape – and were perforated on all eight sides. The common design features the *toughra* of the Sultan and, in the lower part of the central vignette, a view of the railway bridge at Larisa over the river Pinios.

23. Zante, 50 centesimi, 1943

After the Italian collapse in 1943 German troops occupied the Ionian Islands, formerly under Italian control. Italian stamps overprinted 'Isole Jonie' (see plate 16) were issued in the island of Zante (Zakynthos) overprinted in Greek 'Hellas' (Greece) and the date (2 October 1943) of the German takeover. They were overprinted in red or black.

PLATE 18

Great Britain

1. 1 penny, 1840

The celebrated Penny Black, the world's first adhesive postage stamp, was issued with the Twopence Blue in May 1840. The appearance of the stamps was the culmination of a long campaign for postal reform led by Sir Rowland Hill. In 1839 the complicated system of computing postage by the distance and the number of sheets was swept away and a uniform system based on weight alone was substituted. The uniform rate was reduced from 4d. to 1d. in January 1840 and adhesive stamps issued to facilitate prepayment. Hitherto postage was normally recovered from the recipient. The stamps were based on a design by Hill himself. The dies were engraved by Frederick Heath, from the Wyon Guildhall medal of 1838, and the stamps were recess-printed by Perkins Bacon. The letters in the lower corner varied for every stamp in the sheet and were intended as a precaution against forgery. The colour of the 1d. stamp was changed to red in 1841 and this basic design, through permutations of engraving, perforation and paper, remained in use until 1880.

2. 2 shillings, 1867

Although Perkins Bacon retained the lucrative contracts to print the low value stamps (½d. to 2d.) by the recess method until 1880, the higher denominations were typographed by De La Rue, beginning with the 4d. of 1855. Eventually De La Rue were printing all stamps from 3d. to £5 and in 1880 wrested from Perkins Bacon the contract for the lower values. A standard feature of the De La Rue designs was the profile of the youthful Queen Victoria by Jean-Ferdinand Joubert, retained for British stamps till 1902.

3. 10 pence, 1890

De La Rue typographed a bi-coloured series for Britain in 1887 and this is generally known as the Jubilee series, since it appeared in the year of Queen Victoria's Golden Jubilee. The 10d. value was added to the set in 1890.

4. 1 pound, 1902

The highest denomination in the Edwardian series, the £1 stamp retained the format of its Victorian predecessor but introduced a new design. The

Edwardian series was typographed by De La Rue until 1911, but in that year several of the lowest denominations were produced by Harrison & Sons, while the remaining values were printed by the Board of Inland Revenue at Somerset House.

5. 4 pence, 1902

Many of the Edwardian definitive stamps merely followed the design and colour scheme of their Victorian predecessors. Thus the original version of the 4d. stamp portraying King Edward VII was produced in two colours. In 1909, however, the stamp was produced from a single working plate and the colour changed from brown and green to orange over all. This parallels the trend in the colonial stamps typographed by De La Rue in the same period, though this monochrome treatment was not extended to the other bicoloured stamps of the British Edwardian series. Britain did not again use two or more colours in the printing of a definitive stamp until 1967 when the 1s.6d. and 1s.9d. stamps of the Machin series were produced in two-colour photogravure.

6. 1 penny, 1911

One of two stamps released on Coronation Day, 1911, bearing a threequarter profile of King George V. The stamps met with a howl of protest from the public who complained about the 'foreign' appearance of the king, and the lean and hungry look of the lion. This was an inauspicious beginning for the engraver, J. A. C. Harrison, later to equal Schirnböck of Austria as an outstanding portrait engraver. The stamps were re-engraved, opening out the lines of shading in the king's hair and beard, and the lion was given a fatter, healthier appearance by the judicious use of shading.

7. 5 shillings, 1913

The threequarter profile of the king, used for the ½d. and 1d. stamps of 1911, was scrapped in favour of a more formal profile and this was used for all the remaining stamps of this reign. The high value stamps, in denominations of 2s.6d., 5s., 10s. and £1, appeared in 1913 and were recess-printed in a spirited design by Sir Bertram Mackennal. The 'Seahorses' were printed successively by Waterlow Brothers and Layton, De La Rue, and Bradbury Wilkinson and then, in 1934, by Waterlow and Sons. Subtle differences in the products of each company enable philatelists to differentiate the four printings.

8. 1½ pence, 1924

One of a pair issued in April 1924 to mark the British Empire Exhibition at Wembley. These stamps, designed by Harold Nelson, were Britain's first commemoratives. British policy on commemorative issues remained ultra-conservative until the early 1960s. The Wembley stamps were re-issued the following year with the date altered.

9. 1 penny, 1935

One of a set of four stamps issued to celebrate the Silver Jubilee of King George V. Photogravure had been introduced the previous year for the low value definitive stamps, without much success since the same designs, hitherto typographed, had been retained. With the Jubilee series, however, a design had been evolved which was intended to demonstrate the capabilities of photogravure, and this is seen at its best in the delicate tones in the lettering. The stamps were designed by Barnet Freedman and printed by Harrison and Sons who have produced all Britain's photogravure stamps ever since.

10. 1½ pence, 1936

The brief reign of King Edward VIII (later Duke of Windsor) is represented in the stamp album by a handful of issues – four values of a definitive series for Britain and a few of the same stamps suitably overprinted for use in the British post offices in Morocco (see plate 83). From the viewpoint of design these stamps broke new ground, removing the clutter of ornament and lettering which characterized British stamps before (and since) and using a photograph of the king as the basis of the profile. The result was a design of startling simplicity and effectiveness. After the abdication it was thought that the position of the crown on these stamps had been an ill omen. King George VI insisted that, on his stamps, the crown must appear over his head.

11. 1½ pence, 1937
This stamp, released to mark the coronation of King George VI and Queen Elizabeth, was the first British stamp to portray the monarch full-face, and also the first stamp to portray his consort. The design, by Edmund Dulac, set the trend for the omnibus issues of the Crown colonies honouring this event.

12. 10 shillings, 1939
From 1915 to 1948 the highest denomination of the definitive series was 10s., though £1 commemoratives had made a brief appearance in 1929. The high values of George VI featured the royal coat of arms or the heraldic flowers of the United Kingdom. The colour of the 10s. was changed from dark blue to ultramarine in 1942. Several of the photogravure low values were issued in lighter colours in 1941–42 as a wartime economy measure.

13. 2½ pence, 1951
On 3 May 1951, five of the low value definitives were issued in new colours, to conform to the Universal Postal Union's colour code, and on the same day a set of four high value definitives with pictorial designs was also released. To cap the occasion, unprecedented in British philatelic history, two stamps were issued to mark the Festival of Britain, an event which marked the turning point, from postwar austerity to the prosperity of the Fifties. This stamp, designed by Edmund Dulac, symbolized commerce and prosperity. The 4d., by Abram Games, featured the Festival symbol. Despite the pictorialism of the high value definitives, British commemoratives continued to be symbolic rather than pictorial right through to the mid-1960s.

14. 1 shilling 3 pence, 1953
One of a set of four stamps celebrating the coronation of Queen Elizabeth. The other three values used a threequarter profile of the Queen, from a photograph by Dorothy Wilding, but for the 1s.3d. Edmund Dulac chose a somewhat stylized full-face portrait of the Queen in her coronation robes. The Dorothy Wilding portrait was used for the definitives and the majority of the commemoratives from 1952 to 1967.

15. 1 shilling 3 pence, 1966
One of a series of eight stamps issued to mark the 900th anniversary of the Battle of Hastings. Six of the series were 4d. denominations, printed in a se-tenant strip reproducing scenes from the Bayeux Tapestry. The unusually long format of the 1s.3d. accommodated a scene from the tapestry showing Norman horsemen attacking the Saxon huscarls of King Harold. The stamps, designed by David Gentleman, were built up from woodcuts, a technique much favoured by this artist in other forms of minuscule design.

16. 5 pence, 1969
One of a set of four stamps issued in October 1969 to mark the change in status of the Post Office

from a government department to a national corporation. The stamps, featuring aspects of modern postal technology, were designed by David Gentleman and lithographed by De La Rue – the first British stamps produced by this firm since 1911. Note the reduction of the Queen's profile on this, and other commemorative issues, to an insignificant silhouette, often tucked incongruously in a corner. Since 1840 Britain has enjoyed the exclusive privilege of not needing to put the name of the country on its stamps, the monarch's portrait being regarded as sufficient identification. With the advent of pictorial commemoratives, however, this privilege has proved to be a problem, not to say an embarrassment, to stamp designers.

17. 4 pence, 1968
The craze for multicoloured reproductions of famous paintings, prevalent in Europe and the Middle East, spread to Britain in 1967, when a set of three stamps featuring works of art was released. The success of this series induced the Post Office to issue a set of four stamps illustrating paintings by Lawrence, Piper and Constable, as well as this portrait of Queen Elizabeth Tudor by an unknown artist in the following year. Interpretations of the The Adoration of the Shepherds and Madonna and Child themes were used for the Christmas stamps of 1967. Since then, however, Britain has shown less enthusiasm for the postage stamp as a medium for projecting works originally intended for a broader canvas.

18. 4 pence, 1966
Britain issued three stamps to mark the World Cup Football Championship held in England. When the English team defeated West Germany 4–2 to win the championship the 4d. stamp was re-engraved with the words ENGLAND WINNERS. The stamp was sold only in England, the Isle of Man and the Channel Islands and thus may be regarded as the only English 'regional' stamp. A few were also sold in Edinburgh, at the beginning of the annual Festival, and at British Field Post Offices overseas.

19. 1 shilling, 1969
Among the purely thematic sets issued in recent years was a series illustrating the history of British shipping from Elizabethan galleon to modern times. The series coincided with the maiden voyage of the Queen Elizabeth 2 (featured on the 5d. stamp). Three 9d. stamps and two 1s. stamps were produced in se-tenant combinations, and an unusually long format was used for the shilling denominations. The stamps were designed by David Gentleman and printed in multicolour photogravure by Harrison and Sons.

20. Scotland, 6 pence, 1958
One of three stamps released in Scotland in 1958, with suitably Scottish symbolism and heraldic elements. These regional stamps were intended as a sop to nationalist sentiment in the 'regions' of the United Kingdom. Curiously, the largest region of all, England, was omitted from the scheme, presumably on the grounds that nationalist feelings are the prerogative of the Scots, Irish and Welsh. Other denominations appeared in 1966–67 and an entirely new series in 1971, not to mention changes in paper, watermark, gum and phosphor bands.

21. Northern Ireland, 1 shilling 3 pence, 1958
One of the three regional stamps of Northern Ireland, this stamp features a typical Ulster five-barred gate, a flax plant and the red hand of Ulster. As with the other regional issues an attempt was made to cram as much regional symbolism into the limited space as was compatible with the royal portrait.

22. Wales and Monmouthshire, 4 pence, 1966
Like Scotland and Ulster, Wales originally released 3d., 6d. and 1s.3d. stamps, but added a 4d. in value in 1966 when the inland letter rate was raised. The Welsh designs favoured combinations of leeks and dragons to embellish the royal portrait, all three designs being the work of Reynolds Stone.

23. Guernsey, 3 pence, 1958
The three island 'regions' – the Isle of Man, Guernsey and Jersey – issued a 3d. denomination only, but compensated for this by having a 2½d. value in 1964, a value not extended to the three largest regions. The Guernsey 3d., designed by E. A. Piprell, depicted the crown of William the Conqueror and a Guernsey lily. Guernsey's postal administration became fully independent in 1969 and since then British stamps have not been valid in the bailiwick (see plate 19).

24. Jersey, 2½ pence, 1964
This stamp was designed by Edmund Blampied, who was also responsible for the Jersey pictorials of 1943 and one of the two liberation commemoratives of 1948 (see plate 19). Stamps of this denomination were issued in the Channel Islands and the Isle of Man primarily to prepay postage on picture postcards dispatched by tourists. The fact that the volume of tourist postcards dispatched in Scotland, Wales and Northern Ireland far exceeds that in the islands seems to have been completely overlooked by the authorities.

25. Isle of Man, 7½ new pence, 1971
Following the introduction of decimal currency a set of four stamps, in denominations of 2½, 3, 5 and 7½p., was issued in each of the four remaining regions – Scotland, Northern Ireland, Wales and Monmouthshire and the Isle of Man. The designs were uniform in each set and standardization to the group as a whole was imparted by the use of the Machin profile of the Queen on a solid background, with the appropriate national emblem inset in the upper left-hand corner. The Manx postal administration became independent in July 1973 and has since issued its own stamps.

PLATE 19
British Isles Independent Postal Administrations

Fifty years ago there was only one postal administration in the British Isles. Now there are five, the last (the Isle of Man) emerged in July 1973. The first area to become independent of Britain, politically as well as postally, was the Irish Free State, now the Republic of Ireland, in 1922. When the British Post Office ceased to be a government department, in October 1969, responsibility for the postal administration of the Channel Islands was transferred to the individual bailiwicks, both of whom had issued their own stamps during the German occupation of World War II.

1. Provisional Government of Ireland, 1 penny, 1922
The Anglo-Irish Treaty of December 1921, which brought the 'Troubles' to an end, envisaged an independent state in the 26 counties of southern Ireland. A provisional government was established on 16 January 1922, and British stamps suitably overprinted were released the following day. The Gaelic, signifies 'Provisional Government'.

2. Irish Free State, 5 shillings, 1935
Although distinctive stamps inscribed 'Eire' (Ireland) were introduced by the end of 1922 they only

159

covered the denominations up to 1 shilling. The higher values, 2s. 6d. to 10s., continued to consist of the contemporary British 'Seahorses' overprinted 'Saorstat Eireann 1922' (Irish Free State, 1922). High values of the Bradbury Wilkinson printings were used from 1922 till 1935 and then Waterlow printings were used from 1935 to 1937.

3. Eire (Ireland), 1 penny, 1923
Four designs were selected from several hundreds submitted through a public competition and used for the low value definitive series. The map design, by J. Ingrams, provoked considerable protests in Northern Ireland at the time since it ignored the boundary between the Free State and Northern Ireland. This, and the inscription 'Eire' (Ireland) indicated the hopes of the Free State that eventually the northern counties would voluntarily end the partition of the island.

4. Eire, 3 pence, 1923
Another of the four designs chosen, it was used for the 3d. and 10d. denominations. Miss Lily Williams adapted the Celtic Cross motif which had featured on the Sinn Fein publicity labels used on clandestine republican correspondence since 1908. The plates for this series were manufactured at the Royal Mint in London and the stamps typographed at the Government Printing Works, Dublin. The series remained in use until 1968 and underwent changes of watermark (1940) and printing method (1966–67) when photogravure was adopted for 3d. and 5d. denominations.

5. 3 pence, 1929
One of a set of three stamps issued to mark the centenary of Catholic Emancipation, Ireland's first commemorative series. The stamps, designed by Leo Whelan, portrayed Daniel O'Connell, 'The Liberator'. The inscriptions on all Irish stamps since 1922 have been rendered in Gaelic, a language spoken by less than 20 per cent of the population. Since 1952, however, many of the portrait stamps have borne the name of the person in English.

6. 2 pence, 1939
The close ties linking Ireland and the United States were demonstrated by a pair of stamps designed by G. Atkinson and released in March 1939 to celebrate the 150th anniversary of the United States constitution and the installation of George Washington as first president. The Gaelic inscription signifies 'Let the People of Ireland celebrate the 150th year of the American Constitution'. It has been estimated that four-fifths of the population of the American colonies at the time of independence were of Irish stock.

7. 1 penny, 1949
This stamp marked the centenary of the death of James Mangan, the poet who wrote 'My Dark Rosaleen'. By the Republic of Ireland Act, 1949, the status of the country was formally recognized. Two stamps celebrating the new constitution, as well as the Mangan issue, were inscribed 'Republic of Ireland', in English as well as Gaelic, but subsequently the neater form 'Eire' was resumed.

8. 3 pence, 1960
Ireland was one of the many countries which issued stamps to mark World Refugee Year. Whereas most of them chose a symbolic treatment Ireland went back to the Bible. The design, by K. Uhlemann, shows the flight of the Holy Family into Egypt. The stamps were recess-printed in England, by De La Rue.

9. 5 pence, 1964
One of a pair of stamps publicizing Irish participation in the New York World's Fair. The central

feature of the Irish pavilion was a ruined Celtic tower. The stamps, printed in multicolour photogravure by Harrison & Sons of England, along with the Red Cross stamps of the previous year, marked an attempt to improve the appearance of Irish stamps. The stamps were the first to have the inscription given entirely in English.

10. 10 shillings, 1937
Ireland's long-awaited high values finally superseded the overprinted series after fifteen years. R. J. King's vignette of St Patrick invoking a blessing on the Paschal Fire is one of the best examples of Art Deco in stamp design, with overtones of Aubrey Beardsley and the German Bauhaus movement for good measure.

11. 1 shilling 3 pence, 1959
One of a pair of stamps issued to celebrate the bicentenary of the Guinness Breweries, founded by Arthur Guinness in 1759. Significantly these are the only Irish stamps paying tribute to a specific industry. In fairness it should be noted that two stamps, portraying Father Mathew, appeared in 1938 to mark the centenary of the Temperance Crusade.

12. 50 new pence, 1971
The Irish Republic, in common with other countries in the sterling bloc, adopted decimal currency in 1971, and this necessitated a change of definitive stamps. While Britain and other countries changed the symbol for pence from d (denarius) to p, Ireland had to omit the abbreviation altogether since p (pingin) had been adopted as the Gaelic form in 1922. Thus the definitive series of 1971 can only be distinguished from its counterparts of 1968–69 by the absence of the letter. The stamps were designed by a German artist, Heinrich Gerl, after an international competition. The Eagle is from an Irish manuscript now in the library of Corpus Christi College, Cambridge.

13. 4 new pence, 1971
One of a pair of stamps marking the centenary of the birth of the dramatist J. M. Synge, it illustrates the tendency toward stark simplicity in modern Irish stamp design, and the abandonment of Gaelic script in the lettering.

14. 4 new pence, 1972
Austerity of line and form was taken to its ultimate in the pair of stamps honouring 'the patriot dead', and commemorating the fiftieth anniversary of the Troubles (1919–21) and the tragic civil war which followed in 1922–23. Since 1965 all Irish stamps have been printed in photogravure by the Stamping Branch of the Revenue Commissioners, Dublin.

15. Guernsey, 1 penny, 1941
After the occupation of the Channel Islands by German troops in 1940 British stamps continued to be used. When stocks ran out distinctive stamps were produced locally. Guernsey released ½d. and 1d. stamps in 1941 and a 2½d. stamp in 1944. The stamps were designed by E. W. Vaudin and typographed by the Guernsey Press Company. British 2d. stamps were bisected and used as penny stamps pending the introduction of this stamp.

16. Jersey, 2½ pence, 1943
Like Guernsey, Jersey also produced ½d. and 1d. stamps featuring the coat of arms of the bailiwick, but followed this in 1943 by a series of six pictorial stamps, designed by Edmund Blampied and typographed at the French Government Printing Works, Paris. It is interesting to compare the primitive treatment of the subject – Mont Orgueil Castle – on this stamp, with that on the modern definitive series.

17. Channel Islands, 1 penny, 1948
One of a pair of stamps issued in May 1948 to celebrate the third anniversary of the liberation. The stamps were intended primarily for use in the Channel Islands but were also valid for postage in the United Kingdom. Ordinary British stamps were used in the Channel Islands up to 1969.

18. Jersey, 4 pence, 1969
Jersey seized the opportunity provided by postal independence to issue a definitive series designed to attract tourists. Each vignette highlighted an aspect of the island's attractions, while the background featured seagulls, fishing boats and marine life. The series was printed in multicolour photogravure, the low values by Harrison and the higher denominations by Courvoisier.

19. Jersey, 1 shilling 9 pence, 1970
One of four stamps, designed by Rosalind Dease and printed by Courvoisier, which celebrated the 20th anniversary of the liberation. This stamp shows the S.S. Vega, used by the International Red Cross to succour the island in the closing months of World War II.

20. Guernsey, 2 shillings 6 pence, 1969
Guernsey's definitive series also took famous landmarks as its theme, but added an unusual touch by reproducing coin profiles of English monarchs associated with the history of the bailiwick. King John lost the mainland territory of the duchy of Normandy, leaving only the offshore Channel Islands as a dependency of the English crown.

21. Guernsey, 5 new pence, 1971
The same designs were retained for the decimal series, only the value being redrawn. In the original series the location map was shown on the 1d. and 1s.6d. The latitude was given incorrectly as 40° 30′, but was later amended to 49° 30 . The low values of the two sets were printed by Harrison and the higher denominations by Delrieu of Paris.

PLATE 20
British Europe

The British 'empire' in Europe consisted of four island groups and one promontory, maintained at various times for strategic reasons. Of the three territories acquired as a result of the Napoleonic Wars, Heligoland was ceded to Germany in 1890 in exchange for a free hand in East Africa, the Ionian Islands were transferred to Greece in 1864 and Malta attained independence in 1964. Cyprus, under British control by the terms of the Congress of Berlin in 1878, became an independent republic in 1960. Gibraltar, garrisoned by Britain since 1704, retains internal autonomy despite pressure from Spain.

1. Cyprus, 4 pence, 1880
At the beginning of the British occupation ordinary British stamps were used and can only be distinguished by their postmarks. This stamp forms part of a series of British stamps issued in 1880 with a distinguishing overprint. Note the so-called wing-margin, indicating a stamp from the edge of the pane.

2. Cyprus, 30 paras, 1894
Cyprus was one of the first British territories to use a De La Rue keyplate design. This type, with the profile of Queen Victoria, was in use from 1881 till 1903, when it was succeeded by similar

PLATE 20 BRITISH EUROPE

key-plates depicting Edward VII (1903–10) and George V (1912–23).

3. Cyprus, 18 piastres, 1928
Cyprus remained nominally under Turkish suzerainty until 1914 when it was declared a Crown Colony. The golden jubilee of British rule was celebrated by a series of ten stamps tracing the history of the island and emphasizing its Greek rather than Turkish antecedents. One stamp, however, alluded to the period in the twelfth century when it had previously been ruled by an English king. The stamp depicts the statue of Richard the Lion-heart in Westminster, London. This series was recess-printed by Bradbury Wilkinson.

4. Cyprus, 1 piastre, 1934
Cyprus followed the trend toward pictorialism in stamp design by adopting a series of eleven stamps, recess-printed by Waterlow & Sons, in 1934. Like the jubilee series it laid emphasis on the island's antiquities, though a concession to the Turkish community was the inclusion of Bairakdar Mosque and Buyuk Khan on two stamps.

5. Cyprus, 90 piastres, 1938
The definitive series of 1938–51 used the same designs as the 1934 series, with the portrait of King George VI substituted. In addition, however, a fine portrait design was used for the highest denominations, 90p. and £1, and new designs, featuring a map and Othello's Tower in Famagusta, were used for the 4½p. and 9p. denominations respectively.

6. Cyprus, 2 mils, 1960
Decimal currency, based on the pound of 1000 mils, was adopted in 1955 and a pictorial series ranging from 2m. to £1 was issued in August 1955. Cyprus became a republic on 16 August 1960 and a set of three stamps, featuring a map of the island, was issued on that date. At the same time the 1955 series was overprinted in Greek and Turkish to signify 'Cyprus Republic'.

7. Cyprus, 10 mils, 1962
After independence in 1960 the contract to print Cypriot stamps passed from the British companies to the Greek firm of Aspioti-Elka. From 1962 onward Cyprus, as a member of the Council of Europe, has issued stamps in the annual Europa design. This motif, of nineteen doves, was designed by Theo Kurpershoek of the Netherlands. Modern Cypriot stamps are inscribed in Greek, English and Turkish.

8. Cyprus, 15 mils, 1970
Like Greece, Cyprus tends to draw on its classical antiquities for the subjects of its stamps. Thus this stamp, commemorating the 50th anniversary of the General Assembly of the International Vine and Wine Office, depicts a classical mosaic of a vine. In recent years Aspioti-Elka has used multicolour offset-lithography for the majority of Cypriot stamps.

9. Gibraltar, halfpenny, 1886
Prior to 1886 Gibraltar used ordinary British stamps, distinguished by the obliterators G or A 26. Pending the release of distinctive stamps the contemporary series of Bermuda was pressed into service, with a suitable overprint. Both stamps and overprints were the work of De La Rue.

10. Gibraltar, 1 shilling, 1932
This portrait design, featuring either Edward VII or George V, was in use from 1903 till 1938, though four low value stamps depicting the Rock of Gibraltar were introduced in 1931–33. During their relatively long life many denominations of this series changed colour. The shilling stamp, originally typographed in black on various shades of green paper, changed to olive and black in 1932.

11. Gibraltar, 1 shilling, 1938
Pictorial designs were adopted for all but two denominations of the George VI series, issued between 1938 and 1951. The stamps, in two-colour recess, featured prominent landmarks in the colony. The perforations on many of these stamps varied considerably during and after World War II. After the destruction of De La Rue's premises in an air raid the stamps had to be perforated by other firms. Such varieties are known to collectors as the 'blitz perforations'.

12. Gibraltar, 1 pound + 1 pound, 1971
The changeover to decimal currency in 1971 was taken as an opportunity to launch a new definitive series. A novel device, so far unique, was the production of each denomination in pairs, featuring the same view of the Rock in the past and at the present day. Thus the £1 stamps showed Prince Edward's Gate, from an early nineteenth century print and from a present-day photograph. Note also the stylized tower and key emblem and the albino silhouette of the Queen's profile. The series was designed by a local artist, A. G. Ryman, and lithographed by Questa of England.

13. Gibraltar, 5 shillings, 1969
Following the referendum, by which the population voted overwhelmingly in favour of remaining under British rule, Gibraltar was granted a new constitution. A series of four stamps marked the event and made philatelic history by being perforated in the shape of the Rock itself. The portrait and lettering were printed in gold or silver metallic ink. A few examples of the 5d. denomination have been recorded with this printing in both gold and silver ink by mistake.

14. Heligoland, 6 schillings, 1867
Until 1867 Heligoland used the stamps of Hamburg but after that city's absorption into the North German Confederation distinctive stamps with the profile of Queen Victoria were adopted. All the stamps of Heligoland were printed in combinations of green and red on a white ground, alluding to the island's national colours 'green the land, red the strand, white the sand'. The stamps were typographed and embossed at the Imperial German Printing Works, Berlin. The first series was rouletted; the issues from 1869 to 1890 were perforated.

15. Heligoland, 3 pfennigs, 1876
German imperial currency was adopted in Heligoland in 1875, but British sterling currency also circulated on the island. This dual system is reflected in the stamps issued after 1875, with values in German and British currency. H. Gätke, secretary to the Governor and a noted historian and ornithologist, designed the stamps of 1875 portraying Queen Victoria and the set of 1876 depicting the island's coat of arms in denominations ranging from 1pf. (1 farthing) to 50pf. (6 pence). As the farthing was worth slightly more than the pfennig the 3pf. stamp shows the alternative value as 2½ farthings (5/8 of a penny). Distinctive stamps were withdrawn in 1890 after Britain ceded the island to Germany in return for a free hand in Zanzibar.

16. Ionian Islands, orange (halfpenny), 1859
British stamps were used in the Ionian Islands in the 1850s and may be recognized by the Corfu postmark. A set of three undenominated stamps, recess-printed by Perkins Bacon, was released in 1859, the values being recognized by the colours – orange (½d.), blue (1d.) and carmine (2d.) The inscription 'Ionikon Kratos' (Ionian government) was rendered in Greek as a sop to nationalist sentiment. The islands, formerly part of the Venetian Republic, were occupied by Britain during the Napoleonic Wars and were ceded to Greece on 30 May 1864 (see also plate 16).

17. Malta, halfpenny, 1860
Prior to 1885 Malta used ordinary British stamps, distinguished by the M or A 25 obliterators. In 1860, however, an internal rate of a halfpenny was adopted and as there was no British stamp of that value at the time a distinctive Maltese stamp had to be produced. For 25 years the halfpenny stamp, in various shades of orange, buff or yellow, was Malta's only stamp. In that period, however, it underwent numerous changes in shade, paper, watermark and perforation, thus providing philatelists with a surprisingly rich field for study.

18. Malta, 4½ pence, 1899
One of five pictorial stamps issued between 1899 and 1901 to augment the Victorian portrait series, it features a Gozitan fishing boat. Other stamps in this series showed the Grand Harbour at Valletta, an ancient Maltese galley, the allegorical figure of Malta and the shipwreck of St Paul. Malta was one of the very few countries in the nineteenth century to issue pictorial stamps.

19. Malta, 1 shilling, 1922
In recognition of services rendered by the Maltese during World War I the island was granted self-government in 1921 and this fact was celebrated by overprinting the definitive series 'Self-Government' the following year. Stamps with either Crown CA or Script CA watermark were used for this purpose. Self government was withdrawn in 1933 when the Nationalists lent their support to the Italian Fascists, but it was restored in 1947 and the 1948 definitive series was duly overprinted to record the fact.

20. Malta, 10 shillings, 1938
The top value of a series released between 1938 and 1943 featuring scenery, landmarks and historic events. St Paul, patron of Malta, was wrecked on the shore of the island in AD 60. The stamp depicts the wooden statue, sculpted by Melchiore Gafa, borne in procession at the *festa* of St Paul Shipwrecked, which is held on 17 February.

21. Malta, 3 pence, 1950
Bradbury Wilkinson recess-printed a set of three stamps in 1950 to mark the visits of Princess Elizabeth to the island where her husband, the Duke of Edinburgh, was then serving as a lieutenant-commander in the Royal Navy. Note the insignia of the George Cross, awarded to Malta in 1942 and incorporated in many of the stamps issued from 1949 onward.

22. Malta, 1 pound, 1957
A definitive series incorporating a portrait of Queen Elizabeth was issued between January 1956 and January 1957. Waterlow and Sons recess-printed the top values (2s.6d. to £1) while Bradbury Wilkinson recess-printed the lower values. Many of the vignettes alluded to the history of the island under the Knights of St John. The £1 stamp shows the group of statuary known as the Baptism of Christ, by Giuseppe Mazzuoli in the Chapel of the Auvergne.

23. Malta, 3 pence, 1959
The insignia of the award appeared on many Maltese stamps after World War II and still graces the island's flag. Several sets of stamps, between 1957 and 1967, celebrated anniversaries of the award.

161

PLATE 20 BRITISH EUROPE · PLATE 21 HUNGARY

24. Malta, 2 shillings 6 pence, 1966

The vast majority of Maltese stamps since independence have been designed by Chevalier Emmanuel Cremona, whose surrealistic approach is seen at its best in the set of three stamps of June 1966 marking the tenth anniversary of the Malta Trade Fair. The stamps were printed in multicolour photogravure by De La Rue.

25. Malta, 8 pence, 1968

One of three stamps issued for Christmas, 1968, the unusual format of which posed special problems in perforating the sheets. The shortest side at the top and the long side at the bottom both gauge 14½, while the other three sides gauge 14. The stamps were produced in sheets of 60 arranged in ten strips of six, alternately upright and inverted.

26. Malta, 5 pence, 1969

One of a set of five stamps commemorating the fifth anniversary of independence, it shows the Maltese flag and a flight of doves, symbolizing the neutral stance of Malta in Mediterranean politics since independence. Other stamps in the series, printed by Enschedé of the Netherlands, showed the 1919 War monument and allegories of tourism, trade and industry.

27. Malta, 5 pence, 1970

One of a series of eight stamps released to mark the Thirteenth Council of Europe Art Exhibition, held at Valletta in March 1970. This stamp shows the interior of St John's Co-Cathedral in Valletta. Note the increasing use of the Maltese language, the lineal descendant of ancient Phoenician, on the island's stamps.

PLATE 21

Hungary

1. 1 krajczar, newspaper stamp, 1868

Hungary used the stamps of Austria until 1871, but following the *Ausgleich* of 1867 steps were taken to separate the postal administration of Hungary from that of Austria. Newspaper stamps, in denominations of 1 and 2kr., were issued in 1868 – three years before the first stamps for ordinary postage appeared. The stamps were designed by J. Bayer and typographed at the State Printing Office in Budapest where all Hungarian stamps have been produced ever since.

2. 50 filler, 1900

Decimal currency, based on the korona of 100 filler, parallel to the krone of 100 heller in Austria, was introduced in 1900 and a new definitive series became necessary. The filler denominations were designed by J. Böhm and featured the Turul, the mythical bird of the Magyars, and the crown of St Stephen. The korona values portrayed King Ferenc Joszef (Kaiser Franz Josef) wearing the Magyar crown. The stamps underwent several changes of perforation and watermark up to World War I when they were gradually superseded by the Harvesters and Parliament designs.

3. 50 filler, 1918

Hungary became a republic in November 1918 and contemporary stamps of the Harvesters, Parliament, Karl and Zita types were overprinted KÖZTÁRSASÁG (republic) diagonally. The basic 50fl. stamp, portraying Queen Zita, was issued at the end of August 1918.

4. 6 filler, 1919

The republican government of Count Karolyi

resigned in July 1919 and was replaced by a communist regime headed by Bela Kun. The contemporary stamps were overprinted 'Magyar Tanács-Köztársaság' (Hungarian Soviet Republic). The soviet republic was beset on all sides by enemies. The French, Serbs and Rumanians invaded the country and at Szeged the royalists rallied to Admiral Horthy whose National Army overthrew the Kun regime in November 1919.

5. 5 korona, 1920

The Harvesters and Parliament stamps, originally inscribed 'Magyar Kir. Posta' (Hungarian Royal Post) were redrawn with the inscription amended to 'Magyar Posta' (Hungarian Post). This series was overprinted by the communist regime, and then in turn, was overprinted with a wheatsheaf device to blot out the communist overprint. The wheatsheaf emblem was designed by Ferenc Bökrös, who also designed the stamps of the soviet republic and is still active to this day, designing many of the stamps of the people's republic.

6. 100 korona, 1924

One of a series of airmail stamps designed by A. Megyer-Meyer, it depicts the legendary Icarus in flight. The stamps ranged in value from 100 to 10,000k., reflecting the inflation which affected much of Central Europe in the early Twenties. Note the inscription 'Magyarorszag' (Hungary) used on stamps issued during the Regency. The royalist inscription was re-introduced in 1938.

7. 40 filler, 1920

One of a set of three stamps issued with a premium in aid of returned prisoners of war. The stamps, showing returning prisoners, were designed by F. Helbing and were lithographed, a process which had not hitherto been used for Hungarian stamps but which enjoyed a moderate degree of popularity in the 1920s.

8. 50 filler, 1944

One of a set of four stamps marking the 50th anniversary of the death of Lajos Kossuth, leader of the uprising in 1848–49. The stamps, designed by T. Gebhardt and Gyula Toth, featured various portraits of Kossuth and scenes from his life. Note the inscription 'Magyar Kiralyi Posta'.

9. 16 filler, 1930

The inscription 'Magyarorszag' (Hungary) was used on all stamps issued between 1923 and 1937, but subsequently the former inscription signifying 'Hungarian Royal Posts' was resumed. Five stamps were issued in March 1930 with a full-face portrait of the Regent, Admiral Horthy – the admiral without a navy ruling a kingdom without a king. The stamps were designed by F. Helbing and lithographed at the State Printing Works in denominations from 8 to 40fl. and commemorated the tenth anniversary of the regency.

10. 60 filler, 1963

One of a series of nine stamps devoted to provincial costumes, this stamp shows a man in the dress of the Hortobagy district. After the spate of politically slanted stamps in the 1950s Hungary began issuing sets of thematic stamps, aimed at collectors in hard currency areas. The series was designed by Zoltan Nagy and recess-printed.

11. 1 forint, 1964

Seven stamps and a miniature sheet celebrated the opening of the Elisabeth Bridge over the Danube, destroyed during the siege of Budapest in the winter of 1944–45. The stamps, designed by J. Vertel and printed in multicolour photogravure, depicted the various Danube bridges. Many postwar stamps have depicted landmarks in Budapest.

12. 2 filler, 1948

One of a set of ten airmail stamps portraying various writers, including Shakespeare, Voltaire, Goethe and Edgar Allan Poe. A similar airmail series, released earlier the same year, portrayed famous inventors and explorers, ranging from Gutenberg to George Stephenson and Roald Amundsen. Note the inscription 'Magyarorszag', used on some stamps in the postwar period between the end of the regency and the establishment of the people's republic in 1949.

13. 80 filler, 1953

Hungarian composers were the theme of a series of seven airmail stamps issued in December 1953. Zoltan Nagy designed stamps portraying Bihari, Erkel, Liszt, Goldmark, Mosonyi, Bartok and Kodaly, with scenes from their compositions in the background. The stamps were printed in two-colour photogravure, in denominations from 30fl. to 2fo.

14. 1.50 forint, 1965

One of a series of twelve stamps paying tribute to Hungarian medallists at the Tokyo Olympic Games of 1964. The various sporting events were depicted alongside reproductions of the Olympic medals in gold, bronze or silver metallic ink.

15. 2.50 forint, 1968

A set of eight stamps was issued to mark the Congress of the International Council for Bird Preservation in Budapest. The stamps, designed by M. Fule and printed in multicolour photogravure, featured various protected birds such as the Greylag Goose shown on this denomination.

16. Szeged, 40 filler, 1919

Contemporary Hungarian stamps were overprinted to signify 'Hungarian National Government', under the authority of Admiral Horthy at Szeged. It was from Szeged that he directed the campaign against the Soviet republic.

17. Sopron, 30 filler, 1956

During the uprising of October 1956 nineteen denominations of the Buildings definitive series were overprinted by the freedom fighters at Sopron in western Hungary. Some of these stamps were sold at the Sopron post office and did postal duty. The bulk of the stock, however, was confiscated after the uprising. Approximately 14,000 sets of seven denominations were subsequently sold through the Philatelic Agency in Budapest.

18. French occupation, 10 filler, 1919

Various Hungarian stamps were overprinted 'Occupation française' by authority of the French military commander at Arad. Because a letter 'c' with a cedilla was not available an inverted 5 was used in the overprint.

19. Banat Bacska, 10 filler, 1919

Banat Bacska was invaded by Serbia and Rumania in 1919. No fewer than 51 different Hungarian stamps were overprinted by the Rumanian authorities and issued in the area under their control.

20. Debrecen, 15 filler, 1919

Debrecen, in eastern Hungary, was occupied by Rumanian troops between November 1919 and June 1920 when it was relinquished by the terms of the Treaty of Trianon. During that period various Hungarian stamps were overprinted 'Zona de Ocupatie Romana 1919' in an oval. Altogether some 114 stamps were overprinted in this way.

21. Temesvar, 150 on 3 filler, 1919

The Hungarian city of Temesvar was occupied successively by the Rumanians and then the Serbs, and had distinctive stamps under both authorities.

PLATE 21 HUNGARY · PLATE 22 ITALIAN STATES

The Rumanian series consisted of provisional surcharges on Hungarian stamps without any other identifying inscription. Subsequently the overprints of Banat Bacska were used. Temesvar, under the name of Timisoara, was later annexed by Rumania, whose stamps it now uses.

22. Transylvania, 1 leu surcharged on 1 korona, 1919
The Transylvanian province of eastern Hungary was seized by Rumania in 1919 and subsequently annexed. During the transitional period Hungarian stamps were overprinted 'Regatul Romaniei' (Rumanian Kingdom) and surcharged in Rumanian bani and lei. Ordinary Rumanian stamps replaced the overprints at the end of 1919. Approximately 160 Hungarian stamps were overprinted in this way.

23. Transylvania, 6 bani, 1919
Yet another of the Rumanian provisional surcharges circulated in Transylvania in the latter part of 1919. Ordinary Rumanian stamps have been used there ever since.

24. Baranya, 45 filler surcharged on 5 filler, 1919
This district in southern Hungary was invaded by Serbian forces in May 1919. Over 60 different Hungarian stamps were overprinted under the authority of the local commander. The stamps were withdrawn from use in August 1920 when the district was returned to Hungary.

25. Temesvar, 30 filler on 2 filler, 1919
Temesvar was seized by Serbian troops in July 1919 and later handed over by them to the Rumanians. During the brief period when the district was under Serbian control several Hungarian stamps received provisional surcharges converting them in value. These provisional surcharges did not have any other identifying inscription.

PLATE 22
Italian States

Eight Italian kingdoms, duchies and principalities including the Papacy issued their own stamps prior to the unification of the country in 1861. In four cases stamps were also issued by provisional governments during the transitional period between the overthrow of the ancient regimes and the absorption of the states into the kingdom of Italy.

1. Modena, 10 centesimi, 1857
The duchy of Modena introduced adhesive stamps in June 1852. Messrs Rocca, Rinaldi and Algeri engraved the dies and manufactured the electrotypes from which the stamps were typographed at the Modenese State Printing Office. The stamps were printed in black on coloured paper and featured the arms of the ducal house of Este (hence the inscription 'Poste Estensi'). A 10c. stamp printed on lilac instead of rose paper was issued in November 1857 for use on newspapers transmitted by post.

2. Modena, 40 centesimi, 1859
The ducal government was overthrown in 1859 and a provisional government established pending the adherence of Modena to the kingdom of Italy. A series of stamps for the province of Modena, bearing the coat of arms of the house of Savoy, was issued in October 1859. Carlo Setti engraved the dies and made the electrotypes, while the stamps were printed by C. Vincenzi of Modena. Reprints of these stamps were made from the original dies using paper of different colours from the originals.

Modena's stamps were superseded by those of Sardinia in 1860.

3. Parma, 10 centesimi, 1852
The duchy of Parma, like Modena, was in the Austrian sphere of influence and joined the German–Austrian Postal Union in 1852. Adhesive stamps were introduced in June that year and were typographed by D. Bentelli in denominations from 5 to 40c. featuring the Bourbon fleur-de-lis. The 10c. was printed in black on white paper; the other denominations were in black on paper of various colours. Stamps printed in different colours on white paper were adopted between 1853 and 1855.

4. Parma, 15 centesimi, 1859
A new design was introduced in 1857 and used for 25 and 40c. stamps. A 15c. stamp was added two years later. The inscription at the top signifies 'Duchy of Parma, Piacenza Etc'. The dies were engraved by Bentelli and the stamps typographed by Rossi Ubaldi of Parma.

5. Parma, 9 centesimi, 1859
A provisional government was established in Parma in 1859 and stamps inscribed 'Stati Parmensi' (Parmesan states) with the value in a utilitarian design were issued in August. The stamps, from 5 to 80c., were typographed in various colours on white paper. A similar design, in black on coloured paper, was used for 6 and 9c. stamps issued between 1853 and 1857. The stamps of Parma were superseded by those of Sardinia in 1860.

6. Romagna, 8 bajocchi, 1859
Adhesive stamps were not introduced in Romagna until September 1859 when a series from ½ to 20 bajocchi were issued. The stamps were typographed by Volpe and del Sassi of Bologna from electrotypes by Amoretti Brothers. These stamps were suppressed in February 1860 when the issues of Sardinia were introduced. Consequently used examples are comparatively rare.

7. Roman States, 1 bajoccho, 1852
Adhesive stamps were adopted in the territory under the temporal rule of the Pope in January 1852. No country name ever appeared on these stamps, the inscription merely signifying 'postage stamp', and thus they are variously described as being issued by the Roman States or the Papacy.

8. Roman States, 2 bajocchi, 1852
The stamps were engraved and typographed by Doublet and Decoppet of Rome and, in most cases, were printed in black on paper of various colours. The Papal tiara and crossed keys of St Peter were illustrated in different vignettes. Oval, circular, polygonal or other fancy shapes were used for the frames as well as the more orthodox rectangular formats though as a guide to separation narrow lines of printer's rule were placed between adjoining stamps in the sheet.

9. Roman States, 4 bajocchi, 1852
Considerable variation may be found in the shade of paper used for these stamps. The 4b., for example, may be found on buff, lemon or bright yellow paper.

10. Roman States, 5 bajocchi, 1852
The eleven denominations of this series, from ½b. to 1s., were released at various times between 1852 and 1864. Nearly every denomination has been recorded as bisected or cut into smaller fractions for use at a corresponding proportion of the original face value.

11. Roman States, 2 centesimi, 1868
Rome resisted the *Risorgimento* of 1859–60 and,

aided by a French garrison, maintained its independence until 1870. The Italian decimal currency was adopted in 1867 and stamps from 2 to 80c. were issued in September of that year. The original dies were altered by M. Montarsolo. Thus the die of the 2b. stamp was re-engraved for the 2c. value. The earliest printings were imperforate but perforation was adopted in March 1868.

12. Roman States, 3 centesimi, 1868
The centesimi series of 1867–68 was printed on coloured glazed paper. 5, 10 and 20c. stamps were produced on unglazed paper but this version was never put into circulation. In 1870 the French garrison was withdrawn for service in the war against Prussia and Italian troops promptly occupied the city, which then became the new capital in place of Turin. Papal stamps were suppressed in 1870 but have been permitted since 1929 when the Vatican City State was established under the Lateran Treaty (see plate 25).

13. Sardinia, 20 centesimi, 1853
Adhesive stamps were adopted by Sardinia in January 1851 in denominations of 5, 20 and 40c. Francisco Matraire designed and lithographed the stamps which portrayed King Victor Emmanuel II. The three denominations were reissued in October 1853 embossed in albino on coloured paper.

14. Sardinia, 20 centesimi, 1854
The series of 1853 proved unsatisfactory and in an attempt to improve the appearance of the stamps they were reprinted in April 1854 by a very complicated process. The frame was lithographed in colour on white paper and on this the design was embossed as before in such a way that the king's profile showed up on the white oval. The colour of the frame varied considerably, prominent shades being recorded for all three denominations.

15. Sardinia, 40 centesimi, 1857
Matraire next experimented with a combination of typography and embossing, with better results. In July 1855 the stamps were produced with the lettering typographed in white with a coloured frame, the profile alone being embossed as before. In 1858 10 and 80c. values were introduced, and a 3l. stamp added to the series in 1861. The colour of the 40c. stamp was changed from vermilion to scarlet in 1857. Similar stamps, with coloured lettering on a white background, were issued by the Neapolitan Provinces (see below), while similar stamps with perforations appeared in 1862 and are regarded as the first issue of Italy.

16. Sardinia, 1 centesimo, 1861
The last stamps of Sardinia consisted of 1 and 2c. stamps for use on newspapers. They were designed and printed by Matraire and released in January 1861. The numeral of value was embossed in the centre, replacing the king's profile, and the frame was typographed in black. Examples are known with the figures inverted, or the numeral '1' used with the 2c. frame and vice versa. From 1859 to 1862 the stamps of Sardinia were gradually extended to other parts of Italy, superseding the states' issues prior to the introduction of Italian stamps in 1862.

17. Naples, 2 grana, 1858
Adhesive stamps were introduced in the kingdom of Naples in January 1858. The central motif consisted of the arms of the Two Sicilies – the horse of Naples, the *trinacria* of Sicily and the Bourbon fleur-de-lis. The seven denominations were engraved by G. Masini who placed a different letter of his name in the outer border of each stamp as a secret mark. The stamps were recess-printed by G. de Maja of Naples.

163

PLATE 22 ITALIAN STATES · PLATE 23 ITALY

18. Naples, 5 grana, 1858
A different design was used for each denomination, from ½g. to 50g., but all seven stamps were printed in the same colour. The earliest printings were in lake and the later printings in rose. The 1, 2, 5 and 10g. stamps have been recorded with printing on both sides.

19. Neapolitan Provinces, ½ tornese, 1861
F. Matraire produced a series from ½t. to 50g. for the Neapolitan Provinces pending the introduction of Italian stamps in 1862. The frames were lithographed in colour and the profile of King Victor Emmanuel II embossed in albino. The ½t., ½, 1, 2, 5 and 20g stamps have been recorded with the head inverted. Examples of the ½t. and 2g. stamps in black instead of green and blue respectively are errors which were issued at Roccagloriosa and Potenza.

20. Sicily, 2 grana, 1859
The Sicilian portion of the kingdom of the Two Sicilies introduced adhesive stamps in January 1859. The dies were engraved by T. Aloisio Juvara of Messina and the stamps recess-printed by F. Lao of Palermo. To prevent the features of King Ferdinand II ('Bomba') being sullied a decorative postmark, in the form of a picture frame, was devised. The stamps of Sicily were superseded by those of Sardinia in 1860.

21. Tuscany, 1 crazia, 1852
The grand duchy of Tuscany introduced postage stamps in April 1851, in denominations from 1 soldo to 9 crazie. Other denominations, from 1 quattrino to 60 crazie, were issued the following year. M. Alessandri of Florence engraved the dies featuring the arms of Tuscany and made the electrotypes for the Grand Ducal Printing Office where the stamps were typographed. The stamps were originally printed on blue or greyish paper with a crown watermark, but between 1857 and 1859 they were reissued on white paper with a mesh watermark.

22. Tuscany, 20 centesimi, 1860
A provisional government was established in April 1859, and a series of stamps featuring the arms of Savoy was introduced in January 1860. The stamps were inscribed in Sardinian currency and ranged from 1c. to 3l. The 40c. is known to have been bisected for use as a 20c. stamp. Sardinian stamps were adopted late in 1860.

23. Tuscany, 2 soldi, 1854
In connection with a tax on newspapers a 2s. stamp was issued in October 1854. The fee covered not only the government tax but the postage on newspapers transmitted by post. The circular stamp was typographed in black on yellowish paper framed with faint pink lines. The tax on newspapers was suppressed by the provisional government in November 1859.

PLATE 23

Italy

1. 15 centesimi, 1862
The first stamps of the united kingdom of Italy consisted of the series of Sardinia with perforations added. F. Matraire of Turin also produced a distinctive 15c. stamp, the first designed specifically for the new kingdom, hence the inscription FRANCO BOLLO ITALIANO (Italian Postage Stamp). The stamp was lithographed pending receipt of a supply of stamps printed by De La Rue. Two versions of the stamp exist. In one the first 'C' in the bottom inscription is almost closed, while in the second the 'C' is open and the line below 'Q' of QUINDICI is broken.

2. 2 lire, 1863
The highest denomination of a series typographed by De La Rue. Subsequently the plates and machinery were dispatched to Turin to form the nucleus of the Government Printing Works.

3. 20 centesimi, 1916
The basic stamp consisted of 15 + 5c. and was released in 1915 to raise funds for the Italian Red Cross. The postal value of the stamp was increased to 20c. by surcharging in January 1916. A few examples have been recorded with the surcharge inverted. The design features the Italian eagle and the arms of Savoy.

4. 40 centesimi, 1921
The top value in a set of three stamps celebrating the annexation of Venezia Giulia by Italy at the end of World War I. The stamps, designed by G. Petronio, featured the ancient seal of the republic of Trieste.

5. 25 centesimi, 1921
The top value in a series of four stamps celebrating Victory after World War I. Italy was one of the very few countries which issued stamps for this event. The inscription refers to the battle of Vittorio Veneto in October 1918, which brought the Italo–Austrian campaign to a close. The stamps were designed and engraved by A. Repettati.

6. 5 lire, 1923
The highest denomination in a series of six stamps celebrating the assumption of power by the Fascists. The fascist emblem, the ancient Roman fasces or axe and rods, was featured on many Italian stamps from 1923 to 1944. The modernistic design, by G. Balla, shows aircraft over the smog-ridden skyline of Rome, a somewhat curious interpretation of the March on Rome.

7. 1 + 1 lira, 1923
One of a set of three charity or semi-postal stamps issued in October 1923 to raise funds for the Camicie Neri (Black Shirts), the Fascist militia. The unusual anaglyptographic treatment of the medallion, by E. Federici, shows militiamen taking the Fascist oath.

8. 50 centesimi, 1924
As an experiment certain denominations of the 1917–23 definitive series were printed se-tenant with commercial advertisements in different colours. This one features Singer sewing machines. The experiment was short-lived and such stamps are now scarce.

9. 60 + 30 centesimi, 1924
One of a set of six stamps issued to mark Holy Year, 1925. The stamps were designed by E. Federici and A. Blasi and featured different churches in Rome. The two highest denominations showed the Pope opening and shutting the Holy Door to mark the beginning and termination of the year. The premium went to religious charities.

10. 30 centesimi, 1942
A lengthy series was introduced in 1929 to celebrate the foundation of Rome and in honour of the Fascist Labour Organization. It was retained in use as the definitive series and various other denominations were added to it up to 1942. The stamps depicted Romulus, Remus and the she-wolf, Julius Caesar, Augustus, Victor Emmanuel III and the allegory of Italy. In 1945 the stamps were reissued with the Fascist emblems removed. In 1942 the 25, 30 and 50c. values were released with labels se-tenant to promote the Italian war effort. These propaganda stamps bore quotations from speeches by Benito Mussolini.

11. 2 lire, 1943
In June 1943 various definitive stamps, airmails, express letter and express airmail stamps were overprinted P.M. (Posta Militare) for the use of forces on active service. A. Ortona designed the basic stamp for express air letters in 1933. Note the typically Art Deco style of lettering and bands of shading.

12. 3 lire, 1945
The postwar definitive series of Italy reflected the movement toward republicanism which brought the monarchy to an end in June 1946. Six designs were used for the series, ranging from 10c. to 50 lire, showing symbols of freedom, justice, enlightenment, peace and the rebirth of the country. This design was the work of P. Paschetto who also designed the 60c. and 1l. stamps showing a gardener tying a sapling to a stake. The stamps were printed in photogravure and appeared between October 1945 and January 1948.

13. 15 lire, 1946
One of a series of eight stamps paying tribute to the medieval Italian republics. The 15l. value depicts an allegorical composition by C. Mezzana symbolizing the Venetian Republic.

14. 30 centesimi, 1944
One of a series produced for the Italian Social Republic, a German puppet government under the rule of Mussolini, after his escape from captivity in 1943. These stamps were used in areas of northern Italy under German occupation in 1944–45. The stamps featured the Loggia di Mercanti in Bologna and the Basilica di San Lorenzo in Rome as well as the drummer calling volunteers to arms. After the downfall of the Social Republic the stamps were reissued with the offending inscriptions obliterated.

15. 1 lira, 1943
One of a series produced by the British and Americans for use in Sicily after the invasion of 1943. The basic design was lithographed and the words ITALY CENTESIMI overprinted in black. It is thought that these 'Allied Military Postage' stamps were originally intended for use in any enemy territory under Allied occupation, and only the name and currency of the country concerned had then to be overprinted. In the event, however, these Allied stamps were only used in Sicily. A few of the Fascist stamps were subsequently overprinted GOVERNO MILITARE ALLEATO (Allied Military Government) for use in southern Italy, in 1943–44.

16. 50 centesimi, 1944
This stamp, lithographed by Richter of Naples, was the first to be issued by the de jure government of Italy, under the regency of Crown Prince Umberto. Appropriately Romulus and Remus with the she-wolf, symbol of ancient Rome, was chosen for this stamp. Umberto became king on 9 May 1946 but abdicated five weeks later.

17. 25 lire, 1954
Tax evasion is a chronic problem in Italy and on two occasions the government has been forced to use stamps to encourage a more public-spirited approach among taxpayers. This stamp, embodying the Italia Turrita motif of the definitive series, signifies 'Everyone must contribute to the public expense'. The following year a similar stamp bore the slogan 'The nation expects a faithful declara-

PLATE 23 ITALY · PLATE 24 ITALIAN DEPENDENCIES AND OCCUPATION ISSUES

tion of your income'. Both stamps were released in March, at a time when Italians have to complete their tax forms. Whether this propaganda campaign was successful is not known, but it was never repeated.

18. 50 lire, 1950

One of the definitive series released in October 1950, this stamp features a blacksmith from the valley of Aosta. This series, showing provincial costumes and occupations, was designed by C. Mezzana. The 100 and 200*l.* values were recess-printed while the remainder were photogravure.

19. 10 lire, 1953

One of Italy's most attractive and enduring designs was the so-called 'Italia Turrita' (Turreted Italy) or 'La Siracusa'. The latter name dervies from the fact that this motif was borrowed from the splendid profile of the nymph Arethusa which graced the dekadrachms of Syracuse in the fifth century BC. V. Grassi produced the design, printed in photogravure (5 to 80*l.*) or recess (100 and 200*l.*) A multiple star watermark was introduced between 1955 and 1966, replacing the winged wheel watermark hitherto used.

20. 55 lire, 1950

C. Mezzana designed the two stamps which marked the inception of Holy Year and depicted the great dome of St Peter's Basilica in Rome. Many of the postwar commemorative issues of Italy have had strong religious themes.

21. 60 lire, 1954

One of two stamps designed by R. Pierbattista and D. Mancini to mark the termination of Marian Year. The 25*l.* reproduced Perugino's Madonna, while the 60*l.* showed a detail from Michelangelo's Pietà. Two-tone photogravure was used in this stamp to simulate the sculptural quality of the original.

22. 90 lire, 1966

Several stamps in the 1960s marked anniversaries of battles in the wars of Italian unification (1860–70) or World War I. F. Zanaro designed this stamp, issued in July 1966, to commemorate the centenary of the Battle of Bezzecca during the Seven Weeks War. As a result of this victory Austria was forced to cede Lombardy to Italy.

23. 50 lire, 1968

This multicoloured stamp, reproducing Canaletto's painting of the Piazza San Marco in Venice, was issued to mark the bicentenary of the artist's death. It typifies the increasing use of multicolour photogravure, in rather muted shades, by the Italian Government Printing Works in Rome.

24. 22 centesimi, surcharged on 20 heller, 1918

One of a series issued by the Austrian military authorities for use in districts of Italy occupied during World War I. The series, consisting of the Austro–Hungarian military series (see plate 2) surcharged in Italian currency, was introduced on 1 June 1918. A subsequent series, prepared late in 1918, was put on sale in Vienna a few days before the Armistice but was never used in Italy.

PLATE 24
Italian Dependencies and Occupation Issues

1. Trentino, 20 heller, 1918

The collapse of the Austrian forces on the Piave at the end of October 1918 was followed by the Italian occupation of the Trentino district. Stocks of Austrian stamps were seized and overprinted by Signor Seiser of Trente on behalf of the occupying forces. The overprint signifies 'Kingdom of Italy–Trentino' and the date is that of the Italian occupation. Stamps are known with double or inverted overprint and the 5, 10 and 20*h.* values have been recorded with the error '8' instead of '3' in the date.

2. Venezia Tridentina, 2 centesimi, 1918

The Austrian overprints were quickly superseded by contemporary Italian stamps overprinted 'Venezia Tridentina' by Seiser, this being the alternative name for Trentino. The stamps were originally released without surcharge, but in January 1919 the 5, 10 and 20*c.* stamps were overprinted for use in Venezia Tridentina and surcharged with the corresponding heller values. Though this overprinting was carried out at Rome it bristled with errors, missing letters and numerals and others inserted by hand at a subsequent operation.

3. Venezia Giulia, 10 centesimi, 1918

Austrian stamps were overprinted 'Regno d'Italia Venezia Giulia 3. XI. 18' by the Printers' Association of Trieste when Italian forces occupied the district. Subsequently contemporary Italian stamps, from 1*c.* to 1*l.*, were overprinted 'Venezia Giulia' at Trieste and released in December 1918. In February 1919 Italian 5 and 20*c.* stamps were additionally surcharged in heller and were on sale for two days during a temporary shortage of Italian currency.

4. Italian occupied districts, 45 centesimi di corona, 1919

The separate issues of Venezia Tridentina and Venezia Giulia were superseded by a general issue in February 1919. Italian stamps from 1*c.* to 1*l.* were surcharged in centesimi di corona, the former Austrian krone currency being retained in this new guise. These stamps were for general use throughout all the liberated areas, though subsequently Dalmatia issued its own surcharged series (see below).

5. Dalmatia, 1 corona, 1919

Ordinary Italian stamps were adopted in Venezia Tridentina and Venezia Giulia in 1919, but Dalmatia continued to be administered separately until 1922. Italian stamps surcharged in corona currency continued to be used in this area and a new type of surcharge, in thinner lettering than that previously used, was introduced in 1921–22. Express letter and postage due stamps were similarly overprinted. In 1922 the district was ceded to Yugoslavia and distinctive stamps were withdrawn.

6. Fiume, 15 filler, 1918

The Adriatic port of Fiume (Rijeka) was occupied by the Allies on 17 November 1918, and administered by them until September 1919. As part of Slovenia Fiume had been administered by Hungary and thus used Hungarian stamps. These were overprinted by Kirchofer and Co. of Fiume and used without surcharge pending the introduction of distinctive stamps. The Harvesters and Parliament definitives, the Karl and Zita issues and various war charity, newspaper and express letter stamps were overprinted in this way.

7. Fiume, 3 centesimi, 1919

Signor Rubinich designed a series of stamps, lithographed by Kirchofer on behalf of the Italian National Council who governed Fiume under the Allies. The first printing, in sheets of 70, was on thin transparent or toned paper. Later printings, in sheets of 100, were on medium white paper with shiny yellow gum or thick paper with white gum. The four designs featured the head of Liberty, the clock tower in Fiume, the port of Fiume and the goddess of victory. The last issue under Allied control was a semi-postal series celebrating 200 days of peace.

8. Fiume Free State, 5 centesimi, 1919

The uneasy peace of Fiume was shattered in the summer of 1919 as fighting broke out between the Italian and Serbian contingents of the Allied occupation forces. On 12 September 1919 the Italian adventurer and poet, Gabriele d'Annunzio, and his Arditi seized power and drove out the Allies, declaring Fiume a Free State. The 200 days charity series was overprinted 'Valore globale' (world-wide value) to cancel the charity premium. These stamps were used as definitives until a distinctive series was prepared.

9. Fiume Free State, 15 centesimi, 1920

The definitive series of the d'Annunzio regime appeared on the first anniversary of the Free State. Stamps from 5*c.* to 10*l.* portrayed d'Annunzio with the Latin motto signifying 'We shall stay here very well'. The stamps were designed by G. Marussig and typographed by Bertieri and Vanzetti of Milan.

10. Fiume Free State, 1 centesimo, 1920

Newspaper stamps, in an inverted triangular format, were issued by the National Council and Free State authorities. The stamp of September 1920 featured an Adriatic steamship and was typographed by Bertieri and Vanzetti.

11. Carnaro, 55 centesimi, 1920

Not content with ruling Fiume d'Annunzio next launched an attack on the Serbian-held coastal island of Carnaro and issued stamps overprinted to signify 'Italian regency of Carnaro' in November 1920. The basic stamps were issued in September 1920 for the use of the Arditi on the day of issue only. The stamps were designed by A. de Carolis from sketches made by d'Annunzio and typographed by Danesi of Rome. The dagger severing the Gordian knot, featured on these stamps, symbolized the drastic steps taken by d'Annunzio to solve the impasse over the future of Fiume which was contested by Italy and Serbia (Yugoslavia).

12. Fiume, 20 centesimi, 1922

The '200 days of peace' commemoratives were overprinted in April 1921 to mark the adoption of a constitution by Fiume. The first anniversary was commemorated by releasing this series with the date '1922' added to the overprint. In both sets the corona values were surcharged in Italian lire.

13. Fiume, 50 centesimi, 1924

The definitive stamps of Fiume were also released with an overprint signifying 'Kingdom of Italy' pending the introduction of ordinary Italian stamps later in the year. The basic stamps used for both of these sets were designed by G. Marussig and typographed by Bertieri and Vanzetti. The four designs featured a medieval Venetian sailing ship, a Roman arch, an Attic column and St Vitus, patron saint of Fiume. The unoverprinted series was released in March 1923.

14. Arbe, 30 centesimi, 1920

The Fiuman Military Post series overprinted for

use in the Carnaro was further overprinted on 28 November 1920 for circulation in the town of Arbe occupied by the Arditi. The stamps were in six denominations from 5 to 55c. The 30 and 50c. express letter stamps were similarly overprinted.

15. Veglia, 50 centesimi, 1920
The same six denominations of the Carnaro overprints and the two express stamps were released in November 1920 with a further overprint to denote use in the Yugoslav town of Veglia, during its brief occupation by the Arditi. Ordinary Yugoslav stamps were used in this district from 1921 onward.

16. Trieste, 2 + 2 lire, 1945
Trieste fell to the Yugoslav partisans on 1 May 1945 and this was commemorated on 15 June by the release of Italian definitive stamps overprinted with the name of the town in Italian and Serbo-Croat (Trst), with a five-pointed star and a surcharge in aid of war victims. These stamps were superseded by the stamps of the Allied Military Government of Venezia Giulia.

17. Fiume, 4 lire, 1945
Italian stamps of the 1944 definitive series were surcharged in new values from 2 to 20l. and overprinted with a five-pointed star and the rising sun to mark the Yugoslav liberation on 3 May 1945. The stamps bore the name of the town in both Italian and Serbo-Croat forms (Rijeka). These stamps were superseded by ordinary Yugoslav stamps in 1946.

18. Istria and Pola, 1.50 lire, 1945
Yugoslav troops occupied the peninsula of Istria at the end of World War II and overprinted contemporary Italian definitive and commemorative stamps 'Istra', pending the release of the distinctive series of the Yugoslav Military Government (see plate 35).

19. Istria and Pola, 75 centisimi, 1945
Italian stamps of the Emanuel III definitive series were overprinted with the Fascist emblem and the inscription 'Republica Sociale Italiana' for use by the puppet regime under the nominal rule of Mussolini in northern Italy. A small quantity of these stamps fell into the hands of the Yugoslav partisans, when they occupied the districts of Istria and Pola, and these stamps were likewise overprinted for use in liberated territory.

20. Venezia Giulia, 10 lire, 1945
Between 1945 and 1947 contemporary Italian express letter and airmail stamps were overprinted A.M.G.V.G. to signify Allied Military Government Venezia Giulia. They were superseded in 1947 by the stamps overprinted for use in Trieste (see below).

21. Trieste, 5 lire, 1947
The city of Trieste and surrounding district were constituted in 1947 as the Free Territory of Trieste and administered as two zones by Anglo-American forces and the Yugoslav military authorities. For the stamps used in Zone B see plate 35. Italian stamps overprinted A.M.G. F.T.T. (Allied Military Government Free Territory of Trieste) were used in Zone A from October 1947 till the end of October 1954 when the territory was formally partitioned between Yugoslavia and Italy. Since then ordinary Italian stamps have been used in the former Zone A.

22. Trieste, 10 lire, 1948
Trieste was a popular venue for philatelic exhibitions and conferences in the period before World War II and one of the earliest Italian commemorative sets consisted of four stamps overprinted in 1922 to mark the ninth Philatelic Congress, held

that year at Trieste. Appropriately Trieste's first indigenous commemorative issue consisted of three ordinary and three airmail stamps overprinted in September 1948 with a posthorn device to mark the Trieste Philatelic Congress. From July 1948 to October 1954 numerous Italian commemorative stamps were overprinted for use in Zone A.

23. Trieste, 55 lire, 1951
Since August 1949 Trieste has been the venue of an international fair and stamps were overprinted in honour of this event between 1950 and 1954. The Italian stamps bore the AMG–FTT overprint and an additional overprint usually arranged in an ornamental setting inscribed 'Fiera di Trieste'.

24. Italian Colonies, 50 centesimi, 1933
Between 1932 and 1934 a number of commemorative sets were produced for use throughout the Italian colonial empire, instead of releasing omnibus issues in each colony. The first of these issues appeared in July 1932 and marked the centenary of the birth of Giuseppe Garibaldi. Several sets of this type were similar to contemporary Italian issues but were inscribed 'Poste Coloniali Italiane'. The first distinctive series appeared in March 1933 to mark the 50th anniversary of the colony of Eritrea. Various scenes and occupations of the colony, designed by P. Morbiducci, were used for the ordinary stamps, while aircraft or eagles were featured on the airmail stamps designed by L. Ferri. Both ordinary and airmail sets were printed in photogravure in Rome.

25. Italian Colonies, 20 centesimi, 1934
A set of four stamps designed by M. Parrini was released in April 1934 to mark the Fifteenth Milan Exhibition. The stamps featured Mercury holding the fasces, emblem of the Fascist movement. The lettering and style of the vignette are typical of the *moderne* trend in art which dominated Italy in the 1930s.

PLATE 25
San Marino and Vatican

Italy is unique in having two independent sovereign states entirely within its territory, the tiny mountain republic of San Marino and the Vatican City State, temporal headquarters of the Catholic Church. Stamps have been issued by San Marino since 1877 and by the Vatican since 1929, though the Papal States had their own stamps in the period from 1852 to 1870 (see plate 22). Both postal administrations derive a considerable income from the sale of stamps to philatelists and tourists and have given a great deal of thought to producing colourful, well-designed and interesting stamps.

1. San Marino, 5 centesimi, 1892
The triple mountains of San Marino, shown on its coat of arms, were featured on the first definitive series, issued in 1877. New values were introduced in 1890 and the colours of the stamps were changed in 1892–94. This stamp belongs to the 1892–94 set. These stamps, like the majority of Sammarinese stamps since then, were produced at the Italian Government Printing Works, Turin or Rome.

2. San Marino, 1 centesimo, 1907
One of a pair of stamps released between 1907 and 1910 in Art Nouveau designs by Ortolani. The earliest printings had clear, heavy lines of shading, while the later edition had fine printing with faint lines of shading. The latter version is by far the commoner of the two.

3. San Marino, 5 centesimi, 1929
Three designs were used for the definitive series of 1929–35. The lowest values featured La Rocca Fortress, the middle value the Government Palace and the highest denominations a statue of Liberty. The designs, by E. Federici, were recess-printed in two-colour combinations by Bradbury Wilkinson of England.

4. San Marino, 5 centesimi, 1934
San Marino reflects Italy in miniature and, like Italy, embraced Fascism in the 1920s. This stamp was one of a series of seven celebrating the twelfth anniversary of the foundation of the San Marino Fascist Party. The design, showing the ascent of Mount Titano, symbolizes the path of Fascism to victory.

5. San Marino, 5 centesimi, 1935
The centenary of the death of the writer Melchiòrre Delfico was marked by a long series of stamps, designed by M. A. Jamieson and recess-printed by Bradbury Wilkinson. The fine quality of design and printing demonstrated by these and other stamps in the inter-war years helped to establish the popularity of Sammarinese stamps throughout the world.

6. San Marino, 2 lire, 1953
One of a series devoted to sporting events. Since the end of World War II San Marino has launched numerous 'thematic' sets of stamps, the majority being printed in multicolour photogravure by the Italian Government Printing Works in Rome.

7. San Marino, 1.25 lire, 1943
One of a series prepared originally to celebrate the twentieth anniversary of the Fascist regime. The collapse of Fascism, however, prevented the stamps being released as planned. Instead the original inscription was blotted out and dates marking the fall of Fascism were overprinted in its place. Note the dates in the Christian calendar and from the foundation of the republic.

8. San Marino, 2 lire, 1953
One of a series of nine stamps featuring flowers, issued in December 1953. San Marino was in the forefront of the thematic movement and having exhausted the more obvious subjects (sports, fauna and flora) moved on to more esoteric themes such as vintage cars and prehistoric monsters – subsequently exploited by other countries as well.

9. San Marino, 2 lire, 1961
Among the numerous thematic sets issued in postwar years were two devoted to hunting scenes. The first series appeared in May 1961 and featured aspects of hunting throughout history. A second series, showing modern hunting scenes, appeared in August 1962. Both sets were designed by C. Mancioli and printed in multicolour photogravure.

10. San Marino, 90 lire, 1967
One of a series of five stamps depicting famous Gothic cathedrals of Europe, it shows Salisbury Cathedral in England. Other stamps in the series featured the cathedrals at Amiens, Siena, Toledo and Cologne.

11. San Marino, 60 lire, 1962
One of a series of ten stamps outlining the early history of aviation, it shows the monoplane of Alberto Santos Dumont, 1909. The other stamps in the series ranged from the first Wright Brothers' biplane of 1903 to the aircraft of Verdon-Roe and Paccioli, the Italian aircraft pioneer.

12. San Marino, 3 lire, 1958
Fruit and agricultural products were the subjects

PLATE 25 SAN MARINO, VATICAN · PLATE 26 POLAND

of a set of ten stamps issued in September 1958. Two denominations were devoted to each subject and the series was designed by R. Franzoni. Tiny vignettes of San Marino were incorporated in the background.

13. San Marino, 50 lire, 1968

This stamp was part of a series of four reproducing details of The Battle of San Romano by Paolo Uccello. Recess-printed in black on lilac-tinted paper this stamp marks a refreshing change from the multicolour confections produced previously by San Marino and provides a contrast with the art reproductions of other countries in the late 1960s.

14. Vatican, 10 centesimi, 1934

One of a set of six stamps issued in honour of the International Juridical Congress in Rome, it depicts Tribonian presenting the Pandects to Justinian. Many of the commemorative and special issues of the Vatican draw on classical or Renaissance subjects for inspiration.

15. Vatican, 2.75 lire, 1940

Four stamps celebrated the first anniversary of the coronation of Pope Pius XII. The stamps were designed by C. Mezzana and the portraits were engraved by Nicastro and Richelli.

16. Vatican, 5 centesimi, 1938

One of the six stamps designed by Mezzana and released to commemorate the International Christian Archaeological Congress held in Rome in October 1938. The stamps featured the crypt of St Cecilia's basilica and the basilica of Saints Nereus and Achilles in the catacombs of Domitilla.

17. Vatican, 1.25 lire, 1943

Though nominally neutral the Vatican was inevitably caught up in the turmoil of World War II. The Papacy was particularly active in the field of refugee and prisoner-of-war relief and in this connection three sets of stamps were issued between 1942 and 1944. G. Rondini produced the motif with Christ's portrait in the background. Each set of three stamps bore the date in Roman numerals. The stamps did not have a premium, but proceeds from philatelic sales went to the prisoners' relief fund.

18. Vatican, 60 lire, 1953

The definitive series of 1953 portrayed various popes and different views of St Peter's Basilica inset. This stamp portrays Pope Urban VIII and the baldaquin in the Basilica.

19. Vatican, 50 lire, 1952

Commemorating the centenary of the first stamps of the Papal States this recess-printed stamp depicts a nineteenth century mail coach and reproduces in miniature a specimen of the 50 bajocchi stamp of 1852. The stamps were also issued in a miniature sheet containing four examples.

20. Vatican, 60 lire, 1954

A set of three stamps marked the termination of Marian Year in December 1954. The Polish artist C. Dabrowska produced a design featuring the Madonna of Ostra Brama in Vilna. The stamps were printed in four-colour photogravure and heralded an era of more colourful stamps from the Vatican.

21. Vatican, 200 lire, 1965

Miss Dabrowska designed a series of four stamps which were issued in May 1965 to mark the 700th anniversary of the birth of Dante. The designs were based on drawings by Botticelli of Inferno (40*l.*), Purgatory (70*l.*) and Paradise (200*l.*). Raphael's portrait of Dante appeared in the 10*l.* value. The

stamps were printed in combined recess and photogravure.

22. Vatican, 70 lire, 1961

One of three stamps, designed by P. Grassellini, marking the centenary of the Catholic newspaper, *L'Osservatore Romano*. Other stamps showed copies of the paper and printing machinery.

PLATE 26
Poland

1. 10 kopeks, 1860

As the result of the partitions of the eighteenth century Poland was divided between Russia, Prussia and Austria. Some semblance of autonomy was maintained in the so-called Congress Kingdom of Poland under the personal rule of the Tsar as King. To this period belongs the famous Poland Number One, the solitary stamp issued between 1860 and 1863, when the kingdom was suppressed after the abortive rebellion and absorbed into the Tsarist empire. The stamp was similar in design to that used in Russia, but had the Polish white eagle superimposed on the breast of the Russian eagle and was inscribed in the Roman alphabet. The stamp was engraved by H. Meyer and typographed at the Government Printing Office in Warsaw. After 1863 only Russian stamps were used in this part of Poland.

2. German occupation of Poland, 10 pfennigs, 1915

One of a set of five stamps of the Germania series overprinted for use in 'Russisch Polen' (Russian Poland) in May 1915, when the Germans occupied much of that district after the victory at Tannenberg.

3. General Government of Warsaw, 2½ pfennigs, 1916

The Germans established a civil administration in former Russian Poland and named it the General Government of Warsaw. Various stamps of the Germania series, from 2½ to 60*pf.*, were overprinted between August 1916 and mid-1917 for use there.

4. Posen (Poznan) issue, 5 pfennigs, 1919

Five stamps of the Germania series were surcharged with new values and overprinted 'Poczta Polska' (Polish Post) at Posen in August 1919. The stamps of the former General Government were similarly overprinted in Warsaw. Posen (Poznan) was the chief city in the part of Poland formerly ruled by Prussia and used ordinary German stamps up to 1919.

5. Austrian Poland, 90 heller, 1919

In the former Austrian part of Poland (Galicia) stamps of the Austrian Military Post were overprinted at Lublin and Austrian stamps were similarly treated at Cracow. The Lublin overprints incorporated the Polish eagle, used to obliterate the features of the Austrian monarch. Surcharges were made in halerzy (hellers) or korony (kronen).

6. Provisional Government of Poland, 10 fenigi, 1918

Stamps prepared for use by the Warsaw Citizens' Post were overprinted 'Poczta Polska' and surcharged in fenigi (German currency). The basic stamps were valued in groszy, the currency subsequently adopted throughout Poland. All four denominations of this series are known with inverted overprint. Various stamps of a local nature were produced in Warsaw and other cities toward the end of World War I.

7. Poland, 2.50 korony, 1919

Stamps, designed by E. Trojanowski and E. Bartlomiejczyk, were typographed in fenigi and marki for Northern Poland and in halerzy and korony for Southern Poland. After 1 February 1920 the marki series was extended for use throughout the whole country. The earliest printings of both sets were imperforate, but latterly perforations gauging 11½ were adopted. The somewhat impressionistic design of this stamp symbolizes swords into ploughshares.

8. 15 fenigi, 1919

This stamp, portraying the pianist and statesman Jan Paderewski, was one of a set of seven issued in 1919–20 to celebrate the first session of the Polish *sejm* (parliament). Paderewski held office as first Prime Minister of independent Poland. Poland was officially declared a republic on 10 January 1920.

9. 4 marki, 1921

A set of six stamps was issued in May 1921 to celebrate the inauguration of the republican constitution. The designs, by Bartlomiejczyk and Husarki, adopted a suitably modernistic approach, which characterized the stamps of Poland and the other successor states of Europe in the 1920s.

10. 1.25 marki, 1922

This design, by E. Trojanowski, was adopted in 1922–23 for a series of stamps circulated in those districts in Upper Silesia which were awarded to Poland as a result of the plebiscite (see plate 14). The design shows a Silesian miner flanked by the eagle emblems of Poland and Silesia. Ordinary Polish stamps were introduced in Upper Silesia in 1924.

11. 1,000,000 marki, 1924

Poland suffered the ill effects of the inflation which hit Germany, Austria and Russia in 1922–23. The eagle definitive series of January–March 1924 ranged in denomination from 10,000 to 2,000,000*m.* before a reformed currency, based on the zloty of 100 groszy, was adopted in May 1924. This typographed series may be found with various perforations gauging from 10 to 13½.

12. German Eastern Post, 1 zloty, 1939

Following the German invasion of Poland in September 1939 contemporary stamps of the Hindenburg series were issued in the Nazi zone of occupation. The stamps were surcharged in Polish currency, using the German version of the unit 'groschen' instead of 'groszy'. No distinctive issue was made in the Soviet zone of occupation.

13. General Government, 10 zloty, 1940

Various Polish stamps were overprinted with the Nazi eagle and swastika emblem and the name 'Generalgouvernement' revived from World War I. These provisional overprints were superseded in 1940–41 by a pictorial series for the 'General Government', printed in photogravure at the State Printing Works in Vienna, from designs by Professor Puchinger. The name of Poland was completely eliminated and the inscriptions on the stamps were rendered entirely in German, as part of the Nazi campaign of germanification. Stamps from 1941 onward incorporated the legend 'Deutsches Reich' (German State) and portrayed Adolf Hitler.

14. Polish Army in Italy, 50 centesimi, 1944

Although Poland ceased to exist as a separate political entity between 1939 and 1944 it continued to exist philatelically to a surprising degree. A 50 kopeks stamp inscribed 'Dojdziemy' (we shall return) was used by Polish troops at Jangi-Jul near Tashkent in 1942 prior to their transfer to Palestine, 167

PLATE 26 POLAND · PLATE 27 PORTUGAL

North Africa and the Italian front on the side of the Allies. Stamps were also issued by the Polish Underground for their clandestine postal service in occupied Poland. This stamp belongs to a series prepared in 1944 for the use of Polish forces in Italy. The quotation 'Z ziemi Wloskiej do Polski' (from Italy to Poland) comes from the Polish national anthem and alludes to the Polish volunteers who served under Dabrowski in Napoleon's Grand Army. The stamp shows Polish infantrymen of 1812 and 1944. The series was printed in photogravure at the Italian State Printing Works, Rome.

15. London Government-in-Exile, 5 groszy, 1941
Two sets of stamps were recess-printed by Bradbury Wilkinson for the Polish government in London, in 1941 and 1943 respectively. This stamp, from the first series, shows the ruins of the American embassy in Warsaw after Nazi bombing and was no doubt intended to inflame public opinion in the United States against the Germans. By the time the stamps were issued, however, on 13 December 1941, the United States had suffered the Japanese attack at Pearl Harbor and had entered the war on the Allied side. These stamps were used on board Polish ships and, on certain days, were used at Polish army camps in the British Isles.

16. Poland, 50 groszy, 1944
The first stamps of the restored Polish republic appeared at Lublin in September 1944 and, appropriately, portrayed Traugutt, Dabrowski and Kościuszko, the heroes of earlier struggles for Polish independence. A week later 25 and 60gr. stamps were issued in the liberated areas of Poland. The stamps were photogravure-printed by Goznak of Moscow and depicted the Polish white eagle and the memorial at Cracow to the battle of Grunwald at which the Poles had defeated the Teutonic Knights in the fifteenth century.

17. 5 zloty, 1950
One of a series of postage due stamps issued in 1950. The stamps were designed by R. Kleczewski, engraved by S. Lukaszewski and recess-printed in Warsaw. Following a revaluation of the Polish currency toward the end of 1950 a large number of definitive, commemorative and postage due stamps were locally overprinted 'groszy' or 'gr' (1 old zloty = 1 new groszy). There are 37 different known types of overprint, the majority applied by handstamp in black or violet. They are ignored by many stamp catalogues but are of great interest to specialist collectors.

18. 10 groszy, 1963
Like many other countries in the Communist bloc Poland issued politically slanted stamps in the immediate postwar years, but gradually adopted a more liberal approach and began issuing thematic sets in the mid 1950s. This stamp is one of a series of eight released in April 1963 with the theme of historic ships. It features a Phoenician merchantman of the fifteenth century BC. The stamps were printed in combined recess and photogravure, a technique favoured by Poland in many of her more recent stamp issues.

19. 7.10 zloty, 1965
In December 1965 Poland issued a series of nine stamps featuring historic carriages in the Lancut Museum of Transport. The stamps were designed by J. Miller and printed in multicolour lithography. The top value of the series, depicting an English brake drawn by a team of six horses, measures 104mm and is one of the longest stamps ever produced.

20. 60 groszy, 1969
To celebrate the 25th anniversary of the People's Republic of Poland a set of nine stamps was released in 1969. All nine stamps were of 60gr. denomination. Four of them (three of which are shown on the plate) were printed in a row, se-tenant, of horizontal designs, while the other five were printed in vertical designs in a similar sheet. The stamps were designed by F. Winiarski and featured aspects of Polish industrial development. The stamps were lithographed in multicolour at the Polish State Printing Works.

21. Central Lithuania, 2 marki, 1920
A Polish army, under General Zeligowski, seized Vilna (Wilno) and the surrounding district on 9 October 1920, in defiance of the Allies. Eventually a plebiscite was held and resulted in Central Lithuania being incorporated in Poland on 8 April 1922. Distinctive stamps were issued in this district between 20 October 1920 and February 1922. This stamp, depicting the Ostra Brama Sanctuary in Wilno, was designed by F. Ruszczyc and lithographed by Laskow of Wilno in December 1920. The series may be found imperforate or perforated 11½.

22. Central Lithuania, 1 marka, 1921
The various locally produced stamps of Central Lithuania were superseded in April 1921 by a series lithographed at the State Printing Works in Warsaw. Several designs alluded to the union of Lithuania and Poland under the Jagiellonian dynasty in the sixteenth century. This stamp depicts St Nicholas Cathedral in Wilno. Ordinary Polish stamps were introduced in April 1922. Following the dismemberment of Poland in October 1939 Wilno and district were given by Russia to Lithuania, but it was incorporated in the Soviet Union in July 1940 as part of the Lithuanian Soviet Socialist Republic.

23. Polish Military Post in Russia, 1 rouble, 1918
The Polish troops stationed in Russia after the Revolution in 1917 formed themselves into a separate army corps. Contemporary Russian stamps were provided for their use and were overprinted to signify 'Polish Corps', with the Polish eagle obliterating the Russian coat of arms. Stamps from 3 to 70 kopeks were issued without a further surcharge, but various stamps were also surcharged with new values from 10k. to 1r. The surcharged stamps may be found perforated or imperforate.

24. Danzig, 5 million marks, 1923
The East Prussian seaport of Danzig was created a Free City by the Treaty of Versailles and remained nominally independent, though under strong opposing pressure from the Germans and the Poles, until the outbreak of World War II. German stamps overprinted 'Danzig' were introduced in 1920 and distinctive issues first appeared the following year. Danzig suffered the hyper-inflation which affected Central Europe in 1923, as this airmail stamp testifies.

25. Danzig, 10 pfennigs, 1939
Though theoretically an independent state Danzig came increasingly under German influence in the 1930s and eventually elected a Nazi government which agitated for reunion with the Third Reich. Many of the stamps in the late 1930s had a strong pro-German element, as, for example, the series of January 1939, marking the 125th anniversary of the annexation of Danzig by Prussia. The subjects depicted were the Teutonic Knights, scourge of the Slav population of the Baltic, the Danzig-Swedish Treaty of neutrality of 1630, the union of Danzig and Prussia in 1814, and the defeat of Stephen Batori, King of Poland, at Wechselmünde in 1577. The swastika watermark of Germany was adopted for the stamps of Danzig in 1938. This stamp, one of a set of three for an anti-cancer campaign, portrayed eminent German scientists.

26. Polish Post in Danzig, 15 groszy, 1938
Various contemporary Polish stamps were overprinted 'Port Gdansk' for use in the Polish post office in the Free City between 1925 and 1939. This stamp is one of a set of four printed specially for this post office and commemorating the 20th anniversary of Polish independence. The design, by W. Boratynski, shows Polish merchants beside the Crane Tower in the sixteenth century. Danzig was incorporated in the Polish people's republic after World War II under the name of Gdansk.

PLATE 27
Portugal

1. 5 reis, 1867
Portugal adopted adhesive stamps in July 1853 with a series of stamps portraying Queen Maria. The frames were recess-printed and the profiles embossed, and this unusual combination was used for the stamps of her successors, Pedro V and Luiz I. A new series portraying Dom Luiz appeared in 1866 and was typographed with an embossed profile. The first printings were imperforate but those from 1867 to 1870 were perforated and then the value tablet was re-engraved with straight instead of curved ends.

2. 10 reis, 1894
This stamp was issued in March 1894 as one of a lengthy series marking the 500th anniversary of the birth of Prince Henry the Navigator. It was the first commemorative series designed specifically for that purpose to come from a European country and Portugal's first essay in pictorialism. The stamps reproduced paintings by J. V. Salgado and were printed by Giesecke and Devrient of Leipzig, the lower denominations being lithographed and the higher values in recess.

3. ¼ centavo, 1912
One of the best-known stamp designs made its début in 1912 when Portugal introduced the Ceres motif. The original version of this popular design was produced by C. Fernandes and engraved by S. de Carvalho e Silva. The stamps were typographed in Lisbon and a modified design was adopted throughout the Portuguese colonial empire two years later. Between 1912 and 1926 this series was produced on different types of paper, with different gauges of perforation. In 1926 the design was redrawn by E. Meronti and typographed by De La Rue. Apart from differences in the shading and lettering the De La Rue version may be recognized by its absence of marginal imprint.

4. 2 escudos, 1923
A set of sixteen stamps, of which this was the top value, appeared in March 1930 to celebrate the flight by Coutinho and Cabral from Portugal to Brazil. The stamps were lithographed by Waterlow and Sons and the designer seems to have crammed as much as possible into a small space. The upper corners contain portraits of the Portuguese and Brazilian presidents, the aviators appear in twin ovals in the centre, beneath them are a sixteenth century galleon and the seaplane used on the flight, while the side panels depict views of Rio de Janeiro and Lisbon. The dates refer to the discovery of Brazil in 1500 and the flight of 1922.

5. 4 escudos, 1924
Waterlows recess-printed a set of 31 stamps to

PLATE 27 PORTUGAL · PLATE 28 SPAIN

mark the quatercentenary of the birth of Luis de Camoens, the Portuguese national poet. The stamps, which depicted scenes from the life and death of Camoens, were designed by Alberto de Souza. Portugal, like Spain, earned a measure of notoriety in the 1920s from the frequency of excessively long commemorative issues.

6. 3 centavos, 1926
The culmination of Portugal's philatelic excesses was the release of three lengthy sets of stamps in 1926–28 to celebrate independence. The stamps were attractively recess-printed in colour with black vignettes by De La Rue and featured historic events and celebrities from the reign of Dom Alfonso I (1140) onward. These stamps were intended for compulsory use on certain days instead of the definitive issue and the money raised from their sale was used for several projects including the establishment of a war museum.

7. 30 centavos, 1928
In May 1928 Portugal issued a 15c. stamp showing a hurdler and inscribed 'Amsterdao' (Amsterdam). The use of this stamp was compulsory on all correspondence on 22–24 May 1928 to raise funds for the Portuguese Olympic team attending the Amsterdam Games. The stamp illustrated here was intended as a postage due stamp, affixed to mail which did not bear the special Olympic stamp.

8. 25 centavos, 1934
P. Guedes designed a new definitive series showing the female allegory of the republic reading Camoens's poem *Lusiad*. The stamps were issued in various denominations from 4c. to 5e. between 1931 and 1938 and remained current until 1943. This quasi-historical design set the pattern for all subsequent Portuguese definitive issues, which tend to hark back to the glories of the Middle Ages when Portugal was a leading world power.

9. 1 escudo, 1935
This modernistic design, with its slogan signifying 'All for the Nation', was typical of the symbolism with which A. Negreiros imbued his stamp designs in the 1930s. The stamps were typographed at the Institut de Gravure in Paris.

10. 1.40 escudos, 1953
The definitive series of 1943–49 depicted a medieval caravel, while the series of 1953 featured a medieval knight. Both designs were the work of Martins Barata and were lithographed at the Mint, Lisbon. Barata designed the majority of Portuguese stamps between 1940 and 1956, using vigorous, angular lines. This stamp, with the 90c. and 2.30e., was reissued in 1967 on thinner paper to complete sets of the definitive series for sale to collectors.

11. 1.75 escudos, 1940
Portugal was one of the many· countries to pay tribute to the centenary of adhesive postage stamps. A set of eight stamps and a miniature sheet were designed by P. Guedes and engraved by A. Fragoso, with a portrait of Sir Rowland Hill.

12. 1 escudo, 1953
The centenary of the first Portuguese stamps was celebrated in October 1953, not, as one might have expected, by a series reproducing the first stamps, but by a set of seven stamps reproducing a portrait of Queen Maria II in the National Gallery, Lisbon. The stamps were designed by Barata and printed in photogravure by Enschedé of Holland. Curiously enough, the portrait has been reversed; in the original painting the Queen faces left.

13. 3.30 escudos, 1958
One of a pair of stamps issued to mark Portuguese

participation in the Brussels Fair, it was designed by Negreiros using his characteristic poster technique. Portugal also produced an omnibus series for each of its colonies in honour of this event.

14. 10 escudos, 1965
Somewhat belatedly the quincentenary of the city of Braganza which occurred in 1964 was celebrated by two stamps released in March 1965. J. Manta designed the vignette showing Dom Fernando I, the second duke of Braganza. The stamps, in denominations of 1 and 10 escudos, were lithographed in two-colour combinations.

15. 2.80 escudos, 1963
Four stamps in a uniform design were issued in July 1963 to mark the tercentenary of the death of St Vincent de Paul. The design was based on a bas-relief by Maria Monsaraz and the series was printed in photogravure by Harrison and Sons.

16. 1 escudos, 1965
One of a set of three stamps issued to commemorate the 900th anniversary of the capture of Coimbra from the Moors. The design, by C. da Costa Pinto, depicts an avenging angel over the gateway of Coimbra. Pinto has designed many Portuguese stamps in recent years and is continuing the tradition for an ascetic approach and economy of line. The stamps were printed in multicolour lithography at the Lisbon Mint.

17. 4 escudos, 1969
A set of four stamps was issued in December 1969 to celebrate the 500th anniversary of the birth of Vasco da Gama. Martins Barata's designs captured the spirit of fifteenth century illuminated manuscripts in portraying the explorer and depicting his ships. An interesting feature of this series was the descriptive caption, in Portuguese, French and English, on the backs of these stamps. According to the caption on this stamp, for example, it shows 'The fleet of Vasco da Gama which reached India in 1498, represented according to the most recent archaeological research'. This device, used on a number of British Commonwealth issues in recent years, is nothing new. A series released by Portugal in 1895 to mark the 700th anniversary of the birth of St Anthony reproduced the text of his prayer, in Latin, on the reverse of each stamp.

18. Azores, 5 reis, 1910
Portuguese stamos overprinted 'Açores' were used in the Azores between 1868 and 1931, and stamps of similar designs but inscribed with the name of the islands appeared in 1898. D. A. do Rego engraved the portrait, and J. S. de Carvalho e Silva the frame for this series of 1910 portraying King Manoel II. The series was diagonally overprinted in December 1910 following the overthrow of the Portuguese monarchy.

19. Azores, 1 centavo, 1915
Between 1911 and 1928 Portugal and the Azores issued several charity tax stamps whose use was compulsory on internal correspondence on certain days of the year. This 1c. stamp, designed by P. Guedes, depicts the female allegory of Portugal protecting the poor. This stamp may be found on ordinary or thick carton paper. The 2c. denomination, intended for use on telegrams, was also bisected and used in lieu of 1c. stamps.

20. Azores, 2 centavos, 1926
Many of the long commemorative sets of the 1920s were also overprinted for use in the Azores. The use of these distinctive stamps came to an end in 1931 and since then the Azores have used ordinary Portuguese stamps without an overprint. Such stamps, with local postmarks, are of special interest.

21. Angra, 65 reis, 1897
This stamp, engraved by E. Mouchon, was one of a series issued in January 1897 for use in Angra, a district of the Azores. Stamps of this type, with the portrait of King Carlos, were used until 1905 when the district reverted to the stamps of the Azores. Ordinary Portuguese stamps have been in use since 1931.

22. Funchal, 5 reis, 1897
The district of Funchal in the island of Madeira had its own stamps from 1892 till 1905. Subsequently it used the stamps of the Azores and then, since 1931, the ordinary issues of Portugal. During the period of its own stamps it used the contemporary Carlos keyplate designs.

23. Madeira, 5 reis, 1898
The island of Madeira used ordinary Portuguese stamps from 1853 till 1868 and these may be recognized by the numeral obliterator 51. In 1868 Portuguese stamps with an experimental cross-roulette were issued in Madeira and subsequently stamps overprinted with the name of the island were used. This stamp was one of a set of eight stamps released in April 1898 to mark the quatercentenary of the discovery of the sea-route to India by Vasco da Gama. Similar stamps, with the inscription suitably altered, were used in Portugal and several other Portuguese territories and thus foreshadowed the colonial omnibus issues favoured by France and Britain until recently.

24. Horta, 80 reis, 1897,
This district in the Azores had its own stamps from 1892 till 1905, and subsequently used the stamps of the Azores till 1931. The only point of interest in what is otherwise a monotonous aspect of Portuguese philately was the official authorization of the 5r. bisected for use as a 2½r. stamp in 1894. Used examples on cover or piece are very rare.

25. Ponta Delgada, 2½ reis, 1897
This district of the Azores, comprising the islands of Sao Miguel and Santa Maria, used the stamps of the Azores from 1868 till 1892 and from 1905 till 1931. Ordinary Portuguese stamps are now in use. A curious feature of the first issue of stamps made in these islands was the layout of the sheets. The first printings were in sheets of 24, each containing 12 stamps of Angra and Horta or 12 of Funchal and Ponta Delgada. Later printings were in sheets of 28 containing the stamps of one district only. After distinctive issues were discontinued in 1905 stamps of this design but inscribed for the Azores were overprinted in the upper right and lower corners with the letters A, H and PD to denote Angra, Horta and Ponta Delgada.

PLATE 28

Spain

1. 6 cuartos, 1850
The Spanish 'penny black' was issued on New Year's Day, 1850. A set of five stamps, in denominations of 6 and 12c., and 5, 6 and 10 reales, was lithographed at the Government Printing Works in Madrid, from dies engraved by Bartolomeo Coromina. To defeat forgers the designs of Spanish stamps were changed each year up to 1879 and in less than 30 years Spain had issued more than 360 different stamps – a formidable array for the early philatelist to cope with. To avoid defacing the homely features of Queen Isabella an unusual postmark was devised which was intended to frame her portrait.

169

PLATE 28 SPAIN

2. ½ ounce, official stamp, 1854

Two sets of stamps for use on government correspondence were released in 1854 and 1855 respectively. Both were engraved by Jose Varela and typographed in black on paper of various colours. A curious feature of these stamps was their inscription in weights instead of value, ranging from ½ onza (ounce) to 1 libra (pound).

3. 1 milesima, 1870

Isabella was deposed in 1868 and a provisional government was appointed in the interregnum prior to the election of the Italian Duke of Aosta as King Amadeo in 1870. During the interregnum stamps of the Isabella series were overprinted 'Habilitado por la Nacion' (valid for the nation). This stamp was one of a series released in January 1870. Note the republican portrait of Liberty and the cryptic inscription 'Communicaciones' without the country's name. The abbreviation at the foot signifies 'milesima de Escudo' (thousandth of an escudo).

4. 1 peseta, 1873

Amadeo abdicated in 1873 and Spain became a republic until the House of Bourbon was restored two years later, in the person of King Alfonso XII. Two republican sets appeared in this period and one denomination of a third. Allegories of Peace (1873) and Justice (1874) formed the subjects of these sets. Note the small hole punched in this stamp, a curious form of cancellation used from 1870 to 1900 for prepayment of telegrams.

5. 20 centimos, 1901

During the long reign of Alfonso XIII, whose father died before he was born, no fewer than five different definitive sets charted his progress from the cradle to manhood. The first of these, known as the Baby type, was in use from 1889 till 1901. This stamp is one of the second series, known to collectors as the 'Curly-heads'. It remained in use until 1909, by which time the king was 23 years old and a more mature portrait became necessary.

6. 10 centimos, 1931

The fifth portrait series of King Alfonso XIII appeared in 1930. After the king's abdication and the establishment of a republic on 14 April 1931 the series was overprinted REPUBLICA in various ways at Madrid and in Catalonia. This type was applied eighteen times in continuous succession, upon each vertical row of ten stamps, so that stamps show varying portions of the overprint.

7. Parliamentary stamp, 1916

Two sets of four stamps were issued in 1916 to mark the tercentenary of the death of Cervantes, each with different designs but no values expressed. These sets were intended for the use of the Chamber of Deputies and the Senate respectively. The two sets differed only in the colours used. This stamp, showing the National Library in Madrid, comes from the Senate series. Special stamps for parliamentary use were provided between 1895 and 1931.

8. 5 centimos, 1928

Spain produced a spate of commemorative and special issues in the last years of the monarchy. In 1928 two sets, each consisting of 16 stamps, were issued at Santiago and Toledo respectively. The proceeds of the philatelic sales were credited to a fund for the restoration of the catacombs. J. A. C. Harrison engraved the portraits of Pope Pius XI and King Alfonso XIII used for these stamps, which were recess-printed by Waterlow and Sons. The 32 different two-colour combinations of this series make it one of the most striking issues ever made.

9. 50 centimos, 1930

Three sets of stamps were produced in 1930 in honour of Christopher Columbus, one for ordinary postage, one for airmail to Africa and Europe and the third for airmail to America and the Philippines. Certain denominations were lithographed but others, including this one, were recess-printed by Waterlow in London. The three-colour combination used for this stamp was almost thirty years ahead of its time.

10. 1 peseta, 1930

A lengthy series of 30 stamps, for ordinary or airmail postage, was also released in 1930 in honour of the painter Goya. Among the works reproduced on these stamps was his famous Naked Maja, allegedly a portrait of the Duchess of Alba and Berwick. Mail bearing this stamp was banned in several countries, and stamp dealers exhibiting it in their windows were prosecuted in the United States. In Spain, however, it provided certain republican factions with ammunition pointing to the permissiveness and decadence of the monarchy and hastened its downfall.

11. 10 centimos, 1936

One of a lengthy series issued to mark the 40th anniversary of the Madrid Press Association. Three sets of four portrayed famous journalists while a set of three featured the House of Nazareth and a rotary press. The stamps were printed in photogravure by Waterlow and Sons. Note the inscription 'Republica Española' (Spanish Republic), which appeared on stamps between 1931 and November 1938.

12. 1 centimo, 1937

Similar stamps, inscribed 'Republica Española' were issued by the republicans in 1931–38. B. Fournier of Burgos redrew the design, changing the inscription to 'Estado Español' (Spanish State). The Fournier series was lithographed, whereas the republican originals were typographed. After the Civil War this stamp was retained in use until 1950. Printings after 1940 were made at the State Printing Works in Madrid, without the Fournier imprint below the design.

13. 35 centimos, 1951

This design, portraying General Franco, was originally used by Fournier at Burgos in 1939 and appeared with his imprint in the margin. Between 1939 and 1948 similar stamps, without imprint, were lithographed in Madrid, and between 1949 and 1953 various denominations were issued with new perforations, and other values added to the series. Note that the earlier form of the inscription ESPAÑA (Spain) was reverted to after the Civil War.

14. 80 centimos, 1954

One of a set of ten stamps honouring Marian Year. The stamps, printed in photogravure by Fabrica Nacional de Moneda y Timbres (the State Printing Works), featured various paintings and statues of the Virgin. This format was popular for many of the commemorative stamps issued by Spain in the 1950s.

15. 3 pesetas, 1958

One of two stamps issued to commemorate the Brussels International Exhibition. Both stamps were also released in small sheets, each containing a single stamp in new colours, sold at 2 and 5p. respectively at a philatelic exhibition in Madrid.

16. 1.80 pesetas, 1960

Bullfighting, Spain's national sport, did not appear on stamps until February 1960, but then made up for this with a series of twelve ordinary and four airmail stamps. The stamps were recess-printed, usually in two shades of a colour, and featured various aspects of the sport.

17. 2.50 pesetas, 1961

The glories of the former Spanish empire were recalled by several sets of stamps issued in the 1960s portraying famous explorers. The first series appeared in October 1961 and concentrated on men who had explored the Americas. Blas de Lezo was portrayed on the 70c. and 2.50p. denominations.

18. 10 pesetas, 1966

This format has been used for numerous sets issued since 1950 to pay tribute to artists and their works. A series of ten stamps was issued on 23 March 1966 (National Stamp Day) in honour of J. M. Sert. Judicious use is made of gold colouring to simulate picture frames.

19. 1 peseta, 1965

In 1964 Spain began issuing occasional sets of stamps aiming at publicizing the tourist attractions of the country. This stamp comes from the series of 1965 and depicts the fishing port of Cudillero. Many Spanish commemorative or thematic issues in recent years have been recess-printed in multi-colour, echoing the Columbus stamps of 1930.

20. 1 peseta, 1966

Spain usually issues a thematic set of stamps (often without any relevance to the subject) to mark national Stamp Day. In 1966, however, a set of three stamps also marked International Stamp Day (May 6 – the anniversary of the Penny Black) and chose reproductions of covers of 1850 bearing the first three Spanish stamps. Reproductions of covers and postmarks – as opposed to stamps on their own – is a relatively new approach to this subject.

21. Carlist government, 1 real, 1873

During the period of the first republic stamps were issued in Biscay, Navarre, Guipuzcoa, Alava, Catalonia and Valencia under the authority of Don Carlos who proclaimed himself King Carlos VII. This stamp was lithographed by J. Cluzeau at Bayonne during the Carlist War. The first printing, in July 1873, had no tilde over the N of ESPAÑA. A second printing, made in September 1873, had the tilde inserted.

22. Andorra, 2 centimos, 1929

Spanish stamps overprinted ANDORRA were introduced in 1928 and were followed by a pictorial definitive series in November 1929. The series was recess-printed in Madrid and depicted landmarks, scenery and the Andorran General Council. The earliest printings, from 1929 to 1938, had blue serial numbers printed on the back, but from 1935 onwards this security device was gradually omitted.

23. Andorra, 6 pesetas, 1964

The top value of a series issued in 1963–64, it features the Madonna of Meritxell. The stamps were recess-printed in two-colour combinations and, like the series of 1929–43 and 1948–53, showed scenery and landmarks of the principality. For stamps issued by the French post office in Andorra see plate 10.

24. Canary Islands, 80 centimos, 1937

Spanish stamps were overprinted in 1936–38 for use on an airmail service linking Las Palmas and Seville. These special issues prepaid a fee on airmail carried by the Lufthansa subsidiary, Europe–South America Airlines. Each issue was supposed to be valid for only two months, pending the resumption of the normal service by the Nationalist Government at the end of the Civil War. About 60 different

PLATE 28 SPAIN · PLATE 29 RUMANIA

stamps were produced in the Canary Islands in this period, and there are countless errors and varieties in the overprints. The Canary Islands now uses ordinary Spanish stamps.

25. Spanish Civil War, 5 centimos, 1936

Many towns, districts and provinces in Spain issued their own stamps at various times during the Civil War (1936–39). In many cases this was done when ordinary stamps ran out, or to raise funds for war charity. In this case, however, a series of six stamps was produced in December 1936 when the provinces of Asturias and Leon seceded from the Republic to form an autonomous state. The stamps were suppressed after Gijon fell to the Nationalists in October 1937. This 5c. stamp bears the slogan 'Anti-Fascists! Sweep away Fascism and make Spain a lighthouse to illumine the world'. The local issues of the Spanish Civil War are ignored by general stamp catalogues but are listed in the specialized works and are a popular field for study.

PLATE 29
Rumania

1. Moldavia, 5 parales, 1858

The Danubian principalities won their independence from Turkey in 1856 and two years later Moldavia began issuing its own stamps. The so-called 'Moldavian Bulls' were struck by hand and featured the national emblem surmounting a post-horn bearing the numerals of value. The stamps were inscribed 'Porto Skrisorei' in the Cyrillic alphabet. New stamps inscribed 'Gazetei' (newspapers) or 'Skrisorei' (letters) appeared in November 1858, the inscriptions being a curious mixture of Roman and Cyrillic lettering. The Moldavian Bulls were superseded in 1862 by the joint issues of Moldavia–Wallachia.

2. Moldavia-Wallachia, 30 parales, 1862

Prince Alexander Cuza was recognized by the European powers as ruler of both principalities in 1861 and this paved the way to the centralization of government services, including posts, culminating in the issue of stamps bearing the bull of Moldavia and the eagle of Wallachia. The earliest versions of these stamps were handstruck, but in 1864 sheets of stamps containing 40 subjects were produced. Each stamp in the sheet varied slightly from its neighbours. The stamps of Moldavia–Wallachia were superseded by the first issue of Rumania in 1865.

3. Rumania, 18 bani, 1868

The first stamps inscribed 'Posta Romana' portrayed Prince Alexander Cuza, but he was deposed the following year. Prince Karl of Hohenzollern-Sigmaringen was elected prince in his stead. In 1881 Karl (or Carol) assumed the title of king. Stamps with his profile were introduced in 1866, printed in black on coloured paper. The currency was changed from parales to bani in 1868 and a similar series, in various colours on white paper, was adopted. Successive issues used similar portraits, but showing the ruler increasingly hirsute.

4. 3 bani, 1908

J. Pompilion designed and engraved the series recess-printed at the Government Printing Works in Bucharest. Rumanian stamps designed by this artist in the decade before World War I were characterized by their excessively ornate frames and idiosyncratic lettering. The shades and perforations of this series, current till 1920, varied considerably.

5. 30 bani, 1928

The boy-king Michael succeeded his grandfather, Ferdinand, in 1927 but abdicated in favour of his father, Carol II, within three years. During Michael's first reign a new definitive series was gradually released between 1928 and 1930. The lowest denominations were typographed, but the lei denominations were printed in photogravure at the Government Printing Works. Previously Rumania had been one of the earliest countries to make use of this process, with a coronation series (1922) and a Ferdinand definitive series (1926) from Bruckmann of Munich, and an independence series (1927) by Vaugirard of Paris.

6. 25 bani, 1935

King Carol II succeeded his son Michael on 8 June 1930, and reigned till 6 September 1940, when he was deposed by a military coup. During that decade Rumania issued over 120 postage and 105 charity stamps, a staggering output for that period. No doubt the fact that Carol II was an ardent philatelist had something to do with it. This stamp was one of a definitive series released between 1935 and 1940 portraying the king in various uniforms.

7. 3 bani, 1906

Rumania was the first European country to issue charity, or semi-postal, stamps, launching four sets each of four stamps in 1906. This curious Art Nouveau design was used for the first of these sets, issued in January 1906 and it shows the queen of Rumania seated at her spinning wheel. The caption signifies 'God guide our hand'. Other designs showed the queen weaving ('Woman weaves the future of the country') and in pensive mood, resting after her labours ('But Glory, Honour and Peace to all that do good'). The stamp illustrated here was sold for 7 bani, but had a postal value of only 3 bani, the balance going to charity.

8. 10 bani, 1907

The charity stamps of Rumania were notorious before World War II and even to this day Rumania shows a remarkable predeliction for stamps with charity premiums. This stamp was one of a set of four, recess-printed by Bradbury Wilkinson, showing Princess Maria and her children receiving a poor family conducted by an angel. Other early charity stamps showed the queen nursing a wounded soldier, with the caption 'the wounds dressed and the tears wiped away'. The schmaltz of these charity stamps has never been surpassed.

9. 15 bani, 1939

One of a lengthy series celebrating the centenary of the birth of Carol I. The stamps depicted various historic scenes connected with his reign. Several denominations were also released in miniature sheet form.

10. 5 lei, 1931

One of a series of five airmail stamps, designed by L. Basarab, it shows a biplane over wooded mountains. Different aircraft and scenic views were used on each denomination. Rumania has issued numerous airmail stamps from 1928 to the present day.

11. 20 bani, Aviation Fund, 1937

In 1931 Rumania introduced postal tax stamps whose use was compulsory at certain times to raise money for the government aviation fund. These stamps were inscribed either 'Timbrul aviatiei' or 'Fondul aviatiei' (aviation stamp or fund). After 1937 these stamps were not used in conjunction with postal matter but were applied as an additional levy to taxable goods.

12. 75 + 125 lei, 1945

One of a set of four stamps issued to raise money

for the Public Library Fund. The stamps portray King Michael and feature the Carol I Foundation in Bucharest. Note the futuristic style of lettering, a feature of many Rumanian stamps of the wartime period.

13. 16 lei, 1940

The definitive series portraying King Michael was introduced soon after the beginning of his second reign. The earliest printings were made on paper with a watermark of crown and monograms. Printings made in 1944 had a watermark of multiple crosses, a reference to the Fascist emblem used in Rumania during the Iron Guard regime.

14. 20 lei, 1950

This stamp was designed by C. Muller and formed part of the definitive series adopted by Rumania after it became a people's republic in 1948. The designs were redrawn in 1952 with white numerals, while a five-pointed star was added to the top of the emblem in 1953.

15. 5 + 5 lei, 1947

The top value of a series issued to mark the 17th Congress of the General Association of Rumanian Engineers (AGIR). The four lower denominations featured a sawmill, tractor, steel mill and an oil refinery, while the top value, intended for airmail postage, showed aircraft over the mountains. This was the first series released after the currency was stabilized (1,000 old lei = 1 new leu).

16. 1.55 lei, 1962

The top value of a set of nine stamps issued in October 1962 to mark the Fourth Sample Fair, Bucharest, it illustrates the postwar trend toward the poster treatment of subjects and the use of multicolour offset lithography. Other stamps featured preserved foodstuffs, pottery, chemical products, leather goods and furniture equipment.

17. 55 bani, 1964

One of a set of six marking Cultural Anniversaries of 1964. Other stamps in the series portrayed Galileo, Shakespeare and Michelangelo, as well as Rumanian celebrities. Rumania issued numerous stamps in the 1950s and early 1960s honouring foreign celebrities. Among the British personages, for example, were George Bernard Shaw, Charles Darwin, Daniel Defoe and Robert Burns, while American ranged from Franklin to Longfellow.

18. 1.20 lei, 1957

Two stamps, of identical denomination and design, but different colours, were issued to commemorate the launching of the dog Laika in an artificial satellite, the first living creature in space. The stamps were designed by I. Dumitrana and printed in two-colour photogravure. Since 1957 Rumania has faithfully recorded Soviet space achievements and more recently has included American exploits as well.

19. 20 bani, 1966

Like many other countries in the 1960s Rumania succumbed to the craze for reproductions of paintings on stamps. This stamp, reproducing 'The Mid-day Rest' by Camil Ressu, comes from a series of six stamps featuring famous paintings in the National Gallery of Bucharest. Other stamps reproduced works by El Greco, Van Eyck and Daumier. The stamps, designed by I. Druga and G. Bozianu, did not attempt full colour reproduction.

20. 55 bani, 1965

Two stamps were issued in May 1965 to mark the inauguration of the Djerdap Hydro-electric Project, jointly sponsored by Rumania and Yugo-

171

PLATE 29 RUMANIA · PLATE 30 RUSSIA

slavia. The 30b. featured the Djerdap Gorge while the 55b. showed the dam. These two stamps introduced an entirely new concept into stamp design. They were the first stamps to be inscribed in two languages and two currencies so that they could be used for postage in two countries simultaneously. They were also released in a miniature sheet containing two of each denomination. The stamps in the miniature sheet had the arms of Rumania and Yugoslavia on alternate stamps, with an outline of the dam superimposed over the four stamps.

21. 1.20 lei, 1967
The centenary of the Rumanian monetary system was celebrated in 1967 by two stamps. The 55b. depicted the reverse of the 1b. and 1l. coins of 1867, while the 1.20l. stamp showed the obverse and reverse of the 1l. coin of 1966. The popularity of this theme induced Rumania to issue a set of six stamps in 1970 featuring the obverse and reverse of various ancient coins.

22. 1 leu, 1968
Paintings on stamps continued to provide the Rumanian postal administration with revenue. Later sets were printed in multicolour photogravure and featured works in Rumanian state galleries, a set appearing annually in this theme from 1968 onward. This stamp of 1968 reproduces 'Old Nicholas the Cobza-player' by S. Luchian.

23. Austrian occupation of Rumania, 60 bani, 1918
One of a series introduced by the Austrians for use in districts of Rumania under their control in World War I. The designs of the Austro-Hungarian Military Post (see plate 2) were re-engraved to clear the value tablet at the foot, and then the Rumanian currency was inserted by typography. The series ranged in value from 3b. to 4l. and portrayed Kaiser Karl of Austria.

24. German Ninth Army, 10 pfennigs, 1918
One of four stamps of the Germania series overprinted 'Gültig 9. Armee' (valid for 9th Army), issued under the authority of the German authorities occupying part of Rumania in March 1918. These stamps were not intended for the use of civilians in the area, but were designed to facilitate the handling of mail from troops at the front.

25. German occupation of Rumania, 5 bani, 1918
Various German and Rumanian stamps were overprinted M.V.I.R. (Militärverwaltung in Rümanien = Military Administration in Rumania) from June 1917 till October 1918. The basic stamps originally appeared in 1916 and were intended as postal tax stamps, whose use was compulsory on correspondence at certain times of the year. The design shows Queen Elisabeth spinning and was a modification of the design used for the charity stamps of 1906.

PLATE 30

Russia

1. 25 kopeks, 1909
F. M. Kepler produced the basic design used for many Russian stamps from 1858 till after the Revolution. The first stamp, a 10k. blue and brown, was issued imperforate, but perforations were introduced later that year. During the latter half of the nineteenth century different paper and watermarks were employed and various denominations introduced. Between 1883 and 1888 the background to the coat of arms was redrawn, substituting a network for horizontal lines. Thunderbolts were added

to the posthorns below the eagle in 1889–94. A network of varnish was applied to the face of stamps in 1909–12 to prevent fraudulent re-use of the stamps by washing off the postmark. During and after the revolution the stamps were issued without perforations and others were overprinted or surcharged by the Bolsheviks and the various White Russian factions during the civil war.

2. 10 kopeks, 1905
One of a set of four stamps issued during the Russo-Japanese War to raise funds for war orphans. This stamp was sold for 13k., but had a postal value of only 10k., the balance going to the relief fund. This stamp shows the monument to Tsar Alexander II and the Kremlin, Moscow. Other stamps featured the statues to Admiral Kornilof at Sebastopol, Minin and Pozharski in Moscow and Peter the Great in St Petersburg (Leningrad).

3. 3 kopeks, 1883
Stamps in denominations from 1 to 7k. were issued in 1883 in a design featuring the imperial eagle in a crowned oval. In the original version the post-horns were shown without thunderbolts. The stamps were reissued between 1889 and 1894 with tiny thunderbolts added.

4. 10 kopeks, 1915
A set of four stamps was issued in November 1914 with a small premium in aid of war charities. The original version was typographed on tinted paper. The series was reissued in 1915 on white paper. Both sets may be found with several different gauges of perforation. The stamps depicted the Russian medieval hero, Ilya Murometz, a cossack soldier, Mother Russia and St George and the Dragon.

5. 3 kopeks, 1909
One of a series of low value stamps designed by R. Zarrin and typographed in 1909. It augmented the arms designs already in use, and likewise underwent numerous vicissitudes during and after the Revolution.

6. 20 kopeks, 1916
The last stamp issued under the Tsarist regime, this 20k. denomination was one of four provisional surcharges made in 1916 to meet increases in postal rates. Ironically the basic stamps, released in 1913, had celebrated the tercentenary of the foundation of the Romanov dynasty. This stamp portrays the Tsarina Katherine the Great. Several stamps of the Romanov series were printed on thick card and given an inscription on the reverse authorizing their use as money during a shortage of coins caused by by the war.

7. 1 rouble, 1917
On account of severe damage to the perforating machines stamps of the 1909–15 series were released in 1917 imperforate. These Tsarist stamps, in an incomplete state, were issued under the authority of the provisional government of Alexander Kerensky.

8. 5 roubles, 1922
Arms stamps of the Tsarist period were often used without any distinguishing overprint during the Revolutionary period. Inflation overtook the Soviet government in 1921 and stamps were often surcharged with new values. This stamp has a surcharge expressed in 1922 roubles, each worth 10,000 of the depreciated paper roubles of 1921. Numerous errors such as double or inverted surcharge have been recorded in this series.

9. 35 kopeks, 1917
One of two stamps prepared in 1917, the only ones

to bear the name of the country 'Rossiya'. Stamps of the Tsarist period were inscribed 'Pochta' (posts) or 'Pochtovaya Marka' (postage stamp), while those of the Bolshevik period were inscribed RSFSR or SSSR in Cyrillic lettering. Though prepared for the provisional regime of Kerensky these stamps were not released till after the collapse of the Kerensky government and the seizure of power by the Bolsheviks.

10. 20 + 5 roubles, 1922
Though undenominated this stamp was sold for 25 roubles, 5 of which went to a famine relief fund. Four stamps, designed by Zarrin and lithographed at the State Printing Works, were released in November 1922 for this purpose. They depicted various types of transport. They were sold without indication of value printed on them owing to the rapid fluctuations in the value of the rouble at the time.

11. 1,000 roubles, 1921
One of a definitive series issued in 1921 for the Russian Socialist Federal Soviet Republic. On account of the Civil War, then at its height, these stamps were only on sale in Moscow, Petrograd and Kharkov. The designs by Kuprianov and Ksidias show the influences of Art Deco.

12. 3 roubles, 1923
Five stamps were released in May 1923 with motifs of workers, peasants or soldiers. The stamps were designed by Y. Schadr and lithographed at the State Printing Works in Petrograd. They incorporate the date to denote the fact that values were expressed in 1923 roubles, each of which was worth 1 million paper roubles.

13. 10 kopeks, 1926
V. K. Kuprianov designed two stamps issued in August 1926 to raise funds for child welfare. The 10k. featured waifs while the 20k. portrayed Lenin as a young child. The stamps were reissued the following year in new colours, with new inscriptions and small charity premiums.

14. 1 kopek, 1933
To publicize the different races of the Soviet Union a set of 21 stamps was issued in April 1933. The stamps ranged from Kazaks (1k.) to Chuvashes (35k.). The series was designed by I. Dubasov, V. Savialov, S. Novsky and D. Goliadkin and printed in photogravure.

15. 10 kopeks, 1939
One of a lengthy series of definitive stamps issued at various times between 1929 and 1957. The custom of depicting workers, soldiers, peasants and farmgirls on Soviet stamps began with the series of 1923 and has continued to the present day. One design in each series, however, bears a portrait of V. I. Lenin, founder of the Soviet state. During the long currency of this series the paper, perforations and shades varied considerably and three processes – typography, lithography and photogravure – were employed at different times in its production.

16. 5 kopeks, 1946
A series of stamps, each of 1 rouble value, appeared in August 1945 to mark Aviation Day. The same designs, but in various denominations from 5 to 60k., were used for a series issued in 1946. Various military aircraft were featured in this series. This stamp shows a Iakovlev-3 fighter destroying a German aircraft.

17. 30 kopeks, 1951
This stamp, showing a map of the Volga-Don canal system, was one of a series designed by E. N. Gundobin and featuring hydro-electric power

PLATE 30 RUSSIA · PLATE 31 RUSSIAN CIVIL WAR

stations, dams and canals, illustrating important projects accomplished since the end of World War II. Many Soviet stamps in the immediate postwar years highlighted achievements in the various Five Year Plans. Multicolour lithography became increasingly popular in the early 1950s. This stamp involves three shades of blue as well as brown.

18. 4 kopeks, 1965
This stamp portrays Otto Grotewohl, the East German statesman and Communist leader. Since World War II Russia has issued many stamps portraying Communist leaders of other countries, ranging from Marcel Cachin (1959) to Harry Pollitt (1971). Russia has also adopted a liberal policy in portraying international celebrities in the arts and sciences and political figures, like Patrice Lumumba and Pandit Nehru, from the non-aligned nations.

19. 4 kopeks, 1968
This stamp, marking the 50th anniversary of the Soviet Fire Services, typifies the rugged, poster approach of Soviet stamp design in recent years.

20. 40 kopeks, 1957
One of a series of six stamps, all of 40k. denomination, issued to publicise regional handicrafts. The stamp depicts lace-making in the Vologda District. The Soviet Union has issued numerous thematic sets in recent years, though not to the same extent as other Communist countries.

21. 20 kopeks, 1965
This stamp, showing rockets and a radio telescope, was issued in 1965 to mark National Cosmonautics Day. The stamp was printed on aluminium foil, a gimmick used by Russia on several occasions. Since the launching of the first sputnik in 1957 Russia has issued numerous stamps publicizing rocketry and space research.

22. 6 kopeks, 1965
Two stamps designed by Y. V. Riachovsky were issued in May 1965 to celebrate the successful flight of Voskhod 2. The stamps were printed in photogravure in shades of violet and silver metallic ink and portrayed the astronauts Leonov and Beliaiev. Both stamps were of 6k. denomination.

23. 50 kopeks, 1966
Victor Savialov, veteran designer of many prewar issues, produced the definitive series issued in 1966. The stamps, in denominations from 1k. to 1r., laid emphasis on Soviet space achievements, though postal communications was the theme of the 50k. The lower values (up to 16k.) were lithographed in a small horizontal format, while the higher denominations (20k. upwards) were printed in photogravure in a larger size.

24. 4 kopeks, 1967
Karl Marx, father of Communism, has appeared on many Russian stamps since 1933 when a set depicted his grave in Highgate Cemetery, London, to commemorate the 50th anniversary of his death. The centenary of the publication of his political manifesto Das Kapital was celebrated by this stamp, portraying the philosopher and the title page of the first edition. The following year a large format 4k. stamp marked the 150th anniversary of Marx's birth.

25. 6 kopeks, 1966
A set of three stamps was issued in 1966 to highlight the latest round of space achievements. The stamps, all of 6k. denomination, featured the dogs Ugolek and Veterok, Venus-3 and Luna-10. The trajectories of the space-craft were depicted in the background.

PLATE 31
Russian Civil War

The period from the October Revolution in 1917 till the emergence of the Union of Soviet Socialist Republics in 1923 was marked by one of the most complex and devastating civil wars in the history of mankind. Various White Russian factions fought the Bolsheviks, splinter groups such as the Don Cossacks, and adventurers like Avalov-Bermondt and Semyonov, attempted to set up their own regimes, the Czech Legion (see plate 6) roamed at will over vast tracts of Siberia, interventionists held much of the far north, the Caucasus and the far east, and various ethnic groups tried to set up their own republics in the Ukraine and the Caucasus. Apart from the Soviet government there were no fewer than 21 different stamp-issuing entities in Russia at various times in this hectic period. The stamps issued by Finland, Poland and the Baltic States, which also achieved independence at this time, are dealt with elsewhere in this book.

1. Northern Army, 10 kopeks, 1919
The Northern Army, under General Rodzianko, was formed in February 1919 and captured Pskov, Gdov and Yamburg in May. A set of five stamps inscribed OKCA (Osobiy Korpus Severnoy Armiya = Special Corps, Northern Army) was lithographed by B. Mans of Reval in September 1919. The stamps may be found on thick, medium or pelure paper, with or without gum. Rodzianko's command was later merged with the North-Western Army.

2. North-Western Army, 5 kopeks, 1919
On 15 June 1919, General Yudenitch was appointed commander in chief of all anti-Bolshevist forces in the Baltic area. His North-Western Army operated southwest of Petrograd from June until its collapse in November 1919. In August various Arms stamps of the Tsarist period were overprinted in Cyrillic to signify 'North-Western Army'. The overprint was carried out by the Matveev Press at Pskov.

3. Western Army, 20 kopeks, 1919
The Western Army was a mixed body of Germans, Balts and White Russians under the command of Colonel Avalov-Bermondt formed in Courland in 1919. Its commander refused to join the forces of General Yudenitch. In October it unsuccessfully attacked the Latvian Army defending Riga and was subsequently driven out of Latvia in disarray. Various stamps of Latvia overprinted z.A. (Zapadnaya Armiya = Western Army) or L.P. (Latwiya Pashparwalac = Independent Latvia) were used between October and November 1919. This stamp is one of a series prepared for the use of the Western Army, but never issued on account of the collapse of Avalov-Bermondt's command.

4. Omsk, 1 rouble, 1919
Admiral Kolchak assumed power as 'Supreme Ruler' in Siberia in November 1918 with his headquarters at Omsk. After the fall of Omsk to the Bolsheviks he resigned in January 1920. During 1919 various Tsarist stamps were surcharged with new values. Inverted or double surcharges have been recorded for most denominations; forgeries are also known to exist.

5. Transbaikal Province, 5 roubles, 1920
After the fall of the Kolchak government the Cossack hetman Semyonov proclaimed himself ruler of Siberia, with his headquarters at Chita, where he remained until the town was captured by partisans of the Far Eastern Republic on 21 Octo-

ber 1920. Various Tsarist stamps were surcharged with new values at the Typographic Department of the National Bank in Chita.

6. Amur Province, 2 roubles, 1920
In February 1920 a People's Revolutionary Committee set up an administration at Blagoveshchensk, which ended two months later when the Far Eastern Republic was established. A set of five stamps with an inscription signifying 'Amur Province Postage Stamp' was lithographed at Blagoveschchensk and issued in February 1920.

7. Far Eastern Republic, 20 kopeks, 1921
The Far Eastern Republic was established on 6 April 1920, as a buffer state between the Soviet Union and the Japanese. Though nominally independent this republic was rent by the intrigues of the Communists and the Japanese. Eventually the Communists won the upper hand and forced the Japanese to evacuate Vladivostok in November 1922 and shortly afterward the republic joined the Soviet Union. Various Tsarist stamps were overprinted DVR (Dalni-Vostochnaya Respublika = Far Eastern Republic), but in December 1921 a series, lithographed at Chita, was issued in denominations from 1 to 50k.

8. Priamur and Maritime Province, 10 kopeks, 1921
On 26 May 1921, the White Guards, with Japanese connivance, staged a coup in Vladivostok and broke away from the Far Eastern Republic to form the Provisional Government of the Priamur. This ephemeral regime was suppressed by Russian and Far Eastern troops in November 1922 following the Japanese withdrawal from Vladivostok. The stamps of Priamur were, in fact, intended for the Far Eastern Republic, as their inscription indicates, but the province had seceded before these stamps could be put into general circulation. Various stamps of Russia and Siberia were also overprinted or surcharged at various times.

9. Soviet issue for the Far East, 5 gold kopeks, 1923
Following the suppression of the Far Eastern Republic in 1923 Soviet stamps were introduced, with surcharges in gold currency, to distinguish them from the worthless paper money then current in the Soviet Union itself. The word 'zolotom' in the overprint signifies 'gold'. Ordinary Russian stamps were introduced toward the end of 1923.

10. Kuban Cossacks, 1 rouble, 1918
The Kuban Cossacks established a republic at the end of 1917 and declared their independence of Russia in the spring of 1918. Their independence was recognized by the White Russian general Denikin, but after he evacuated Novorossiisk on 27 March 1920, the republic quickly succumbed to the Bolsheviks. Between 1918 and 1920 various Tsarist stamps were surcharged with new values at Ekaterinodar.

11. Don Cossacks, 20 kopeks, 1919
The Don Cossacks established a republic at Rostov on 5 June 1918, and enjoyed a measure of independence under the protection of General Denikin until February 1920, when he was forced to withdraw from Rostov. Various Tsarist stamps were surcharged with new values in this period. This stamp, portraying the sixteenth-century hetman Ermak, was lithographed by the State Bank, Rostov, on thick carton paper with a seven-line inscription on the reverse to signify its use as a form of currency during a shortage of coin. This practice was also used in Tsarist Russia and the Ukraine.

12. Crimea, 35 kopeks, 1919
The Germans set up a Tartar nationalist government in the Crimea in June 1918 but this was

173

PLATE 31 RUSSIAN CIVIL WAR · PLATE 32 SWITZERLAND, LIECHTENSTEIN

followed by a provisional government in November 1918. The peninsula was successively occupied by the French, the Bolsheviks and General Denikin's army. During the provisional regime the 1*k*. Tsarist stamp was surcharged for use as a 35*k*. value and a 50*k*. 'currency stamp' on thick carton paper was also released.

13. Denikin regime, 10 roubles, 1919
General Denikin became commander in chief of the Volunteer Army on 8 October 1918, and during 1919 recaptured much of southern Russia from the Bolsheviks until halted at Tsaritsyn (Stalingrad or Volgograd) in October. He was driven back by the Red Army and forced to abandon all of southern Russia except the Crimea which he handed over to General Wrangel in April 1920. In May 1919 a series inscribed 'Edinaya Rossiya' (One Russia) and featuring St George and the Dragon was lithographed at Novocherkassk for use in southern Russia. These stamps were also used in the territories of the Don and Kuban Cossacks.

14. Denikin regime, 70 kopeks, 1919
Two designs featuring St George and the Dragon were used for the series of 1919. The kopek denominations were in a small upright design and printed in monochrome, while the rouble values were in a larger size and printed in two colour combinations.

15. Wrangel regime, 5 roubles, 1920
The Volunteer Army was reorganized under General Baron von Wrangel, who re-occupied much of southern Russia between June and October 1920. Various stamps of Russia were surcharged with new values or overprinted 'Yug Rossiy' (South Russia) in this period. Wrangel's army evacuated Sebastapol in November 1920 and was subsequently interned in Turkey.

16. Russian Refugees Post, 10,000 roubles, 1920
After the withdrawal of the remnants of Wrangel's forces various stamps of Russia, the Ukraine and South Russia were overprinted and surcharged with new values for use in the various refugee camps set up in Turkey. About 180 different varieties have been recorded in the period up to June 1921, when these camps were dispersed. This stamp consists of a Tsarist 3 kopek stamp, overprinted with the trident emblem of the Ukraine, and subsequently overprinted RUSSKAYA POCHTA (Russian Post) with a new value reflecting the inflation of Russian currency at that time.

17. White Russia, 1 rouble, 1920
This stamp was one of a series alleged to have been produced for the use of troops in White Russia operating under the command of General Bulak-Balakhovitch. The stamps, showing a peasant couple, were inscribed 'Asobni Atrad' (special section) with BNR at the foot signifying Byelorussian National Republic. The stamps are said to have been issued by the Special Section (military forces) of Byelorussia during operations in the neighbourhood of Dzvinsk in 1920.

18. Armenia, 5 roubles, 1921
A national republic of Armenia was proclaimed at Erivan in May 1918 and lasted until December 1920, when it was overthrown by the Bolsheviks. It made a brief reappearance in February 1921 but was finally suppressed in April 1921. During that period various Tsarist stamps were surcharged with new values. A pictorial series, recess-printed by the French Government Printing Works in Paris, was ordered by the Armenian National Government but was not issued since the Bolsheviks had seized power. The stamps featured a woman spinning, the eagle emblem of Armenia and a view of Mount Ararat.

19. Armenia, 10,000 roubles, 1922
A pictorial series lithographed at Erivan, was prepared in denominations from 1 to 25,000*r*., but before they were released the currency was reformed and the stamps had therefore to be surcharged in new values from 1 to 50*k*. Stamps without the surcharge are from part of the original consignment left with the printer in lieu of payment. He subsequently circulated them to the philatelic market abroad. This stamp shows a typical street scene in Erivan. The stamps of Armenia were superseded by those of the Transcaucasian Federation on 1 October 1923.

20. Armenia, 1 rouble, 1922
Another stamp from the series of 1922, not regularly issued without a surcharge to convert it from roubles to kopeks. The series was released imperforate or perforated 11½. The surcharges may be found in various different colours.

21. Armenia, 1,000 roubles, 1923
A series of stamps was prepared in 1923 for use in Armenia under the government of the Transcaucasian Federation. The stamps featured Mount Ararat and Soviet emblems or aspects of industry and agriculture. The series ranged from 50 to 10,000*r*., but before issue the stamps were surcharged with new values from 10,000 to 500,000*r*. This set was not regularly issued without these surcharges.

22. Azerbaijan, 10 roubles, 1919
One of a series of ten stamps lithographed by Demidoff of Baku for the National Republic of Azerbaijan, which functioned between May 1918 and April 1920. Four designs were used, featuring a standard-bearer, the temple of Eternal Fires, a reaper and the citadel at Baku. Note the use of Persic script on the stamps and the French inscription at the foot. Azerbaijan became a soviet republic in April 1920 and subsequently issued a new series inscribed in Cyrillic and Persic. The stamps of the Transcaucasian Federation were adopted in October 1923.

23. Batum, 10 roubles, 1920
Batum, centre of the Black Sea oil industry, was captured by the Turks in March 1918 and by the British in December of the same year. From then until April 1920, when the British evacuated the town, distinctive stamps inscribed 'Batumskaya Pochta' were used. This stamp belongs to the series of 1920 printed in new colours with the words 'British Occupation' across the middle, shortly before the withdrawal of British and White Russian troops. Batum has used Soviet Russian stamps ever since.

24. Georgia, 60 kopeks, 1919
A National Republic was established in Georgia in May 1918 and issued a series of stamps, lithographed at the State Printing Works, Tiflis, between May 1919 and mid-1920. The kopek values featured St George, while the rouble denomination portrayed Queen Tamara (1184–1212). The stamps may be found imperforate or perforated 11½ and vary considerably in shade, gum and paper. Various freak 'errors' were perpetrated and given in lieu of payment to the mechanic who repaired the machinery.

25. Georgian Soviet Republic, 80,000 roubles, 1923
Georgia was taken over by the Bolsheviks on 25 February 1921, and a series of Soviet stamps, lithographed at the State Printing Works, was introduced in February 1922. The stamps were subsequently revalued by means of a handstamp in black or violet in February 1923, reflecting the tide of inflation which overtook the republic. The

stamps of the Transcaucasian Federation superseded this series in October 1923.

26. Transcaucasian Federation, 350,000 roubles, 1923
This federation, comprising the soviet republics of Armenia, Azerbaijan and Georgia, was formed in March 1922, but did not release its own stamps till April 1923. In September a series lithographed in two designs showing Mount Ararat and oil-wells was introduced in denominations ranging from 40,000 to 500,000*r*.

27. Transcaucasian Federation, 9 gold kopeks, 1923
In October 1923 the currency was reformed and the stamps were reissued with values expressed in *kopek chervonetz* (gold kopeks). The ordinary stamps of the Soviet Union superseded these issues early in 1924.

28. Ukraine, 1 rouble, 1918
The Ukraine became an independent republic in 1917 and at first stamps of the Tsarist regime were overprinted with the trident emblem. Numerous different types of trident were used at Kiev, Odessa, Yekaterinoslav, Kharkov, Poltava and Podolia, applied by machine or by hand, in various colours.

29. Ukraine, 20 shagiv, 1918
A general series, in Ukrainian currency, appeared in July 1918. These stamps may be found imperforate on thin paper, or perforated on thick carton with an inscription on the reverse denoting their use as currency. The Ukraine was absorbed by the Soviet Union in 1923.

30. West Ukraine, 10 heller, 1919
Various stamps of Austria, the Austro-Hungarian Military Post and Bosnia-Herzegovina were over-overprinted in 1918–19 for use in the provisional regime of West Ukraine, formerly part of the provinces of Galicia and Bukovina. Before the government could link up with the Ukraine it was invaded by the Poles and forcibly incorporated in Poland. The trident overprint on this Austrian stamp bears the Cyrillic initials signifying West Ukraine National Republic. It was invaded by Germany in 1941, recaptured by the Red Army in 1944 and now uses ordinary Russian stamps.

31. Ukraine, 40 pfennigs, 1941
One of the Hitler Head series overprinted for use in the Ukraine and South Russia following the Nazi occupation in World War II.

PLATE 32

Switzerland and Liechtenstein

Three of the Swiss cantons were among the earliest countries in the world to issue adhesive stamps and these now rank among the most coveted rarities in philately. Modern Swiss philately is distinguished by the various special issues provided for the use of the agencies of the United Nations, and its interwar forerunner, the League of Nations. Allied to Switzerland postally is the diminutive principality of Liechtenstein, which formerly derived much of its revenue from philatelic sales but now relies on its position as a business tax haven for much of its prosperity.

1. Basle, 2½ rappen, 1845
The third of the Swiss cantons to adopt stamps, Basle (Basel) produced the most ambitious of designs. The stamp was printed in three colours —

PLATE 32 SWITZERLAND, LIECHTENSTEIN

carmine, black and blue – and had the dove embossed in the middle. The 'Basle Dove' was the first stamp to be printed extra-nationally, being produced by Krebs of Frankfurt-am-Main. Similar stamps, in green, black and vermilion, are colour proofs.

2. Geneva, 5 + 5 centimes, 1843
Geneva followed Zürich in October 1843. The first stamps are known to collectors as the 'Double Geneva', from the fact that the 10c. stamp consisted of two parts, each of which could be used as a 5c. stamp. Each half bore the inscription 'Poste Genève – Port Local', while the entire unit was inscribed across the top 'Port Cantonal', indicating the relative usages of the 5 and 10c. rates. The stamps were lithographed by M. Schmidt of Geneva in black on green-coloured paper.

3. Zürich, 4 rappen, 1843
Orell, Füssli & Co. of Zürich lithographed the 4 and 6 rappen stamps introduced in March 1843. These stamps were, in fact, the first government stamps to appear anywhere in the world outside the British Isles, though the United States (see plate 91) had had a private postal service using adhesive stamps since February 1842. The stamps were printed in black, with a background of horizontal red lines, and thus they can be regarded as the world's first bicoloured stamps.

4. Switzerland, 2½ rappen, 1850
The earliest federal issues were inscribed in German ('Ortspost') or French ('Poste locale') and were lithographed by M. Durheim of Berne. To this series belong the stamps inscribed Rayon I, II or III, indicating the radius whose postage they covered.

5. Transitional Stamps, 5 centimes, 1850
The federal authorities took over the cantonal posts in 1849, but pending the introduction of stamps for use throughout the country Geneva and Zürich issued 'transitional' stamps, depicting the Swiss cross and merely inscribed 'Poste Locale'. Early philatelists were puzzled by these stamps, attributing them to the cantons of Vaud, Neuchâtel or Winterthur. All of the transitional stamps were printed in black with the background to the cross shown in red.

6. 2 rappen, 1854
Vogt of Munich was responsible for the series known to collectors as the 'Strubelis' (tousle-haired) from the dishevelled appearance of the hair on the figure of Helvetia. The multi-national character of Switzerland was demonstrated by the inscription of the currency in three languages – centimes, centesimi and rappen. The stamps were printed in combined embossing and typography, first by J. G. Weiss of Munich and then, from October 1854 onwards, at the Mint, Berne. The stamps were distinguished by the incorporation of a thin silk thread, embedded in the paper as a security device. The printings of 1855–59 had threads of different colours for each denomination.

7. 1 franc, 1902
The so-called 'standing Helvetia' design was introduced in 1882 and remained in use till 1908. During that period it was first recess-printed by Müllhaupt of Berne, and subsequently by Max Girardet of Berne (1886–1904), and Benziger of Einsiedeln (1907). The paper, perforation and colours of the stamps varied enormously over that period, and the design of the 40c. denomination was redrawn in 1904.

8. 5 centimes, 1900
One of a set of three stamps celebrating the 25th anniversary of the Universal Postal Union. The Union has its permanent headquarters at Berne and now has its own distinctive stamps (see below). The stamps were designed by E. Grasset, better known for his stamps of French Indochina (see plate 61) and recess-printed by Girardet at Berne. In the original version the figure of value was solid, but in August the design was redrawn with the numerals lined.

9. 30 centimes, 1924
R. Kissling's design showing William Tell, the Swiss national hero, was used for Swiss definitive stamps from 1914 to 1936 and during that period went through numerous changes of colour and denomination as postal rates fluctuated. The dies were engraved by J. Sprenger and the stamps typographed at the Mint, Berne.

10. 20 francs, 1961
The highest denomination ever issued in Switzerland, this stamp formed one of a set of four featuring the four evangelists, Matthew (3f), Mark (5f.), Luke (10f.) and John (20f.). The stamps were designed by Agathe Bagnoud, engraved by H. Heusser and recess-printed on granite paper at the headquarters of the Swiss PTT in Berne. The designs are based on medieval wood-carvings from the church of St Oswald at Zug and are now in the Swiss National Museum in Zürich.

11. 1 franc, 1924
The top value of three airmail stamps designed by P. E. Vibert and typographed at the PTT Printing Bureau in Berne. The stamps feature the mythical figure of Icarus, a popular subject with designers of airmail stamps in the 1920s (compare this design with the treatment of the same subject by Hungary, plate 21). Switzerland first issued air stamps in 1919 and on many occasions has released special 'Pro Aero' stamps in connection with important flights.

12. 10 centimes, 1921
Since 1913 Switzerland has issued stamps each year with premiums in aid of children's charities. These stamps are known to collectors as Pro Juventutes from the Latin inscription 'pro Juventute' (on behalf of youth). Prior to 1937 the charity premium was not expressed on these stamps, but stamps with a postal value of 10c., for example, were sold for 15c. and the balance given to charity. A strong feature of these stamps has been their thematic nature. In the earlier years the coats of arms of the cantons were depicted. In more recent years flowers, animals, butterflies and birds have been depicted, and usually one stamp in each series portrays a famous Swiss.

13. 30 centimes, 1939
To avoid national feeling Swiss stamps are usually inscribed in Latin and where one of the four national languages is favoured French is used, on account of its international, rather than national status. In 1939, however, stamps were produced for the National Exhibition at Zürich and released in French, German and Italian versions. The 30c. denomination of these sets was printed in photogravure by Courvoisier, better known for their high quality printing of the stamps for other countries.

14. 5 centimes, 1963
Rather than make a number of commemorative issues each year the Swiss economize by releasing a single series of five or six denominations publicizing important current events. The series of 1963, for example, contained stamps honouring the centenary of the Swiss Alpine Club, the centenaries of the Red Cross and the Paris Postal Conference and the golden jubilees of scouting in Switzerland and the Lötschberg Railway. Note the German, French and Italian words for Boy Scout, inscribed on this stamp. The Publicity series usually appears in March or April each year.

15. League of Nations, 15 centimes, 1927
Swiss stamps overprinted 'Société des Nations' were provided for the use of the League headquarters from 1922 onward. Prior to 1944 these stamps were not available to the general public in unused condition, though examples of most denominations leaked on to the philatelic market.

16. International Labour Office, 10 centimes, 1923
Swiss stamps overprinted 'Bureau International du Travail' were provided for the ILO secretariat from 1923 onwards. These stamps were not available in mint condition until 1944. Distinctive stamps featuring miners or emblems of industry were introduced between 1956 and 1960.

17. International Education Office, 5 centimes, 1958
Various issues of Switzerland overprinted 'Courrier du Bureau International d'Éducation' were released in 1944. A distinctive series depicting the Pestalozzi Monument at Yverdon or a globe on books was introduced in 1958–60, the designs being by D. Brun.

18. International Refugees Organization, 1 franc, 1950
Contemporary Swiss stamps, from 5c. to 2f., were overprinted 'Organisation Internationale pour les Réfugiés' and issued in February 1950. These stamps were in use for a relatively short period only.

19. World Health Organization, 40 centimes, 1948
Swiss stamps overprinted 'Organisation Mondiale de la Santé' were introduced in 1948 for the headquarters of WHO. A definitive series, designed by H. Thöni and engraved by A. Yersin, was adopted in September 1957 and shows the staff of Aesculapius surmounting the globe.

20. World Meteorological Organization, 10 centimes, 1956
Stamps featuring a weathervane or a symbolic design of the elements were released between October 1956 and October 1960 for the use of the WMO headquarters.

21. Universal Postal Union, 5 centimes, 1957
Two designs were used for the series provided for the use of the UPU headquarters in Berne, one showing the UPU monument outside the Ständehaus, by H. Thöni, and the other, by E. Poncy, showing a statue of Pegasus.

22. United Nations, 3 francs, 1968
Swiss stamps suitably overprinted 'Nations Unies Office Européen' were introduced in February 1950 and were followed by various distinctive issues between 1955 and 1963, following the same pattern as those of the other international organisations in Switzerland. Since 1968, however, stamps of designs similar to those of the New York office, but inscribed in French and with values in Swiss currency, have been provided for the Geneva headquarters of the organization. This stamp reproduces the statue by Henrik Starcke in the Trusteeship Council Chamber. (see plate 92).

23. International Telecommunications Union, 40 centimes, 1958
A series of nine stamps was released between September 1958 and October 1960 for the ITU headquarters. Two designs were adopted, showing a transmitting aerial (by D. Brun) and receiving aerial (by H. Thöni).

24. Liechtenstein, 40 heller, 1920
Liechtenstein formerly used Austrian stamps but

PLATE 32 SWITZERLAND, LIECHTENSTEIN · PLATE 33 TURKEY

attained limited postal authority in 1912 and began issuing its own stamps portraying Prince Johan II and the coat of arms of the principality. After World War I Liechtenstein threw off the remaining controls of the Austrian postal administration and introduced a full-length definitive series featuring the coat of arms, historic landmarks and portraits of Johan I and Johan II. The stamps were designed by L. Kasimir and recess-printed by Paulussen & Co. of Vienna.

25. Liechtenstein, 2 krone, 1920
The 80th birthday of Prince Johan II was marked by a set of three stamps in October 1920. The common design showed the Madonna and Child over a Liechtenstein landscape. The stamps, in denominations of 50h., 80h. and 2k., were recess-printed by Paulussen & Co. of Vienna and were issued imperforate or perforated 12½.

26. Liechtenstein, 1 franc, 1954
The termination of the Marian Year was celebrated by 20 and 40r., and 1f. stamps depicting the Madonna and Child. The stamps were designed and engraved by Karl Bickel and recess-printed by the Swiss PTT Bureau in Berne.

27. Liechtenstein, 1 franc, 1959
Since 1959 Liechtenstein has issued Christmas stamps at sporadic intervals. The first series was designed by M. Frommelt and featured sculpture and carvings from the belfries and towers of churches in the principality. This stamp shows a sculpture from the tower of the Church of St Lucius.

28. Liechtenstein, 50 rappen, 1959
Liechtenstein adopted Swiss rappen and francs in 1921 and henceforward was linked postally and economically to Switzerland. Many of the stamps in recent years have been printed in photogravure by Courvoisier of Chaux de Fonds. This stamp featuring Vaduz Castle is one of a series issued between 1959 and 1961 featuring landmarks in the principality.

29. Liechtenstein, 80 rappen, 1969
Liechtenstein, which formerly derived much of its revenue from the sale of stamps, acknowledged its debt to the hobby with two sets of stamps in 1968-69 portraying Sir Rowland Hill and famous philatelists such as Maurice Burrus and Count Philipp von Ferrary. This stamp, from the set of 1969, portrays the famous Swedish philatelist Carl Lindenberg. The stamps were all designed by Adalbert Pilch, engraved by A. Nefe and recess-printed at the Austrian State Printing Works in Vienna. In recent years the vast majority of Liechtenstein stamps have been printed either by Courvoisier or by the Austrian State Printing Works.

PLATE 33

Turkey

1. 20 paras, 1863
One of a series in denominations of 20pa., 1, 2 and 5pi. with which Turkey introduced adhesive stamps. The principal motif is the *toughra*, or sign manual, of the Sultan Abdul Aziz (1861-76). The stamps were lithographed at Constantinople in black on coloured paper, with a contrasting band of colour containing an albino inscription in Turkish signifying 'Ministry of Finance of the Sublime Government'. The stamps were printed with each alternate row inverted in respect to the adjacent rows. All

values of this series are known without the coloured band.

2. 20 paras, 1876
The basic design of this stamp, showing the crescent and star in an upright oval, was adopted in 1865. Between that date and 1876 it was released with no fewer than six different overprints signifying 'Posts of the Government of Turkey', with the value at the foot. The earliest printings of this series were typographed by Poitevin of Paris, but in 1868 the plates were sent to Constantinople and subsequent printings were made there. The earliest and latest versions of the overprints were typographed but those of the period 1868-74 were lithographed. There are numerous examples of inverted or omitted overprint.

3. 5 paras, 1915
The basic 10pa. stamp was part of a series released in 1895, surcharged two years later to create a 5pa. denomination. The central motif consists of the *toughra* surrounded by a trophy of arms. Note that the denomination of the basic stamp and the surcharge is rendered in French as well as Turkish. A shortage of the definitive stamps printed by Bradbury Wilkinson, after the outbreak of World War I, led to the reintroduction of various obsolete issues, overprinted with a crescent and star and the date 1331 (AD 1915) to revalidate them.

4. 50 paras, 1917
One of a set of six stamps issued in 1917-18 to celebrate Turkish victories in World War I. Two designs featured a map of Gallipoli and the Dardanelles. Previous issues of Turkey had been produced in England or, after the outbreak of World War I, Austria, but latterly the design and production of stamps were carried out in Turkey itself. The Gallipoli map stamp, with its heavy reliance on traditional motifs and decorative forms, represents the acme of indigenous stamp design.

5. 5 piastres, 1919
The basic stamp was the top value of the victory series of 1917-18 and shows the pyramids of Egypt. The stamp was originally produced in anticipation of a Turkish victory leading to the conquest of Egypt. The overprint, with the *toughra* of Sultan Mohamed VI, signifies the first anniversary of the sultan's accession.

6. 5 paras, 1920
This series originally appeared in January 1914, but was reissued in 1920 in new colours and with the *toughra* of Mohammed VI in place of that of Mohammed V. The stamps, featuring famous landmarks of the Ottoman Empire, were designed by Oskan Effendi and printed by Bradbury Wilkinson. The lowest values, from 2 to 6pa., were lithographed, while the higher values were recess-printed. This stamp features Leander's Tower on the Hellespont.

7. 3 piastres, 1922
The top value of a set of six stamps issued under the authority of the Nationalists at Angora (Ankara). The stamps were typographed by I. G. A. Barbarino of Genoa and featured the Parliament House in Ankara. These stamps were used in the districts under the control of the Kemalist troops during the civil war which culminated in the abdication of the sultan and the emergence of the Turkish republic.

8. 10 paras, 1926
One of a series recess-printed by Bradbury Wilkinson, it depicts the legendary blacksmith and the grey wolf Boz Kurt, symbolizing the rebirth of Turkey. This series was the first to be inscribed in Turkish using the Roman alphabet. Hitherto the

Roman alphabet had been confined to denominations and, occasionally, the name of the country rendered in French. In 1929 the series was issued with the inscriptions redrawn: the Arabic script was dropped and the words TURKIYE CUMHURIYETI (Turkish Republic) substituted at the top, with POSTA at the foot. The gradual transition from the Roman script reflects the sweeping educational and social reforms introduced by the Kemalist government.

9. 200 kurus, 1943
The top value of a series printed in photogravure by the State Printing Works, Vienna. The stamps featured scenery, landmarks, industry and agriculture, but the place of honour on the highest denomination was reserved for the portrait of President Inönü, colleague and successor of Kemal. The majority of Turkish stamps in this period were printed in Turkey, but this series, produced in Nazi-occupied Vienna, illustrates the equivocal nature of Turkey's neutrality during World War II.

10. 1 kurus, 1956
One of a series of seventeen definitive stamps released between July 1956 and January 1957 and lithographed by Klisecilik ve Matbaacilik in Istanbul. Various portraits of Kemal Ataturk (Mustapha Kemal) have been used on almost every definitive series of Turkey since 1926.

11. 5 kurus, 1958
Turkey astounded the philatelic world in 1958 by embarking on a series of stamps of 5 or 20k. denominations, featuring all the major towns and cities of the country. The stamps were released at various times between 5 January, 1958 and 4 July 1960. The 134 different stamps, ranging from Adana to Zonguldak, were printed in photogravure by Courvoisier.

12. 500 kurus, 1959
This high value stamp, with a profile of Kemal Ataturk, marked the 31st anniversary of his death. The background was lithographed and the profile embossed by the State Printing Works in Berlin, the only occasion on which the contract for a Turkish stamp was awarded to them. The stamp was issued in sheet form, perforated and printed in deep blue. It was also released imperforate in brown-red in a commemorative miniature sheet.

13. 1 kurus, 1954
Since 1910 Turkey has issued stamps which, though possessing no postal validity in themselves, are obligatory on correspondence posted on national and religious holidays. The money raised from the sale of these stamps is given to the Turkish Red Crescent Society and various child welfare organizations. These stamps are ignored by some catalogues, but listed in others.

14. 50 kurus, 1963
One of a set of three stamps marking the centenary of the Turkish Agricultural Bank. The stamps portrayed the founder, Mithat Pasha, a ploughing scene and a view of the bank's headquarters in Ankara. The series was printed in photogravure by Matbaacilik Sanayi of Istanbul and illustrates the Turkish penchant for bleeding the design into the perforations.

15. 50 piastres, 1916
One of a series engraved and recess-printed at the Imperial Austrian Printing Works, Vienna for Turkey during World War I when supplies of stamps from the English printers, Bradbury Wilkinson, were unobtainable. The stamp portrays the Sultan Mohammed V. This stamp was released in carmine, green or indigo.

PLATE 33 TURKEY · PLATE 34 FOREIGN POST OFFICES IN TURKEY

16. 25 kurus, 1958
One of two stamps issued by Turkey in the Europa theme. Unlike other countries which released stamps for that purpose Turkey chose a distinctive motif, a tree-stump sprouting a fresh shoot, symbolizing the rebirth of a new Europe. Note the Turkish form 'Avrupa'. The stamps were lithographed by Guzel Sanatlar Matbaasi of Ankara. Since 1960 Turkey has adopted the uniform design used by other member countries of the Council of Europe for the annual Europa stamps.

17. 90 + 5 kurus, 1960
One of four stamps issued to mark the Manisa Fair, with a small premium in aid of local charities. This stamp depicts the Sultan Mosque in Manisa. Other stamps in the series portrayed Merkez Muchlihiddin Effendi and the Manisa lunatic asylum.

18. 40 + 5 kurus, 1963
Two stamps were originally intended for release in 1960 to commemorate the agricultural census. They were not issued at that time, but were eventually put on sale in April 1963, with the inscription 'Kasim 1960' obliterated. The stamps were printed by Courvoisier and showed wheat with a graph or a census chart.

19. 60 kurus, 1963
One of two stamps commemorating the 25th anniversary of the death of Kemal Ataturk. The stamps were produced by Matbaacilik Sanayi of Istanbul and were the first indigenous attempts at multi-colour photogravure. Note the Turkish word in the marginal imprint – 'Tifdruk'. The German word 'Tiefdruck' means recess-printing, and photogravure (*rastertiefdruck*) is, in effect, a modern version of recess.

20. 60 kurus, 1955
The top value in a series of four publicizing the National Census. A set of four stamps, featuring a map and population figures, had been released for the National Census in 1940. This series, lithographed by Yeni Desen Matbaasi of Ankara, illustrates graphically the population growth, from 13 millions in 1927 to 21 millions in 1950.

21. 130 kurus, 1968
Two stamps lithographed by Ajans-Turk Matbaasi of Ankara were issued in honour of the Independence Medal. The 50*k.* depicted the battle of Sakarya, while the 130*k.* reproduced the text of the National Anthem. Both stamps featured obverse and reverse of the medal. To simulate the relief engraving on the medal a novel process, involving plastic-surfaced die-stamping, was employed.

22. 60 kurus, 1967
One of a pair of stamps, lithographed by Ajans-Turk, to mark the 125th anniversary of the Turkish Veterinary Medical Service. The 50*k.* showed a little girl cuddling a cat, while the 60*k.* showed a horse in a paddock. These stamps are typical of the multicolour offset printing used for many Turkish stamps in recent years.

23. 0.25 kurus, 1953
Stamps inscribed 'Resmi' were introduced in 1947 for use on official correspondence. In 1951 several denominations of the 1948 definitive series, portraying President Inönü, were overprinted 'Resmi' with the crescent and star emblem. Further overprints on the definitive series appeared in 1953–54 and a new style of overprint was adopted in 1955–57. Distinctive official stamps were reintroduced in 1957.

24. 20 paras, 1929
Between 1926 and 1934 stamps for compulsory use

on air letters were issued. These stamps had to be used on airmail on certain national and religious holidays, especially the Aerial Fête (29–31 August). The stamps were produced by the Turkish Air League, who supplied them to the Post Office. The series of 1926 showing a biplane was reissued in a smaller format in 1929 and then surcharged with values in the Roman alphabet in 1930–31. The last issue, made in 1934, consisted of contemporary definitive stamps overprinted with an aircraft and surcharged with new values from 7½ to 40 kurus. The issues of the Turkish Air League are ignored by all but the specialized catalogues, though they are not uncommon and frequently puzzle collectors by their outlandish appearance.

25. 5 paras, 1914
Bradbury Wilkinson recess-printed a set of four postage due stamps for Turkey, issued in February 1914. Each denomination, 5 and 20*pa.*, 1 and 2*pi*, had a different design, with Arabesque foliate patterns in the spandrels and the *toughra* and crescent emblems as a means of identification.

PLATE 34
Foreign Post Offices in Turkey

The chaotic state of the postal services in the Ottoman Empire induced no fewer than ten other countries to operate their own postal systems in the more important cities and seaports of the empire. The first of these post offices was established by Austria in 1721 and by the early years of this century all the major European powers with commercial interests in the Levant were operating post offices or agencies with the tacit approval of the Ottoman authorities. Turkey seized the opportunity presented by the outbreak of World War I to close down the foreign post offices (including those of her allies Germany and Austria). Nevertheless Poland and Rumania contrived to open consular post offices in Constantinople after World War I, the French post office in Beirut survived as late as 1923 and Britain issued stamps overprinted 'Levant' during the British occupation of Turkey after World War I. The stamps fall into two groups: those inscribed 'Levant' (a generic term for the Mediterranean coast of the Ottoman Empire) and/or valued in Turkish currency, and those overprinted with the name of a specific town. In the latter category the stamps overprinted for use in towns now outside Turkey (such as Salonika and Jerusalem) are dealt with under their respective countries.

1. Austria, 3 soldi, 1867
Austria introduced stamps for use in the Levantine post offices in 1867, in the same designs as the contemporary Austro-Hungraian series but with values in soldi currency. The series was re-engraved between 1876 and 1883, with the emperor's whiskers finely drawn. In the original series the whiskers were coarsely delineated.

2. Austria, 10 paras, 1888
This stamp was one of a series of six introduced in August 1883, with the imperial arms typographed in various colours and the lettering and value printed in black. The inscription is the abbreviated form of the Latin signifying 'imperial and royal Austrian post' – an early example of the use of Latin on stamps as an international language.

3. Austria, 1 piastre, 1890
The Austrian post offices in the Levant adopted

Turkish currency in 1886 and four years later the contemporary definitive series of Austria was surcharged with values from 8*pa.* to 20*pi.* Five different gauges of perforation have been recorded in this series over the period of ten years in which it was current. Note the fine particles of hair embedded in the paper, the so-called granite paper used by Austrian stamps at this period.

4. Austria, 10 paras, 1908
This stamp comes from one of the very few commemorative issues released in any of the European post offices in Turkey. Several designs of the 1908 Diamond Jubilee series were re-engraved with Turkish currency and printed on paper of various colours. A similar series, with values in centimes and francs, was used in the Austrian post offices in Crete (see plate 16).

5. France, 15 piastres, 1921
French stamps of the Peace and Commerce series were issued in 1885, with values surcharged in Turkish currency. Previously ordinary French stamps were used in the Levantine post offices and can only be identified by their postmarks. French stamps surcharged in Turkish currency were withdrawn in 1914 but were resumed in 1921 and finally withdrawn in 1923.

6. France, 1 centime, 1902
The 'Blanc', 'Mouchon' and 'Merson' designs of France were released in 1902–06 with the inscriptions modified to include the word 'Levant'. This series, with values in French currency, was intended for use on printed matter, postcards and parcels. Other denominations, surcharged in Turkish currency, were used on letter mail.

7. Great Britain, 2 pence, 1905
One of a series of ten British stamps released in August 1905 with the overprint 'Levant'. The company conveying the British parcel post to and from Turkey received a percentage of the stamps' total face value. As the Turkish currency fluctuated considerably the charges had to be calculated in sterling. Stamps for use on letters continued to be surcharged in Turkish currency as before.

8. Great Britain, 2½ piastres, 1910
One of three Edwardian stamps issued in 1910 with values surcharged in piastres for use on letter mail from the Levantine post offices. They were followed by various stamps portraying King George V, which remained in use until August 1914 when the Turkish authorities closed the post offices.

9. Great Britain, 3 pence, 1921
British stamps surcharged in Turkish currency or overprinted LEVANT were reintroduced in 1921 for the use of troops serving in Constantinople after World War I. For similar stamps overprinted 'Levant' in upper and lower case lettering, see under Salonika (plate 16).

10. Germany, 10 paras, 1889
German stamps surcharged in paras or piastres were introduced in 1884 and remained in use till the outbreak of World War I, when the post offices were closed by the Turks. The first German post office was opened at Constantinople in 1870 and at first used ordinary stamps of the North German Confederation, distinguishable only by the postmark. Ordinary German stamps were then used, from 1872 till 1884.

11. Germany, 5 centimes, 1908
Five denominations of the Germania definitive series were surcharged in French currency and issued in August 1908 in the German post offices in the Levant, primarily for use on printed matter. 177

PLATE 34 FOREIGN POST OFFICES IN TURKEY · PLATE 35 YUGOSLAVIA

French currency was adopted since the mail was conveyed by a French shipping company and the charged had to be computed in centimes and francs.

12. Italy, 1 centisino, 1874

Stamps of the definitive series of 1863 were overprinted 'Estero' (foreign) and issued on 1 January 1874, for use in the Italian post offices and postal agencies overseas. For this purpose the design of the basic stamps was subtly modified as a precaution against the forging of the overprint. The corner ornaments of these stamps were modified, with white spaces in place of the original spandrels. Though these stamps are commonly classed under the Levant they were in fact intended for use in the Italian overseas post offices in Alexandria, Assab, La Goletta, Massaouah, Susa, Tripoli and Tunis as well as at the consular postal agencies in Buenos Aires and Montevideo. They were superseded by distinctive overprints for use in the major offices between 1902 and 1908.

13. Italy, 40 paras, 1908

Italian stamps of the 1908 series were surcharged in Turkish currency for use as 40 or 80*pa.* stamps and released in June 1908. These stamps were intended for use in all the Italian post offices in the Turkish empire, other than those in the Albanian seaports of Durazzo and Scutari, for which separate issues were provided.

14. Italy, 1 piastre, 1908

Italian express letter stamps were overprinted 'Levante' and surcharged in Turkish currency for use in all Italian post offices in the Turkish Empire other than Durazzo and Scutari in Albania which were provided with similar stamps overprinted 'Albania'. (See plate 1). The 25*c.* express letter stamp was subsequently overprinted for airmail use but never issued. Two or three examples are known to exist.

15. Poland, 2 marek, 1919

In May 1919 contemporary Polish stamps overprinted 'Levant' were introduced for use on correspondence handed in at the Polish consulate in Constantinople for onward transmission. This practice was speedily suppressed by the Turkish authorities and used examples of these stamps, especially on genuine covers, are scarce. A second overprint, with the word placed diagonally in a fancy frame, was produced in May 1921 but was never used postally.

16. Rumania, 20 paras, 1896

Rumanian stamps surcharged in Turkish currency were issued in 1896 to prepay postage on mail carried by the Rumanian steamship company between Constantinople and Constanta on the Black Sea. The Turkish authorities refused to permit Rumania to open a post office in Constantinople and as a result a postal agency was set up in one of the steamship company's ships moored in Constantinople. The service operated from 15 March to 25 May 1896 when the mail on board the steamer was seized by the Turkish police, who alleged that it had been franked illegally in order to defraud the Ottoman Post Office.

17. Russia, 10 kopeks, 1872

Russia began issuing distinctive stamps for use in the Levant in 1863, with a large square 6*k.* stamp inscribed in Cyrillic to signify 'Dispatch under wrapper to the East'. Subsequently stamps depicting a steamship were provided for the use of ROPiT (from the initials of Russian Company for Navigation and Trade), which held the mail contract from Turkey to Russia. This stamp is one of a set of four, originally issued in 1868, but reissued in new colours at various times between 1872 and

1894. The inscription 'Vostochnaya Korrespondentsia' signifies eastern correspondence.

18. Russia, 2½ piastres on 20 paras on 4 kopeks, 1918

Though the European post offices in Turkey were closed in 1914 the Russians resumed their mail service across the Black Sea to Odessa in 1918. Various stamps of the Levant, as well as contemporary Tsarist issues of Russia itself, were overprinted with the initials of the steamship company and new values. These stamps, surcharged in paras, without the initials of ROPiT, were originally released between 1900 and 1910.

19. Russia, 5 paras, 1913

The Romanov tercentenary series of 1913 was also released with surcharges in Turkish currency, for use in the Levantine post offices. This stamp portrays Peter the Great. These stamps were suppressed by the Turkish authorities in August 1914.

20. Constantinople, 10 paras, 1909

Italian stamps overprinted 'Costantinopoli' were issued between 1909 and 1914 and were reintroduced between November 1921 and March 1923 for the use of Italian troops on garrison duty in the Turkish capital.

21. Constantinople, 5 paras, 1909

The definitive stamps of the Russian Levantine postal administration were released in 1909–10, overprinted 'Constantinople'. Apart from inverted overprints various mis-spellings have been recorded, such as 'Constantinopie' or 'Consnantinople', on this series.

22. Constantinople, 15 bani, 1919

Rumanian troops occupied Constantinople at the end of World War I and contemporary stamps overprinted 'Posta Romana Constantinopol' with the emblem of the Rumanian PTT in the centre, were issued for their convenience. They were withdrawn at the end of 1919.

23. Dardanelles, 35 piastres, 1909

Russian Levant stamps of the 1900 definitive series and the 1909 commemorative set marking the ROPiT golden jubilee, were overprinted for use in the Russian post office at the Dardanelles. The 20*pa.* on 4*k.* denomination has been recorded with the overprint inverted.

24. Kerassunde, 5 paras, 1909

Nine of the contemporary Russian Levantine stamps were similarly overprinted for use at Kerassunde in 1909–14. The three lowest denominations, 5, 10 and 20*pa.*, are known with the overprint inverted.

25. Smyrna, 10 paras, 1909

Various Italian stamps were overprinted 'Smirne' for use at Smyrna between 1909 and 1914. Similar stamps overprinted 'Smirne' in 1922 were intended for the use of Italian occupation forces but were never issued.

26. Smyrna, 5 paras, 1909

Nine stamps of the Russian Levant were overprinted 'Smyrne' for use in the Russian post office in Smyrna between 1909 and 1914. The six lower denominations are known with the spelling error 'Smyrn', while the 5, 10 and 20 paras values have been recorded with the overprint inverted.

27. Rizeh, 5 paras, 1909

The same nine stamps were likewise overprinted for use in Rizeh between 1909 and 1912. The only variety of note is the inverted overprint found on the three lowest denominations of the series.

28. Long Island, 2 pence, 1916

The island of Cheustan or Makronisi (in English 'long island') situated in the Gulf of Smyrna, was occupied by a British naval detachment in 1916. During the brief occupation the administrator overprinted Turkish fiscal stamps 'G.R.I. Postage' and surcharged them in British currency. These stamps were followed by a curious series, produced by typewriting, in denominations from ½*d.* to 1*s.* Each stamp bears the initials of the administrator, Lieutenant-Commander H. Pirie-Gordon, in red ink or indelible pencil.

29. Trebizonde, 10 paras, 1909

The last of the sets issued in 1909–12 for use in individual Russian post offices in the Ottoman Empire. Again, the only errors of note are the inverted overprints found on the 5, 10 and 20*pa.* values. For similar stamps overprinted for use in Jaffa and Jerusalem see plate 36, for those in Metelin, Mount Athos and Salonika see plate 17, and for those overprinted 'Beyrouth' see plate 38.

PLATE 35
Yugoslavia

The federative nature of Yugoslavia is well illustrated by the stamps used in this country, ranging from the distinctive issues of Serbia and Montenegro and the Austrian-controlled districts of Bosnia and Herzegovina, the transitional period of the early Twenties which culminated in the emergence of Yugoslavia, the kingdom of the southern Slavs, under Serb leadership, the Italian and German occupations of World War II and the temporary dismemberment of the country into Nazi puppet states, to the re-emergence of the country as a federative socialist republic under Tito. Plebiscite, military occupation, exile and political partition are all reflected in the stamps of this frequently turbulent area.

1. Serbia, 1 para, 1866

Under the enlightened rule of Prince Michael Obrenovich Serbia adopted postage stamps in 1866. 1 and 2 para stamps were typographed in Belgrade and showed the coat of arms of the principality, while 1, 2, 10, 20 and 40*pa.* stamps with the portrait of Prince Michael, were typographed at the Imperial Printing Works in Vienna. The Cyrillic inscription 'K. Srbska Pochta' signified Royal Serb Post.

2. 25 paras, 1903

The basic stamps, portraying Prince Alexander I Obrenovich, were designed and engraved by Mouchon and typographed at the French Government Printing Works in Paris. Alexander and his wife, Draga Mashin, were brutally murdered in a coup on 15 June 1903. The stamps were promptly overprinted with the coat of arms to obliterate the features of the dead king. Members of the rival Obrenovich and Karageorgevich families ruled Serbia alternately, their reigns punctuated by rebellions, coups, assassination and murder.

3. Montenegro, 7 novi, 1893

Montenegro has the dubious distinction of having been the first European country to issue commemorative stamps, the definitive series being overprinted to mark the quatercentenary of printing in Montenegro. The basic stamps were typographed at Vienna, where all Montenegrin stamps were produced. The series was introduced in 1874, when Montenegro adopted stamps, and remained in use, with changes in colour, paper and perforation,

PLATE 35 YUGOSLAVIA

until 1902, when the currency was changed to the Austrian system of the krone of 100 heller.

4. Montenegro, 25 heller, 1905

Prince Nikita, who governed Montenegro as if it were his private estate, was forced to grant a constitution in 1905. The 1902 definitive stamps were overprinted in English and Serb to celebrate the occasion. Numerous errors and misspellings are noted in these overprints. In addition, this 25h. stamp, intended for acknowledgment of receipt, was overprinted. Montenegro was the only European country to issue stamps for this purpose. Note the initials AR in the Roman alphabet, denoting this service.

5. Bosnia and Herzegovina, 5 heller, 1900

By the Treaty of Berlin Austria-Hungary was authorized to occupy Bosnia and Herzegovina, which remained nominally part of the Ottoman Empire. From then until 1906 the Austrian authorities issued stamps featuring the imperial coat of arms and inscribed in Austrian currency, but without any other identifying inscription, in view of the multi-national composition of the population. The first series, with values in kreuzer currency, had the numerals in the upper corners of the design, while the second series, nominally in heller and kronen, had the numerals in the lower corners. This series underwent numerous changes in perforation, colour and method of production: in lithography (1879–94) and typography (1895–1906).

6. Serbia under Austrian occupation, 10 heller, 1916

The increasingly military nature of the Austrian occupation of Bosnia and Herzegovina in the years immediately preceding World War I is indicated by the inscription 'Militär Post' found on stamps issued from 1912 onward. Austria-Hungary annexed the provinces in 1908, despite the protests of Russia and Serbia, and this action eventually precipitated World War I. Following the occupation of Serbia in 1914 by Austrian troops the contemporary series of Bosnia was overprinted for use in the captured districts.

7. Montenegro under Austrian occupation, 15 heller, 1917

Following the Austrian occupation of Montenegro, Fieldpost stamps were overprinted K.U.K. VERWALTUNG MILIT. MONTENEGRO (Royal and Imperial Military Administration). Subsequently stamps merely overprinted 'Montenegro' were prepared but never issued on account of the Austrian withdrawal from that territory.

8. Bosnia and Herzegovina, 2 heller, 1906

One of a lengthy series, the first stamps to bear the name of the provinces. Although released two years before the annexation it is significant that these stamps bore the German versions of the names. This stamp shows a view of Mostar. Others in the series featured landmarks and scenery in the provinces, but portrayed Kaiser Franz Josef on the top value, 5 krone.

9. Bosnia and Herzegovina, 45 heller, 1918

The basic stamps of this series were released in 1910 to celebrate the eightieth birthday of Kaiser Franz Josef and were modified from the definitive designs of 1906. This stamp shows the Moslem bazaar in Sarajevo, capital of Bosnia and scene of the assassination of Archduke Franz Ferdinand, which brought about World War I. The Slav population seized power in November 1918 and overprinted the stamps with the names of the provinces in Cyrillic. The inscription 'Drzava s.H.s.' rendered in Cyrillic at the top signifies the union of Serbs, Hrvats (Croats) and Slovenes.

10. Carinthia, 5 paras, 1920

A plebiscite was held in Carinthia in October 1920 to decide whether the district should go to Yugoslavia or remain with Austria. Both governments issued stamps for the plebiscite (for the Austrian series see plate 2). The Yugoslav issues consisted of five newspaper stamps of Slovenia overprinted K.G.C.A. (Karinthian Government Commission, [zone] A) and surcharged in Serbian currency. The district reverted to Austria.

11. Slovenia, 20 vinar, 1919

I. Vavpotic designed the series, lithographed by I. Blaznik of Ljubljana, for use in Slovenia after it had seceded from Austria-Hungary and joined the southern Slavs. The stamps are popularly known to philatelists as the 'Chainbreakers' from the design symbolizing freedom from Austrian rule. Subsequent printings, distinguished by their zigzag roulette, were made by the Government Printing Works in Ljubljana and then, in 1919–20, by A. Reisser in Vienna. Each of these printings exhibited considerable variation in shade, fineness of impression, perforation and type of paper used.

12. Croatia, 10 filler, 1918

Hungarian stamps, of the Karl, Zita, Harvesters and Parliament designs, were seized by the Croat nationalists and overprinted on 18 November, 1918, to signify their adherence to the union of Serbs, Croats and Slovenes. Distinctive stamps inscribed 'Hrvatska' (Croatia) were produced in 1918–19 prior to the introduction of the unified series in 1921.

13. Kingdom of the Serbs, Croats and Slovenes, 15 + 15 paras, 1921

One of a set of three stamps issued to raise funds for the disabled soldiers' fund, the design shows a wounded soldier typifying the retreat through Albania during World War I. Other designs show the battlefield of Kosovo (when the Serbs were annihilated by the Turks in 1389) and the symbol of national unity. The stamps, like the definitive series released the same year, were recess-printed by the American Bank Note Company in New York, a rare instance of work by this firm for a European country. Note the use of both Cyrillic and Roman alphabets in the inscriptions of this series. The Roman alphabet was used in those districts formerly under Austrian rule while Cyrillic was used in Serbia and Montenegro.

14. Yugoslavia, 20 dinars, 1931

One of a series issued between 1931 and 1933 portraying King Alexander. The country officially adopted the name 'Yugoslavia' in 1929 but two years elapsed before the new name began to appear on stamps. This series was designed by P. Stojicevic and engraved by D. Wagner. All stamps of the kingdom of Yugoslavia were produced at the Government Printing Works in Belgrade. The series was reissued in October 1934, with black borders in mourning for the king, following his assassination at Marseilles on 9 October of that year.

15. Yugoslav Government in Exile, 5 dinars, 1943

Between 1941 and 1945 Yugoslavia ceased to exist as a stamp-issuing entity, but fourteen stamps and a miniature sheet were printed by Waterlow and Sons for the use of the government-in-exile at its London headquarters and on board ships of the Yugoslav Merchant Navy working with the Allies. This stamp was one of a series, portraying King Peter II, issued to celebrate the 2nd anniversary of the overthrow of the regency of Prince Paul.

16. Croatia, 25 banicas, 1941

Croat nationalists, under Dr Ante Pavelitch, were

encouraged by Nazi Germany to establish a separate republic, ostensibly an independent state but actually under Nazi and Fascist control. This stamp is one of a definitive series, designed by O. Antonini and printed in photogravure at Zagreb, issued in 1941–42. The stamps featured views of Croatia. Croatia maintained an uneasy independence until June 1945, when it was reabsorbed into Yugoslavia. The currency used during the period of independence was based on the kuna of 100 banicas.

17. Montenegro, 1 lira, 1942

Yugoslav or Italian stamps overprinted 'Montenegro' or 'Crna Gora' (the equivalent in Cyrillic) were used in the former kingdom after it was occupied by the Italians in April 1941. The Italians issued a series in 1943 celebrating the centenary of Montenegro's national anthem. The stamps featured scenery with a portrait of Prince Bishop Peter Njegosh inset. After the Italian surrender in 1943 Montenegro was occupied by German troops who overprinted various stamps of Yugoslavia or Montenegro in German to mark the German Military Administration and the National Administrative Committee which followed.

18. Serbia, 1 dinar, 1941

Distinctive stamps were issued in the puppet state of Serbia set up by the Nazis after the invasion of Yugoslavia in 1941. At first Yugoslav stamps overprinted SERBIEN were used, but distinctive stamps inscribed 'Srbija' (Serbia) were adopted in September 1941. The German-sponsored stamps of Serbia were superseded by Yugoslav partisan issues in late 1944.

19. Slovenia, 2 dinars, 1941

Slovenia was under Italian control from April 1941 till the Italian surrender in 1943. At first Yugoslav stamps overprinted in Italian were used, but from July 1941 onwards ordinary Italian stamps were employed.

20. Slovenia, 20 centesimi, 1944

Following the Italian collapse the Germans took over the administration, renaming the district as the province of Laibach (Ljubljana) and overprinted Italian stamps for that purpose. A distinctive pictorial series, inscribed in Serbo-Croat and German, was released in 1945. Slovenia now uses ordinary Yugoslav stamps.

21. Trieste, 20 dinars, 1949

The city of Trieste and adjacent territory was administered as a Free City under joint control of the Allies and Yugoslavia. Distinctive stamps for use in Zone B, under Yugoslav control, were issued from 1948 to 1954. In that year the territory was divided between Italy and Yugoslavia and the ordinary stamps of these countries introduced. Stamps overprinted or inscribed STT VUJA signify Yugoslav Military Government. In many cases contemporary Yugoslav stamps used in Trieste were printed in new colours. For the stamps issued under Allied military occupation see plate 24.

22. Venezia Giulia and Istria, 1 lira, 1946

The districts of Venezia Giulia and Istria, including the cities of Fiume and Trieste and the naval base of Pola, were occupied by British and American troops and Yugoslav partisans at the end of World War II. For the stamps issued by the Allies see plate 24. In the areas administered by the Yugoslavs Italian stamps were overprinted 'Istra', 'Trieste-Trst' or 'Fiume-Rijeka' in June-July 1945 (see plate 24). Subsequently a pictorial series inscribed in Serbo-Croat and Italian to signify 'Istria-Slovenian Coast' were issued in 1945–46. Stamps perforated 10½ by 11½ were lithographed at

179

PLATE 35 YUGOSLAVIA

Ljubljana, while those perforated 12 were printed at Zagreb.

23. Yugoslavia, 4 + 21 dinars, 1945

The first stamps issued by Yugoslavia after it was liberated by Tito's partisans appeared in December 1944 and January 1945. Stamps of the puppet regime in Serbia were overprinted with the republican arms and an overprint signifying 'Democratic Federative Yugoslavia'. Stamps portraying Marshal Tito appeared later in 1945.

24. Yugoslavia, 50 paras, 1951

Yugoslavia reappeared as a stamp-issuing country in 1944 when stamps were released by Tito's partisans for areas under their control. The earliest stamps were inscribed 'Demokratska Federativna Jugoslavija' (Democratic Federative Yugoslavia), though the abbreviation FNR (Federative People's Republic) began to appear in 1946. Since World War II the stamps of Yugoslavia have been inscribed wholly in either Roman or Cyrillic, sometimes in both scripts and sometimes partly in one and partly in the other. Since 1944 stamps have appeared annually for Red Cross or Children's Week, their use being compulsory on all correspondence. Special postage due stamps, for taxing mail not franked by these stamps, have also been produced.

25. Yugoslavia, 300 dinars, 1958

One of two stamps recess-printed in 1958 to honour International Geophysical Year, it shows the moon, earth and orbital tracks of the early sputniks. This stamp, designed by B. Krsic and engraved by S. Babic, was one of the earliest with the theme of space exploration and, as such, is highly regarded by thematic collectors.

26. Yugoslavia, 50 dinars, 1963

The 20th anniversary of the battle of the Sutjeska River was marked by three stamps, issued in July 1963. Two stamps, featuring partisans in action, reproduced wood-carvings by D. Andrejevic-Kun in combined recess and lithography, while the 25d. stamp, reproducing B. Sotra's painting of the Sutjeska Gorge, was printed entirely by lithography.

27. Yugoslavia, 200 dinars, 1964

The top value in a set of six stamps publicizing various aspects of Yugoslav art. This stamp, designed by D. Kazic and S. Fileki, reproduces a detail from a 14th century manuscript in Herman Priory at Bistrica. It typifies the increasing use of multicolour photogravure by Yugoslavia in the past decade.

28. Yugoslavia, 200 dinars, 1965

The top value in a series celebrating the 20th anniversary of the liberation. Each denomination in the series depicted one of the six capitals, Belgrade being featured on this stamp, designed by A. Milenkovic and engraved by S. Babic.

ASIA

PLATE 36 PALESTINE, ISRAEL

PLATE 36

Palestine, Israel

1. Jerusalem (Italian Post Office), 10 paras, 1909
Contemporary Italian definitive stamps, in denominations from 5 centesimi to 5 lire, were overprinted 'Gerusalemme' and surcharged in Turkish currency from 10 paras to 20 piastres. The series went on sale at the Italian post office in Jerusalem in February 1909. Two years later a higher value, 40*pi*. on 10*l.*, was added to the set. The Italian post office closed down shortly afterward, on account of the outbreak of the Italo-Turkish War.

2. Jerusalem (Russian Post Office), 20 paras, 1909
Before 1909 the Russian post office in Jerusalem used the stamps of the Russian Levant series. In 1909 nine values of the 50th anniversary series was overprinted 'Ierusalem' and surcharged with values from 5*pa*. to 70*pi*. The low values up to 7*pi*. are known with the error 'erusalem'. Inverted overprints are recorded on the 5, 10 and 20*pa.*, and the 7*pi*. is known with the value omitted.

3. Jaffa (Russian Post Office), 10 paras, 1909
A similar series was adopted at the Russian post office in Jaffa. Inverted overprints are known on the three lowest denominations and the 5*pa*. has also been recorded with a blue instead of black overprint.

4. Egyptian Expeditionary Force, 1 piastre, 1918
Turkish stamps were used in Palestine until 1918, when the Egyptian Expeditionary Force under General Allenby drove out the Turks. A 1*pi*. stamp was photo-lithographed at the Typographical Department of the Survey of Egypt in Giza for use in the occupied territories of Transjordan, Cilicia, northern Egypt and Syria as well as Palestine. The first printing was in indigo on ungummed paper and appeared in February 1918. The following month the stamp was printed in ultramarine on gummed paper. Subsequently a series from 1 millième to 20 piastres was typographed at at Somerset House, London, in a similar design.

5. Palestine, 1 millième, 1920
A civil administration, under a British High Commissioner, was established in Palestine in July 1920. In September the E.E.F. series was released with an overprint 'Palestine' in English, Arabic and Hebrew. The stamps were overprinted at the Greek Orthodox Convent in Jerusalem. Numerous errors and varieties are recorded in this issue, with the lettering misplaced or Arabic or Hebrew characters transposed. Overprints of this type were subsequently produced at Somerset House or by Waterlow and Sons.

6. Palestine, 500 millièmes, 1941
Britain received a mandate from the League of Nations over Palestine in September 1923 but the overprinted stamps continued in use until 1927. F. Taylor produced four designs for a series typographed by Harrison and Sons in 1927. The low values featured Rachel's tomb, the Dome of the Rock or the Citadel in Jerusalem, while the high values showed the Sea of Galilee. New colours were introduced between 1932 and 1944 and the 250 and 500*m*. and £1 stamps were added to the series in 1941. These stamps remained in use until the end of the mandatory period in 1948.

7. Palestine Interim Period, 10 millièmes, 1948
The British mandate came to an end on 14 May 1948, and stamps of the Hebrew Post came into use on 16 May. In the last months of the mandate, as law and order disintegrated into open warfare between Arabs and Israelis, numerous postal services sprang into being. This stamp, showing an immigrant ship, was one of a series issued at Nahariya during the interim period.

8. Israel, 1,000 millièmes, 1948
The first stamps of Israel were inscribed in Hebrew 'Doar Ivri' (Hebrew Post) and featured coins issued by the Jewish authorities at the time of the first and second Jewish revolts against the Romans, or in the reign of the Hebrew king, Alexander Jannaeus. The stamps were designed by O. Wallish and typographed by the Haaretz Printing Press in Sarona.

9. Israel, 100 pruta, 1949
The second definitive series appeared between 1949 and 1952. Coins continued to provide the subject matter for most denominations, but four large pictorial designs were also introduced. This stamp was designed initially to commemorate the 25th anniversary of the establishment of Jerusalem University but was retained as part of the definitive range. It was designed by F. Krausz and lithographed by Lewin-Epstein of Bat-Yam. The currency was changed to the Israeli pound of 1,000 pruta in 1949.

10. Israel, 125 pruta, 1954
Ancient coins formed the basis of the definitive sets of 1950, 1954, and 1960. It is interesting to note that the motifs of these ancient Hebrew coins were also adapted for the modern Israeli currency. The stamps were designed by O. Wallish and lithographed by Lewin-Epstein.

11. Israel, 80 pruta, 1951
This stamp of April 1951 was issued to publicize the Independence Bonds Campaign. The design, symbolizing a worker supporting Israel, was the work of Abram Games, a British-Jewish artist who made his philatelic début with the 3*d* stamp in the British Olympic Games set of 1948, and was subsequently a member of the British Post Office advisory committee on stamp design.

12. Israel, 25 agora, 1960
The currency was reformed in 1960 and the pound of 100 agora (singular: agorot) adopted. O. Adler designed this stamp of December 1960 to mark the centenary of the birth of Henrietta Szold, founder of the Youth Immigration Scheme. The stamp was printed in photogravure by the Israeli Government Printer at Hakirya, Tel Aviv.

13. Israel, 10 agora, 1968
Adler also designed the definitive series of 1968, which took as its theme Israeli exports. A tailor's dummy and draped cloth symbolized the textile industry. Other designs symbolized electronics, diamonds, fruit, flowers, telecommunications equipment, atomic isotopes and fashion modelling.

14. Israel, 55 agora, 1967
The memorial to the War of Independence formed the subject of this stamp, issued in May 1967 to mark Memorial Day. Many of the Israeli commemorative stamps in recent years allude to the struggles against the Arab world for national survival.

15. Israel, 30 agora, 1970
The 20th anniversary of Operation 'Magic Carpet', the evacuation of Jewish communities from the Yemen, was celebrated by this stamp showing an aircraft with a carpet motif. Allied to the symbolism of this design is the tab attached to stamps in the bottom row of the sheet, with a quotation from Exodus 19, 4: 'I bore you on eagles' wings and

181

PLATE 36 PALESTINE, ISRAEL · PLATE 37 JORDAN AND IRAQ

brought you to myself.' Marginal inscriptions, known to collectors as tabs, are a unique feature of Israeli stamps.

16. Israel, 12 agora, 1964
The first anniversary of the death of President Izhak Ben-Zvi was marked by this stamp issued in April 1964. It was designed by M. Krup from a photograph, and was printed in photogravure by the Israeli Government Printer.

17. Israel, 25 agora, 1964
The brothers M. and G. Shamir produced this stamp to mark the 'Year of the Blockade Runners', lithographed by Lewin-Epstein. Compare the treatment of the crowded 'hell-ship' with the motif of the Nahariya stamp. Again an apt Biblical quotation provided the tab inscription.

18. Israel, 55 agora, 1968
Several stamps appeared on 24 April 1968, two of them marking Independence Day, while this stamp marked Memorial Day. Other stamps released on the same day honoured Zahal (the Israeli Defence Forces) and the 25th anniversary of the Rising in the Warsaw Ghetto. A martial flavour underlay all five designs, linking the past with the present. E. Weishoff designed the Memorial Day stamp, which, with its motif of crossed rifles, banner and steel helmet, alluded to the recently concluded June War of 1967. The black border symbolizes mourning for those who were killed in action.

19. Israel, 60 agora, 1969
Even sporting stamps are imbued with a martial atmosphere. There is something ruggedly aggressive about the bold outline and sharp colours of this stamp, issued in 1969 to mark the 8th Maccabiah or national games, named after the Hebrew hero, Alexander Maccabaeus, who led the Jews in revolt against the Romans.

20. Israel, 35 agora, 1970
The influence of Hebrew mosaics is very strong on contemporary Israeli stamp design, with bold primary colours and metallic ink simulating the *cloisonné* effect of ancient enamel decoration. This stamp marked the 50th anniversary of Histradut, the General Federation of Labour.

21. Israel, 25 agora, 1965
The definitive sets of recent years have had a thematic character – signs of the zodiac (1961), birds (1963) and civic coats of arms (1965). The last-named series was designed by M. and G. Shamir and printed in photogravure by the Government Printer in denominations from 1 agorot to 3 pounds. A second series featuring civic arms (2 to 80a.) was released in 1969.

22. Indian Forces in Gaza, 15 paise, 1965
Indian troops formed part of the United Nations Emergency Force stationed in the Gaza strip to prevent war between Israel and Egypt. The Nehru commemorative stamp of 1965 was overprinted UNEF for the use of military personnel serving with the UN force. The peace-keeping force was withdrawn in 1967, shortly before the June War. No special stamps were provided by any other contingent.

23. Jordanian occupation of Palestine, 200 mils, 1948
Jordanian stamps overprinted 'Palestine' in English and Arabic, were provided for the use of troops occupying parts of Palestine on the west bank of the Jordan after the withdrawal of the British in 1948. The definitive series, from 1 mil to £1, was overprinted in this way. Inverted or double overprints have been recorded on the 2, 3 and 10m. denominations.

24. Jordanian occupation of Palestine, 10 mils, 1949
The set of five stamps marking the 75th anniversary of the Universal Postal Union was similarly overprinted for use in the occupied territories of Palestine. The 4 and 40m. stamps are known with the error 'Plaestine'. Ordinary Jordanian stamps were introduced in the territories on the west bank in 1949 and were used until 1967, when these districts were taken over by Israel.

25. Egyptian occupation of Palestine, 1 millième, 1958
Egyptian stamps overprinted 'Palestine' in Arabic and English were issued in the Gaza Strip from 1948 to 1967. Those issued after 1960 were similar to contemporary stamps of the United Arab Republic but were inscribed 'Palestine' and were often printed in different colours. These stamps were withdrawn from use following the Israeli occupation of Gaza in June 1967.

PLATE 37
Jordan and Iraq

---

1. East of Jordan, 4 mils, 1920
The British received a mandate from the League of Nations over the Arab territory on the east bank of the River Jordan. Stamps of the Egyptian Expeditionary Force issued in Palestine (see plate 36) were overprinted in Arabic to signify 'East of Jordan' and issued in November 1920. The overprinting was done by the Greek Orthodox Convent in Jerusalem. The 1m. stamp is known with the overprint inverted.

2. Arab Government of the East, 5 piastres, 1925
Stamps of the EEF series and various contemporary issues of Hejaz (see plate 39) were overprinted in Arabic to signify 'Arab Government of the East' between 1921 and 1925. Numerous different types of overprint, often incorporating the date in Arabic numerals, were used in this period. The close family ties between Jordan and Arabia (the Emir Abdullah was the son of King Hussein of Hejaz) are reflected in the use of Hejaz stamps by Jordan at this time.

3. Transjordan, 50 mils, 1930
Perkins Bacon recess-printed a series of stamps portraying the Emir Abdullah. The stamps ranged from 2 to 1000m. and were released between 1927 and 1929. The series was re-engraved between 1930 and 1939 with the figures of value expressed at the left instead of both sides as formerly. A 1m. denomination was introduced in 1934. A version of this series, lithographed in Cairo, appeared in 1942, while Bradbury Wilkinson recess-printed the series in 1943–44, using a different gauge of perforation. Colour changes and new values appeared in 1947.

4. Transjordan, 12 mils, 1946
Transjordan became an independent kingdom in 1946, the emir being elevated to the status of a king. To celebrate independence a series of nine stamps was lithographed at the Catholic Printery in Beirut and issued in May 1946. The common design featured a map of Jordan, the torch of enlightenment and the dove of peace.

5. Transjordan, 200 mils, 1947
De La Rue recess-printed a set of nine stamps, in denominations from 1 to 200m., to mark the inauguration of the first national parliament in November 1947. The stamps featured the parliament building in Amman and were curiously inscribed with the hyphenated form 'Trans-Jordan'.

The country officially became the Hashemite Kingdom of Jordan at the time of independence but continued to use the archaic name on stamps until 1947.

6. Jordan, 15 fils, 1960
Since independence Jordan has had an uneasy relationship with the Arab world in general and Egypt in particular. From time to time stamps in an Arab omnibus design have been issued to demonstrate Arab solidarity. In May 1960 this 15 fils stamp was issued to mark the inauguration of the Arab League Centre in Cairo. The same design was used by all the participating countries, with the appropriate portrait inset and an overprint adding the name of the country and the value. Jordan adopted the dinar of 1000 fils in 1950. Note the spelling error 'fills' instead of 'fils' on this stamp.

7. Jordan, 35 fils, 1962
The modernization of Jordan has been publicized by many sets of stamps in recent years. This was one of a pair recess-printed by Bradbury Wilkinson and issued in December 1962 to mark the opening of the port of Aqaba.

8. Jordan, 15 fils, 1964
A surprising number of stamps from this Moslem country have a Christian motif, emphasizing Jordan's role as preserver of many of the holy places of the Christian religion. A series of 1963 depicted these holy shrines and included Christian churches and Moslem mosques. Stamps of 1965–66 featured other Christian shrines and a long series depicted the fourteen stations of the Cross. Jordan's claim as a preserver of Jewish antiquities was shown in a series of 1965 featuring the Dead Sea Scrolls. This stamp was one of a series of four issued in January 1964 to commemorate the visit of Pope Paul VI to the Holy Land. It shows El Aqsa Mosque flanked by portraits of the Pope and King Hussein. Other stamps depicted mosques and churches. The stamps were designed by P. Koroless and lithographed by Yacoub Slim Press, Beirut.

9. Jordan, 10 fils, 1964
The second birthday of Crown Prince Abdullah was celebrated by a set of three stamps issued in March 1964. Rectangular formats were used for the 5 and 35f. stamps and a large diamond shape for the 10f. The stamps featured various portraits of the prince and were printed in multicolour photogravure by Harrison and Sons.

10. Jordan, 80 fils, 1964
The continuing hostility between the Arab world and Israel is graphically demonstrated by the series of five stamps issued by Jordan in September 1964 to mark the Arab Summit Conference. The stamps featured a map of Jordan showing its territory as including the whole of Israel, with no indication that an independent Jewish state existed. The issue of stamps of this nature by her Arab neighbours is unlikely to reduce the level of national paranoia in Israel concerning the intentions of the Arab world.

11. Jordan, 10 fils, 1965
Many of the stamps of Jordan in recent years have been inspired by an external philatelic agency, and this accounts for the spate of issues commemorating famous people and events beyond the Arab world. A set of four stamps was issued in June 1965 in memory of the late John F. Kennedy, belatedly marking the first anniversay of his assassination. The stamps were lithographed in Beirut.

12. Mosul, 4 annas, 1919
Troops of the Indian Expeditionary Force 'D' occupied the Mosul district of Mesopotamia at the

PLATE 37 JORDAN AND IRAQ · PLATE 38 SYRIA AND LEBANON

end of World War I and used Turkish fiscal stamps suitably overprinted and surcharged in Indian currency. The stamps ranged from ½a. on 1pi. to 8a. on 10pa. Numerous errors and varieties have been recorded in these overprints.

13. Baghdad, ¼ anna, 1917
British troops of the Egyptian Expeditionary Force occupied Baghdad in September 1917 and stocks of Turkish stamps were overprinted 'Baghdad in British Occupation' for use by the civil population. The stamps were surcharged in Indian currency from ¼ to 2a. Several stamps are recorded with words or the value omitted from the overprint.

14. Iraq, 8 annas, 1920
Turkish stamps of the 1913 series, overprinted 'Iraq in British Occupation' were adopted in September 1918. The series, additionally overprinted 'On State Service' was released for official purposes in 1920–21. Later issues of these stamps, recess-printed by Bradbury Wilkinson, were produced on paper with the standard colonial watermark, though the original Turkish series had been unwatermarked.

15. Iraq, ½ anna, 1923
The overprinted Turkish stamps were superseded in 1923 by a pictorial series recess-printed by Bradbury Wilkinson. Two women were responsible for the ten designs of this series – Miss Edith Cheesman and Mrs C. C. Garbett. The thirteen denominations, from ½a. to 10r., featured Babylonian antiquities, modern mosques, camels and water transport. A 1r. stamp portraying King Faisal I was added to the series in 1927.

16. Iraq, ½ dinar, 1934
A new currency system based on the dinar of 1000 fils was adopted in 1932. In October of that year Iraq ceased to be under British mandate from the League of Nations and became an independent kingdom. King Ghazi succeeded Faisal I in September 1933 and a series bearing his portrait was introduced in June 1934. The stamps were recess-printed by Bradbury Wilkinson in denominations from 1f. to 1d., using three different formats and frame designs.

17. Iraq, 12 fils, 1942
King Faisal II succeeded his father in April 1939, after the latter was killed in a car crash. Stamps portraying the young king did not appear until 1942, when a set of eight denominations, from 1 to 12f., was released. The portraits were printed in photogravure and the frames lithographed by the Survey Department in Cairo. Stamps of this and the preceding sets, together with the later definitives portraying King Faisal II, were overprinted in 1958 after the overthrow of the monarchy.

18. Iraq, 40 fils, 1959
Significantly the first distinctive stamps issued by the republican regime consisted of three stamps celebrating Army Day. Ironically the first stamps issued for that purpose appeared in January 1958 and portrayed King Faisal, who was overthrown by an army coup. Since 1959 the majority of stamps issued by Iraq have had a martial flavour.

19. Iraq, 50 fils, 1963
During the first phase of the republic the country was governed by the military dictator General Kassem, who instituted a cult of the personality by having himself portrayed on stamps at every opportunity. The Army Day series of 1963 provides a typical example, with Kassem portrayed above an array of guns, and lengthy extracts from his speeches quoted in the lower part of the design.

Many of the stamps of Iraq in this period were printed in photogravure by Courvoisier of Switzerland.

20. Iraq, 15 fils, 1969
Since the overthrow of Kassem in the 14th Ramadan Revolution of 1963 the military flavour of Iraqi stamps has been somewhat toned down, though still apparent. Many stamps mark the anniversaries of the revolutions of 1920, 1958, 1963 and more recently, of 17 July 1968. In between, however, a few stamps have commemorated religious events such as the Hajeer Year (1969). This multicoloured triangular stamp depicts a mosque and worshippers.

21. Iraq, 15 fils, 1971
The golden jubilee of Army Day, instituted in 1921 by the Emir Faisal, was celebrated by two stamps issued in January 1971. The design of the 15f. stamp marks a break with traditional Iraqi realism, by adopting a more whimsical approach. Outlines of a tank and a delta-winged aircraft are superimposed on stylized figures of marching infantry.

PLATE 38
Syria and Lebanon

1. Beirut, 5 paras, 1909
Post offices were maintained in Beirut by several European powers from the late nineteenth century to World War I and stamps of the appropriate Levantine series were used. In 1905–06 during temporary shortages of the normal issues, both France and Britain produced 1 piastre provisional stamps which were limited in use to Beirut. In 1909 the Russian post office adopted a series overprinted 'Beyrouth' in French, but reverted to the Russian Levant general series the following year.

2. Rouad Island, 3 centimes, 1916
Rouad Island, off the coast of Syria, was occupied by French forces in January 1916 and various French stamps, suitably overprinted, were introduced that year. The stamps up to 40c. were issued without a further surcharge, but higher denominations were surcharged from 1 to 20pi. for use on letter mail. After World War I the island was transferred to the territory of the Alaouites (see 24, below).

3. Cilicia, 20 paras, 1919
This district of Asia Minor on the borders of Syria and Turkey was occupied by French troops at the end of World War I. Various Turkish postage and fiscal stamps of 1901–17 were overprinted 'Cilicie' in block letters or cursive script and released between March and May 1919. Subsequently stamps were overprinted to denote 'French Military Occupation'.

4. Cilicia, 20 paras, 1920
Contemporary French stamps were overprinted O.M.F. (Occupation Militaire Française) or T.E.O. (Territoires Ennemis Occupés = Occupied Enemy Territory), with values surcharged in Turkish currency. The 10c. of the former French Levant was overprinted T.E.O. and surcharged 20 paras at Beirut in 1920. Examples are known with the 's' of PARAS inverted. Cilicia was returned to Turkey in 1921 and distinctive stamps withdrawn.

5. Syria, 2.50 piastres, 1922
French and French Levantine stamps overprinted T.E.O. or O.M.F. were issued in Syria in 1919–20, surcharged in Egyptian currency (millièmes and

piastres) or Syrian currency (centièmes and piastres). The last stamp issued under the military occupation was this 2.50pi., the surcharge being printed by the Capuchin Fathers in Beirut.

6. Syria and Great Lebanon, 1.50 piastres, 1923
In 1923 France received a mandate from the League of Nations over Syria and the area then known as Great Lebanon. Various French stamps were overprinted by the Capuchin Fathers 'Syrie – Grand Liban' and surcharged in Syrian centièmes and piastres. These stamps were issued between September and December 1923 and were withdrawn when separate issues were adopted for each territory at the beginning of 1924.

7. Syria, 1 piastre, 1925
The first distinctive series of Syria was issued in March 1925. J. de la Nézière produced various designs featuring famous landmarks in the cities of Syria and the stamps were printed in photogravure by Vaugirard of Paris. Various provisional surcharges were made in 1926 and several stamps were overprinted in 1929 for airmail purposes.

8. Syria, 20 centièmes, 1930
Vaugirard produced a similar pictorial series between 1930 and 1936, but used lithography for the lower denominations and photogravure for the higher values. Several stamps were issued in new colours between 1932 and 1936 and in those cases the designs were redrawn in minor details.

9. Syria, 12.50 piastres, 1938
Syria became a republic under French mandate in 1934 and stamps denoting the change in status were issued in August of that year, recess-printed at the Institut de Gravure in Paris. A new pictorial series was recess-printed at the French Government Printing Works in 1940. In between, however, Vaugirard continued to print stamps by photogravure. This stamp, portraying President Atasi, was produced as a 10 piastre denomination but was surcharged 12.50p. before issue.

10. Syria, 12.50 piastres, 1946
Syria became an independent republic in April 1942. The stamps continued to be inscribed in French but were printed either in Cairo or Beirut and were inscribed either 'République Syrienne' or reverted to the earlier form 'Syrie'. This stamp was one of a series issued in 1946–47 portraying President Shukri Bey al-Quwatli. The stamps were printed in photogravure or offset-lithography in Cairo.

11. United Arab Republic, 50 piastres, 1959
Syria and Egypt joined in February 1958 to form the United Arab Republic. At first stamps continued to include the word 'Syrie' and for a short time the form 'République Arabe Unie' was used, but from the end of 1958 till October 1961 the stamps were inscribed in English and the simple abbreviation UAR was adopted. The stamps of Syria continued to be different from those used in Egypt, and where a joint issue was made the Syrian version may be identified by the use of the piastre currency, whereas Egypt used milliemes.

12. Syrian Arab Republic, 55 piastres, 1964
The union with Egypt was dissolved in November 1961 but left its legacy in the use of English instead of French on the stamps of Syria and the form of title subsequently adopted, 'Syrian Arab Republic'. In some recent stamps the abbreviated form SAR has been used instead. This stamp was one of a definitive series introduced between March and September 1954. The lower values featured the head of Princess Ugharit, while the higher values depicted a mosaic from Chahba. Many recent

183

Syrian stamps have featured classical and medieval antiquities of the country.

13. **Syrian Arab Republic, 15 piastres, 1971**
To publicize the referendum held in September 1971 on the question of Arab federation this 15*p*. stamp was released. Designed by M. Hammad and printed in multicolour lithography, it features a flag and a map of the proposed Federation of Egypt, Libya and Syria.

14. **Great Lebanon, 2 piastres, 1924**
French stamps overprinted 'Grand Liban' were adopted in Great Lebanon in January 1924. The overprints were in capitals at first, but in July an overprint in upper and lower case lettering was introduced. The stamps were surcharged in centiemes and piastres and numerous errors and varieties have been noted in these overprints.

15. **Lebanon, 10 centièmes, 1927**
A republic under French tutelage was proclaimed in 1927 and stamps overprinted 'République Libanaise' were introduced between July and October of that year. The basic series was designed by J. de la Nézière and printed by Vaugirard in lithography or photogravure in 1925. The low values featured the famous cedars of Lebanon, a recurring motif on Lebanese stamps over the past fifty years.

16. **Lebanon, 25 centièmes, 1930**
The overprinted series was superseded in May 1930 by a pictorial definitive set. The low values, up to 25*c*., were lithographed, while the higher denominations, up to 100*pi*., were printed in photogravure. The stamps featured views of Beirut, country scenery and the classical ruins of Baalbeck, Tyre, Sidon and other ancient ports.

17. **Lebanon, 50 centièmes, 1931**
Vaugirard printed a photogravure airmail series for Lebanon in 1931, featuring aircraft over various cities. The stamps were designed by J. de la Nézière in the style characteristic of his work for Morocco, Syria and other Moslem countries, with elaborate Saracenic patterns and Arabesque ornament.

18. **Lebanon, 25 centièmes, 1940**
Between 1937 and 1940 a new series designed by P. Mourani was issued. The three designs featured the ubiquitous cedars, a Lebanese landscape and a portrait of President Edde. The 'cedars' stamps were typographed and the others recess-printed by the French Government Printing Works. P. Mourani designed the majority of Lebanese stamps between 1936 and 1940.

19. **Lebanon, 50 piastres, 1945**
The Lebanon began issuing postage due stamps in 1924 and has since followed the French colonial tradition of using pictorial designs for this purpose. A set of four stamps printed by Imprimerie Catholique on coloured paper was issued in 1945. The design by P. Koroleff showed the National Museum in Beirut. The Lebanon became an independent republic in 1941 but there was no change in the inscription of the stamps to denote this fact.

20. **Lebanon, 45 piastres, 1964**
Since 1947 the form 'Liban' gradually supplanted 'République Libanaise' on the stamps of this country. Multicolour lithography, either by local firms such as Cortbawi or Saikali, or foreign firms such as De La Rue, has become increasingly used, coinciding with the policy of releasing thematic sets at regular intervals. This stamp was one of sixteen postage and airmail stamps lithographed by De La Rue in 1964 with the theme of flowers.

21. **Lebanon, 200 piastres, 1965**
The series of March–August 1965 featured birds (ordinary postage) and butterflies (airmail). The majority of the stamps were recess-printed in multicolour by the French Government Printing Works, but the 500*pi*. value was printed in combined recess and lithography at the Austrian Government Printing Works in Vienna.

22. **Lebanon, 25 piastres, 1967**
To mark International Tourist Year the Lebanon issued two sets of stamps featuring scenery and landmarks. The seventeen stamps, both ordinary and airmail, were subsequently retained as a definitive series. The stamps were printed in multicolour offset lithography by the State Printing Office in Budapest, which has produced most Lebanese stamps since 1966.

23. **French Forces in the Levant, 10 francs, 1942**
After the defeat of the Vichy French forces in the Middle East in 1942 Free French troops took over garrison duties in Syria and the Lebanon. Contemporary stamps of both countries were overprinted with the Cross of Lorraine and the inscription 'Forces Françaises Libres Levant' or with the initials of the F.A.F.L. airline. Subsequently a series of stamps designed by R. Soriano and offset-lithographed in Beirut was introduced. The ordinary postage stamps featured camelry and the ruins of Palmyra while the air stamps depicted wings bearing the Cross of Lorraine.

24. **Alaouites, 5 centièmes, 1926**
In 1925 the mandated territory of Syria was divided and the Jebel Druse and territory of the Alawi tribe were given autonomy. No stamps were issued by the Jebel Druse but Syrian stamps overprinted 'Alaouites' were introduced in that district and remained current until September 1930, when the territory was renamed Latakia.

25. **Latakia, 50 centièmes, 1931**
The territory of the Alawi tribe was formally renamed in September 1930 but it was not until July 1931 that Syrian stamps thus inscribed were put into circulation. The airmail series, from 50*c*. to 100*pi*., was overprinted 'Lattaquie' in French and Arabic and issued between November 1931 and August 1933.

26. **Latakia, 10 centièmes, 1933**
The definitive series of Syria was similarly overprinted and issued between July 1931 and 1934. The colour of the 10*c*. was changed from magenta to purple and issued with the overprint in August 1933. In accordance with the Franco-Syrian Treaty of 1937 Latakia was re-absorbed by Syria and distinctive stamps were withdrawn at the end of February.

27. **Alexandretta, 2.50 piastres, 1938**
The sandjak (district) of Alexandretta, formerly part of Syria, was detached in April 1938 and administered by the French, pending a decision on its future. Syrian stamps were overprinted 'Sandjak d'Alexandrette' and issued between April and December 1938. Following a decision of the League of Nations, Alexandretta was ceded to Turkey.

28. **Hatay, 5 kurus, 1939**
Turkish stamps overprinted 'Hatay Devleti' were issued in Alexandretta, renamed Hatay, at the beginning of 1939. A pictorial definitive series, from 10*pa*. to 50*k*., was issued in July. Hatay was annexed to Turkey in June 1939 and ordinary Turkish stamps were introduced shortly afterwards.

PLATE 39

Arabia

1. **Hejaz, 2 piastres, 1917**
The Arabs of the Hejaz rose against the Turks during World War I and, with the help of Colonel T. E. Lawrence, established their own kingdom in 1916. Distinctive stamps were introduced in August 1916 and were typographed at the Survey of Egypt in Cairo. Further stamps appeared in December 1916 and between May and August 1917. The stamps were designed by Agami Effendi (though Lawrence of Arabia is said to have had some say in the matter) and took as their model the inscriptions and ornaments on various mosques and other buildings in Egypt or from historic copies of the Koran.

2. **Hejaz, $\frac{1}{8}$ piastre,** 1917.
This stamp was issued in February 1917. The earliest printings were rouletted with a very fine gauge of 20, but later printings (October 1917) had a zigzag roulette, giving the severed stamps a saw-toothed appearance. These stamps were superseded in 1922 by a series lithographed locally. Various stamps of the Hejaz were also overprinted for use in neighbouring Transjordan (see plate 37).

3. **Nejd, $\frac{1}{2}$ piastre, 1925**
The Wahabi sultanate of Nejd, though originally more backward than the Hejaz, fought with it for mastery of Arabia and finally drove out the Caliph of Hejaz. Stamps were not adopted in Nejd until March 1925 and at first various postage or fiscal stamps of Turkey and the Hejaz were used, with suitable overprints in Arabic. This stamp was originally lithographed at the State Printing Works in Mecca for use in the Hejaz, but was overprinted to signify 'Nejd Sultanate Post' in June 1925. Postage and fiscal stamps were subsequently overprinted in a similar fashion to celebrate the capture of Medina and Jeddah by Nejd forces.

4. **Hejaz-Nejd, 3 piastres, 1926**
The defeat of the Hejaz Arabs and the unification of the two sultanates was marked by a series of stamps issued in 1926 in denominations from $\frac{1}{4}$ to 5*pi*. All six stamps were reissued in new colours later the same year, and then overprinted in Arabic to mark the Grand Moslem Conference of June 1926.

5. **Saudi Arabia, 20 guerches, 1934**
Hejaz-Nejd was declared a kingdom under Ibn Saud in 1927 and seven years later changed its name to the kingdom of Saudi Arabia. In that year (1934) the currency was devalued from 110*g*. (piastres) to 880*g*. to the gold sovereign and a new definitive series, from $\frac{1}{8}$ to 200*g*., introduced. The stamps bore the name of the country in Arabic and French, with the *toughra* or sign manual of King Saud as the sole form of decoration. Various denominations were added up to 1957.

6. **Saudi Arabia, 5 guerches, 1939**
A set of six stamps, from 3 to 200*g*., was typographed at Mecca and introduced in 1939 for use on government correspondence. These stamps remained in use until 1961, when they were superseded by a similar series featuring the palms and crossed swords emblem of the state. In 1964 the size of the stamps was increased.

7. **Saudi Arabia, 3 guerches, 1949**
The first airmail stamps of Saudi Arabia were issued in October 1949, a set of six stamps, from 1 to 100*g*., featuring a modern airliner. There seems to have been some confusion over the trans-

PLATE 39 ARABIA · PLATE 40 SOUTHERN ARABIA

literation of the name into French. Stamps up to and including this series gave the name as 'Soudite', but subsequent issues were inscribed 'Saoudite'.

8. Saudi Arabia, 9 piastres, 1960
The currency was revalued in 1960 at 800 piastres to the gold sovereign, and the expression 'guerche' was dropped. From this date onward Saudi Arabia began issuing stamps more frequently, and many of these were printed in Cairo, reflecting the closer ties between Egypt and Arabia at that time. A lengthy definitive series was prepared at the Survey Department in Cairo and issued in 1960–61. The frames were lithographed and the vignettes printed in photogravure. The cartouche at the right contained the signature of King Saud, but between 1963 and 1965 the stamps were reissued with the signature of King Faisal instead.

9. Saudi Arabia, 4 piastres, 1968
Since 1967 all stamps of Saudi Arabia have been lithographed by the Government Printer in Riyadh. A set of eight stamps (four 4*pi.* and four 10*pi.*) was released in September 1968 to stimulate the tourist industry and featured notable buildings in Mecca. This stamp depicts the extension to the Prophet's Mosque in Mecca. In subsequent years other denominations, from 3 to 20*pi.* have been issued in the same style.

10. Saudi Arabia, 4 piastres, 1971
In recent years Saudi Arabia has taken part in the various international issues sponsored by the United Nations. This stamp was issued in 1971 to mark International Education Year and featured the IEY emblem. Note the use of English instead of French, and the shorter form of the name with the word 'kingdom' omitted.

11. Saudi Arabia, 10 piastres, 1971
In connection with Arab Propaganda Week this stamp was released in November 1971. The date '1967' refers to the establishment of the Arab Information Office in Cairo. The stamp features the Arab League emblem and motto 'Unity is strength'. Nonetheless Saudi Arabia has followed an independent line on many occasions in recent years, in defiance of Egypt, especially over the Yemen.

12. Saudi Arabia, 4 piastres, 1971
The tenth anniversary of the Organization of Petroleum Exporting Countries was marked by this stamp featuring the emblem of the organization in the form of stylized letters.

13. Yemen, 6 bogaches, 1930
Adhesive stamps were adopted by the Yemen in 1926, the earliest issue being crudely typographed at Sana with an Arabic inscription signifying 'Sana. Government of the Yemen by the will of God. Yahya. May God grant him success.' Subsequent issues in the same vein were typographed in Berlin or lithographed by Waterlow and Sons up to 1951. Thereafter stamps were produced in New York, Paris, Rome and Vienna at infrequent intervals. A series of 1948–50 marked admission to the United Nations, but is regarded by many catalogues as being speculative. Both Harrison and Courvoisier produced photogravure sets for the Yemen in the early 1960s before the overthrow of the Imam.

14. Yemen Arab Republic, 4 bogaches, 1965
The death of the Imam Ahmad in September 1962 was followed by a military coup establishing a republican government in Sana. Stamps of the royalist regime were overprinted Y.A.R. in Arabic and English to denote the Yemen Arab Republic and this inscription appeared on subsequent issues.

The majority of the stamps of the republic have pandered to collectors, particularly in the Western world. Significantly John F. Kennedy features on numerous stamps of the republic. Eight stamps and two miniature sheets were issued in November 1965, portraying Kennedy and publicizing the American space programme.

15. Yemen Arab Republic, ¼ bogache, 1964
A set of six diamond-shaped stamps ostensibly marking American space achievements appeared in December 1963. The lower part of the design was left suspiciously blank, but when the stamps were reissued in May 1964 a portrait of Kennedy was superimposed in this convenient space.

16. Yemen Arab Republic, ¼ bogache, 1967
Numerous thematic sets have been issued by the Yemen Arab Republic since 1963. A significant feature of these sets is the very low denominations used – ⅛, ¼, ⅓ or ½*b.* – though no postal rates exist for which such values could be employed. This indicates that many of the ultra-low value stamps of the Yemen are destined for the juvenile packet trade where large, colourful stamps of minimal value are a boon to the packet merchants. The bogache is roughly on a par with the United States cent.

17. Mutawakelite Kingdom of Yemen, 4 bogaches, 1965
The royalists, under the Imam Mohammed al Badr, carried on a guerrilla campaign against the republicans and their Egyptian allies until 1969. During the period from 1963 to 1969 stamps were produced by the 'Mutawakelite Kingdom' for use in those areas under royalist control. Harrison and Sons lithographed this stamp, issued in March 1965 in honour of Prince Seif, a guerrilla leader killed in action against the republicans. The stamp was overprinted the following month with an inscription in Arabic and English in memory of Sir Winston Churchill – a procedure which many regard as an insult to the memories of both men.

18. Mutawakelite Kingdom of Yemen, ¼ bogache, 1965
The royalists also cashed in on the current fashions and embarked on a prolific policy of thematic issues extolling space achievements, sporting events, and notable personalities as well as the more pedestrian subjects such as cats, flowers, birds and fishes. The appearance of very low value stamps indicates the same connection with the juvenile stamp trade as has been noted for the republicans. The stamp depicted shows President Kennedy as a naval officer during World War II. Long after the royalist faction ceased to exist, stamps in the name of the Mutawakelite Kingdom continued to be produced.

19. People's Democratic Republic of Yemen, 80 fils, 1971
A definitive series was introduced in 1971 in denominations from 5*f.* to 1 *d.* The lower denominations up to 80*f.* depicted a map of Arabia, showing the location of the republic. The national flag and an anchor symbolizing the harbour of Aden were included for good measure. The four highest denominations depicted the Dam-al-Akhawain tree, emblem of the republic.

20. People's Democratic Republic of Yemen, 65 fils, 1971
Though the Mutawakelite Kingdom is no more there are still two Yemens. The People's Republic of Southern Yemen (see plate 40) changed its name in November 1970 to the People's Democratic Republic of Yemen and stamps thus inscribed began appearing in 1971. Stamps issued during

that year includes sets commemorating the UNESCO campaign to save the Temples of Nubia, the new constitution and Racial Equality Year. In June 1971 a set of three stamps celebrated the 'Corrective Move' but the somewhat symbolic designs of industry and agriculture do not reveal what this corrective move consisted of. Curiously the production and distribution of the stamps of this left-wing country continue to be the responsibility of the Crown Agents in England.

PLATE 40
Southern Arabia

British interest in Arabia began in 1839, when the rock of Aden was captured by an expedition of the Honourable East India Company to suppress the pirates tyrannizing over the Indian Ocean. Similar expeditions stamped out piracy in the Persian Gulf and led to the creation of the Trucial States (see plate 41). The postal services in this British sphere of influence were, for many years, in the hands of the Indian authorities and ordinary Indian stamps were used, distinguished only by their postmarks. Kuwait (1923), Bahrain (1933) and Muscat (1944) began using Indian stamps suitably overprinted, while Aden (1937), in view of its status as a British crown colony, introduced stamps in distinctive designs. From then onward the usual pattern of former colonies and protectorates moving toward complete independence has been faithfully recorded in the stamps of the area.

1. Aden, 1 rupee, 1937
De La Rue recess-printed a set of twelve stamps in the uniform design featuring an Arab dhow, flanked by Arab knives and Islamic decorative motifs. The series had a relatively short life since it was felt that the king's portrait ought to be included and consequently the 'Dhows' were withdrawn after twenty months.

2. Aden, 2½ annas, 1939
A slightly larger format was used by Waterlow and Sons for the series of 1939 incorporating the royal portrait. Six different designs were used, ranging from views of Mukalla (shown on this stamp) and Aden Harbour, to a dhow and a patrolman of the Camel Corps. Three values, 3 and 14*a.*, and 10*r.*, depicted the capture of Aden by troops of the Honourable East India Company in 1839. The series was reissued in 1951, surcharged in the decimal currency of 100 cents to the East African shilling.

3. Aden, 5 cents, 1953
This stamp was the lowest value in a series introduced in June 1953 – one of the first colonial definitive sets portraying Queen Elizabeth. The stamps were recess-printed by Waterlow and Sons until 1961 and from then onwards by De La Rue. The colours were deepened in shade in 1955 and the vignettes of the higher values were changed from the original sepia to black. A new gauge of perforation was introduced in 1956 and finally the watermark was changed in 1964–65. All of these changes added up to one of the most complex sets released in recent decades.

4. Aden, 1.25 shillings, 1959
The move toward self-government was foreshadowed in the revised constitution granted in 1959. To mark the occasion two stamps of the definitive series were overprinted, the 15*c.* being entirely in Arabic and the 1.25*s.* in English. The stamps of Aden were withdrawn on 31 March 1965, 185

PLATE 40 SOUTHERN ARABIA

and were superseded by the issues of the Federation of South Arabia.

5. Federation of South Arabia, 15 cents, 1963
The Federation of South Arabia consisted of the former Aden colony, most of the territories of the former Western Aden Protectorate and one sheikdom from the former Eastern Aden Protectorate. The federation continued to use ordinary Adenese stamps for two years and in that period the only distinctive stamps of the federation were the two stamps issued in November to mark the centenary of the Red Cross. The federation used the British colonial omnibus design, but modified it to omit the portrait of Queen Elizabeth. Subsequent colonial omnibus issues of the federation had the entwined crescent and star emblem substituted for the royal portrait.

6. Federation of South Arabia, 100 fils, 1965
The currency was changed to the dinar of 1000 fils in 1965 and this necessitated the introduction of a distinctive definitive series. Victor Whiteley produced two designs, a small format showing the federal crest for the low values and a horizontal format showing the South Arabian flag for the higher denominations. The series was printed in photogravure by Harrison and Sons. The Federation of South Arabia became fully independent on 30 November 1967, and subsequently changed its name to the People's Republic of Southern Yemen, whose stamps were then introduced.

7. Southern Yemen, 50 fils, 1970
One of a set of three stamps released in 1970 to mark the seventh anniversary of the revolution of 14 October 1963 – the date on which the rebellion against British rule in Aden began. The design contrasts the terrorist activities of 1963 with the peaceful agricultural pursuits of 1970. The first stamps of Southern Yemen consisted of the Southern Arabia definitives suitably overprinted. Subsequent issues of the people's republic emphasized the revolutionary and left-wing nature of the regime. The country changed its name to the People's Democratic Republic of the Yemen on 30 November 1970. Stamps issued since that date will be found on plate 39.

8. Kathiri State of Seiyun, 1½ annas, 1946
Theoretically the stamps of Aden were also valid in the Eastern and Western Aden protectorates though postal services were not established in these areas until 1942. In July of that year distinctive sets were issued in two of the states, both recess-printed by De La Rue in standard formats, colours and denominations, but differing in designs and inscriptions. The series of the Kathiri State of Seiyun portrayed Sultan Ali bin Mansur al Kathiri. The three lowest denominations portrayed the Sultan, while the remaining values, from 1½a. to 5r., depicted scenery in Seiyun and Tarim. This stamp was one of two overprinted in October 1946 to celebrate victory in World War II.

9. Kathiri State of Seiyun, 50 cents, 1954
The original series was surcharged in decimal currency in October 1951 and was superseded by an entirely new series in January 1954 after the accession of Sultan Hussein. As before, the stamps were recess-printed by De La Rue who used the same designs with the portrait of the new sultan inset.

10. Qu'aiti State of Shihr and Mukalla, 2½ annas, 1946
During the early twentieth century the Qu'aiti and Kathiri sultans were in a state of perpetual feud, both occupying territory in the Hadhramaut area of the Eastern Aden Protectorate. For political reasons it was deemed expedient to grant them

both distinctive issues of stamps. The first issues of the Qu'aiti state bore the names of Shihr and Mukalla, the two chief ports of the Hadhramaut. The stamps portrayed Sultan Sir Saleh. The designs were produced by Harold Ingrams, the British resident, and Freya Stark, the novelist and traveller. This stamp was one of two overprinted to celebrate victory after World War II.

11. Qu'aiti State in Hadhramaut, 1 shilling, 1955
The inscription on the stamps of the Qu'aiti State was changed in 1955 to emphasize the claims of the Qu'aiti sultan to overlordship of the entire Hadhramaut. This pictorial definitive series was recess-printed by De La Rue, using designs by Madame de Sturler Raemaekers. A similar series, but with the portrait of Sultan Awadh, was adopted in 1963.

12. Bahrain, 5 rupees, 1933
This stamp was the top value of a series of Indian stamps overprinted for use in Bahrain in August 1933, when that sheikhdom adopted its own stamps. India continued to be postally responsible for Bahrain until 1948 when, India and Pakistan having gained their independence, responsibility was transferred to Britain.

13. Bahrain, 2 annas, 1948
As a result of the transfer of the postal administration to Britain, British stamps were introduced, with surcharges in Indian currency. British definitive and commemorative stamps overprinted and surcharged in this way continued in use till 1960.

14. Bahrain, 75 naye paise, 1960
In 1953 three low-value stamps portraying Sheikh Sulman bin Hamed al-Khalifa were introduced for internal local mail. These local stamps continued in use until 1961. In 1960, however, a series for external mail was adopted, using a similar portrait and bearing values in Indian decimal currency. The stamps were designed by Michael Farrar-Bell and photogravure-printed by Harrison and Sons. The rupee denominations, with the same portrait, were designed by O. C. Meronti and recess-printed by De La Rue. Bahrain took over the running of its postal services on 1 January 1966.

15. Kuwait, 6 annas, 1923
Kuwait was the first of the sheikhdoms to adopt its own stamps. This series, released in 1923–24, ranged from ½ anna to 10 rupees. A similar series overprinted 'Koweit' was prepared but never issued. Examples of these stamps are known but are very rare.

16. Kuwait, 6 annas, 1948
Britain assumed responsibility for Kuwait's postal affairs in 1948 and introduced British definitive stamps overprinted and surcharged in Indian currency. Various British commemorative stamps were likewise overprinted, including the series of four marking the Olympic Games in London. Distinctive stamps, portraying Sheikh Abdullah, appeared in 1959. Kuwait became an independent state in 1961.

17. Kuwait, 50 fils, 1965
One of a definitive series recess-printed by De La Rue and issued in December 1965. A common design featuring a peregrine falcon was used for this series, ranging in value from 8 to 90f. The inscription 'State of Kuwait' was adopted in 1962. Since independence Kuwait has issued numerous stamps, printed by Harrisons, Enschedé, Courvoisier, and the state printing works of Cairo, Berlin, Vienna and Karachi.

18. Kuwait, 8 fils, 1965
Many of the countries in the Arab world issued an

omnibus series of stamps in June 1965 to commemorate the burning of the Algiers Library. Kuwait's issue consisted of 8 and 15f. stamps and, like the other stamps produced for this event, were printed in three-colour photogravure by the Postal Authority Press in Cairo.

19. Kuwait, 45 fils, 1966
The majority of the commemorative stamps issued by Kuwait consist of 'hardy annuals'. Since June 1962 the anniversary of independence has been marked by National Day stamps, invariably depicting the national flag, map, coat of arms and other patriotic motifs. Enschedé of Holland lithographed the series of three stamps issued in 1966 showing an eagle balancing the scales of justice.

20. Kuwait, 20 fils, 1966
Harrison and Sons produced a set of three stamps in multicolour photogravure to mark Education Day (10 January) in 1966. The motif of an open book in a laurel wreath typifies the somewhat hackneyed approach to this and other annual subjects. Among the other events for which Kuwait has regularly produced stamps may be mentioned Mothers' Day, World Health Day, Traffic Day, Blood Bank Day, United Nations Day, Teachers' Day, Palestine Day, International Literacy Day and Arab Week.

21. Muscat, 2 rupees, 1944
Muscat began issuing stamps in November 1944 with the contemporary Indian series, from 3 pies to 2 rupees, overprinted in Arabic to signify 'Al-Busaid 1363'. These stamps commemorated the bicentenary of the foundation of the Al-Busaid dynasty, rulers of Muscat and Zanzibar. This commemorative issue was retained as a definitive series until India relinquished postal control of the sheikhdom in 1948. From then until 1966 British stamps surcharged in Indian currency, without any other identifying overprint, were used in Muscat, Dubai, Doha and Umm Said (see plate 41).

22. Muscat and Oman, 10 rupees, 1966
An independent Muscat postal department was created on 29 April 1966, and the use of distinctive stamps, waived since 1948, was resumed the following day. Stamps inscribed in local currency (64 baizas = 1 rupee) were designed by L. Morland and printed by Harrisons in photogravure. The low values featured the sultan's crest while the higher values featured different forts in the sultanate. This stamp, the highest denomination of the series, depicts Mirani Fort. The same designs, inscribed in decimal currency (100 baizas = 1 rupee), were released in 1970.

23. Oman, 1½ baizas, 1967
Stamps purporting to be issued by the 'state of Oman' appeared in 1967 and are known on covers passing through the post via Baghdad and Amman. They were issued in territory under the rule of the Imam, or religious leader, of Oman, who has been in revolt against the sultan of Muscat for many years. In 1970 a coup d'état in Muscat led to the overthrow of the sultan. The new sultan decided to change the name of the state and in 1971 stamps of Muscat and Oman were released, overprinted 'Sultanate of Oman' to counter the claims of the Imamate.

24. Sultanate of Oman, 20 baizas, 1971
For political reasons the territory previously known as the Sultanate of Muscat and Oman was renamed in 1971 and the name Muscat dropped from the title. The contemporary definitive series was released with an overprint showing the new name, pending the production of stamps thus inscribed.

PLATE 40 SOUTHERN ARABIA · PLATE 41 TRUCIAL STATES

25. Mahra Sultanate of Qishn and Socotra, 20 fils, 1967

Distinctive stamps, designed and lithographed by Harrison and Sons, were provided for this sultanate in March 1967 in denominations from 5 to 500f. The National Liberation Front gained control of the Mahra sultanate in October 1967 and suppressed the stamps of all three states. Between March and September, however the Mahra sultanate allegedly contrived to issue numerous stamps in honour of the Scout Jamboree, Idaho, the Mexico Olympic Games and John F. Kennedy, all of which are regarded as entirely speculative and therefore ignored by most catalogues. Since November 1967 only the stamps of the republic of Southern Yemen or the Democratic Republic of the Yemen have been used in these states.

PLATE 41
Trucial States

The Arab sheikhdoms of the Persian Gulf are known collectively as the Trucial States, from the treaties made with the United Kingdom in the nineteenth century for the suppression of piracy. Postal arrangements were apparently unnecessary until after World War II, when the stamps surcharged in Indian currency for use in Muscat (see plate 40) were extended also to Dubai, Doha and Umm Said. Gradually, however, each of the component states has attained postal independence or, in some cases, established a postal service where none existed before. With the exception of Abu Dhabi, all of the states have come under the aegis, at some time or another, of philatelic agencies based in the Lebanon and the United States and this has resulted in the spate of unnecessary issues designed to mulct stamp collectors rather than perform any genuine postal service.

1. Qatar, 15 naye paise, 1957

The surcharged British stamps provided for Muscat were used at the British post office in Doha, capital of Qatar, until April 1957, when a separate series, overprinted 'Qatar', was adopted. British definitive and commemorative stamps overprinted in this way, with values surcharged in Indian currency, continued to be issued until September 1961, when a series portraying Sheik Ahmad was released. Since then Qatar has produced a considerable number of stamps, though compared with other sheikhdoms its policy has been moderate (see also 19 below).

2. Persian Gulf Agencies, 15 naye paise, 1957

British stamps surcharged in Indian currency were adopted in Muscat (see plate 40) in 1948 but were subsequently extended to other parts of the Persian Gulf area served by British post offices. They were used in Dubai, Doha, Das Island, Umm Said and Abu Dhabi at various times up to 1961, when the stamps of the Trucial States were introduced. British definitive stamps with values in naye paise may be found with either the E2R or multiple-crowns watermarks.

3. Trucial States, 40 naye paise, 1961

Stamps bearing this inscription were issued in Dubai in January 1961 and were intended for use throughout the Trucial States, if and when the various sheikhdoms established a postal service. In the event, however, their use was confined to Dubai and they were withdrawn from use in June 1963, when that state took control of its own postal administration (see below). The naye paise denominations were designed by Michael Goaman and featured seven palm trees, symbolizing the states. The rupee denominations were designed by Michael Farrar-Bell and featured an Arab dhow. The naye paise stamps were printed by Harrisons, using photogravure, while the rupee stamps were recess-printed by De La Rue.

4. Ajman, 2 riyals, 1968

The sheikhdom of Ajman began issuing stamps in 1964 and in less than a decade has succeeded in catching up with many old-established countries of much greater size and commercial importance. Like its neighbours, Ajman has a predilection for subjects of little relevance to the Persian Gulf but more likely to appeal to the passing fancy of collectors on the other side of the world. One of its earliest issues was a series depicting historic stamp catalogues and rare stamps, to promote the Stanley Gibbons Catalogue Centenary Exhibition in London. The death of Robert Kennedy provoked a pair of mourning stamps in 1968, portraying him and his elder brother John.

5. Manama, 1 dirham, 1970

Not content with issuing stamps in its own name, Ajman began issuing stamps for its 'dependency' of Manama, a diminutive fishing village on the other side of the peninsula. The first issues, consisting of Ajman stamps overprinted, were artificially controlled by the American philatelic agency in order to work up a demand for the stamps, but after they became available on the world stamp market they quickly depreciated in both interest and aesthetic appeal. Like Ajman itself, Manama has run the entire gamut of world events and personalities, from the Olympic Games to Expo 70, from Churchill and Kennedy to Lord Baden-Powell and the astronaut White.

6. Abu Dhabi, 60 fils, 1969

The anniversary of the accession of Sheikh Zaid is the pretext for an annual issue of stamps highlighting developments in Abu Dhabi. The first anniversary (1967) was belatedly marked by stamps the following year showing the coat of arms. Later, in 1968, the second anniversary was marked by stamps showing modern developments, and this set the tone for the issues of subsequent years. The series of 1969 concentrated on progress in the petroleum industry.

7. Abu Dhabi, 35 fils, 1970

Abu Dhabi is alphabetically the first country in the world, and is also the largest of the Trucial States. Its first stamps, issued in 1964, were controlled by the British Post Office and were in restrained designs portraying Sheikh Shakhbut and views of the sheikhdom. The British contract expired in January 1967 and since then Abu Dhabi has adopted a more liberal and colourful policy but, under the watchful aegis of the Crown Agents, has avoided the excesses of its neighbours.

8. Dubai, 1 rupee, 1964

Dubai took over control of its own postal affairs from Britain in June 1963 and became the first of the Trucial States to embark on a prolific stamp programme. Many of the earlier issues were lithographed in the Lebanon and included a set of three stamps and a miniature sheet issued in January 1964 in memory of President Kennedy. The unsold remainders of this series were subsequently overprinted to mark the late president's 50th birthday.

9. Dubai, 1.25 riyals, 1970

Under the auspices of various philatelic agents Dubia's output of stamps escalated until 1967, when most catalogues decided to boycott its more questionable issues. In 1969 the sheikhdom revoked the contracts with its philatelic agent and placed them with the Crown Agents in London. Since 1969 a more restrained policy has been adopted, though the stamps continue to pander to the 'sports-space-Old Masters' enthusiasts as before. This stamp, featuring a Tiros weather satellite, was one of a set of four issued in March 1970 to mark World Meteorological Day.

10. Dubai, 60 dirhams, 1969

A set of four stamps was released in 1969 to honour four European explorers who opened up Arabia. The stamps portrayed Sir Richard Burton, Charles Doughty, J. L. Burckhardt and Wilfrid Thesiger, together with a map of Arabia.

11. Fujeira, 75 dirhams, 1970

Fujeira began issuing stamps in September 1964, with an attractive definitive series portraying Sheikh Mohammed bin Hamad and wildlife of the Persian Gulf area. A taste of things to come, however, was provided by the sumptuous John F. Kennedy series of 1965, with portraits of the late president from early childhood onwards. Subsequently the same biographical treatment was accorded to other world leaders, including Winston Churchill, General Eisenhower and President De Gaulle. Since 1967 few catalogues have bothered to list the stamps of this tiny state, though, for the record, it should be noted that in 1969 Fujeira led the world new-issue stakes by producing 130 stamps. In the same period Britain issued 50 and the United States 26.

12. Ras al Khaima, 4 rupees, 1965

The last of the Trucial States to adopt stamps, Ras al Khaima introduced a definitive series in December 1964, portraying Sheikh Saqr bin Mohammed as Qasimi. Unlike most of its neighbours this sheikhdom began under the aegis of the Crown Agents but cancelled the agreement a few months later. The last issue made in the Crown Agents' period was a set of three stamps in memory of Winston Churchill. The stamps were printed in photogravure by Harrison and Sons and great ingenuity was shown in the selection of unusual photographs. The 4r. stamp, for example, featured various heads of state attending Churchill's funeral. Since 1965 Ras al Khaima has produced a vast number of stamps few of which have any relevance to the Arab world.

13. Sharjah, 40 naye paise, 1965

Sharjah's first stamps in memory of John Kennedy consisted of a hastily applied overprint on the airmail overprints of 1963, issued barely six weeks after the assassination. The first anniversary of Kennedy's death was marked more stylishly by a set of three stamps and a miniature sheet bearing his portrait and the statue of Liberty. Following the death of Sir Winston Churchill at the end of of January 1965 Sharjah was again very quick off the mark, with overprints applied to the recent Kennedy stamps. This was felt, at the time, to have been something of an insult to the memory of both statesmen. Sharjah, however, has made ample amends for this by issuing many other stamps dedicated to both men.

14. Sharjah, 55 naye paise, 1965

Sharjah began issuing stamps in July 1963, less than a month after Dubai. Apart from a brief period in 1966, when the Crown Agents had some say in the matter, Sharjah's philatelic affairs have been in the hands of various American and Middle Eastern agencies. One of the few issues to have any bearing on the area was the set of four stamps issued in September 1965 to promote the UNESCO campaign for the preservation of the temples of Nubia. The stamps, appropriately enough, were printed by the Postal Authority Press in Cairo.

187

PLATE 41 TRUCIAL STATES · PLATE 42 IRAN

15. Khor Fakkan, 80 naye paise, 1966
Like Ajman, Sharjah has resorted to the subterfuge of issuing stamps for its dependency, the coastal village of Khor Fakkan. The majority of these stamps have consisted of Sharjah stamps overprinted in English and Arabic, or produced in different colours. In this way it was hoped to sell two sets for the outlay of one, but most catalogues have refused to list the stamps of this territory.

16. Umm al Qiwain, 25 dirhams, 1969
Umm al Qiwain began issuing stamps in June 1964 and its subsequent career closely paralleled that of Ajman and Fujeira with a spate of issues which were totally irrelevant and unnecessary but were aimed solely at the occidental thematic market. The zenith of philatelic activity was reached in 1969 with fourteen lengthy and expensive sets. The provision of a 16mm film projector for the few thousand inhabitants of the sheikhdom was celebrated by a set of twelve stamps reproducing stills from vintage Hollywood films. This was followed by a marathon series of 48 stamps featuring veteran and vintage cars. In the hands of Umm al Qiwain the stamp came near to attaining the status and purpose of cigarette and trade cards.

17. Umm al Qiwain, 20 dirhams, 1970
In 1969 the sheikh cancelled the contract with the American and Lebanese agencies then handling the production and distribution of his stamps and invited the Crown Agents to salvage the reputation of Umm al Qiwain. Since the end of 1969 a more moderate policy has been adopted, though a strong thematic element has persisted. This is one of a series of 1970 in honour of Expo 70 in Japan.

18. Umm al Qiwain, 75 dirhams, 1970
The 150th anniversary of the British invasion of the Trucial Coast seems a thin pretext for a series of stamps depicting historic uniforms of the British Army and Navy. This formula had proved successful with the stamps of Gibraltar and Ascension, but it seems rather incongruous and untimely on the stamps of the Arab world, where colonialism and militarism have a pejorative ring.

19. Qatar, 1 dirham, 1968
After flirting with various firms all over the world, Qatar eventually awarded stamp contracts to Bradbury Wilkinson, who have designed and produced all the stamps of this sheikhdom since 1967. International Human Rights Year was marked in April 1968 by a set of six stamps with different designs symbolizing freedom from injustice and oppression.

PLATE 42

Iran (Persia)

1. 1 chahi, 1868
One of the many reforms instituted by Shah Nasr-ed-Din was a postal service on European lines, introduced in 1868. Despite the crude appearance of the stamps they were actually engraved in Paris by Albert Barre. Copper *clichés* were made from the original dies and the stamps were typographed in Teheran on paper of varying thickness. The majority of the stamps have very coarse impressions. The stamps were in denominations from 1 to 8 chahis and the values were expressed in Arabic numerals. In 1875 the design was modified to include European numerals in the lower corners.

2. 5 chahis, 1889
A series from 1 chahi to 5 krans was typographed in Paris and released in November 1889. The values from 1 to 7c. took the value (in Persian script) as the principal motif, relegating the lion and sun emblems to a secondary role. The higher values portrayed the Shah.

3. 5 chahis, 1891
The Austrian Government Printing Office in Vienna typographed the stamps of Persia from 1876 to 1894, six definitive sets being produced in this period. In most cases the lower values depicted the sun or lion emblems while the higher values portrayed Shah Nasr-ed-Din. From 1881 onward the inscription 'Poste Persane' (Persian Post) in French provided some indication of the country of origin.

4. 5 chahis, 1894
Enschedé and Sons of Haarlem typographed the series issued in 1894. The lion and sun symbols were featured on the small-format low values, while the Shah was depicted on the values from 10c. to 50k.

5. 5 chahis, 1882
The sun was featured on a series issued between June 1881 and November 1882. The first printings were lithographed in Vienna in single colours. In January 1882, however, a recess-printed version, with frames and vignettes in contrasting colours, was introduced and this was superseded toward the end of the year by similar stamps in which the frames and vignettes were in different shades of the same colour. The perforations of these three sets vary considerably.

6. 1 kran, 1899
Edouard Mouchon engraved the dies for a series, portraying Shah Muzaffer-ed-Din, which was typographed by Enschedé and released in 1898 in denominations from 1 to 50k. The lower denominations continued to portray his predecessor but for this purpose the designs of the 1894 series was released in new colours. To counteract looting of post office stock the stamps were given a variety of control overprints in 1899 and then reissued in new colours. In 1900 the overprinted series of 1899 was given yet another control overprint consisting of a white lion on a violet background, applied across the middle of each block of four.

7. 13 chahis, 1906
The political chaos of Persia at the turn of the century is reflected in the spate of provisional overprints and surcharges between 1897 and 1925. In some cases provisional surcharges became necessary when stock of stamps ran out; in others, however, control marks were overprinted in order to invalidate stocks looted by bandits. Occasionally local postmasters produced distinctive overprints with an eye to philatelic sales. In most instances the stamps thus treated were the various definitive sets printed in Europe. In 1906, however, a locally printed series was issued in denominations from 1 to 13c., and given a control overprint as a matter of course. Overprinted stamps had become so commonplace that the appearance of an *unoverprinted* series might have caused suspicion! The stamps were issued imperforate, though some are known with irregular perforations by sewing machine.

8. 2 chahis, 1909
Enschedé typographed a series from 1c. to 30k. in 1909. The uniform design featured the lion and sunrise emblem – in maroon (chahi values) or sepia (kran values) with various coloured frames. Several stamps of this series may be found with an overprint 'Relais' in French and Persian. These stamps were used on letters posted in boxes at the horse-posting stages (*relais*) between Resht and Teheran. They were sold to the keepers of these stages at a discount of 10 per cent. The overprint was intended to prevent the stamps being resold to merchants in the towns. This experimental service was not a success and after a few years was stopped.

9. 3 tomans, 1915
Although Shah Ahmed ascended the peacock throne in 1909 his coronation did not take place until 1914. The occasion was marked by a series of seventeen stamps in three designs featuring the imperial crown (chahi values), King Darius on his throne (kran values) and the gateway of the Palace of Persepolis (toman denominations), released the following year. Two colour combinations were used for each stamp, but an added refinement was the use of silver ink on the kran values and gold ink on the toman stamps. Stamps with inverted centres were deliberately produced for sale to collectors.

10. 6 chahis, 1915
The Coronation series of 1914 was reissued the following year with overprints in French (Colis Postaux) and Persian to signify parcel post. Examples of the stamps of 1907–08 may be found with similar inscriptions but these are merely forms of postmarks and not distinctive stamps as such.

11. 3 chahis, 1924
The Mejliss Press in Teheran produced a series portraying Shah Ahmed in 1919. The value tablets were left blank and the various denominations were inserted by overprinting at a subsequent operation. Surcharges of this sort were produced in 1919 and 1924–25, the appropriate date being incorporated in the overprint. Numerous errors and varieties have been noted in these overprints. Stamps of this series may be found with the portrait obliterated, after the Kajar Dynasty was deposed in 1925.

12. 8 chahis, 1930
Riza Khan Pahlavi led the coup which deposed Shah Ahmed in 1925 and the following year he assumed the title of Shah. Under his rule Persia was rapidly reformed and modernized. An airmail service was introduced in 1927 and overprinted stamps were used at first. Enschedé produced a series of handsome two-colour pictorials for this purpose in 1930. The stamps from 1c. to 1k. were printed in photogravure while those from 2k. to 3 tomans were recess-printed. The vignette shows an eagle with the Elburz Mountains in the background.

13. 1 rial, 1935
To symbolize the reform of the country Shah Reza dropped the Greek name Persia and adopted the more ancient form Iran ('land of the Aryan'). Stamps were overprinted with this name in 1935 and superseded later the same year by a distinctive series thus inscribed. The stamps were printed in photogravure by the Mejliss Press in the new currency based on the rial of 100 dinars.

14. 10 + 5 rials, 1949
The majority of Persian stamps over the past fifty years have been printed in Teheran. Among the few exceptions were the sets recess-printed by Bradbury Wilkinson between 1948 and 1954 with premiums for the National Monuments Protection Fund. In that period five sets, each of five different stamps, were produced and showed sculpture, artifacts and architecture dating from the time of Darius to the Middle Ages. This stamp was the top value in the third series (1949) and features a coin of the Sassanid dynasty.

PLATE 42 IRAN · PLATE 43 CENTRAL ASIA

15. 5 rials, 1956
Two stamps were issued in August 1956 to publicize the national Boy Scout movement. The 2.50r. denomination showed reveille at a scout camp, while the 5r. portrayed the Shah in scout uniform and reproduced the scout badge. Part of the policy of promoting the public image of the Shah has been to portray him on stamps in different poses and uniforms.

16. 6 rials, 1958
Since the late 1950s Persia has issued stamps in connection with various international events. The turning point came in April 1958 when two stamps were issued to commemorate the Brussels World Fair. The stamps were in denominations of 2.50 and 6r. and both featured the Fair emblem. They were printed in two-tone photogravure by the Mejliss Press.

17. 20 rials, 1960
Since 1944 the various definitive issues of Persia have portrayed Shah Muhammed, the sets being changed at regular intervals to update the portraits used. The longest-lived of these series first appeared in 1958, with changes of colour and new values added at various times up to 1964.

18. 6 rials, 1961
Since 1956 Persia has honoured visiting heads of state by issuing stamps bearing their portrait with the Shah. The first of these issues appeared in late 1956 and portrayed President Mirza of Pakistan. Subsequent issues, showing portraits flanked by the appropriate national flags, honoured President Gronchi of Italy, King Faisal of Iraq (both 1957), President Khan of Pakistan (1959) and King Hussein of Jordan (1960). The visit of Queen Elizabeth in 1961 was marked by 1 and 6r. stamps reproducing portraits without the national flags. More recent stamps have honoured visits by King Frederick of Denmark and Queen Juliana of the Netherlands, President Lübke of West Germany and Brezhnev of the Soviet Union.

19. 3 rials, 1965
This stamp was issued in October 1965 to mark the Iranian Industrial Exhibition in Teheran. The unusual 'arches' motif symbolizes industrial progress. The stamp was lithographed in multicolour by the Mejliss Press.

20. 6 rials, 1969
Most commemorative stamps are for anniversaries but in 1969 Persia issued this stamp to mark the 10,000th day of the Shah's reign. The people's affection for their ruler was expressed by the portrait enshrined in a heart, against a background picture of a crowd scene.

21. 10 rials, 1969
The majority of Iranian stamps in recent years have consisted of single stamps, many of them publicizing current events. This stamp, with its stylized flower and birds motif, was released in 1969 to mark Handicrafts Week.

22. 2 rials, 1971
In 1970 the Shah inaugurated his so-called White Revolution, instituting a new wave of much-needed reforms. The campaign was launched with two stamps portraying the Shah surrounded with symbols of reform in housing, medicine, education, industry, agriculture and social welfare. The first anniversary of the White Revolution was celebrated by a giant-sized 2r. stamp portraying the Shah in full colour, resplendent in ceremonial uniform. The linked circles represent the provinces of Persia and their solidarity behind the monarchy. In 1972 the monarchy celebrated its 2,500th anniversary.

23. 4 rials, 1969
The government campaign to stamp out illiteracy received impetus from this 4r. stamp. The thumbprint, mark of the illiterate who use this method of making their 'signature', was an unusual, but effective way of conveying the message, though the significance of the space-craft orbiting the earth is obscure. Stamps publicizing the anti-illiteracy campaign have been issued annually since 1967.

24. Bushire, 6 chahis, 1915
The seaport of Bushire was occupied by British and Indian forces on 8 August 1915, to forestall the influence of German and Austrian agents in that part of Persia threatening Britain's oil supplies. On 15 August, stocks of Persian stamps found in the Bushire post office were issued with a three-line overprint 'Bushire Under British Occupation'. The Coronation commemoratives were released in September with the same overprint. Most denominations of the Shah Ahmed series are known with the full-stop omitted and there are numerous minor varieties in the lettering. The 5 krans value of the Coronation series has been recorded with the overprint inverted. The Persian authorities resumed control of the postal services in Bushire on 16 October, 1915, and the overprinted stamps were then withdrawn from use.

PLATE 43
Central Asia

The philately of Central Asia, the remote area beyond the Himalayas and the Karakorums, provides an interesting contrast between extreme crudity of design and production and various attempts at gimmickry and exploitation of the philatelic market by entrepreneurs whose link with the countries concerned often seems remote.

1. Afghanistan, 1 abasi, 1893
All the stamps of Afghanistan, from 1870 till 1892, were circular in design, with Arabic inscriptions encircling a lion's head, the state emblem. For some inexplicable reason philatelists persist in calling these stamps the 'Afghan Tigers'. Stamps of different denominations were printed together in the same sheet and a different colour was used for the stamps of each major town. The outlandish appearance of these stamps was completed by the method of cancellation: the postmaster lifted a corner of the stamp on the envelope and tore or bit a piece out of it. Thus, used Afghan stamps of the early period are not known in perfect condition. The first rectangular stamps appeared in 1892-93 and featured the state coat of arms. They were crudely lithographed in black on paper of various colours. These exceedingly primitive stamps continued until the late 1920s.

2. Afghanistan, 2 paisa, 1913.
A series of stamps from 1 abasi to 1 rupee was designed and engraved by Mahmud Masi and released in 1909. A 2pa. value was added in 1913. The stamps were recess-printed in Kabul on paper with a sheet watermark 'Howard & Jones, London'.

3. Afghanistan, undenominated official stamp, 1909
This curiosity was introduced in 1909 for use on government correspondence. The colour was changed from red to carmine in 1922 and it remained in use until 1939, when a series bearing values from 15 puls to 1 afghani was released.

4. Afghanistan, 2 puls, 1939
One of a lengthy definitive series designed by Abdul

Gafour Brishna and typographed locally. This series has remained in use to the present day, despite occasional attempts to introduce more professional designs and productions at various times in the intervening years. Note the use of the Arabic and European numerals intertwined and the curious mixture of French ('poste') and English ('Afghanistan'). Over the long period of currency this series has varied considerably in paper, colour and perforation.

5. Afghanistan, 10 puls, 1952
The majority of Afghan commemorative issues have marked anniversaries of independence, Pashtunistan Day and the Red Crescent with monotonous regularity. Crudity of design has been equalled by sloppiness in execution, little attention being given to niceties of spelling and neatness of layout and balance. This stamp was lithographed in Kabul and issued in 1952 on behalf of the Red Crescent. It depicts a medical orderly (in German-style helmet) bandaging a wounded soldier.

6. Afghanistan, 12 afghanis, 1963
Between April 1961 and March 1964 Afghanistan permitted an American philatelic agency to produce and market stamps, only token supplies of which were actually available in Kabul. The stamps were attractively printed, usually in multicolour photogravure, but were intended for sale to collectors and were therefore subject to heavy speculation. This stamp is from a series of 1963 honouring the Girl Scouts of Afghanistan. The contract was revoked in 1964 and since then Afghanistan has exercised strict control over stamp issues.

7. Afghanistan, 1 afghani + 50 puls, 1964
This stamp, marking Red Crescent Day, was lithographed locally, though there is a noticeable improvement over other locally produced stamps of the pre-agency era. Many stamps since 1964, however, have been printed in multicolour photogravure at the Austrian State Printing Works on behalf of the Afghan authorities.

8. Afghanistan, 5 afghanis, 1971
For many years Afghanistan has waged a propaganda campaign against neighbouring Pakistan over the Pathan district (Pakhtunistan). Stamps marking Pakhtunistan Day have been issued regularly since 1952, invariably featuring the flags of Afghanistan or Pakhtunistan (or both), sometimes in conjunction with recognizable landmarks in the disputed territory.

9. Bhutan, 150 nultrums, 1970
Since 1967 Bhutan has experimented with various materials to create unusual effects in stamp production. The first of these was a set of space stamps printed with a laminated prismatic-ribbed plastic surface to create a three-dimensional effect. Subsequently stamps have been printed on silk, metal foil and even thin steel plates (commemorating the steel industry of America!). This stamp is one of a series of Art stamps whose plastic surface simulates the appearance of oil paint on canvas.

10. Bhutan, 10 chentrums, 1968
The Himalayan state of Bhutan was content with a series of four revenue stamps, for postal as well as fiscal purposes, from 1954 onwards, but since 1962 has issued numerous stamps of a highly questionable nature. The majority of these are handled by the Bhutan Trust of Nassau, Bahamas and are designed for events and personalities which are hardly relevant to Bhutan. Occasionally, however, Bhutan issues a stamp more in keeping with the nature of the country and these are printed at the Indian Security Printing Press, Nasik. This stamp,

PLATE 43 CENTRAL ASIA · PLATE 44 PAKISTAN, BANGLADESH

depicting the Tashichho Dzong monastery, was designed from a photograph by L. Wangchuck.

11. Bhutan, 10 chentrums, 1972

This stamp, depicting the funerary mask of Tutankhamun, was one of a series of plastic stamps die-stamped in high relief to create the effect of sculpture. The stamp was provided with a self-adhesive backing, similar to that pioneered by Sierra Leone in 1963 (see plate 71).

12. Mongolia, 25 mung, 1932

Victor Savialov, the well-known Soviet artist, designed a pictorial definitive for Mongolia in 1932. The stamps were printed in photogravure at the State Printing Works in Moscow and featured the people, occupations, landmarks and scenery of the country. The appearance of the inscriptions in English gives a clue to the main purpose of these and subsequent issues – to earn hard currency in the Western stamp market, principally in Britain and the United States.

13. Mongolia, 60 mung, 1969

One of a set of eight stamps depicting the costumes of different Mongol tribes. These stamps, like most modern Mongol stamps, were lithographed in multicolour by the Hungarian State Printing Office, Budapest. Mongolia, a socialist republic between China and Russia, has been independent since 1921 and began issuing stamps in 1924. Many of the prewar issues were printed in Moscow and designed for the western philatelic market. English inscriptions appeared on the stamps between 1924 and 1941 and from 1958 onwards, alongside Russian and Mongol.

14. Tuva, 1 kopek, 1926

Tuva (otherwise known as North Mongolia) adopted postage stamps in 1926, using a design featuring the wheel of eternity. The inscription on these stamps was entirely in Mongol script, but a series inscribed in English appeared the following year. This series was lithographed in Moscow. Tuva was absorbed into the Soviet Union in October 1944 and now uses the stamps of Russia.

15. Tuva, 5 kopeks, 1927

The pictorial definitive series released in July 1927 was designed by Madame O. F. Amossova and lithographed in two-colour combinations at the State Printing Works in Moscow.

16. Tuva, 1 tugrik, 1934

Like Mongolia, Tuva issued numerous stamps in the period before World War II, intended for the western philatelic market. The stamps were printed in photogravure in Moscow, using unusual formats and pictorial designs. The inscriptions were almost entirely in English, with little concession to Mongol or Russian. Covers and used stamps bearing Tuvan cancellations often emanated from Moscow where duplicate sets of cancellers were kept. The speculative nature of these stamps denied them catalogue status for many years, but they are now recognized as having served a genuine – albeit limited – function.

17. Tibet, ⅓ trangka, 1912

Tibet adopted adhesive stamps in 1912 and issued a series in denominations of ⅙, ⅓, ½, ⅔t. and 1 sang (6⅔ trangkas = 1 sang). The crude, rubber-necked lion and the uneven lettering of 'Tibet Postage' and its Tibetan equivalent, were matched by the primitive typography. This series remained in use into the 1950s and varied considerably in paper and ink. The paper was hand-made, of varying thickness and texture, and either ink or shiny enamel paint were used for the printing. The Chinese occupied eastern Tibet in 1950 and gradu-

ally extended the network of Chinese posts to cover the entire country. Native stamps survived as late as 1965, when Tibet became an autonomous region of the Chinese People's Republic. Ordinary Chinese stamps are now used.

18. Nepal, 2 annas, 1881

The Himalayan kingdom of Nepal adopted adhesive stamps in 1881, issuing a series of 1, 2, and 4a. stamps in a primitive design. This series continued in use up to 1907 and was then reissued in 1917–18. During its long life this set was issued imperforate, perforated in various gauges and printed on different types of paper or in different colours.

19. Nepal, 32 pice, 1949

Although adopting adhesive stamps in 1881, Nepal used crudely typographed native stamps as late as 1918. Recess-printed stamps, by Perkins Bacon, were introduced in 1907 and featured the deity Siva Mahadeva seated among the Himalayas. The Siva series was reprinted at various times, the last version being typographed by the Gurkha Patra Press in Kathmandu in 1942–46. This stamp is one of a series offset-lithographed at Nasik for Nepal in 1949. All stamps of Nepal until 1959 had local validity only and Indian stamps had to be used on all external mail. Since 1959, when Nepal joined the Universal Postal Union, her stamps have been valid on all outgoing mail.

20. Nepal, 15 pice, 1962

A perennial excuse for commemorative stamps is the birthday of King Mahendra. Stamps for this purpose first appeared in 1960 and have appeared annually ever since. An equestrian portrait of the king was used for the four diamond-shaped stamps issued in June 1962. The stamps were printed in photogravure at Nasik.

PLATE 44
Pakistan and Bangladesh

1. Pakistan, 10 rupees, 1947

The Indian sub-continent was partitioned in August 1947, the predominantly Moslem areas becoming the dominion of Pakistan. Contemporary Indian stamps were overprinted 'Pakistan' pending the production of distinctive stamps. The majority of the overprints were carried out at the Indian Security Printing Press, Nasik, but provisional overprints were also applied by local postmasters. These were hand-struck or machine printed and vary enormously in size, style and colour.

2. Pakistan, 1 rupee, 1948

A pictorial definitive series was released in August 1948, coinciding with the first anniversary of independence. The stamps, in denominations from 3 pies to 25 rupees, were recess-printed by De La Rue but later printings, made between 1951 and 1954, were produced by the Pakistan Security Printing Corporation in Karachi. The De La Rue printings were perforated 12½ whereas the Karachi printings were perforated 13 or 13½.

3. Pakistan, 12 annas, 1951

The fourth anniversary of independence was marked by a set of eight stamps issued in August 1951. The stamps bore no commemorative inscription and were retained for definitive purposes. The four designs, by A. R. Chughtai, featured pottery, a Saracenic leaf pattern, an archway and lamp, and an aircraft and hour glass. Initial printings were made by De La Rue, who then shipped the plates off to Karachi as before, but there is no

appreciable difference in the two printings. The 3½a. value, with the Arabic value re-engraved, was issued in December 1956.

4. Pakistan, 12 annas, 1952

The first distinctive Asian stamps were issued in territory now forming part of Pakistan (see below) and the centenary of these stamps was celebrated on Independence Day 1952 by two stamps recess-printed by De La Rue. The 3 and 12a. stamps showed aircraft and a camel train, representing old and new methods of transport, and had a reproduction of the 'Scinde Dawk' stamp inset.

5. Pakistan, 9 pies, 1954

The seventh anniversary of independence was marked by a set of seven stamps which, like their predecessors, were retained for definitive use. Stamps were also released with a 'Service' overprint for use on government correspondence. Scenery was the subject of this series and the 9p. value was used to promote Pakistan's claim to the disputed territory of Kashmir, in Indian hands since 1947 though it possessed a predominantly Moslem population. The stamp shows the Pakistani flag flying in a Kashmiri valley with the mountains of Gilgit in the background.

6. Pakistan, 12 annas, 1955

Four stamps marking the eighth anniversary of independence appeared in August 1955 and took as their theme modern industrial developments in Pakistan. They were retained for permanent usage like their predecessors. The 12a. denomination, and the 1½a. value of the 1954 independence series, were overprinted in October 1955 to mark the tenth anniversary of the United Nations.

7. Pakistan, 2 annas, 1956

Pakistan dropped dominion status and became the independent 'Islamic Republic of Pakistan' on 23 March 1956. To mark the occasion this stamp, lithographed by De La Rue, was released on that date. It features the Constituent Assembly Building in Karachi. This was the only stamp to bear the full title of the republic. All other stamps have continued to be inscribed 'Pakistan' as before.

8. Pakistan, 10 rupees, 1957

A set of three stamps was issued in March 1957 to mark the first anniversary of the republic and, like the independence issues of previous years, was retained as part of the definitive range. An interesting feature of these stamps was the incorporation of the word for Pakistan in Bengali as well as Arabic script, reflecting the growing voice of the East Pakistan Bengalis for equal status in the Islamic republic. The 2½ and 3½a. stamps of this set were, in fact, re-engraved versions of earlier stamps with the Bengali inscription incorporated.

9. Pakistan, 2 annas, 1960

A pair of stamps featuring the emblem of the armed forces was issued in January 1960 to mark Armed Forces Day. The stamps were lithographed in three colours by De La Rue. A few stamps of Pakistan have subsequently been produced by this firm though the majority were printed in Karachi.

10. Pakistan, 13 paisa, 1961

Pakistan adopted the rupee of 100 paisa in 1961 and various definitive and commemorative stamps were surcharged with the new values, either by the Security Printing Corporation or by The Times Press of Karachi. The surcharge was also applied to those stamps overprinted for official use. This stamp is one of a set of four originally issued in March 1960, ostensibly marking the fourth anniversary of the republic but actually publicizing the Pakistani claim to Jammu and Kashmir – yet

PLATE 44 PAKISTAN, BANGLADESH · PLATE 45 INDIA

another example of the way in which stamps featuring maps have been used for political ends.

11. Pakistan, 25 paisa, 1962
Pakistan began issuing short thematic sets in August 1962. The first series consisted of four stamps devoted to various sports. Each stamp showed the equipment, field layout and sports trophy associated with football, hockey, squash and cricket, the most popular sporting pastimes in the country.

12. Pakistan, 15 paisa, 1965
This stamp, issued in August 1965, was the first stamp lithographed by the Security Printing Corporation and all stamps issued since that date have been produced by this process. A. Chughtai designed this stamp, issued as part of a government campaign on behalf of blind welfare. The majority of Pakistani commemoratives and special issues since that date have consisted of pairs or single stamps.

13. Pakistan, 15 paisa, 1964
This stamp, issued in December 1964, marked the end of the recess-printing era of Pakistani philately. It commemorated the first convocation of the West Pakistan University of Engineering and Technology in Lahore. Note the lettering of the country's name in Urdu, Bengali and English in equal size, though the value and captions are entirely in English – thus avoiding the cultural conflict between East and West which escalated in the late 1960s.

14. Pakistan, 15 paisa, 1966
The medieval Arab physician Hakim ibn Sina (Avicenna) was portrayed on this stamp, issued in December 1966 to mark the opening of the Tibbi Research Institute of herbal medicine. Many of the stamps lithographed at Karachi in recent years have been in pale pastel shades, giving them a rather washed-out appearance.

15. Pakistan, 15 paisa, 1967
A single stamp marking the twentieth anniversary of independence was a far cry from the recess-printed pictorials of earlier years, in its bold use of a radiant star on a solid ground. The attempt to make a decorative motif out of the numerals, however, was only partially successful.

16. Scinde, ½ anna, 1852
The curious circular, embossed stamps of Scinde were the first stamps to appear in Asia. According to Sir Bartle Frere, governor of Scinde, they were produced for him by De La Rue, but this seems unlikely since De La Rue's earliest venture into stamp printing came a year later and embossing is not a process this firm has favoured to any extent (the Gambia 'Cameos' being the sole exception). It seems more likely that they were of local manufacture and this would account for their unusual appearance. The central motif was the monogram of the Honourable East India Company. The Scinde 'Dawks' were suppressed in 1854, when adhesive stamps were introduced for general use throughout British India.

17. Las Bela, ½ anna, 1899
The state of Las Bela in Baluchistan issued its own stamps between 1897 and 1907. During that decade ½a. stamps, lithographed in black on white or coloured paper, were produced by Thacker and Co. of Bombay. The stamps were roughly pin-perforated and partially imperforate examples have been recorded. A new design, for ½ and 1a. stamps, was introduced in 1901. The numerous different settings of these stamps adds greatly to their interest for the specialist collector. Stamps of British India were introduced in Las Bela in 1907 and the state series was withdrawn.

18. Bahawalpur, 1½ annas, 1946
The princely state of Bahawalpur began issuing stamps for use on official mail in January 1945, a pictorial series with a red Arabic overprint being recess-printed by De La Rue for that purpose. Subsequently stamps with the name of the state rendered in English were produced by the same firm. E. Meronti designed this stamp, issued in May 1946 to celebrate victory in World War II. The stamp was recess-printed in green on a grey background previously lithographed and its attractive motif of the Allied flags resulted in a more pleasing design than the Victory stamp produced by rival Hyderabad (see plate 46).

19. Bahawalpur, 9 pies, 1949
Stamps for the use of the general public appeared in 1948 – three years after the official stamps were introduced. A definitive series recess-printed in two-colour combinations emphasized the history and cultural background of Bahawalpur, three generations of rulers being portrayed on the 10r. denomination. Several commemorative sets were also released. This stamp was one of four issued in March 1949 to celebrate the Silver Jubilee of His Highness the Ameer. The vignettes featured wheat, cotton, cattle and irrigation, with a portrait of the Ameer inset.

20. Bahawalpur, 9 pies, 1949
The last issue of Bahawalpur was a set of four in October 1949 to mark the 75th anniversary of the Universal Postal Union. The stamps featured the UPU monument in Berne, Switzerland. The stamps may be found perforated 13 all round or 17½ by 17 – an unusually high gauge which De La Rue seems to have favoured also for the Malayan stamps they produced at this period. Ordinary Pakistani stamps have been used in Bahawalpur since 1950.

21. Bangladesh, 1 paisa, 1971
Civil war between the Bengalis of East Pakistan and the Moslems of West Pakistan led to the establishment of East Bengal as the Republic of Bangladesh. Support for Bengal by India led to war between India and Pakistan, resulting in a victory for the forces of India and Bangladesh. In the areas liberated by Indian troops and Bangladesh Irregulars the contemporary stamps of Pakistan were overprinted with the name of the country in various styles of lettering. Numerous different types of overprint, both machine and handstruck, have been recorded. They were superseded in July 1971 by a definitive series lithographed by Format International and designed by Biman Mullick.

22. Bangladesh, 20 paisa, 1972
The series featured a map (10p.), the massacre at Dacca University (20p.), the symbol of 75 million people (50p.), the national flag (1r.), a ballot box (2r.), the broken chain symbolizing independence (3r.), a portrait of Sheikh Mujibur Rahman (5r.) and a symbol of international support for the new state (10r.). A 10p. stamp, inscribed entirely in Bengali, was issued in 1972 in memory of victims of the war.

PLATE 45
India

1. 1 anna, 1854
Adhesive stamps were adopted by the East India Company in 1854, the stamps being lithographed in denominations of ½, 1 and 4a. at the office of the Surveyor-General in Calcutta. Printings of the 1a. began in July and continued through August 1855.

Three dies were used in the printing of this value. This stamp, with rounded bust and a white vertical line on the chignon, belongs to Die II, from printings made in August-September 1854.

2. ½ anna, 1873
Stamps in this design, with the inscription 'East India Postage', were gradually introduced from 1855 onwards. These, and all other Indian stamps up to 1926, were typographed by De La Rue. The half anna first appeared in 1856 but dissatisfaction with the engraving of the profile led to the adoption of a new die in 1873 in which the features were more clearly delineated. These stamps continued in use till 1882.

3. 5 rupees, 1895
The East India Company relinquished control of India in 1877 when Queen Victoria was proclaimed Empress of India. The 'East India' series of stamps continued in use for a further five years. A new series, in similar designs but omitting the word 'East', was issued between 1882 and 1888. High values, from 2 to 5r., were released in 1895 and reproduced the portrait of the queen by Baron von Angeli. This large format was retained for the high value stamps of succeeding reigns up to 1947.

4. 1 rupee, 1902
The accession of King Edward VII in 1901 necessitated a new definitive series. De La Rue retained the Victorian frames, with the Emil Fuchs profile of the king substituted. Many different shades of these stamps were produced in the nine years in which the series was current.

5. ¼ anna, 1931
A set of six stamps was issued in February 1931 to mark the inauguration of New Delhi as the new capital of India. The stamps, featuring famous landmarks in the city, were designed by H. W. Barr and printed by offset-lithography at the Security Printing Press, Nasik, which has produced all Indian stamps since 1926. This was the first commemorative issue from British India, and by a curious coincidence both Jaipur (March) and Travancore (November) issued commemorative stamps later the same year.

6. 2 annas, 1911
One of a series typographed by De La Rue between 1911 and 1922 with the portrait of the King Emperor in his Durbar robes. One of the decorations shown on the king's breast is an elephant, but Hindu agitators put about the story that it was a pig – no doubt hoping to repeat the furore which sparked off the Indian Mutiny of 1857. The allegation was promptly scotched by the authorities and there was no necessity to withdraw the offending design. The original printings had a single star watermark, but from 1926 to 1933 it was printed at Nasik on paper with a watermark of multiple stars.

7. 8 annas, 1935
The top value in a series of seven, this stamp depicts a pagoda in Mandalay, a reminder that until 1937 Burma was administered as part of the Empire of India. The stamps were offset-lithographed and commemorated the Silver Jubilee of King George V, the most interesting and colourful of all the issues made to celebrate that event. The stamps followed the pattern established by the New Delhi series of 1931, and featured characteristic landmarks from various parts of India. The king's portrait is framed by coronation regalia and the collar of the Star of India.

8. 14 annas, 1940
The George VI definitive series was released in

191

PLATE 45 INDIA · PLATE 46 INDIAN PRINCELY STATES

1937, the middle denominations depicting various methods of mail transport. An increase in the air-mail rate in 1940, from 12 to 14*a*., led to the release of this stamp in a similar design but with a larger profile of the king. The series was typographed at Nasik.

9. 12 annas, 1947

The division of the Indian sub-continent into the dominions of India and Pakistan had important repercussions on philately. Pakistan (see plate 44) was a new name in the stamp album, but India continued as before, the main difference being the incorporation of the name of the country in Sanskrit lettering as well as English for the first time. This stamp was one of a set of three, released between August and December 1947, to celebrate independence. The stamps depicted the Asokan capital, the national flag and a Douglas DC–4 airliner. A somewhat similar design, featuring a Lockheed Constellation, was issued the following year to mark the inauguration of Air India's India-Britain air service.

10. 1½ annas, 1948

The dramatic assassination of Mahatma Gandhi on 30 January 1948, shocked the infant dominion and led to the release of four stamps on 15 August 1948 – the first anniversary of independence. The stamps were printed in photogravure by Courvoisier of Switzerland, a marked contrast to the typography and offset-lithography used by Nasik at that time. A small quantity of these stamps was also overprinted 'Service' for official use and now constitute the rarest Indian stamps to have been regularly issued.

11. 4½ annas, 1952

Nasik imported machinery for photogravure printing in 1952 and, from this series onwards, the vast majority of Indian stamps have been produced by this process. This stamp was one of a series of six portraying Indian saints and poets, ranging from Tulsidas to Rabindranath Tagore. The stamp illustrated depicts the nineteenth century poet, Mirza Ghalib.

12. 6 annas, 1955

The first definitive series of independent India had been typographed (low values) and offset-lithographed (rupee denominations) and depicted examples of ancient Indian culture. By contrast the theme of the definitive series of 1955 was the republic's first Five Year Plan. The majority of the eighteen denominations featured industry and agriculture, but three middle values showed aircraft over scenic views and this 6 annas stamp highlighted the government campaign for the control of malaria. The rupee denominations were reissued in 1959 on paper with a watermark of Asokan capitals in place of the five-pointed star of the original series.

13. 2 rupees, 1950

Following in the traditions of the British Raj the republic of India has issued stamps for official use. All issues since 1950 have depicted the capital of Asoka, legendary hero of medieval India. The stamps were produced in two sizes, the anna values being typographed and the rupee denominations being lithographed. The lower values were replaced by similar stamps, inscribed in naye paise, in 1957 and the watermark was changed from stars to Asokan capitals in 1958. New shades of several denominations appeared in 1969.

14. 90 naye paise, 1958

India adopted a decimal currency system, based on the rupee of 100 naye paise, in April 1957. As a result a new low-value definitive series was issued,

featuring a map of India. The inclusion of the disputed territories of Jammu and Kashmir in the design led to protests from neighbouring Pakistan. Star watermarked paper was used at first, but between 1958 and 1963 the series was reissued on paper with the Asokan capital watermark. The 5, 10, 15, 20, 25 and 50*np*. denominations may be found with serial numbers on the reverse. These were coil stamps intended for use in experimental vending machines. In the event the vending machines were not purchased and the stamps were sold normally over the counter.

15. 90 naye paise, 1957

Both India and Pakistan issued stamps in 1957 to mark the centenary of the 'war of independence', commonly known in the history books as the Indian or Sepoy Mutiny, since it was confined mainly to native troops of the Indian Army. India's stamps portrayed the Rani of Jhansi (15*np*.), a female warrior in the best traditions of Boadicea, and a shrine symbolizing national remembrance. From this date onward, incidentally, purely Indian inscriptions became increasingly common on the stamps of India, though English continues to be used predominantly to this day.

16. 15 naye paise, 1963

In the past twenty years the republic of India has issued a number of stamps commemorating important international events. Henri Dunant, founder of the Red Cross, was the first non-Indian to appear on stamps of this country. A portrait of him as an old man appeared on a 15*np*. stamp issued in 1957 to mark the 19th International Red Cross Conference at New Delhi. This stamp, showing a much younger portrait, was issued to mark the centenary of the movement. A few examples are known with the Red Cross accidentally omitted.

17. 5 paisa, 1967

This stamp, depicting Pandit Nehru leading a group of Naga tribesmen, was issued in December 1967 as part of the government propaganda campaign for the pacification of Nagaland. Various sets of labels, purporting to be stamps of Nagaland, have come on the philatelic market in recent years but their status is highly questionable.

18. 5 paisa, 1965

The adjective 'naya' (new) was dropped from currency notation in 1964 and stamps from that date are valued in paise only. A definitive series was issued between August 1965 and May 1968 in denominations from 2*p*. to 10*r*. The designs covered a wide range of topics, from agriculture and industry to medieval sculpture and wildlife. The 5*p*., depicting the ideal family unit, publicized the government's family planning campaign. On 15 November 1971, the Indian authorities instituted a levy of 5*p*. on all correspondence to raise money for the relief of refugees from East Pakistan. The 5*p*. stamp was overprinted 'Refugee Relief'. Apart from the official overprint, postmasters were authorized to overprint the stamp locally and a wide variety of different hand-struck marks were used.

19. Indian Expeditionary Force, 1 rupee, 1914

Indian stamps, overprinted for the use of troops, were issued at the time of the Boxer Rebellion (see plate 57). This set the precedent for the release of the George V series overprinted for the use of the Indian Expeditionary Force which served in World War I. These stamps were used by Indian troops stationed in Europe, Mesopotamia and East Africa. Most denominations up to 12*a*. are known with the stop omitted after the F, while the 3*p*. value is known with the overprint double. Turkish fiscal stamps overprinted I.E.F. 'D' were used by Force D at Mosul in 1919 (see plate 37).

20. Chamba, 1 anna, 1943

Chamba, Gwalior and the four Cis-Sutlej Sikh states of Faridkot, Jind, Nabha and Patiala, are known to philatelists as the Convention States, from the Postal Conventions between British India and these states established in 1886. By the terms of these conventions British Indian stamps were overprinted for use in each state. These stamps were recognized as valid for postage, not only in the respective territories, but in each other's territories and had franking power throughout British India as well. They were replaced by the stamps of the republic of India on 1 April 1950.

21. Faridkot, 2 annas

Faridkot replaced its own indigenous issues with the overprinted series in January 1887 but replaced them by ordinary, unoverprinted stamps of British India in March 1901. A few examples are known with the error 'Aridkot'.

22. Gwalior, 3 pies, 1927

Gwalior introduced overprinted stamps in May 1885 and continued to use them up to 1950. Stamps intended for ordinary postage bore the name of the state in English and Hindi, but between 1895 and 1948 those intended for official use were issued with the overprint entirely in Sanskrit.

23. Jind, 1 anna, 1914

Jind began using the convention overprints in 1885, superseding the issues of the princely administration. There seems to have been some doubt about the orthography of the name. On the first overprints it appeared as 'Jhind', but subsequently 'Jeend' was used. The form 'Jind' was not adopted until 1914.

24. Nabha, 3 pies, 1900

Nabha began using the convention overprints in May 1885 and continued up to 1950. A few examples are known with spelling errors 'ABHA' or 'NBHA'.

25. Patiala, 1 anna, 1903

The first stamps with Convention overprints were issued in 1884 and bore the spelling 'Puttialla'. The error 'Auttialla' is not uncommon on stamps of 1884–85. The more correct form 'Patiala' was adopted in 1891 and continued in use until 1950. During this period stamps overprinted 'Service' were provided for official mail.

PLATE 46
Indian Princely States

1. Alwar, ¼ anna, 1877

Alwar, in the Rajputana district, issued ¼ and 1 anna stamps in 1877, lithographed locally and rouletted. Perforations were adopted in 1899 and stamps were discontinued in 1902. The rouletting of these stamps is believed to have been done with a toothed strip of bone. Alwar (3144 square miles, population about 825,000) had eighteen state post offices, which closed at the end of 1902.

2. Bamra, 1890, ¼ anna

The first stamps of Bamra were crudely type-set at the Jagannata Ballabh Press in Deogarh in 1888. A more elaborate design, with a double-lined frame, was adopted two years later and typographed in black on paper of various colours. In the earliest printings (1890–93) the word 'Postage' was printed with a capital 'P', but in later printings (1891–93) it was spelled with a small 'p'. This state in the Central Provinces (area 1988 square miles, population 280,000) ceased to issue stamps in 1894 when the postal service was taken over by the British Indian authorities.

3. **Barwani, ½ anna, 1921**
Barwani began issuing stamps in 1921 and continued to do so until India became independent and the last of the princely postal services were suppressed in 1948. The stamps of Barwani were typographed locally, with half-tone portraits of the rulers. This method of portraiture seems to have been confined to the issues of the Indian states. Barwani had an area of 1332 square miles and a population of about 177,000.

4. **Bhopal, ¼ anna, 1889**
This important Moslem state of Central India issued its own postage stamps from 1876 till 1908, and continued to issue stamps for official correspondence till 1949. The earliest stamps were lithographed with Hindi script embossed in the centre. The correct inscription on these stamps should read 'H.H. Nawab Shah Jahan Begam', the title of the female ruler. This stamp shows the error 'Began', current on the stamps of 1886–89, and other errors, such as 'Nawah', 'Bbegam' or 'Eegam' are not uncommon. The embossed and lithographed stamps continued in use till 1895.

5. **Bhopal, ¼ anna, 1896**
Upright rectangular designs, lithographed without embossing, were used on various stamps from 1878 onward, in conjunction with the above type. This stamp belongs to a series released in 1896. Again, there are numerous errors in the spelling of the inscription. These locally lithographed stamps continued, with variations, up to 1908, when distinctive stamps for public use were replaced by the ordinary Indian stamps.

6. **Bhopal, ½ anna, 1908**
This stamp, recess-printed by Perkins Bacon, was issued in 1908 for ordinary postage. When ordinary stamps were discontinued on 1 July, it was overprinted 'Service' for use on official correspondence. Stamps are known with double or inverted overprint, or in pairs, one with and the other without overprint.

7. **Bhopal, ½ anna, 1936**
This stamp formed part of a series typographed at Nasik for the Bhopal state government in 1936. It depicts the Moti Mahal and the crest of the Bhopal government. Other denominations in the series featured the Taj Mahal, Rait Ghat and various palaces. Various values were added to the series up to 1938 and the style of the overprint changed at various times up to 1949, when the stamps were withdrawn.

8. **Bhor, ½ anna, 1879**
This small state (925 square miles, population 156,000) south of Bombay issued its own stamps between 1879 and 1901. The stamps consisted of crudely handstruck ½ and 1*a.* values on native paper which varied enormously in thickness and quality. The state post office closed in 1895, but six years later a ½*a.* stamp, portraying the ruler, Pant Sachiv Shankarro Chimnaji, appeared. Used copies were probably cancelled by favour at the Indian Government Post Office.

9. **Bijawar, 6 pies, 1935**
This state in Central India (area 973 square miles, population 120,000) issued its own stamps between 1935 and 1937, with portraits of the ruler Maharaja Sir Sarwant Singh Bahadur. In the first issue the portrait was rather crudely engraved, but in the series of 1937 a half-tone portrait was used. All stamps were typographed by Beerindra Kumar & Co.

10. **Bundi, 1 anna, 1898**
The Rajput state of Bundi (area 2220 square miles, population 250,000) issued its own stamps from 1894 till 1948. The early issues, from 1894 till 1898, were crudely lithographed, each stamp in the sheet differing in some detail from its neighbours. The stamps of Bundi were discontinued in 1902, but were revived in 1914 when a large design portraying Maharao Raja Sir Raghubir Singh, flanked by two sacred cows, was introduced. This curious design remained in use until 1941.

11. **Bundi, ½ anna, 1918**
Stamps portraying Maharao Raja Sir Raghubir Singh flanked by holy cows were issued between 1914 and 1941. During that period the lettering in the panels and the top and bottom of the stamps was altered on several occasions. Stamps overprinted in Sanskrit or English for use on government correspondence were introduced in 1918. Various colours were used for these overprints.

12. **Bundi, ½ anna, 1947**
One of the last series of Bundi, released in 1947, with various portraits of the ruler, Maharao Rajah Bahadur Singh. The stamps of Bundi were also overprinted 'Service' or its Hindi equivalent, for use on official mail from 1918 onwards. Bundi used the Rajasthan overprinted series in 1948–49 and since then has used ordinary Indian stamps.

13. **Bussahir, ½ anna, 1900**
The state of Bussahir (area 3320 square miles, population 750,000) in the Simla Hills of the Punjab issued its own stamps between 1895 and 1901. A wide variety of different designs, all featuring the lion emblem of the state, were lithographed at the Bussahir Press by Maulvi Karam Bakhsh and overprinted with a monogram RS (the initials of Ragunath Singh, son of the raja and postmaster of Bussahir). The stamps may be found imperforate, rouletted, or pin-perforated by sewing machine.

14. **Charkari, ¼ anna, 1894**
This Central Indian state (area 703 square miles, population 124,000) issued its own stamps from 1894 till 1940. The steel die for this stamp was kept in the Maharaja's personal custody and stamps were printed singly by hand, as and when required. The values and the letter S (for the plural form of anna) were inserted in slots in the die. In the earliest printings of the denominations from ¼ to 4*a* the word was shown in the singular form, but moveable plugs in new types were produced in 1905–07. Most denominations are known in various colours, the ¼*a.*, for example, being recorded in rose, magenta, purple or violet.

15. **Charkari, 1 pice, 1912**
A more elaborate series, in values from 1 pice to 1 rupee, was issued in 1909–11. The stamps were lithographed and the values were inserted by hand on the stones, thus giving rise to many interesting varieties. The value in native characters on this stamp was redrawn in 1912 in heavier lines (immediately above the word INDIA).

16. **Charkari, ½ anna, 1931**
This was one of a series issued in June 1931 and subject to manipulation by philatelic entrepreneurs. The series ranged in denomination from ½ anna to 5*r.* and had some limited postal use, though large numbers were subsequently postmarked to order and retailed on the philatelic market at a few annas for the entire set. Numerous errors, probably clandestine, exist. The issue was eventually withdrawn by the state and the previous type reissued.

17. **Cochin, 2 pies, 1909**
The Malayalam state of Cochin (area 1362 square miles, population 1,425,000) in south-western India, began issuing stamps in 1892 and continued until 1949. The first issue, showing the emblems of the state, was engraved by P. Orr and Sons of Madras and typographed by the Cochin Government Press at Ernakulam, in denominations of ½ and 1 puttam. Indian currency was adopted in 1898 for a series of large-format stamps with the numeral of value as the principal motif. This stamp, originally issued in blue in 1898, was reprinted in rosy mauve and surcharged to convert it to a 2 pies stamp in 1909.

18. **Cochin, 8 pies, 1911**
Perkins Bacon recess-printed a series for Cochin portraying the ruler, Raja Sir Rama Varma I, between 1911 and 1923. Subsequent definitive sets, portraying the rulers of Cochin, appeared in 1918 and 1933 and were likewise recess-printed by Perkins Bacon, but the latter series was lithographed locally in 1938. Various crudely lithographed issues were made locally between 1943 and 1949. Cochin subsequently used the stamps of Travancore-Cochin (see plate 47) and now uses ordinary Indian stamps.

19. **Dhar, ½ anna, 1897**
This central Indian state (area 1775 square miles, population 170,000) issued stamps between 1897 and 1901. The first series was typeset and printed in black on coloured paper. An oval handstamp was added as a security measure. Numerous error and varieties are recorded in the setting of the ornaments and the Hindi characters.

20. **Dhar, ½ anna, 1900**
A more ambitious series, featuring the state coat of arms, was typographed and perforated locally in denominations of ½, 1 and 2*a*. Used examples are rare, since the postal service of Dhar was suppressed in March 1901.

21. **Duttia, ½ anna, 1916**
Duttia consisted of a number of scattered districts in the Bundelkhand totalling about 846 square miles, with a population of 160,000. Stamps were introduced in 1893 and were withdrawn about 1920. All stamps of Duttia were crudely typeset and were impressed with the Maharaja's personal seal before issue in order to authenticate them. In some printings (1897) the name of the state is spelled 'Datia'. The motif on the stamps of Duttia is the Hindu deity Ganesh, patron of shopkeepers and merchants.

22. **Faridkot, 1 folus, 1879**
The Cis-Sutlej state of Faridkot (area 637 square miles, population 199,000) issued stamps between 1879 and 1886, when overprinted stamps of British India (see plate 45) were adopted. The folus stamps were normally printed in ultramarine, but impressions were made in other colours after the stamps became obsolete.

23. **Faridkot, 1 paisa, 1879**
The paisa denomination of Faridkot was produced in this design between 1879 and 1886 but printed in ultramarine. Like the folus stamp it was subsequently reprinted in various colours, with or without perforations, for sale to collectors.

24. **Hyderabad, 1 anna, 1871**
This large state in the Deccan (area 82,313 square miles, population 16,500,000) began issuing stamps in 1869. The Arabesque design, entirely inscribed in native characters, was actually engraved by a Mr Rapkin and recess-printed by Nissen and Parker of London. In 1871 it was superseded by this design, which was used with variations in the inscription till the 1930s. During that long period

various printers, including Bradbury Wilkinson, produced the stamps. This was, in fact, the first series produced by this famous firm of security printers.

25. Hyderabad, 4 pies, 1937

This stamp was one of a set of four, printed by offset-lithography at the Indian Government Printing Works, Nasik, to mark the silver jubilee of the Nizam. The stamps featured hospitals, Osmania University and the Jubilee Hall. The abbreviation H.E.H. on this stamp alludes to the title of His Exalted Highness, conferred on the Nizam by the British for outstanding services to the Raj in World War I.

26. Hyderabad, 1 anna, 1946

This stamp, typographed at the Government Press, was released in 1946 to celebrate victory in World War II and was printed on either laid or wove paper. It contains a curious error in design. The soldier is shown carrying a rifle – contrary to Indian Army regulations which forbade troops to take arms with them on leave. Hyderabad continued to issue its own stamps till 1950, when the the state was invaded by Indian troops and forcibly incorporated in the dominion of India, despite the vacillation of its Moslem ruler. Indian stamps have been used in Hyderabad ever since.

27. Hyderabad, 1 anna, 1947

One of the last stamps issued by Hyderabad was released in February 1947 to mark the establishment of the reformed legislature. The stamp, lithographed by the Government Press, depicts the Town Hall in Hyderabad City. Examples are known imperforate between adjoining stamps.

28. Idar, ½ anna, 1944

This west Indian state (area 1669 square miles, population 270,000) issued its own stamps between 1939 and 1944. A curious feature of them was that they were all issued in booklets containing panes of four stamps, producing singles which were imperforate on one or more adjacent sides. The first issue consisted of a ½a. stamp, typographed by M. N. Kothari of Bombay. P. G. Mehta & Co. of Himmatnagar typographed ½, 1, 2 and 4a. stamps in 1944. Both issues had half-tone portraits of Maharaja Shri Himatsinhji.

PLATE 47
Indian Princely States (Continued)

1. Indore (Holkar), ½ anna, 1889

The confusion of inscriptions on the stamps of this state may be dispelled when it is realized that Holkar was the name of the ruling dynasty, while the real name of the state was Indore (area 9934 square miles, population 1,514,000). The first stamps appeared in 1888 and were lithographed by Waterlow and Sons. This stamp belongs to the series of 1889–92, recess-printed by Waterlows with the portrait of Maharaja Shaivaji Rao Holkar XII. The stamp may be found in dull violet or brown purple.

2. Indore, ½ anna, 1904

Perkins Bacon recess-printed the basic series of stamps, in denominations from ½ to 4a., in 1904 for ordinary postage. At the same time the series was overprinted 'Service' for use on official mail. From 1 March 1908, the use of Indore stamps was restricted to official correspondence, but subsequent issues did not have a 'Service' inscription or overprint. The last series of Indore appeared

between 1941 and 1947. Since then only Indian stamps have been used.

3. Jaipur, 8 annas, 1905.

Jaipur (15,610 square miles, population 3,100,000) began issuing stamps in 1904 with a crudely executed series showing the chariot of the sun-god. Later the same year a horizontal-format series was recess-printed by Perkins Bacon with the same subject. During temporary shortages of these attractive London printings locally produced stamps in more or less the same design were used.

4. Jaipur, ½ anna, 1913

A very crude ¼a. stamp was typographed at the Jail Press in Jaipur City in 1911 and two years later a rather more ambitious version was typographed in values from ¼ to 4a. Perkins Bacon recess-printed similar stamps, in new colours and a different gauge of perforation, in 1928.

5. Jaipur, 2 rupees, 1931

The investiture of the Maharaja Sir Man Singh Bahadur was celebrated in March 1931 by a series of twelve stamps offset-lithographed by the Security Printing Press, Nasik. The vignettes of these stamps portrayed the Maharaja and featured palaces, state emblems and regalia. Eighteen sets of these stamps were overprinted 'Investiture – March 14, 1931' and presented to high officials and guests at the investiture.

6. Jaipur, 1 rupee, 1948

This stamp, the last to be issued by the independent postal administration of Jaipur, was one of a series released between December 1947 and May 1948 to celebrate the silver jubilee of Maharaja Sir Man Singh Bahadur. The series, in denominations from ¼a. to 1r., was recess-printed by De La Rue and depicted scenery and symbolism connected with Jaipur. Jaipur subsequently used the stamps of Rajasthan before adopting Indian stamps in 1950.

7. Jammu and Kashmir, 1 anna, 1869

Circular stamps, handstamped and printed in water-colours, were first issued in Jammu and Kashmir in 1866. This stamp was one of the series reissued three years later for use in Jammu alone. The stamps were all printed in red whereas the set of 1866 had been printed in black or blue. The circular stamps were in use till 1878 and were afterward reprinted in various fancy colours for sale to collectors.

8. Jammu and Kashmir, ¼ anna, 1883

A disconcerting feature of the stamps of this state was the tendency to issue all the denominations of each series in the same colours. The value is shown by the characters in the bottom row of the central inscription. The stamps of Jammu and Kashmir were withdrawn from use in 1894.

9. Jasdan, 1 anna, 1942

This small state on the Kathiawar peninsula (area 296 square miles, population 35,000) issued a solitary stamp in 1942, typographed by L. V. Indap & Co. of Bombay. It may be found in various shades of green, but examples in carmine were intended for fiscal purposes.

10. Jhalawar, ¼ anna, 1887

This state in Rajputana (area 824 square miles, population 123,000) issued stamps in denominations of 1 pice and ¼a. between 1887 and 1890 in various shades of green. The stamps were withdrawn in November 1900 when the state post office was taken over by the imperial authorities. The stamp depicts the Apsara Rhemba, a dancing nymph of the Hindu paradise.

11. Jind, ¼ anna, 1882

This Sikh state (area 1299 square miles, population 362,000) began issuing stamps in 1874, but abandoned distinctive issues in 1886, when the overprints of the Indian Postal Convention were adopted (see plate 45). All of the stamps issued in this period were lithographed at the Raja's Press, Sungroor. The capital letter R in the design is the initial of Raghbir Singh, Raja of Jind.

12. Kishangarh, ¼ anna, 1904

Inevitably Perkins Bacon secured a contract to recess-print stamps, with the portrait of Maharaja Madan Singh. This attractive series contrasted strongly with the locally typographed issues which preceded and followed it.

13. Kishangarh, ¼ anna, 1899

This Rajput state (area 837 square miles, population 105,000) issued its own stamps between 1899 and 1949, when the stamps of Rajasthan were adopted. The series of 1899–1901 bore the name of the state in the spelling 'Kishengarh', though Kishangarh was later adopted as more correct. Not all denominations of this series had the value expressed, but different frame designs and colours served to identify them. The stamps, in denominations from ¼a. to 5r., were issued imperforate or pin-perforated. The lower values were released in several different colours.

14. Kishangarh, ¼ anna, 1912

Kishangarh soon fell back on locally printed stamps, though there was a marked improvement over the previous issues. From 1912 onwards stamps were produced at the Diamond Soap Works, Kishangarh, using type-set inscriptions and half-tone portraits of the rulers. This stamp was reissued in 1913 with small ornaments added to the Hindi version of the value at the foot of the design.

15. Morvi, 3 pies, 1934

This western Indian state (area 822 square miles, population 115,000) began issuing stamps in 1931. The local printings were in sheets of four or eight and were typographed with portraits of Maharaja Sir Lakhdirji Waghji. A new series, typographed by an unidentified London printer, appeared in 1934. The stamps were subsequently typographed by the Morvi Press and may be distinguished from the London printings by their rough perforations and duller colours. Morvi's stamps were withdrawn from use in 1949.

16. Nandgaon, ½ anna, 1893

Nandgaon, or Rajnandgam, a state of Central India (area 871 square miles, population 190,000) issued its own stamps between 1892 and 1895. The first were in a large format inscribed 'Feudatory State Raj Nandgam' with the initials C.P. (Central Provinces) below. Subsequent stamps in a smaller design were inscribed entirely in Hindi characters, but were overprinted M.B.D. in an oval prior to issue. The initials are those of the Raja Machant Balram Das. As many examples of these stamps are known without this 'security endorsement' it has been argued that it may have served to indicate mail intended for official use.

17. Nawanagar, 1 docra, 1877

Nawanagar, or Nowanuggur (as it appears on the first series), had an area of 3791 square miles and a population of half a million. The first stamps, featuring a native dagger, appeared in 1877 but were almost immediately superseded by a crudely type-set series. No fewer than nineteen different settings of the type-set issues have been recorded.

18. Nawanagar, 1 docra, 1893

A highly professional series, by an unidentified

PLATE 47 INDIAN PRINCELY STATES · PLATE 48 INDIAN SUB-CONTINENT

printer, appeared in 1893 in denominations of 1, 2 and 3d. Distinctive stamps were discontinued two years later.

19. Orchha, 1 anna, 1914
This central Indian state (area 2080 square miles, population 320,000) issued its own stamps from 1913 till 1942. A set of four, similar to the stamp illustrated here, was produced by a European jeweller in 1897, but the authenticity of this issue has been denied. The first stamps were inscribed 'Orcha', and featured the state coat of arms.

20. Orchha, 1¼ annas, 1939
One of a series offset-lithographed by the Indian Government Printing Works, Nasik, for Orchha in denominations from ¼a. to 10r. A series of 21 stamps, portraying the Maharaja in European dress was issued in 1935 but owing to lack of proper state control it was offered to dealers and collectors at less than face value. As this set was subject to speculation it is ignored by most catalogues.

21. Poonch, 1 pice, 1884
This state, a tributary of Jammu and Kashmir, issued its own stamps between 1876 and 1894. The stamps were printed singly, with inscriptions entirely in Hindi and Arabic characters. This stamp belongs to the notorious series of 1884–87 in which stamps of various denominations from 1p. to 4a. were printed singly in red on a wide variety of different papers. More than fifteen different kinds or colours of paper have been recorded. This example was printed on blue wove bâtonné, exhibiting a faint pattern of horizontal lines on the reverse.

22. Rajpipla, 1 pice, 1880
The state of Rajpipla near Bombay (1517 square miles, population 215,000) issued stamps between 1880 and 1886. A different format and design was used for each denomination (1p., 2a. and 4a.) and the stamps were lithographed locally.

23, Rajasthan, 8 annas, 1949
Stamps of Bundi, Jaipur and Kishangarh were overprinted to denote the new state of Rajasthan, created in 1948 from a number of Rajput states. The postal service of Rajasthan was closed down by the Indian government on 1 April 1950, and ordinary Indian stamps have been used there ever since.

24. Sirmoor, 1 pice, 1892
This state in the Simla Hills (area 1091 square miles, population 157,000) issued its own stamps from 1879 to 1902. The first issue consisted of a 1p. stamp in green, reissued the following year in blue. The stamp illustrated here was originally made as a reprint in 1891–92 for sale to collectors. The design was taken (perforations and all) from an illustration in a dealer's price list, and is therefore regarded by thematic collectors as the earliest example of a stamp reproduced on a stamp.

25. Sirmoor, 2 annas, 1885
A series from 3p. to 2a. was lithographed by Waterlow and Sons in 1885, portraying Raja Sir Shamsher Parkash. As many as seven printings were made of certain denominations between 1885 and 1896, each differing slightly from its predecessors.

26. Sirmoor, 4 annas, 1899
Waterlow and Sons recess-printed two sets for Sirmoor. The series of 1895 featured an elephant, while the series of 1899 portrayed Raja Sir Surendar Bikram Parkash. These stamps were also overprinted by hand 'On S.S.S.' for use on Sirmoor State Service correspondence.

27. Soruth, 1 anna, 1913
The name 'Soruth' is applied to the territory subsequently known as Kathiawar, and sometimes referred to as 'Saurashtra', but in point of fact should have been given only to a section of Kathiawar including the state of Junagadh. The earliest stamps, from 1864 to 1915, were only used in Junagadh. The basic stamp was first issued in 1877 and was reprinted, with perforations, in 1886. Various denominations were surcharged with new values in 1913–15. Numerous errors and varieties have been recorded in these surcharges.

28. Saurashtra, 3 pies, 1929
The spelling on the stamps of this locality changed from 'Soruth' to 'Sourashtra' in 1923 and then appeared as 'Saurashtra' on a pictorial series issued in 1929. The stamps were produced at Nasik and remained current until 1950, when ordinary Indian stamps were introduced. The series was also overprinted 'Sarkari' in 1929 to denote its use on government correspondence.

29. Travancore, 8 cash, 1943
This southern Indian state (area 7120 square miles, population 3 millions) issued stamps from 1888 until 1949, when they were superseded by the joint issues of Travancore-Cochin. All stamps up to 1931 had a conch shell as their principal motif, but subsequently a number of crudely typographed sets of a commemorative nature were produced. The first of these sets, released in 1931, celebrated the Maharaja's coronation. Subsequent issues celebrated his 27th, 29th and 34th birthdays – at different dates ranging from 20 October to 9 November. This stamp, originally issued in October 1941 for the Maharaja's 29th birthday, was reprinted in 1943 in red instead of violet and surcharged to convert it to 8 cash. The letters BRV signify Maharaja Bala Rama Varma.

30. Travancore-Cochin, 2 pies, 1950
Stamps of Travancore and Cochin were issued in 1949 overprinted U.S.T.C. (United States of Travan- and Cochin) and these were followed in 1950 by a pair of stamps offset-lithographed at Nasik. The 2p. featured a conch shell, a traditional emblem in both states, while the 4p. depicted palm trees on the south Indian coast. Stamps overprinted 'Service' for official mail survived as late as 1951, the last of the princely issues.

31. Wadhwan, ½ pice, 1888
Wadhwan, with an area of 238 square miles and a population of 47,000, was the smallest of the Indian states to issue its own stamps. A solitary ½p. stamp, featuring the state coat of arms, was issued between 1888 and 1894, but several different kinds of paper and gauges of perforation were employed in that period. The stamps were lithographed from seven basic stones in different settings, ranging from 20 to 42 subjects per sheet.

PLATE 48
Indian Sub-Continent

For the sake of convenience only the stamps of four territories are grouped here. Burma formed part of the British Empire of India, but had postal autonomy from 1937 onwards and became an independent republic in 1948. Ceylon, formerly ruled by the Portuguese and then the Dutch, passed to Britain during the Napoleonic Wars and was administered as a crown colony until 1947 when it became an independent dominion. In 1972 it became a republic under the indigenous name of Sri Lanka. Stamps were also provided for the French and Portuguese settlements in India, remnants of the once mighty colonial empires broken by the East India Company. The republic of India gave the *coup de grâce* by annexing these territories in the 1950s.

1. Burma, 5 rupees, 1937
Burma used ordinary Indian stamps from 1854 until 1937, when the country received the status of a dominion in its own right. The first stamps of Burma consisted of the contemporary Indian series, up to 5r., overprinted. These provisional stamps were superseded in 1938 by a pictorial definitive series.

2. Burma, 8 annas, 1938
The defininitive series of the dominion of Burma consisted of eight designs by local artists produced by offset-lithography at Nasik. The Durbar portrait of King George VI was used on these stamps, flanked by Burmese chinthes and nagas (lowest denominations), nats or peacocks (rupee values) and featuring Burmese scenes on the middle denominations. The 2a.6p. denomination was surcharged for use as a 1a. stamp and overprinted to commemorate the centenary of the Penny Black in May 1940. This series went out of general use following the Japanese invasion of 1942, though a few examples with a typewritten 'Service' overprint were used by guerrilla units at Falam and Tiddim during World War II.

3. Burma, 15 cents, 1943
The stamps of Burma were overprinted with various peacock devices to obliterate the features of King George, during the Japanese occupation from March 1942 onwards. Subsequently distinctive stamps, inscribed in decimal currency (100 cents = 1 rupee) were issued under Japanese authority. The first stamps were crudely typographed at Rangoon, but in 1943 two sets, for use in Burma proper and the Shan states, were typographed by G. Kolff & Co. of Batavia. This stamp, showing an elephant carrying a log, was one of the Burmese series issued in October 1943.

4. Burma, 10 rupees, 1945
After the liberation of Burma in 1945 the 1938 definitive series was reintroduced with an overprint to denote the British Military Administration. The government was handed over to the civil authorities on 1 January 1946, and ordinary definitives, printed in new colours, were released on that date. The Military Administration series was the subject of heavy speculation by British troops serving in Burma and when these were unloaded on the London stamp market they slumped heavily in value.

5. Burma, 3 annas 6 pies, 1946
A. G. I. McGeogh designed a set of four stamps to celebrate victory in World War II. The stamps, offset-litho printed at Nasik, were the last stamps issued under British rule. The stamps featured Burmese people, an elephant and a chinthe, with a map of the country in the background.

6. Burma, 4 annas, 1947
On 1 October 1947 the British handed over control to a provisional government which administered the country until 4 January 1948, when Burma became an independent republic and left the British Commonwealth. During this short interim period the 1946 definitive series was overprinted in Burmese to signify 'Interim Government'. The 3p., 6p., 2a., 2a.6p. and 3a.6p. denominations are known with the overprint inverted.

7. Burma, 1 rupee, 1949
The new republic began inauspiciously with the

PLATE 48 INDIAN SUB-CONTINENT · PLATE 49 THAILAND

assassination of several prominent politicians, which started a civil war between the Burmese government and the Karen (communist) rebels. De La Rue recess-printed a lengthy series marking the first anniversary of the death of the Burmese leaders and featured the Martyrs' Memorial in Rangoon. The stamps were in denomications from 3p. to 5r. and, though commemorative in nature, were retained as a definitive series pending the introduction of a permanent series the following year. The stamps were overprinted in 1949 for use on official correspondence.

8. Burma, 3 annas, 1949

De La Rue recess-printed a pictorial definitive series for the Union of Burma in January 1949, the stamps commemorating the first anniversary of independence. Despite their commemorative nature they were retained as a definitive series till 1952. A similar series, but offset-lithographed instead of recess-printed, was gradually released between July 1952 and 1953. On 4 January 1954, the sixth anniversary of independence, the series was re-issued with values in the new currency.

9. Burma, 2 pyas, 1964

The 1954 series remained in use for ten years and was superseded by a set, from 1p. to 5k., printed in photogravure by the Government Printing Works in Tokyo. Twelve designs were used, each featuring a different bird of Burma. The series was reissued four year later, printed in the same colours but new sizes and formats by the German Bank Note Printing Co. of Leipzig. In the Tokyo printings the stamps were perforated 13½, 13 or a compound of these gauges, while the Leipzig printings were uniformly perforated 14.

10. Burma, 25 pyas, 1961

Since independence Burma has pursued a fairly conservative policy with regard to new issues of stamps. This stamp was one of a set issued in December 1961 to commemorate the second South East Asia and Pacific Games. The four stamps featuring sporting events were printed in two-colour photogravure by Enschedé of Holland

11. Ceylon, 5 pence, 1857

Ceylon adopted adhesive stamps in 1857, the first series being recess-printed by Perkins Bacon in various denominations from 1d. to 2s. At the same time De La Rue typographed a halfpenny stamp. De La Rue took over the Perkins Bacon contract in 1862 and continued to print the stamps by the recess method till 1867. Perforation was adopted in 1861 and the watermark of the stamps changed on several occasions during the life of this series.

12. Ceylon, 10 cents, 1910

Ceylon abandoned sterling currency in 1872 and introduced the rupee of 100 cents. All the stamps of Ceylon from 1862 onward were produced by De La Rue, those from 1866 onward being typographed. The series with the portrait of King Edward VII was issued in 1903, printed on paper watermarked single Crown CA. It was reissued in 1904–05 on paper watermarked Multiple Crown CA, while colour changes and new denominations were released in 1910–11.

13. Ceylon, 20 cents, 1935

Ceylon adopted a pictorial definitive series in 1935. De La Rue recess-printed the 2, 3, 20 and 50c. denominations while Bradbury Wilkinson printed the remaining values. Various landmarks, scenery and occupations of the island were featured, and inset, a portrait of King George V in the uniform of the Black Watch. The same designs, with a portrait of King George VI substituted, were used for the series of 1938–49.

14. Ceylon, 15 cents, 1947

Ceylon was granted a new constitution in November 1947, paving the way to full dominion status. A set of four stamps was recess-printed by Bradbury Wilkinson to mark the occasion. The stamps, designed by R. Tenison and M. S. V. Rodrigo, depicted the parliament building, Adam's Peak, Anuradhapura and the temple of the Tooth.

15. Ceylon, 25 cents, 1949

This stamp was one of a set of four issued in February–April 1949 to mark the first anniversary of independence. Two stamps depicted the national flag while the others portrayed Dudley Senanayake, the first Prime Minister. The stamps were recess-printed (the flag being typographed) by Bradbury Wilkinson on paper having the lotus and 'sri' watermark adopted by Ceylon for all subsequent issues.

16. Ceylon, 25 cents, 1960

One of a pair of stamps, photogravure-printed by Courvoisier, commemorating World Refugee Year. The stamps were designed by W. A. Ariyasena, who produced many of the designs for Ceylonese stamps after independence. Note that English is relegated to a subsidiary role in the inscription, alongside Tamil, while Sinhala is shown in the more prominent position. In the definitive series of 1950–54 English was shown predominantly with Sinhala and Tamil in secondary positions, but in 1958–59 the series was reissued with the inscriptions re-engraved reversing the roles of English and Sinhala. After an experiment with bilingual pairs, showing Tamil on one, English on the other, and Sinhala on both, Ceylon settled for equal treatment for all three languages.

17. Ceylon, 1 rupee, 1967

One of a set of four stamps issued to mark the centenary of the Ceylon Tea Industry. The stamps were lithographed in multicolour by Rosenbaum Brothers of Vienna, who have printed a number of stamps for the island in recent years. Note that English, Sinhala and Tamil are now accorded equal treatment on these stamps.

18. Ceylon, 5 cents, 1968

A high proportion of the commemorative issues of Ceylon since independence has been devoted to Buddhism. This stamp was released in December 1968 to mark the golden jubilee of the All Ceylon Buddhist Congress. A 50 cents stamp showing the sacred footprint of the Buddha was also prepared but its release was cancelled the day before it was due to go on sale. A few examples, however, were sold in error.

19. Sri Lanka, 15 cents, 1972

Ceylon became the republic of Sri Lanka on 22 May 1972, and marked the occasion by issuing a 15 cents stamp inscribed with the new name in Roman lettering, as well as in Tamil and Sinhala as previously. The stamp was produced by De La Rue, using the delacryl process, and shows the rays of the rising sun behind the mountain of the Illustrious Foot (Sri Pada) with a lotus in full bloom in the foreground.

20. French Indian Settlements, 1 centime, 1914

The French settlement of Pondicherry used the colonial keyplate series of the French colonies up to 1914, when a series, depicting Brahma, was introduced. The series was designed and engraved by E. Froment and the stamps were typographed at the French Government Printing Works, Paris, in denominations from 1 centime to 5 francs. New colours were adopted in 1922 and between 1923 and 1928 the series was surcharged in new currency (caches, fanons and rupees). A series using this

design, with new currency engraved, appeared in 1929. The stamps were overprinted 'France Libre' (Free France) by the Gaullists in 1941 and 1942–43, pending the introduction of a distinctive Free French series.

21. French Indian Settlements, 2 caches, 1942

This stamp, featuring lotus flowers, was one of a series designed by Edmund Dulac and printed in photogravure by Harrison and Sons.

22. French Indian Settlements, 2 caches, 1948

Messrs Rolland and Dassonville designed a pictorial series for the French Indian Settlements, printed in photogravure by Vaugirard and issued between June 1948 and June 1952. The stamps featured Indian deities and mythological figures, such as the Apsara (dancing nymph) featured on the lowest denominations. A 3r. airmail stamp issued with this series depicted an aircraft over a Hindu temple. The French Indian Settlements were voluntarily surrendered to India on 1 November 1954 and ordinary Indian stamps have been used there ever since.

23. Portuguese India, 4½ reis, 1882

The Portuguese colonies of Goa, Diu and Damao began issuing their own stamps in 1871, using a primitive locally produced series. The Portuguese colonial 'crown' keytype was introduced six years later and remained in use until 1886. During that nine-year period changes of perforation, colour, variations in the design and provisional surcharges added up to a formidable total of 198 different stamps – prolific even by present-day standards. The 4½r. denomination was introduced in 1882 and exists in three different forms varying in perforation or the presence or absence of a tiny pearl in the centre of the cross at the top of the orb.

24. Portuguese India, 1 reis, 1946

The majority of the stamps issued by Portuguese India conformed to the various Portuguese colonial keyplates. Among the few exceptions were sets of stamps issued in 1931 and 1946 in honour of St Francis Xavier. This stamp, lithographed by Litografia Nacional, Oporto, featured national heroes. A second series with similar historical portraits appeared two years later.

25. Portuguese India, 2 escudos, 1959

The basic stamp was one of a series issued in 1957, depicting a map of Damao, Dadra and Nagar Aveli. A new currency, based on the escudo of 100 centavos, was introduced in 1959 and these stamps were surcharged with new denominations. The stamps were lithographed at the Mint, Lisbon. The Portuguese territories in India were invaded by Indian troops in 1960 and since then ordinary Indian stamps have been used. The 1962 sports and malaria sets were printed but never issued.

PLATE 49
Thailand

1. 1 salung, 1883

Thailand's first postage stamps appeared in August 1883, Waterlow and Sons recess-printing different designs and using different colours to denote the various values – solot (½ att), att, sio (2 atts), sik (4 atts) and salung (16 atts). The stamps portrayed King Chulalongkorn, the king of 'The King and I'. In 1885 the value of this stamp was reduced to 12a. but no surcharge denoted this change. The 1s. stamp was surcharged in July 1885 to create a 1 tical denomination.

PLATE 49 THAILAND

2. 1 att, 1894

De La Rue typographed a series for Thailand in April 1887 with a full-face portrait of King Chulalongkorn. The stamps were in denominations from 1 to 64a. but from 1889 to 1899 numerous provisional surcharges were made on this series. Approximately fifty different surcharges were made, and numerous errors and varieties have been recorded.

3. 10 atts, 1902

Giesecke and Devrient of Leipzig typographed similar sets for Thailand in 1899, using either full-face or profile portraits of the king. A shortage of 2 and 10a. stamps was met by the postmaster of Battambang in September 1902 by surcharging 3 and 12a. stamps with new values in Siamese characters, applied by typewriting in violet ink.

4. 5 atts, 1905

C. Ferro produced a design featuring King Chulalongkorn and a view of the Wat Cheng 'Temple of Light' for Thailand's first pictorial series. The stamps were recess-printed by Giesecke and Devrient in values from 1a. to 1t. New values and changes of colour were introduced in 1908.

5. 3 satangs, 1918

The accession of King Vajiravudh in 1910 necessitated a change of definitive series. C. Tamagno of Bangkok designed a series, recess-printed by the Imperial Printing Works in Vienna and issued in October 1912 in denominations from 2 satangs to 20 bahts. A full-length portrait was used for the baht denominations. On account of World War I further supplies of the stamps could not be procured from Vienna and in 1917 Waterlow and Sons produced a series differing in perforation and minor details of the engraving. This series was over-printed in January 1918 with a red cross emblem, to raise funds for the Red Cross, and appeared the following December with an overprint in English and Thai to celebrate victory.

6. 5 satangs, 1925

A series of stamps, from 2s. to 1b., was issued in 1925 for airmail postage. The stamps were recess-printed by Waterlow and Sons and featured the mythical Garuda bird. The first printings were perforated 14–15 but stamps perforated 12½ were issued between 1930 and 1937. Stamps of this series with a Thai overprint signifying 'Government Museum 2468' were prepared in connection with a fair to raise funds for a Government Museum. The fair was cancelled on account of the king's death and the stamps never put on sale.

7. 5 satangs, 1928

Although King Prajadhipok ascended the throne in November 1925 stamps bearing his portrait did not appear until April 1928. The satang denominations bore a profile of the king, from a design by Khun Thep Laksanlehka, while a vertical format showing a three-quarter length portrait of the king, designed by Captain M. C. Gunvudhi Prija, was used for the baht denominations. The series was recess-printed by Waterlow and Sons.

8. 15 satangs, 1932

Apart from overprinted issues Thailand did not produce a distinctive commemorative series until 1932, when a set of eight stamps was released to celebrate the foundation of Bangkok and the Chakri dynasty. Three designs were produced by Prince Narisara, two (satang values) showing conjoined profiles of Chao Phya Chakri and King Prajadhipok, while the third (1 baht) showed the statue of Chao Phya Chakri. The stamps were engraved by J. A. C. Harrison and recess-printed by Waterlow and Sons.

9. 2 satangs, 1941

The boy king Ananda Mahidol succeeded his father in March 1935 but more than six years elapsed before stamps bearing his portrait were issued. On 17 April 1941, a series from 2s. to 10b. was released. The king was portrayed on the four lowest denominations while vignettes of a rice field and the Ban Pa'im Palace, Ayuthia, were used for the higher denominations. The stamps were designed by the Fine Arts Department in Bangkok and recess-printed by Waterlow and Sons. The outbreak of the war in the Far East cut off further supplies of these stamps and subsequent definitives were produced by the Defence Ministry in Bangkok up to the end of World War II.

10. 2 satangs, 1943

The Defence Ministry in Bangkok lithographed several stamps for Thailand during World War II, including a pair of stamps (2 and 10s.) in November 1943 featuring the Bangkaen Monument. Ears of rice provided the ornamental motifs for the vertical panels. Similar stamps, inscribed in Malayan currency, were issued the following year in the four Malay states occupied by Thailand during World War II (see below).

11. 5 satangs, 1951

Waterlow and Sons resumed their contracts in 1947, recess-printing a series portraying King Bhumibol, who succeeded his brother in June 1946. A more mature portrait of the king was used for a series introduced in June 1951 and recess-printed by Waterlows. Various values were added to this series up to 1960 and the following year stamps from these plates were printed by De La Rue, using a different gauge of perforation.

12. 25 satangs, 1955

The quatercentenary of the birth of King Naresuan was celebrated by a series of five stamps recess-printed by Waterlow and Sons and issued between February and April 1955. The common design featured a processional elephant. The majority of Thai commemoratives were recess-printed by Waterlows up to the end of 1956.

13. 25 satangs, 1957

Since 1957 many Thai commemoratives have been printed in photogravure, mainly by the Japanese Government Printing Bureau in Tokyo. A feature of postwar Thai philately has been the annual issue of stamps for United Nations Day. The first of these stamps appeared in 1951 and single stamps have been issued in October each year since then. This stamp features the UN emblem.

14. 25 satangs, 1960

An awareness of events beyond the national frontiers is reflected in stamps issued since 1960. This stamp, for example, commemorated the Fifth World Forestry Congress, held in Seattle, USA. Forestry continues to yield a large part of Thailand's revenue and appropriately this stamp features an elephant hauling timber. Other stamps issued that year included a pair marking World Refugee Year and single for S.E.A.T.O. Day.

15. 50 satangs, 1962

Thailand has participated in the various United Nations campaigns marked by special issues of stamps since 1960. The Anti-Malaria Campaign of 1962 was publicized by a set of eight stamps using two designs. The four satang values featured the campaign emblem and a Thai temple, while the four baht values showed a Siamese fighting mosquitoes.

16. 2 bahts, 1963

The Japanese Government Printing Bureau prod-uced a definitive series in photogravure with a portrait of King Bhumibol. The satang denominations were printed in one colour while the baht values were printed in contrasting frame and vignette colours. Various denominations were added to the series between 1964 and 1968. Curiously enough, a large format portrait series, recess-printed by De La Rue, was current simultaneously, in the same denominations from 5s. to 40b., and also had extra denominations introduced at the same time up to 1968.

17. 20 satangs, 1963

Stamps in denominations from 10s. to 2b. were used compulsorily by government departments between 1 October 1963 and 31 January 1964 to determine the amount of mail sent out by each department. This was used to estimate the relative costs of postage to be charged to the respective departments in future. The stamps were designed by Nai Chao Thongma and rather crudely typographed by the Infantry Printing Centre, Lopburi. The inscription signifies 'for Government Service Statistical Research'. The first printings were produced in two-colour combinations but the registration of the colours was very poor and subsequently the stamps were printed in a single colour.

18. 50 satangs, 1964

The seventeenth anniversary of UNICEF was marked by 50s. and 2b. stamps, issued in January 1964. The stamps reproduced the mother and child emblem of UNICEF and were designed and printed in photogravure by the Japanese Government Printing Bureau, Tokyo.

19. 25 satangs, 1968

Since 1967 Thailand has produced a number of colourful thematic sets. The first of these depicted fishes and appeared in January 1967. In June 1968 a second series devoted to the same subject was released. Subsequent sets have featured butterflies, flowers, architecture and Thai art.

20. 1 baht, 1970

An abstract design symbolizing households and statistical data was used for a 1b. stamp issued in April 1970 to publicize the National Census. Note the inclusion of the date 2513 in the Thai calendar.

21. 1 baht, 1970

The Sixth Asian Games were held in Bangkok in 1970 and were marked by two issues of stamps. A set of four featuring the venues of the sporting events was followed by this stamp, released at the commencement of the Games. It depicts King Bhumibol lighting the ceremonial flame at the inauguration of the Games. Note the increasing use of English in the inscriptions on Thai stamps, especially commemorative issues, in recent years.

22. 2 bahts, 1971

The most recent thematic sets have concentrated on the ethnography of Thailand. Sets have featured Thai ceremonies and festivals, dances, musicians and musical instruments and regional costumes of different periods.

23. British Post Office in Bangkok, 10 cents, 1882

From about 1860 onward it was customary to entrust outgoing mail from Bangkok to the British Consulate, for onward transmission to Singapore. The stamps of the Straits Settlements (see plate 51) were used for this purpose. A consular post office was formally established in April 1882 and henceforward the Straits stamps were overprinted with the initial 'B' to denote use in Bangkok. The need for these stamps diminished after the Thai postal service was inaugurated in August 1883 and their use ceased at the end of June 1885.

PLATE 49 THAILAND · PLATE 50 MALAY STATES

24. Thai Occupation of Malaya, 15 cents, 1944
The four Malay states of Kedah, Kelantan, Perlis and Trengganu were ceded by Japan to Thailand on 19 October 1943. A distinctive series featuring a coat of arms was released in Kelantan in November 1943, while various Malayan stamps were subsequently overprinted for use in Trengganu. A general series, lithographed at the Survey Department in Bangkok, was issued in January 1944 for use in the four occupied states. The stamps were similar to the contemporary Thai series, but featured the War Memorial and were inscribed in Malayan currency from 1 to 15c. At the end of World War II the four states reverted to British control.

PLATE 50
The Malay States

The philately of Malaysia often confuses the uninitiated. To this day the component states reserve the right to issue their own stamps, the majority of which are now printed in uniform designs. Higher denominations, and most commemorative stamps, are issued throughout the federation and are represented on plate 52. Three of the states were formerly grouped together as the Straits Settlements and were governed directly as British crown colonies (see plate 51). Of the remaining states four – Negri Sembilan, Pahang, Perak and Selangor – at one time formed the Federated Malay States and issued stamps thus inscribed between 1900 and 1935, and of the rest, Sungei Ujong was incorporated with Negri Sembilan in 1895, while the unfederated states – Johore, Kedah, Kelantan and Trengganu – have always maintained some semblance of postal autonomy. Perlis has only issued stamps since 1948. Further confusion is created by the adoption of new spelling in recent years – Johor (Johore) and Negeri Sembilan (Negri Sembilan).

1. Johore, 1 cent, 1896
Johore began issuing stamps in 1876 when contemporary 2c. stamps of the Straits Settlements were overprinted for local postage. De La Rue typographed a distinctive series portraying Sultan Aboubaker in 1891. The series was overprinted 'Kemahkotaan' (coronation) in 1896 in honour of Sultan Sir Ibrahim. All seven values have been recorded with the error 'Ketahkotaan'.

2. Johore, 5 dollars, 1949
Since 1949 Johore has used the uniform designs of Malaya for its stamps, with the portraits of Sultan Ibrahim (1949–60) or Sultan Sir Ismail (since 1960) inset. This stamp was the top value of a series issued between 1949 and 1955.

3. Johore, 5 dollars, 1960
A series of pictorial stamps was introduced in the Malay States in 1957 but Johore alone refused to adopt it. It has been suggested that Sultan Sir Ibrahim objected to the design of the 10c. stamp, showing a tiger, because it gave the world at large a false impression of Malaya's backwardness. The uniform designs were, however, adopted for the definitive series portraying his successor.

4. Kedah, 5 cents, 1912
Kedah adopted adhesive stamps in 1912 and issued a series recess-printed by De La Rue. The low values depicted a sheaf of rice, the state emblem, while higher denominations showed a ploughman or the council chamber. Between 1919 and 1940 this design was reissued with the stamps printed in

one colour, from single plates. Numerous variations in colour, watermark and engraving occurred in that period.

5. Kedah, 5 dollars, 1937
Waterlow and Sons recess-printed a new series for Kedah in denominations from 10c. to $5, portraying the sultan Abdul Hamid Halimshah. These stamps remained in use until the Japanese occupation in 1942.

6. Kelantan, 10 cents, 1911
Kelantan introduced adhesive stamps in 1911. The stamps were typographed by De La Rue in values from 1c. to $25 and featured the state emblem. The watermark used on this series was changed in 1921 and the series was overprinted the following year in honour of the Malaya–Borneo Exhibition. The series was withdrawn from use in 1937.

7. Kelantan, 40 cents, 1937
Bradbury Wilkinson recess-printed a new series for Kelantan between July 1937 and March 1940, portraying Sultan Ismail. Various denominations of this series were overprinted during the Japanese occupation.

8. Negri Sembilan, 1 dollar, 1936
Negri Sembilan ('nine states') began issuing stamps in 1891 when the Straits Settlements 2c. value was overprinted for local usage. Subsequently it used the uniform designs of the Federated Malay States. When distinctive issues were resumed in 1935, following the establishment of the Malayan Postal Union, Negri Sembilan chose the states' emblem, a group of nine spears, for the central motif. This series bore the states' name in Arabic alone, a feature peculiar to it and the stamps of Selangor.

9. Negri Sembilan, 8 cents, 1957
The uniform series of the Malay states was adapted for Negri Sembilan, with the nine spears emblem inset instead of a portrait. The colours and perforations of certain denominations were altered between 1960 and 1963. Since 1965 the stamps of this area have been inscribed 'Negeri Sembilan'.

10. Pahang, 2 cents, 1889
The first stamps of Pahang consisted of contemporary Straits Settlements' issues suitably overprinted. The keyplate designs common to the other Federated Malay States were introduced in 1891 and the 'leaping tiger' series superseded the individual state issues between 1900 and 1935.

11. Pahang, 2 dollars, 1935
When Pahang resumed its own stamp issues in 1935 a distinctive series portraying Sultan Sir Abu Bakar was typographed by De La Rue in denominations from 1c. to $5. 2c. grey and 6c. orange in this design were prepared for use but never issued.

12. Perak, 3 cents, 1900
Perak's first stamp consisted of the Straits 2c. stamp overprinted with a P, a crescent and star in an upright oval, intended for local use in 1878. Two years later Straits' issues overprinted 'Perak' were issued. Between 1892 and 1899 the various keyplate designs of the Federated Malay States were issued with the name of the state inscribed on them. This stamp was one of a series of provisional surcharges made in 1900 during a temporary shortage of 1 and 3c. stamps. The unified series of the Federated Malay States superseded these stamps later in 1900.

13. Perak, 5 dollars, 1941
Perak resumed distinctive stamp issues in 1935 with a series featuring a left-facing profile of Sultan Iskandar. A similar series, with a full-face portrait

of the sultan, was released in 1938 and various denominations up to $5 were released over a period up to October 1941. The stamp illustrated had a very short life, since Perak was overrun by the Japanese five months later and the state stamps were suppressed.

14. Perak, 20 cents, 1965
In 1965 a series of seven low-value stamps, in uniform designs depicting orchids, was introduced in each of the Malay states. The higher values were provided by the definitive issues of Malaysia. The Perak series portrayed Sultan Idris. The series was designed by A. Fraser-Brunner and printed in multicolour photogravure by Harrison and Sons. This stamp has been found with the bright purple colour (the blooms) accidentally omitted.

15. Perlis, 30 cents, 1955
The state of Perlis did not issue its own stamps until 1948. The first two sets consisted of colonial omnibus issues for the Royal Silver Wedding and the 75th anniversary of the Universal Postal Union. The first definitive series, portraying Raja Syed Putra, did not appear until March 1951. Various denominations, including the 30c., were added to the series between 1952 and 1955.

16. Perlis, 5 cents, 1957
The recess-printed definitive series of Malaya was gradually issued in Perlis between June and August 1957. The 50c. denomination was reissued in May 1962 with a different gauge of perforation.

17. Selangor, 2 dollars, 1941
Selangor issued its first stamps in 1881, when Straits' stamps suitably overprinted were put on sale. Subsequently Selangor used the keyplate designs of the Federated Malay States and ceased to issue its own stamps between 1900 and 1935. The series of 1935–41 was inscribed in Arabic and depicted the mosque at Klang Palace (low values) and a portrait of Sultan Suleiman (dollar values). On the accession of Sultan Hisamud-din Alam Shah new dollar denominations became necessary. The 1 and 2 dollar stamps were typographed by De La Rue and released in July 1941. A $5 stamp in the same design was prepared but never issued on account of the Japanese invasion.

18. Selangor, 10 cents, 1957
The recess-printed definitive series was released in 1957. The perforations of the higher denominations were altered in 1960 and the colour of this stamp was changed from brown to deep maroon in May 1961. The series was reissued in 1961–62 with the portrait of Sultan Salahuddin substituted for that of Sultan Hisamud.

19. Selangor, 2 cents, 1971
Victor Whiteley designed a new low-value definitive series for the Malay states, depicting various butterflies. The stamps, with the appropriate inscriptions and rulers' portraits, were lithographed by Bradbury Wilkinson.

20. Sungei Ujong, 3 cents, 1894
Sungei Ujong issued its own stamps from 1878 to 1895 when the state was incorporated in Negri Sembilan. The first issue consisted of the Straits 2c. stamp overprinted with a crescent and star surmounting the letters su in an oval. From 1881 till 1891 various Straits' issues were overprinted 'Sungei Ujong' and in 1891 the 'tiger in the undergrowth' design, common to all the Federated Malay States, was issued with the name abbreviated to 'S. Ujong'. An increase in the inland rate from 2 to 3 cents in 1894 led to the release of the 5c. stamp, printed in new colours (green or red instead of blue) with surcharges of 1 and 3c. respectively.

198

PLATE 50 MALAY STATES · PLATE 51 STRAITS SETTLEMENTS

21. Sungei Ujong, 3 cents, 1895
The provisional surcharges were superseded by a 1 cent stamp showing a tiger's head. The distinctive stamps of Sungei Ujong were withdrawn shortly afterwards.

22. Trengganu, 10 cents, 1910
Trengganu was one of the Malay states, hitherto under Thai suzerainty, which came under British protection in 1909 and began issuing its own stamps shortly afterward. The first series, introduced gradually between 1910 and 1919, portrayed Sultan Zain ul-ab-din and was typographed by De La Rue in two sizes, for cents and dollar denominations respectively.

23. Trengganu, 1 cent, 1965
The low-value definitive series of 1965 portrayed Sultan Ismail Nasiruddin Shah. A few examples of the 2c. have been recorded with the black (Trengganu) omitted.

24. Trengganu, 15 cents, 1971
This stamp, featuring a Blue Pansy Butterfly, was issued in the standard designs common to all the Malay states.

25. Trengganu, 50 cents, 1970
The Malay states have issued very few commemorative stamps distinctive to themselves. So far these commemoratives have been confined to single stamps commemorating the accession of a new sultan. Trengganu broke new ground with a series of three stamps celebrating the 25th anniversary of the installation of Tuanku Ismail Nasiruddin Shah. The stamps were designed by Enche Nik Zainal Abidin and printed in multicolour photogravure by Harrison and Sons.

PLATE 51
Straits Settlements

1. Straits Settlements, 1½ cents, 1867
The three Straits Settlements of Malacca, Penang and Singapore used the stamps of India from 1854 till 1867. The postal administration of this crown colony was separated from that of India in 1867 and Indian stamps surcharged in Malay currency and overprinted with a crown were issued on 1 September, pending the production of a distinctive series by De La Rue.

2. Straits Settlements, 2 cents, 1868
The first distinctive series of the Straits was introduced in December 1868, but the 2, 4 and 6c. values were not released till the following year. This series remained in use until 1892 and during the ensuing period was subject to numerous surcharges during temporary shortages of certain denominations. The 2c. stamps were also overprinted for use in several of the Malay states.

3. Straits Settlements, 10 cents, 1907
The crown colony of Labuan was incorporated in the Straits Settlements on 30 October 1906. Stocks of Labuan stamps then on hand were subsequently overprinted 'Straits Settlements' and put into circulation in 1907. Several denominations were surcharged to convert them to the most commonly used 4c. value. Numerous errors and varieties occurred in the surcharges and overprints. For Labuan stamps see plate 62.

4. Straits Settlements, 6 cents, 1920
A series of four stamps, with profiles of King Edward VII in different frames, was introduced in

1903. These frames were retained for the series of King George V released between 1912 and 1923. The designs incorporated symbolism alluding to each component of the colony: coconut palms (Singapore), betlenut or pinang palms (Penang), nipah palms (Malacca) and Malay daggers or kris (Malaya).

5. Straits Settlements, 2 dollars, 1936
After the establishment of the Malayan Postal Union in 1935 each state of the union adopted a uniform definitive series showing the state ruler flanked by palm trees. King George V, as ruler of the crown colony of the Straits Settlements, thus appeared on the series of this colony. The majority of the series appeared in 1936 but 1c. and $5 values were added the following year.

6. Straits Settlements, 5 dollars, 1937
The uniform series, with the profile of King George VI substituted, was gradually released between November 1937 and October 1941. In the earliest issues the stamps were printed at two operations, head and frame being separate even when the stamps were printed in only one colour. The monochrome low-values were subsequently printed from single working dies, at one operation. Specialists distinguish the two printings by minute differences in the lines of shading in the oval. An 8c. stamp in scarlet instead of grey was prepared in 1941 but never issued, on account of the Japanese invasion.

7. Malacca, 20 cents, 1949
After World War II Straits Settlements stamps overprinted B.M.A. MALAYA were used throughout Malaya. Individual issues were not resumed until 1948 when the colonial omnibus series marking the Silver Wedding were issued. Distinctive definitive sets, in standard Malayan designs, appeared in 1949. The former crown colony of the Straits Settlements was broken up into its components, each of which has issued its own stamps since then.

8. Malacca, 50 cents, 1957
In 1954–55 and 1957 Malacca issued definitive sets portraying Queen Elizabeth using the uniform Malayan designs. At the same time the first stamps of the Malayan Federation were released and were used alongside the state issues.

9. Malacca, 20 cents, 1960
The anomalous situation of Queen Elizabeth, as ruler of Malacca, being subordinate to the Yang di Pertuan Agong (king) of Malaya, was eliminated in 1960 and her portrait removed from the stamps. The state emblem was substituted on the series released in March 1960.

10. Melaka, 15 cents, 1971
The spelling of the name was altered to the more correct Malay form of Melaka on the orchid series of 1971 and this form was retained on the butterfly definitives of 1971. On both sets the state coat of arms replaced the ruler's portrait standard on the other sets.

11. Penang, 1 dollar, 1949
Penang likewise began issuing its own stamps in 1948, with the Royal Silver Wedding series, and introduced a definitive series the following year. The stamps were similar to the prewar Straits Settlements series, but with the name of the state substituted. The set of twenty stamps, in denominations from 1c. to $5, remained in use till 1954, when it was superseded by a similar issue, with the profile of Queen Elizabeth substituted.

12. Penang, 4 cents, 1957
The first version of the Penang pictorial series, like Malacca, had the profile of Queen Elizabeth inset.

The set was reissued in 1960 with the state coat of arms substituted.

13. Pulau Pinang, 15 cents, 1965
For the orchid definitive series of 1965 the orthography of the Malay names was corrected, and this applied also to Penang which henceforward appeared at Pulau Pinang. This 15c. stamp has been recorded with the green colour (value and leaves) omitted. The 5c. denomination is known with the blue (background and inscription) missing.

14. Singapore, 2 dollars, 1949
Singapore was established as a separate crown colony in 1948, though closely associated with Malaya. This is reflected in the fact that the definitive set of 1949–52 conformed to the standard design of the Malayan Postal Union. Two versions exist of this series. The first, released between 1 September and 25 October 1948, was perforated 14 all round, while the second, released between July 1949 and December 1952, was perforated 17½ by 18, an unusually high gauge of perforation.

15. Singapore, 1 cent, 1955
Singapore asserted its independence, postally at least, by adopting entirely new designs for the Elizabethan definitive series of 1955. The twelve low-value stamps depicted various methods of waterborne transport (except the 25c., designated mainly for airmail, which featured an Argonaut aircraft), while the dollar values featured the statue of Raffles, a view of Singapore River and the colony's coat of arms. The cents values were printed in photogravure by Harrison while the dollar values were recess-printed by Bradbury Wilkinson. Later printings of the 10 and 50c. stamps were produced with a finer screen, of 250 dots per inch instead of the normal 200.

16. Singapore, 50 cents, 1959
On 1 August 1958, Singapore became an internally self-governing territory under the name of the State of Singapore. In belated commemoration of the new constitution a set of six stamps was released in June 1959. The stamps, printed in three-colour photogravure by Harrison, depicted the Singapore state emblem. The name 'Singapore' means 'lion's gateway'.

17. Singapore, 10 cents, 1961
The inscription 'State of Singapore' was confined to those stamps released annually to mark National Day (June 3). The majority of these issues tried to emphasize the multinational aspects of the state and the spirit of cooperation between the different communities. This stamp was one of a pair printed in photogravure by Enschedé of Holland.

18. Singapore, 12 cents, 1963
Between March 1962 and March 1963 Singapore issued a new definitive series in three phases and in three themes. Five of the lower values depicted various orchids, another seven depicted fishes, and the four highest denominations showed various birds. A 15c. stamp, for airmail use, was issued in 1966 and featured a black-naped tern. This series echoed the Malay state definitive low values (orchids) and the Malaysian Federation high values (birds) which appeared in 1965. Between August 1963 and August 1965 Singapore was, in fact, a component state of the Malaysian Federation but since then has become an independent republic within the Commonwealth.

19. Singapore, 50 cents, 1967
A set of three stamps was issued on 9 August 1967, to mark the inauguration of Singapore as an independent sovereign republic. The stamps depicted a flag procession with the caption 'Build a vigorous

199

PLATE 51 STRAITS SETTLEMENTS · PLATE 52 MALAYSIA

Singapore' at the foot in English and with the equivalent in Chinese, Malay and Tamil on the respective denominations. This interesting precedent was retained for the National Day stamps of 1968 but has been dropped in subsequent years.

20. Singapore, 10 dollars, 1969
A republican definitive series was introduced between November 1968 and December 1970, with the theme of dances and musical instruments. The denominations from 1c. to $1 were printed by De La Rue while the 2, 5 and 10 dollar values were produced by the Japanese Government Printing Bureau, Tokyo. This stamp depicts a drum known as a *ta ku*.

21. Singapore, 1 dollar, 1971
Singapore was host to the meeting of the Commonwealth heads of government in January 1971 and for the occasion a series of four stamps was issued. The stamps were designed by the local artist, W. Lee, and were lithographed in multicolour by De La Rue. Each stamp succeeded in including in its design elements connected with every independent Commonwealth country. On the 15c. value all 32 country names were featured in a circle, while the other three stamps contrived to show all 32 national flags, linked to that of Singapore in the centre.

22. Singapore, 10 dollars, 1969
A set of six stamps and a miniature sheet were issued in August 1969 (National Day under the republican system) to celebrate the 150th anniversary of the foundation of Singapore. The stamps took as their subjects various episodes in the long and colourful history of the island. Much criticism was levelled at the postal administration for including an excessively high denomination stamp in the series. The $10 features the head of Sir Stamford Raffles, founder of the city. The stamps were designed by Eng Siak Loy and Han Kuan Cheng, and were lithographed by Bradbury Wilkinson.

23. Singapore, 15 cents, 1968
The National Day series of August 1968 continued the practice of inscriptions in the various languages of Singapore. Stamps in denominations of 6, 15 and 50c. showed a symbolic figure wielding a hammer and were inscribed at the top in Chinese, Malay and Tamil respectively. The stamps were printed in three-colour photogravure by Harrison and Sons.

24. Singapore, 75 cents, 1969
Eng Siak Loy designed the three diamond-format stamps issued in April 1969 to mark the 25th Plenary Session of the UN Economic Commission for Asia and the Far East. The stamps, featuring the ECAFE emblem, were printed in photogravure at the Japanese Government Printing Bureau, Tokyo.

25. Singapore, 25 cents, 1969.
Tay Siew Chiah cunningly adapted the slogan '100,000 Homes for the People' to make a symbolic block of apartments as the basis of the two stamps lithographed by Bradbury Wilkinson and issued in July 1969 to mark the completion of the 100,000 Homes project.

PLATE 52
Malaysia

The various attempts to unite the Malay states over the past eighty years are reflected in the stamps of that period. Political unity manifested itself in the Federated Malay States at the turn of the century. Later the Malayan Postal Union brought about the standardization of the states' stamps which led inevitably to monotony in their issues (see plate 50). The Japanese occupation and the subsequent British military administration were both, in their own way, forces for unity in Malaya and the various constitutional developments since World War II, leading to the Federation of Malaya and then the establishment of Malaysia are vividly illustrated by the stamps of these regimes. Even today, however, the individual states retain the privilege of issuing their own stamps and these are often used in conjunction with the stamps of Malaysia.

1. Federated Malay States, 2 cents, 1900
Pending the introduction of a distinctive series the Federated Malay States first made use of obsolete issues of Negri Sembilan and Perak suitably overprinted. Eight stamps of Negri Sembilan, from 1 to 50c., and six of Perak, from 5c. to $25, were overprinted for use throughout these states as well as Pahang and Selangor. The 10c. of Perak overprinted in this way has been recorded with the bar omitted.

2. Federated Malay States, 10 cents, 1900
The overprinted stamps were superseded in 1900–01 by a series typographed in two-colour combinations by De La Rue. The cents values featured a leaping tiger while the dollar values showed a group of elephants, the latter design being similar to that previously used by the individual states for their higher denominations. These stamps remained in use until 1935, when separate issues were resumed. During that comparatively long period the stamps underwent numerous changes in shade and colour and single working plates were adopted for certain lower values in 1906, whereby the entire design was printed in one colour. The watermark was changed from single to multiple crown CA in 1904 and then to the script watermark between 1922 and 1934.

3. Malayan Postal Union, 1 cent, 1938
The Malayan Postal Union came into being in 1935 and led to the standardization of postal services throughout Malaya. As a result each of the member states began issuing definitive sets in a uniform design, and this practice has continued to the present day. A unified series of postage due stamps, however, was also introduced and bore the inscription 'Malayan Postal Union'. These stamps, typographed by Waterlow and Sons, appeared in 1936 and at first were confined to the former Federated Malay States and the Straits Settlements. Distinctive postage due stamps of the other states were retained where possible. The series was reintroduced in 1945 and extended to the whole of Malaya. Similar stamps inscribed 'Malaysia' were adopted in 1968.

4. Japanese Occupation, 3 cents, 1942
Following the Japanese invasion and occupation of Malaya in 1941–42 stocks of stamps were seized by the military authorities and overprinted in various ways. In the majority of cases these overprinted stamps could be used anywhere in occupied territory, but in some cases they were confined to the state from which they originally emanated. The first stamps to be thus treated were

the George VI series of the Straits Settlements which received an octagonal handstamp in Japanese characters signifying 'Seal of Post Office of Malayan Military Department'. In other districts the stamps were overprinted by hand with the personal chop, or seal, of the local military commander. Machine-overprinted stamps appeared towards the end of 1942 and included a series of Straits Settlements stamps overprinted to commemorate the Selangor Agri-Horticultural Exhibition.

5. Japanese Occupation, 15 cents, 1943
A distinctive definitive series replaced the various overprinted stamps in 1943. The stamps were printed by G. Kolff of Batavia by offset-lithography and featured scenery, landmarks and occupations of Malaya. The inscriptions on these stamps were rendered entirely in Japanese. Two distinctive commemorative pairs were issued under the Japanese regime in 1943 and 1944 to publicise the savings campaign and the rebirth of Malaya respectively.

6. British Military Administration, 8 cents, 1945
Following the liberation of Malaya the prewar series of the Straits Settlements was reintroduced, with an overprint to signify 'British Military Administration'. The 8c. stamp was due to change colour from grey to scarlet in 1941, but the new colour was not issued on account of the war. Stamps in this colour were never issued without the BMA overprint, though a few examples eventually came into the hands of collectors.

7. Federation of Malaya, 30 cents, 1957
The Federation of Malaya was formed on 31 August 1957. Four months earlier, however, a set of four definitive stamps was released for use throughout Malaya. De La Rue printed the stamps, using combined recess and lithography for the three lower values and recess alone for the 30c. denomination. The stamps featured rubber-tapping, tin-dredging, the Federation's coat of arms and a map of Malaya. These stamps were originally perforated 13 by 12½, but a new printing perforated 13 all round and in somewhat deeper colours appeared in 1961. These were the only definitive stamps issued by the Federation of Malaya.

8. 30 cents, 1958
One of a pair of stamps celebrating the first anniversary of independence. The stamps, portraying the Yang di Pertuan Agong, or king of Malaya, were printed in multicolour photogravure by Harrison and Sons.

9. 30 sen, 1960
Up to 1960 the stamps of Malaya had always included the word 'Malaya' in the inscription. On 19 September 1960, a pair of stamps was issued to mark the Natural Rubber Research Conference and the 15th International Rubber Study Group Meeting held at Kuala Lumpur. For the first time the Malay form 'Persekutuan Tanah Melayu' (Federation of Malaya) was rendered in Malay alone. The stamps were printed in photogravure by the Japanese Government Printing Bureau, Tokyo, and were the first Commonwealth issues to be printed there since World War II – an event which caused considerable furore in philatelic circles at the time. Note the use of the Malay form 'sen' instead of 'cents'.

10. 10 sen, 1962
One of a set of three stamps issued in July 1962 to publicize National Language Month. The stamps were printed in multicolour photogravure by Harrison and Sons in *tête-bêche* combinations. The motif is a palmyra leaf, used as writing material in the Far East, and therefore an apt symbol for literacy.

PLATE 52 MALAYSIA · PLATE 53 INDIAN OCEAN ISLANDS

11. **30 sen, 1963**

Three stamps in a common design were issued in March 1963 to mark the United Nations Freedom from Hunger campaign. The stamps were printed in two-colour photogravure by Courvoisier and featured a harvester and fishermen. These were the first stamps printed by Courvoisier for Malaya.

12. **30 sen, 1963**

One of a pair of stamps issued in June 1963 to commemorate the inauguration of the Cameron Highlands Hydro-electric project. The stamps, printed by Harrisons, depict the dam and a pylon.

13. **Malaysia, 30 sen, 1963**

Victor Whiteley designed 20 and 30s. stamps issued in November 1963 in honour of the Ninth Commonwealth Parliamentary Conference, held at Kuala Lumpur. The stamps, in a large diamond format, featured the Parliament House in Kuala Lumpur. The stamps were printed in photogravure by Harrison and Sons, using gold ink for the lettering on a dark background of magenta or green.

14. **Malaysia, 50 sen, 1963**

The Federation of Malaysia was inaugurated on 16 September, and a set of three stamps, produced by Harrisons, was released in honour of the occasion. The design shows the sunrise over a map of the Federation, but it was criticized at the time for its striking resemblance to the Japanese national flag – an ill-omen, or an untimely reminder of the wartime occupation.

15. **2 sen, 1965**

A set of three stamps was printed in multicolour photogravure by Courvoisier and issued in May 1965 to mark the centenary of the International Telecommunications Union. While most countries were content to use symbolic designs Malaysia chose a micro-wave tower in Malaya for its series. Note the use of the $\mathcal{C}$ symbol to denote 'sen'. This has been used on Malaysian stamps ever since.

16. **30 sen, 1967**

Malaysia celebrated the centenary of its first stamps (those of the former Straits Settlements) by issuing three multicoloured stamps in December 1967. Each denomination reproduced an early Straits stamp and a modern Malaysian stamp for comparison, the latter being of the same denomination as the commemorative stamp. The stamps were designed by Enche Ng Peng Nam using an unusual trapezoid format and were printed in Tokyo.

17. **50 sen, 1966**

Two stamps were photogravure-printed by De La Rue and released in October 1966 to mark the 150th anniversary of the Penang Free School. The 20 sen value bore the caption in English only while the 50s. denomination was inscribed in both Malay and English.

18. **75 sen, 1969**

Two stamps appeared in December 1969 to mark National Rice Year. The design by Enche Hossein Anas, shows a peasant girl with sheaves of paddy. Striking use was made by Harrisons of a gold metallic frame in conjunction with multicolour photogravure.

19. **15 sen, 1970**

Enschedé en Zonen printed a set of three stamps to commemorate the launching of the satellite earth station Intelsat III. Two of the stamps were 30s. values and were identical in every respect except their lettering, which was in white or gold respectively. The 15s. denomination, showing a satellite tracking aerial, was in a curious trapezoid format. These stamps were issued in sheets horizontally *tête-bêche*.

20. **15 sen, 1966**

Five stamps, each of 15 sen denomination, were released in December 1966 to publicize the first Malaysia Plan. The stamps were designed by Enche Ng Peng Nam and printed in multicolour photogravure by the Japanese Government Printing Bureau. Each stamp highlighted an aspect of the plan – agriculture, rural health, communications, education and irrigation.

21. **75 sen, 1970**

In keeping with the low-value definitive stamps of the individual states the Malaysian unified definitive stamps of 1970 depicted butterflies. Eight vertical designs by Victor Whiteley were lithographed by Bradbury Wilkinson in denominations from 25s. to $10.

22. **Malaysia, 75 sen, 1968**

Bradbury Wilkinson lithographed two stamps in multicolour to mark the Mexico Olympic Games. The 30s. stamp showed a Mexican sombrero and blanket, while the 75s. depicted Mexican embroidery.

23. **Malaysia, 15 sen, 1969**

To publicize Solidarity Week a set of three stamps, in multicolour photogravure by the Japanese Government Printing Bureau, was issued in February 1969. Different portraits of Tunku Abdul Rahman, against pandanus weave patterns, were used for these stamps.

24. **Malaysia, 25 sen, 1968**

The Natural Rubber Conference at Kuala Lumpur was marked by three stamps issued in August 1968. The stamps were lithographed by Bradbury Wilkinson and depicted rubber tapping alongside a molecular unit (25s.), an export consignment (30s.) and aircraft tyres (50s.).

PLATE 53
Indian Ocean Islands

The four territories dealt with on this plate have had a chequered career. Both Christmas Island and the Cocos-Keeling group were formerly administered by the Straits Settlements and subsequently by Singapore before being transferred to Australian control in the 1950s. The Maldive Islands were formerly administered by Ceylon, while the islands which now constitute the British Indian Ocean Territory were formerly administered by Mauritius and the Seychelles.

1. **Christmas Island, 1 dollar, 1958**

Responsibility for Christmas Island was transferred from Singapore to Australia on 18 October 1958. A series of stamps was introduced three days earlier and consisted of the Australian 1s.0½d. stamp of 1955 in various colours, with new values in Malayan currency and the name of the island overprinted typographically. The stamps, in denominations from 2c. to $1, were recess-printed by the Note Printing Branch of the Commonwealth Bank of Australia in Melbourne. Christmas Island was formally annexed to the Straits Settlements in 1900 and used the stamps of that territory until 1942, when it was overrun by the Japanese. After World War II the stamps of the British Military Administration of Malaya and then those of Singapore were in use.

2. **Christmas Island, 10 cents, 1963**

A pictorial series, recess-printed by the Reserve Bank of Australia, was issued in August 1963 in denominations from 2c. to $1. A map, scenery, fauna and flora, and aspects of the phosphate industry provided material for the ten designs.

3. **Christmas Island, 1 dollar, 1968**

Following the adoption of Australian currency a definitive series in denominations from 1c. to $1 was issued in May 1968. The ten stamps featured fishes of the Indian Ocean and were designed by George Hamori. In December 1970, 15 and 30c. stamps were added to the series. The stamps were printed in multicolour photogravure in Melbourne by the Reserve Bank of Australia.

4. **Christmas Island, 5 cents, 1970**

Appropriately, Christmas stamps were introduced by Christmas Island in 1969, the first stamp featuring a mosaic of an angel. Harrison and Sons designed and produced 3 and 4c. stamps in October 1970, reproducing Old Master paintings – Raphael's *Ansidei Madonna* and Morando's *Virgin and Child with St John the Baptist*.

5. **Christmas Island, 20 cents, 1972**

A definitive series featuring ships associated with the island was introduced in February 1972. The stamps were designed by Victor Whiteley and printed in multicolour photogravure by Harrison and Sons. The stamp illustrated shows the East Indiaman *Thomas*, which discovered the island in 1615. The stamps, in denominations up to $1, were released in batches of four during 1972.

6. **Cocos Islands, 3 pence, 1963**

The Cocos (Keeling) Islands formed part of the colony of Singapore until 1955, when they were transferred to Australia. Ordinary Australian stamps were in use until 1963, when a series of pictorial stamps was adopted. The six stamps, from 3d. to 2s.3d., featured palms, the copra industry, a map of the islands, an airliner, a native sailing boat and a white tern. They were recess-printed by the Reserve Bank of Australia, Melbourne.

7. **Cocos Islands, 5 pence, 1965**

The first (and so far, the only) commemorative stamp issued by the Cocos Islands appeared in April 1965 to mark the 50th anniversary of the Gallipoli landings by ANZAC troops. Australia and her dependencies in the Pacific and Indian Oceans issued stamps in an omnibus design by C. Andrew, reproducing the statue of Simpson and his Donkey in the Shrine of Remembrance, Melbourne. Two printings were made of the Cocos Islands stamp, differing markedly in shade. With the introduction of Australian decimal currency in February 1966 Australian stamps were used in the Cocos Islands until July 1969.

8. **Cocos Islands, 1 dollar, 1969**

Distinctive stamps were reintroduced in the Cocos Islands in July 1969. The six lowest denominations (1c. to 6c.) featured seashells and fishes and were designed by L. Annois, while the six higher values (10c. to $1) were designed by Peter Jones and featured birds of the islands. The series was printed in multicolour photogravure by the Reserve Bank of Australia.

9. **Maldive Islands, 3 cents, 1909**

A postal service having been established at Malé, the chief island, in 1906, contemporary stamps of Ceylon overprinted 'Maldives' were issued in denominations from 2 to 25c. Three years later De La Rue recess-printed a series showing the minaret of Juma Mosque in Malé. Four denominations – 2, 3, 5 and 10c. – sufficed until 1933 when a photogravure version of the design was made by Harrison and Sons in denominations from 2c. to 1 rupee. The photogravure series remained in use till 1950.

PLATE 53 INDIAN OCEAN ISLANDS · PLATE 54 CHINA

10. Maldive Islands, 25 larees, 1956
The currency of the Maldives was changed to the rupee of 100 larees in 1950 and this necessitated a new definitive series, which was recess-printed by Bradbury Wilkinson with a motif of palm trees and a dhow. Bradbury Wilkinson also recess-printed the pictorial series of February 1956. The laree denominations depicted Malé Harbour while the three-rupee values showed the fort and administrative buildings.

11. Maldive Islands, 2 rupees, 1965
On 26 July 1965, the Maldive Islands left the British Commonwealth and became an independent sultanate. Since independence the output of stamps has been greatly increased and issues have been made to commemorate all manner of people and events with little or no direct connection with the island. The Austrian State Printing Works photogravure-printed a series of five stamps and a miniature sheet, issued in October 1965 in memory of John F. Kennedy. The stamps, featuring Kennedy and peace doves, may be found imperforate as well as perforated.

12. Maldive Islands, 1 rupee, 1968
A set of four stamps, lithographed in multicolour, was issued in January 1968 to further the Maldivian scout movement. Lord Baden-Powell's portrait was shown with scout and cub activities. The set was reissued the following August with an overprint commemorating the Scout Jamboree in Idaho.

13. Maldive Islands, 2 rupees, 1968
Every bandwagon, every passing philatelic craze, was duly noted by the Maldives and stamps issued accordingly. Thus a set of four stamps appeared in April 1968 reproducing famous landscape paintings by European artists. M. Shamir adapted the paintings and designed the frames while the stamps were lithographed by the Israeli Government Printer. The 2r. showed Monet's *Sailing Boat at Argenteuil*.

14. Maldive Islands, 2 rupees, 1970
The islands became a republic in November 1968 and stamps issued since that date have been appropriately inscribed. An unusual 'stained-glass' treatment was used by M. Shamir for sets of stamps issued in 1969–70 to commemorate the first Apollo moon landing and the 25th anniversary of the United Nations respectively. The six stamps marking the latter anniversary featured the emblems and aspects of work by the major UN agencies.

15. Maldive Islands, 25 larees, 1971
The problems and attitudes of the Third World are faithfully mirrored in the stamps of the Maldive Islands. Thus 10 and 25*l.* stamps were released in 1971 to mark Racial Equality Year. Shamir's stylized flower and globe motif in bold pastel colours was used for both stamps. Shamir has been responsible for virtually every design used by the Maldives since independence.

16. British Indian Ocean Territory, 10 rupees, 1968
The crown colony of the British Indian Ocean Territory was created in November 1967 and comprises the Chagos archipelago previously administered by Mauritius, together with the islands of Aldabra, Farquhar and Desroches formerly under the control of the Seychelles. The first stamps consisted of the contemporary definitive series of the Seychelles overprinted B.I.O.T. and released in January 1968. Most of the fifteen denominations (5*c*. to 10*r*.) have been recorded with missing stop varieties.

17. British Indian Ocean Territory, 10 rupees, 1968
A distinctive definitive series was issued in October

1968. Gordon Drummond adapted original sketches of Indian Ocean wild-life by Mrs W. Veevers-Carter and the stamps were lithographed in multicolour by De La Rue. 30, 60 and 85*c*. values in new designs were added to the series in December 1970 to meet increases in postal rates.

18. British Indian Ocean Territory, 1 rupee, 1971
The definitive series has been augmented at regular intervals by short thematic sets. The first of these appeared in December 1969 and illustrated ships connected with the islands. The second set of four was released in February 1971 and featured aspects of the Aldabra Nature Reserve. The stamps were designed by Gordon Drummond and lithographed in multicolour by Format International.

19. British Indian Ocean Territory, 3.50 rupees, 1971
The first commemorative stamp issued by the British Indian Ocean Territory appeared in June 1971 and marked the opening of the Royal Society Research Station on Aldabra. Victor Whiteley produced the design showing the arms of the Society and a flightless rail. The stamps were lithographed in multicolour by John Waddington of Kirkstall.

20. British Indian Ocean Territory, 1.50 rupees, 1969
Mrs M. Hayward produced the original drawings, from which Victor Whiteley did the final artwork, for the series of four stamps showing vessels connected with the islands. An outrigger canoe, sailing priogue, motor vessel *Nordvaer* and the schooner *Isle of Farquhar* formed the subjects of this set, lithographed in multicolour by De La Rue and issued in December 1969.

PLATE 54

China

1. 1 candarin, 1878
A westernized postal service was organized by the Chinese Imperial Customs and introduced adhesive stamps in October 1878 in denominations from 1 to 5*c*. Various types of paper, such as pelure, transparent and thick opaque were used for printings of this series between 1878 and 1883. The stamps, featuring an imperial dragon, were typographed at the Customs Statistical Department in Shanghai.

2. 1 candarin, 1885
A smaller, more compact design was adopted for the series issued between 1885 and 1894, also typographed by the Customs in Shanghai. The earliest printings (November 1885) were perforated 12½, and numerous varieties of partially imperforate stamps have been recorded. The printings of 1888 were perforated 11½ or 12.

3. 2 cents, 1897
Control of the postal services was transferred in 1897 to the Chinese Imperial Post, a separate government department. At the same time the currency of China was changed to the dollar or yuan of 100 cents. Stamps of the 1888 and 1894 series were surcharged with the new values in Chinese and English. This stamp was one of a series introduced in 1894, designed by R. A. de Villard and lithographed in Shanghai by transfers from stereotyped plates made by the Tokyo Tsukiji Foundry of Japan.

4. 4 cents, 1898
Stamps inscribed 'Imperial Chinese Post' were

introduced in August 1897. Six different designs were used for the values up to 10*c*., each having a dragon as the principal motif. The two designs used for the higher denominations featured carp and a flying goose. The stamps were designed by R. A. de Villard and typographed by the Tokyo Tsukiji company of Japan. The inscription on these stamps was emended the following year to read 'Chinese Imperial Post'. Paper without a watermark was adopted in 1902 and the colours of many stamps were changed between 1905 and 1910, new denominations being issued in the same period.

5. 2 cents, 1909
China's first commemorative issue consisted of three stamps, released in September 1909 to celebrate the first year of the reign of the boy emperor Hsuan T'ung. The stamps, illustrating the Temple of Heaven in Peking, were designed and engraved by L. J. Hatch and recess-printed by Waterlow and Sons. These stamps were the last to be issued by the Chinese Empire. Hsuan T'ung re-emerged in the 1930s as President Pu Yi of Manchukuo and subsequently became Emperor Kangteh (see plate 56).

6. 2 cents, 1912
The Manchu dynasty was toppled by a military revolt, backed by the republican movement of Dr Sun Yat-sen in October 1911. In January 1912 the stamps of the imperial series were released with a vertical overprint in Chinese characters signifying 'Provisional Neutrality', followed by similar overprints meaning 'Republic of China'. Overprints were applied to stamps in Foochow, Hankow, Nanking and Changsha and then a general series, overprinted in Shanghai or by Waterlows in London, was released later in the year. Numerous other overprints of a purely local nature have been recorded.

7. 4 cents, 1923
Waterlow and Sons recess-printed a republican definitive series in May 1913. The three designs featured a Chinese junk, a rice-cutter and the gateway to the Imperial Academy in Peking. The following year the designs were re-engraved by William A. Grant and stamps recess-printed by the Chinese Bureau of Engraving and Printing in Peking. The Chinese version differs from the London printing in paper, shade and minor details of the designs. The designs were again redrawn between 1923 and 1933 and in many cases new colours were adopted.

8. ½ cent, 1932
A set of twelve stamps was issued between 1932 and 1934 to commemorate martyrs of the 1912 revolution. Though primarily designated as a commemorative series this set was retained as a definitive issue and several denominations were subsequently reprinted by the Nationalists or by the Japanese occupying North China. The plates were manufactured by De La Rue and the stamps recess-printed by the Bureau of Engraving and Printing in Peking. The later versions differ in perforation, shade and watermark from the 1932 printing.

9. 300 yuan, 1946
Inflation overtook the Chinese economy at the end of World War II and stamps of obsolete issues were surcharged in Chinese National Currency (C.N.C.) in 1945–48. Stamps of the 1931–46 Sun Yat-sen definitive series were surcharged by the Union Printing Company of Shanghai in June 1946 in denominations from 20 to 5000 CNC yuan, but were rapidly superseded by even higher denominations as the inflation escalated. The basic stamps were typographed by the Chung Hwa Book Co. of

PLATE 54 CHINA · PLATE 55 PEOPLE'S REPUBLIC OF CHINA

Chungking in June 1944, at the wartime head-quarters of the Chinese National government.

10. 10 cents, 1948
The currency of Nationalist China was reformed in 1948 when the gold yuan of 100 cents was intro-duced. Stamps of preceding sets were overprinted with four Chinese characters to signify the re-valuation, from ½c. to 1y. Unfortunately the gold yuan collapsed even more rapidly than the CNC yuan and within a few months stamps with values as high as 5,000,000 gold yuan were being issued. The basic stamp illustrated here was typographed by the Dah Tung Book Co. of Chungking in 1945–46 in denominations from 2 to 20y.

11. 100 yuan, 1949
The thirteenth Chinese definitive series to portray the founder of the republic, Dr Sun Yat-sen, ap-peared in January 1949. The stamps, in denomina-tions from 1 to 1000 gold yuan, were originally recess-printed by the Dah Tung Book Co. of Shanghai. Subsequently this series was recess-printed by the Central Trust of Shanghai and lithographed by the Dah Tung Book Co. of Shanghai or the Hwa Nam Printing Co. of Chungking. Apart from the characteristics of the various printing processes there are minor differences in the details, impressions and colours of these stamps.

12. 250 yuan, 1947
A set of five stamps was recess-printed by the Central Trust, Peking, and issued on 5 May 1947, to mark the first anniversary of the return of the government to Nanking. The stamps showed the entrance to the mausoleum of Dr Sun Yat-sen. Similar stamps, with the inscription on the left altered, were also issued in the Chinese provinces of Formosa and the northeast.

13. 500 yuan, 1947
Four stamps were released between August and October 1947 to commemorate the philosopher Confucius. The stamps bore his portrait and also included the lecture school, temple and tomb of Confucius. The 500y. stamp was lithographed and the other three values recess-printed by the Dah Tung Book Co. of Shanghai.

14. 1,800 yuan, 1947
The modern developments of the postal services were highlighted in a series of four stamps issued in November 1947. The 500 and 1250y. denomina-tions featured a mobile post office while the 1000 and 18,000y. denominations showed a postal kiosk equipped with automatic vending machines. The stamps were recess-printed by the Central Trust in Peking.

15. 3,000 yuan, 1947
The last of the many commemorative sets released in 1947 consisted of three stamps celebrating the introduction of a new constitution. The Dah Tung Co. of Shanghai recess-printed the stamps in a common design showing the Book of the Consti-tution and the National Assembly building. Like many other Chinese stamps of this and later periods the stamps were released without gum.

16. 1.60 yuan, 1957
A new currency based on the silver yuan of 100c. was adopted in 1949, shortly after the Nationalist government withdrew from the mainland to For-mosa. This stamp was the top value in a series of three issued to mark the 50th anniversary of the Boy Scout movement. The stamps, having rosettes bearing the initials of Lord Baden-Powell and the Chinese Scout emblem, were designed by Liang Li-yu and recess-printed by the China Engraving and Printing Works, in Taipeh.

17. 40 cents, 1960
The Chü Kwang tower in Quemoy, symbol of Nationalist defiance of the Communist mainland, has appeared on three of the definitive sets issued since 1959. This stamp belongs to the second series, issued between 1960 and 1963. The stamps were lithographed on ordinary or granite paper in denominations from 3c. to 4.50y. The third series, issued in 1964–66, had a smaller vignette and an unshaded background.

18. 3.60 yuan, 1962
Before they evacuated the mainland the Nationalists succeeded in removing the bulk of China's art treasures to Formosa and these have provided the subject for many of the stamps issued in recent years. This stamp was the top value of the third series devoted to ancient Chinese artifacts and appeared in January 1962. The stamps were printed in multicolour photogravure at the Govern-ment Printing Works, Tokyo.

19. 80 cents, 1963
Two stamps were issued in September 1963 to mark the centenary of the International Red Cross. The 80c. showed a Red Cross nurse and the emblem, while the 10y. stamp featured a globe and a scroll. Before 1961 Chinese stamps of the nationalist regime seldom bore an identifying inscription in English but since that date it has been customary to incorporate the words 'Republic of China' in the design or in the margin.

20. 2 yuan, 1965
The close ties between the Nationalist regime and the United States are reflected in the many stamps with an American theme. Stamps were issued in May 1965 in honour of the New York World's Fair and featured the Unisphere and the Formosan pavilion (2y.) and a traditional picture of a hundred birds paying tribute to Queen Phoenix.

21. 10 yuan, 1966
In recent years Formosa has issued many stamps projecting a cosmopolitan outlook, unlike the stamps of the earlier period, which were intro-spective in character. A typical example of the modern approach is this stamp, issued in July 1966 to celebrate the 150th anniversary of Argentina's independence.

22. 1 yuan, 1969
Although photogravure is used for the majority of modern Chinese stamps recess still makes an occasional appearance. Two stamps of 1969 marked the tenth anniversary of the Forces' Savings Services and illustrated a soldier, sailor and airman with the savings emblem.

23. 4.50 yuan, 1971
Since 1968 Formosa has issued stamps for use on greetings cards at the Lunar New Year and, like the stamps of Hong Kong, Japan and the Ryukyu Islands, takes the zodiacal calendar system for its subjects. For the Year of the Squirrel a block of four stamps featuring squirrels was issued in a se-tenant formation. Each stamp is a self-contained unit but the four make up a composite design. The stamps, printed in deep-etched multicolour offset, were released in October 1971.

24. 3 yuan, 1972
In October 1971 the United Nations General Assembly voted for the expulsion of Nationalist China. This action inspired a definitive series, released in May 1972, bearing a motif of four Chinese characters signifying 'Dignity with Self-reliance' – the new motto of the Nationalists as they face increasing isolation from the rest of the world. The vermilion border round the central

vignette has been treated to react electronically to automatic facer-cancelling equipment, sorting do-mestic ordinary letters, while the green border of the 2.50y. (express letter mail) serves a similar purpose.

PLATE 55
People's Republic of China

Between 1929 and 1946 stamps were issued in many parts of China under the temporary control of the Communists after they broke away from the Kuomintang and began the series of guerrilla campaigns, first against the Nationalists and then against the Japanese. These stamps had only local validity, however, and are therefore outside the scope of this volume. At the end of World War II the Communists were in control of large areas of the Chinese mainland and gradually extended their dominion over all of the mainland, culminating with the expulsion of the Nationalists in 1949. During the period from 1945 to 1950 the political and economic upheavals were reflected in the issue of stamps in the various areas and provinces. In some cases these provincial issues remained in use until 1951, though a general series for use in the People's Republic as a whole was introduced in October 1949.

1. North East China, 1,500 yuan, 1949
Stamps were issued in North East China under Communist control from February 1946 till 1951. From November 1948 onward this area included the whole of Manchuria. The majority of these stamps portrayed Mao Tse-tung or featured sym-bolism of a political nature. This stamp was one of a set of five issued to mark Labour Day. The stamps were lithographed in two-colour combinations and depicted workers with banners.

2. North East China, 50,000 yuan, 1949
A vignette symbolizing production in field and industry was used for a definitive series ranging from 5,000 to 100,000y. The perforation of this series varies from 10 to 11 and the quality of the lithography is poor, reflecting the primitive con-ditions under which all aspects of government laboured at that time.

3. North East China, 1,500 yuan, 1949
Numerous commemorative issues appeared in this part of China during the brief period when it produced its own stamps. The stamps celebrated anniversaries of the Communist movement and the struggle against the Japanese or the Nationalists. This stamp was one of a set of three issued in August 1949 to mark the fourth anniversary of the Japanese surrender. It features the North East Heroes monument. The last commemorative issue appeared in December 1950 to mark the Sino-Soviet Treaty.

4. Port Arthur and Dairen, 100 yuan, 1949
The Communists occupied the Port Arthur and Dairen district in 1946, when the area was handed over to them by the Soviet troops who invaded Manchuria at the end of World War II. At first various stamps of Manchuria or Japan were over-printed, but in 1949 distinctive stamps inscribed in Chinese to signify 'Kwantung Postal and Tele-graphic General Administration' were released. Similar stamps inscribed to denote 'Port Arthur' appeared in July 1949.

5. Shensi-Kansu-Ninghsia, 1 yuan, 1948
Stamps were issued by the Communists in the large Shensi-Kansu-Ninghsia area from 1935 onwards

PLATE 55 PEOPLE'S REPUBLIC OF CHINA

but little is known of them outside their country of origin. The stamps issued from 1946 to 1949, however, have received catalogue status. All the stamps of this period showed the Yenan Pagoda and four different versions of this design, differing in minor details, were produced.

6. Central China, 80 yuan, 1949
After the Communists took Hankow stamps of the Nationalist Sun Yat-sen series were overprinted for use in Central China. Subsequently a series depicting a peasant, soldier and worker was lithographed by the Kuo Kwang Printing Co. of Hankow in denominations from 1 to 220y. A subsequent series portraying Chairman Mao was released in Honan.

7. Central China 290 yuan, 1949
A definitive series in values from 110 to 10,000 yuan was lithographed by the Kuo Kwang Printing Company of Hankow and released in July 1949. The common design featured a five-pointed star enclosing a map of the Hankow area. Similar stamps with four Chinese characters inscribed in the side panels were issued in November 1949 for parcel postage.

8. East China, 1 yuan, 1949
A large number of stamps was issued in East China between April 1949 and January 1950. Various stamps of the Nationalist government were surcharged with new values. This 10 yuan stamp of the Sun Yat-sen series was surcharged for use as a 1y. stamp at Nanking and issued in May 1949.

9. East China, 5 yuan, 1949
The victory of the Communists over the Nationalists at Hwai-Hai in January 1949 was celebrated by a series of stamps, lithographed at Tientsin in denominations from 1 to 100y. The design shows victorious troops and a map of the battle. Subsequent issues of East China celebrated the liberation of Shanghai and Nanking and portrayed Mao Tse-tung.

10. East China, 5 yuan, 1949
The liberation of Nanking and Shanghai by the Communists was celebrated in May 1949 by a series of nine stamps featuring maps of the two cities. The progress of the Communists in their bid to drive the Nationalists from the Chinese mainland was lavishly illustrated by special issues of stamps such as this.

11. East China, 500 yuan, 1949
The San Yih Printing Company of Shanghai lithographed a small format definitive series for East China in October 1949. The stamps, from 10 to 20,000y., portrayed Mao Tse-tung. These stamps surcharged with new values were subsequently used by the Chinese People's Republic.

12. North China, 6 yuan, 1949
Stamps were issued in North China between January and November 1949. Various stamps of China or North Eastern Provinces were overprinted to signify 'People's Postal Service North China'. In addition several distinctive sets marked Labour Day and the 28th anniversary of the Chinese Communist Party were issued as commemoratives and functioned as definitive sets. The last series, depicting the Gate of Heavenly Peace, Peking, was subsequently modified for use by the People's Republic.

13. North West China, 100 yuan, 1949
The Kwang Hwa Press in Sian lithographed a set of four stamps for use in North West China in October 1949. The 50 and 200y. portrayed Chairman Mao while the 100 and 400y. depicted the Great Wall of China. The 200y. is known in pink (the colour of the 50y.) instead of orange.

14. South China, 100 yuan, 1949
A set of five stamps, in denominations from 10 to 100y., was issued in November 1949 in South China to celebrate the liberation of Canton. The stamps featured the Ho Nam Bridge in Canton and were lithographed and imperforate. Subsequently these stamps were surcharged with new values, from 300 to 1000y.

15. South West China, 20 yuan, 1950
Stamps were issued in South West China between December 1949 and February 1950. The first series, portraying Mao Tse-tung, General Chu Teh and marching troops, was lithographed by the San Yih Printing Co. of Shanghai in denominations from 10 to 5,000y. Similar stamps, in other values, had been produced in East China the previous August by the Dah Tung Book Co. of Shanghai. Subsequently South West China issued this series additionally overprinted for use in East or West Szechwan. One of the last issues was a set of four stamps, issued in January 1950, celebrating the liberation of the South West and showing the Communist flag over a map of the area.

16. Chinese People's Republic, 100 yuan, 1949
The first stamps issued for use throughout the People's Republic appeared in October 1949 and consisted of a set of four celebrating the first session of the Chinese People's Political Conference. The stamps, featuring the Gate of Heavenly Peace, were lithographed by the Commercial Press, Shanghai. These and many other Chinese stamps up to 1952 were reprinted for sale to collectors in 1955–56 but could be used postally. The reprints differ in minor detail from the original printings.

17. 50 yuan, 1950
Various stamps of East China were overprinted for general use, and surcharged with new values in December 1950. This stamp, one of a series portraying Chairman Mao, was originally lithographed by the San Yih Printing Co. of Shanghai and issued in October 1949. Many provincial issues were surcharged in this way and revalidated for use throughout the People's Republic in 1949–50.

18. 1,000 yuan, 1951
The People's Printing Works, Shanghai, recess-printed a set of five stamps for airmail purposes in May 1951. The common design of the series, from 1,000 to 30,000y., showed an aircraft over the Temple of Heaven in Peking. The majority of Chinese stamps, from 1951 to 1961, were either lithographed or recess-printed.

19. 800 yuan, 1952
A set of four stamps was issued in August 1952 to mark the 25th anniversary of the People's Liberation Army. All four stamps were of 800y. value – a feature of commemorative issues in China and North Vietnam which has now begun to spread to other countries in recent years. The stamps of this series depicted servicemen and weapons of the different branches of the armed forces.

20. 800 yuan, 1952
The Asia and Pacific Ocean Peace Conference held in October 1952 was celebrated by a set of four stamps recess-printed by the Dayeh Printing Company of Shanghai. Two stamps featured a map of the Pacific area and two a globe of the world. All four stamps incorporated a reproduction of the Dove of Peace painted by Pablo Picasso.

21. 400 yuan, 1952
Postage stamps have been put to some curious uses, but none more so than that to which the Chinese series of 1952 was applied. Between 20 June and 23 July 1952, 400y. stamps were issued in ten different colours. Each colour represented a block of four stamps each of which showed a different stage of a gymnastic exercise. These 40 different stamps were designed to be used in conjunction with a radio programme of exercises. The stamps were lithographed by the East China Revenue Office, Shanghai.

22. 8 fen, 1960
The currency was reformed in 1955 and the yuan of 100 fen introduced. From the late 1950s onwards the People's Republic has issued numerous thematic sets. In June 1960 a set of five stamps, all of 8f. denomination, illustrated aspects of pig-breeding. The stamps were printed in two-colour photogravure by the People's Printing Works, Shanghai.

23. 50 fen, 1963
A set of twenty stamps, depicting butterflies, was released between April and July 1963. Five stamps were issued in denominations of 4, 8 and 10f., two at 20f. and one each at 22, 30 and 50f. A useful feature of these stamps, which aids identification in cases where several stamps are issued in the same denomination, is the serial number which appears alongside the date in the margin of the design.

24. 8 fen, 1967
Whereas the stamps of most Communist countries have become more thematic and less political with the passage of time, those of the Chinese People's Republic have become more political and less thematic, particularly since the Cultural Revolution of 1966. This stamp was one of a pair of 8f. stamps issued in April 1967 to publicize the third Five Year Plan. Its motif of red flags, increased industrial and agricultural output and workers brandishing weapons and the Thoughts of Chairman Mao typify current Chinese stamp design. Though printed in multicolour photogravure the predominant colour is always red.

25. 8 fen, 1968
From 1967 onward the vast majority of Chinese stamps have had two subjects only – portraits of Chairman Mao and quotations from his poems, his speeches and his thoughts. In many cases the stamps have had no other pretension to a design other than epigrams of Mao. Ironically several of these sets have borne epigrams on Mao by the late Lin Piao, who paid with his life, in 1971, for attempting to oust the Chairman. This stamp, issued in 1968, belongs to the second series of the Chairman's thoughts and was the last stamp freely available to the international stamp trade. Subsequently the official export agency was closed down and the supply of stamps has become exceedingly irregular. Significantly it is only within recent years that trading in the stamps of the Chinese People's Republic has been permitted in the United States.

PLATE 56 CHINESE PROVINCES

PLATE 56
Chinese Provinces

The stamps grouped on this plate are those issued in the provinces of China at various times since 1915, other than those noted in the previous plate as having been issued under the authority of the Communists. The provincial issues may be divided into three broad categories – those issued between 1915 and World War II, those issued under Japanese authority and those issued between 1945 and 1949 during the closing phases of the civil war between the Communists and the Nationalists.

1. Sinkiang, 1 dollar, 1915
Because the currency used in Sinkiang (Chinese Turkestan) had a different value from that in other parts of China the definitive issues for that province had to be overprinted from 1915 onwards. The first overprint had the top character out of alignment, but this was corrected the following year. The 1 dollar stamp (first overprint) has also been recorded with the second and third characters transposed. Sinkiang continued to use Chinese stamps with a distinctive overprint until 1949, when the province was absorbed by the People's Republic.

2. Yunnan, 1 dollar, 1929
For the same reason stamps with a distinctive overprint were issued in Yunnan from 1926 to 1934. As well as the definitive series various commemoratives were treated in this way, including the Sun Yat-sen memorial series of 1929.

3. Szechwan, 40 cents, 1933
Chinese stamps with a five-character overprint were issued in the province of Szechwan in 1933–34 only. Among the stamps thus treated were the Martyrs series of 1933–34 in denominations from ½ to 50c. This stamp portrays General Huang Hsing, who lost his life in the interminable civil wars which had rent China since the revolution of 1912. Ordinary Chinese stamps were used in Szechwan after 1934.

4. Kirin and Heilungchang, 4 cents, 1929
Chinese definitives with a five-character overprint were introduced in this part of Manchuria in 1927 and continued in use until 1931, when the Japanese overran this area. As well as the definitive series three commemorative sets were issued. the latter with an overprint of four characters. These stamps commemorated Chang Tso-lin (1928), the unification of China and the Sun Yat-sen memorial (both 1929). Manchurian stamps were adopted in 1932 and subsequently the stamps of North-East China and the People's Republic were used.

5. Manchukuo, 3 fen, 1934
Manchuria was invaded by Japanese troops in 1931 and the following year the puppet republic of Manchukuo was established under the presidency of Pu Yi, who, as a little boy, had been the last Manchu emperor of China. In 1934 Manchukuo became an empire and Pu Yi ascended the throne a second time, under the title of the Emperor Kangteh. A pictorial definitive series was introduced in July 1932. The first printings were lithographed but in February 1934 a recess-printed version appeared. Later the same year the inscription was re-engraved to incorporate an extra character signifying 'Imperial', after the Empire had been proclaimed.

6. Manchukuo, 13 fen, 1937
The early stamps of Manchukuo were produced in Tokyo, but from 1935 onward many stamps were lithographed at the Central Bank Printing Bureau in Hsinking. Four stamps were issued in 1935 to prepay postage on mail to China and featured either the orchids of Kaoliang or the Sacred White Mountains and Black Waters. Various denominations were added to this series up to 1945. Those stamps issued after 1936 were recess-printed.

7. Manchukuo, 39 fen, 1937
The Central Bank Printing Bureau recess-printed a new definitive series in December 1936 of various landscapes. An aeroplane was incorporated in the design of the 18 and 19f. stamps featuring a shepherd (inland airmail), and a similar motif, with the railway bridge over the River Sungari, was used on the 38 and 39f. stamps prepaying airmail correspondence to Japan. All stamps of Manchukuo issued from 1935 onward incorporated an orchid emblem as a guide to identification.

8. Manchukuo, 2½ fen, 1937
The orchids of Kaoliang were featured on the low-value stamps for mail going to China. In 1937 the rate was increased from 2 to 2½f. and various obsolete stamps were surcharged in Chinese characters to signify 'Temporarily to make two fen five li'. In July 1937 the 2f. stamp was re-engraved to convert it to a 2½f. stamp and was printed in violet instead of green.

9. Manchukuo, 2 fen, 1940
A set of four stamps was issued in 1935 to celebrate the first visit of the Emperor Kangteh to Japan. Five years later his second visit rated only two stamps. Yo-ai Ohta designed 2 and 4f. stamps showing storks flying over the Manchu flag, a delicate motif in the best traditions of Japanese natural symbolism. The stamps were printed in photogravure at the Japanese Government Printing Bureau, Tokyo.

10. Manchukuo, 40 fen, 1944
Several commemorative sets appeared during World War II, mostly emphasizing the alignment of Manchukuo with Japan and anniversaries of the Greater East Asia War. In 1944, 10 and 40f. stamps were issued to mark friendship between Japan and Manchukuo. The stamps were printed in Japanese and Chinese characters alternately throughout the sheet.

11. Kwangtung, 3 sen, 1936
Japan issued a set of three stamps in September 1936 to celebrate the 30th anniversary of the lease. As these stamps were only valid for postage in the leased territory and in the South Manchurian Railway Zone they should be regarded as the first stamps of Kwangtung, though they are invariably catalogued under Japan proper.

12. Kwangtung, 30 cents, 1942
Japanese forces occupied Kwangtung in 1906 after the Russo-Japanese War and leased the territory from the Chinese government until the outbreak of World War II, when the entire Kwangtung area was taken over. Contemporary Chinese stamps were given a four-character overprint in an ornamental frame to signify 'Special for Kwangtung'. Subsequently an overprint of four characters, one in each corner, was applied to various Chinese stamps in denominations from 2c. to 20y. Provisional surcharges of 200 or 400y. were made at Canton and Swatow for use in Kwangtung in 1945.

13. Mengkiang, 4 cents, 1943
Japanese and Manchu troops invaded Mengkiang (Inner Mongolia) in 1937 and established the autonomous state of the Mongolian Marches in November of that year. Distinctive stamps did not appear, however, until July 1941, when contemporary Chinese stamps were overprinted with two characters to signify 'Mengkiang'. A similar overprint, with two additional characters signifying the value, was applied to Chinese stamps in June 1942. Distinctive stamps marking anniversaries of the Mengkiang postal service and the federation of autonomous provinces of Mongolia appeared in 1943 and subsequent issues celebrated the second anniversary of the war in Asia and publicized the government's campaign for increased production.

14. North China, 4 cents, 1942
At first the Japanese authorities in North China were content to use contemporary Chinese stamps of the Sun Yat-sen and Martyrs series and in 1941 went so far as to have printings made of these stamps. The so-called 'New Peking Printings' differ from the originals in many respects, being generally of a poorer quality in paper, ink and production. In July 1941 these stamps were issued with provincial overprints, consisting of two characters signifying Honan, Hopei, Shansi, Shantung and Supeh. Similar overprints were also issued in Mengkiang (see above). In June 1942 the stamps were issued with a four-character overprint, the upper characters signifying 'North China' and the lower characters denoting half the original face value. Distinctive stamps commemorating North China's autonomy appeared in 1945.

15. Shanghai and Nanking, 5 yuan, 1944
The famous Purple Mountain of Nanking was selected as the motif for two stamps issued in March 1944, to celebrate the fourth anniversary of the establishment of the Chinese Puppet Government under Japanese control. The design of these stamps demonstrates the extent to which the puppet regime eschewed everything Occidental – even to the extent of doing away with European numerals to express the value.

16. Shanghai and Nanking, 20 sen, 1941
Stamps were issued between 1941 and 1945 for use in the areas along the River Yangtze under Japanese occupation but nominally controlled by the puppet Nanking government. The first issue consisted of prewar Chinese airmail stamps surcharged in Japanese currency from 10 to 35s. Subsequent issues were surcharged in Chinese currency.

17. Shanghai and Nanking, 30 yuan, 1945
The only distinctive stamps issued by the regime in Shanghai and Nanking appeared in 1944–45 to mark the fourth and fifth anniversaries of the establishment of the puppet government. Four stamps marking the fourth anniversary featured wheat and a cotton flower or the Purple Mountain, Nanking. The fifth anniversary set consisted of the previous issue surcharged in new values from 15 to 200y., to take account of the galloping inflation which overtook China at the end of the war. Ironically the last issue of the Shanghai government consisted of stamps overprinted with a bomb to publicize air raid precautions.

18. Formosa, 5 sen, 1946
The island of Formosa (Taiwan) was ceded by China to Japan after the Sino-Japanese War of 1895 and was returned to China in 1945 at the end of World War II. Japanese stamps were prepared for issue in Formosa in a numeral and chrysanthemum motif but were not issued on account of the Japanese surrender. Subsequently, however, these stamps were overprinted in Chinese characters to signify 'Taiwan Province, Chinese Republic'. Chinese stamps with a distinctive overprint and surcharged in Japanese currency were introduced in 1946.

PLATE 56 CHINESE PROVINCES · PLATE 57 FOREIGN POST OFFICES IN CHINA

19. Formosa, 10 yuan, 1947
From 1947 to 1949 Chinese definitive and commemorative sets were re-designed for use in Formosa because Japanese currency continued to circulate there. Among the sets issued in this period were the commemoratives marking Chiang Kai-shek's 60th birthday and the first anniversary of the return of the government to Nanking. Definitive issues were similar in design to those used in China proper but the value tablets had small underlined noughts to denote 'sen'. From November 1949 Formosa was directly controlled by the remnants of the Nationalist forces. Subsequent issues of Formosa will be found in plate 54.

20. North-Eastern Provinces, 100 yuan, 1947
Because of differences in the value of money after World War II separate issues of stamps had to be provided for the north-eastern provinces. Contemporary stamps of China were overprinted to signify 'limited for use in the North East' and surcharged with new values. Definitive stamps similarly inscribed were released in 1946–47 and the Chiang Birthday and Nanking Government commemoratives were likewise released with distinctive inscriptions. These stamps were superseded by the Communist issues of North East China in November 1948 (see plate 55).

21. North-Eastern Provinces, 1 yuan, 1947
The North-eastern Provinces possessed the only provincial postal administration to issue its own distinctive postage due stamps. A set of six, from 10c. to 5y., was recess-printed in 1947 and reissued the following year with surcharges from 10 to 50y.

22. Chinese Post Office in Tibet, 2 annas, 1911
Chinese post offices were established at Gyantse, Lhasa, Phari Jong, Shigatse and Yatung in 1911 and contemporary Chinese stamps were overprinted in Chinese, English and Tibetan to denote the value in Indian currency. The stamps ranged from 3 pies on 1 cent, to 2 rupees on 2 yuan. The 3 annas on 16 cents is known with a large inverted 's' in 'Annas'. These stamps were in use for a very short time, the Chinese post offices being suppressed in 1912.

PLATE 57

Foreign Post Offices in China

The commercial exploitation of China in modern times stemmed from the Treaty of Nanking (1842), which permitted Britain, and later other occidental powers, to trade in certain seaports. By the end of the nineteenth century post offices were maintained in the major cities and seaports by Britain, France, Germany, Italy and Russia and, in addition, both Japan and the United States were competing in this field. The Boxer Rebellion did little to check foreign encroachment but during and immediately after World War I the foreign post offices were gradually suppressed. For the sake of convenience the International Post Office in Shanghai is also included in this group, since it was organized by, and for the use of, the foreign mercantile community.

1. British Post Offices in China, 50 cents, 1917
British consular post offices were established at Amoy, Canton, Foochow and Ningpo in 1844 and handstruck stamps were used till 1862, when the adhesive stamps of Hong Kong were adopted. These may be recognized by the distinctive postmarks of the Chinese offices. Control of the British post offices was transferred from Hong Kong to London in 1917 and as a result distinctive stamps

were adopted. These consisted of the contemporary Hong Kong series overprinted 'CHINA'. Both Multiple Crown CA and Multiple Script CA watermarked sets were used. These stamps were withdrawn in October 1930, when the British post offices in China were suppressed.

2. French Post Offices in China, 5 centimes, 1894
A French post office was established in Shanghai in the mid-nineteenth century and used ordinary French stamps, distinguished by the numeral obliterator 5104 (large figures). Contemporary French stamps overprinted 'Chine' were introduced in 1894. This series, from 5c. to 5f., was released without surcharge, though various provisional surcharges appeared at Tientsin, Shanghai and Peking between 1900 and 1903.

3. French Post Offices in China, 6 cents, 1915
The Blanc, Mouchon and Merson keytype designs inscribed 'Chine' were issued in 1902–03. The values in Chinese currency were surcharged from 1907 onwards in both French and Chinese. The French post offices (with the exception of Kouang-Tcheou) were closed on 31 December 1922, and the distinctive stamps withdrawn from use.

4. Canton, 4 cents, 1908
The French general series continued to be used in Peking, Shanghai and Tientsin, but the remaining seven post offices were given sets with distinctive overprints, beginning with Canton in 1901. Contemporary stamps of Indochina were overprinted with the name of the office in French and Chinese, and, from 1919, were additionally surcharged in Chinese currency. These stamps were withdrawn at the end of 1922.

5. Hoi-Hao, 1⅗ cents, 1919
Indochinese stamps overprinted 'Hoi Hao' in French and Chinese were introduced in 1902 in denominations from 1c. to 5f. In 1903–04 the value was surcharged in Chinese characters and this was retained in successive sets issued in 1906 and 1908. In 1919 the series was further surcharged in Chinese currency, but in Western numerals and lettering. This series ranged from ⅗ cent on 1 centime, to 4 piastres on 10 francs. These stamps were likewise withdrawn at the end of 1922.

6. Kouang-Tcheou-Wan, 25 centimes, 1906
Indochinese stamps of the 'Tablet' keyplate series and the 'Grasset' series were issued in this city in October 1906, overprinted 'Kouang Tchéou-Wan' and surcharged with the value in Chinese characters. The series ranged from 1c. to 10f. The Chinese subsequently leased Kouang-Tcheou and surrounding district to France, and new overprints, omitting the suffix 'Wan', were released in 1908.

7. Kouang-Tcheou, ⅕ cent, 1927
Kouang-Tcheou used overprinted Indochinese stamps on the same lines as the other French post offices in China, but being a leased territory continued to use distinctive stamps after the other French post offices were closed in 1922. The Indochinese pictorial definitive series of 1927, from 1/10th centime to 2 piastres, was issued with a distinctive overprint in September of that year.

8. Kouang-Tcheou, 3 cents, 1941
The 1931–41 definitive series of Indochina was released in Kouang-Tcheou with a larger overprint. The stamps ranged from 3 to 70c. and appeared in 1941–42. The district was occupied by Japanese troops in 1942 and though nominally allied to the Vichy French administration they gradually took over all public services including the posts. Various stamps of Indochina, issued under the authority of the Vichy regime, were overprinted 'Kouang-

'Tcheou' between 1942 and 1944 but it is doubtful whether any were used postally. Kouang-Tcheou was surrendered to the Chinese authorities in 1945 and has used the stamps of China ever since.

9. Mongtze, 1 franc, 1903
The 'Tablet' series of Indochina, from 1c. to 5f., was overprinted 'Mongtze' and surcharged in Chinese characters. This series was issued in 1903, and the 25 and 50c. in new colours were added in 1906.

10. Mong-Tseu, 1 centime, 1908
Indochinese stamps with the name spelled 'Mong-Tseu' according to French orthography were released in October 1906. The 'Grasset' series was superseded in 1908 by the series designed by J. Puyplat depicting Indochinese women. The surcharges in Chinese currency appeared in 1919 and three years later the stamps were discontinued.

11. Pakhoi, 2 centimes, 1908
Indochinese stamps with a distinctive overprint were adopted in Pakhoi in April 1903. The 'Tablet' series had the name rendered as 'Packhoi', while the 'Grasset' series bore the spelling 'Pak-Hoi'. The Puyplat series of 1908–19 used the spelling 'Pakhoi'. These stamps were withdrawn at the end of 1922.

12. Tchongking, 1 centime, 1906
Stamps with a distinctive overprint were adopted in this post office in 1903, the 'Tablet' series of Indochina being overprinted 'Tchongking' and surcharged in Chinese characters. The 'Grasset' series was released in October 1906 with the overprint rendered as 'Tch'ong K'ing'.

13. Tchongking, 4 centimes, 1908
The more modern spelling was resumed in 1908 when the pictorial series was issued. The series additionally surcharged with values in Chinese currency appeared in January 1919. The stamps of Tchongking were suppressed in December 1922.

14. Yunnansen, 10 centimes, 1903
The 'Tablet' series was released with the overprint 'Yunnansen' and values in Chinese characters in 1903–04. The 75c. value of this series is known with the name in the label inverted. This error is also recorded on the corresponding denomination overprinted for Canton, Hoi-Hao, and Mong-Tseu. The city of Yunnan was elevated in status in 1905 and this was denoted by the change in name from Yunnansen to Yunnan-Fou. Stamps from 1906 onwards were thus overprinted.

15. Yunnan-Fou, 1 centime, 1908
The pictorial series of Indochina overprinted 'Yunnanfou' was released in 1908, replacing the series of October 1906, in which the name had been rendered as 'Yunnan-Fou'. The 2, 5 and 10f. denominations of the 1908 series are known with the error 'Yunannfou' in the overprint. The Chinese currency surcharge appeared in January 1919 and the series was withdrawn three years later.

16. German Post Offices in China, 20 pfennigs, 1901
A German post office was opened in Shanghai in 1886 and offices were eventually established in eleven other Chinese cities. Ordinary German stamps were used until 1898 and may be recognized by their postmarks. Stamps with a diagonal overprint 'China' were issued between 1898 and 1901, followed by the Reichspost 'Germania' series with horizontal overprint in January 1901. This series ranged from 3pf. to 5m. and was released gradually between 1901 and 1904.

17. German Post Offices in China, 1 cent, 1905
The 'Deutsches Reich' Germania series was released

in October 1905 additionally surcharged in Chinese currency from 1c. to $2½. The original printings were unwatermarked, but between 1905 and 1911 the lozenge watermark was introduced. The German post offices in China were suppressed in 1917.

18. **Peking, 40 centesimi, 1917**
Italian post offices were established in Peking and Tientsin in 1917, taking advantage of the suppression of the German agencies. Contemporary Italian stamps were overprinted 'Pechino' in September 1917. A handstruck overprint included surcharges in Chinese currency, but a typographed overprint made at Turin was merely inscribed 'Pechino' in upper and lower case lettering. In 1918–19 these stamps were issued with the surcharge in Chinese values. Express letter and postage due stamps were similarly overprinted for use in Peking.

19. **Tientsin, 1 centesimo, 1917**
The Italian stamps issued at Tientsin followed the same pattern as those issued in Peking. Numerous errors and varieties exist in the first, handstruck overprints. The Turin overprints, without surcharge, were released in December 1917 and were followed in 1918–19 with stamps additionally surcharged from ½ cent to 2 dollari. The Italian post offices, like the French, were closed down at the end of 1922.

20. **Japanese Post Offices in China, 5 rin, 1900**
Japanese post offices were established in China in the 1890s and used ordinary Japanese stamps with distinctive postmarks. Contemporary Japanese stamps were released in 1900 with two characters overprinted at the foot of the design to denote usage in China. The series of 1900–08, like the stamps current in Japan itself at that time, vary considerably in shade and perforation.

21. **Japanese Post Offices in China, 3 sen, 1900**
Apart from the definitive series Japan issued the 3s. stamp commemorating the wedding of the Prince Imperial with the two-character overprint for use in China. Subsequently stamps of the 1913 and 1914–19 definitive sets were similarly overprinted. Japanese stamps overprinted for use in China were withdrawn at the end of 1922.

22. **Russian Post Offices in China, 1 kopek, 1899**
Russian stamps of the 1899–1904 definitive series were released between 1899 and 1908 with a diagonal overprint 'Kitai' in Cyrillic to denote usage in China. Stamps of the 1909–12 definitive series were similarly overprinted between 1910 and 1917. Numerous instances of inverted overprint have been recorded in the 1910–17 series.

23. **Russian Post Offices in China, 2 cents, 1917**
The 'Kitai' overprints were superseded in 1917 by contemporary Russian stamps surcharged in Chinese currency in English, without any overprint to designate the country itself. The kopek denominations were surcharged with corresponding values in cents, and the rouble values with their dollar counterparts. The surcharges were applied diagonally in capital lettering, but a new series appeared in 1920 with the surcharges in upper and lower case lettering applied horizontally. These were withdrawn at the end of 1922.

24. **United States Post Offices in Shanghai, 4 cents, 1919**
Ordinary American stamps were used in the American post offices in China until July 1919, when the contemporary definitive series was overprinted 'Shanghai China' with values in Chinese currency. These overprints became necessary, owing to the confusion between American and Chinese

cents, the latter being worth only half the former. These stamps were withdrawn at the end of 1922.

25. **Shanghai, 20 cash, 1884**
The first postal service on European lines in China was established in Shanghai in 1865 for the convenience of the foreign mercantile community and a further thirteen years elapsed before the Imperial authorities followed suit. The definitive issues of the International Post Office in Shanghai featured the Chinese dragon and were valued in candareens (1865–66 and 1867–77) or cents (1866–72). Stamps surcharged in cash appeared in 1879–84 and were superseded by stamps inscribed in this currency. The stamps from 1866 to 1893 were lithographed by Nissen and Parker (later Nissen and Arnold) of London.

26. **Shanghai, 2 cents, 1893**
The jubilee of the first European settlement in Shanghai was marked by this stamp released in December 1893. The design, by R. de Villard, shows the female figure of Commerce, the rising sun and a winged wheel symbolizing communications. After the establishment of the Chinese Imperial Post Office in 1878 the postal service of Shanghai had local status, though continuing to be recognized internationally until 1898, when the Chinese authorities suppressed the postal service.

27. **Shanghai, 1 cent, 1893**
A new definitive series, typographed by Barclay and Fry of London, was introduced in 1893. The stamps, from ½ to 20c., featured the coat of arms of the Shanghai municipality.

28. **Shanghai, ½ cent, 1893**
The series was subsequently overprinted diagonally in Gothic script to celebrate the 50th anniversary of the European settlement. The 1c. is known with this overprint double.

29. **Chefoo, 5 cents, 1893**
Following the example of Shanghai, the European merchant communities in the other treaty ports established their own postal services. Unlike Shanghai these services never enjoyed international recognition and the stamps had local status only. Their heyday was the 1890s, when attractive pictorial sets were produced with increasing frequency, with an eye to philatelic revenue rather than the performance of a real postal service.

30. **Chinese Expeditionary Force, 3 pies, 1900**
During the Boxer Rebellion of 1900 Indian stamps overprinted C.E.F. were provided for the use of the Chinese Expeditionary Force, the British Imperial troops who took part in the suppression of the rising. Stamps with the profile of King Edward VII were similarly overprinted in 1904–09 and the Georgian series was likewise issued between 1913 and 1921. These stamps were used by British and Indian garrisons in China up to 1922, when distinctive stamps were withdrawn.

PLATE 58

European Colonies in China

---

1. **Hong Kong, 48 cents, 1862**
Hong Kong must rank as one of the most philatelically conservative countries in the world. Adhesive stamps were adopted in 1862 and for forty years had the same design, with a profile of Queen Victoria in a simple frame inscribed in Chinese and English. The stamps were typographed by De La Rue, who held the Hong Kong contracts, with one

exception, for exactly a century. The Victorian series went through variations of watermark (1863 and 1882) and countless nuances of shade, but it was the plethora of provisional surcharges which relieved what might otherwise have been a very monotonous period.

2. **Hong Kong, 2 cents, 1891**
Hong Kong was one of the earliest British colonies to issue a commemorative stamp. The 2c. definitive stamp was released in January 1891 with a four-line overprint to celebrate the 50th anniversary of the British occupation. Apart from double overprints, examples with misshapen letters have been recorded. The overprint was applied to one row of stamps at a time and thus there are twelve varieties differing in minor details.

3. **Hong Kong, 1 cent, 1903**
For the definitive series portraying King Edward VII De La Rue abandoned the Victorian design and adopted a more elaborate style of frame and vignette. Many of the stamps were enlivened by printing the frame and vignette in different colours, though single working plates were adopted between 1907 and 1911. The first printings were on single watermarked paper but the multiple Crown CA watermark was introduced in 1904.

4. **Hong Kong, 2 cents, 1912**
De La Rue modified the Edwardian series in 1912 to show a profile of King George V. At the same time the inscriptions were redrawn and in some cases the numerals of value were placed in the lower corners, replacing the swastika-shaped ornaments of the previous series. The original series, released between 1912 and 1921, was printed on multiple Crown CA paper, but the multiple Script CA paper was gradually adopted between 1921 and 1937. For stamps of this series overprinted 'China' see plate 57.

5. **Hong Kong, 8 cents, 1941**
De La Rue revived the simple Victorian design for the definitive series of 1938 portraying King George VI. The frame was modified to include two small crowns in the upper corners but otherwise the design was unchanged. A number of stamps were issued with new perforations in 1941, after De La Rue's premises had been bombed. An increase in postal rates led to the introduction of this 8c. denomination in November 1941. A month later Hong Kong was invaded by the Japanese and British colonial stamps were withdrawn. The Georgian series was re-introduced after World War II and, with various changes of colour, was issued up to 1952.

6. **Hong Kong, 1 dollar, 30 cents, 1960**
The first Elizabethan definitive series retained the Georgian frame and substituted a profile of Queen Elizabeth. The original series, from 5c. to $10, was released in January 1954, but 65c. and $1.30 denominations were added in June 1960.

7. **Hong Kong, 2 cents, 1941**
Hong Kong took part in the various colonial omnibus sets of 1935–37 but did not produce a distinctive commemorative series until February 1941, when a set of six stamps was issued to celebrate the centenary of the British occupation. The stamps, depicting views of the city and harbour, were designed by the local artist, W. E. Jones, and recess-printed by Bradbury Wilkinson.

8. **Hong Kong, 1 dollar, 1946**
Hong Kong did not participate in the colonial omnibus issue marking victory after World War II, but, as a special dispensation, was permitted to issue stamps in a distinctive design. The 30c. and $1

PLATE 58 EUROPEAN COLONIES IN CHINA · PLATE 59 KOREA

stamps were designed by W. E. Jones while in a Japanese internment camp and show the phoenix rising from the flames of enemy occupation. The stamps were recess-printed by De La Rue.

9. Hong Kong, 20 cents, 1962

De La Rue's century-old monopoly of Hong Kong stamp production was broken in 1961 when Harrison and Sons printed a $1 stamp in photogravure to mark the golden jubilee of Hong Kong University. The following year a set of three stamps marked the centenary of the first stamps. One might have expected a motif reproducing the Victorian series of 1862 would be printed by De La Rue, but instead the contract went to Harrisons, who illustrated the statue of Queen Victoria and an inset portrait of Queen Elizabeth.

10. Hong Kong, 20 dollars, 1962

A new definitive series was issued in October 1962 and broke entirely with tradition by reproducing the Annigoni portrait of the Queen in a simple design. The stamps up to $1 were in a small monochrome design, but the higher denominations, from $1.30 to $20, were printed in multicolour. Between 1966 and 1970 the stamps were reissued on paper with the watermark sideways. Stamps of this series may also be found with either gum arabic or polyvinyl alcohol gum.

11. Hong Kong, 1 dollar, 30 cents, 1967

Victor Whiteley designed 10c. and $1.30 stamps issued in January 1967 to mark the lunar new year. Since then an issue of stamps has appeared annually for this occasion. The series of 1967, marking the Year of the Ram, depicted ram's-head lanterns (10c.) and three rams ($1.30). The stamps were printed in three-colour photogravure by Harrison and Sons.

12. Hong Kong, 1 dollar, 30 cents, 1967

This stamp was issued in March 1967 to mark the completion of the Malaysia–Hong Kong link in the SEACOM telephone cable. Whiteley's design shows the silhouette of a telephone enclosing a map of the cable route—a neat way of putting across the message.

13. Hong Kong, 20 cents, 1968

A series of six stamps, designed and lithographed be De La Rue, was issued in April 1968 with the theme of sea craft. The Queen's profile was silhouetted against a Chinese bamboo lattice effect and the vignettes were of traditional and occidental forms of shipping. This interesting entry into the purely thematic field has not so far been followed up.

14. Hong Kong, 1 dollar, 1968

The 65c. and $1 denominations of the Annigoni portrait series were replaced in September 1968 by stamps designed by Victor Whiteley. The 65c. illustrated the flower *Bauhinia blakeana* while the $1 showed the coat of arms. The Annigoni portrait was inset on the lower value but the royal monogram was used on the $1 denomination.

15. Hong Kong, 1 dollar 30 cents, 1969

To mark the Year of the Cock, the lunar new year stamps of February 1969 featured cockerels. Both designs were produced by Richard Granger-Barrett and printed in multicolour photogravure by Enschedé.

16. Hong Kong, 1 dollar, 1969

Cashing in on the worldwide popularity of stamps with a space theme Hong Kong issued this stamp in September 1969 to mark the opening of the satellite tracking station. The stamp, designed by Whiteley and printed in multicolour photogravure

by Harrisons, shows the earth station and a communications satellite.

17. Hong Kong, 15 cents, 1970

Bradbury Wilkinson designed and lithographed in multicolour stamps in denominations of 15 and 25c. to mark the Osaka World's Fair of 1970. A relatively simple design incorporating the Expo emblem was used for the 15c. stamp, while the 25c. denomination had Chinese junks and the emblem in a horizontal design.

18. Hong Kong, 2 dollars, 1971

The Chinese system of anniversaries prefers the figure 60 to the European system of 100 and thus it was fitting that stamps should be issued in 1971 to mark the diamond jubilee of the Hong Kong Boy Scouts' Association. Three stamps, in a common design featuring the numerals and the fleur-de-lis emblem, were designed by staff artists of Harrison and Sons, who printed the stamps in multicolour lithography.

19. Kiautschou, 3 pfennigs, 1901

Germany seized the Chinese port of Kiautschou (Kiao-Tcheou) in 1897 after the murder of some German missionaries by the local populace. German stamps overprinted for use in China were used until 1901, when the Hohenzollern keytype series was introduced. In 1900, however, a shortage of 5pf. stamps was met by surcharging the 10pf. denomination of the Chinese overprinted series at Tsingtau, and these provisionals are therefore regarded as the first stamps of Kiautschou. The currency inscribed on the 'yacht' series was changed to Chinese cents and dollars in 1905, while the lozenge watermark was introduced between 1905 and 1909. Kiautschou was occupied by the Japanese at the beginning of World War I. Chinese stamps have been used there ever since.

20. Macao, 5 reis, 1884

Adhesive stamps were adopted by the Portuguese colony of Macao in March 1884. The stamps, in the 'crown' keyplate design, were issued in denominations from 5 to 300r. New values and colours appeared in 1885 and provisional surcharges between 1885 and 1887. The stamps of this series may be found perforated 12½ or 13½.

21. Macao, 5 reis, 1887

Apart from surcharges on postage stamps provisional stamps were created in October 1887 by surcharging various fiscal stamps in denominations from 5 to 40 reis. The original fiscal stamps were in a long vertical format, but in many cases the upper and lower horizontal panels, containing the original value, were removed by reperforation before the stamps were put on sale.

22. Macao, 1 avo, 1950

After using Portuguese keyplate designs for more than sixty years Macao issued a pictorial definitive series in 1948. Stamps from 1 avo to 5 patacas depicted prominent landmarks in the colony. The stamps were designed by A. de Sousa and lithographed by Litografia Nacional, Oporto. The colour of the 1 pataca was changed from green to ultramarine in 1950. A dragon motif was adopted in 1950, for a series lithographed by Sin Chun Printing Co. of Macao.

23. Macao, 1 avo, 1956

Since 1953 Macao has produced a number of thematic issues, in accordance with current Portuguese colonial policy. This stamp was one of a series of eight released in March 1956, with a map of the colony. Similar sets, lithographed in multicolour by Enschedé and Sons, were issued by other colonial territories about the same time.

24. Macao, 20 avos, 1964

The centenary of the National Overseas Bank was marked by stamps issued throughout the Portuguese colonial empire, but a different design was used in each case. This 20a. stamp depicts a view of the bank's headquarters in Lisbon.

25. Macao, 5 avos, 1970

Similarly the centenary of the birth of Marshal Carmona was commemorated in 1970 by a stamp from each territory, using distinctive designs and different portraits in each case.

26. Japanese Occupation of Hong Kong, 3 yen, 1945

Ordinary Japanese stamps were used in Hong Kong from 1941 till the end of World War II. In March 1945, however, three Japanese stamps (1, 2 and 5s.) were surcharged in Japanese characters, revaluing them for use as 1.50, 3 and 5y. stamps. The stamps showed a girl factory worker, General Nogi and Admiral Togo.

PLATE 59
Korea

1. Kingdom of Korea, 5 mon, 1884

A postal service on western lines, complete with postage stamps, was introduced in Korea in November 1884. The stamps, in denominations of 5 and 10 mon, were designed by C. Saito and typographed at the Stamp Bureau of the Ministry of Finance in Tokyo. Four different gauges of perforation were used, ranging from 8½ to 11½. Shortly after these stamps were issued there was a revolution in Korea and the Seoul post office was destroyed. Eleven years elapsed before postage stamps were reintroduced.

2. Empire of Korea, 2 re, 1900

Korea was declared an empire in October 1897 and stamps inscribed 'Imperial Korean Post' in emulation of the contemporary issues of Japan were issued in January 1900. The stamps, ranging in value from 2 re to 20 cheun, were designed by Chi Chang Han and typographed by the Printing Bureau of the Ministry of Agriculture, Commerce and Industry in Seoul. Higher values, of 50 cheun and 1 won, were added in 1901–03. The stamps featured the hibiscus flower and *teaguk* emblem of Korea.

3. Empire of Korea, 2 cheun, 1903

The last stamps issued by an independent Korea appeared in June 1903. They were designed by E. Clemencet and typographed by the French Government Printing Works in Paris in denominations from 2 rin to 2 won. The standard design had a falcon holding the sceptre and orb of imperial power. By this time, however, Korean sovereignty was more imaginary than real as Japan and Russia jostled for control of the country. In the aftermath of the Russo-Japanese War the Korean postal system was merged into that of Japan on 1 June 1905, and ordinary Japanese stamps were introduced. Korea remained nominally independent of Japan until August 1910, when it was formally annexed.

4. South Korea, 15 won, 1950

The 50th anniversary of Korea's admission to the Universal Postal Union was marked by two stamps issued in January 1950. The 15 and 65w. stamps, bearing a post-horse warrant, were lithographed on granite paper. This design was subsequently modified for use as a definitive 100w. stamp in 1951.

PLATE 59 KOREA · PLATE 60 JAPAN, RYUKYUS

5. South Korea, 100 hwan, 1954
On account of the Korean War the currency of South Korea depreciated rapidly. In 1953 it was reformed, 100 old won being worth one new hwan. This brought about a change of definitive series, which appeared in 1954–55 in denominations from 5 to 1000h. The six designs used for this series featured deer, antiquities and symbols of reconstruction after the war. The series was printed on watermarked paper between April 1954 and October 1955 but thereafter unwatermarked paper was adopted.

6. South Korea, 35 hwan, 1954
This stamp was one of a series of five airmail stamps issued in July 1954 in denominations from 25 to 71h. The stamps were lithographed by the Korean Government Printing Agency, who have produced the majority of South Korean stamps since 1952. The common design showed an aircraft over the East Gate in Seoul.

7. South Korea, 55 hwan, 1956
Dr Syngman Rhee became president of the republic in 1948 and held office till May 1961, when he was overthrown by a military coup. Many of the stamps issued in the 1950s bore his portrait, commemorating his birthday or his various terms of office. This stamp, and a 20h. in the same design, were issued in August 1956 to celebrate his election for a third term of office.

8. South Korea, 55 hwan, 1957
Two stamps were released in February 1957 to mark the 50th anniversary of the Boy Scout movement. The 40 and 55h. stamps featured a Korean scout and the fleur-de-lis emblem. The social and cultural influence of the United States on the postwar development of South Korea was reflected on many stamps such as this in the 1950s.

9. South Korea, 40 hwan, 1960
This stamp, and a miniature sheet of the same denomination, were released in June 1960 to commemorate the visit of President Eisenhower to South Korea. Eisenhower had previously appeared on a set of three stamps, issued in December 1954 to mark the Korea–United States mutual defence treaty. Subsequent stamps celebrated the state visits of Lyndon Johnson (1966), Lübke of West Germany (1967), the Emperor Haile Selassie (1968), the Yang di-Pertuan Agong of Malaysia and Hamani of Niger (1969) and Hernandez of Salvador (1970) – the latter usually in company with President Park.

10. South Korea, 40 hwan, 1960
Two stamps and a miniature sheet were released in August 1960 to mark the Rome Olympic Games. The 20h. stamp showed a weight-lifter – a Korean speciality – while the 40h. depicted the South Gate, Seoul, and the Games emblem. South Korea has been an enthusiastic supporter of international sporting events, judging by the range of stamps issued for that purpose in the past two decades.

11. South Korea, 40 hwan, 1962
The first anniversary of the overthrow of Syngman Rhee was celebrated by a set of three stamps featuring industrial progress (30h.), soldiers crossing the Han River bridge (40h.) and an industrial skyline (200h.). In addition each stamp was also produced in a miniature sheet printed in English or Korean versions giving the text of the revolutionary manifesto.

12. South Korea, 10 chon, 1971
The currency of South Korea was again reformed in 1962, 100 chon being equal to 10 old hwan or 1 new won. Stylistically the stamps of South Korea

have varied little since the early 1960s and in subject they are still largely used for political or economic propaganda. This stamp is one of several released in 1971 with the theme of economic development, featuring in symbolic manner various aspects of agriculture and industry. Other stamps released about the same time marked Policeman's Day, Homeland Reserve Forces' Day and Anti-Espionage Month.

13. North Korea, 20 chon, 1946
Stamps were introduced in the Soviet zone of Korea in March 1946, portraying Marshal Kim Il-sung or commemorating land reform. The Russians withdrew in 1948, following the establishment of the People's Republic of North Korea. The stamps from 1946 to 1956 were reprinted in 1957–58 for sale to collectors and differ in minute details from the original versions. These reprints could, and often were, used for postal purposes and are thus of interest to the specialist.

14. North Korea, 10 chon, 1960
The stamps of North Korea have conformed to the Communist pattern since World War II, with strong emphasis on portraiture of Communist leaders. This stamp marked the 43rd anniversary of the Russian October Revolution and depicted Soviet and Korean workers with Lenin's portrait in the background. Numerous stamps have portrayed Lenin, on the anniversary of his birthday, and others have recorded international (Communist) events.

15. North Korea, 10 chon, 1961
The fifteenth anniversary of the Land Reform law was celebrated in March 1961 by this stamp lithographed in green on yellow-tinted paper. The progress of Korean agriculture is illustrated by the modern tractor and the man-plough of pre-Communist times. Agricultural mechanization is a recurring theme on North Korean stamps up to the present time.

16. North Korea, 10 chon, 1961
This stamp was released in November 1961 with the theme of agriculture and industry. It was neither commemorative nor definitive in scope, but was intended merely to publicize developments in agriculture and industry. A number of stamps in the early 1960s came into this category and were designed to strengthen morale. The practice of dating stamps, borrowed from China, began in 1961 and has continued down to the present time.

17. North Korea, 10 chon, 1963
Although stamps with a political message have continued to dominate North Korean philately it is significant that a thematic approach has been adopted since the early 1960s. This stamp was the top value in a series of September 1963 devoted to traditional musical instruments. Subsequent issues have covered almost every conceivable aspect of Korean fauna and flora, culture and traditions. At the same time multicolour lithography was used increasingly.

18. North Korea, 10 chon, 1964
The fifth anniversary of the International Red Cross scheme for the repatriation of people from the North was marked by two stamps, issued in December 1964. The 10c. stamp showed a repatriation ship, with the Red Cross and North Korean flags. The 30c. stamp depicted the return of repatriates. A number of stamps from 1960 onward has emphasized aspects of north-south co-operation and the moves towards the reunification of Korea.

19. North Korea, 40 chon, 1965
This stamp, the top value in a set of three, portrayed

An Hagyong, a hero of the Korean War, and the incident in which he lost his life in action. Since June 1965 North Korea has issued a number of short sets portraying other war heroes. These stamps have been recess-printed, a process which North Korea has used increasingly in the past decade.

20. North Korea, 10 chon, 1965
This stamp, in multicolour lithography, is typical of the poster-type stamps of recent years, designed to stimulate public interest in government policies. Its subject was the 'ten major tasks of the Seven Year Plan' and it shows furnacemen and workers, with the legendary figure of Chulima, the Korean counterpart of Pegasus. The title 'Chulima-rider' is conferred on those who have performed outstanding services to the community.

21. North Korea, 10 chon, 1966
The 30th anniversary of the Fatherland Association was marked by this stamp issued in May 1966. The Association was a subversive organization dedicated to the liberation of Korea from Japanese rule. This stamp was printed in photogravure, a process which North Korea has since used as an alternative to lithography.

22. North Korea, 10 chon, 1969
North Korea has waged a continuous war against the United States by means of postage stamps. This provocative stamp of 1969 is supposed to show the American imperialist hyena being stabbed by Vietnamese bayonets. A similar design was used for another 10 chon stamp of 1969. The International Journalists' Conference in Pyongyang was marked by a stamp in which the prostrate figure of President Nixon was substituted for the hyena, and the pens of world journalism were substituted for the bayonets.

23. Indian Custodian Forces in Korea, 1 rupee, 1953
At the end of the Korean War the demarcation line between North and South Korea was patrolled by an international custodian force drawn from neutral countries. India alone issued special stamps for the use of her troops. Twelve stamps of the 1949 definitive series, from 3pi. to 1r., were overprinted in Hindi in three lines to signify 'Indian Custodian Forces in Korea'. Subsequently Indian stamps were similarly overprinted for the use of custodian forces in Palestine, Indochina and the Congo (see plates 36, 61 and 81).

24. Japanese Post Offices in Korea, 15 sen, 1900
Japanese post offices functioned briefly in the Korean Empire in 1900–01 and contemporary stamps were overprinted with two characters to denote such usage. They were withdrawn in April 1901. Ordinary Japanese stamps were used in Korea from 1905 till 1945.

PLATE 60
Japan and Ryukyus

1. 48 mon, 1871
The Westernization of Japan, following the Meiji Restoration of 1868, included the introduction of a postal service and postage stamps. The first series was engraved and recess-printed by Matsuda of Kyoto in denominations of 48, 100, 200 and 500m. and released in April 1871. The stamps were printed on ungummed laid or wove paper. Different colours were used for the frames and the values were inscribed in black. The stamps are popularly known as the 'Dragon' series.

209

PLATE 60 JAPAN, RYUKYUS

2. ½ sen, 1872

Decimal currency, based on the yen of 100 sen, was adopted in 1871 and later printings of the 'dragon' series were inscribed in this currency. In August 1872 Matsuda produced a new series, known to philatelists as the 'cherry blossom' issue, from the motif in the central vignette. The earliest printings were made by Matsuda but later printings were produced at the Government Printing Bureau, Tokyo. The two versions differ in the shade, type of paper and perforations.

3. 10 sen, 1876

The 'koban' definitive series adopted in 1876 was designed by E. Chiosso'ne and typographed by the Government Printing Works, which produced the vast majority of Japanese stamps since that date. In previous issues the value alone had been rendered in English, but now the complete inscription was given in both Japanese and English. The stamps were inscribed either 'Imperial Japanese Post' or 'Japanese Empire Post'. Five different gauges of perforation were employed in this series, three major types of paper and three different printings distinguished by the shade and minor details in the design. The resulting permutations and combinations add up to one of the most complicated sets ever issued. The stamps were in use from 1876 to 1899.

4. 2 sen, 1894

Japan was one of the first countries to issue commemorative stamps, the first series consisting of 2 and 5s. stamps celebrating the silver wedding of the Emperor Mutsohito. The stamps were designed by T. Honda, engraved by T. Saito and typographed. The common design featured the imperial chrysanthemum crest flanked by cranes. Many of the early commemorative issues marked events of particular interest to the Royal Family.

5. 3 sen, 1905

The amalgamation of the Japanese and Korean postal services was commemorated in July 1905 by this stamp, designed by T. Isobe and engraved by T. Hosogai. The circular motif shows doves flying between the hibiscus of Korea and the chrysanthemum of Japan, an excellent example of the way in which floral motifs were used to convey the message on early Japanese stamps. Korea continued to be nominally independent until 1910.

6. 3 sen, 1921

At the end of World War I the crown prince (now the Emperor Hirohito) made a tour of Europe. His return to Japan in September 1921 was celebrated by a set of four stamps, from 1½ to 10s., featuring the warships *Katori* and *Kashima*. Y. Yoshida designed the series, engraved by S. Morimoto and lithographed at the Government Printing Bureau.

7. 3 sen, 1929

Yoshida, who designed the majority of Japanese stamps in the 1920s, produced a vignette featuring the shrine of Ise for 1½ and 3s. stamps released in October 1929 to mark the 58th vicennial (period of twenty years) of the removal of the shrine. The dies were engraved by M. Aoki and the stamps were recess-printed. Japanese chauvinism in this period was manifest in the rejection of all forms of occidental inscription on the stamps, though this was the only issue which went to the extreme of omitting even the numerals in Western notation.

8. 2 sen, 1937

A recess-printed definitive series was issued between 1937 and 1940 in denominations from ½s. to 10y. The first stamp to appear was this 2s. value, portraying General Nogi, victor in the Russo-Japanese War of 1905. The 4s. stamp in the same series portrayed his naval counterpart, Admiral Togo, while the 12s. featured a modern fighter aircraft. Other subjects in the series concentrated on agricultural pursuits or scenery. The colours of many denominations were changed in 1942–45 and the deterioration in paper, ink and perforation of the later printings reflects wartime shortages.

9. 1 sen, 1943

Twelve new designs were used for the wartime definitive series, issued between 1942 and 1945, as well as the existing designs retained in new colours. The stamps of this series struck a more bellicose note, with pictures of a girl war-worker (1s.), fighter pilot (15s.) and the slogan 'The enemy will surrender' (10s.). The other designs illustrated shrines, monuments and scenery as before and were retained as part of the postwar series (1945–48) issued ungummed and imperforate.

10. 5 yen, 1954

Two 5y. stamps were issued in August 1954 to mark the Ninth National Athletic Meeting. The stamps featured archery and table-tennis and were printed alternately throughout the same sheet. The stamps were designed by M. Hisano and Saburo Watanabe respectively and were recess-printed.

11. 10 sen, 1958

The flame of freedom was the principal element in the stamp designed by M. Hisano to mark the tenth anniversary of the declaration of Human Rights. The stamp was printed in four-colour photogravure and issued on 10 December 1958. Multicolour photogravure was used increasingly for Japanese stamps from 1955 onwards.

12. 10 sen, 1961

Since 1936 Japan has issued numerous stamps publicizing the national parks of the country. The first series consisted of four stamps showing the Fuji-Hakone National Park, with views of Mount Fuji from different vantage points. Since World War II these occasional issues have normally been confined to single stamps or pairs. This stamp was released in April 1961 to publicize the Lake Biwa quasi-national park. It was designed by Hideo Hasebe, one of Japan's foremost postwar designers.

13. 5 + 5 yen, 1961

Since 1950 Japan has issued stamps annually in honour of the National Athletic Meeting. At first a single stamp was released and then a pair, often of the same denomination printed *se-tenant*. Since 1967, however, the practice of issuing a single stamp has been reverted to. The pair of 1961 had gymnastics and rowing as subjects. The stamps were designed by Hasebe and Hisano respectively and were recess-printed.

14. 10 yen, 1962

A series of four multicoloured 10 yen stamps was released between March 1962 and February 1963 marking various children's festivals. The stamps were designed by H. Otsuka and featured the doll festival, the star festival, the seven-five-three festival and the spring festival. Japan also issues stamps regularly for New Year's greetings and in recent years these have reproduced motifs connected with the animals after whom the year is named.

15. 10 yen, 1964

The International Monetary Fund Convention was held in Tokyo in 1964 and this stamp, designed by M. Hisano, was issued on 7 September 1964 to mark the occasion. The stamp features 'coins' inscribed with the initials of the IMF and other international financial organizations.

16. 10 yen, 1965

Mount Fuji has appeared on countless Japanese stamps since 1922, usually viewed from a distance. This stamp of March 1965, however, depicts the summit of this extinct volcano. The golf-ball structure is a radar station erected for meteorological purposes and this stamp was issued to mark its completion. The stamp was designed by H. Otsuka and printed in multicolour photogravure.

17. 15 yen, 1967

The Sobo-Katamuki quasi-national park was the subject of two stamps, designed by Hisano and released in December 1967. This stamp shows Mount Sobo while the other 15y. stamp features Takachiho Gorge. All Japanese stamps since 1966 have been inscribed 'Nippon' in European lettering as well as Japanese.

18. 15 yen, 1971

Since 1910 Japan has taken an active part in the exploration of the Antarctic and, though having no territorial claims in that continent, was a signatory of the Antarctic Treaty of 1961. This stamp was released in June 1971 to mark the tenth anniversary of the treaty and depicts penguins in a style reminiscent of the eighteenth century prints of Hokusai.

19. 50 yen, 1972

Since World War II many Japanese stamps have depicted the art of the country. In more recent years attention has been focused on the theatrical traditions of Japan. This stamp was one of a set of three issued in March 1972 devoted to the Bunraku puppet theatre. It features Awa-no-Naruto, from a photograph by Kakichi Hayashi. The two 20y. denominations were printed in photogravure while the 50y. was recess-printed.

20. British Occupation of Japan, ½ penny, 1946

Australian ½, 1 and 3d. stamps, overprinted 'B.C.O.F. Japan 1946', were issued on 11 October 1946, but were withdrawn for political reasons two days later. They were, however, reissued on 8 May 1947, along with 6d., 1s., 2s. and 5s. denominations similarly overprinted. The initials represent British Commonwealth Occupation Force. The stamps were normally overprinted in black but trial overprints in various other colours were produced as proofs and examples of these are known to have been used postally. These stamps were discontinued on 28 March 1949. No other occupying force in Japan issued its own stamps.

21. Ryukyu Islands, 1 yen, 1952

The Ryukyu Islands, formerly part of Japan, were under American military government from 1945 till 1952 and were then transferred to an American civil administration. K. Oshiro designed a series of eight stamps, printed in photogravure by the Japanese Government Printing Works, Tokyo. The stamps featured bridges, temples and other landmarks in the islands.

22. Ryukyu Islands, 3 cents, 1968

S. Isagawa designed this stamp, issued in May 1968 to mark Library Week. Many of the single commemorative stamps issued by the Ryukyus mark annual events such as philatelic week, press week, afforestation week, old people's day and mothers' day.

23. Ryukyu Islands, 1½ cents, 1969

Another of the hardy annuals from this territory were stamps for New Year's greetings, beginning with a 2y. stamp in 1956 depicting a traditional garland of pine, bamboo and plum. In 1969 this stamp was issued to mark the Year of the Dog and reproduced a Bingata textile pattern showing dogs.

PLATE 60 JAPAN, RYUKYUS · PLATE 61 INDOCHINA

24. Ryukyu Islands, 4 cents, 1971

The 25th anniversary of the nurses' training scheme was commemorated by this stamp, issued in December 1971. K. Miyagi designed the motif showing a student nurse and a lighted candle symbolizing knowledge. This design has an uncanny resemblance to a stamp issued by China in 1964 for Nurses' Day showing nurses holding a candlelight ceremony.

PLATE 61
Indochina

1. Cochin-China, 5 centimes, 1886

The French colonial general series was used in French Indochina until 1892. The first distinctive stamps to appear in this area, however, consisted of 5c. provisional surcharges made in Cochin-China in 1886–87. Stamps of the 'Commerce' keytypes were surcharged with a numeral 5, with or without the abbreviation C.CH. In 1888 30c. stamps were surcharged with two 15s. and a diagonal line to facilitate the bisection of the stamps. These provisionals were superseded by the stamps of Indochina in 1892.

2. Annam and Tonquin, 1 centime, 1888

Provisional surcharges of 1 or 5c. were produced in Annam and Tonquin in January 1888 by surcharging various colonial keytype stamps with the appropriate numeral and the initials A & T. The colonial series was replaced in 1892 by the Indochina series in the 'Tablet' design.

3. Indochina, 5 centimes, 1904

The 'Tablet' series inscribed 'Indo-chine' was used from 1892 to 1904, when a series distinctive to the territory was adopted. Known to collectors as the Grasset series (from its designer, E. Grasset) it featured the female allegory of France clutching a sword and an olive branch. The stamps were inscribed 'Indochine Française' though all subsequent issues omitted the word for French. Every denomination, from 1c. to 10f., was typographed on tinted paper, a fashion much favoured in France at that period.

4. Indochina, $\frac{1}{10}$ cent, 1922

The Grasset series was superseded by a set designed by A. Puyplat and typographed in black and a contrasting colour. Three designs were used, two of which portrayed Cambodian women while the third showed an Annamite girl. With the usual colour and value changes this series remained in use until 1927 and was the one used mainly for the overprints of the French post offices in China (see plate 57). The stamps were reissued in 1922 with values expressed in cents and piastres instead of centimes and francs, thus giving rise to some of the most diminutive fractions of value ever found on stamps.

5. Indochina, $\frac{1}{10}$ cent, 1931

Pictorial sets appeared in 1927 and 1931, both being designed by local artists though engraved and printed in France. The 1927 series was typographed at the Government Printing Works whereas the 1931 series was printed in photogravure by Vaugirard. Three small designs were used for the lower values, depicting a junk, the ruins of Angkor and rice fields, while a double-sized design showing an Apsara (dancing nymph) was used for the higher denominations. Various denominations were added to the series up to 1941.

6. Indochina, 9 cents, 1939

Indochina took part in the various French omnibus series of the 1930s. Two stamps appeared in May 1931 to mark the New York World's Fair and in this instance Indochina used the omnibus design of the other French territories. In June of the same year, however, a set of four stamps was issued in honour of the San Francisco International exhibition and a distinctive design, featuring the Mot Cot Pagoda in Hanoi was used. The stamps were designed by Feltesse, engraved by Cerutti Maori and recess-printed in Paris.

7. Vietnam Democratic Republic, 50 cents, 1945

The Democratic Republic of Vietnam was proclaimed on 2 September 1945, under Ho Chi-minh and recognized by the French on 6 March 1946, as a free state within the Indochinese Federation. During the period of Franco-Vietnamese amity stamps of Indochina were overprinted 'Viet-Nam Dan-Chu Cong-Hoa' (Vietnam Democratic Republic) and latterly surcharged in a new currency of the dong of 100xu. Fighting broke out between the French and the Viet Minh in December 1946 and the latter withdrew to northern Tongking, now known as North Vietnam or the Vietnam Democratic Republic.

8. Vietnam, 10 cents, 1951

After the withdrawal of Ho Chi-minh the French began negotiating with Bao Dai, formerly emperor of Annam, and as a result the state of Vietnam was formed in June 1949 out of Annam, Cochin China and southern Tongking. Stamps inscribed 'Viet-nam' were introduced in June 1951 and featured scenery or portrayed Bao Dai. The series was printed in photogravure by Vaugirard. By the Geneva Declaration of 21 July 1954, Vietnam was partitioned near the 17th Parallel, districts to the north being ceded to the Democratic Republic. South Vietnam became an independent republic in October 1955.

9. South Vietnam, 7 dong, 1966

Not surprisingly a large proportion of the stamps issued by South Vietnam since independence have been directly concerned with the interminable conflict with the north. Nguyen-Ming-Hoang designed 3 and 7d. stamps issued in July 1966 in aid of refugees from the war. A curious relic of the former French connection is that up to 1967 the great majority of South Vietnamese stamps were recess-printed at the Government Printing Works in Paris.

10. South Vietnam, 2 dong, 1971

Many of the more recent stamps have been designed to boost public morale or publicize the much-needed reforms now being instituted. A set of three stamps was issued in August 1971 to mark the first anniversary of the Agrarian Reforms. The stamps showed peasants and the Agrarian Law (2d.), a tractor and the Law (3d.) and peasants ringing the Law (16d.). Since 1967 the majority of South Vietnam's stamps have been printed in multicolour photogravure at the Japanese Government Printing Bureau in Tokyo.

11. South Vietnam, 1 dong, 1965

Interspersed with political and military propaganda issues the short thematic sets come as welcome relief. Flowers were the subject of five stamps issued in September 1965 to mark the Mid-Autumn Festival. More recent sets have had fruits, arts and crafts as their subjects.

12. North Vietnam, 2,000 dong, 1958

Since 1946 the stamps of North Vietnam have continued to use the inscriptions introduced by the Democratic Republic in 1945, and may be recognized by the words 'Dan-Chu' (democratic). A high proportion of these since 1946 have been politically slanted, with portraits of the Communist pantheon. However, perhaps a higher proportion of stamps than in the south have had non-political subjects. Two stamps were issued in June 1958 to mark the Arts and Crafts Fair in Hanoi and featured a cup, basket and lace. The stamps were designed by M. V. Khanh and lithographed in Hanoi.

13. North Vietnam, 12 xu, 1971

The more prolific output of stamps in the north includes a large number of thematic sets. The first of these, featuring fruits of Vietnam, appeared in 1959 and since then every type of Vietnamese fauna, flora and culture has been explored philatelically. The traditional way of life is reflected in the numerous stamps featuring costume, customs and folklore. This stamp was one of a series of six in multicolour lithography issued in 1971 with traditional tiger motifs.

14. North Vietnam, 12 xu, 1972

A set of four stamps was issued in May 1972 to mark the 25th anniversary of national resistance – the withdrawal of the Viet Minh to the north in December 1946. All four stamps were of 12xu. denomination and were printed in multicolour offset. Three designs were pictorial and featured a farmer, industrial worker and girl partisan, but the fourth, taking a leaf out of Chairman Mao's book, bore a lengthy quotation from an appeal by the late Ho Chi-minh: 'We would rather make every sacrifice than return to slavery'. Verbal stamp designs, now commonplace in Communist China, are seldom used in North Vietnam.

15. Laos, 20 cents, 1958

Stamps for the kingdom of Laos were introduced in November 1951 and from then until 1953 they included the inscription 'Union Française', to denote Laotian membership of the French Union. Laos left the Union on 7 December 1956, and became an independent kingdom. Nevertheless the great majority of stamps since then have been engraved and recess-printed in Paris. The use of traditional motifs in the framework of the stamps, together with the emphasis on indigenous subjects, gives Laotian stamps a distinctive quality. This stamp was one of a series designed by Chamnane Prisayane and issued in March 1958 with the theme of Laotian elephants. Since independence short thematic sets have been issued at regular intervals in lieu of a full-length definitive series.

16. Laos, 4 kip, 1963

The test of a country's individuality is in how it interprets international themes on its stamps and in this respect Laos has seldom been content to rely on the stock motifs used by most issuing countries. For the Human Rights issues of December 1963, for example, Laos produced a Daliesque montage of a Laotian supporting the UN emblem. A. Frères, who engraved the dies, is usually credited also with designing this stamp, though one senses the hand of a Laotian artist in this work.

17. Laos, 20 + 5 kip, 1967

The tenth anniversary of the Laotian Red Cross was celebrated in October 1967 by a set of three stamps and a miniature sheet. The common design, by S. Rodboon, showed a harvesting scene with an Apsara stone sculpture as a frame ornament. The only allusion to the movement commemorated was the red cross tucked in one corner of the vignette. The stamps were engraved by Prisayane and recess-printed in Paris.

18. Cambodia, 30 cents, 1951

Like Laos, Cambodia began issuing its own stamps in 1951. The three designs featured an Apsara, a

211

PLATE 61 INDOCHINA · PLATE 62 BRITISH BORNEO

portrait of King Norodom Sihanouk and the throne room at Pnomh-Penh. The monogram UF incorporated in the frame signifies the French Union to which Cambodia belonged until September 1955. Subsequent stamps have been similar in design and content to those produced for Laos.

19. Khmer, 10 cents, 1972
Paradoxically the ultra left-wing government of Prince Norodom Sihanouk was overthrown in 1970 by a right-wing military coup. The prince fled into exile in the People's Republic of China and Cambodia ceased to be a kingdom, assuming the name of the Republic of Khmer, reviving the ancient name used by the original inhabitants. Stamps bearing the new name were introduced in 1971.

20. Indian Forces in Cambodia, 12 annas, 1954
A set of five Indian stamps were issued in December 1954 with a two-line inscription in Hindi to denote usage by the Indian forces in Cambodia as part of the international commission. These stamps were superseded in 1957 by similar denominations in the map series. Separate issues for Cambodia, Laos and Vietnam were superseded in 1965–68 by a unified series overprinted with the initials of the International Commission in Indochina.

21. Indian Forces in Laos, 8 annas, 1954
The same five values – 3 pies, 1, 2, 8 and 12 annas – were overprinted for use in Laos and Vietnam. The map stamps were adopted in April 1957 and may be found with both types of watermark.

22. Indian Forces in Vietnam, 75 naye paise, 1957
The change to decimal currency led to a map definitive series being introduced by India in April 1957. Simultaneously five denominations, from 2 to 75np., were overprinted for use in Cambodia, Laos and Vietnam. Between 1962 and 1965 the same denominations on Asoka watermarked paper were issued and a 1np. denomination issued in Vietnam alone in 1962.

23. International Commission in Indochina, 15 paise, 1965
From January 1965 onwards the separate issues for the three countries of Indochina were gradually phased out and Indian stamps, from 2 paise to 2 rupees, issued in October 1968, overprinted with the initials of the Commission in English and Hindi. The first general issue appeared in January 1965 and consisted of the Nehru commemorative stamp overprinted ICC. India is the only country in the International Commission to have produced distinctive stamps for the use of its contingent.

24. South Vietnam Provisional Revolutionary Government, 40 xu, 1971
The South Vietnam Liberation Front issued stamps with the inscription 'Mat Tran Dan Toc Giai Phong Mien Nam Viet Nam' for use in the districts which it controlled. These stamps appeared from 1963 onward but as they had only local validity they have never been recognized by stamp catalogues. In June 1971, however, a series of five stamps was produced in Hanoi on behalf of the 'provisional revolutionary government' of the republic of South Vietnam to commemorate the second anniversary of this provisional administration. The stamps may be distinguished from the issues of the other two regimes in Vietnam by their inscription 'Cong Hoa Mien Nam Viet Nam'. The stamps featured various activities of the provisional government in the 'liberated' areas. The stamp illustrated here, for example, shows men erecting a stockade round a fortified village.

PLATE 62
British Borneo

1. Labuan, 2 cents, 1885
The island of Labuan, off the northwest coast of Borneo, was ceded to Britain in 1846 and became a crown colony. Stamps were introduced in May 1879 and consisted of 2, 6, 12 and 16 cents recess-printed by De La Rue in small sheets containing ten subjects. This design remained in use until 1894 and during that period underwent changes of watermark. The colonial watermark was omitted in printings after the island was transferred to the British North Borneo Company in 1890, though still remaining a crown colony. Provisional surcharges and new denominations were produced between 1880 and 1894.

2. Labuan, 3 cents, 1897
The transfer of the administration in 1890 was reflected in the stamps issued by Labuan after that date. In 1894 the contemporary pictorial series of North Borneo was issued in the island, in new colours and overprinted 'Labuan'. The same practice was carried out in the pictorial definitive series of April 1897. The stamps were recess-printed by Waterlow and Sons.

3. Labuan, 25 cents, 1902
Waterlows recess-printed a series from 1c. to $1 in 1902–03 to emphasize Labuan's status as a crown colony. In October 1906 Labuan was transferred to the administration of the Straits Settlements (see plate 51) and henceforward used the stamps of that territory. At the end of World War II it became part of the colony of North Borneo and now uses the stamps of Sabah.

4. British North Borneo, 10 cents, 1886
Postage stamps were introduced in the territory of the British North Borneo Company in 1883 and at first were inscribed 'North Borneo'. The designs were emended three years later to include the word 'British'. The designs were again emended in 1888 to include the inscription 'Postage & Revenue'. All of the stamps issued in British North Borneo between 1883 and 1894 were designed and engraved by Thomas Macdonald, and lithographed by Blades, East and Blades of London.

5. State of North Borneo, 5 cents, 1909
North Borneo became a British protectorate in 1888, but thirteen years elapsed before the stamps were overprinted to denote the change in status. Subsequently the words 'British Protectorate' were incorporated in the inscription of all stamps up to World War II. Waterlow and Sons recess-printed a pictorial series for this territory in 1894. A second series of wildlife, native types and scenery on stamps appeared in 1897–1902 and a third between 1909 and 1922. The spate of handsome pictorial stamps in a period of under thirty years bore little relation to actual postal requirements and caused the unpopularity of North Borneo with collectors at the time, though there has been a re-appraisal of these stamps in recent years.

6. North Borneo, 4 + 2 cents, 1918
North Borneo did little to enhance its popularity with philatelists by producing lengthy Red Cross sets during World War I. In May 1916 the entire definitive series was overprinted with a cross, in either vermilion or carmine. In 1918 the series was overprinted 'Red Cross Two Cents' indicating a charity premium on each denomination, and later the same year the stamps were overprinted with a red cross and surcharged with a 4 cents premium. The stamp illustrated here shows a curious mis-

placement of the overprint: 'Red Cross' should appear at the top and 'Two Cents' at the foot, but was reversed on this stamp by accident. The basic stamp, from the series of 1909, shows the Sultan of Sulu, his staff and W. C. Cowie, the first Chairman of the Company.

7. North Borneo, 2 cents, 1941
Waterlow and Sons recess-printed a pictorial definitive series in 1939. In February 1941 the 1 and 2 cents values were overprinted to denote a wartime levy on correspondence. These were the last stamps issued by North Borneo before the Japanese invasion in 1942.

8. North Borneo, 5 dollars, 1947
At the end of World War II the series of 1939 was reintroduced but overprinted BMA to signify the British Military Administration. These stamps and similarly overprinted stamps of Sarawak, could be used anywhere in British Borneo (Brunei, Labuan, North Borneo and Sarawak). In 1947 civil government was resumed, but North Borneo was elevated in status from a protectorate under Company rule, to a crown colony. This was signified by overprinting the 1939 series with the royal monogram and obliterating the words 'State of' and 'British Protectorate' in the inscription.

9. North Borneo, 50 cents, 1954
The overprinted series was replaced in July 1950 by a pictorial set printed in monochrome photogravure by Harrison and Sons, with a full-face portrait of King George VI inset. The same designs were used, with the portrait of Queen Elizabeth substituted, for the definitive series of 1954–57. In the Georgian series the name inscribed on this stamp was incorrectly rendered 'Jessleton'. A corrected version appeared in 1952 and also appeared in the Elizabethan series.

10. North Borneo, 10 dollars, 1961
Chong Yun Fatt designed the sixteen denominations of the definitive series issued in February 1961. After a decade of photogravure stamps North Borneo surprisingly reverted to recess-printing, adhering to the tradition of engraved pictorials established almost seventy years previously. The stamps were the same mixture as before – wildlife and native types with a dash of scenery and the coat of arms on the top value.

11. Sabah, 5 dollars, 1964
North Borneo ceased to be a British crown colony in July 1964 and changed its name to Sabah. The definitive series was overprinted with the new name. This series was originally recess-printed by Waterlow and Sons but from 1962 onwards it was produced by De La Rue, using the original Waterlow plates. Stocks of both Waterlow and De La Rue printings were used for the 1964 Sabah overprints. This series was superseded in 1965 by the general series of Malaysia (see plate 52) and the orchid low-value definitives in the standard Malaysian designs.

12. Sabah, 10 cents, 1971
The orchid series was replaced in February 1971 by the standard butterfly designs of the Malaysian federation. The series used in Sabah depicted the coat of arms of the state in place of the ruler's portrait normally shown on these stamps.

13. Japanese occupation of North Borneo, 4 sen, 1945
Stamps of North Borneo were overprinted in 1942 with seven Japanese characters to signify 'Imperial Japanese Government'. Similar overprints were applied to the stamps of Brunei and Sarawak and were interchangeable between all three territories. Two distinctive stamps, featuring Mount Kinabalu

PLATE 62 BRITISH BORNEO · PLATE 63 DUTCH AND PORTUGUESE INDIES

(4c.) and a Borneo scene (8c.) were offset-lithographed by Kolff of Batavia in 1943. Subsequently, contemporary Japanese definitive stamps were overprinted for use throughout North Borneo.

14. Sarawak, 3 cents, 1871
The territory of Sarawak was ceded by the Sultan of Brunei to James Brooke in 1841 for services rendered in rooting out rebellion and piracy in the sultan's dominions. Stamps were introduced in 1869 when a 3c. stamp portraying Sir James Brooke was issued posthumously. Two years later a similar stamp portraying Charles Brooke was produced. Both stamps were engraved by William Ridgway and lithographed by Maclure, Macdonald & Company of Glasgow. Other denominations, from 2 to 12c., were added in 1875. These stamps exist imperforate, rouletted or perforated in various ways, and partially imperforate varieties are not uncommon.

15. Sarawak, 1 cent, 1901
The state of Sarawak was placed under British protection in 1888. In November of that year a new definitive series, from 1c. to $1, was typographed by De La Rue. Higher denominations, of 2, 5 and 10 dollars, were prepared for use but never issued. This design, with the inscription emended to read 'Postage Postage' instead of 'Postage & Revenue', was used for a series issued between 1899 and 1908. A 5c. denomination in the emended design was prepared but never issued.

16. Sarawak, 1 dollar, 1918
The accession of Sir Charles Vyner Brooke as rajah of Sarawak in May 1917 necessitated a change of definitive series. The series was typographed by De La Rue in the same denominations as before. A 1c. in slate-blue and slate, instead of slate-blue and red, was prepared but never released. New colours and denominations were introduced in 1922–23 following increases in postal rates.

17. Sarawak, 50 cents, 1946
Bradbury Wilkinson recess-printed a set of four stamps intended for issue in 1941 to celebrate the centenary of the 'white rajahs'. Because of the Japanese invasion the stamps were not released until May 1946 during the period of the military administration. The stamps portray Sir James Brooke, Sir Charles Vyner Brooke and Sir Charles Brooke.

18. Sarawak, 5 dollars, 1947
Stamps of North Borneo or Sarawak overprinted B.M.A. were used in Sarawak after the liberation in 1945. Distinctive definitive stamps were resumed in April 1947 when the prewar series portraying Sir Charles Vyner Brooke was reissued with an overprint to signify Sarawak's crown colonial status. The royal monogram was typographed by Bradbury Wilkinson who had recess-printed the original stamps.

19. Sarawak, 6 cents, 1957
Sarawak became a British crown colony in 1947 and a pictorial series, with the portrait of King George VI inset, was recess-printed by Bradbury Wilkinson in January 1950. The same designs were retained for the Elizabethan series issued between June 1955 and October 1957. In 1964–65 the series was reissued on Block CA paper instead of the original Multiple Script CA paper. Since 1965 Sarawak has used the stamps of Malaysia and the orchid or butterfly uniform designs of the Malaysian states.

20. Brunei, 5 dollars, 1948
The first stamps of Brunei consisted of the contemporary series of Labuan suitably overprinted.

This issue of 1906 was superseded the following year by a series recess-printed by De La Rue showing a canoe and waterside dwellings on Brunei River. This design remained in use for the Brunei definitive stamps up to 1952, undergoing changes of colour (1908–12, 1916 and 1947–51) and watermark (1924–37). The stamps were overprinted in Japanese in 1942 to signify 'Imperial Japanese Government' but were reintroduced in 1947. The top values of 5 and 10 dollars were added to the series in February 1948.

21. Brunei, 50 cents, 1949
Apart from overprinting several of the definitive series in 1922 for the Malaya-Borneo Exhibition, Brunei did not issue any commemorative stamps until September 1949, when three stamps were recess-printed by De La Rue to mark the silver jubilee of Sultan Ahmed Tajuddin. The stamps, in denominations of 8, 25 and 50c., portrayed the sultan and showed an aerial view of Brunei Town.

22. Brunei, 50 cents, 1952
The accession of Sultan Omar Ali Saifuddin was taken as the opportunity to introduce a new definitive series. The stamps were recess-printed by De La Rue and issued in March 1952. The series was printed on Multiple Script CA paper, but between 1964 and 1970 was gradually reprinted on the Block CA watermark.

23. Brunei, 25 cents, 1967
Brunei's stamp policy, hitherto ultra-conservative, became more liberal in 1967 with the issue of a set of four stamps to commemorate the 1400th anniversary of the descent of Al-Quran (the Koran) to the Universe. The stamps were printed in multicolour photogravure by Harrisons and have the state arms, the sultan's portrait and Brunei Mosque.

24. Brunei, 12 cents, 1968
Since the late 1960s Brunei has shown an increasing awareness of world affairs and their philatelic application. Victor Whiteley designed a set of three stamps, released in December 1968 to mark Human Rights Year, with the common motif of the flame emblem and a struggling man. The stamps were lithographed in three colours by Harrison and Sons.

25. Brunei, 40 sen, 1969
Three large-format stamps appeared in July 1969 to celebrate the installation, on 9 May, of Pengiran Shah-bandar as Y.T.M. Seri Paduka Duli Pengiran Di-Gadong Sahibol Mal (prime minister). They were designed by Victor Whiteley from artwork produced by a local artist and allude to the offshore oil-drilling, which it is hoped will revitalize the Brunei economy. They were printed in multicolour photogravure by Enschedé.

26. Brunei, 10 sen, 1971
Since 1967 Brunei also has made increasing use of Malay instead of English in the inscriptions on stamps, and has adopted the Malay spelling of 'sen' for 'cents'. A set of three stamps was issued in May 1971 honouring the Brunei armed forces and depicted a soldier (10c.) helicopter (15c.) and the coastal defence vessel Pahlawan (75c.), with the emblem of the armed forces and the sultan's portrait inset.

27. Brunei under Japanese occupation, 5 cents, 1942
Consequent on the Japanese occupation of Brunei in 1942 the contemporary definitive series was reissued with an overprint in Japanese characters to signify 'Imperial Japanese Government'. These stamps were valid for postage not only in Brunei, but also in Labuan, North Borneo and Sarawak.

PLATE 63
Dutch and Portuguese Indies

1. Netherlands Indies, 25 cents, 1874
Adhesive postage stamps were introduced in the Netherlands Indies in April 1864, the first, with a value of 10c. bearing a full-face portrait of King Willem III. The stamp was issued imperforate till 1868 when perforations gauging 12½ by 12 were adopted. Typographed stamps with a profile of the king were introduced in 1870 and remained in use till 1883. The 25c. denomination was added to the series in 1874. Numerous types and gauges of perforation were used in this period.

2. Netherlands Indies, ½ cent, 1902
The basic stamp in the numeral design was issued in 1883–84 and was subsequently used for low denominations, from 1 to 5c., the monarch being portrayed on the higher values. A reduction in the internal rate from 3 to 2½c. in 1902 led to provisional ½ and 2½c. surcharges on the 2 and 3c. stamps respectively. The upright numeral series was superseded later that year by a horizontal numeral design with the name of the territory expressed in full.

3. Netherlands Indies, 15 cents, 1909
Professor Jan Veth designed a series of stamps in 1902 portraying Queen Wilhelmina and ranging in value from 10 to 50c. Some confusion was caused by the colours of the 15 and 50c. stamps (brown and lake-brown respectively), so two horizontal bars were overprinted on the 15c. in 1909 to make it more distinctive. The stamps were typographed by Enschedé, who was responsible for the majority of Netherlands Indies stamps from 1870 to 1948, when the territory became independent.

4. Netherlands Indies (Java), ½ cent, 1908
As an experiment stamps were introduced in June 1908 with the overprint 'Java' for use in the islands of Java and Madura only. The entire series, from ½c. to 2½ guilders, was overprinted in this way. Most denominations are known with the overprint inverted, while the 5 and 10c. stamps have been found with the final A of JAVA omitted.

5. Netherlands Indies (Outer Islands), 5 cents, 1908
At the same time as the Javanese overprints, stamps were overprinted 'Buiten Bezit.' to denote usage in the outer islands of the Netherlands Indies. Double or inverted overprints have been noted for most denominations and the guilder values are known with this overprint in different gauges of perforation. The experiment was short-lived and ordinary unoverprinted stamps were reintroduced at the end of 1909.

6. Netherlands Indies, 20 cents, 1915
Between 1912 and 1915 Enschedé introduced a new series. The numeral low values were similar to the preceding series, but with unshaded ovals behind the numerals. A new portrait of Queen Wilhelmina was used for the denominations from 10 to 50c., with a background symbolizing Dutch maritime power.

7. Netherlands Indies, 30 cents, 1930
In 1928 Koppen and Van der Hoop made their pioneer flight from Holland to the Far East and mail carried on the return flight was prepaid with stamps overprinted 'Luchtpost' (airmail) and the outline of a monoplane. In December that year a set of five air stamps, designed by Fokko Mees and lithographed, was released in denominations from 10c. to 1.50g. These were the first stamps of the Netherlands Indies to draw on Javanese art forms

213

PLATE 63 DUTCH AND PORTUGUESE INDIES · PLATE 64 INDONESIA

for inspiration. A 30c. denomination was created two years later by surcharging the 40c. value, first in black and then (1932) in green.

8. Netherlands Indies, 2 + 1 cents, 1930
Like the mother country the Netherlands Indies regularly issued semi-postal stamps with premiums in aid of child welfare. The first of these issues appeared in December 1930 and featured a Balinese temple (2c.), a watch-tower (5c.), a Miningkabaus compound (12½c.) and a Buddhist temple at Boroboedoer (15c.). The stamps were printed in two-colour photogravure. Subsequent sets were also thematic in character.

9. Netherlands Indies, 12½ + 2½ cents, 1937
A. Kreisler designed two stamps, issued on 1 May 1937, with premiums to assist the Indies contingent of scouts attending the World Jamboree in Holland that year. This was the first occasion on which Scout Jamboree stamps were issued by a country other than the host-country. The stamps show two scouts against a globe and the Jamboree emblem.

10. Netherlands Indies, 2 + 1 cents, 1937
The charity stamps of December 1937 were issued on behalf of the ASIB, the Indies Native Relief Fund, and featured the people of the Indies in various agricultural pursuits. Among the other organizations for which charity stamps were issued in the interwar period were the Salvation Army, the Christian Military Association, the Protestant Church and the leper colony. In 1941 stamps were issued to raise funds for Spitfire fighter aircraft.

11. Netherlands Indies, 5 cents, 1941
The last definitive series before the Japanese invasion took the theme of native dancers and was designed by J. F. Dickhoff in denominations from 2½ to 7½c. A 2c. stamp was added in 1945, after the liberation. The stamps of the Indies, from May to September 1941, were printed by Kolff & Co. of Batavia, after Holland had been overrun and stamps could no longer be supplied by Enschedé.

12. Japanese Occupation of Java, 3½ cents, 1943
The Japanese occupied the Netherlands Indies at the end of 1941 and early 1942 and subsequently divided the islands into separate administrative areas, each using distinctive stamps. Stamps were lithographed by Kolff for use in Java between March 1943 and April 1944. The definitive series was designed by G. Ruhl and featured native art and artifacts, scenery and agriculture. Commemorative sets marked the first anniversary of the Japanese occupation and the savings campaign.

13. Japanese Occupation of Sumatra, 10 cents, 1944
Netherlands Indies stamps were overprinted locally at the outset of the Japanese occupation but until 1943 the island was administered as part of Malaya and used the Japanese stamps of that territory. Sumatra was separated from Malaya in May 1943 and resumed distinctive stamps, a series of pictorial designs being lithographed by Kolff. These stamps were superseded in January 1944 by the 1933 and 1941 definitive sets of the Netherlands Indies overprinted in Japanese and with the portrait of Queen Wilhelmina obliterated by a pattern of diagonal lines.

14. Japanese Naval Control Area, 20 cents, 1943
The Japanese Naval Control Area consisted of Borneo, Celebes, Moluccas and Lesser Sunda Islands, each island or group having its own distinctive overprint on Netherlands Indies stamps at first, superseded by a general overprint consisting of an anchor and Japanese characters. A series was typographed and introduced in May 1943. The

stamps from 10 to 20c. depicted the Japanese flag and palm trees, while the stamps from 25c. to 1g. showed Mount Fuji and a bird.

15. Netherlands Indies, 1 cent, 1945
The American Bank Note Co. recess-printed a pictorial series for the Netherlands Indies, released at the time of the liberation. The five lowest denominations featured scenery, while the higher denominations, from 10c. to 2½g., portrayed Queen Wilhelmina. Other stamps in the immediate postwar period were typographed at the Netherlands Indies Government Printing Works' temporary premises in Melbourne, Australia. For later issues, under Dutch authority but inscribed 'Indonesia' see plate 64.

16. Netherlands New Guinea, 1 cent, 1950
Stamps inscribed 'Indonesia' were used throughout the Netherlands Indies between 1948 and 1950 when the territory became independent. Western New Guinea, however, remained under Dutch control and distinctive stamps inscribed 'Nieuw Guinea', in the contemporary Dutch colonial keyplate designs, were issued in 1950. Jan van Krimpen designed the numeral low values, from 1 to 12½c., while S. L. Hartz designed the higher denominations portraying Queen Juliana. All of the stamps of Netherlands New Guinea were produced by Enschedé.

17. Netherlands New Guinea, 10 cents, 1954
The traditional numeral and royal portrait definitive series was replaced between 1954 and 1959 with a series in multicolour photogravure depicting birds of New Guinea. Three designs, by A. van der Vossen, featured birds of paradise and a crown pigeon. In this series, and subsequent charity and commemorative sets, the inscription was 'Nederlands Nieuw Guinea'.

18. Netherlands New Guinea, 25 + 10 cents, 1958
The Netherlands Indies tradition of prolific issues of charity stamps was continued by New Guinea, beginning with a set of three overprinted in 1953 with premiums in aid of Netherlands flood relief. A. van der Vossen designed the four stamps of 1958 on behalf of the Red Cross fund, the stamps featuring native idols and wood-carvings.

19. Netherlands New Guinea, 55 cents, 1962
New Guinea participated in the Dutch omnibus issue of April 1962 to celebrate the Silver Wedding of Queen Juliana and Prince Bernhard. Both Holland and the Netherlands Antilles issued two stamps each, while Surinam and New Guinea contented themselves with one. The stamps were designed by S. Schroder and printed in photogravure. On 1 October 1962, control of New Guinea was transferred to the United Nations, pending its handover to Indonesia. For later stamps see West New Guinea and West Irian (plate 64).

20. Timor, 5 reis, 1886
Adhesive stamps were adopted by the Portuguese colony of Timor in February 1886, the first series consisting of contemporary 'crown' keyplate stamps of Macao suitably overprinted. They were superseded the following year by the Carlos keyplate designs with the appropriate inscription.

21. Timor, 1 avo, 1898
A currency based on the pataca of 100 avos was adopted in 1894 and stamps of the Carlos series were surcharged in new values. Timor took part in the Portuguese colonial omnibus series of April 1898 commemorating the quincentenary of Vasco de Gama's voyage to India. The eight stamps ranged from ½ to 24a. The series was reissued with a republican overprint in 1913.

22. Timor, ½ avo, 1914
The Ceres keyplates of the Portuguese republic were introduced in 1914 with suitable inscriptions and values. Chalk-surfaced paper was used for the earliest printings, but unsurfaced paper was adopted in 1919–20 and glazed paper in 1923. The Ceres types were superseded in 1935 by the San Gabriel series introduced the previous year in Macao.

23. Timor, 4 avos, 1948
Timor had been using stamps for over sixty years before it adopted distinctive designs. During World War II the island was occupied by the Japanese although Portugal was nominally neutral. In 1947 stamps of the prewar series overprinted to celebrate the liberation were issued. The first distinctive stamps consisted of a set of eight and a miniature sheet issued in September 1948. The stamps, designed by A. de Sousa and lithographed in two-colour combinations by Litografia Maia, Oporto, featured native types and occupations.

24. Timor, 10 avos, 1954
The centenary of the first Portuguese stamps (1953) was belatedly marked in March of the following year by a stamp issued in each of the colonial territories in an omnibus design showing a Donna Maria stamp of 1853 flanked by the coats of arms of the colonies. The stamps were printed in multicolour lithography by Litografia Maia of Oporto.

25. Timor, 40 avos, 1958
Many of the postwar issues of Timor have conformed to the Portuguese colonial omnibus designs as, for example, this one issued in September 1958 marking the Brussels World Fair. The few distinctive stamps have tended to fall into the stereotyped Portuguese colonial pattern, using the standard themes such as sports (1962) and military uniforms (1967).

PLATE 64
Indonesia

1. Indonesia, 15 cents, 1948
In September 1948 the Netherlands East Indies was formally renamed Indonesia and contemporary stamps of the Wilhelmina series were issued with the new name overprinted. The overprints were typographed in glossy black ink by G. C. T. van Dorp of Batavia, or by photogravure in dull black ink by G. Kolff of Batavia. The 1 gulden stamp has been recorded with a double overprint.

2. Indonesia, 1 rupiah, 1949
The currency of Indonesia changed to the rupiah of 100 sen in 1949 and a definitive series in this currency was released in February 1949. A numeral design was used for the lowest values (1 to 10s.) while pictorial motifs showing temples, sculpture and scenery, were used for the higher denominations. The stamps were designed by H. G. Smelt and printed in photogravure by Kolff & Co.

3. Indonesia, 15 sen, 1949
Smelt also designed the 15 and 25s. stamps issued in October 1949 to mark the 75th anniversary of the Universal Postal Union. The common design shows the globe and the civic arms of Berne. Indonesia became independent on 27 December 1949, when the stamps of the United States of Indonesia were adopted.

4. Indonesian Republic, 40 sen, 1946
An independent republic was proclaimed in August 1945 at the time of the Japanese surrender, in

PLATE 64 INDONESIA · PLATE 65 PHILIPPINES

defiance of the Dutch. The republicans controlled central Java and most of Sumatra and issued distinctive stamps in these areas. The Dutch controlled the rest of the islands, which they renamed Indonesia in 1948. This stamp was one of a series issued in Sumatra in 1946–47. Originally the stamps had been issued with an inscription 'Fonds Kemerdekaan' (liberation fund) and were sold at a heavy premium over postal value, but the charity inscription was subsequently erased and the stamps reissued as a definitive series.

5. United States of Indonesia, 15 sen, 1950
On 27 December 1949, Indonesia, comprising the former Dutch territory of that name, together with the republican areas, became an independent state in the Netherlands-Indonesian Union with the title of the United States of Indonesia (Republik Indonesia Serikat). Stamps of the Netherlands Indies overprinted RIS (the initials of the name) were issued in January 1950. A 15s. stamp celebrating the inauguration of the United States was printed in photogravure by Kolff and showed the Indonesian flag.

6. Indonesian Republic, 40 sen, 1949
The period of open warfare between the Netherlands and the republicans over Indonesia enabled various outside parties to profit from the situation. An agency based in the United States of America arranged to have stamps printed for the republican faction. The stamps were printed in photogravure by the Austrian State Printing Works in Vienna. That they were quite blatantly aimed at collectors in America is born out by the frequency of American portraits on them – Washington, Franklin, Lincoln and Jefferson being shown along with Indonesian leaders. The stamps were later overprinted 'Merdeka' (liberation) with the date of the attainment of independence. After Indonesia had thrown off Dutch colonial control these stamps were put on sale in Java and Sumatra, but it is believed that only nominal supplies were available and for that reason they have been boycotted by many stamp catalogues.

7. Indonesia, 75 + 25 sen, 1955
A unitary state, known as the Indonesian Republic, was proclaimed in August 1950 and remained within the Netherlands-Indonesian Union until August 1954, when that union was dissolved. All stamps issued since 1950 have been inscribed 'Republik Indonesia'. A set of five stamps, designed by Koernia, was printed by Kolff and issued in June 1955 to mark the National Scout Jamboree.

8. Indonesia, 50 sen, 1958
From the mid-fifties onward Indonesia has closely watched international events and been quick to issue stamps in support of them. Five stamps appeared in October 1958 to mark International Geophysical Year. The stamps, designed by K. R. Soeplanto, depicted a satellite encircling the globe, an allusion to the early sputnik experiments by the Soviet Union.

9. Indonesia, 10 sen, 1960
A set of eight stamps, illustrating agricultural products, was issued in August–October 1960 and initiated the Indonesian policy of thematic sets issued at frequent intervals. The stamps featured oil-palms, sugar cane, coffee, rubber, rice, tobacco and tea.

10. Indonesia, 5 rupiahs, 1964
The thematic set of 1964 concentrated on aspects of transport and communications, ranging from the ox-cart (1r.) to a telephone operator (35r.). The stamps were designed by the artist Soeroso and printed in photogravure by the Indonesian government printers, Pertjetakan Kebajoran of Djakarta.

11. Indonesia, 75 sen, 1961
Many of the stamps issued in the 1950s and early 1960s portrayed President Sukarno and promoted his image as the nation-builder. This stamp, issued in February 1961, publicized the National Development Plan and showed the president and workers hoeing crops.

12. Indonesia, 50 sen, 1961
A set of twenty stamps was released between November 1961 and October 1962 portraying historic heroes, ranging from Abdul Muis (20s.) to Dr Soetomo (15r.). The portraits were shown in sepia against a coloured background.

13. Indonesia, 25 sen, 1962
The Fourth Asian Games were staged at Djakarta in 1962 and the occasion was marked by the release of a set of 24 stamps – the longest commemorative series issued by Indonesia. The majority of the stamps, in vertical designs, showed different sporting events, but three horizontal designs illustrated the main stadium (15s.), the Hotel Indonesia (25s.) and road improvement (30s.). The stamps were partially inscribed in English – a practice which was originally confined to stamps commemorating international sporting events, but later extended to cover other occasions.

14. Indonesia, 30 sen, 1962
Messrs Mardio and Junalies designed a set of six stamps, issued in January 1962 in honour of the Ramayana ballet dancers. The stamps depicted different characters from the Ramayana ballet.

15. Indonesia, 1 rupiah, 1963
Djakarta was the venue of the twelfth Pacific Area Travel Association Conference in 1963 and a series of four stamps was released in March for the occasion. The stamps, designed by Messrs Hasto, Mahriajub and Soemarsono, featured famous tourist landmarks or the conference emblem.

16. Indonesia, 100 sen, 1965
The Indonesian rupiah, hard hit by inflation, was revalued in December 1965. Stamps of the definitive series were overprinted 'Sen' and the last two digits of the date, to convert then from old rupiahs to new sen. Similar overprints, with the dates '1966' or '1967' were issued in the ensuing years. The definitive series, portraying President Sukarno, was designed by Junalies and issued in 1964.

17. Indonesia, 20 + 5 sen, 1966
Two sets of stamps depicting flowers were issued with a premium in aid of charity. The first, dated 1965, appeared in December of that year in denominations from 30 to 100r. The second, dated 1966, appeared the following February in values from 10 to 40s., together with a miniature sheet containing one of each value. A third set appeared in May 1966 with an additional overprint in connection with the National Disaster Fund (Bentjana Alam Nasional).

18. Indonesia, 25 rupiahs, 1964
The one sport in which Indonesians lead the world is badminton, and not surprisingly this has resulted in a number of commemorative stamps. A set of three appeared in August 1964 to mark the Thomas Cup World Badminton Championship. The stamps, designed by K. R. Soeplanto, depicted the trophy. Similar stamps, in denominations of 5 and 12r., appeared in 1967 to mark the same event.

19. Riau-Lingga, 5 sen, 1958
A separate issue of stamps was made for the Riau-Lingga islands between 1954 and 1960. Contemporary commemorative and definitive stamps of Indonesia were overprinted 'Riau' in various

styles of lettering. The series issued in January 1954 included obsolete stamps of the Netherlands Indies, but from 1957 to 1960 only Indonesian stamps were thus overprinted. Ordinary Indonesian stamps have been used since May 1960.

20. West New Guinea, 40 cents, 1962
The Dutch relinquished control of West New Guinea to a United Nations Temporary Executive Authority in 1962, pending the cession of the territory to Indonesia. Contemporary stamps of Netherlands New Guinea were overprinted UNTEA, the initials of the authority, and issued in 1962–63. Overprints made locally at Hollandia (later renamed Kota Baru) used dull ink, while subsequent overprints by Enschedé used shiny ink. West New Guinea passed to Indonesia on 1 May 1963, and was renamed West Irian (Irian Barat). (Stamp reproduced by permission of the National Postal Museum).

21. West Irian, 10 sen, 1968
Following the cession of West New Guinea to Indonesia various stamps of Indonesia were overprinted 'Irian Barat' for use in that territory. At the same time the Indonesian series celebrating the liberation of West Irian was released in that area with the inscriptions suitably modified. Subsequently a distinctive definitive series depicting fauna and flora of New Guinea was issued in August 1968 and simultaneously two stamps commemorated the West Irian People's Pledge of May 1964. No further stamps were issued and ordinary Indonesian stamps are now in use.

22. Pakistan Forces in West Irian, 13 paisa, 1963
Pakistani troops garrisoned West Irian under the UN Temporary Executive Authority until May 1963. In February of that year the Pakistan 13p. stamp, prepaying the ordinary and forces letter rate, was overprinted for the use of troops serving in West Irian. This stamp is analogous to those issues of India for use in Gaza, the Congo, Korea and Indochina. Though overprinted 'U.N. Force W. Irian' this stamp was confined to the Pakistani contingent.

PLATE 65
Philippines

---

1. 5 cuartos, 1861
Adhesive stamps were adopted by the Philippine Islands in February 1854, the stamps being printed in Manila from locally engraved plates. All stamps up to 1864 portrayed Queen Isabella of Spain and, as in the mother country, new designs were introduced at frequent intervals. None of the stamps up to 1874 bore the name of the islands.

2. 2½ centimos, 1880
Between 1880 and 1890 the Philippines had a rash of provisional surcharges unequalled anywhere else in the nineteenth century. Postage stamps, newspaper stamps, fiscals and telegraph stamps were overprinted in various ways and surcharged with new values and more than sixty different varieties have been recorded. The ⅛c. printed-matter stamp, portraying King Alfonso XII, was overprinted 'Recargo de Consumos' (extra tax on provisions). Double or inverted surcharges are not uncommon.

3. 2⅜ centimos, 1891
From 1864 onward the stamps issued in the Philippines under Spanish rule conformed to the colonial keytypes. The 'Baby' types were in use

PLATE 65 PHILIPPINES

from 1890 to 1898, the colours being changed at more or less annual intervals. The 2⅝c. denomination appeared originally in deep blue but changed to grey in 1891 and was dropped from subsequent sets.

4. 5 milesimas, 1898

The 'Curly Head' type was adopted in 1898 in denominations ranging from 1 milesima to 2 pesos. Dated 1898–99 the stamps had a rather briefer life than the dates indicate, since the Philippine Islands were ceded to the United States in April 1899 at the end of the Spanish–American War.

5. 1 cent, 1899

Although the cession took place on 11 April no provision for postage stamps was made until 30 June, when contemporary American stamps overprinted 'Philippines' were introduced. The series of 1902 was adopted in 1903–04 with a similar overprint, and remained in use until 1906. The 5c. (1899) is known with inverted overprint, while the 10c. (1903) has been found with the overprint omitted, in pair with a normal stamp.

6. 1 peso, 1928

The first distinctive series of the Philippines appeared in September 1906 in denominations from 1 centavo to 10 pesos. The stamps were recess-printed at the U.S. Bureau of Engraving and Printing in Washington. The centavo denominations portrayed various people, ranging from Magellan, who discovered the islands, and Dr Rizal, the martyr of Filipino independence, to American presidents such as Lincoln and Washington. The peso values featured the arms of the city of Manila. The colours were changed between 1909 and 1913 and the watermarks were altered in 1911–14 and 1914–26; in 1917–28 they were omitted altogether. The series up to 1p. was overprinted L.O.F. to commemorate the London–Orient Flight by a squadron of British seaplanes. The Philippines were an important staging post on all the major world flights of the twenties and thirties and the definitive series was overprinted in connection with these events on no fewer than six occasions between 1926 and 1936.

7. 24 centavos, 1932

A pictorial series was issued in May 1932 to supplement the portrait definitives. Seven designs were used for stamps ranging between 2 and 32c. The 18c. allegedly depicted the Pagsanjan Falls but in fact showed, by mistake, the Vernal Falls in the Yosemite National Park, California. The stamps were recess-printed in Washington as before.

8. 1 peso, 1941

The Philippines attained self-governing status in November 1935 as a Commonwealth of the United States. The definitive series appeared the following year overprinted 'Commonwealth' and stamps issued subsequently incorporated this word in their inscriptions. The last stamps issued in the Philippines before the Japanese invasion appeared at the end of June 1941 and consisted of four airmail stamps with a motif by O. Spirito showing a traditional sailing vessel and a modern four-engined clipper.

9. 2 centavos, 1941

A 2c. stamp portraying Dr Rizal was introduced in April 1941. It was produced at the U.S. Bureau of Engraving and Printing on either rotary or flat-plate presses, the latter producing slightly smaller stamps. Simultaneously the rotary press version was overprinted O.B. (Official Business). Stamps with a handstruck or machine-overprint have been used on official mail since the early days of the United States administration up to the present day.

10. 16 centavos, 1943

The Philippine Islands were overrun by the Japanese by April 1942 and stamps of the Commonwealth were overprinted to obliterate the American inscriptions. In 1943 a pictorial series inscribed entirely in Japanese was issued, the four designs showing a nipa hut, a rice planter, a native prahu or sailing boat and a view of Mount Mayon and Fuji. The stamps were produced by the Japanese Government Printing Works in Tokyo. Subsequently stamps inscribed 'Republika ng Pilipinas' were issued, after the Japanese had recognized a Filipino republic as part of the 'Co-Prosperity' campaign for Greater East Asia.

11. 2 centavos, 1945

Various stamps of the prewar series were overprinted 'Victory' by hand and issued at Tacloban on the island of Leyte in November–December 1944 under the authority of the Secretary of National Defense and Communications. In January 1945 the prewar series was machine overprinted and released generally throughout the Philippines. Stamps from 2c. to 20p. were overprinted 'Victory Commonwealth'.

12. 1 centavo, 1947

The Philippines became an independent republic on 4 July 1946 and a set of three stamps symbolizing independence appeared on that date. One of the earliest commemoratives issued by the republic was a 1c. stamp in memory of Manuel Quezon, the prewar Filipino leader, who died in 1944. The stamp, typographed in Manila, was also released in a miniature sheet of four imperforate stamps.

13. 3 centavos, 1948

Changes in postal rates led to the introduction of a 3c. stamp in December 1948. Previous definitives had been recess-printed by the American Bank Note Co. but this stamp was typographed locally, and it depicts the Sampaguita, the Filipino national flower. Very few stamps were produced in Manila, the Philippines having preferred to get its stamps printed in the United States or Europe.

14. 2 + 2 centavos, 1950

Two stamps were issued in November 1950 with 100 per cent premiums in aid of war victims. The 2c. stamp featured a war widow and orphaned children, the 4c. a disabled war veteran. Comparatively few charity or semi-postal stamps have been issued by the Philippines.

15. 6 centavos, 1953

The visit of President Quirino to Indonesia in 1953 was marked by 5 and 6c. stamps issued in October of that year. The stamps reflect the mood of conciliation and rapprochement by the Philippines toward Indonesia despite the latter's claim to Filipino territory. The American Bank Note Co. produced the stamps, recess-printing the inscriptions in black and lithographing the multicoloured portions of the design. The stamps show Presidents Quirino and Sukarno and the national flags of both countries.

16. 5 centavos, 1956

Dr Jose P. Rizal, leader of the Filipino independence movement in the 1890s, has left an indelible mark on the stamps of the Philippines. Apart from the numerous issues which bear his portrait are those stamps which refer to him indirectly. In November 1956 5 and 20c. stamps were issued to mark the second National Eucharistic Congress and the centenary of the Feast of the Sacred Heart. The common motif was a reproduction of a statuette of the Sacred Heart carved by Dr Rizal while in prison under sentence of death.

17. 5 centavos, 1957

Quezon City was the venue for the Girl Guides' Pacific World Camp in January 1957 and a 5c.

stamp was issued to mark the occasion. The stamp, showing a Girl Guide, the trefoil emblem and stylized tents, was lithographed in Manila and was released imperforate or perforated 12½. The dates in the vertical panels allude to the centenary of the birth of Lord Baden-Powell. The 48th stamp in each sheet had an error in the date – '1357' instead of '1857'. This was noticed and the error cancelled with bars. All but a few of these defective stamps were removed and destroyed before the sheets were issued.

18. 5 centavos, 1957

The centenary of the birth of the painter Juan Luna was marked by this stamp, issued in October 1957. It reproduces his painting 'The Spoliarium', with his portrait inset. The majority of recent Filipino commemoratives have been single stamps.

19. 6 + 5 centavos, 1961

Between 1958 and 1965 the Philippines issued compulsory tax stamps with premiums in aid of the anti-tuberculosis campaign. The stamps showed various hospitals and sanatoria. All of these stamps were printed in monochrome photogravure, with the Cross of Lorraine emblem in red.

20. 30 centavos, 1961

The Philippines departed from normal procedure by issuing a set of five stamps in honour of the centenary of the birth of Jose Rizal. The stamps, in multicolour photogravure, showed episodes in Rizal's life, from birthplace (5c.) to execution (30c.).

21. 70 centavos, 1966

Filipino inscriptions replaced English on stamps issued from May 1962 onwards and the country name was rendered as 'Pilipinas'. At the same time the notation for the currency was changed to s. (sen) though the unit continues to be known as the centavo. The definitive series of 1962–69 was recess-printed by Bradbury Wilkinson and portrayed famous Filipinos.

22. 6 centavos, 1966

The 6c. stamp was overprinted in May 1966 to publicize the government's campaign against smuggling. The quotation, from a speech by President Marcos, is ambiguous, to say the least!

23. 6 centavos, 1959

A set of three stamps and a miniature sheet were issued in 1949 to mark the 75th anniversary of the Universal Postal Union and featured the UPU monument in Berne, Switzerland. The 18c. stamp was reissued ten years later, surcharged for use as a 6c. stamp, and overprinted for United Nations Day.

24. 6 centavos, 1966

The 50th anniversary of the Philippines National Bank was celebrated in July 1966 by two stamps and a miniature sheet lithographed by De La Rue. The stamps featured a 1 peso coin (6c.) and old and new bank buildings (10c.) while the 70c. stamp symbolizing progress was inset in a reproduction of a banknote to form the miniature sheet. Stamps in recent years have been produced in photogravure by Courvoisier, Enschedé or Harrison or lithographed by De La Rue.

25. 40 centavos, 1971

Two stamps in multicolour photogravure were released in December 1971 to mark three related events – the sixth Asia Electronics Conference, the second General Assembly of the Electronics Union and the fourth National Electronics and Telecommunications Week. Remarkably the unknown designer managed to fit into the stamps the inscriptions concerning all three events in a neat and relatively unobtrusive manner.

AFRICA

PLATE 66 SOUTH AFRICA

PLATE 66
South Africa

1. Cape of Good Hope, 4 pence, 1853

The first stamps to appear anywhere in the African continent were the 1d. and 4d. of the Cape of Good Hope, the celebrated 'Cape Triangulars' issued in September 1853. The design, featuring the seated figure of Hope, was produced by the Surveyor-General, Charles Bell, dies were engraved by William Humphrys and the stamps recess-printed by Perkins Bacon. The stamps were printed on blued paper at first, but subsequent printings were on white paper. In 1863 Perkins Bacon handed over the plates to De La Rue, who made a printing in 1863–64. Higher denominations, of 6d. and 1s., in the same design were introduced in 1858. A crude version of the 1d. and 4d. values was typographed locally in 1861 and known erroneously to philatelists as the 'Woodblocks'.

2. Cape of Good Hope, 1 shilling, 1871

In 1864 De La Rue introduced a rectangular design, again featuring the seated figure of Hope designed by Charles Bell. The earliest versions of this design had a thin frame line enclosing the whole design, but when the dies were re-engraved in 1871 the line was removed. Stamps in this design, from $\frac{1}{2}$d. to 5s., were current between 1864 and 1900.

3. Cape of Good Hope, 1 penny, 1893

A new design, showing Hope standing in front of Table Bay, was produced by a Mr Mountford and typographed by De La Rue, thus combining allegory with pictorialism. $\frac{1}{2}$d. and 3d. stamps in this design were issued between 1898 and 1902.

4. Cape of Good Hope, 1 penny, 1900

Heraldry and pictorialism were again combined when E. Sturman designed this stamp, typographed by De La Rue in 1900. Originally it was planned to issue it in two-colour combinations, like the Bermuda 'Dock' series (see plate 110) but eventually it was issued in monochrome. The stamp shows a view of Table Mountain and Cape Town, surmounted by the coat of arms of the colony.

5. Cape of Good Hope, 2½ pence, 1903

The accession of King Edward VII was taken as the opportunity to issue an entirely new definitive series. Stamps in values from $\frac{1}{2}$d. to 5s. were typographed by De La Rue and issued at intervals between December 1902 and October 1904. The stamps of the Cape were superseded by those of the Union of South Africa in 1913. Between the founding of the Union in 1910 and 31 December 1937, Cape stamps were valid for postage in any part of the Union. Stamps used in this period are known as 'Inter-provincials'.

6. Natal, 1 penny, 1869

The first stamps of Natal, issued in 1857, were embossed in plain relief on coloured wove paper. They were followed in 1859 by a series recess-printed by Perkins Bacon reproducing the Chalon portrait of Queen Victoria. After 1863 these stamps were produced by De La Rue. Separate stamps for fiscal purposes were introduced in 1869 and consequently the Chalon stamps then in use were overprinted 'Postage' to denote their specific purpose. Eight different types of overprint have been recorded, not to mention numerous minor flaws and varieties in the setting of the overprints. These stamps were superseded by a typographed issue in 1874.

7. Natal, ½ penny, 1895

Between 1877 and 1895 Natal seems to have suffered a chronic shortage of halfpenny stamps, judging by the frequency of provisional surcharges in this period. The last of these makeshifts appeared in March 1895 and consisted of the penny stamp of the 1874 series overprinted HALF. Stamps are known with a double overprint. Each alternate stamp in the first vertical row of the right-hand pane has the variety showing a long left limb of the H. This variety was soon corrected.

8. Natal, 3 pence, 1902

De La Rue typographed a series portraying King Edward VII, using two-colour combinations in values from $\frac{1}{2}$d. to 4s. Higher denominations, from 5s. to £20, were produced in a larger format. The series was issued on Crown CA paper in 1902–03, reprinted on Multiple Crown CA paper in 1904–05 and reissued in 1908–09 with the inscription redrawn to read 'Postage' on both sides instead of 'Postage Revenue'. Natal now uses the stamps of the Republic of South Africa.

9. Orange Free State, 1 penny, 1866

Adhesive stamps were adopted by the Orange Free State in January 1866, when De La Rue typographed 1d., 6d. and 1s. stamps depicting the orange-tree emblem of the republic. In 1878 4d. and 5s. stamps in the same design were issued and $\frac{1}{2}$d., 2d. and 3d. in 1883–84. The colours of the $\frac{1}{2}$d., 1d. and 1s. stamps were changed between 1894 and 1900. Between 1877 and 1900 a vast range of temporary surcharges were used to create new values as and when they were required. Otherwise the orange-tree stamps remained virtually unchanged for almost forty years.

10. Orange Free State, 4 pence, 1900

During the Boer War the British occupied much of the Orange Free State and overprinted the stamps with the V.R.I. monogram and surcharged them with sterling equivalents. Hitherto the values had been expressed only in Dutch though it is interesting to note that the words 'penny' and 'pence' were used by the Afrikaaners. The overprints were made by Messrs Curling of Bloemfontein and bristle with errors and varieties. Three different major settings of the overprints were made.

11. Orange River Colony, 2½ pence, 1900

After the republican government was overthrown by the British the country became a crown colony and changed its name. The contemporary $\frac{1}{2}$, 1 and 2½d. stamps of the Cape of Good Hope were overprinted in August 1900, pending the introduction of a distinctive series.

12. Orange River Colony, 6 pence, 1903

De La Rue typographed a series from $\frac{1}{2}$d. to 5s. in 1903–04 portraying King Edward VII and depicting a springbok and a gnu. Between 1905 and 1907 the stamps were reprinted on Multiple Crown CA paper. Examples overprinted CSAR were used on official correspondence of the Central South African Railways.

13. Transvaal, 1 penny, 1869

The Transvaal, otherwise known as the South African Republic, adopted adhesive stamps in 1869. Stamps in denominations of 1d., 6d. and 1s. were typographed by Adolph Otto of Gustrow, Mecklenburg-Schwerin, in 1869 and shipped out to South Africa. Stamps of this printing were sold to collectors but few, if any, were generally used on mail. A 3d. denomination was added to the series in July 1871. In April 1870 M. J. Viljoen of Pretoria printed similar stamps, distinguished from the Otto printings by their relatively coarse and defective impressions. Subsequently versions of this design were produced by P. Davis & Son of Pietermaritzburg and the Government Stamp Commission in

Pretoria. The stamps may be found imperforate, rouletted or perforated in various gauges. Following the first British occupation in 1877 they were overprinted V. R. TRANSVAAL.

14. Transvaal, 1 penny, 1882
The V.R. overprints of 1877 were followed by a distinctive series recess-printed by Bradbury Wilkinson in denominations from ½d. to 2s. with a profile of Queen Victoria. A shortage of 1d. stamps led to the provisional surcharge of 6d. stamps with the new value in 1879. Seven different types of overprint were used. Discontent with the administration by the British who had taken over the country to stave off anarchy and bankruptcy in 1877, led to the First Boer War and the defeat of the British in 1881. The first issue of the Second Republic consisted of the 4d. colonial stamp surcharged 'Een Penny' in Afrikaans. Subsequently the Arms stamps were reissued.

15. Transvaal, 5 pounds, 1892
A distinctive series, designed by J. Vurtheim and typographed by Enschedé, was issued between March 1885 and 1893 in values from ½d. to £5. This series was notorious for the numerous reprints made for sale to collectors. Specialists differentiate the reprints of 1885–93, 1894–95, 1895–96 and 1896–97 by means of their colour, paper and perforation though they cannot be readily distinguished from the stamps actually sold for postage.

16. Transvaal, 2 shillings 6 pence, 1896
Enschedé typographed a new series for the Transvaal in 1894–95. In the first version the wagon in the coat of arms was depicted incorrectly with twin shafts. The design was emended the following year to show the wagon with the characteristic *disselboom* (single shaft) favoured by the Boers. In 1896–97 the series was reissued in new colours and a 2s.6d. denomination was added at this time.

17. Transvaal, 2 pence, 1900
After the second British occupation, which resulted from the Anglo-Boer War of 1899–1902, stamps were again overprinted with the British royal monogram. Several denominations are known with the error V.I.R. which occurred on the 34th stamp of the sheet in the first batch to be overprinted. Stamps were similarly overprinted in 1901–02 with the E.R.I. monogram of King Edward VII.

18. Transvaal, 6 pence, 1895
During a temporary shortage of 6d. postage stamps the corresponding value of the fiscal series was overprinted 'Postzegel' (postage stamp) and pressed into service. Examples of these stamps are known vertically imperforate.

19. Transvaal, 1 penny, 1895
In 1895 the South African Republic introduced penny postage and to celebrate the lowering of postal rates a double-sized commemorative stamp was issued. The stamp was lithographed by the Printing Press and Publishing Company of Pretoria and depicted the coat of arms flanked by a mail coach and a locomotive. This stamp was the first commemorative issue to appear anywhere in Africa.

20. Transvaal, 6 pence, 1902
The name 'Transvaal' reappeared in 1902 when De La Rue typographed a series portraying King Edward VII. The series ranged from ½d. to £5 and appeared on single, then multiple, crown watermarked paper. Between 1905 and 1909 the four lowest denominations (½, 1, 2 and 2½d.) were reissued in single colours. Many of these stamps were likewise overprinted for the use of the Central South African Railways.

21. Stellaland, 1 penny, 1884
Several ephemeral Boer republics existed in the late nineteenth century but only Stellaland achieved the distinction of having its own stamps. Five denominations, from 1d. to 1s., were typographed by Van der Sandt, de Villiers and Co. of Cape Town and issued in February 1884. A British expeditionary force, led by Sir Charles Warren, suppressed this republic in 1884 and its stamps were withdrawn from use in December 1885. It subsequently formed part of Griqualand West (see below) and then Cape Province.

22. New Republic, 6 pence, 1886
The New Republic was an ephemeral state, formerly part of Zululand, which was established by the Boers in 1895. Stamps were adopted in January 1886 and were printed with a rubber handstamp on paper procured in Europe and despatched to South Africa already gummed and perforated. There is considerable variation in these stamps, numerous different dates being found in combination with different types of paper and errors in the embossed coat of arms. The Republic was annexed by the Transvaal in 1887 and renamed as the district of Vrijheid. Subsequently the stamps of the Transvaal were used.

23. British Bechuanaland, ½ penny, 1887
The district of British Bechuanaland became a crown colony in 1885 and began using the stamps of the Cape of Good Hope overprinted. In October 1887 contemporary British stamps, similarly overprinted, were introduced. This stamp has been recorded with the overprint double.

24. British Bechuanaland, 3 pence, 1887
The so-called 'unappropriated dies', normally used for various British fiscal stamps, were typographed by De La Rue with inscriptions for use in British Bechuanaland and released, in values from 1d. to £5, in 1887. The following year several denominations were reissued with the value in numerals additionally overprinted.

25. British Bechuanaland, ½ penny, 1897
At various times Cape of Good Hope stamps, with a distinctive overprint, were used, during temporary shortages of the De La Rue 'fiscal' series. On 16 November 1895 the colony of British Bechuanaland was annexed to the Cape of Good Hope, but stamps with this inscription continued to be used in the Bechuanaland Protectorate (see plate 68) until 1897.

26. Griqualand West, ½ penny, 1877
This district in the Vaal River valley was awarded to the Griqua chief, Nicholas Waterboer, in 1871, after the area had been contested by the Orange Free State and the Griquas. Cape of Good Hope stamps were used in this area from 1871 onwards and were given an overprint, either G.W. or G., in 1877 to simplify accountancy problems. Seventeen different types of capital G were used on Cape stamps between April 1877 and 1879 on various denominations from ½d. to 5s. Griqualand West was incorporated in the Cape of Good Hope in October 1880 and distinctive stamps then became superfluous.

27. Zululand, 2½ pence, 1888
Attempts by the Germans to infiltrate south-east Africa led the British to annexe Zululand in May 1887. The following year British stamps, from ½d. to 5s., were overprinted 'Zululand'. Subsequently various stamps of Natal were similarly treated, the overprinting in both cases being carried out by De La Rue. The 2d. stamp is known with the overprint inverted, while the Natal ½d. is recorded with the overprint double.

28. Zululand, ½ penny, 1894
The overprinted series was superseded by the colonial keyplate designs, typographed by De La Rue between 1894 and 1896 in values from ½d. to £5. At the same time Natal fiscal stamps, from 1d. to £20, were overprinted 'Zululand' and authorized for postal use. Zululand was annexed to Natal on 30 December 1897, and separate issues of stamps were henceforth discontinued.

29. Mafeking, 6 pence, 1900
The Boer War of 1899–1902 resulted in a number of provisional war issues. The most famous of these are the stamps issued in the town of Mafeking during the siege by the Boers. Distinctive stamps were released between March and May 1900. At first stamps of the Cape of Good Hope, Bechuanaland Protectorate and British Bechuanaland were overprinted 'Mafeking Besieged' and surcharged with new values. Subsequently, however, distinctive 1d. and 3d. stamps were produced locally by a photographic process. The 1d. showed Cadet Sergeant Major Warner Goodyear on a bicycle while the 3d. portrayed Colonel Baden-Powell, the Commander of the garrison. Provisional stamps were also produced in several other towns by both sides, while Cape stamps overprinted Z.A.R. were issued during the temporary Boer occupation of Vryburg.

PLATE 67
South Africa (Continued)

1. 2½ pence, 1910
The four provinces of Cape of Good Hope, Natal, Orange River Colony and Transvaal amalgamated in 1910 to form the Union of South Africa. To mark the occasion a 2½d. stamp portraying King George V was designed by H. S. Wilkinson recess-printed by De La Rue. This florid design is notable for several reasons. It was one of the earliest stamps in the reign of George V to bear his portrait, it was inscribed bilingually, in English and Dutch, and it featured the coats of arms of the four provinces. Note that the older name of Orange Free State was resumed for that territory, after it had ceased to be a crown colony.

2. 3 + 3 pence, 1933
The first definitive series of South Africa appeared in 1913 in a small format inscribed in Dutch and English. In 1926 Afrikaans replaced Dutch as the official language of the Union along with English, and in that year the first denominations of a pictorial series were introduced. These were the springbok (½d.), Van Riebeeck's ship (1d.) and orange tree (6d.) designs which were to remain in use until 1954, at first being typographed and then, from 1930, being printed by the rotogravure process. Bradbury Wilkinson recess-printed other denominations in 1927–28 and these likewise appeared in rotogravure versions from 1930. In the printings from 1930 to 1945 the word 'Suidafrika' was used, but in printings from 1933 to 1948 the word appeared in hyphenated form 'Suid-Afrika'. All definitive stamps of South Africa from 1926 to 1954 were printed in bilingual pairs, each stamp being alternatively inscribed in English or Afrikaans.

3. 1 + 1 penny, 1938
South Africa issued several sets of stamps from 1933 with premiums in aid of a fund to construct a memorial to the Voortrekkers, the Boer pioneers of the Great Trek. As well as the semi-postal issues two stamps marked the centenary of the trek (1938) and a further three the inauguration of the memorial

PLATE 67 SOUTH AFRICA · PLATE 68 SOUTHERN AFRICA

(1949). All but the last of these were printed in bilingual pairs. This pair of stamps, from the 1938 series, shows a Boer wagon crossing the Drakensberg Mountains. Note the use of chains and cartwheels to form a decorative border to the design.

4. 4 + 4 pence, 1941
The pictorial series was temporarily displaced by a wartime definitive set ranging in value from ½d. to 1s. The stamps publicized the South African war effort and depicted aspects of the military forces of the Union. The 2d. and 1s. stamps were inscribed bilingually, while the remaining denominations were printed alternately in English and Afrikaans.

5. 1 + 1 shilling, 1942
South Africa adopted the novel measure of printing stamps in a greatly reduced size as a means of saving paper during World War II. The stamps were printed in pairs or triplets, each subject being divided by rouletting, while orthodox perforation separated each pair or triplet from the others in the sheet. Although intended as a wartime economy measure it was retained in the immediate postwar years and even extended, in 1948, to a reduced format edition of the 1½d. (gold-mine) design of the prewar pictorial series.

6. 4 pence, 1953
The centenary of the first adhesive postage stamps in Africa was celebrated by a pair of stamps reproducing the appropriate denomination of the Cape triangulars. The postal centenaries of Natal and the Orange Free State were allowed to pass unnoticed, but two stamps appeared in 1969 to mark the postal centenary of the Transvaal.

7. 10 shillings, 1954
The majority of commemorative stamps from 1952 onwards were inscribed bilingually and this practice was extended to the definitive series, introduced in October 1954. A single theme, the rich and varied wildlife of South Africa, was used for all fourteen denominations from ½d. to 10s. Apart from the four lowest denominations two-colour combinations were used for this series. In the early printings a multiple springbok watermark was used, but from 1959 to 1961 a watermark showing the coat of arms was adopted. The series reappeared in February 1961 with values inscribed in cents and rands.

8. 2 pence, 1958
Several stamps of South Africa have commemorated the arrival of settlers from countries other than the Netherlands. In 1949 the centenary of the British settlement of Natal was commemorated by a 1½d. stamp and this was also the theme of two stamps issued in 1962. In July 1958 a 2d. stamp was issued to mark the centenary of the arrival of German colonists. The design shows a settlers' block-wagon and homestead.

9. 3 pence, 1960
The golden jubilee of the Union was celebrated by a set of four stamps featuring the national flag, coat of arms and symbolic designs. Four weeks later, on 31 May, a 3d. stamp was issued to mark Union Day; it depicted the profiles of Botha, Smuts, Hertzog, Malan, Strijdom and Verwoerd, the prime ministers of South Africa since 1910. Exactly one year later South Africa left the British Commonwealth and became an independent republic.

10. 2½ cents, 1964
A republican definitive series, inscribed bilingually, appeared on 31 May 1961, the thirteen denominations from ½c. to 1r. featuring wildlife, scenery, industries, agriculture and landmarks. The series was reissued in 1961-63 on unwatermarked paper and then, between 1963 and 1967, on paper with

a triangular watermark enclosing the letters RSA (Republic of South Africa). Between 1964 and 1969, however, the designs of the series were gradually redrawn, mainly to make the inscriptions more prominent. In 1969-70 the redrawn series was issued with horizontal phosphor bands to facilitate automatic letter facing and cancellation.

11. 12½ cents, 1970
Two stamps were issued in August 1970 to mark the centenary of the Bible Society of South Africa. The 2½ cents featured a stylized figure of a sower, while the 12½ cents had a symbolic representation of an open book inscribed 'Biblia' in gold die-stamped lettering. These stamps had phosphor lines applied on all four sides like a frame, a curious feature of all South African stamps issued from this time onwards.

12. South Africa, 2½ cents, 1963
As part of its policy of separate development (apartheid) the South African Government established a number of 'Bantustans' or areas reserved for the native population. These areas were granted internal self-government and the inauguration of the Transkei Legislative Assembly in December 1963 was marked by this stamp featuring the assembly building in Umtata.

13. South Africa, 2½ cents, 1967
South Africa has close cultural ties with Europe, in particular the Netherlands, from which many of the Afrikaaner population emanated. Two stamps were issued in 1965 for the tercentenary of the Dutch Reformed Church, and two years later a pair of stamps celebrated the 450th anniversary of the Reformation. Martin Luther was portrayed on the 2½c. while the 12½c. depicted the door of the church in Wittenberg to which Luther nailed his famous theses in 1517.

14. German South-West Africa, 5 pfennigs, 1900
Ordinary German stamps were used in South West Africa from 1884 till 1897 and can only be identified by the postmark. The contemporary German series, diagonally overprinted 'Deutsch-Südwest-Afrika', was introduced in 1897 and was followed by the Hohenzollern keyplate designs in 1900. Ordinary South African stamps were used in South West Africa after the Germans were defeated in 1914-15. After World War I a League of Nations mandate was conferred on South Africa and stamps overprinted in English or Dutch were introduced in 1923.

15. South West Africa, 1 + 1 pound, 1923
Although the basic stamps of South Africa were inscribed bilingually overprints were applied alternately in Dutch and English, so that these stamps are best collected in pairs. In the original version of the Dutch overprint the word was hyphenated but subsequently it was rendered as 'Zuidwest'. The Afrikaans form 'Suidwes' was adopted three years later. These overprints of 1923-24 were produced typographically or lithographically, in several different settings, so that no fewer than eight different versions exist.

16. South West Africa, 2 shillings 6 pence + 2 shillings 6 pence, 1931
The overprinted stamps of South Africa were superseded in March 1931 by a pictorial series recess-printed by Bradbury Wilkinson in bilingual pairs. The fourteen denominations, from ½d. to 20s., featured scenery and wildlife.

17. South West Africa, 1 penny, 1949
Apart from sets marking the Silver Jubilee of King George V (1935) and the coronations of 1937 and 1953, South West Africa did not produce any

distinctive commemorative stamps, but was content to make use of South African stamps overprinted SWA. This overprint obviated the problem of using English and Afrikaans alternately. This stamp was one of the set of three issues released in December 1949 to mark the inauguration of the Voortrekker memorial.

18. South West Africa, 1 shilling, 1954
O. Schroeder and M. Vandeneschen designed a pictorial series, printed in rotogravure by the South African Government Printing Works, and issued in November 1954. The twelve values, from 1d. to 10s., illustrated prehistoric rock paintings, native types and wildlife. The stamps were inscribed bilingually, instead of alternately in English and Afrikaans and thus followed the South African pattern adopted the same year.

19. South West Africa, 3 cents, 1962
With the introduction of South African decimal currency South West Africa issued a pictorial definitive series from ½c. to 1r. in February 1961. Following changes in postal rates a 3c. denomination was introduced in October 1962. The stamp featured flamingoes beside Swakopmund lighthouse. A 15c. depicting the Hardap dam was released in March 1963. The series was originally issued on unsurfaced paper with the standard South African watermark. Between 1962 and 1966 several values were reissued on unwatermarked paper and between 1966 and 1970 the stamps from ½ to 20c. were reissued on chalk surfaced paper with the South African watermark.

20. South West Africa, 3 cents, 1968
South West Africa adopted the South African decimal system of 100 cents to the rand in 1961 and all stamps since then have been inscribed in this currency. Two denominations, 3 and 15c., were used for a set of stamps issued in January 1968 in memory of President Swart of South Africa. They were issued in strips of three, each inscribed in English, Afrikaans or German, the three official languages of South West Africa. This expensive practice has not been continued with subsequent issues.

21. South West Africa, 15 cents, 1965
Comparatively few commemorative stamps have been issued by South West Africa in recent years. Two stamps were issued in October 1965 to celebrate the 75th anniversary of Windhoek, the capital. The 3c. depicted a native mail runner of 1890 while the 15c. portrayed General Kurt von François who founded the city. The stamps were designed by D. Aschenborn and printed in photogravure by the Government Printer in Pretoria. This territory is now known internationally as Namibia.

PLATE 68
Southern Africa

The three countries grouped on this plate were formerly known as the High Commission Territories, from the fact that they continued to be administered by the British High Commissioner in South Africa after that country became an independent dominion, and subsequently a republic. Basutoland and Swaziland are enclaves within the territory of the republic, while Bechuanaland lies between South Africa and Rhodesia. On attaining independence, Basutoland changed its name to Lesotho, and Bechuanaland to Botswana; only Swaziland retains the Anglo-Saxon name conferred in colonial days.

PLATE 68 SOUTHERN AFRICA

1. Bechuanaland, ½ penny, 1888

The first stamps used in the Bechuanaland Protectorate consisted of the stamps previously overprinted for use in British Bechuanaland but additionally overprinted 'Protectorate'. Until 1897 both British and Cape stamps were overprinted for this purpose by the administration of British Bechuanaland. Numerous errors in the overprinting have been recorded.

2. Bechuanaland, 6 pence, 1897

In 1895 British Bechuanaland was incorporated in the Cape of Good Hope and the stamps of that territory continued to be used in the protectorate till October 1897, when they were superseded by British stamps overprinted 'Bechuanaland Protectorate'. Between 1897 and 1902 stamps of the 'Jubilee' series, from ½d. to 6d., were thus overprinted.

3. Bechuanaland, ½ penny, 1908

Low-value British stamps of the King Edward VII series were overprinted for use in the protectorate between 1904 and 1913. The colour of the halfpenny stamp was changed from blue-green to yellow-green in November 1908. The majority of these overprints were made at Somerset House, London.

4. Bechuanaland, 5 shillings, 1920

The first high-value stamps consisted of the British 'Seahorses' 2s.6d. and 5s. of the Waterlow printings, issued with the overprint in 1914. The De La Rue printings of these denominations were issued between 1916 and 1920 and the Bradbury Wilkinson printings between 1920 and 1923. These British overprinted stamps continued in use until December 1932 when stamps showing cattle drinking at a waterhole beside a baobab tree were recess-printed by Waterlow and Sons.

5. Bechuanaland, 3 pence, 1947

A 'mini-omnibus' issue was made by the three British High Commission territories in Southern Africa to mark the visit of the British Royal Family in February 1947. The stamps portrayed King George VI (1d.), the King and Queen (2d.), the Princesses Elizabeth and Margaret (3d.) and the entire Royal Family (1s.). All three sets of stamps were recess-printed by Waterlow & Sons.

6. Bechuanaland, 6 pence, 1960

Apart from colonial omnibus designs and overprinted South African stamps Bechuanaland did not issue any distinctive commemorative stamps of its own until January 1960, when a set of three, printed in photogravure by Harrisons, celebrated the 75th anniversary of the British protectorate. The stamps, in denominations of 1, 3 and 6d., portrayed Queen Victoria and Queen Elizabeth with a typical Bechuana landscape in the background.

7. Bechuanaland, 12½ cents, 1961

The famous 'thirsty cattle' design was used for all the definitive sets of Bechuanaland from 1932 to 1961. The design was adapted from a photograph taken by the Resident Commissioner of Ngamiland and recess-printed by Waterlow and Sons with portraits of George V (1932), George VI (1938–43) and Queen Elizabeth (1955–58). The Elizabethan series was surcharged with South African decimal currency in February 1961. Considerable excitement arose in philatelic circles when it was discovered that certain settings of the surcharges were exceedingly rare. They had been overlooked by dealers who circulated them to their customers as part of their new issue service before their rarity was appreciated. A photogravure pictorial series, featuring the birds and scenery, replaced the decimal surcharges in October 1961.

8. Botswana, 35 cents, 1966

Bechuanaland attained self-government in 1965 and became an independent republic, under the name of Botswana, in September 1966. Richard Granger Barrett designed a series of four stamps, printed in multicolour photogravure by Harrison and Sons, featuring the National Assembly, the abbatoir at Lobatsi, a National Airways Dakota and the State House in Gaberones.

9. Botswana, 25 cents, 1970

Since 1968 Botswana has issued stamps for Christmas greetings and has aimed at keeping clear of the hackneyed Old Master image found on the similar issues of other countries. Such themes as the Star of Bethlehem over an African village or an African woman and child were used for the earlier issues. The series of 1970, however, illustrated toy versions of African animals. The stamps were designed by A. A. Vale and lithographed in multicolour by Questa.

10. Botswana, 15 cents, 1968

Four stamps and a miniature sheet were issued in September 1968 to mark the opening of the National Museum and Art Gallery. The three lower values, in orthodox shapes and sizes, featured rock paintings, a girl wearing ceremonial beads and a painting of baobab trees by Thomas Baines. The curiously long, narrow format was used for the top value with its stylized impression of the museum buildings. The series was lithographed by De La Rue.

11. Basutoland, 10 shillings, 1933

Up to 1933 Basutoland used the stamps of South Africa, but for political reasons a separate issue of stamps was introduced in December of that year. Waterlow and Sons recess-printed a series in a common design which echoed the 'thirsty cattle' design of Bechuanaland, but with the king's portrait and a typical Basuto scene underneath. In this case a crocodile and the Drakensberg Mountains was selected for stamps from ½d. to 10s. The same design, with the portrait of King George VI substituted, was used for the series of 1938.

12. Basutoland, 1 shilling, 1954

An entirely new series, with different designs for each denomination, was adopted for the Elizabethan series of October 1954. The stamps were recess-printed by De La Rue and illustrated scenery, wildlife and native occupations of Basutoland. The 2d. was surcharged for use as a halfpenny stamp in 1959 and the entire series was surcharged in cents and rands in February 1961. Subsequently a similar series, with values inscribed in South African currency, was used between 1961 and 1966. The series was then overprinted 'Lesotho' pending the release of a new series for that country.

13. Basutoland, 1 shilling, 1959

The inauguration of the Basuto National Council was commemorated by three stamps issued in December 1959. The stamps were designed by James Walton and recess-printed by Waterlow and Sons. For the first time the native name 'Lesotho' appeared on the stamps in conjunction with the European name. A series of four stamps issued in 1965 to celebrate the new constitution was similarly inscribed with the dual names.

14. Lesotho, 1 rand, 1967

A series designed and printed by Harrison and Sons was introduced in April 1967. King Moshoeshoe II was portrayed on the 2r. denomination and inset on the pictorial designs used for the lower denominations, which featured the natural products of the country. Initial printings of this series were on unwatermarked paper, but in 1968–69 the

stamps were reissued on paper with a watermark of multiple Basotho hats. Shortly afterwards King Moshoeshoe was deposed by the Prime Minister, Chief Leabua Jonathan, and the definitive series was reissued in 1971 with the royal portrait omitted and the designs redrawn.

15. Lesotho, 15 cents, 1968

Jennifer Toombs designed a set of seven stamps for Lesotho containing the rock paintings for which the country is world-famous. In this set the technique of bleeding the design into the perforations was used effectively to capture the atmosphere of the caves in which these paintings were made. The same technique was repeated two years later, less satisfactorily, in a series of five stamps depicting prehistoric monsters and their petrified footprints. Both sets were printed in photogravure by Harrison and Sons.

16. Lesotho, 25 cents, 1969

C. R. Househam and Gordon Drummond collaborated on the designs of a set of four stamps, issued in March 1969, to mark the centenary of Maseru, the national capital. The stamps were lithographed by Perkins Bacon (making a comeback in the field of stamp production) and featured the Queen Elizabeth II Hospital, the Lesotho radio station, the Leabua Jonathan Airport and the royal palace.

17. Lesotho, 1 rand, 1971

Shortly after the introduction of the 1967 definitive series Moshoeshoe II was deposed by Chief Jonathan the Prime Minister who has ruled Lesotho ever since. Nevertheless the definitive stamps continued to bear the portrait of the deposed ruler and even appeared in 1968–69 with a new watermark. In January 1971, however, the series was reissued with similar designs but in a slightly longer format and omitting the portrait of Moshoeshoe II. The stamps were designed by staff artists of Harrison & Sons (who printed the original version) but were lithographed in multicolour by Questa.

18. Swaziland, 1 penny, 1889

The native kingdom of Swaziland was placed under the joint protection of the South African Republic (Transvaal) and Great Britain in 1890. Post offices established the previous year and contemporary Transvaal stamps, overprinted 'Swazieland' (sic), were issued in denominations from ½d. to 10s. Apart from inverted or double overprints several denominations are known with the misspelling 'Swazielan'. Reprints for sale to collectors were made in 1894–95 and may be distinguished from the originals by the inclusion of a full stop after the name. Britain transferred its responsibilities to the South African Republic in 1894 and the overprinted stamps were superseded by ordinary Transvaal stamps on 7 November of that year. Control of Swaziland was confirmed in the government of the Transvaal in 1903, but three years later the territory was again placed under British protection, though it continued to use Transvaal and South African stamps until 1933.

19. Swaziland, ½ penny, 1933

Distinctive stamps were revived in January 1933 when a series recess-printed by De La Rue was released. The stamps were in a common design by the Rev. C. C. Tugman and portrayed King George V, flanked by Zulu shields. Beneath is a typical Swazi landscape of mountains, with a *kraal* in the foreground. The map of the country served as a background to the value tablet. This ingenious design was marred only by the lettering, in which the w of SWAZILAND, is incorrectly shaded. The design was retained for the George VI series of 1938–54.

PLATE 68 SOUTHERN AFRICA · PLATE 69 RHODESIA, NYASALAND

20. Swaziland, 50 cents, 1961
Bradbury Wilkinson recess-printed a pictorial series in 1956 depicting Swazi men and women, a highland landscape and the Havelock asbestos mine. The series was surcharged in cents and rands in February 1961 and superseded by a similar series inscribed in this currency. The re-engraved series appeared almost simultaneously, thereby demonstrating that there was no necessity for the surcharged series – other than to mulct stamp collectors.

21. Swaziland, 4 cents, 1962
Hard on the heels of the re-engraved series came a new set, designed by Mrs C. Hughes and printed in multicolour photogravure by Enschedé. This stamp has a montage of subjects symbolizing modern irrigation methods. Other denominations depicted ceremonial head-dress, musical instruments, flowers, birds and animals of Swaziland.

22. Swaziland, 25 cents, 1964
The opening of the Swaziland Railway in November 1964 was marked by a set of four stamps designed by R. A. H. Street and recess-printed by Bradbury Wilkinson. The stamps depicted a locomotive and a map of the country showing the rail network. This was Swaziland's first distinctive commemorative series, other than colonial omnibus and South African overprinted issues.

23. Swaziland, 2½ cents, 1967
A set of four stamps designed and printed in photogravure by Harrison & Sons was released in April 1967 to celebrate the change in status from a British Protectorate to a Protected State. Two designs were used for this set, both of which portrayed King Sobhuza II. This traditional status paved the way to complete independence the following year.

24. Swaziland, 25 cents, 1971
Swaziland, since the attainment of full independence has embarked on a policy of short thematic sets at frequent intervals. This stamp is one of a set of four released in February 1971 which illustrated flowers of southern Africa. The stamps incorporate a portrait of King Sobhuza II and were designed by L. D. Curtis and lithographed by Questa.

25. Swaziland, 25 cents, 1970
A set of four stamps, designed by L. D. Curtis and printed in multicolour lithography by Format International, was issued in July 1970 to mark the Ninth Commonwealth Games, held in Edinburgh. The three lower denominations featured an athlete, runner and hurdler, while the top value showed the Swazi national team parading in the stadium.

26. Swaziland, 25 cents, 1968
The attainment of complete independence in September 1968 was celebrated by overprinting the entire definitive series from ½c. to 2 rands. Stamps with both upright and sideways watermark may be found with this overprint.

PLATE 69
Rhodesia and Nyasaland

1. British South Africa Company, ½ penny, 1892
A British expedition sponsored by Cecil Rhodes took part in the 'scramble for Africa' in the late 1880s and resulted in the annexation of vast tracts of southern and central Africa in the name of the British South Africa Company in 1890. A distinctive series, recess-printed by Bradbury Wilkinson, was issued in January 1892 for use in this territory. Certain denominations of this series were produced at two operations, with a recess-printed design and a typographed value tablet. A printing of 2d. and 4d. stamps was made in 1895 by Perkins Bacon, using the original Bradbury Wilkinson plates.

2. British South Africa Company, 1 penny, 1896
In March 1896 the Matabele rose in revolt against the British and swiftly overran all the trading posts except Bulawayo, Gwelo and Belingwe. Fighting continued till August, when Rhodes personally arranged a peace treaty with the Matabele chiefs. During the rebellion a shortage of stamps was first met by surcharging little-used values at Bulawayo and then, in May, a consignment of Cape of Good Hope stamps, overprinted by the Argus Printing Co. of Cape Town, was employed.

3. British South Africa Company, 8 pence, 1897
Large-format stamps featuring the company's coat of arms were first produced by Perkins Bacon, with their centres recess-printed and the values typographed. Two dies, differing in the shading of the lion's body, were used for these stamps issued in 1896–97. In 1897 Waterlow and Sons recess-printed a similar series. The main difference between the Waterlow and Perkins Bacon versions was the ends of the scrolls – between the legs of the springboks (Waterlow) and behind the legs of the animals (Perkins Bacon).

4. Rhodesia, 1 penny, 1909
Although the name Rhodesia was adopted in 1895 the stamps continued to bear the name of the company alone until 1909, when the definitive series of 1898 was overprinted by Waterlow and Sons. Most values are known with the stop after RHODESIA omitted. Several of the overprinted series were subsequently surcharged with new values between 1909 and 1911.

5. Rhodesia, 1 shilling, 1910
The definitive series recess-printed by Waterlow and Sons and introduced in November 1910 was one of the first sets to portray King George V and the only series to portray Queen Mary. The set is popularly known to collectors as the 'Double-heads' and has been the subject of intensive study, on account of its many different shades and perforations. This stamp shows the flaw known as the gash in the Queen's ear, a constant variety on all denominations printed from double working plates, and occurring on the second stamp in each sheet.

6. Southern Rhodesia, 1 shilling, 1924
Stamps portraying King George V in the undress uniform of an admiral were issued by Rhodesia in 1913. In 1924 the territory of the former British South Africa Company was divided into Northern and Southern Rhodesia and distinctive sets of stamps were issued in each territory. The series of Southern Rhodesia retained the Admiral design, but the inscriptions were redrawn. This series, in values from ½d. to 5s., was notorious for the frequency of partially imperforate varieties.

7. Southern Rhodesia, 3 pence, 1931
Bradbury Wilkinson recess-printed a new series in 1931, with a bare-headed portrait of the king. At the same time, however, Waterlow and Sons typographed 2d. and 3d. stamps in a small horizontal design showing the Victoria Falls. The typographed stamps were not regarded as satisfactory and were superseded a year later by much larger stamps depicting the falls.

8. Southern Rhodesia, 6 pence, 1937
For the Silver Jubilee (1935) and the Coronation (1937) Southern Rhodesia opted out of the colonial omnibus issues and produced distinctive designs, both of which illustrated the Victoria Falls. The Silver Jubilee series showed wildlife in the foreground, while the Coronation series depicted the railway bridge over the falls. Both sets were recess-printed by Waterlow and Sons in denominations of 1, 2, 3 and 6d.

9. Southern Rhodesia, 3 pence, 1947
A patriotic note was struck by the set of four stamps issued in May 1947 to celebrate victory after World War II. King George VI, Queen Elizabeth and the two princesses were portrayed on the four stamps. A month earlier the Royal Family had visited Southern Rhodesia and on that occasion two stamps, portraying the king and queen (1d.) and the two princesses (½d.), were released. Both sets were recess-printed by Waterlows.

10. Southern Rhodesia, 1 penny, 1953
Bradbury Wilkinson recess-printed a definitive series issued in August 1953. The fourteen denominations, from ½d. to £1, depicted scenery, wildlife and occupations of the country. The stamps were printed in two-colour combinations, with the exception of the 4d. (flame lily), whose vignette was typographed in two colours, in conjunction with a recess-printed frame. The stamps of Southern Rhodesia were superseded by the joint issues of Rhodesia and Nyasaland on 1 July 1954.

11. Rhodesia and Nyasaland, 1 pound, 1954
The three British territories in Central Africa formed a federation in 1954 and substituted a joint definitive series for the separate sets hitherto used. The stamps were in three designs, each portraying Queen Elizabeth, and were recess-printed by Waterlow and Sons. Examples of the ½d. and 1d., intended for use in coils and differing from the sheet stamps in the gauge of perforation, were printed by Imprimerie Belge de Sécurité, a Belgian subsidiary of Waterlows, in 1955.

12. Southern Rhodesia, 2 shillings, 1964
After the breakup of the federation of Rhodesia and Nyasaland Southern Rhodesia reverted to its own distinctive stamps. Victor Whiteley designed a series of fourteen denominations, printed in multicolour photogravure by Harrison and Sons, released in February 1964. The theme of the series was industries and agricultural pursuits of the country, with pictures of animals, birds, agricultural produce and minerals. The 2s. stamp, depicting Lake Kyle, reflected the growing tourist industry. In October 1964 the country was renamed simply Rhodesia and subsequent printings of the definitive series were thus inscribed.

13. Rhodesia, 2½ cents, 1970
The stamps issued since 1965 have reflected the changing status of Rhodesia. The unilateral declaration of independence was celebrated in December 1965 by a locally lithographed 2s.6d. stamp portraying the Queen and showing the Rhodesian coat of arms. Subsequently the 'Southern Rhodesia' definitive series and the Churchill commemorative were overprinted to mark independence. Both of these issues were declared illegal by the British authorities and mail bearing these stamps was treated as unpaid. Subsequently the definitive series was printed by Harrisons, with the word 'Southern' omitted, but after the applications of sanctions in 1966 Mardon Printers of Salisbury produced lithographed versions. A republican series was introduced in 1970 and various denominations added to it in 1971.

14. Rhodesia, 15 cents, 1971
Rhodesia was the venue of a geological symposium

221

PLATE 69 RHODESIA, NYASALAND · PLATE 70 EAST AFRICA

entitled 'Granite 71' and a set of four stamps, lithographed by Mardons, was issued to mark the event. The stamps depicted different types of granite, while the top value, 15c., showed a geological map of Rhodesia.

15. British Central Africa, 8 pence
A British expedition led by Sir Harry Johnston occupied Nyasaland in 1890 to forestall attempts by the Portuguese to link Angola in the west with Mozambique in the east. The first stamps used in this territory consisted of the contemporary series of the British South Africa Company overprinted B.C.A. The values from 1d. to £10 were thus treated. There are numerous minor variations in the thickness and style of the lettering of the overprints.

16. British Central Africa, 1 penny, 1895
The indefatigable Johnston not only governed the country but wrote the standard reference work on Central Africa and designed its first distinctive stamps, lithographed by De La Rue. When the territory was taken over by the Colonial Office a new series was commissioned by the Crown Agents, in which Johnston's design was considerably modified and typographed by De La Rue. The stamps were printed in two sizes, for values from 1d. to 1s. and from 2s.6d. to £10 respectively.

17. Nyasaland, 2 shillings 6 pence, 1918
In July 1907 the name of the territory was changed to Nyasaland Protectorate and stamps thus inscribed, with a profile of King Edward VII, were issued in July 1908. Similar stamps, with the profile of King George V substituted, were introduced between 1913 and 1918. Both sets were typographed by De La Rue. The series was reissued between 1921 and 1930 on Script watermarked paper instead of the original Multiple Crown paper.

18. Nyasaland, 20 shillings, 1953
A pictorial definitive series, recess-printed by Bradbury Wilkinson, was introduced in September 1945 with a full-face portrait of King George VI inset. The same designs, with a profile of Queen Elizabeth, were used in the series issued in September 1953 in denominations from ½d. to 20s. Eight designs were used for the fifteen denominations and showed agricultural pursuits, the protectorate's emblem, a map and the coat of arms.

19. Nyasaland, 1 pound, 1963
Between 1954 and 1963 Nyasland used the stamps inscribed 'Rhodesia & Nyasaland' but after the breakup of the Central African Federation distinctive stamps were reintroduced. Pending the production of a pictorial series a set of revenue stamps, recess-printed by Bradbury Wilkinson, was issued for postal use in November 1963. The word 'Revenue' was obliterated and the word 'Postage' was overprinted. A ½d. denomination was created by printing the 1d. revenue stamp in a different colour and surcharging it with the new value. These stamps had a very short life, being superseded on 1 January 1964 by a pictorial series.

20. Malawi, 2 shillings 6 pence, 1964
Nyasaland achieved independence in 1964 and adopted the ancient name of Malawi. A set of four stamps thus inscribed was issued on 6 July 1964 to celebrate independence ('Ufulu') and portrayed Dr Hastings Banda, the prime minister (later president of the republic). The stamps were designed by Michael Goaman and printed in multicolour photogravure by Harrison and Sons. The stamps featured the independence monument, the rising sun, the national flag and the coat of arms.

21. Malawi, 2 pence, 1969
Malawi was the first Commonwealth country in Africa to issue special Christmas stamps, a set of four by Victor Whiteley being released in 1964. The series of 1969 consisted of five values, issued in normal sheet form, and also in a miniature sheet embellished with the Praying Hands by Albrecht Dürer. The stamps, showing the dove of peace over Bethlehem, were designed by Jennifer Toombs and printed by Harrisons.

22. Malawi, 2 kwachas, 1971
Malawi used sterling currency until September 1970, when the kwacha of 100 tambalas was adopted. A definitive series inscribed in this currency was introduced in February 1971. The stamps ranged from 1t. to 4k., featured different types of antelope and were designed and lithographed in multicolour by John Waddington Ltd.

23. Northern Rhodesia, 1 shilling
The stamps of Rhodesia were superseded by the series of Northern Rhodesia in April 1925. W. G. Fairweather engraved the vignette showing a giraffe and elephants, while J. A. C. Harrison engraved the profile of King George V. The stamps were recess-printed by Waterlow and Sons in values from ½d. to 20s. The same designs were retained for the sets of 1938 and 1953 portraying King George VI and Queen Elizabeth respectively. The latter series was superseded by the joint issue of Rhodesia and Nyasaland in 1954.

24. Northern Rhodesia, 3 pence, 1963
Distinctive stamps were reintroduced in Northern Rhodesia in December 1963 after the dissolution of the Central African Federation. The stamps were printed in multicolour photogravure by Harrison & Sons and featured the national coat of arms and the Anthony Buckley portrait of Queen Elizabeth. The stamps from ½d. to 1s.3d. were in small format while a larger size was used for the higher denominations, from 2 to 20s. Several denominations have been recorded with the value omitted. These stamps were superseded in October 1964 by the stamps of Zambia.

25. Zambia, 1 ngwee, 1968
Northern Rhodesia adopted the ancient name of Zambia on the attainment of independence in October 1964. The currency was changed to the kwacha of 100 ngwee in 1968 and this led to the issue of a new definitive series from 1n. to 2k. The majority of Zambian stamps since independence have been designed by Mrs Gabrielle Ellison and printed in multicolour photogravure by Harrison and Sons. An unusual feature of most Zambian stamps is the use of copper metallic ink in the design – an allusion to the mineral from which the country's wealth is derived.

26. Zambia, 25 ngwee, 1970
Since 1970 many stamps have been lithographed by other printers, but Mrs Ellison still enjoys a monopoly of Zambian stamp design. This stamp comes from a set of four issued in November 1970 to publicize traditional crafts and ceremonies. The stamps were lithographed by De La Rue. An unusually long, narrow format was used for the 25n. featuring a Kuomboka ceremony.

27. Zambia, 25 ngwee, 1971
The International Year for African Tourism was the subject of 5 and 25n. stamps issued by Zambia in 1971. The common design featured a map of the continent with the territory of Zambia delineated. Since independence Zambia has pursued a relatively conservative policy with regard to new issues.

PLATE 70
East Africa

1. British East Africa Company, 5 annas, 1894
British stamps of the Jubilee series were overprinted for use in the territory administered by the Imperial British East Africa Company and issued in May 1890, pending the supply of a distinctive series, which were lithographed by Bradbury Wilkinson in October 1890. Changes in postal rates led to the issue of 5 and 7½a. values in December 1894. When the territory (now known as Kenya) was taken over by the British government in 1895 the stamps were overprinted 'British East Africa'.

2. Uganda, 5 cowries, 1896
The first stamps of Uganda rank among the world's most primitive issues. A postal service was organized in 1895 by George Wilson, but as there was no printing press in the country the services of a missionary, the Rev. Ernest Millar, were enlisted. Millar produced the stamps on a Barlock typewriter, on the thin foolscap paper he used for sermons. The first series was inscribed merely UG (Uganda Government) but the issue of the following year included the royal monogram and the last two digits of the date. Values were expressed in cowries which, at the rate of 200 to the rupee, were the commonest form of currency in East Africa during the nineteenth century.

3. Uganda, 1 rupee, 1898
The locally typewritten or typeset stamps were superseded in 1898 by a series, recess-printed by De La Rue, in denominations from 1a. to 5r. The large design used for the rupee values reproduced the Von Angeli portrait of Queen Victoria, flanked by lions and spears surmounted by tropical foliage.

4. East Africa and Uganda Protectorates, 20 rupees, 1902
The postal services of Uganda and British East Africa were amalgamated in 1902 and in the following year the separate issues of each protectorate were superseded by a unified series bearing the Emil Fuchs profile of King Edward VII. In denominations from ½a. to 50r., they were typographed in two-colour combinations by De La Rue. Similar designs, but with the portrait of King George V, were in use from 1912 till 1920.

5. Kenya and Uganda, 1 cent, 1922
The British East Africa (except for a coastal strip, including Mombasa) protectorate was raised to the status of a crown colony in 1920 and the name changed to Kenya, after the country's highest mountain. Two years elapsed, however, before stamps bearing this name were introduced. The low values, from 1 to 75c., bore a profile of King George V flanked by palm trees. The higher denominations, in a larger size, had the portrait flanked by cotton plants. This series included higher values from £2 to £100, the last-named being the highest denomination ever issued by any country.

6. Zanzibar, 1 rupee, 1896
An Indian post office functioned in Zanzibar from 1868 to 1869 and from 1875 to 1895, when control of the posts was transferred to British East African administration. Contemporary Indian stamps were overprinted 'Zanzibar' in 1895–96 pending the introduction of the sultanate's own stamps. The first distinctive series was recess-printed by De La Rue in two sizes, both portraying the Sultan Seyyid Hamid-bin-Thwain. The stamps were released a month after the sultan's death and a further three years elapsed before stamps portraying his succes-

PLATE 70 EAST AFRICA · PLATE 71 WEST AFRICA

sor, Seyyid Hamoud-bin-Mahommed, were released.

7. German East Africa, 7½ heller, 1905
German stamps, with a suitable overprint and surcharged in pesa currency, were adopted in German East Africa in 1893, and three years later similar stamps overprinted 'Deutsch-Ostafrika' were introduced. The Yacht key-types thus inscribed were issued between 1901 and 1916. A similar series, in heller currency, was adopted in 1905.

8. Mafia Island, 3 pies, 1915
Mafia Island, in the Rufiji Delta, was occupied by British troops in December 1914. Captured stocks of German East African stamps were overprinted 'G.R. Mafia' in black or violet in January 1915 and the following July various denominations were additionally surcharged 6 cents in East African currency. Subsequently German fiscal stamps and Indian stamps overprinted for the Indian Expeditionary Force (see plate 45) were overprinted for use in Mafia. In August 1918 the island was transferred to the administration of Tanganyika (now Tanzania) whose stamps have been used there ever since.

9. Nyasaland Field Force, ½ penny, 1916
The Nyasaland Field Force consisted of British troops drawn from Rhodesia, Nyasaland and South Africa, engaged in the campaign of 1916–18 against General von Lettow-Vorbeck in Tanganyika. Contemporary Nyasaland stamps, from ½d. to 1s., were overprinted for use by this force. Originally it was intended to overprint them N.F.F., but a shortage of the letter F resulted in the overprint being abbreviated.

10. German East Africa under British Administration, 12 cents, 1917
Civil administration of the former German East Africa was organized in November 1917 and postal services resumed. Contemporary stamps of East Africa and Uganda were introduced with the overprint G.E.A. (German East Africa). The stamps ranged from 1 cent to 50 rupees. A new overprint on the 1 and 10c. stamps was made by the Government Printer, Dar-es-Salaam, in 1922, using thinner, seriffed capitals. These stamps were superseded in 1922 by the issues inscribed Tanganyika.

11. Tanganyika, 5 cents, 1922
Tanganyika's first distinctive stamps were recessprinted by Bradbury Wilkinson in two designs, both bearing a giraffe. Commercial depression in East Africa after the war resulted in a change of currency in 1922 from rupees (15 to the £ sterling) to florins (10 to the £) and then to shillings (20 to the £). Essays for the 'giraffe' stamps inscribed in florins exist, but none were issued.

12. Tanganyika, 15 cents, 1927
De La Rue typographed a series for Tanganyika in 1927, using their colonial key-plate designs and inscribed 'Mandated Territory of Tanganyika', to denote the status of the country. These stamps were in two formats, and ranged from 5c. to £1.

13. Kenya, Uganda and Tanganyika, 5 shillings, 1935
The postal services of Kenya, Uganda and Tanganyika were amalgamated in 1935, under the terms of the East African Customs and Postal Union of that year. Separate issues were superseded by a pictorial series bearing the names of the three countries. Seven pictorial designs, each incorporating a profile of King George V, were used for the fourteen stamps, from 1c. to £1. The 30c. and 5s. stamps, showing Jinja Bridge over the Nile, had a curious error: the approach to the road under the bridge is

shown on the right side, but is missing on the left. This was rectified in the corresponding denominations portraying King George VI, issued in 1938

14. South African stamps overprinted for use in East Africa, 70 cents, 1942
A curious wartime makeshift was the set of four South African stamps overprinted and surcharged for use in East Africa, as a result of a shortage of the stamps normally supplied from London by De La Rue, whose premises were destroyed during the Blitz in 1941. These stamps are usually collected in bilingual pairs, to show both English and Afrikaans versions.

15. Zanzibar, 8 cents, 1926
Zanzibar continued to issue its own stamps until 1967 and the majority of these, prior to the overthrow of the Arab sultanate, portrayed the ruler. Sultan Khalif bin Harub was portrayed on the low-value definitive stamps between 1913 and 1961. The stamp illustrated was part of the 1926 series.

16. Zanzibar, 10 cents, 1944
Ahmed bin Said, Imam of Muscat, founded the Al-Busaid dynasty in 1744. This powerful Arab family eventually ruled over much of the coast of Arabia and East Africa as well as Zanzibar. Both Muscat and Zanzibar celebrated the bicentenary in 1944, the latter with four stamps showing a map of the western Indian Ocean and an Arab dhow.

17. Kenya, Uganda and Tanganyika, 1.30 shillings, 1960
A series of fourteen stamps, from 5c. to 20s., was designed by Michael Goaman and printed by De La Rue in 1960. The cents denominations were produced in a small upright format, featuring Queen Elizabeth and the animal emblems of the three countries. The higher denominations were in a larger size and depicted scenery and wildlife. The cents stamps were printed in photogravure while the shilling denominations were recess-printed.

18. Tanganyika, 5 shillings, 1961
Tanganyika was the first of the East African countries to become independent and was thus the first to resume separate issues of stamps. A photogravure series inscribed 'Uhuru' (Independence) was released on 9 December 1961. The designs by Victor Whiteley featured various aspects of the life and scenery of the country.

19. Uganda, 5 shillings, 1965
Uganda reintroduced its own stamps in October 1962, with a series by Victor Whiteley in the same genre as the Tanganyika set. This was superseded in 1965 by a series featuring birds of East Africa, designed by Mrs Rena Fennessy and printed in multicolour photogravure by Harrison and Sons.

20. Kenya, 1.30 shillings, 1964
Kenya resumed the issue of distinctive stamps on the attainment of independence in December 1963, producing an 'Uhuru' series similar to those of Tanganyika and Uganda. On the first anniversary of independence Kenya was declared a sovereign republic, with Jomo Kenyatta as first president. A set of five stamps celebrated the occasion. President Kenyatta appeared on the 30c. stamp, while the other denominations showed the heraldic flower (Nandi Flame), the lion, and birds.

21. United Republic of Tanganyika and Zanzibar, 2.50 shillings, 1964
Following the overthrow of the Arab sultanate of Zanzibar and the establishment of a republic, a union of Zanzibar with neighbouring Tanganyika was proclaimed in April 1964. Michael Goaman

designed a set of four stamps, printed in photogravure by Harrison and Sons, to signalize this union. These stamps were valid in Tanganyika (as well as Uganda and Kenya), but not in Zanzibar, whose postal services continued to function separately till 1967.

22. East Africa, 2.50 shillings, 1964
Since 1963 commemorative stamps have been made jointly by the countries operating the East African Posts and Telecommunications Corporation and such stamps have borne the names of the countries concerned. The Olympic series of 1964 was the only one to bear the inscription 'Kenya, Uganda, Tanganyika, Zanzibar' in the transitional period before the name Tanzania was adopted.

23. Tanzania (Zanzibar), 2.50 shillings, 1966
Until 1967 Zanzibar continued to issue its own stamps which, though inscribed 'Tanzania', were not valid outside the islands of Pemba and Zanzibar. The second anniversary of the union of Zanzibar and Tanganyika was marked by four stamps printed by Enschedé. The 30c. and 2.50s. stamps, designed by a schoolboy, J. O. Ahmed, showed President Nyerere and Vice-President Karume embracing.

24. Tanzania, 20 shillings, 1967
Stamps inscribed 'Tanzania' were adopted by Tanganyika in 1965, but it was not until the end of 1967 that distinctive issues were withdrawn in Zanzibar, and Tanzanian stamps substituted. The first series used throughout the united republic was the fishes series, released on 9 December 1967. The stamps were designed by Mrs Fennessy and printed in multicolour photogravure by Harrisons.

25. East Africa, 5 shillings, 1967
Mrs Fennessy also designed this stamp, issued on 1 December 1967 to mark the foundation of the East African Community. In the fields of commerce, customs, telecommunications and postal services cooperation among the East African countries has long been close. The tree and pyramid motif, with the emblems of the three member countries, symbolizes progress through mutual cooperation.

26. East Africa, 30 cents, 1969
Since April 1965, when a set of four stamps publicized the East African Safari Rally, the commemorative stamps issued jointy by the countries of the East African Posts and Telecommunications Corporation have been inscribed with the names of the three countries. Great care is taken to vary the order of precedence in which these names are inscribed. Since 1967 these stamps have also been valid in Zanzibar.

PLATE 71

West Africa

1. Sierra Leone, 4 pence, 1884
Sierra Leone began issuing stamps in 1859 – the first territory in West Africa to do so. The first stamp, a 6d. purple, remained in use until 1896, undergoing several changes in paper, watermark, shade and perforation. This was the only denomination issued until 1872, when 1d., 3d., 4d. and 1s. stamps were introduced. The 4d. stamp changed from blue to brown in 1884. Up to 1932 all stamps of Sierra Leone were typographed by De La Rue.

2. Gold Coast, 2½ pence, 1891
Stamps in this design were adopted in 1875, when

PLATE 71 WEST AFRICA

the Gold Coast began issuing stamps. A revision in postal rates, after the Gold Coast joined the Universal Postal Union, led to the issue of a 2½d. stamp, the first stamp of this territory to have the value tablet inscribed in a second colour. Until 1928 all the stamps of the Gold Coast were typographed by De La Rue.

3. The Gambia, halfpenny, 1880
All stamps of The Gambia, from their inception in 1869 till 1898, were produced in combined typography and embossing by De La Rue, and are popularly known to collectors as the 'Cameos'. Over this period of thirty years they changed in perforation, watermark, paper and colour, and various denominations, such as the ½d., were added to the basic series as required.

4. Gold Coast, 1 penny, 1908
The Gold Coast used the various colonial key-plate designs from 1889 till 1928. The sole exception was the penny stamp introduced in 1908, which had a distinctive design. The same design, with a profile of King George V instead of King Edward VII, was retained for the series of 1913–23.

5. Gold Coast, 2 shillings, 1928
This stamp was one of a series of ten issued in 1928, the first British Commonwealth stamps to be printed by the photogravure method. The higher denominations, from 6d. to 5s., were printed in two-colour combinations. For the first time also, the Gold Coast introduced a pictorial element (Christiansborg Castle, Accra) beneath the king's portrait. Curiously, having made such a promising beginning, the Gold Coast reverted to the more traditional recess method from 1938 to 1954.

6. The Gambia, 1½ pence, 1938
The George VI definitive series of 1938–46 presented a curious compromise between the trend toward greater pictorialism and the desire to retain a more formal heraldic approach. Thus the colony's elephant and palm tree emblem was depicted in a naturalistic setting. This design was used for all sixteen denominations of the series, recess-printed by Bradbury Wilkinson.

7. Sierra Leone, 2 shillings, 1932
The contract to print the 1932 definitives was split between Waterlow and Sons, who produced the lower values, and Bradbury Wilkinson, who printed the higher denominations, from 2s. to £1. The low values were of a rice field while the higher values showed palms and a kola tree. This series was among the first of the pictorial sets which were a popular feature of British colonial stamps before World War II.

8. Sierra Leone, 4 pence, 1938
For the George VI definitive series of 1938 two designs were adopted, one showing rice harvesting, the other a view of Freetown from the harbour. The frame of the latter design shows some of the fruit produced in this area. Because of increases in postal rates the colours of the 1½d. and 2d. were changed in 1941 and a 1s.3d. was added to the series in 1944. The stamps were recess-printed by Waterlow.

9. Gold Coast, 5 shillings, 1948
Bradbury Wilkinson recess-printed a new series for the Gold Coast, using different vignettes for each denomination. The subjects included native types, landmarks, industry and agriculture.

10. Sierra Leone, ½ penny, 1961
One of a series of thirteen stamps released in 1961 to celebrate independence. Though primarily commemorative, the series was retained as definitive

stamps for almost two years, a practice adopted by many of the emergent nations of British Africa. A new watermark was introduced for this series, showing the monogram SL and the British imperial crown, reflecting Sierra Leone's position as an independent state within the Commonwealth. The queen's portrait, however, was replaced by the emblem of the new state, a lion and mountains, alluding to the Spanish name of the country.

11. Sierra Leone, ½ penny, 1963
A definitive series, designed by Michael Goaman, and printed in multicolour photogravure by Harrison and Sons, was released in January 1961. The stamps illustrated flowers of the country in full natural colour, reflecting the tendency of the African states toward exuberant colours in their stamps.

12. Sierra Leone, 9 pence, airmail, 1964
In 1964 Sierra Leone made philatelic history by issuing two sets of stamps of a novel shape and composition. The stamps were 'free-form' following the outline of the country. Secondly they were provided with a self-adhesive backing and the peelable backing paper bore an advertisement for the paper manufacturers, Samuel Jones. The stamps were printed in a combination of recess and lithography by the Walsall Lithographic Company, a newcomer to stamp production. Since 1964 Sierra Leone has issued many free-form, self-adhesive stamps, many of which have had commercial advertisements on the back, but, with the exception of Tonga (see plate 120), this idea has not been adopted elsewhere so far.

13. The Gambia, 1 shilling and 3 pence, 1963
Victor Whiteley designed a series of stamps depicting birds of The Gambia, printed in multicolour photogravure by Harrison and Sons and released in November 1963. Four stamps in the series were issued a few days later with an overprint 'Self Government 1963' to mark the adoption of a New Constitution.

14. The Gambia, 6 pence, 1969
The centenary of the first stamps of the Gambia was celebrated in January 1969 by a set of three stamps designed by Gordon Drummond. They reproduced the first stamps of The Gambia flanked with portraits of Queen Victoria and Queen Elizabeth. They were printed in photogravure by Harrison and Sons but the famous 'Cameo' was embossed in each case.

15. The Gambia, 2 pence, 1970
The Gambia became an independent state in 1965 and a republic within the British Commonwealth in 1970. To mark this occasion a set of three stamps portraying President Dauda Jawara and the State House in Bathurst was designed by George Vasarhelyi and lithographed in multicolour by Questa of London.

16. Ghana, 2½ pence, 1958
In July 1958 Dr Nkrumah, the Prime Minister of Ghana, paid a visit to the United States and Canada and his transatlantic journey was subsequently marked by two sets of stamps. The four denominations of the Independence series of 1957 were overprinted in July 1958 'Prime Minister's Visit, U.S.A. and Canada' and in February 1959 a set of three stamps and a miniature sheet featured Dr Nkrumah posing in front of the Lincoln Memorial statue in Washington. The latter series marked the 150th anniversary of the birth of Abraham Lincoln.

17. Ghana, 8½ pence, 1959
One of a pair marking Africa Freedom Day, 15 April 1959. Ghana acted as host to the first confer-

ence of Independent African states in 1958 and henceforward designated 15 April as the date for the promotion of African independence. Stamps thus issued were embellished with the flags of the independent states. It is interesting to note the increase in the number of flags depicted over the years.

18. Ghana, 20 new pesewas, 1969
Ghana adopted a decimal currency based on the cedi of 100 pesewas in 1965. The value of the cedi, however, was revised in 1967 and a system of 100 new pesewas to the new cedi was then introduced. The third anniversary of the revolution which deposed Dr Nkrumah was celebrated in September 1969 by a set of four stamps and a miniature sheet. Two stamps showed the Constituent Assembly Building while the other two depicted the coat of arms of Ghana.

19. Ghana, 12½ new pesewas, 1970
Many stamps issued by Ghana in recent years have pandered to the thematic collector and by now all of the more popular themes have been covered. A. Medina and George Vasarhelyi designed a set of four stamps and a miniature sheet lithographed by De La Rue and issued in June 1970 in honour of the first Apollo moon landing. The stamps depicted the lunar module and the astronauts. Remainders of this series were subsequently overprinted 'Philympia London 1970' but only a token quantity of 900 sets is believed to have been available for postal duty in Ghana itself, the rest of the stock being dispatched to the philatelic trade.

20. Liberia, 10 cents, 1903
The republic of Liberia began issuing stamps in 1860, using a design curiously reminiscent of the reverse side of a British penny – complete with a seated figure of Liberty looking suspiciously like Britannia! Liberia issued special stamps for use on registered mail from 1893 to 1941. This stamp is one of a set of five 10c. stamps issued in 1903 portraying President Gibson and each bearing the name of a different Liberian town. All five stamps are known with the portrait upside down.

21. Liberia, 10 cents, 1909
One of a colourful definitive series recess-printed by Perkins Bacon in 1909, it shows the seated figure of Commerce in a design and format suspiciously like the Cape of Good Hope triangulars of 1853 (see plate 66). Perkins Bacon had a genius for plagiarizing their own designs, particularly in the classic period of the 1850s and 1860s, when they printed stamps for many foreign and Commonwealth countries.

22. Liberia, 1 cent, 1918
A type of antelope known as a bongo was the subject of this stamp, one of a series recess-printed by Perkins Bacon in 1918. Other stamps in the series depicted the coat of arms, scenery and wildlife of the country. Eye-catching pictorial stamps of this sort were produced at frequent intervals by Liberia between 1892 and 1923. Unsold remainders were often surcharged or revalidated for use at later dates.

23. Liberia, 1 cent, 1936
Before the advent of the Goodyear Rubber Company, Liberia derived much of its income from the sale of attractive pictorial stamps to collectors. At various times remaindered stocks would be revalidated by the time-honoured expedient of overprinting. This stamp was originally issued for ordinary postage in 1918, and subsequently issued in a new colour (red instead of rose) with an overprint OS to signify official stamp for government correspondence, and then converted back to

PLATE 71 WEST AFRICA · PLATE 72 NIGERIA

ordinary postal service again, in 1936, by obliterating the OS with a star, surcharging a new value and the new date.

24. Liberia, 15 cents, 1966
Ever since its foundation the Republic of Liberia has enjoyed close cultural ties with the United States and not surprisingly this is reflected in the many stamps which portrayed prominent Americans or aspects of the American way of life. Several sets were issued in the mid-1960s in honour of President Kennedy. This stamp is one of a series of four issued in August 1966, prematurely commemorating the third anniversary of Kennedy's assassination. It shows him taking the Presidential Oath.

25. Liberian Field Force, 1 cent, 1916
In this year the Liberian Government dispatched a punitive expedition up country to quell a revolt. Special stamps were provided for the use of troops on active service and bore an overprint 'L.F.F.' (Liberian Field Force). Numerous errors exist in these overprints with transposed and inverted letters.

PLATE 72
Nigeria

---

1. Oil Rivers, 2½ pence, 1892
A British protectorate was proclaimed over the Oil Rivers district on the coast of Nigeria in June 1885 but six years elapsed before a postal service was established at Old Calabar, the capital. Ordinary British stamps were used between November 1891 and July 1892, when the overprinted stamps were adopted in denominations from ½d. to 1s. Numerous provisional surcharges appeared between September and December 1893.

2. Niger Coast, 1 penny, 1894
The territory changed its name to the Niger Coast Protectorate in May 1893. In November that year a series of stamps inscribed 'Oil Rivers', but with the name obliterated and the new name engraved above, was produced by Waterlow and Sons. In May 1894 similar designs inscribed 'Niger Coast' were released. The stamps, from ½d. to 1s., were designed by G. D. Drummond and portrayed Queen Victoria in widow's weeds. The original version was printed on unwatermarked paper, but the Crown CA colonial watermark was adopted in 1897–98. The Niger Coast Protectorate was abolished in 1899 and subsequently the stamps of Southern Nigeria were adopted.

3. Lagos, 6 pence, 1887
Adhesive stamps were introduced in the colony of Lagos in June 1874, the stamps being typographed by De La Rue in a design which may be regarded as the forerunner of the colonial keyplates, since it was also modified for use in St Christopher and Tobago. The first version consisted of stamps printed in various colours, the perforations being altered in 1876 and the watermark in 1882. New values and colours were adopted in 1884–86 and then the standard dull mauve (low values) and green (shilling denominations) fugitive colours were introduced between 1887 and 1902.

4. Lagos, 2½ pence, 1904
A series portraying King Edward VII superseded the Victorian set in January 1904. The watermark was changed from single to multiple Crown CA in 1904–05. The colony of Lagos was amalgamated with the protectorate of Southern Nigeria in

February 1906 and stamps of the latter replaced the separate issues of Lagos.

5. Southern Nigeria, 2 pence, 1901
Ordinary British stamps were used in the territory administered by the Royal Niger Company from 1888 to 1901. In 1899 the company's territory, and the protectorate of the Niger Coast were brought directly under British control and divided into the protectorates of Northern and Southern Nigeria. Distinctive stamps for the latter were typographed by De La Rue and introduced in March 1901. The stamps, from ½d. to 10s., reproduced the von Angeli portrait of Queen Victoria.

6. Southern Nigeria, 1 penny, 1903
A definitive series with similar frames but portraying King Edward VII was typographed by De La Rue and released in March 1903. A 2½d. stamp was added to the series in 1904. The multiple watermark gradually replaced the single watermark between June 1904 and 1911. The shades of these stamps also varied considerably. Two dies were used for the frame of the 1d., differing in the thickness of the numeral of value, and two dies were used for the portrait, varying in the lines of shading on the king's cheek. A similar series portraying King George V was issued in 1912–14.

7. Northern Nigeria, 2 shillings 6 pence, 1900
De La Rue stuck rigidly to the contemporary colonial keyplate designs for the stamps of Northern Nigeria issued between 1900 and 1912. The Victorian series appeared in March 1900 in denominations from ½d. to 10s., dull mauve being used for the pence values and green for the shilling denominations, with distinctive colours in the inscription and value tablet.

8. Northern Nigeria, 1 pound, 1912
The keyplates with the profile of King Edward VII substituted were issued in July 1902 on single watermarked paper. The multiple Crown CA watermark was issued in 1904–05 and new colours adopted in 1910–11. Similar stamps portraying King George V were issued in 1912 in denominations from ½d. to £1. The distinctive issues of Northern and Southern Nigeria were withdrawn on 1 January 1914 when the stamps of the Federation of Nigeria were adopted.

9. Nigeria, 1 shilling, 1936
From 1914 to 1936 Nigeria used the colonial keyplate designs typographed by De La Rue with the profile of King George V, but a pictorial definitive series was introduced in February 1936. Eight different vertical designs were used for the values from ½d. to 1s., while two-coloured horizontal designs were used for the four higher denominations. The vignettes were of the industries and agriculture of Nigeria, and landmarks such as the Habe minaret (6d.), and the Victoria–Buea road (2s.6d.). De La Rue recess-printed this series with an inset portrait of King George V in Black Watch uniform.

10. Nigeria, 2 shillings 6 pence, 1938
The vignettes showing the Victoria–Buea road and the River Niger at Jebba were retained for the 2s.6d. and 5s. stamps portraying King George VI. Numerous shades and wartime changes of perforation occasioned by the Blitz add considerably to the interest of these two stamps. No higher denominations were issued during this reign.

11. Nigeria, 1 shilling 3 pence, 1940
The fifty-year-old De La Rue monopoly of Nigerian stamps was broken in 1938 when Bradbury Wilkinson were given the contract to produce the lower denominations of the George VI series. A small-

format standard design, with the king's profile flanked by oil-palms, was used for the stamps from ½d. to 1s. A 1s.3d. stamp was added in 1940, following increases in postal rates. Further increases in 1941–44 led to the introduction of a 2½d. stamp and changes in the colour of other low values.

12. Nigeria, 6 pence, 1953
Maurice Fievet designed a series of thirteen stamps, from ½d. to £1, recess-printed by Waterlow and Sons and issued in September 1953. Only four of the designs incorporated a profile of Queen Elizabeth. The series was a hotch-potch of scenery, native types and occupations, the bold lettering and stylized vignettes reflecting postwar trends in stamp design. The outstanding design of the series, however, was that used for the 6d. stamp, reproducing a bronze head from Ife.

13. Nigeria, 2 pence, 1956
Apart from the colonial omnibus stamps Nigeria did not produce a distinctive commemorative until January 1956, when the 2d. definitive stamp was overprinted in honour of the visit of the Queen and Duke of Edinburgh – a somewhat disappointing beginning. The basic stamp, featuring the tin industry, was originally printed in black and ochre, but was reprinted in various shades of slate or grey in 1956–57. The monochrome version was recess-printed by Waterlow's subsidiary company Imprimerie Belge de Sécurité, who also produced 1d. and 3d. stamps on rotary machines.

14. Nigeria, 3 pence, 1959
In December 1958 Nigeria issued a 3d. stamp marking the centenary of Victoria and showing a view of the harbour. A similar frame, with different vignettes, was used in March 1959 for two stamps celebrating the attainment of self-government in the Northern Region of Nigeria. Both issues were recess-printed by Waterlow. The 3d. featured Lugard Hall and the 1s. the mosque at Kano.

15. Nigeria, 1½ pence, 1961
Nigeria became an independent federation in October 1960 and adopted a new definitive series in January 1961. The series, like the vast majority of Nigerian stamps from 1961 to the end of 1967, was printed in photogravure by Harrison and Sons. Small upright formats were used for the stamps from ½d. to 1s.3d. and double-sized horizontal designs for those from 2s. 6d. to £1. The stamps illustrated occupations, wildlife, art, communications and buildings.

16. Nigeria, ½ penny, 1965
A pictorial definitive series in multicolour photogravure was introduced between November 1965 and October 1966. The fourteen denominations, from ½d. to £1, were designed by Maurice Fievet but production was split between Harrison and Sons (1, 2, 3, 4 and 9d.) and the French firm of Delrieu (the remaining values). A single theme was used, featuring mammals and birds, and most designs also incorporated the tracks made by the respective animal. Several denominations were overprinted F.G.N. (Federal Government of Nigeria) for use on official correspondence but were never actually issued for that purpose, though a few were sold to the general public in error.

17. Nigeria, 5 shillings, 1964
Three stamps and a miniature sheet were issued in August 1964 in memory of John F. Kennedy. The stamps, bearing various portraits of the late president, were produced in Israel, the 1s.3d. being printed in photogravure by the Israeli Government Printer, while the 2s.6d. and 5s. were lithographed by Lewin-Epstein of Bat Yam. Several other Nigerian stamps of 1963–65 were printed by De

225

PLATE 72 NIGERIA · PLATE 73 ST HELENA AND DEPENDENCIES

La Rue or Enschedé, though the majority continued to be produced by Harrisons.

18. Nigeria, 1 shilling 6 pence, 1968
Nigeria issued stamps marking the 15th and 20th anniversaries of the Declaration of Human Rights in 1963 and 1968 respectively. Jennifer Toombs designed the 4d. (map and enchained hands) and 1s.6d. (national flag and flame emblem) to emphasize Nigerian national unity, at a time when the breakaway eastern region was struggling for national survival as the republic of Biafra.

19. Nigeria, 1 shilling 6 pence, 1968
George Vasarhelyi designed the 4d. and 1s.6d. stamps which were issued in October 1968 to mark the fifth anniversary of the Federal Republic. These stamps, and the majority of issues from 1968 to the present day, were printed in multicolour photogravure by the Niegerian Security Printing and Minting Co. of Lagos. The motif showing a hand grasping at doves of peace was intended to symbolize conciliation towards Biafra, before the situation deteriorated into full-scale war.

20. Nigeria, 4 pence, 1970
The end of the civil war was celebrated in May 1970 by a set of four stamps printed in multicolour photogravure by Enschedé. The 4d. 1 and 2s. stamps were designed by E. Emokpae and the 1s.6d. by B. Onobrakpeya, using symbolism to promote the image of a reunified country and the slogan 'One people, one destiny'.

21. Nigeria, 1 shilling 3 pence, 1972
Nigeria issued three stamps in February 1972 to publicize the first All-Africa Trade Fair, held in Nairobi, Kenya. The stamps were printed in multicolour lithography by De La Rue. The 1s.3d. and 1s.9d. stamps, with appropriate symbolism, were designed by Austin Onwudimegwu, while the 4d. was the work of Erabor Emokpae who, between them, have produced the majority of Nigerian stamp designs in recent years.

22. Biafra, 4 pence, 1968
A set of four stamps showing butterflies and plants of Biafra was lithographed at the Mint, Lisbon, and issued in September 1968. This series was subsequently reissued with an overprint to mark the Mexico Olympic Games. It is obvious that had Biafra continued to exist as a stamp-issuing entity the number of sets pandering to popular thematic themes might have proliferated.

23. Biafra, 9 pence, 1969
Biafra's philatelic sales were handled by a French agency in 1969–70 and it is doubtful whether some of the later issues were actually released in the shrinking territory of Biafra itself. The Christmas issue of 1969 overprinted 'Peace on earth and goodwill to all men' struck a particularly poignant note. Nigerian stamps were reintroduced in Biafra in January 1970.

24. Biafra, 1 shilling + 6 pence, 1968
Nigerian federal stamps overprinted 'Sovereign Biafra' were issued in the breakaway eastern region in 1968. Various commemorative issues were lithographed at the Mint, Lisbon, on behalf of the Biafran regime. The first anniversary of independence was marked by a set of five stamps highlighting the horrors of the civil war. The 1s. stamp, showing the decapitated victim of a tribal atrocity, bears the statistics of Ibos massacred in other parts of Nigeria in the background. The stamps were surcharged in May 1968 to raise funds for orphaned children.

PLATE 73
St Helena and Dependencies

1. St Helena, 1 penny, 1863
Adhesive stamps were introduced in 1856. At first only a 6d. stamp was used, to prepay the postage on letters going from the island to Cape Town or England, and as subsequent denominations were required De La Rue hit upon the expedient of printing the 6d. stamps in various colours and surcharging them with new values. These makeshifts continued in use until 1894, when they finally gave way to the colonial keyplate designs typographed by that firm.

2. St Helena, 1 shilling, 1903
Although the keyplate design was retained for certain denominations of the Edwardian series an attempt to introduce pictorialism resulted in two designs featuring Government House and the wharf at Jamestown. These incorporated the king's profile and were typographed, but with the usual indifferent result. Nevertheless these designs were retained for the George V series of 1912–16.

3. St Helena, 1 penny, 1934
The centenary of British colonization was celebrated in April 1934 by a lengthy series, from ½d. to £1, recess-printed by Bradbury Wilkinson. Six of the ten denominations incorporated portraits of the British sovereigns in whose reigns the island had been occupied. The vignettes were of scenery and a map of the island, but a vertical design, used for the 2s.6d. stamp, portrayed St Helena, the island's Roman namesake.

4. St Helena, 1 shilling, 1953
De La Rue recess-printed a series of thirteen denominations, from ½d. to 10s., issued in August 1953 with the profile of Queen Elizabeth inset. The stamps depicted the industries and occupations of the islanders as well as scenery and historic landmarks such as Napoleon's house at Longwood. This series replaced definitive issues of George V and George VI in which the colony's emblem had been the sole pictorial motif.

5. St Helena, 1 shilling, 1959
The tercentenary of the British settlement of the island was celebrated in May 1959 by three stamps recess-printed by Waterlow & Sons. The stamps featured the coat of arms of the Honourable East India Company (3d.), the East Indiaman *London* off James Bay in 1659 (6d.) and a carved stone commemorating the foundation of the British fort on the island by Captain John Dutton (1s.).

6. St Helena, 2 shillings 6 pence, 1969
Since 1969 St Helena has exploited the growing interest of collectors in stamps having a military theme, with sets of stamps of uniforms and regimental insignia. The first set of four stamps, designed by Rene North and lithographed by Format, were of infantrymen and artillerymen in uniforms from 1815 to 1920, with the dates of their garrison duty in St Helena.

7. St Helena, 2 shillings 6 pence, 1967
Internal self-government was granted to St Helena in May 1967 and two stamps, printed by Harrisons, marked the occasion. The stamps were designed by W. H. Brown and featured the island's coat of arms. The 2s.6d. denomination has been recorded with the red colour (the ribbon and the cross on the flag) omitted.

8. St Helena, 1 pound, 1961
Victor Whiteley designed a definitive series issued

in December 1961. The values up to 10s. illustrated birds, flowers and marine life, against a background of St Helena lace, while the ultra-large £1 stamp used lace as a decorative border. The stamp reproduced a portrait of Queen Elizabeth with the baby Prince Andrew, from a photograph by Cecil Beaton. The early printings were on ordinary paper, but several values, including the £1, were reissued in November 1965 on chalky paper.

9. St Helena, 1 pound, 1968
Sylvia Goaman's rather austere designs for the definitive series of 1968 aroused considerable criticism because of their generally vapid appearance and because the queen's profile was shown rising out of various forms of plant-life. A different plant appeared on each stamp, in an appeal to thematic collectors, but different subjects were selected for the principal vignettes, with the emphasis on modern development and improved facilities.

10. Ascension, 3 pence, 1924
Before 1922 ordinary British stamps were used in Ascension and can be identified by their postmark. In 1922 the contemporary series of St Helena was overprinted 'Ascension' and issued in the island, after it was transferred from the Admiralty to the Colonial Office. The same design, with the inscription re-engraved, was used for the series issued between 1924 and 1934. The stamps were typographed by De La Rue in denominations from ½d. to 3s.

11. Ascension, 2 shillings 6 pence, 1934
The uniform typographed series was superseded by a pictorial set, recess-printed by De La Rue and issued in July 1934. Six designs, incorporating a profile of King George V, were used for the five denominations. The five horizontal designs featured scenery while the vertical design (1, 2 and 8d. and 2s.6d.) showed a turtle and a map of the island. The radio masts in the side panels allude to the island's importance as a staging post for the Cable and Wireless international telecommunications network.

12. Ascension, 10 shillings, 1938
The George V horizontal designs were retained in a modified form for the definitive series of 1938 portraying King George VI. The series, from ½d. to 10s., underwent several changes of colour, as a result of increases in postal rates, and also exhibited a number of 'Blitz perfs', as a result of the emergency perforation of partly finished stamps elsewhere after De La Rue's premises were bombed.

13. Ascension, 1 shilling, 1956
Bradbury Wilkinson recess-printed a pictorial series for Ascension released in November 1956. The stamps depicted the scenery and wildlife of the island. A map of the island appeared on the 1d. denomination while a map of the south Atlantic showing Ascension's position in regard to the international cable network was depicted on the 2d. value.

14. Ascension, 2 shillings 3 pence, 1969
Since 1967 Ascension has issued short thematic sets at frequent intervals, featuring fishes and naval badges. The first series of naval crests appeared in October 1969 and were designed by L. D. Curtis. The date at the top of the design denotes the visit of the ship to Ascension.

15. Ascension, 2½ pence, 1971
Ascension adopted the new British decimal currency in February 1971 and issued a definitive series with the theme of the evolution of space travel. The stamps ranged from a ½p. showing a

PLATE 73 ST HELENA AND DEPENDENCIES · PLATE 74 MAURITIUS, SEYCHELLES

medieval Chinese rocket to the £1 giving an artist's impression of a future space research station. Isaac Newton's scientific instruments and an apple were depicted on the 2½p., the apple being an allusion to the dramatic incident which gave Sir Isaac Newton the clue to the law of gravity. The stamps were designed by Victor Whiteley and lithographed in multicolour by Format International.

16. Tristan da Cunha, 2 + 2 pence, 1922
British stamps and an overprint inscribed 'Tristan da Cunha' were supplied by the British Post Office to Sir Ernest Shackleton for use on the Shackleton-Rowett Expedition to the Antarctic in 1921–22, following the precedent set by New Zealand for King Edward VII Land and Victoria Land in 1908–11 (see plate 117). The expedition was prematurely abandoned after Shackleton's death at South Georgia. The overprinted stamps were postmarked at Tristan da Cunha in May 1922 as a souvenir of the expedition's visit to the island on the homeward journey, but such stamps were never used postally. They are regarded as the forerunner of Tristan stamps and, as such, were reproduced on stamps of 1971 celebrating the 50th anniversary of the expedition.

17. Tristan da Cunha, 6 pence, 1952
A post office was established on Tristan da Cunha in January 1952 and contemporary stamps of St Helena suitably overprinted were put on sale. Previously letters from the island were dispatched either unstamped or bearing British adhesives cancelled by various unofficial cachets. Examples of covers from the 'pre-adhesive' period are now highly sought after by collectors.

18. Tristan da Cunha, 7½ cents, 1961
A definitive series, from ½d. to 10s., depicting marine life, was issued in February 1960. The fourteen denominations were designed by Mr and Mrs G. F. Harris and recess-printed by Waterlow and Sons. In April 1961 the series was reissued with values in South African cents and rands. This set had a very short life, being withdrawn from sale on 10 October 1961, when Tristan da Cunha was evacuated after the volcano erupted. Four denominations of this series were subsequently overprinted at St Helena (where reserve stocks were held) and surcharged, in sterling, to raise money for a relief fund.

19. Tristan da Cunha, 1 shilling 6 pence, 1969
From 1853 to 1950 the United Society for the Propagation of the Gospel supplied the island with the only outside agency, in the form of a resident missionary, and took a close interest in the island's welfare. A set of four stamps was issued in November 1969 paying tribute to the work of the Society and illustrating landmarks in the religious history of the island. The stamps were designed by Jennifer Toombs and lithographed by Format. The somewhat whimsical design of this stamp, and its curious caption, refer to the arrival of the Rev. Erwin H. Dodgson (brother of Lewis Carroll) in 1881. The schooner *Edward Vittery* was wrecked and Mr Dodgson's books and baggage were lost.

20. Tristan da Cunha, 6 pence, 1963
After eighteen months in refugee camps in England the islanders decided to return to Tristan. The island was officially resettled on 12 April 1963, and the contemporary St Helena definitive series (½d to 10s.) was overprinted for use at Tristan. The 'Resettlement' series was superseded by a ships' thematic series in February 1965.

21. Tristan da Cunha, 2 shillings 6 pence, 1966
The 150th anniversary of the settlement of the island by a British garrison was marked by four

stamps designed by Victor Whiteley and lithographed in multicolour by Harrison and Sons. The common design showed a sailing ship of the Napoleonic period and an artilleryman of 1816. The island was temporarily garrisoned to forestall attempts by Bonapartists to release Napoleon from St Helena. The garrison was withdrawn in 1817, but Corporal Glass and his family elected to remain behind to form the nucleus of the present colony.

22. Tristan da Cunha, 50 pence, 1971
In common with the other countries of the sterling bloc Tristan da Cunha adopted decimal currency in February 1971. The definitive series up to 10s. was surcharged in new pence. The basic stamp, featuring the South African research vessel *R.S.A.*, was recess-printed by Bradbury Wilkinson and was added to the ships' series in September 1967. An entirely new series, illustrating flowers of the island, was issued in 1972 to replace the surcharged set.

PLATE 74
Mauritius and Seychelles

1. Mauritius, undenominated, 1858
The early philately of Mauritius is a curious example of perversity. While the colonial authorities were supplying the island with attractive Britannia stamps recess-printed by Perkins Bacon the local administration neglected to put them into circulation and persisted with a series of locally produced stamps, whose ugliness and crudity have seldom been surpassed. To Mauritius goes the honour of being the first British colony to issue its own stamps. To Mauritius also the Crown Agents owe their first contract for the supply of stamps, the order having been placed with them in 1848. Stamps in the Britannia design, subsequently used in Barbados and Trinidad, were prepared in 1848 and shipped off to the island, where they languished for several years. Eventually green (4d.), vermilion (6d.) and magenta (9d.) stamps were issued between 1854 and 1859, but the red-brown and blue stamps were never put on sale. Eventually they were remaindered and many of them were overprinted as souvenirs of the London Philatelic Exhibition of 1890.

2. Mauritius, 4 cents, 1885
Mauritius changed to the rupee of 100 cents in 1878, producing a spate of surcharges which persisted down to the end of the century. De La Rue typographed the stamps of Mauritius from 1860 onwards, using different frames with a standard profile of Queen Victoria.

3. Mauritius, 3 cents, 1895
Royal portraiture gave way to heraldry in 1895, when De La Rue typographed a series from 1 to 18c., bearing the island's coat of arms. Stamps in a similar design, but including the words 'Postage Revenue', were issued in 1910.

4. Mauritius, 15 cents, 1899
The glorious era of French colonial rule, under Admiral Mahé de Labourdonnais (1735–46) was recalled by this large-format stamp issued in December 1899 to mark the bicentenary of his birth. The stamp was recess-printed by De La Rue and is in the florid style favoured for the early commemorative stamps of the British Empire.

5. Mauritius, 15 cents, 1899
The Diamond Jubilee of Queen Victoria was

belatedly marked by a 36c. stamp in May 1898, almost a year after the event had taken place. The stamp was typographed by De La Rue, who unimaginatively adapted their coat of arms design for the purpose. Only the inclusion of the VR monogram in the lower corners gives an indication of whose jubilee was being celebrated. There seems to have been little demand for the stamp, and used copies are much scarcer than unused. The following year it was revalued by surcharging and used as a 15c. stamp. Examples are known in which the surcharge bar is omitted.

6. Mauritius, 12 cents, 1938
The colonial keyplate designs were introduced in 1910, when a series portraying King Edward VII was typographed by De La Rue. The keyplates were subsequently adapted for the series of 1913–34 and 1938–48 portraying George V and George VI. The shades and perforations of the George VI series varied considerably, especially during World War II. Mauritius was the last colony (apart from the Leeward Islands) to use the keyplate designs pioneered by De La Rue in 1879.

7. Mauritius, 1 rupee, 1948
The centenary of the island's first stamps was somewhat tardily celebrated (a year after the event) by a set of four stamps recess-printed by Bradbury Wilkinson and issued in March 1948. The stamps reproduced the 1d. and 2d. Mauritius 'Post Office' stamps issued in September 1847. The original stamps were engraved singly on a copper plate by James Barnard, a half-blind watchmaker and jeweler of Port Louis. Only 500 of each denomination were printed, for which Barnard received £10 – more than the face value of the stamps! The stamps were a copy (one might almost say a parody) of the contemporary British 1d. red and 2d. blue stamps.

8. Mauritius, 35 cents, 1954
After retaining the keyplate stamps for so long Mauritius was one of the first colonies in the post-war period to adopt a photogravure pictorial series. Stamps in denominations from 1c. to 10 rupees were issued in July 1950 in various designs featuring scenery, wildlife and occupations of the island. The same designs, with the portrait of Queen Elizabeth substituted, were reissued in 1953–54.

9. Mauritius, 20 cents, 1961
A set of four stamps, lithographed by Enschedé, was issued in January 1961 to celebrate the 150th anniversary of the establishment of a British post office in the island. The stamps, in denominations of 10, 20 and 35c., and 1r., reproduced the Lawrence portrait of King George III and the Annigoni portrait of Queen Elizabeth and the form of crown used in 1811 and 1961.

10. Mauritius, 60 cents, 1967
David Reid-Henry, an authority on the birds of Mauritius, designed a definitive series printed in multicolour photogravure by Harrisons in 1965. Similar designs, with a new profile of Queen Elizabeth, were used for a set of four stamps celebrating the attainment of self-government in September 1967. Subsequently the entire definitive series was overprinted 'Self Government 1967'.

11. Mauritius, 15 cents, 1968
The bicentenary of the visit of Bernardin de Saint-Pierre to Mauritius was commemorated by a set of six stamps issued in December 1968. The stamps were lithographed by Format and designed by Victor Whiteley, who adapted eighteenth century illustrations from Saint-Pierre's book *Paul et Virginie*, a romantic tragedy set in Mauritius. A

PLATE 74 MAURITIUS, SEYCHELLES · PLATE 75 EQUATORIAL AFRICA

portrait of Saint-Pierre, from a contemporary miniature, appeared on the 2.50 rupee stamp.

12. Mauritius, 2.50 rupees, 1969
The 150th anniversary of Telfair's improvements to the sugar industry was marked by a set of five stamps and a miniature sheet, designed by Whiteley and printed in multicolour photogravure by Enschedé. The stamps depicted cane-crushing and sugar refining machinery of the eighteenth and nineteenth centuries. The top value reproduced a contemporary portrait of Dr Charles Telfair, whose improvements revolutionized the sugar industry, source of Mauritius' wealth. The series was also released in a miniature sheet containing one stamp of each denomination, a practice adopted for many Mauritian commemorative sets in recent years.

13. Mauritius, 15 cents, 1970
Two stamps were issued in May 1970 to celebrate the centenary of the birth of V. I. Lenin. The stamps were printed in blackish green and silver (15c.) or gold (75c.) by the State Printing Works in Moscow and were presented free of cost to the people of Mauritius by the Soviet authorities. These were the first stamps produced in the Soviet Union to be issued in a British Commonwealth country.

14. Seychelles, 3 cents, 1893
British or Mauritian stamps were used in the Seychelles prior to 1890 and may be identified by the B 64 numeral obliterator of that island. The postal administration was separated from Mauritius in April 1890 and the De La Rue colonial key-type series introduced. Changes in postal rates led to provisional surcharges in January 1893, followed by new denominations including the 3c. value.

15. Seychelles, 2 cents, 1917
The various colonial keyplates were used for sets portraying King Edward VII (1903–06) and King George V (1912–13 and 1917–32). The frames were modified in 1917 for a series inscribed 'Postage & Revenue'. Previous issues had been inscribed for postal use only. The 1917–22 series was originally printed on Multiple Crown CA paper, but was reissued between 1921 and 1932 on the Multiple Script CA paper.

16. Seychelles, 5 rupees, 1938
The Seychelles was one of the first colonies to use photogravure for a pictorial definitive series. Between January 1938 and June 1949 various changes of colour and new denominations were introduced, making this (24 values) one of the longest British Commonwealth definitive sets issued in modern times. Three designs were employed, the coco-de-mer palm, the giant tortoise and a fishing pirogue. The stamps were produced by Harrison and Sons.

17. Seychelles, 3 cents, 1952
The same designs were retained for a series with a more mature portrait of King George VI inset. Harrison and Sons added two new designs to the series, featuring a sailfish and a map of the Indian Ocean giving the position of the colony. Most stamps of this series are recorded with the watermark errors, missing crown, and St Edward's crown substituted for a Tudor crown.

18. Seychelles, 5 cents, 1957
The definitive series of February 1954 retained the previous designs, merely substituting a portrait of Queen Elizabeth for that of King George. An increase in local postal rates in 1957, however, led to the introduction of a new design, illustrating a flying fox (fruit bat). In the previous month the 45c. stamp was locally surcharged 5c.

19. Seychelles, 2.25 rupees, 1961
The centenary of the establishment of a post office in the Seychelles was marked in December 1961 by a set of three stamps, recess-printed by Bradbury Wilkinson. They reproduced a Mauritian 6d. stamp of 1861 with the B 64 obliterator of the Seychelles; the 'postmark' was typographed. The stamps were among the first to make use of the Annigoni portrait, subsequently modified for the pictorial definitive series of 1962.

20. Seychelles, 15 cents, 1962
Just as the Seychelles was one of the first colonies to use photogravure for its definitive stamps, so also was it in the forefront of the fashion for multi-colour photogravure. As many as seven colours were used in the production of certain denominations of the series designed by Victor Whiteley and issued in February 1962. Changes in postal rates led to the addition of 45 and 75c. values in 1966 and a 30c. stamp in 1968. The stamps were the usual colonial medley of birds, fishes, flowers, landmarks and occupations of the islanders.

21. Seychelles, 2.25 rupees, 1967
After pursuing a conservative policy on stamp issues the Seychelles began issuing short thematic sets at regular intervals. The first of these consisted of four stamps issued in December 1967 and featuring sea-shells of the islands. The stamps were issued ostensibly in connection with International Tourist Year, whose emblem was incorporated in the design. The stamps were designed by Victor Whiteley and printed in multicolour photogravure by Harrison and Sons.

22. Seychelles, 15 cents, 1969
For the definitive series, lithographed by Enschedé and issued in November 1969, Mrs M. Hayward chose ships connected with the Seychelles. The designs ranged chronologically from the landing of Picault in 1742 to the visit of the Duke of Edinburgh in 1956. The 15c. stamp purports to show the German warship *Koenigsberg* at Aldabra in 1915. In fact it was 1914 that this famous raider visited Aldabra, and, moreover, the wrong *Koenigsberg* was depicted on the stamp. This is yet another example of those blunders in stamp design which delight the heart of the philatelist.

23. Seychelles, 85 cents, 1968
A set of four stamps, designed by Mrs Mary Hayward and lithographed by Harrison and Sons, was released in December 1968 to mark the bicentenary of the first landing on the island of Praslin. The stamps depicted sailing vessels and island wildlife.

24. Seychelles, 85 cents, 1969
The importance of the Seychelles as a tracking station in connection with the American Apollo moon projects was alluded to in a set of five stamps designed by Victor Whiteley and lithographed in multicolour by Format International. The stamps depicted the Apollo launching, astronauts on the moon, the lunar module leaving the mother ship and a lunar landscape. The 85c. stamp featured the tracking station in the Seychelles.

25. Seychelles, 3.50 rupees, 1971
The completion of the Seychelles International Airport in 1971 was the excuse for a set of six stamps tracing the development of aviation in the islands and they showed different types of aircraft used in the Seychelles; the one illustrated is the Vickers Supermarine Walrus flying-boat.

PLATE 75
Equatorial Africa

1. French Congo, 10 centimes, 1900
The French colonial general series overprinted 'Congo français' was introduced in 1891 and was superseded the following year by the 'Tablet' series suitably inscribed. Paul Merwart produced the famous design of a leopard in ambush for a set of six stamps, from 1 to 15c., typographed by M. Chassepot and issued in May 1900. The 1c. is recorded with inverted background, and the 2 and 4c. with the wrong colour of background. Higher denominations featured a woman of the Bakalois tribe or a grove of coconut palms. In February 1906 French Congo was divided into four administrative regions – Gaboon, Middle Congo, Oubangui-Chari and Tchad and the distinctive stamps of these territories were subsequently issued using similar designs.

2. Gaboon, 25 centimes, 1910
Gaboon issued its own stamps from 1886 to 1889, mainly consisting of provisional surcharges on the colonial general series or typeset 15 and 25c. stamps produced locally. From 1889 till 1904 Gaboon formed part of the French Congo but then became a separate colony, using the 'Tablet' series appropriately inscribed. Distinctive pictorial stamps appeared in 1910. The original version incorporated the words 'Congo Français', but the designs were redrawn in December 1910 with the caption changed to 'Afrique Equatoriale'. The three designs were a native warrior, woman, and a view of Libreville.

3. Gaboon, 1 centime, 1932
C. Hourriez produced three designs, used for a recess-printed series issued in 1932–33 which replaced the previous typographed set. The designs featured a raft on the River Ogowe, a Gabonese village, and the Comte de Brazza. Stamps of French Equatorial Africa superseded the stamps of Gaboon in 1937.

4. Gaboon, 50 centimes, 1961
Gaboon became a republic within the French Community in November 1958, but apart from several commemorative stamps did not reintroduce a distinctive definitive series until 1961. The low values were of flowers while the high values (used for airmail) were of birds. The stamps were recess-printed in multicolour at the French Government Printing Works in Paris.

5. Gaboon, 4 centimes, 1924
The pictorial series of 1910–17, designed by L. Colmet Daage, was issued between 1924 and 1931 with a three-line overprint 'Afrique Equatoriale Française', reflecting the closer political grouping of the four territories in Equatorial Africa. This was also denoted by the monogram AEF incorporated in the 1932 series.

6. Gaboon, 50 + 50 centimes, 1962
A triangular format was adopted by many of the French African territories for their postage due stamps, each denomination being released in two designs *se-tenant*. The Gaboon series took the theme of fruits, the two 50c. stamps showing mangoes and pineapple. The series was designed by G. François and recess-printed in three-colour combinations.

7. Gaboon, 50 francs, 1971
The Europafrique movement, reinforcing the ties between France and her former African colonies, was founded in 1963 and since then Gaboon has

PLATE 75 EQUATORIAL AFRICA · PLATE 76 FRENCH WEST AFRICA

issued a number of stamps to publicize it. The 1971 stamp was designed by P. Bequet and printed in photogravure by Delrieu. Many Gabonese stamps since independence have emphasized the connection with the motherland.

8. Gaboon, 25 francs, 1959
The first stamps issued by Gaboon after attaining independence consisted of 15 and 25f. stamps with full-face or profile portraits of Prime Minister Léon Mba. The stamps were designed and engraved by Meunier and recess-printed at the French Government Printing Works, which have continued to produce many Gabonese stamps to this day.

9. Middle Congo, 20 centimes, 1907
After the division of the French Congo in 1906 distinctive stamps were adopted by Middle Congo. J. Puyplat adapted the leopard design of 1900 and it is interesting to note that Paul Merwart's name appears in the lower left-hand corner of the design as the 'inventor'. The Bakalois and Libreville designs were similarly adapted and the stamps typographed in two-colour combinations by the French Government Printing Works. The 10c. was surcharged 5c. in aid of the Red Cross in 1916. New colours and values appeared in 1922 and the series was overprinted 'Afrique Équatoriale Française' in 1924–30. In 1937 it was superseded by French Equatorial African stamps.

10. Congo, 15 francs, 1960
The former Middle Congo attained independence as the Congo republic in November 1958 but, like Gaboon, continued to use the stamps of Equatorial Africa until 1961. One of the earliest distinctive issues, however, consisted of two stamps designed by Meunier which portrayed Fulbert Youlou, the abbé turned president. The 15 and 85f. stamps were issued in December 1960 as the precursor of a flower and fish definitive series.

11. Congo, 50 centimes, 1961
Tropical fishes formed the theme of the first independent definitive series, released in November 1961. Various denominations were added to this series in October 1964. Though independent, Congo has remained within the French Community and all its stamps down to the present time have been designed and printed in France.

12. Congo, 80 francs, 1965
Though entirely distinctive designs have always been used there is a certain parallel between the stamps of many of the French Community countries in Africa. Thus the Congo's set of June 1965 honouring famous men had its counterpart elsewhere, especially in its portraiture of Kennedy and Churchill. The Congo series also portrayed Patrice Lumumba and Barthélemy Boganda, the first president, killed in an accident shortly after taking office in 1959. The stamps were printed in two-colour photogravure by Delrieu.

13. Congo, 50 centimes, 1961
A series of postage due stamps in triangular format was issued in December 1961. Each denomination consisted of two designs printed alternately throughout the sheet. The two 50c. denominations featured a native letter-carrier with a letter in a cleft stick and by contrast a modern Brossard monoplane. The stamps featured various old and new forms of mail transportation.

14. Oubangui-Chari-Tchad, 10 centimes, 1915
The stamps of Middle Congo were used in this area till 1915, when a distinctive overprint 'Oubangui-Chari-Tchad' was introduced. New colours were issued in 1922 and later that year separate issues were adopted in Oubangui-Chari and Tchad.

15. Oubangui-Chari, 1 centime, 1924
Stamps of Middle Congo overprinted 'Oubangui-Chari' were issued in November 1922 in denominations from 1c. to 5f. Between October 1924 and September 1933 the stamps were additionally overprinted 'Afrique Equatoriale Française'. These stamps were withdrawn in 1937 when the general series of Equatorial Africa was adopted.

16. Central African Republic, 100 francs, 1967
Oubangui-Chari became an independent republic within the French Community in 1958 and assumed the name of the Central African Republic. The pattern of stamp design and production has followed that of the other Equatorial states, with the same blend of thematic definitives, commemoratives for international events and personalities and pictorial triangular postage dues. C. Guillaume designed and engraved this 100f. stamp issued to mark the inauguration of Bangui M'Poko airport.

17. Central African Republic, 50 centimes, 1962
The Central African Republic has likewise adopted a triangular format for its postage dues. A series designed by R. Serres and engraved by G. Bétemps was released in October 1962. The various designs featured different types of beetles. Each denomination consists of two designs printed in tête-bêche pairs throughout the sheet.

18. Tchad, 1 centime, 1924
Stamps of Middle Congo, in new colours, were overprinted 'Tchad' when this territory began issuing its own stamps in November 1922. The 1c. stamp is known with the overprint omitted but is regarded as an error of Tchad, since it was never issued in those colours in Middle Congo. The Equatorial overprint was introduced in September 1924 and new colours and denominations added to the series between then and 1933. Provisional surcharges appeared in 1925–27 and the stamps were superseded by the general series of Equatorial Africa in 1937.

19. Tchad, 100 francs, 1964
Tchad became a republic within the French Community in 1958 and began issuing its own stamps the following year. R. Aubry designed this stamp in memory of John F. Kennedy, printed in multicolour photogravure by Delrieu in 1964. Among the other international figures portrayed on recent issues of Tchad are Dr Albert Schweitzer, Abraham Lincoln and Conrad Adenauer.

20. Tchad, 25 francs, 1965
The majority of Tchad's commemorative stamps have consisted of single denominations and a high proportion have been devoted to matters of local importance. P. Lambert designed this stamp, issued in July 1965, in honour of the National Gendarmerie. The stamps are invariably produced in France, by Delrieu, So. Ge. Im. or the Government Printing Works in Paris.

21. French Equatorial Africa, 5 centimes, 1942
Stamps of French Equatorial Africa were used in Gaboon, Middle Congo, Oubangui-Chari and Tchad from 1937 till 1961. The colony went over to the Gaullists in 1940 and the definitive series of 1937 was overprinted 'Afrique Française Libre' (Free French Africa). Subsequently a definitive series showing the phoenix was designed by Edmund Dulac and printed in photogravure by Harrison and Sons in 1942. Various stamps of the 1937 series were also overprinted to commemorate the arrival of General de Gaulle in Equatorial Africa in October 1940.

22. French Equatorial Africa, 10 centimes, 1946
A recess-printed definitive series was released between 1946 and 1953. The stamps, designed and engraved by Pierre Gandon or R. Serres, featured scenery, wildlife and native types, while the four airmail stamps (50 to 500f.) showed aircraft. The stamps were recess-printed at the Institut de Gravure in Paris. Multicoloured recess-printed stamps in the same subjects were released gradually between 1955 and 1957. The separate issues of the four republics gradually superseded the stamps of Equatorial Africa between 1959 and 1961.

PLATE 76
French West Africa

---

1. French West Africa, 30 centimes, 1947
Separate issues of stamps in the French colonies of Dahomey, French Guinea, French Sudan, Ivory Coast, Mauritania, Niger, Senegal and Upper Volta were superseded in 1944 by stamps inscribed 'Afrique Occidentale Française'. Hitherto stamps with this inscription or the abbreviation AOF had been used in these territories, but distinctive designs and the names of the colonies had been featured. A series lithographed by De La Rue for the Free French was followed in 1947 by a recess-printed series, produced at the Institut de Gravure in Paris and depicting scenery and the peoples of the various regions. The 30c. stamp shows a girl beside the submersible bridge over the Bamako River in the French Sudan. The stamps of French West Africa were gradually phased out in 1958–59 as the component territories became independent and resumed separate issues of stamps.

2. Dahomey, 4 centimes, 1913
Dahomey issued its own stamps from 1899 to 1944 while under French colonial administration. The colonial keyplates of 1899–1900 were superseded by the West African omnibus designs in 1906–07 and these, in turn, gave way to a distinctive series showing a native climbing a palm-tree. The series, from 1c. to 5f., was designed by J. de la Nezière and typographed in two-colour combinations. A recess-printed pictorial series replaced this issue in 1941.

3. Dahomey, 50 centimes, 1963
Dahomey began issuing stamps in 1960 as a republic within the French Community, but left the French union in August of that year. Nevertheless all the stamps issued since independence, without exception, have been designed and printed in France. This stamp was one of a set of six issued in April 1963 in honour of the Dakar Games. The three designs, featuring boxing, running and football, were produced by Durrens and recess-printed at the Government Printing Works, Paris.

4. Benin, 4 centimes, 1894
French post offices were established on the gulf of Benin in 1892 and contemporary French colonial general issues were overprinted BENIN in September of that year. Subsequently the colonial keyplate 'Tablet' design was used, either inscribed 'Golfe de Benin' (1893) or simply 'Benin' (1894). These were superseded by the stamps of Dahomey in 1899.

5. French Guinea, 15 centimes, 1904
The 'Tablet' series inscribed 'Guinée Française' was introduced in November 1892, but gave way to a distinctive series, depicting a Fulas shepherd. The series was typographed in values from 1c. to 5f. and issued in December 1904. The West African omnibus designs were adopted in 1906.

229

PLATE 76 FRENCH WEST AFRICA

6. French Guinea, 1 centime, 1913

Following the pattern of the French colonies in West Africa Guinea adopted a series in 1913 with a distinctive vignette designed by J. de la Nezière and engraved by M. J. Puyplat. The stamps, in denominations from 1c. to 5f., showed the ford at Kitim. New values, changes of colour and provisional surcharges appeared between 1916 and 1933. A recess-printed pictorial series appeared in 1938–40. The various colonial omnibus sets were issued, but no distinctive commemoratives.

7. Guinea, 75 francs, 1964

Guinea became an independent republic in October 1958 but did not begin issuing its own stamps till the following year. Unlike the majority of the former French colonies Guinea has preferred to go elsewhere for its stamps and these have been printed by De La Rue, Courvoisier, Fournier and, most of all, by the E. A. Wright Bank Note Co. of Philadelphia. The last-named firm recess-printed a set of four stamps and two miniature sheets, issued in October 1964 to mark the New York World's Fair. The stamps depicted the Guinea pavilion while the miniature sheets depicted the Unisphere, with the Guinea pavilion in the background. The stamps were reissued the following year in new colours, with the date '1965' incorporated in the design.

8. Guinea, 200 francs, 1971

Since independence Guinea has changed its definitive series at frequent intervals, using various themes. That of 1971 illustrates various fishes in denominations from 5 to 200f. The stamps were printed in multicolour photogravure by Heraclio Fournier of Vittoria.

9. French Soudan, 10 centimes, 1931

Stamps inscribed 'Soudan Français' were used between 1894 and 1899, when the colony was abolished and its territories divided between Senegal, Guinea, Ivory Coast, Dahomey and Senegambia and Niger. The colony was reconstituted in 1921 and the stamps of Upper Senegal and Niger were issued with an appropriate overprint. A decade elapsed, however, before a distinctive series was introduced. Three designs were used for the series issued in March 1931, and depicted a Sudanese woman, the Bamako gateway and a Niger boatman. The dies were designed and engraved by À. Delzers, J. Piel and G. Hourriez respectively.

10. Mauritania, 15 centimes, 1913

The first stamps of Mauritania appeared in 1906 and consisted of the West African omnibus designs suitably inscribed. A distinctive series in a uniform design showing merchants crossing the desert appeared in 1913, providing yet another example of the remarkable partnership of de la Nezière and Puyplat in French colonial stamp production in the period before World War II. The series, after numerous changes of colour and additional denominations, was replaced by a recess-printed pictorial set in 1938–40 which was, in turn, superseded by the general series of French West Africa in 1944.

11. Mauritania, 50 francs, 1968

The independent Islamic republic of Mauritania began issuing its own stamps in 1960 and these, without exception, have been designed and printed in France. The stamps reflect a catholicity of taste and interest, ranging from Soviet space achievements to Old Master paintings. This stamp, portraying Dr Martin Luther King, was one of a pair of November 1968 dedicated to 'Apostles of Peace'. The other stamp portrayed Mahatma Gandhi. Both stamps were printed in photogravure by Delrieu of Paris.

12. Upper Volta, 4 centimes, 1928

The colony of Upper Volta had a relatively brief existence between 1920 and 1933. The first stamps consisted of the series of Upper Senegal and Niger overprinted 'Haute-Volta'. This was superseded in 1928 by a series using three designs, a Hausa warrior (1 to 20c.), a Hausa woman (25 to 90c.) and a Hausa horseman (1 to 20f.). The stamps were designed by Becker and engraved by G. Daussy, and typographed in the usual two-colour garish combinations so beloved of the French colonial administrations in the 'twenties. The stamps were withdrawn at the end of 1932 when the territory was divided between Niger, French Soudan and Ivory Coast.

13. Upper Volta, 1 franc, 1960

Upper Volta was reconstituted as an independent republic in December 1958 and introduced a distinctive definitive series in April 1960. The stamps, recess-printed in values from 30 centimes to 85 francs, illustrated various animals, and the native masks which represented them. This stamp, designed and engraved by Cottet, features a warthog mask.

14. Ivory Coast, 50 centimes, 1960

A definitive series featuring native masks was designed by G. Francois and recess-printed at the French Government Printing Works in Paris. Each denomination from 50c. to 85f. featured a different type of mask from each region of the country.

15. Mauritania, 1 franc, 1965

Since independence Mauritania has issued numerous short thematic sets. This stamp from a series of June 1965 devoted to tourism and archaeology featured a grove of palm trees in the Adrar district. The stamps were designed and engraved by Pierre Gandon and recess-printed in Paris.

16. Mali, 100 francs, 1964

The former French Soudan and Senegal formed the federation of Mali, within the French Community, in 1959. In August 1960, however, Senegal seceded from the federation while the Soudan, retaining the name Mali, left the Community. The numerous stamps of the republic of Mali since 1960 have all been printed in France. The stamps cover a very wide field of subjects, reflecting current fashions in stamp-collecting rather than events and personalities of specific interest to Mali.

17. Niger, 1 franc, 1962

Stamps for use on government correspondence were introduced in January 1962. A series designed and engraved by A. Barre was typographed in Paris in denominations from 1 to 200f. The common design featured a Djerma woman. A 30f. denomination was added to the series in 1965.

18. Ivory Coast, 1 centime, 1913

The Ivory Coast went through the various phases in French colonial philately: 'Tablet' series (1892), West African omnibus designs (1906) and a two-tone series by de la Nezière (1913). The stamps, from 1c. to 5f., featured a native canoe on the Ebrie Lagoon. Carved idols decorate the side panels. After the predictable mutations of colour and denomination between 1916 and 1936 this set was replaced by a recess-printed pictorial series issued between 1936 and 1942. French West African stamps were used from 1944 to 1959 and subsequently stamps of the independent republic of the Ivory Coast.

19. Senegambia and Niger, 2 centimes, 1903

The remnants of the former French Soudan, partitioned in 1902, formed the colony of Senegambia and Niger and the 'Tablet' series thus inscribed was issued in July 1903. Three years later the name of this territory was changed to Upper Senegal and Niger and stamps with that inscription superseded the 'Tablet' series.

20. Senegal, 5 centimes, 1915

The first stamps of Senegal consisted of the French colonial general series surcharged 5, 10 or 15c. in 1887. Similar stamps overprinted 'Sénégal' were issued in 1892 and later that year the 'Tablet' series was released with a suitable inscription 'Sénégal et Dépendances'. From then until 1944 Senegal passed through the various phases of the French West African colonies. This stamp was one of a series of postage due stamps issued in the standard West African design in 1915.

21. Senegal, 10 francs, 1965

Senegal resumed stamp-issuing in 1960, as a republic within the French Community. In many respects the stamps of this country have adhered more closely in style and subject matter to the mother country than those of most other ex-French colonies, and reflect the close economic and political ties with France. This stamp, designed by A. Spitz and engraved by J. Piel, was issued in April 1965 to commemorate the centenary of postal services in Senegal. It portrays Abdoulaye Seck, director of posts from 1873 to 1931.

22. Niger, 10 centimes, 1926

The first stamps of this territory appeared in December 1921 and consisted of the stamps of Upper Senegal and Niger overprinted 'Territoire du Niger'. A distinctive series designed by Jules Kerhor, was typographed in 1926. The three designs featured a native drawing water from a well (1 to 15c.), Zinder Fort (20 to 90c.) and a native craft on the River Niger (franc denominations). Distinctive stamps were reintroduced in 1959 for the republic of Niger.

23. Niger, 50 centimes, 1962

Although it attained independence in 1958 the Republic of Niger did not resume issuing its own stamps until December 1959, when a definitive series was gradually released between that date and January 1962. All sixteen stamps made some reference to nature conservation or to the National Park. It was engraved by various French artists and recess-printed by the French Government Printing Works, Paris.

24. Senegal, 25 francs, 1963

The third anniversary of the death of Professor Gaston Berger the educationalist was marked by this 25f. stamp depicting his portrait, an owl and his book 'Prospective'. The stamp was designed by J. Combet and printed in multicolour photogravure.

25. Upper Senegal and Niger, 2 centimes, 1906

The name of the territory Senegambia and Niger was changed in 1906 and the French West African omnibus designs, inscribed 'Ht. Sénégal et Niger', were issued. Three designs were used throughout French West Africa between 1906 and 1913. The lowest values portrayed General Faidherbe, with Pont Faidherbe, the bridge over the Senegal River, in the background. The middle values depicted palm trees and the franc denomination portrayed Governor-General Noel-Eugéne Ballay, with a native village in the background. The stamps were engraved by J. Puyplat and typographed in monochrome, with the name of the territory in red or blue. J. de la Nezière designed a series for Upper Senegal and Niger in 1914 featuring a Touareg tribesman. The stamps of this territory were superseded by the separate issues of Niger and French Soudan in 1921.

PLATE 77 CAMEROUN, TOGO

PLATE 77
Cameroun and Togo

1. Kamerun, 5 pfennigs, 1900
German stamps diagonally overprinted 'Kamerun' were issued in this territory in 1897, followed three years later by the colonial keyplate designs featuring the imperial yacht *Hohenzollern*. The first printings of these stamps, from 3pf. to 5m., were on unwatermarked paper, but between 1905 and 1914 the lozenge watermarked paper was adopted. The 1 and 5m. stamps on watermarked paper were produced in 1915–18 but were on sale only at the philatelic bureau in Berlin, since the colony had, by that time, fallen to the Allies.

2. Kamerun, ½ penny, 1915
After the British occupation of Kamerun the contemporary German colonial stamps were overprinted C.E.F. (Cameroons Expeditionary Force) and surcharged with values in sterling from ½d. to 5s. Numerous errors and varieties have been recorded in this overprint. These stamps were superseded by the ordinary issues of Nigeria after the incorporation of the British held territory in the federation of Nigeria.

3. Cameroun, 5 centimes, 1916
Stamps of Gaboon, overprinted 'Corps Expéditionnaire Franco-Anglais CAMEROUN' were issued in November 1915 and were followed in January 1916 by stamps of the French Congo overprinted 'Occupation Française du Cameroun'. These, in turn, were superseded by stamps of Middle Congo overprinted 'CAMEROUN Occupation Française' later in 1916. Most denominations, from 1c. to 5f., have been recorded without a stop after 'Française' or an inverted 's' in 'Française'.

4. Cameroun, 30 centimes, 1921
After World War I France was granted a mandate over Cameroun by the League of Nations and stamps of Middle Congo were overprinted for use in 1921. The southern portion of the former German colony, under British occupation, was absorbed into Nigeria, and used ordinary Nigerian stamps until 1960.

5. Cameroun, 2 centimes, 1925
J. Kerhor designed a distinctive series for Cameroun which was issued in May 1925. Three designs were used, featuring cattle fording a river (1 to 15c.), tapping rubber trees (20 to 85c.) and a liana suspension bridge (1 to 5f.). New values and colours were introduced between 1926 and 1938.

6. Cameroun, 2 centimes, 1925
A series of pictorial postage due stamps was issued in 1925 in denominations from 2c. to 1f. High denominations of 2 and 3f. were released two years later. The common design by J. Kerhor and engraved by G. Daussy depicted the felling of mahogany trees. The stamps were typographed in two-colour combinations by the French Government Printing Works.

7. Cameroun, 25 centimes, 1942
In August 1940 Cameroon gave its allegiance to the Free French movement of General De Gaulle and various contemporary stamps were overprinted 'Cameroun Français' with the date 27.8.40. A distinctive Free French issue was released in 1942. The stamps, designed by Edmund Dulac and printed in photogravure by Harrison & Sons, featured the Cross of Lorraine, a sword and shield.

8. Cameroun, 10 centimes, 1946
The pastoral economy of Cameroun was emphasized in the pictorial definitive series, recess-printed at the Institut de Gravure, Paris, and issued between 1946 and 1953. G. Barlangue, Pierre Gandon and Georges Betemps designed and engraved the eleven designs used for this series depicting scenery, agricultural pursuits and warriors.

9. Cameroun, 10 centimes, 1947
A uniform series from 10c. to 20f., was issued in 1947 for unpaid and underpaid items. The numeral design, with a *guilloche* background, was recess-printed at the Institut de Gravure. Cameroun became an autonomous state within the French Community in 1958 and an independent republic in January 1960.

10. Southern Cameroons, 1 pound, 1960
After the independence of Nigeria, stamps of the obsolescent series from ½d. to £1 were overprinted for use in the United Kingdom Trust Territory of the Cameroons – the area taken over from Germany under a mandate of the League of Nations in 1920. These stamps were used in Northern Cameroons before that territory voted to join the Federation of Nigeria, but are generally regarded as issues of Southern Cameroons, since they were used there after that district became an autonomous state on 1 October 1960. As a result of a second plebiscite, however, Southern Cameroons voted to join the former French territory of Cameroun. The union took place on 30 September 1961. Stamps of Cameroun, surcharged in sterling, were used in this area pending the introduction of the Cameroun franc in 1962.

11. Cameroun, 12 + 18 francs, 1965
Cameroun, with its close British connection, had better reasons than most of the former French territories for issuing stamps in honour of Sir Winston Churchill. This triptych, designed by J. Combet and printed in multicolour photogravure by Delrieu, was issued in May 1965. Curiously enough, bilingual inscriptions were not used on these stamps. Since independence Cameroun has issued numerous stamps portraying world celebrities and marking international, rather than national, events.

12. Cameroun, 15 francs, 1965
In 1961 the former British trust territory of the Southern Cameroons joined the state of Cameroun to form the federal republic of Cameroun. The union of the two areas is reflected in the use of English as well as French in the inscriptions of several stamps issued between 1961 and 1966. This stamp was one of three designed and engraved by J. Combet after a schools' design competition. Note the misspelling of the English word 'Scholar'. The stamps were issued in June 1965 to promote the national savings campaign.

13. Togo, 3 pfennigs, 1897
Following the German colonization of Togo in 1884 ordinary German stamps were used and can only be identified by their postmarks. The contemporary definitive series, diagonally overprinted 'Togo', was introduced in 1897–98 in denominations from 3 to 50pf. These overprints were superseded by the Hohenzollern colonial keytypes in 1900. Watermarks were adopted in 1909 but only 5 and 10pf. stamps were actually issued before the territory was occupied by the Allies in 1914.

14. Togo, 4 centimes, 1916
An Anglo-French force invaded Togo in September 1914 and rapidly overran the colony. The German colonial stamps were overprinted 'TOGO Occupation franco-anglaise' at Porto Novo, Dahomey, and issued in October 1914. Subsequently stamps were overprinted at the Catholic mission in Lome. Stamps of Dahomey were introduced with a distinctive overprint in 1916. The plate illustrates a stamp from the last of these sets.

15. Togo, 2 pence, 1915
German colonial stamps were also overprinted in English and subsequently the contemporary series of the Gold Coast was similarly overprinted. Local overprints appeared in May 1915 and similar stamps overprinted in London followed in April 1916. The overprints may be differentiated by the length of the word 'Occupation' – 14½mm long (local) and 15mm long (London version). The London overprints were in heavier type which shows through on the back of the stamps. British Togo was incorporated with the Gold Coast at the end of World War I. The stamps of the Gold Coast (now Ghana) have been used there ever since.

16. Togo, 1.25 francs, 1926
A distinctive series in the prevailing French colonial *genre* was introduced in December 1924. J. Kerhor designed and A. Delzers engraved the series ranging from 1c. to 5f. Other denominations up to 20f. were added between 1926 and 1938. Surprisingly only one provisional surcharge was ever required, the 1f. value surcharged in June 1926 for use as a 1.25f. denomination. Kerhor produced three designs for this series, illustrating coconut palms, cocoa trees and oil-palm trees.

17. Togo, 10 centimes, 1947
The postage due stamps of Togo like those of other French territories favoured a pictorial motif. A series issued in 1940 was designed and engraved by Pierre Gandon and featured a native mask. A similar series recess-printed at the Institut de Gravure in Paris was released in 1947 and featured native idols.

18. Togo, 100 francs, 1962
Togo became an autonomous republic within the French Community in June 1957 but left in April 1960. The majority of the stamps issued between 1960 and 1963 were lithographed by De La Rue, but since that date most stamps have been printed in multicolour by the Israeli Government Printer. From the De La Rue period dates the series of six stamps and a miniature sheet marking the visit of President Sylvanus Olympio to the United States. The design, by C. Bottiau, portrayed Olympio and John F. Kennedy beside the Capitol in Washington. Apart from a stamp of Mexico issued a few days earlier (see plate 93) these were the only stamps to portray Kennedy in his lifetime. Ironically President Olympio was felled by an assassin's bullet a year later.

19. Togo, 25 francs, 1965
The neutral position of Togo in relation to the super powers of the world is demonstrated by the depiction of American and Russian subjects with equal impartiality. Famous Americans such as Abraham Lincoln, John F. Kennedy and even Duke Ellington the jazz musician are balanced by such stamps as the pair of 1970 portraying Lenin. Two stamps issued in 1965 paid tribute to Man's achievement in outer space. The 25f. depicted the Soviet astronaut Leonov with a camera, while the 50f. stamp depicted the American astronaut White with a rocket gun.

20. Togo, 10 centimes, 1947
A lengthy series, recess-printed at the Institut de Gravure in Paris, was released in October 1947. The denominations up to 25f., for ordinary postage, depicted natives and wildlife, while the higher values, from 40 to 200f., intended for airmail postage, featured landscapes with different types

231

PLATE 77 CAMEROUN, TOGO · PLATE 78 FRENCH INDIAN OCEAN

of aircraft. The low values showed Togolese extracting oil from palms. This design was produced and engraved by Christian Hertenberger.

21. Togo, 30 francs, 1969

The fiftieth anniversary of the Togolese Red Cross was celebrated by a series of six stamps, designed by M. Shamir and printed in Israel, portraying famous scientists and depicting aspects of Red Cross work. This stamp portrays Sir Alexander Fleming, the Scottish pioneer of penicillin, and a stylized composition representing flood control. Other stamps portrayed Louis Pasteur, Konrad Röntgen and Henri Dunant, founder of the Red Cross.

PLATE 78
French Indian Ocean

1. Diego Suarez, 1 centime, 1894

The district of Diego Suarez in Madagascar began issuing its own stamps in 1890 and in 1892 the 'Tablet' series inscribed 'Diego Suarez et Dépendances' was introduced. Two years later this was replaced by three separate issues of the 'Tablet' series, inscribed for use in Diego Suarez, Nossi Bé and Ste Marie de Madagascar. The stamps of Madagascar superseded these issues in 1896.

2. Nossi Bé, 4 centimes, 1894

Prior to the 'Tablet' series various stamps of the French colonial general series were surcharged or overprinted for use in this district. The earlier surcharges (1889) merely bore the numerals of the value, but those issued in 1890 were overprinted NSB as a means of identification. Further overprints (1893) had the name inscribed in full. The 'Tablet' series of 1894–96 was withdrawn when the stamps of Madagascar were introduced.

3. Ste Marie de Madagascar, 4 centimes, 1894

The 'Tablet' series, from 1 centime to 1 franc, inscribed for use in this seaport, appeared in April 1894. This keyplate series was quite undistinguished in every sense and no varieties of consequence have been recorded. The series gave way in 1896 to the similar issue inscribed for use in Madagascar and Dependencies.

4. Réunion, 4 centimes, 1907

Réunion had the distinction of issuing its own typeset stamps as early as 1852 but they were quickly suppressed by the imperial government and thereafter the colonial general series was used until 1885, when the provisional surcharges which afflicted many of the French colonies that year were issued. Subsequently the various keyplate issues were produced and it was not until 1907 that a distinctive pictorial series was released. A. Chauvet produced three designs, engraved by Puyplat and typographed in two-colour combinations, featuring a map of the island and views of St Denis and St Pierre. These stamps, with numerous changes of colour, provisional surcharges and new values, remained in use until 1933.

5. Réunion, 5 centimes, 1843

Réunion went over to the Gaullists in 1943 and signified this change of allegiance by overprinting the definitive series 'France Libre'. Subsequently a series designed by Dulac and printed in photogravure by Harrison and Sons was released in December that year. The common design depicted the chief products of the colony.

6. Réunion, 5 centimes, 1933

A recess-printed series was adopted in September 1933, designed by R. Caulet and C. Abadie and printed at the Institut de Gravure. The three designs were an island waterfall, the Anchain Peak at Salazie and the Leon Dierx Museum. Four airmail stamps with an aircraft over mountain scenery followed in 1938. Since World War II Réunion has used French stamps surcharged in CFA (Colonies Françaises Africaines) currency.

7. Madagascar, 1 centime, 1908

L. Dumoulin designed a series for Madagascar showing the Malagasy version of a sedan chair, and the stamps were typographed in the usual gaudy two-colour combinations. The series appeared in July 1908, but various new colours and values were added between 1916 and 1928 and provisional surcharges between 1921 and 1932.

8. Madagascar, 2 centimes, 1930

The definitive series of 1930–38 was unusual, as French colonial sets went, in that four of its designs were typographed while the fifth was recess-printed. A Sakalava chief, Betsileo woman, Hova girl and zebu cattle formed the subjects of the typographed designs while the recess design portrayed General Gallieni, hero of the Marne and a former governor of Madagascar. Between 1936 and 1940 a photogravure version of the Gallieni design was produced in values from 3c. to 3fr.

9. Madagascar, 5 centimes, 1943

The island switched allegiance from the Vichy government to the Gaullists in 1941 and subsequently overprinted its stamps 'France Libre'. In due course a series by Dulac featuring a traveller's tree was printed in photogravure and released in 1943. A number of provisional surcharges appeared in 1945.

10. Madagascar, 40 centimes, 1946

Native types and former colonial administrators were the subjects of the postwar definitive series printed in photogravure by Vaugirard. In addition to Galliéni, General Duchesne and Marshal Joffre (the latter as a lieutenant-colonel) were portrayed in company with a southern dancer, Sakalava natives and a Betsimisaraka mother and child. The airmail stamps showed an aerial view of Tamatave or an allegorical figure of Flight.

11. Malagasy Republic, 40 centimes, 1960

Madagascar became a republic within the French Community in 1958. From then until the end of 1960 stamps were inscribed in French 'République Malgache'. The definitive series released between January and May 1960 illustrated butterflies and agricultural pursuits. A concession to national sentiment was the inclusion of the Malagasy designation of the republic in smaller lettering below the French name.

12. Malagasy Republic, 20 francs, 1962

Since 1961 the stamps of the republic have been inscribed 'Repoblika Malagasy' in the indigenous language, though subsidiary inscriptions are invariably rendered in French. Without exception the stamps since independence have been printed in France and though occasionally the artwork is initiated by local artists the finished work has been left to French designers. This stamp, photogravure-printed by Delrieu, was issued in September 1962 to mark the UNESCO Conference on Higher Education held at Tananarive.

13. Malagasy Republic, 20 francs, 1963

This was the first in a series reproducing the coats of arms of Malagasy cities, issued between December 1963 and January 1968. The stamps were designed by S. Gauthier and R. Louis and lithographed in multicolour by So.Ge.Im. of Paris.

14. Malagasy Republic, 25 francs, 1966

A custom borrowed from France is the issue of an annual stamp in honour of Stamp Day (8 May). The majority of these stamps have shown aspects of mail communications old and new but the 25f. stamp of 1966, designed and engraved by C. Durrens, reproduced Madagascar's first distinctive stamp, the 1c. of 1903 showing a zebu bull and a lemur beneath a traveller's tree.

15. Malagasy Republic, 5 francs, 1967

Occasional short thematic sets have been issued since 1962 to augment the definitive series. Three stamps of April 1967 took the theme of the development of Malagasy aviation and featured historic aircraft ranging from Jean Raoult's monoplane of 1911 to Dagnaux-Dufert's biplane of 1927. The series was designed by Gandon and recess-printed by the French Government Printing Works.

16. Anjouan, 1 centime, 1892

The first stamps issued in the Comoro Islands were the 'Tablet' keytypes which appeared in the 1890s variously inscribed for the different islands of the archipelago. The first series, for use in the sultanate of Anjouan, was released in November 1892 in denominations from 1c. to 1f. New colours and values appeared between 1900 and 1907 and provisional surcharges of 5 and 10c. in 1912. The distinctive series was withdrawn in February 1914 when the islands were attached to Madagascar.

17. Grand Comoro, 15 centimes, 1897

The 'Tablet' series inscribed 'Grande Comoro' was issued in 1897 and thereafter underwent the same history of new colours, values and provisional surcharges described for Anjouan. It was superseded by the stamps of Madagascar in February 1914.

18. Mayotte, 2 centimes, 1892

The same remarks apply to the stamps of Mayotte, which appeared between November 1892 and February 1914. No errors or varieties appeared to lighten the monotony of these rather uninteresting stamps.

19. Moheli, 10 centimes, 1912

Moheli, the fourth island of the Comoros, did not adopt its own stamps until 1906 and therefore avoided many of the permutations which characterized the other islands' issues. Like the others, however, it had a rash of provisional 5 and 10c. surcharges in November 1912. Two sets can be made of these provisionals, with the numerals spaced wide or close together, the former being by far the scarcer.

20. Comoro Islands, 1 franc, 1950

Stamps of Madagascar were used in the Comoro Islands until May 1950, when they began issuing their own distinctive series. In addition to a pictorial definitive series they produced 50c. and 1f. postage due stamps featuring the mosque in Anjouan. The definitive series featured scenery, landmarks and native types. The postage stamps were designed by Barlangue and the postage dues by Giat, both issues being recess-printed by the French Government Printing Works.

21. Comoro Islands, 40 francs, 1954

The coelacanth, the prehistoric fish thought to have been long extinct but discovered in the Indian Ocean near the Comoros since World War II, was the subject of the 40f. stamp added to the definitive series in 1954. Whereas the other stamps had been printed in single colours this one was produced in indigo and turquoise. Pierre Gandon both designed and engraved this stamp, which marks the transition from monochrome recess-printing to the multicolour processes favoured in recent years.

PLATE 78 FRENCH INDIAN OCEAN · PLATE 79 PORTUGUESE EAST AFRICA

22. Comoro Islands, 50 centimes, 1962
The rather staid monochrome series of 1950 gave way to a multicoloured series featuring different types of seashells. The stamps were designed by R. Chapelet and printed in photogravure by Helio-Comy and released between January and October 1962. Large vertical designs featuring marine plants and coral were used for the 100 and 500f. airmail stamps issued at the same time. Relatively few stamps have been issued by the Comoros in recent years, but they show a marked preference for bright multicolour combinations and are mainly thematic in character, showing flowers, birds, fishes and views of the islands.

23. French Southern and Antarctic Territories, 10 francs, 1971
Before 1955 stamps of Madagascar were used in the French sub-Antarctic islands of the Indian Ocean (St Paul, Crozet and Kerguelen archipelagoes) and by scientists manning stations in Adelie Land. In that year the 15f. stamp of Madagascar was overprinted 'Terres Australes et Antarctiques Françaises' and the following year a distinctive pictorial series was recess-printed with views of the islands and their wildlife. Various stamps were added piecemeal to the series up to 1969, augmented by occasional commemorative or thematic sets. This stamp was one of a set of five released in 1971 with the theme of fishes of the southern Indian Ocean. A further fish series appeared in 1972. All but one stamp of this territory have been recess-printed, the exception being a solitary 10f. stamp of 1959 depicting flora in multicolour photogravure.

24. French Southern and Antarctic Territories, 40 centimes, 1959
The artist and engraver Cottet designed this stamp, featuring Skuas, which formed part of the definitive series issued between 1956 and 1960. No fewer than ten different artists were involved in the engraving of the dies for this series.

25. French Post Office in Zanzibar, ½ anna, 1896
A French post office operated on the island of Zanzibar between 1894 and 1904 and a surprisingly large number of different stamps was issued in that decade. The first stamps consisted of contemporary French stamps surcharged in Indian currency. Subsequently the name 'Zanzibar' also appeared in the overprint. A curious feature of these stamps was the makeshift issue of 1897 in which the overprints were applied to the blank margins and gutters of sheets of stamps, so that the overprinted pieces of paper themselves became valid as postage stamps. The Blanc, Mouchon and Merson keytypes appeared in 1902 suitably inscribed. These stamps were withdrawn from use at the end of July 1904 when the French post office was closed.

26. British Post Office in Madagascar, 4 pence, 1895
A British consular postal service operated in Madagascar from 1884 till 1899 and issued its own stamps in that period. The stamp belongs to the series of 1895, lithographed by John Haddon of London, and depicts Malagasy postal runners. The word at the foot is the value rendered in Malagasy.

PLATE 79
Portuguese East Africa

1. Portuguese Africa, 2½ reis, 1898
Stamps for general use in the Portuguese colonies in Africa have been issued on three occasions. In 1898 a set of eight stamps, recess-printed by Waterlow and Sons, commemorated the quatercentenary of Vasco da Gama's discovery of the sea route to India. Fiscal stamps (see below) appeared in 1919 and since 1945 a general series inscribed 'Imperio Colonial Portugues' has been used in Portuguese Africa.

2. Portuguese Africa, 1 centavo, 1919
Portuguese colonial fiscal stamps were diagonally overprinted 'Taxa de Guerra' (War Tax) and issued in 1919, in all the Portuguese colonies in Africa, with the exception of Mozambique. The 1c. denomination was intended for compulsory use on letter mail, while 4 and 5c. stamps with this overprint were for use on receipts and telegrams respectively. The money raised by the use of these stamps was credited to war relief funds.

3. Inhambane, 2½ reis, 1911
The district of Inhambane began issuing its own stamps in 1895, when the St Anthony commemorative series of Mozambique was overprinted with the name of the territory. Subsequently, however, the Carlos and Ceres keytypes were issued with a suitable inscription. The Carlos series of 1903 was diagonally overprinted 'Republica' in 1911. At the end of World War I the stamps of Mozambique were reintroduced in Inhambane.

4. Kionga, 5 centavos, 1916
During World War I Portuguese troops occupied a strip of German East Africa along the River Tuvuma known as Kionga. Stamps of Lourenço Marques were overprinted for use in this territory and surcharged in centavos. The stamps were in use for a short time in 1916 but subsequently the stamps of Mozambique were adopted.

5. Lourenço Marques, 7½ centavos, 1914
Before 1895 the port of Lourenço Marques used the stamps of Mozambique but in that year it began using colonial keytype stamps suitably inscribed. Between 1895 and 1921 various colonial keytype designs were used. The Ceres design was introduced in 1914, the earliest printings being on chalk-surfaced paper and those from 1915 to 1918 on unsurfaced paper. The stamps of Mozambique were reintroduced in 1921.

6. Lourenço Marques, 1.50 escudos, 1952
Although Lourenço Marques has used the stamps of Mozambique since 1921 several examples are known of stamps with the distinctive inscription 'Lourenzo Marques' which were not confined to that city. Several stamps of Lourenço Marques were surcharged with new values in January 1922 and despite the name were in fact used throughout Mozambique. This stamp issued in September 1952 to mark the 4th African Tourist Congress is inscribed 'Lourenzo Marques' but was valid for postage throughout Mozambique.

7. Mozambique, 60 centavos, 1922
From their inception in 1876 to 1930 the stamps of Mozambique followed the Portuguese colonial keytype pattern. The Ceres types were issued in 1914 and thereafter went through the various permutations and combinations of paper, perforation and colour common to all the colonies which used this series. Between 1920 and 1926 the colours were changed and new values, such as this 60c., were

8. Mozambique, 5 centavos, 1916
To raise funds for the prosecution of the war in East Africa, 1 and 5c. stamps were issued in July 1916 for compulsory use on all correspondence at certain times of the year. The 1c. contained the arms of Portugal and Mozambique while the 5c. showed the prow of a galley and allegorical figures symbolizing the declaration of war. The stamps were designed by J. C. P. Ferreira da Costa and lithographed by Hortor Ltd of Johannesburg. A subsequent version, with solid frame instead of a shaded frame, was lithographed by the Argus Printing and Publishing Company of Johannesburg in 1918.

9. Mozambique, 5 escudos, 1933
The first definitive series to break with the keyplate tradition of the colonies appeared in July 1933. Nevertheless it was identical in all but inscription with that introduced in Portugal two years earlier, and in 1938 Mozambique reverted to a keytype series. It was not until 1948 that a series that was wholly distinctive to Mozambique was released. The 1933–47 series depicted the allegory of Portugal reading the heroic poem 'Lusiad' by Camoens. The stamps were designed by P. Guedes, engraved by A. Fragoso and typographed at the Mint, Lisbon.

10. Mozambique, 80 centavos, 1948
The first distinctive definitive series of Mozambique was issued in 1948–49 and featured scenery and landmarks of the colony. The stamps were typographed in denominations from 5c. to 20e. by the Portuguese Mint in Lisbon.

11. Mozambique, 40 centavos, 1953
A series featuring scenery and landmarks was adopted in 1948, but since 1951 Mozambique has issued lengthy sets at frequent intervals having a single theme. The butterflies series issued in May 1953 was produced in multicolour photogravure by Enschedé. Other sets have included fishes (1951), maps (1954), coats of arms (1961), ships (1963), military uniforms (1967) and minerals (1971) as their themes.

12. Mozambique, 1 escudo, 1961
J. de Moura designed the definitive series released in January 1961 with the theme of coats of arms of the cities of Mozambique. The arms were depicted in full colour against a coloured ground, varying for each denomination of the series. The stamps ranged from 5c. to 50e. and were lithographed in Portugal.

13. Mozambique Company, 10 reis, 1892
A large tract of territory in East Africa was granted to the Mozambique Company in 1892 and stamps of Mozambique were overprinted for use in this area. The Carlos profile series was overprinted 'Compª de Mocambique' and released in 1892–93 pending the production of a set featuring the arms of the Company. This series may be found on chalk-surfaced or enamel-glazed paper, the latter being produced to meet philatelic demand after the original version had become obsolete.

14. Mozambique Company, 25 reis, 1895
The first distinctive series used by the Mozambique Company appeared between 1895 and 1902. The stamps were designed and engraved by J. S. de Carvalho e Silva and typographed in Lisbon. The stamps ranged from 2½ to 1000r. and featured the company's coat of arms. These stamps remained in use until 1918 and during that lengthy period were subject to numerous changes in perforation, type of paper, surcharges and overprints.

PLATE 79 PORTUGUESE EAST AFRICA · PLATE 80 PORTUGUESE WEST AFRICA

15. Mozambique Company, 5 centavos, 1919

A series of postage due stamps, containing the Company's arms, was recess-printed by Waterlow and Sons and introduced in November 1919. Two gauges of perforation may be found, either 12½ or 14–15. The stamps ranged from ½ to 50c. and superseded the utilitarian numeral series of 1906.

16. Mozambique Company, 10 centavos, 1918

In the spirit of the other chartered companies of the time, for which they had also printed stamps (Nyassa and North Borneo), Waterlow and Sons produced a handsome series for the Mozambique Company in 1918, featuring scenery, native types and agricultural products. The majority of the stamps, from ½c. to 1e., were recess-printed in two-colour combinations. The earliest printings were perforated 14, but those issued in 1924 were perforated 12½. Additional denominations were recess-printed in the same *genre* by Bradbury Wilkinson in 1925–31 or lithographed by De La Rue in 1931.

17. Mozambique Company, 20 centavos, 1935

The inauguration of the Blantyre–Beira–Salisbury air route was celebrated by a series of ten airmail stamps in a triangular format showing a monoplane over Beira. The stamps, in denominations from 5 to 80c., were recess-printed by Waterlow and Sons. The vignette was subsequently used for a smaller format rectangular series of air stamps released in November 1935.

18. Mozambique Company, 15 centavos, 1937

J. Webb designed a pictorial definitive series which was recess-printed by Waterlow and Sons and released in May 1937. The stamps, from 1c. to 20e., featured wildlife, scenery and people of the area in the same tradition as the 1918–31 issues, though lettering and frame layout were subtly modernized. In 1941 the charter of the Company was revoked and its territory absorbed by Mozambique, whose stamps have been used in that area ever since.

19. Nyassa Company, 300 reis, 1911

Stamps of Mozambique overprinted 'Nyassa' were released in 1897 for use in the territory administered by the Nyassa Company. They were superseded in 1901 by a series designed by Sir Robert Edgcumbe, engraved by Herbert Bourne and recess-printed by Waterlow and Sons. The stamps illustrated a giraffe or camels and had a portrait of King Carlos inset. A similar series portraying King Manoel was prepared but not issued without the 'Republica' overprint. This set appeared in March 1911 in denominations from 2½ to 500r. Two new vignettes were introduced, featuring a zebra and the *San Gabriel*, flagship of Vasco da Gama.

20. Nyassa Company, 1 escudo, 1921

Waterlows produced a series in 1921–23 using the vignettes of the 1911 series with new frames. The escudo of 100 centavos was adopted in 1918 and the 1911 series was then surcharged with new values. For the 1921–24 series a new design (an Arab dhow) was used for the 2 and 5e values.

21. Nyassa Company, 6 centavos, 1921

Vasco da Gama discovered the coast of East Africa and laid the foundations of the colonial empire which reached its zenith in the sixteenth century. It was appropriate therefore that his portrait should appear on stamps of every definitive series of Nyassa from 1911 onwards. The earliest printings of the 1921 series were perforated 14 or 15, but later printings were perforated 12½.

22. Nyassa Company, 50 centavos, 1924

Waterlow and Sons also recess-printed a series of triangular postage due stamps, issued in 1924. The vignettes of the postage series were modified for

this set ranging in value from ½ to 50c. Nyassa was incorporated in Mozambique in 1929 and since then has used the stamps of that territory.

23. Quelimane, ¼ centavo, 1914

The district of Quelimane used the stamps of Mozambique until 1913, when the Vasco da Gama stamps of 1898 were overprinted 'Republica' and 'Quelimane' and surcharged in centavo currency. The following year the Ceres keytypes were introduced, chalk-surfaced paper being used for the first printings and unsurfaced paper for those stamps printed in 1916. The separate issues of Quelimane were withdrawn at the end of World War I and ordinary Mozambique stamps have been used there ever since.

24. Tete, ½ centavo, 1914

The philately of the district of Tete is identical with that of Quelimane in every respect, except that unsurfaced paper was never adopted. One printing alone seems to have sufficed for these unappealing stamps. After a few years Tete returned to philatelic oblivion, Mozambique stamps being reintroduced in 1918.

25. Zambezia, 5 reis, 1898

The Zambezia province of Mozambique had its own stamps from 1894 to 1918 but used the various colonial keytypes portraying King Carlos (1894 and 1898–1903) and the 'Republica' overprints (1911–17). Curiously enough the Ceres stamps, prevalent everywhere else, were never adopted in this territory. Since 1918 Mozambique stamps have been used in Zambezia.

PLATE 80

Portuguese West Africa

---

1. Angola, 2½ reis, 1893

Angola began issuing stamps in 1870, introducing the 'Crown' keytypes suitably inscribed. Thereafter the various colonial keytype designs were used up to 1948. E. C. Azedo Gneco designed and engraved the 2½r. newspaper stamp issued in July 1893. Though intended primarily for newspapers this stamp could be, and often was, used to prepay ordinary postage on correspondence.

2. Angola, 300 reis, 1912

A series portraying King Manoel was prepared but never issued, on account of the overthrow of the monarchy in 1910. The series appeared two years later with a diagonal republican overprint. The stamps ranged from 2½ to 300r. The lower values were typographed on white paper and the three highest denominations on coloured paper.

3. Angola, 10 angolars, 1932

The Ceres keytype design was used in Angola from 1914 onwards, with an appropriate inscription. In 1932 the currency of Angola changed to the angolar or escudo of 100 centavos and a distinctive form of the Ceres design was adopted. C. Fernandes modified the design, engraved by A. Fragoso and typographed in Lisbon in denominations from 1c. to 20a. In 1946 35c. and 1.75a. denominations were added to the set.

4. Angola, 1.75 angolars, 1938

A handsome series extolling the past glories of the Portuguese empire was released in July 1938. A. R. Garcia designed the six vignettes and Bradbury Wilkinson recess-printed the stamps in denominations from 1 to 20c. (ordinary) and 10c. to 10a. (airmail). The name and value were added

in black. The same designs were adopted by other Portuguese colonies at the same time. The stamps portrayed Vasco da Gama, Prince Henry the Navigator and other illustrious explorers, with the names of the places they discovered or annexed inscribed on the pillars at the side of the design.

5. Angola, 5 centavos, 1948

The first series entirely distinctive to Angola appeared in May 1948 and commemorated the tercentenary of the restoration of Angola to Portugal. The ten stamps, designed by A. de Sousa and lithographed by Litografia Maia in Oporto, were of landmarks in the colony and portraits of historic personalities. The stamps were also released in a miniature sheet containing one of each.

6. Angola, 30 centavos, 1953

Angola's first distinctive definitive series appeared in 1949 and featured scenery. Thereafter new sets appeared at two-yearly intervals and became increasingly colourful. Courvoisier printed a birds series in 1951 in multicolour photogravure and two years later a series of animal stamps was lithographed at Oporto in denominations from 5c. (leopard) to 20a. (giraffe).

7. Angola, 5 centavos, 1955

By way of contrast, the definitive series issued in August 1955 stuck to a single design, a map of the colony. The design was produced by J. de Moura and the series lithographed at the Mint, Lisbon. Though the stamps were printed in multicolour a different colour was used as the background to Angolan territory for each denomination.

8. Angola, 20 centavos, 1957

Courvoisier printed the series of January 1957 in multicolour photogravure. Messrs Neves and Sousa designed the stamps, featuring various native types, chiefs, dancers and musicians. Subsequent sets depicted Angolan women (1961), coats of arms, and Angolan churches (1963), dams and bridges (1965), military uniforms (1966), medals and decorations (1967) and fossils and minerals (1970).

9. Angola, 1 escudo, 1966

With few exceptions, commemorative issues since 1949 have been confined to single stamps and the vast majority of such issues have been concerned with persons and events of Portuguese, if not Angolan interest, rather than those of the international scene. This stamp was issued in August 1966 to mark the centenary of the Brotherhood of the Holy Spirit and features its emblem.

10. Cape Verde Islands, ½ centavo, 1921

The Cape Verde Islands adopted their own stamps in 1877 and from then until 1948 used the prevailing Portuguese colonial keytype designs. Postage due stamps were introduced in the standard colonial design in 1904 and were typographed in various colours with the name and value in black. The first series was inscribed in reis currency; in 1911 it was issued with the republican overprint, and then in 1921 it reappeared with denominations from ½ to 50c. Since 1952 the postage due stamps have been in the keytype design introduced throughout the Portuguese colonies in that year.

11. Cape Verde Islands, 10 centavos, 1952

The philatelic history of the islands parallels that of the other Portuguses colonies. A pictorial definitive series was issued in 1948 and depicted views of the islands. Thereafter thematic sets appeared at regular intervals. The series of May 1952 portrayed Portuguese explorers and navigators and historic maps of the islands. The series was designed by R. Preto Pacheco and lithographed in multicolour by Litografia Nacional, Oporto.

12. Cape Verde Islands, 4.50 escudos, 1962
In common with the other colonies the Cape Verde Islands issued a set of six diamond-shaped stamps in January 1962 with sporting themes. This colony has the doubtful honour of having issued the first stamp to depict the ancient English sport of cricket (1.50e.) and the ancient Scottish pastime of golf (12.50e.). Other stamps in the series featured sports which are probably played in these islands.

13. Cape Verde Islands, 2.50 escudos, 1970
In recent years the Portuguese colonies have issued stamps for a particular event but have used distinctive designs in each territory. Thus the centenary of the birth of Marshal Carmona, former president of the republic, was celebrated in 1970 by a single stamp in each colony, using a different portrait in each case.

14. Portuguese Guinea, 1 escudo, 1951
Portuguese Guinea began issuing stamps in 1881 but it was not until 1946 that any distinctive designs were used. In that year a set of seven stamps and a miniature sheet commemorated the quincentenary of the discovery of the colony. Distinctive definitive sets have been issued at frequent intervals since 1948. Many of the early commemorative issues conformed to Portuguese colonial omnibus designs. This stamp was released in October 1951 to mark the termination of Holy Year and showed Out Lady of Fatima. The only touch of individualism was provided by the se-tenant coupon which bore a quotation from Pope Pius XII; different quotations were used for each colony.

15. Portuguese Guinea, 10 centavos, 1953
The first definitive series of Guinea to have indigenous designs appeared in April 1948 and illustrated native types and occupations. The second series, of insects in the natural colours, was issued in 1953. Both sets were printed by Courvoisier. The only saving grace, so far as Guinea was concerned, was that definitive sets were rotated far less frequently than in most of the other colonies.

16. Portuguese Guinea, 2.50 escudos, 1965
St Gabriel, patron saint of postmen and philatelists, appeared on this stamp of May 1965, marking the centenary of the International Telecommunications Union. The stamp was lithographed by Litografia Nacional of Oporto and was in the omnibus design used by all the Portuguese colonies for this event. The few stamps issued by this colony in recent years have either conformed to the prevailing omnibus design or used a distinctive design for an occasion shared by the other territories. The only exception was a 2.50e. stamp of 1970 celebrating the centenary of the Bolama arbitrational judgment by Ulysses Grant.

17. Portuguese Guinea, 20 escudos, 1963
Ten years elapsed before Guinea got another definitive set. In January 1963 a series in diamond-format was lithographed at Oporto with the theme of reptiles of West Africa. Ten vertical and two horizontal designs were used in denominations from 20c. to 20e. Having exhausted the insect and reptile denizens of the colony Guinea has not (at the time of writing) produced a further definitive set, though short thematic sets of 1962 (sports) and 1966 (military uniforms) have appeared in the standard colonial style.

18. St Thomas and Prince Islands, 1 escudo, 1962
Six diamond-shaped stamps with sporting subjects were issued in January 1962 and conformed to the colonial pattern. The stamps illustrated fishing, gymnastics, handball, yachting, running and skindiving. Since then very few stamps have been produced which are entirely distinctive to the colony.

The quincentenary of the discovery of the islands was celebrated by a stamp in 1969 portraying Pero Escobar and Joao de Santarem, while the centenary of the colony's first stamps was marked in 1970 by a set of three, reproducing stamps in conjunction with a coffee plant (1e.) and views of the head post office in St Thomas (1.50e.) and the Cathedral (2.50e.).

19. Portuguese Congo, 2½ reis, 1898
Stamps were issued by the Portuguese Congo between 1894 and 1920. Predictably the stamps all conformed to the current colonial keytypes. Stamps portraying King Carlos were in use between 1894 and 1913, the only variety being provided by the welter of provisional surcharges in 1902 and the 'Republica' overprints of 1911-13.

20. Portuguese Congo, 7½ centavos, 1914
The adoption of decimal currency led to the introduction of the 'Ceres' keytypes in 1914. The series inscribed for use in the Congo was printed on chalk-surfaced paper, but ¼ and 2c. denominations appeared in 1920 on unsurfaced paper. In 1920 Portuguese Congo was absorbed by neighbouring Angola, whose stamps have been used by the former ever since.

21. St Thomas and Prince Islands, 25 reis, 1885
Adhesive postage stamps were adopted by St Thomas and Prince in 1870, the contemporary 'Crown' keytype design being used. The earliest printings were on thick paper, perforated 12½, but thinner paper was adopted in 1875 and subsequently the gauge of perforation was altered to 13½. Between 1881 and 1885 the values up to 50 reis were reissued in new colours. The first distinctive series did not appear until 1948, when a set featuring native fruits was released.

22. St Thomas and Prince Islands, 10 centavos, 1952
Like Cape Verde Islands, St Thomas and Prince chose famous navigators as the theme of its definitive series in 1952. A. de Sousa produced six designs for a series ranging in value from 10c. to 3.50e. The portraits were reproduced in vertical frames and the stamps were lithographed in multicolour by Litografia Maia of Oporto. Subsequently St Thomas and Prince has been even less enterprising than Guinea and has produced no distinctive issues, other than the short thematic sets using subjects common to the other colonies.

PLATE 81
Belgian Territories in Africa

---

1. Congo Free State, 25 centimes, 1894
The Congo Free State was established in May 1885 under the personal rule of King Leopold II of the Belgians. Stamps bearing his portrait were introduced in 1886, but were superseded eight years later by a pictorial series recess-printed by Waterlow and Sons. The vignettes of the stamps were taken from a diorama by R. Mols and P. van Engelen shown at the Antwerp Exhibition in 1894. The stamps, in denominations from 5c. to 5f., included scenery, wildlife and native types. Note the inscription 'État Indépendant du Congo' (Independent State of the Congo) inscribed on the stamps of this territory from 1886 to 1909.

2. Belgian Congo, 1 franc, 1915
After the exposure of corruption and brutality in the Free State the Belgian government annexed the territory and renamed it the Belgian Congo. The preceding series was overprinted 'Congo Belge' in

1909 and was superseded by similar designs with the new name in June of that year. Bilingual inscriptions were adopted for pictorial definitive stamps in 1910; in 1915 they were reissued in new colours. The philatelic history of the Belgian Congo curiously parallels that of North Borneo (see plate 62), whose attractive pictorials were also produced by Waterlow and Sons.

3. Belgian Congo, 50 centimes, 1920
Bradbury Wilkinson recess-printed a set of four airmail stamps after the successful flight by Fabry and van der Linden between Belgium and the Congo. The stamps showed a Congo river wharf, district stores, a river landscape and the provincial prison.

4. Belgian Congo, 10 centimes, 1923
Between 1923 and 1927 a lengthy definitive series was gradually released, featuring animals, tribal types and various indigenous occupations. It was designed by Émile Vloors and recess-printed by the American Bank Note Co. The same themes were explored in the definitive sets of 1931-37 and 1942-43.

5. Belgian Congo, 5 centimes, 1938
The Belgian government printing works at Malines produced a photogravure series illustrating national parks of the Congo. Six stamps and a miniature sheet were issued in March 1938 and featured scenery on the Molindi, Suza and Ratshuru rivers and Mount Karisimbi. The vignettes were printed in black or brown, and various colours were used for the frames. The later issues of the Belgian Congo closely paralleled the issues of Ruanda-Urundi (see below). The stamps of the Belgian Congo were withdrawn in 1960 when the Congo became an independent republic.

6. Belgian Congo, 70 cents, 1947
The first postwar definitive series issued by the Belgian Congo took as its theme various native masks and carvings. Stamps in denominations from 10c. to 100f., were designed, engraved and recess-printed by the Institut de Gravure in Paris. Various stamps were added to the series between December 1947 and April 1946. Similar stamps with revised inscriptions were released simultaneously in Ruanda Urundi.

7. Congo Republic, 2 francs, 1963
The former Belgian Congo becoming independent in 1960, its stamps were overprinted 'Congo'. The stamps of the republic have been printed in various countries, but not in Belgium. This stamp was one of a series issued originally in January 1963 to mark the entry of the Congo into the Universal Postal Union, but was reissued with an overprint the following December to mark the fifteenth anniversary of the Declaration of Human Rights. The stamps were designed by Jean van Noten, engraved by J. Devos and recess-printed by Enschedé.

8. Congo, 5 kuta, 1967
A new currency based on the zaire of 100 kuta or 10,000 sengi was introduced in 1967. Several stamps of the 1964 definitive series, showing the National Palace in Leopoldville, were surcharged in new values and overprinted in September 1967 to commemorate the fourth conference of the African Unity Organization at Kinshasa. The basic series was designed by Jean van Noten and printed in photogravure by Courvoisier.

9. Congo, 100 kuta, 1969
A definitive series in the new currency was not released until 1969. Stamps in denominations from 10 to 90s. featured the republican coat of arms, while the higher values, from 1 to 100k., reproduced a portrait of President Mobutu. The stamps

235

PLATE 81 BELGIAN TERRITORIES IN AFRICA · PLATE 82 SPANISH AFRICA

were printed by De La Rue in photogravure, the low values in two-colour combinations, the portrait stamps in multicolour. Note the inclusion of the adjective 'Démocratique' in the inscription, to distinguish this country from the Republic of Congo (formerly French Congo).

10. Congo, 10 kuta, 1970

The tenth anniversary of independence was celebrated in June 1970 by a set of seven stamps featuring the map and national flag and portraying President Mobutu. The stamps were lithographed in multicolour.

11. Congo, 6 kuta, 1971

Since the attainment of independence in 1960 the former Belgian Congo was known as the Republic of Congo. To avoid confusion with the neighbouring Republic of Congo (the former French or Middle Congo) the name of this country was emended in 1964 to the Democratic Republic of the Congo and stamps thus inscribed in French were used until 1971. The name of the country was again changed in 1971 to Zaire and stamps thus inscribed were introduced the following year.

12. Belgian occupation of German East Africa, 5 centimes, 1916

German East Africa was invaded from the northwest by Belgian forces in September 1914 and within a year the Germans had been driven out of the districts of Ruanda and Urundi at the north of Lake Tanganyika. Stamps of Belgian Congo were overprinted 'Ruanda' or 'Urundi' for use in these areas in July 1916. Similar stamps are known with markings 'Karema', 'Kigoma' or 'Tabora' but these are only postmarks. In November 1916 the same series was overprinted in French and Flemish to signify 'German East Africa – Belgian Occupation'. The 5c. denomination is known with the overprint inverted.

13. Ruanda-Urundi, 20 centimes, 1942

Belgium received a mandate from the League of Nations over Ruanda-Urundi in 1920 and Congolese stamps thus overprinted were introduced in 1924. The majority of stamps issued in this territory from then until 1961 were identical with the stamps of the Belgian Congo, either overprinted or redrawn with the appropriate inscription. Waterlow and Sons recess-printed a definitive series for the Congo and Ruanda-Urundi in 1942, featuring palm trees, wildlife and native types. Four denominations of this series were printed by the Belgian government exiled in London and distributed with copies of the Belgian political periodical *Message* in 1944.

14. Ruanda-Urundi, 15 centimes, 1953

In the postwar period both the Belgian Congo and Ruanda-Urundi issued thematic definitive sets illustrating native masks (1948), flowers (1953) and animals (1959). The floral series ranged from 10c. to 20f. and was printed in multicolour photogravure by Courvoisier.

15. Ruanda-Urundi, 5 + 2 francs, 1961

Apart from a single definitive series in 1931, depicting scenery and native types, Ruanda-Urundi did not issue any wholly distinctive stamps till 1961. Following the independence of the Congo 20 and 50f. definitive high values, featuring a leopard and lions respectively, were issued, followed by a set of six stamps with premiums in aid of the fund for the completion of Usumbura Cathedral. The stamps were printed in multicolour photogravure and had various views of the cathedral. These were the last stamps issued by the territory before it achieved independence as the republic of Rwanda and the kingdom of Burundi.

16. Rwanda, 20 francs, 1963

The first stamps of Rwanda appeared in 1962, showing President Kayibanda against a map of Africa. The definitives of Ruanda-Urundi were overprinted 'République Rwandaise' in 1963 and a set of four stamps was issued to mark Rwanda's admission to the Universal Postal Union. The stamps were designed by Jean van Noten and printed in multicolour photogravure by Courvoisier.

17. Rwanda, 100 francs, 1970

Since independence Rwanda has issued numerous thematic sets covering a wide variety of subjects: animals of Kagera National Park, butterflies, snakes, flowers, waterfalls, native dances and Old Master paintings, among others. This stamp was the top value in a series of 1970, designed by Jean van Noten and depicting animals of Rwanda.

18. Rwanda, 100 francs, 1971

As a member of the African and Malagasy Posts and Telecommunications Union Rwanda was one of the countries which issued stamps in 1971 to celebrate the tenth anniversary of this organization. This stamp was designed by Quillivic and printed in multicolour photogravure by Delrieu of Paris. It depicts a Rwandan woman and child, the headquarters of the Union in Brazzaville (Congo) and the Union emblem.

19. Burundi, 50 francs, 1962

The first stamps of Burundi consisted of the Ruanda-Urundi definitive series overprinted 'Royaume du Burundi' in July 1962. Several denominations are known with the curious error 'Royaume du Royaume'. The provisional overprints were superseded by a series portraying King Mwambutsa IV in September 1962.

20. Burundi, 10 + 1 franc, 1966

Prince Louis Rwagasore, first prime minister of Burundi, was assassinated in 1962. Stamps were issued in 1963 and 1966 to raise funds for a memorial library and sports stadium. The series of January 1966 was linked to commemoration of the late President John F. Kennedy, no doubt with an eye to bigger philatelic sales, especially in the United States. Four stamps and a miniature sheet portrayed the two statesmen, with views of the proposed memorials in the background. The 40fr. value showed King Mwambutsa visiting Kennedy's grave.

21. Burundi, 40 francs, 1968

In February 1967, while the king was absent on a tour of Europe, a military coup overthrew the monarchy and established a republic. The two previous definitive sets, featuring birds and flowers, were overprinted 'République du Burundi' pending the release of a republican series depicting fishes. Subsequent lengthy thematic definitive sets have appeared at annual intervals. The commemorative stamps of the republic are mainly concerned with events outside the republic, such as the World's Fair, Montreal, Expo 70 at Osaka and the Apollo moon-landings. This stamp was one of a series of ten issued in 1968 in connection with the Olympic Games in Mexico City.

22. Katanga, 50 centimes, 1961

Following the independence of the Congo the province of Katanga, source of the republic's vast mineral wealth, seceded from the union under the leadership of Moise Tshombe. Various stamps of the former Belgian Congo were at first overprinted 'Katanga' and then a series depicting Katangan art was printed in photogravure by Courvoisier. The Tshombe regime was overthrown after United Nations intervention and Katanga was reunited with the Congolese republic in 1963.

23. Katanga, 8 francs, 1960

The animals definitive series of the Belgian Congo were among the many stamps which were overprinted for use in Katanga following the secession of the province in 1960. The 50c. denomination has been recorded with the overprint inverted while the 8f. stamp (normally overprinted at the foot of the design) has been found with the overprint at the top.

24. South Kasai, 10 francs, 1960

In the period of anarchy which followed the attainment of independence several ephemeral regimes were established in the Congo. In the district of South Kasai a former storekeeper, 'King' Albert Kalonji, established himself as dictator and issued Congolese stamps with an appropriate overprint. Subsequently a series featuring a leopard was printed in multicolour photogravure by Courvoisier for use in South Kasai. The separatist regime was suppressed shortly afterward.

25. Indian U.N. Force in Congo, 13 naye paise, 1962

The United Nations dispatched troops to the Congo in 1961 to quell the internecine strife and to restore law and order. Of all of the contingents which formed the U.N. forces only the Indian had its own special stamps. Contemporary Indian definitive stamps from 1 to 50np. were issued in January 1962 with the overprint 'U.N. Force (India) Congo'.

PLATE 82

Spanish Africa

1. Fernando Póo, 10 centavos, 1900

The earliest stamps used in Fernando Póo were British (between 1860 and 1877) and may be recognized by the numeral obliterator 247. A Spanish post office was established in 1868 and issued a distinctive 20 centimos de escudo stamp portraying Queen Isabella, but this was quickly superseded by the 'Ultramar' series of Cuba and Puerto Rico and distinctive stamps were not reintroduced until 1879. Thereafter Fernando Póo followed the usual pattern of colonial keytypes with changes of series at more or less annual intervals. The Alfonso XIII 'Curly head' series was issued in 1899 and reissued the following year in new colours and with the date changed.

2. Fernando Póo, 1 centimo, 1907

The currency of the island was changed to the peseta of 100 centimos in 1901 and later versions of the 'Curly head' type are inscribed in that currency (1901–05). Fernando Póo's last keyplate issue appeared in a new design in 1907, with a more mature portrait of Alfonso XIII. Separate issues of stamps were withdrawn in 1909 and thereafter the stamps of Spanish Guinea were in use.

3. Fernando Póo, 4 pesetas, 1929

Although the stamps of Spanish Guinea were in general use in Fernando Póo from 1909 till 1960 there was one exception. In 1929 the Spanish stamps commemorating the Seville and Barcelona Exhibitions were overprinted for use in the island, the denominations ranging from 5c. to 10p.

4. Fernando Póo, 50 centimos, 1960

The territory of Spanish Guinea was partitioned in 1960, into the island of Fernando Póo and the mainland territory of Rio Muni. Distinctive stamps were introduced in both territories and all were produced in photogravure at the Mint in Madrid. A single design, showing a woman at prayer, was used for the Fernando Póo definitive series issued

PLATE 82 SPANISH AFRICA

in February 1960 in denominations from 25c. to 10p. In October 1968 Fernando Póo and Rio Muni were reunited to form the independent republic of Equatorial Guinea (see below), and distinctive stamps were gradually phased out.

5. Elobey, Annobon and Corisco, 3 centimos, 1907
These three islands originally used the stamps of Fernando Póo but received keytype stamps with a distinctive inscription in 1903. The 'Curly head' stamps were issued in 1903 and 1905 and surcharged with new values in 1906. A new series appeared in 1907 and various provisional surcharges in 1908–09. The stamps of these islands were superseded by the general series of Spanish Guinea in 1909. From 1960 to 1968 the stamps of Fernando Póo were again in use and since then the issues of Equatorial Guinea have been used.

6. Spanish Guinea, 4 centimos, 1905
The 'Curly head' design inscribed 'Guinea Contial Española' was adopted in 1902 for the mainland (continental) area of Spanish Guinea. Stamps of Elobey overprinted 'Guinea Continental' were used in 1906 and the new portrait was adopted in 1907. The stamps of Continental Guinea (later renamed Rio Muni) were superseded by the general series of the Gulf of Guinea in 1909.

7. Spanish Guinea, 2 centimos, 1909
The separate issues of Fernando Póo, Elobey and Continental Guinea were replaced in 1909 by a single series inscribed for use in the Spanish Territories of the Gulf of Guinea. The stamps from 1c. to 10p. were designed and engraved by G. Carrascu and A. Morago and were typographed at the Mint in Madrid. The stamps were reissued two years later with an oval control mark inscribed 'Guinea 1911', applied by hand. The first stamp in each row of a sheet had the date '1911' omitted.

8. Spanish Guinea, 30 centimos, 1931
A series depicting a Nipa house was issued in 1924 and introduced a pictorial element in place of the rather monotonous royal portraiture. This series remained in use for five years – exceptional longevity by Spanish standards – and was replaced by a recess-printed series using three designs showing a native porter, drummers and the King and Queen. The original versions had control serial numbers on the reverse but in 1934–36 they were reissued without numbers. The 5, 20 and 40c. values were reprinted lithographically in 1941.

9. Spanish Guinea, 40 centimos, 1914
Up to 1924 Spanish Guinea had a new definitive series virtually every year, with different portraits of King Alfonso, or printed in new colours, or overprinted with the new date. Examples of the obsolete 'Curly head' type overprinted 1914 are regarded as bogus.

10. Spanish Guinea, 10 centimos, 1949
Relatively few stamps appeared in the 1940s and most of these consisted of provisional surcharges or stamps of Spain suitably overprinted. A pictorial series designed by Nunez de Celis and printed in photogravure was released in December 1949 showing scenery in the colony with a portrait of General Franco inset. An airmail series in the same style appeared two years later. The stamps of Spanish Guinea were superseded by the issue of Fernando Póo and Rio Muni in 1960.

11. Rio de Oro, 10 centimos, 1921
The first post office in Spanish north-west Africa was established at Rio de Oro in 1905 and the 'Curly head' series suitably inscribed was introduced that year. Thereafter the philately of Rio de Oro followed the predictable pattern of the other Spanish colonies. The last series, portraying King Alfonso XIII, was dated 1921–22, but remained in use until 1924, when Rio de Oro was incorporated in Spanish Sahara, whose stamps have been in use ever since.

12. La Aguera, 4 pesetas, 1923
A separate issue of stamps was introduced in 1920 in the district of La Aguera in the southern part of the province of Rio de Oro. Stamps of Rio de Oro were overprinted 'La Agüera' in 1920 and followed by the colonial keyplate design with an appropriate inscription in June 1923. The stamps were withdrawn the following year when La Aguera was incorporated in Spanish Sahara.

13. Cape Juby, 15 centimos, 1919
The district of Cape Juby was administered as a separate province from 1916 to 1950 and during that period issued its own stamps. The first series consisted of stamps of Rio de Oro overprinted 'Cabo Jubi' and surcharged with new values. In 1919 the contemporary Spanish definitive series was diagonally overprinted 'Cabo Juby'. Spanish stamps with this overprint continued in use until 1934, when the overprint was applied to the stamps of Spanish Morocco. The undistinguished philately of Cape Juby is remarkable only in a negative sense. At no time during the 34 years of its separate identity did this territory produce a single indigenous stamp; all stamps consisted of overprints on the stamps of other countries or territories. In 1950 Cape Juby was incorporated with Spanish Sahara, whose stamps it now uses.

14. Cape Juby, 2 centimos, 1935
This stamp was one of the 1933–35 series of Spanish Morocco overprinted between 1935 and 1936 for use in Cape Juby. The only relief from monotony was provided by the different styles and lettering used for these overprints; apart from the spelling already noted, variety was imported by occasional hyphenation, different sizes of capitals and the use of upper and lower case lettering.

15. Spanish Sahara, 10 centimos, 1924
The stamps of Rio de Oro and La Aguera were replaced in 1924 by a series whose inscription signified 'Spanish possessions in Western Sahara'. The stamps, from 5c. to 10p., featured a tribesman and camel. After this promising beginning Spanish Sahara settled down to a diet of overprinted Spanish stamps and nineteen years elapsed before another distinctive pictorial series appeared. The stamps of Spanish Sahara were withdrawn between 1949 and 1950 when general issues of Spanish West Africa were in use.

16. Spanish Sahara, 5 centimos, 1953
Since 1950 Spanish Sahara's philatelic output has consisted mainly of stamps for Child Welfare or Colonial Stamp Day, interspersed by short thematic sets. Among the few genuinely commemorative issues was a set of three, released in March 1953 to mark the 75th anniversary of the Royal Geographical Society of Spain. The common design by R. L. Prieto depicted the allegorical figure of Geography. Like all postwar issues of Spanish Sahara this series was printed in photogravure at the Mint, Madrid.

17. Spanish Sahara, 15 + 5 centimos, 1956
Stamps have been issued annually by Spanish Sahara since 1950 in aid of child welfare funds. The series of 1956 was designed by R. Lozano Prieto and depicted flowers of the Sahara Desert.

18. Rio Muni, 50 + 20 centimos, 1960
The territory formerly known as Continental Guinea was constituted a separate administrative unit in 1960 under the name of Rio Muni and stamps thus inscribed were introduced in April 1960. The only definitive series issued in the period 1960–68 depicted a boy reading a book. Occasional commemoratives were augmented by regular issues marking Stamp Day or bearing surcharges in aid of Child Welfare funds. Since 1968 Rio Muni has used the stamps of Equatorial Guinea.

19. Ifni, 20 centimos, 9141
Separate issues of stamps for the district of Ifni were adopted in 1941, the first series consisting of contemporary Spanish definitives overprinted 'Territorio de Ifni'. The district of Ifni is a coastal enclave in southern Morocco that still remains in Spanish hands.

20. Ifni, 2 centimos, 1949
The Franco definitive series, lithographed in Madrid in 1939, was also overprinted for use in Ifni. Both Franco and numeral designs were released in Ifni in 1949–50 with a smaller, neater overprint in denominations from 2c. to 10p.

21. Ifni, 25 centimos, 1950
The Juan de la Cierva airmail series of 1939, lithographed by Fournier of Burgos, was overprinted 'Ifni' in 1947 and three years later was released with the full overprint 'Territori de Ifni'.

22. Ifni, 5 + 5 centimos, 1951
This stamp was one of a set of three, depicting a fennec, issued in November 1951 to mark Colonial Stamp Day. Since then these semi-postal stamps have been a regular feature of Ifni philately, along with the ubiquitous Child Welfare series. The series of 1951 was designed by E. Serra and S. Quintana. The charity premiums on these stamps have been dropped since 1962.

23. Spanish West Africa, 2 centimos, 1950
Joint issues inscribed 'Africa Occidental Española' (Spanish West Africa) were produced for Spanish Sahara and Ifni between October 1949 and March 1951, but the attempt to rationalize the stamp output of the Spanish colonies in this area was short-lived. During that period a definitive series, airmail and express letter stamps were issued with views of the territory and a portrait of General Franco inset, all designed by Nunez de Celis. Single stamps were also released in 1949 commemorating the 75th anniversary of the Universal Postal Union and Colonial Stamp Day respectively.

24. Equatorial Guinea, 8 pesetas, 1972
Very few stamps have been released by Equatorial Guinea since independence, and these have been confined to sets marking the anniversaries of independence. Independence Day was marked by three stamps depicting clasped hands. President Nguema was portrayed on the series of 1970 marking the first anniversary, and the President and a cockerel appeared on the stamps of 1971 celebrating the second anniversary. A native archer was depicted on the series of 1972 honouring the third anniversary.

25. Equatorial Guinea, 1.50 pesetas, 1970
The former Spanish overseas provinces of Fernando Póo and Rio Muni united on 12 October 1968, to form the independent Republic of Equatorial Guinea. A set of three stamps inscribed 'Republica de Guinea Ecuatorial' appeared in 1968 to celebrate independence, but the stamps of Fernando Póo and Rio Muni continued for definitive purposes until 1970, when a series, from 50c. to 25p., belatedly marked the first anniversary of independence. The stamps, portraying President F. M. Nguema, were printed in photogravure at the Mint, Madrid.

PLATE 83 MOROCCO

PLATE 83
Morocco

1. French Post Offices, 2 centimos, 1902
French consular post offices were established in Morocco in 1891 and between that date and 1917 contemporary French stamps surcharged in Spanish centimos or pesetas were used. Between 1902 and 1910 the French Blanc, Mouchon and Merson designs inscribed 'Maroc' were introduced. Following the proclamation of the French protectorate in 1912 the stamps were overprinted 'Protectorat Français'.

2. German Post Offices, 60 centimos, 1900
German post offices were opened in Morocco in 1899 and used contemporary German stamps overprinted diagonally 'Marocco' and surcharged in Spanish currency. In 1900 the Germania series was introduced and given a horizontal overprint, which was changed to 'Marokko' in 1911. The German post offices were suppressed at the beginning of World War I.

3. Spanish Post Offices, ¼ centimo, 1903
Contemporary Spanish stamps overprinted 'Correo Español Marruecos' (Spanish Post Morocco) were issued in 1903. In 1908–09 stamps of this series were also issued with a handstruck overprint 'Tetuan'. These stamps remained in use till 1914, when they were superseded by the issues of the Spanish Protectorate.

4. Gibraltarian Post Offices, 20 centimos, 1898
A British post office was established in Tangier in 1857. All mail was taken to Gibraltar, where British stamps were postmarked with the A 26 obliterator of that port. Gibraltarian stamps were introduced in 1886 and can only be identified by the postmarks of Tangier, Casablanca, Alcazar, Tetuan and other Moroccan towns in which these post offices were situated. Stamps of Gibraltar overprinted 'Morocco Agencies' were adopted in 1898. The overprints were applied by the Gibraltar *Chronicle*, but subsequent stocks were overprinted by De La Rue. In 1907 control of these post offices was transferred from Gibraltar to the General Post Office in London and the Gibraltarian stamps were withdrawn from use.

5. British Post Offices, 20 centimos, 1907
British stamps of the Edwardian series were issued in 1907, surcharged in Spanish currency. These stamps were sold at British post offices throughout Morocco until the establishment of the French Zone and the Tangier International Zone. Thereafter their use was confined to the Spanish Zone. Stamps of this type and surcharge were withdrawn from sale on 31 December 1956.

6. British Post Offices, 2 pence, 1936
British stamps overprinted 'Morocco Agencies' but without a surcharge in Spanish currency were issued from 1907 to 1937 for use on parcels, and subsequently airmail correspondence. Ordinary British stamps, without an overprint, were introduced in 1937. In 1949, however, overprinted stamps without a surcharge were reintroduced for use in the British post office at Tetuan in the Spanish Zone. These stamps were withdrawn at the end of 1956 when Morocco became an independent kingdom.

7. British Post Offices, 5 centimes, 1937
Stamps overprinted 'Morocco Agencies' and surcharged in French centimes and francs were introduced in 1917, for sale at the post offices in the French Zone. These stamps were withdrawn from sale on 8 January 1938. The only stamps portraying King Edward VIII issued outside the United Kingdom were those British stamps overprinted for use in the post offices in Morocco and Tangier.

8. Tangier (French Post Office), 3 centimes, 1917
Although the French had established a protectorate over part of Morocco the status of Tangier was not clearly defined until 1924, when it was established as an international zone. Nevertheless, from 1917 onwards France issued occasional sets of stamps for use in the French post office in that city. The first series consisted of the obsolete Blanc, Mouchon and Merson types overprinted in capitals. In 1929 contemporary issues of French Morocco were overprinted 'Tanger' in upper and lower case lettering.

9. Tangier (Spanish Post Office), 10 centimos, 1948
After the establishment of the Spanish Zone in 1914 contemporary Spanish stamps overprinted 'Correo Español Marruecos' continued to be used in Tangier only. They were replaced by similar stamps overprinted 'Tanger' in 1926. Overprinted stamps continued in use until 1948 when they were superseded by a distinctive pictorial series, recess-printed at the Government Printing Works in Madrid. The stamps ranged from 1c. to 10p. and showed scenery and people of Morocco. The 30c. and 1.35p. denominations featured a map of the city. These stamps were withdrawn at the end of 1956, when Morocco became independent and the international zone of Tangier was abolished.

10. Tangier (British Post Office), 10 shillings, 1957
British stamps overprinted 'Tangier' without a surcharge in French or Spanish currency, were introduced in 1927, three years after the establishment of the international zone. The international zone was abolished when Morocco became independent in January 1957 but the British post office was allowed to remain open until 30 April 1957, in order to celebrate its centenary. The entire Elizabethan series (½d. to 10s.) was given a commemorative overprint and released on 1 April. The 9d. stamp is known with the word 'Tangier' omitted, while the three Castles high values are known with missing hyphen or hyphen inserted by hand.

11. Morocco (Cherifian Post), 2 moussonats, 1912
A Moorish post was established in 1885 and used handstruck marks on official, or Cherifian, mail from then until 1912, when a series of six stamps was introduced. The stamps, in denominations from 1 to 50m., were designed by P. Legat and featured the Aissouas Mosque in Tangier. They were lithographed by Lecocq Mathorel and Chr. Bernard. The first stamps, released in May 1912, were printed on white paper with narrow margins. A second printing, in 1913, was made on tinted paper with wide margin.

12. French Zone, 1 centime, 1914
The Blanc, Mouchon and Merson stamps of the French post offices in Morocco were surcharged in Arabic in 1911. Three years later, on the establishment of the French Zone, they were overprinted 'Protectorat Français'. Most denominations are known with the 's' of 'Français' inverted.

13. French Zone, 3 centimes, 1923
A pictorial series, recess-printed by A. Oelzer and Co. was released in September 1917. The six designs illustrated prominent landmarks in the principal cities of the French protectorate. The designs were substantially redrawn and printed in photogravure by Vaugirard in 1923. New colours and denominations were added to the set in 1927. The lowest denominations in both 1917 and 1923 sets showed the Tower of Hassan in Rabat.

14. French Zone, 80 centimes, 1933
Distinctive stamps for airmail postage were adopted in 1922, the first series featuring a biplane over Casablanca. A new definitive series in 1933 was accompanied by a set of six stamps for airmail. The three lowest values featured an aerial view of Rabat, the higher denominations Casablanca. The stamps were designed by R. Belliot and recess-printed by the French Government Printing Works.

15. French Morocco, 1 centime, 1939
The definitive series issued by Morocco between 1939 and 1942 was recess-printed but reflects the trend towards simplicity in stamp design compared with the series of 1933–34. Scenery, landmarks and wildlife continued to provide the subjects for these pictorials.

16. French Morocco, 50 centimes, 1947
C. Josso designed a series engraved by Pierre Gandon and recess-printed by Lugat of Casablanca between 1947 and 1954. As with the previous sets the emphasis was placed on scenery and landmarks. The centime denominations all featured the terraces in Casablanca.

17. French Morocco, 15 + 5 francs, 1952
Like France, the French Post Offices in Morocco issued stamps each year to mark Stamp Day. The first of these issues appearing in 1947. The majority depicted aspects of the postal service or historic developments. The stamp of 1952 had the head post office in Casablanca with a reproduction of the airmail stamps of 1922 and marked the 30th anniversary of the first Moroccan airmail stamps.

18. Spanish Zone, 1 centimo, 1928
From 1914 to 1928 Spanish stamps overprinted 'Protectorado Español' or 'Marruecos' were used in the Spanish zone. A distinctive series, designed by M. Bertuchi and recess-printed by De La Rue, was introduced in 1928. Five designs were used, featuring the Mosque at Alcazarquivir, the Moorish gateway at Larache, the well at Alhucemas and views of Xauen and Tetuan. In the original version of the 1c. stamp the plural abbreviation 'Cs' was inadvertently used. The correct form 'Ct' was substituted four years later. Bertuchi designed all the stamps of the Spanish protectorate up to 1956.

19. Spanish Zone, 10 centimos, 1937
The revolt of the Spanish nationalists against the republican regime began in Morocco and owed its initial success to the colonial troops brought from North Africa to Spain by General Franco. The first anniversary of the Civil War was celebrated by a lengthy series, from 1c. to 10p., printed in photogravure by Waterlows. The stamps depicted legionaries, Cherifian guards, Cape Juby Camel Corps and Falangist volunteers. General Franco himself was portrayed on the 10c. denomination.

20. French Morocco, 50 francs, 1955
The last definitive series issued in Morocco under French protection appeared in 1955 and like its predecessors concentrated on prominent landmarks of the country. The 50f. stamp depicted the Portuguese cistern at Mazagan. The stamps were designed, engraved and recess-printed in Paris.

21. Spanish Zone, 25 centimos, 1966
Rieusset of Barcelona lithographed many of the stamps of the Spanish protectorate from 1944 onward. The first definitive series printed by this firm took as its theme the agricultural occupations of Morocco with vignettes of ploughing, harvesting, threshing, gathering oranges and tending flocks of sheep. Two years later a similar series in the same denominations depicted urban arts and crafts, and in 1948 was replaced by a series devoted to various

PLATE 83 MOROCCO · PLATE 84 ALGERIA, TUNISIA

forms of transport. Similar scenic designs were used for the anti-T.B. semi-postal stamps of 1946.

22. Spanish Zone, 5 centimos, 1950
The 75th anniversary of the Universal Postal Union in 1949 was seized as the opportunity for yet another lengthy series of stamps from the partnership of Bertuchi and Rieusset, showing postmen of different periods, a mail-coach, a mail-van and a mail-train.

23. Spanish Zone, 10 centimos, 1954
Interspersed with the various pictorial definitive sets, a number of semi-postal or charity sets were issued by the Spanish protectorate. Obligatory tax stamps, for use on all correspondence at certain times of the year, were issued between 1941 and 1946 to raise money for wounded ex-soldiers of the Civil War and North African campaigns. From 1946 to 1954 sets of stamps appeared annually with premiums in aid of the Anti-Tuberculosis Fund. For this purpose the Cross of Lorraine (used on similar Spanish stamps) was adapted to a double crescent motif and appeared on these stamps. Otherwise the vignettes of these stamps were very much in the Bertuchi idiom, with scenery and aspects of Moroccan life.

24. Morocco, 30 francs, 1958
Stamps inscribed in Spanish or French currency continued to appear in the independent kingdom of Morocco until 1959, when the dirham of 100 francs was adopted. The stamps in Spanish currency continued to be printed in Spain while those in French currency were recess-printed in Paris. This stamp was one of a set of three issued in April 1958 to mark the participation of Morocco at the Brussels World Fair. It depicts the Moroccan pavilion with the Expo emblem inset. The stamps were designed and engraved by the French artist Fenneteaux.

25. Morocco, 25 francs, 1971
The 25th anniversary of the SOFAR Conference and the foundation of the Arab Postal Union was celebrated in December 1971 by a 25f. stamp with the A.P.U. emblem. The stamp was lithographed by De La Rue. The Arab Postal Union was formed under the aegis of Egypt in 1946 and now extends throughout the Middle East to encompass all the Arab countries.

26. Morocco, 30 francs, 1963
Since independence Morocco has gone to printers other than the French and Spanish government printing works. A series of three stamps, released in July 1963 to publicize the UNESCO campaign for the preservation of the Nubian temples, was recess-printed by Zavod za Izradu Novcanica of Belgrade. The stamps showed the colossi of Abu Simbel (20f.), the bas-relief of Isis (30f.) and the Temple of Philae (50f.).

PLATE 84
Algeria and Tunisia

---

1. Algeria, 30 centimes, 1924
Ordinary French stamps were used in Algeria until May 1924, when the postal administration was separated from metropolitan France and French stamps with a suitable overprint were adopted. Between then and December 1925 more than thirty different contemporary French stamps were released with the 'Algérie' overprint, and included the Blanc, Mouchon, Merson, Sower and Pasteur definitives. Several cases of double or triple overprint have

been recorded, while the 60c. is known with overprint inverted.

2. Algeria, 65 centimes, 1927
A distinctive definitive series superseded the overprinted stamps in 1926, various denominations and changes of colour being introduced up to 1941. Three small-format designs were used for the centime values, showing a street in the Casbah, the mosque of Sidi Abderahman and the Grand Mosque. The franc denominations had the Bay of Algiers seen from the arches of Mustapha Supérieur. This design was subsequently used for a 50c. stamp issued by France in 1930 to mark the centenary of French occupation. Several stamps of this series were reissued in 1942 with the words 'République Française' omitted.

3. Algeria, 1 centime, 1936
As elsewhere in the French colonial empire, the typographed definitives gave way to recess-printed stamps in the mid-1930s. Eight double-sized designs were used for the series issued between 1936 and 1940. Prominent landmarks in the cities of Algeria formed the subjects of seven designs, but for the eighth H. Cheffer produced a vignette, 'A halt in the Sahara', which managed to convey the vastness and emptiness of the desert.

4. Algeria, 2.40 francs, 1943
Under the Vichy regime of World War II stamps were issued without the republican inscription or monogram. An entirely new definitive series was released in 1942–43 in denominations from 40c. to 5f. The stamps were printed in photogravure by Berliot of Algiers and had the coats of arms of Algiers, Oran and Constantine. After the liberation of France a typographed version was produced in Paris. The typographed stamps omitted the imprint found in the bottom left hand corner of the Berliot stamps.

5. Algeria, 10 centimes, 1944
Algeria was liberated at the end of 1943 and stamps were produced under the auspices of the Free French. Stamps designed by L. Fernez and engraved by C. Herve were lithographed between December 1943 and early 1945, with such symbolic subjects as victory, the V sign, the head of Marianne and a Gallic cock. These were followed by contemporary French stamps overprinted 'Algérie' in the manner of 1924–25.

6. Algeria, 40 francs, 1954
The postwar stamps of Algeria reflected the military nature of the French administration. The majority of the commemorative issues had some military connection. This stamp was one of a set of three issued in January 1954 to publicize the military health service and commemorate the 150th anniversary of the birth of Dr Maillot, pioneer of anti-malaria treatment. They were designed and engraved by R. Serres and printed in two-colour recess.

7. Algeria, 15 francs, 1956
The centenary of Marshal Franchet d'Esperey, a hero of World War I, was marked by this stamp, issued in May 1956. Designed and engraved by J. Ebstein, it has as its background the marshal's birthplace at Mostaganem. Other stamps issued in the same period portrayed Marshal Leclerc and Colonel Ornano or they raised money for the Foreign Legion and Army welfare funds. The last stamp issued under French auspices appeared in July 1958 in aid of the Marshal de Lattre Foundation.

8. Algeria, 25 centimes, 1963
The early stamps of the Algerian republic were pro-

duced in France but from 1963 onwards Algeria has taken an independent line of stamp production. This stamp, printed by Courvoisier and issued in December 1963, commemorated the fifteenth anniversary of the Declaration of Human Rights. The majority of Algerian commemoratives have been single stamps, covering a wide range of national and international events.

9. Algeria, 1 dinar, 1966
Algeria adopted a currency based on the dinar of 100 centimes in 1964. The 30th anniversary of the Algerian Scout movement coincided with the seventh Arab Scout Jamboree, held at Jedaid, Tripoli, and was marked by two stamps designed by M. Bouzid. The 30c. showed the Mohammedan Scout banner and emblem, the 1d. stamp the Jamboree badge. The stamps were printed in multicolour photogravure by the Central Bank of Algeria, which has produced most Algerian stamps in the past decade.

10. Tunisia, 1 centime, 1888
Adhesive postage stamps were adopted by the Regency of Tunis, as Tunisia was then known, in July 1888. The stamps, featuring the coat of arms, were designed and engraved by E. Casse and typographed at the French Government Printing Works. In October a re-engraved version, by E. Mouchon, was issued. The original Casse series had an unshaded background to the coat of arms, whereas the Mouchon version was shaded. New colours and denominations were added to the series between 1893 and 1901.

11. Tunisia, 2 francs, 1926
A pictorial series was introduced in 1906, with small-format designs for the low values and double-sized designs for the higher ones. A similar series replaced it in 1926. The centimes denominations featured an Arab woman, the Grand Mosque and the mosque in the Place Halfaouine, Tunis, while the franc denominations showed the Amphitheatre at El Djem. This design was produced by Dabadie and engraved by Hourriez. The stamps were typographed in denominations from 1c. to 20f., various changes of colour and value being introduced up to 1941.

12. Tunisia, 2 centimes, 1931
The same four designs were retained for a series recess-printed by the Institut de Gravure and released in January 1931. Apart from the different characteristics of the two processes the designs differ in major details, principally in the engraving of the value tablets and the position of the crescent and star emblem. A number of provisional surcharges were applied to this series between 1937 and 1941.

13. Tunisia, 1.50 + 8.50 francs, 1943
Tunisia was under the control of the Vichy authorities and the Germans from 1940 till 1943. Following the North Africa landings in late 1942 the country was liberated by Allied troops. C. Herve designed this stamp, issued at the end of 1943 to celebrate the liberation and to raise funds for war charities. The stamp depicts soldiers wearing British, Tunisian and American helmets. Several stamps appeared soon afterwards with premiums in aid of the fighting forces and war veterans.

14. Tunisia, 50 centimes, 1951
The prewar definitive series (1926–41 designs) was reintroduced in 1945, the various denominations being printed in new colours. This series was superseded between 1950 and 1953 by a set in a uniform design featuring a Carthaginian intaglio of a horse. The stamps were designed by Besson, engraved by Cortot and printed in Paris, the lower

PLATE 84 ALGERIA, TUNISIA · PLATE 85 LIBYA

values being typographed and the higher denominations recess-printed.

15. Tunisia, 5 francs, 1949
The 75th anniversary of the Universal Postal Union was marked in October 1949 by 5 and 15*f.* stamps for ordinary postage and a 25*f.* for airmail. They were designed by Besson and engraved by Dufresne and recess-printed on blue tinted paper, an unusual feature for postwar stamps of this country.

16. Tunisia, 15 francs, 1955
Cottet engraved and designed a series portraying the Bey of Tunisia which was issued in October 1954 in denominations from 8 to 30*f.* A similar portrait, but in a smaller format, was adopted for a 15*f.* stamp released in July 1955. The portrayal of the Bey reflected the move toward independence, which was granted in March 1956. Tunisia was a sovereign kingdom from 26 March 1956 to 25 July 1957, when it became a republic.

17. Tunisia, 5 francs, 1955
The last stamps issued under French auspices were a set of six publicizing the Tunis International Fair. Three designs were used showing embroidery, pottery and jasmin sellers. Pierre Gandon adapted the original designs of Gorgi and also engraved the dies. The stamps were recess-printed in Paris in denominations from 5 to 30*f.*

18. Tunisia, 30 francs, 1958
Pierre Gandon designed and engraved this stamp, issued in April 1958 to mark the Brussels International Fair. Unlike the other stamps issued all over the world to celebrate this event the Tunisian stamp struck a novel, if faintly irrelevant, note. Symbols of medicine were flanked by portraits of the medieval physicians André Vesalius and Abderahman ibn Khaldoun.

19. Tunisia, ½ millième, 1959
French currency was scrapped in favour of the Tunisian dinar of 1000 millièmes at the beginning of 1959. A republican definitive series was introduced between March 1959 and December 1961. A wide range of subjects was depicted on the stamps from ½*m.* to 1*d.* The birdlife of Tunisia was represented by the Ain Draham on this stamp, designed by Hatem Elmekki – one of the few designs by this artist in which realism has triumphed over surrealism. The stamps were engraved by French craftsmen and recess-printed in Paris.

20. Tunisia, 2 millièmes, 1959
Yahia Turki designed four of the stamps in the 1959–61 series, including this one featuring a camel driver. Other designs were produced by Tunisian artists Abdallah, Gamra, Farhat and Morand, though the majority were by Elmekki. No fewer than thirteen leading French engravers, representing the cream of the profession, had a hand in the dies of these stamps.

21. Tunisia, 50 millièmes, 1959
This stamp was released in November 1959 to mark the first anniversary of the Tunisian Central Bank. Elmekki's whimsical approach to stamp design is seen at its best in this motif, with a dancing girl balancing on a coin. The coin itself is an Arab dinar of the medieval Caliphate – a gold coin which served as the model of many European coins, including those of Russia and England.

22. Tunisia, 20 millièmes, 1967
The Mediterranean Games were held in Tunis in September 1967 and two stamps appeared the previous March to provide advance publicity. They were designed by Hatem Elmekki to symbolize athletics. Note his clever adaptation of the Olym-

pic rings motif and overlapping figures to convey the impression of action. The stamps were recess-printed in Paris. The Games themselves were marked by five stamps issued in September, illustrating various aspects of sport.

23. Tunisia, 25 millièmes, 1970
The Sixth North African Maghreb Medical Seminar held in Tunis in 1970 was honoured by this stamp. A nurse, caduceus and flags of the participating countries were combined by Elmekki into one of his characteristic designs.

PLATE 85

Libya

---

1. Bengasi, 1 piastre, 1911
An Italian post office was established in the North African port of Bengasi in the mid-nineteenth century, with the permission of the Turkish authorities then governing Libya. Ordinary Italian stamps were used, followed by the Levant overprints in 1874 (see plate 34). The Italian 25 centesimi stamp was overprinted for use in this office in July 1901 and surcharged 1 piastre local currency. It was replaced by the 25*c.* of the 1908 series in December 1911. This post office was temporarily closed during the Italo-Turkish War and subsequently used the stamps of Libya.

2. Tripoli, 10 centesimi, 1909
The contemporary Italian definitive series, without surcharge in local currency, was overprinted 'Tripoli di Barberia' and issued in the Italian post office in December 1909. These stamps were likewise withdrawn in 1912, when the series overprinted for use throughout Libya was introduced.

3. Libya, 2 centesimi, 1912
Following the withdrawal of the Turks from North Africa as a result of the war with Italy stamps overprinted 'Libia' were adopted throughout the country. Upper and lower case lettering was used for the overprints, except in the case of the 15*c.*, which was overprinted in capitals. There are two types of the overprint, varying in the shapes of the letters. The 5*c.* is known with the overprint double. This overprinted set was replaced in 1921 by a pictorial series emphasizing the historic Roman connection between Italy and Libya.

4. Libya, 10 + 5 centesimi, 1915
The basic stamp was one of a series issued by Italy in 1915–16 to raise funds for the Red Cross war effort. The majority of stamps issued for general use in Libya up to 1942 consisted of Italian stamps either overprinted or inscribed 'Libia'.

5. Libya, 1.25 lire, 1939
Among the few distinctive issues of Libya under Italian rule was the set of April 1939 publicizing the thirteenth Tripoli Fair. Stamps marking this annual event were marked by the Italian colony of Libya from 1936 to 1939, though Tripolitania (see below) issued sets to mark the fair from its inception. The Libyan series of 1939 was designed by G. Rondini and printed in photogravure by the Italian State Printing Works. Three stamps showed an agricultural landscape, the other two a view of Ghadames.

6. Cyrenaica, 60 centesimi, 1925
Separate issues of stamps were made in the provinces of Cyrenaica and Tripolitania between 1923 and 1939. In the majority of instances they consisted of contemporary Italian stamps suitably overprinted. This stamp was one of a set of three issued

in 1925–26 to celebrate the jubilee of King Victor Emmanuel III.

7. Cyrenaica, 50 centesimi, 1932
Although Cyrenaica was content to use Italian stamps with an overprint a distinctive airmail series was issued in August 1932. The six stamps were printed in photogravure, using two designs by L. de Rosa. The 3*c.* denominations showed a camel rider, the lire values depicted an aeroplane flying over Roman ruins.

8. Cyrenaica, 80 centesimi, 1934
Both Cyrenaica and Tripolitania issued sets of large-sized stamps in October 1934 to mark the second International Colonial Exhibition, held at Naples. They were designed by G. Rondini and printed in two-colour photogravure, the vignettes being distinctive in each case. The ordinary series of six stamps had an Arab horseman, the three lower values of the airmail series (25, 50 and 75*c.*) the arrival of a mail-plane, while the top three denominations the Venus of Cyrene. Note the notation of the date in the Christian calendar (1934) and according to the Fascist era (A. XII = year twelve). The use of distinctive stamps in Cyrenaica was discontinued in 1939, when stamps of Libya were resumed.

9. Cyrenaica, 20 centesimi, 1930
Like the other Italian colonies Cyrenaica issued five denominations of the Italian series of 1930 commemorating the quatercentenary of the death of Francesco Ferrucci. The stamps were in new colours and suitably overprinted.

10. Tripolitania, 60 centesimi, 1926
Italian stamps overprinted 'Tripolitania' were adopted in October 1923 and provided the bulk of the issues of that territory from then until 1939. In 1926 a set of six semi-postal stamps was issued in both Cyrenaica and Tripolitania, with identical designs. The stamps were designed by A. Calcagnadoro, and symbolized Italia armed with sword and spade to represent the colonizing mission of the Italian empire. The premiums from the sale of these stamps went to the Italian Colonial Institute.

11. Tripolitania, 25 centesimi, 1927
The first Fair was held in February 1927 and appropriately was marked by the first distinctive series of stamps issued in the colony. Six postage and two express letters stamps were designed by N. D'Urso and depicted various views of Tripoli. They were lithographed with black vignettes and coloured frames. Annual sets were issued for the Tripoli Fair by Tripolitania until 1935 and by Libya in subsequent years up to the present day.

12. Tripolitania, 1.25 lire, 1930
The year 1930 marked the high-tide of Tripolitania's philatelic activity, no fewer than five sets (40 stamps) being released between February and December. In the main they consisted of contemporary Italian issues with a distinctive overprint and they were mostly printed in new colours. This stamp was one of five ordinary and three airmail stamps released on 26 July, to mark the quatercentenary of the death of Francesco Ferrucci.

13. Tripolitania, 1 lira, 1930
Italian commemorative stamps, printed in new colours, were overprinted for use in Tripolitania between 1930 and 1934. This stamp was one of a set of four airmail stamps issued in December 1930 to mark the bimillenary of the poet Virgil. The basic stamps were designed by C. Mezzana and featured scenes from the *Aeneid* and other epic poems.

14. Tripolitania, 1.25 lire, 1931
The seventh centenary of St Anthony was marked

PLATE 85 LIBYA · PLATE 86 EGYPT

by a set of seven stamps issued in Italy. The series was subsequently overprinted for use in several colonies, including Tripolitania; illustrating scenes from the life of the saint, it was designed by C. Vincenti. The 75c. and 5 + 2l. values were recess-printed, but the remaining denominations were produced in photogravure.

15. Middle East Forces, 3 pence, 1943
Contemporary British stamps overprinted M.E.F. were used by the Middle East Forces in areas under their control. They were first used in Eritrea and Italian Somaliland in 1942 and extended to Cyrenaica and Tripolitania in 1943. Subsequently they were used in the Dodecanese Islands in 1945, between the surrender of these islands by the Italians and Germans and the annexation of the archipelago by Greece (see plate 15). The overprints were made in London and Cairo. The London version, by Harrison and Sons, has sharp lettering and upright oblong stops, while the Cairo printing, by the Army Printing Service, was characterized by rough lettering and rounded stops.

16. Tripolitania, 12 M.A.L., 1948
Contemporary British stamps, from ½d. to 10s. were overprinted 'B.M.A. Tripolitania' and released in July 1948 for use in territory under British Military Administration. The stamps were surcharged in M.A.L. (Military Administration lire) currency. Following the transfer of government to a civil administration in 1950 the stamps were reissued with the overprint 'B.A. Tripolitania'. They were withdrawn in 1951, when Tripolitania became a part of the kingdom of Libya.

17. Fezzan and Ghadames, 10 centimes, 1946
Free French forces invaded southern Libya in 1942 and occupied the districts of Fezzan and Ghadames. Stamps of Italy and Libya were overprinted by V. Heintz of Algiers 'Fezzan Occupation Française' and surcharged in French currency. From April 1944 till October 1946 ordinary Algerian stamps were in use, but were then superseded by a pictorial series inscribed 'Fezzan. Ghadamés'. A. Boutet designed the three vignettes used for this series, showing the fort at Sebha, the Turkish fort and mosque at Mourzouk and a map of the district. This joint series was succeeded three years later by separate issues for both districts.

18. Fezzan, 4 francs, 1949
A pictorial series inscribed 'Territoire Militaire du Fezzan' was issued in 1949. The five designs, by A. Boutet, featured scenery of the district and portraits of Colonel d'Ornano and General Leclerc, who led the Free French forces in the North African campaign. In 1951 government was handed over to the civil authorities and this was reflected in a new pictorial series in which the word 'Militaire' was deleted. On 24 December 1951, Fezzan became part of the kingdom of Libya whose stamps it now uses.

19. Ghadames, 100 francs, 1949
The administration of Ghadames was separated from Fezzan in 1949 and a distinctive set of stamps introduced in April of that year. The eight ordinary and two airmail stamps were produced in a uniform design by M. Besson and depicted the cross of Agadem in a decorative frame. They were engraved by Cortot and recess-printed in Paris. Ghadames became part of Libya on the same date as Fezzan and since then has used Libyan stamps.

20. Cyrenaica, 200 mils, 1950
The M.E.F. overprinted stamps of Britain were replaced by a distinctive series in January 1950, pending the transfer of the district to the kingdom of Libya. A mounted warrior formed the subject of

the stamps, recess-printed by Waterlow and Sons in denominations from 1 to 500m. A larger format was used for the denominations from 50 to 500m., and a series of postage due stamps was introduced at the same time.

21. Libya, 20 M.A.L., 1951
In December 1951 the stamps of Cyrenaica were overprinted 'Libya' in English and Arabic for use in Cyrenaica, and additionally surcharged in M.A.L. or French currency for use in Tripolitania and Fezzan-Ghadamés respectively, pending the release of a distinctive series the following year.

22. Libya, 25 mils, 1952
The first series of the independent kingdom of Libya was recess-printed by Bradbury Wilkinson and issued in April 1952. Two formats were used, the small size for the low values (2 to 25m.) and the large size for the 50 to 500m. denominations. Both depicted King Idris I al Senussi, king of Libya. Stamps from 1955 to 1960 were usually inscribed 'United Kingdom of Libya', but the form 'Libya' was subsequently adopted.

23. Libya, 45 mils, 1963
Libya pursued a fairly moderate policy with regard to stamp issues in the decade following independence but since then has produced stamps at more frequent intervals, using printers in many different countries. Courvoisier produced a set of three multicolour photogravure stamps in February 1963 to mark the Freedom from Hunger campaign; a date palm and well, camel and sheep and a farmer and tractor were illustrated.

24. Libya, 75 mils, 1967
This stamp was one of a series issued in 1967 to mark the Mediterranean Sports Contest, held in neighbouring Tunisia. Note the resumption of the full title, 'Kingdom of Libya', which appeared on stamps from 1968 to the end of 1969, when the monarchy was overthrown.

25. Libyan Arab Republic, 20 mils, 1970
The monarchy came to an end in September 1969 in a coup led by elements of the Libyan Army. Stamps issued since the end of 1969 have been inscribed L.A.R. (Libyan Arab Republic), emulating the styles adopted by Egypt, Syria and the Yemen. This stamp was one of a set of six issued in 1970 to mark the inauguration of the new headquarters of the Universal Postal Union.

26. Libyan Arab Republic, 15 mils, 1972
Many countries throughout the world issued stamps in 1972 to mark International Books Year. The stamp illustrated, with the suitable symbolic motif, was Libya's contribution to the theme.

PLATE 86
Egypt

---

1. 5 paras, 1866
Adhesive stamps were introduced in January 1866 and were lithographed or typographed by Pellas Brothers of Genoa. Various designs were used for the ornamental background, on which five lines of Arabic script were overprinted. The stamps ranged from 5pa. to 10pi. and may be found imperforate or perforated in various gauges. The watermark used for this series showed a pyramid surmounted by the rising sun.

2. 10 paras, 1867
The staid designs of the first issue were rapidly

superseded by a pictorial series designed by F. Hoff of Hirschberg in Silesia and lithographed by V. Penasson of Alexandria. The central oval featured the Pyramid and Sphinx, while the side panels showed a pillar and an obelisk. The Sphinx and Pyramid motif was retained, in various poses, for all Egyptian stamps up to World War I. The stamps were printed on crescent and star watermarked paper in denominations from 5pa. to 5pi.

3. 1 millième, 1888
The Egyptian currency was revised in 1887, when the piastre of 10 milliemes was adopted. This necessitated a change of definitive series. The pyramid and sphinx designs used since 1879 were redrawn with new values in the side panels. A 3m. denomination was added to the series in 1892 and between that date and 1906 the colours of other denominations were changed. All the pyramid and sphinx stamps from 1879 to 1906 were typographed by De La Rue.

4. 200 milliemes, 1914
The Sphinx and Pyramid stamps were replaced by a pictorial series in January 1914, typographed by De La Rue. The stamps ranged from 1 to 200m. and illustrated antiquities such as the pyramids of Giza, the rock temples of Abu Simbel and the pylon of Karnak. The top value, however, depicted the Aswan Dam to emphasize the rapid modernization of the country. The series was typographed by Harrison and Sons (1 to 100m.) in 1921–22 on multiple crescent paper, whereas the De La Rue version was on single crescent paper. Note the use of English in the captions, reflecting growing British influence at that time. Egypt became a British protectorate in December 1914.

5. 5 milliemes, 1923
The first set of stamps printed by Harrisons in the photogravure process was the Egyptian definitive series of 1923, in values from 1m. to £1. Five years later the same method was used for stamps of the Gold Coast (see plate 71) and by Britain from 1934 onward. A curious feature of the series of 1923 was the absence of any inscription in a European script. Egypt became an independent kingdom in March 1922 and these stamps reflect the prevailing mood of nationalism at the time.

6. 5 milliemes, 1926
The Survey Department in Cairo took over responsibility for the production of Egyptian stamps in 1925. Occasional sets were subsequently printed by Harrisons but the vast majority were printed locally. Offset-lithography was used at first, and this stamp, one of a set of six issued in 1926, is a good example of the Egyptian commemoratives of the period, printed by this method. The stamps, in values from 5 to 200m., marked the 12th Agricultural Exhibition. Note the use of French as the alternative language in the inscriptions. This practice continued up to the end of 1956.

7. 20 milliemes, 1929
Prince Farouk made his first appearance on a set of four stamps issued in February 1929 to mark his ninth birthday. The stamps were printed in photogravure with centres in slate and frames in various colours. A special printing was made in which the centres were in brown or black and the portrait was very much clearer. This was the beginning of those special printings – and latterly, deliberately contrived errors – produced for Farouk, who counted philately among his many collecting manias.

8. 1 millième, 1933
A trick question in philatelic quizzes used to be 'on which stamps would you find Hannibal crossing

PLATE 86 EGYPT · PLATE 87 ETHIOPIA, SUDAN

the Pyramids?' The answer is on the Egyptian airmail series of 1933–38, which shows the Imperial Airways liner *Hannibal* flying over the pyramids. The stamps were offset-lithographed in two-colour combinations, from 1 to 200*m*. A photogravure version of this design (5 to 30*m*.) appeared between 1941 and 1946. The latter stamps were printed in single colours and have a screened background, instead of the horizontal lines of the original series.

9. 20 millièmes, 1938

The top value of a set of three stamps issued in March 1938 in honour of the Leprosy Research Congress, this stamp illustrates the way in which Egyptian commemorative stamps in the period before World War II drew on natural or antiquarian subjects · for inspiration. The vignette depicts the flower *Hydnocarpus*.

10. 5 millièmes, 1936

A set of three stamps was issued in December 1936 to mark the signing of the Anglo-Egyptian Treaty, negotiating, among other things, the British military occupation of the Canal Zone and the regulation of international traffic through the Suez Canal. The common design shows Nahas Pasha, the British foreign secretary Anthony Eden and the treaty delegates. Ironically it was Egypt's repudiation of the treaty and the nationalization of the Canal in 1956 which led to the Suez venture and the downfall of Anthony Eden, the prime minister who sanctioned the punitive invasion of Egypt. Eden was the only British politician to appear on Egyptian stamps.

11. 30 millièmes, 1939

A portrait of the eighteen-year-old King Farouk was used for the pictorial high values of 1939. The lower denominations, from 1 to 20*m*., had appeared in 1937 to mark his investiture and were retained as a definitive issue. The higher values, from 30 to 200*m*., showed various landmarks in the background. The colour of this stamp was changed from grey to blue-grey in 1945 and then to yellow-green the following year.

12. 22 + 22 millièmes, 1946

Four stamps, each bearing 100 per cent premiums, were released in February 1946 to celebrate the 80th anniversary of the first Egyptian postage stamps. The 1 + 1*m*. stamp reproduced the 5*pa*. stamp of 1866, while the other denominations portrayed Khedive Ismail Pasha, King Fuad and King Farouk. The stamps were also issued in miniature sheets, both perforated and imperforate, in connection with an international philatelic exhibition held in Cairo.

13. 10 millièmes, 1963

The building of the Aswan High Dam in the 1960s created immense problems in the preservation of the Nubian temples. International effort, organized by UNESCO, saved the temples for posterity and publicity was given to the campaign by stamps issued in many countries. From 1959 onwards Egypt issued numerous stamps in connection with the temple preservation programme. This stamp, from the series of 1963, shows the Great Hall of Pillars at Abu Simbel.

14. 10 millièmes, 1956

The Suez Canal was nationalized in July 1956 and a joint Anglo-French expedition invaded Suez in November. World opinion, rather than Egyptian military prowess, halted the invading forces and eventually obliged them to withdraw. Egypt promptly issued this stamp, on 20 December 1956, giving a highly coloured version of the repulse of the invaders at Port Said. The soldier, worker and housewife, clutching rifles and a grenade, contrast

with the pathetic shambles on the beach-head, the tattered parachutes and the sinking ship. Two days later the British and French troops evacuated Port Said and the stamp was immediately reissued with a celebratory overprint. All Egyptian stamps from then onwards were inscribed in English, such was the animosity against anything French as a result of the campaign. When it was pointed out that the British were equally to blame the Egyptian authorities explained that the captions were not really in English – they were in American!

15. 60 millièmes, 1960

Many of the commemorative and definitive stamps in the era since the establishment of the republic in 1953 have had a solid background bled into the perforations, though this tendency was also noticeable in isolated cases from 1947 onward. Egypt and Syria merged in February 1958 to form the United Arab Republic. Although Syria left the union in 1961 Egypt retained the title, and all Egyptian stamps from 1958 onwards have been inscribed UAR. This stamp is one of the series issued in 1959–60 following this political change.

16. 15 millièmes, 1964

A new definitive series was issued between 1964 and 1967, the emphasis being laid on the antiquities of Egypt throughout its long and colourful history. The stamps ranged from 1*m*. (fourteenth century glass vase) to 500*m*. (Tutankhamun). The 15*m*. stamp shows a decorated window from the Ahmed ibn Toulon mosque. That this series was designed to boost the tourist industry is borne out by the inclusion of the Nile Hilton Hotel on the 20*m*. denomination.

17. 15 millièmes, 1934

Stamps inscribed 'Service de l'État' (Service of the State) were adopted by Egypt for official correspondence in 1893. Between 1907 and 1926 contemporary postage stamps were overprinted O.H.H.S. (On His Highness's Service) or O.H.E.M.S. (On His Egyptian Majesty's Service). Distinctive stamps inscribed in French were reintroduced in 1926 and were printed by offset lithography at the Survey Department in Cairo. The colours of certain denominations were changed in 1934–35 and the size of the stamps was increased in 1938. Stamps inscribed entirely in Arabic were used between 1958 and 1967 but since then stamps have been inscribed 'Official' in English.

18. 35 + 15 millièmes, 1956

Egypt has issued relatively few charity stamps. Among the exceptions was a set of three stamps and two miniature sheets (either perforated or imperforate) released in July 1956 to mark the second Arab Scout Jamboree. Each of the three stamps bore the emblems of the boy scouts, sea scouts and air scouts.

19. Egyptian Arab Republic, 30 millièmes, 1971

Between 1958 and 1971 the stamps of Egypt have been inscribed UAR. The federation of Egypt, Libya and Syria proposed in 1971 resulted in a change in the designation of the stamps and the name Egypt has been reintroduced with the abbreviation AR (Arab Republic). This stamp was one of a pair issued in 1971 to mark the proposed federation.

20. French Post Office in Alexandria, 3 centimes, 1902

A French post office was established in Alexandria in the 1860s. Ordinary French stamps were used up to 1899 and may be identified, by the numeral obliterators 3702 (small figures) and 5080 (large figures). Stamps overprinted 'Alexandrie' were put on sale in 1899 and followed in 1902 by the Blanc,

Mouchon and Merson designs of France suitably inscribed. The French post office closed in 1931.

21. French Post Office in Port Said, 4 millièmes, 1921

The French post office was established at Port Said in 1867 and used ordinary French stamps, identifiable by the numeral postmark 5129 (large figures). The French keyplate designs inscribed 'Levant', used throughout the Turkish Empire, were introduced in 1879. Twenty years later French stamps overprinted 'Port-Saïd' were issued and in 1902 the contemporary French designs, with emended inscriptions, were adopted. The series was surcharged in Egyptian currency in 1921 either locally (in lower case lettering) or in Paris (in capital letters). The French post office at Port Said closed in 1931.

22. British Post Office in Suez, 6 pence, 1874

British post offices were established at Alexandria and Suez in 1860 and closed in 1879. During that period ordinary British stamps were used and can only be identified by their numeral obliterators – B01 (Alexandria) or B02 (Suez).

23. Suez Canal Company, 20 centimes, 1868

A set of four stamps, in denominations from 1 to 40 centimes, was issued by the Suez Canal Company in July 1868, for the prepayment of postage on mail carried by its ships along the canal. The stamps featured a steamship and were lithographed by Chezaud, Ain & Tavernier of Paris. The stamps were withdrawn from sale on 31 August 1868, and are thus scarce used, especially on entire envelopes.

24. British Forces Post, 10 millièmes, 1939

The first stamps used by British troops in Egypt were ordinary British stamps of the Queen Victoria series with a postmark inscribed 'British Army Post Office Egypt', during the campaign of 1882 to suppress the rebellion of Arabi Pasha. Subsequently British stamps, with field post cancellations, were employed. The first 3 and 10*m*. stamps appeared in 1936 with portraits of King Fuad. Similar stamps, in a smaller format portraying King Farouk, were issued in 1939. The sale of these stamps came to an end in October 1951 following the abrogation of the Anglo-Egyptian Treaty.

25. British Forces in Egypt, 1 piastre, 1934

A special concession was introduced in 1932, whereby British military personnel and their families were permitted to send mail at reduced rates, using seals sold in NAAFI canteens instead of Egyptian stamps. This concession was discontinued in March 1936 and from then onwards the Egyptian postal authorities issued special stamps inscribed 'Army Post' for the use of the British troops.

PLATE 87

Ethiopia and Sudan

1. Ethiopia, 8 guerches, 1894

Adhesive stamps were introduced by Ethiopia in 1894 and a series typographed at the French Government Printing Works in Paris. E. Mouchon designed and engraved two types, portraying Menelik II (¼ to 2*g*.) and showing the Lion of the Tribe of Judah (4, 8 and 16*g*.) – alluding to the descent of the Ethiopian royal family from Solomon and the Queen of Sheba. The stamps were subsequently overprinted in a diagonal scroll with Amharic lettering for use as postage dues (1896) and then with the word 'Éthiopie' in 1901. Further overprints and surcharges in European or Amharic script appeared between 1902 and 1908.

PLATE 87 ETHIOPIA, SUDAN

2. Ethiopia, 8 guerches, 1917

A series of vertical double-sized stamps appeared in 1909. The designs, by M. V. Marec, were reminiscent of contemporary French colonial stamps, with their penchant for gaudy two-colour typography; they portrayed the Negus Menelik II in various costumes. The series was overprinted in February 1917 to celebrate the coronation of the Empress Zauditu (Judith). The stamps are known with double, inverted or double and inverted overprints.

3. Ethiopia, 2 guerches, 1919

Haile Selassie made his philatelic début in the definitive series typographed by Busag of Berne in 1919. He appeared in the robes of Crown Prince on the 1, 2 and 4g. low values. The stamps, designed by W. Plattner, were notable for the wealth of detail – fauna, flora, weapons and artifacts, all crammed into the decorative framework.

4. Ethiopia, 1 thaler, 1936

A definitive series, recess-printed at the Institut de Gravure in Paris, was released in July 1931. The stamps portrayed the Emperor Haile Selassie I and his wife, the Empress Menen, the Crown Prince Ras Makonnen and the equestrian statue of Menelik I. They ranged in value from $\frac{1}{8}g.$ to 5t. The use of thaler currency is a reminder that, until recently, the Maria Theresa thaler of Austria (dated 1782) was the immutable, eternal unit of currency in Ethiopia and much of the Middle East. In February 1936, at the height of the Italo-Abyssinian War, several values from 1g. to 1t. were overprinted with a red cross and sold at double face value, the premium going to the Red Cross war effort. Stamps of the independent empire of Ethiopia were suppressed by the Italian invaders shortly afterwards.

5. Eritrea, 2 centesimi, 1893

Italian stamps overprinted 'Colonia Eritrea' were introduced in January 1893, following the Italian annexation of this district on the Red Sea coast of Ethiopia. It was the expansion of Italian colonial interests into the heart of Ethiopia which led to the defeat of the Italians at Adowa the following year. Overprinted Italian stamps were used exclusively in this colony until 1910 and this practice continued intermittently up to 1931.

6. Eritrea, 2 centesimi, 1930

A series of stamps designed by Cossio and lithographed at the Government Printing Works in Rome was released in April 1930. The four vertical designs were a native lancer, rifleman, postman and telegraph linesman. The four horizontal designs featured scenery, and aspects of communications such as camel transport and locomotives.

7. Eritrea, 25 centesimi, 1910

Apart from overprinted Italian stamps the only distinctive stamps issued by Eritrea from 1893 to 1930 consisted of four values, from 5 to 25c., issued in 1910–14. They depicted a ploughman and the Government Palace at Massaouah in various frames, and were recess-printed by the Italian Government Printing Works. Originally the set was perforated 14, but in 1928–29 the three lower values were perforated 11.

8. Eritrea, 2 lire + 20 centesimi, 1934

The air flight of King Victor Emmanuel III from Rome to Mogadishu in Somalia in 1934 was celebrated by sets of stamps in the various Italian African colonies. The series from Eritrea consisted of ten stamps designed by G. Rondini, showing the king in military uniform. The top value was also printed in carmine instead of green and overprinted 'Servizio di Stato' for official use.

9. Italian Occupation of Ethiopia, 20 centesimi, 1936

Following the Italian occupation of Ethiopia in 1936 a set of seven stamps portraying Victor Emmanuel III was introduced. They were inscribed with the date of the annexation (9 May, 1936) and included the notation in the Fascist calendar. Ethiopia was subsequently incorporated in Italian East Africa, whose stamps it used from 1938 till 1942, when the issues of the independent empire were resumed.

10. Italian East Africa, 10 centesimi, 1941

Stamps inscribed 'Africa Orientale Italiana' superseded the separate issues of Eritrea, Ethiopia and Italian Somaliland in February 1938. A lengthy definitive series, printed in recess or photogravure, and featuring scenery in the Italian colonial empire, was issued and was followed by various airmail and commemorative sets. The last series issued in the ephemeral empire appeared in June 1941 and marked the solidarity of the Axis partnership. The seven stamps, designed by G. Rondini, portrayed Hitler and Mussolini, with the emblems of Fascism and National Socialism and the slogan 'Two peoples, one war'.

11. Eritrea under British occupation, 65 cents, 1949

British stamps, from $\frac{1}{2}d.$ to 10s., were overprinted 'B.M.A. Eritrea' and surcharged in East African cents and shillings for use in the former Italian colony of Eritrea in 1948–49. As with Tripolitania (see plate 85) a new overprint 'B.A. Eritrea' was adopted in February 1950, after the government had been handed over to the civilian authorities. These stamps were withdrawn in September 1952 after Eritrea had been ceded to Ethiopia. Ordinary Ethiopian stamps have been used there ever since.

12. Ethiopia, 10 centimes, 1942

By the end of 1941 the Italian forces had been driven out of most of Ethiopia and the government of Haile Selassie restored. A decimal currency, based on the thaler or talari of 100 centimes, had been introduced in 1936 shortly before the collapse of the empire. This was now revived and stamps in values of 4, 10 and 20c. were issued in March 1942. Portraying Haile Selassie in ceremonial robes, they were lithographed at the Indian Security Printing Press, Nasik. In the first printings the value in French and Amharic was added typographically at Khartoum. Later printings of the stamps were entirely lithographed at Nasik. The Khartoum values were expressed in upper and lower case lettering, whereas the later Nasik values were in capital lettering.

13. Ethiopia, 2 cents, 1947

The first postwar definitive series issued by Ethiopia was recess-printed by Bradbury Wilkinson and issued between 1947 and 1955. The stamps bore a portrait of the Emperor Haile Selassie inset and depicted scenery and landmarks of the country.

14. Ethiopia, 1 thaler, 1965

Most European security printers have produced stamps for Ethiopia since World War II, including Aspioti-Elka of Athens and the State Printing Works in Prague. Courvoisier of Switzerland printed the definitive series of 1965 in multicolour photogravure featuring scenery, occupations and wildlife of the country. Each of the seven ordinary and eight airmail stamps incorporated a portrait of Haile Selassie. A curious error was perpetrated on the 15c. stamp. Although depicting sisal cultivation it is captioned 'sugar canes'.

15. Ethiopia, 30 centimes, 1965

A set of three stamps was issued in November 1965 in honour of the Ethiopian National and Commercial Banks. Featuring bank emblems and

buildings, they were designed by staff artists of the Bureau d'Études Henri Chomette in Paris, and were printed in three-colour photogravure by De La Rue. The majority of modern commemorative sets consist of three values, while thematic sets appear at frequent intervals.

16. Sudan, 1 millième, 1897

Adhesive stamps were adopted after the reconquest of the Sudan by Anglo-Egyptian forces in 1897. The contemporary series of Egypt was overprinted in Arabic and French. There are six distinct varieties of each overprint and specialists prefer to collect these stamps in strips of six to display these differences.

17. Sudan, 3 piastres, 1927

De La Rue printed all the stamps of the Sudan from 1898 till the country gained independence in 1956. The first distinctive series was designed by Colonel E. A. Stanton, later to become a notable philatelist. His native bearer posed as the camel postman for this design, and Stanton added the names of Khartoum and Berber (then in enemy hands) to the saddle-bags. De La Rue faithfully reproduced these names on the stamps and they continued to appear on all the variations of this design up to 1954, though they had long ceased to have any topical significance. The camel postman formed the subject of the definitive sets of 1898, 1921–22, 1927–40 and 1948, and was used on several commemorative stamps, including a 2p. of October 1948 honouring the golden jubilee of the design.

18. Sudan, 5 piastres, 1931

Following the establishment of a regular air service in 1931 a set of twelve air stamps was recess-printed and introduced on 22 August. The uniform design features the statue of General Gordon at Khartoum. The perforations of several denominations were altered in 1937, from 14 all round to $11\frac{1}{2}$ by $12\frac{1}{2}$.

19. Sudan, 20 piastres, 1941

The camel postman went into temporary retirement during World War II. Between March and August 1941 a series, from 1m. to 20p., was lithographed at the Security Printing Press, Nasik, picturing palms on Tuti Island on the Nile near Khartoum. The 'Palms' series was designed by Miss H. M. Hebbert. Inexplicably this series never captured the popularity of its predecessor and the camel postman reappeared on the postwar definitive series.

20. Sudan, 3 piastres, 1954

Significantly the camel postman was used for the set of three stamps issued in January 1954 to mark the attainment of self-government. Similar stamps, but dated 1953, were prepared but never issued for postal purposes, though a few were inadvertently released at the Sudan Agency in London. The ubiquitous postman was also incorporated in the design of two stamps issued in December 1948 to mark the opening of the Sudanese legislative assembly. Stanton's camel postman was used for the 50p. and £1 stamps of 1951 and 1962 respectively, the latter being still current at the time of writing (1972).

21. Sudan, 5 piastres, 1956

The attainment of independence was celebrated on 15 September 1956 by a set of three stamps, recess-printed by De La Rue. The uniform design consisted of a map of the country with wings symbolizing its independent status. Since independence the Sudan has maintained its conservative policy on stamp issues, with a single definitive set (1962) and relatively few commemorative sets.

22. Sudan, 55 millièmes, 1963

To mark the United Nations Freedom from

243

PLATE 87 ETHIOPIA, SUDAN · PLATE 88 SOMALILAND

Hunger campaign, the Sudan issued two stamps in March 1963. The design, by S. Baghdadi, showed the campaign emblem and a hand holding millet cobs. The vast majority of Sudanese stamps since 1962 have been designed by Baghdadi and printed in lithography or photogravure by De La Rue or the Survey Department in Cairo.

23. Sudan, 15 millièmes, 1964
A set of three stamps designed by S. Baghdadi was issued in April 1964 in honour of the New York World's Fair. The 3p. stamp had the Sudanese pavilion at the fair but the other two designs were irrelevant to the event, depicting the Khashm el Girba dam (15m.) and a map of the country (55m.). Since independence Sudan has issued relatively few stamps, mostly commemorating events and personalities of Sudanese interest rather than international events. In recent years most of them have been lithographed or printed in photogravure by the Postal Authority Press in Cairo.

PLATE 88
Somaliland

The northeast corner of Africa, occupied by the Somali people, was formerly governed by three colonial powers – Britain, Italy and France. The British and Italian territories now constitute the independent republic of Somalia, but colonial rule is still in force in the French Somali Coast, renamed the French Territory of the Afars and Issas since 1967. Much of the East African campaign was fought over this area in World War II and left its mark on the philately of that region.

1. Obock, 1 centime, 1892
The first distinctive stamps to appear in any part of Somaliland were issued in the French seaport of Obock in 1892. At first the French colonial general series was overprinted 'Obock' but later that year the 'Tablet' keytype series was released with a suitable inscription.

2. Obock, 1 centime, 1894
The stamps used in Obock between 1894 and 1902 are among the most unusual ever produced. They were issued imperforate, although an imitation perforation was printed as a border round the frame. The stamps were typographed on paper with a faint quadrille pattern. Arabic and Amharic lettering completed the outlandish appearance of these stamps. From 1c. to 1f. they were rectangular and depicted Somali warriors, while the higher values were triangular and featured camels. The stamps of Obock were superseded by those of French Somali Coast in 1902.

3. Djibouti, 5 centimes, 1894
'Tablet' stamps of Obock overprinted DJ or 'Djibouti' were adopted in this seaport in 1893, pending the release of a distinctive pictorial series. They were in the same curious style as those of Obock, with the addition of a diamond-shaped design showing a camel train crossing the desert (25 and 50f.). The low values depicted a view of Djibouti, the triangular middle denominations a French gunboat. The rectangular design was modified in 1938 and used for 5, 10 and 20f. stamps of French Somali Coast. The stamps of Djibouti were superseded by the general series of French Somali Coast in 1902.

4. French Somali Coast, 2 centimes, 1909
Stamps inscribed 'Côte Française des Somalis' were adopted in July 1902, recess-printed by Chasse-

pot of Paris from designs by Paul Merwart. Seven years later similar vignettes in larger designs were typographed by the French Government Printing Works. The low values showed the mosque at Tajurah, the middle values mounted Somalis and the franc denominations Somali warriors.

5. French Somali Coast, 1 centime, 1915
Three designs by A. Montader were used for the series introduced in July 1915. Vertical designs showed a drummer and a Somali woman, while the franc denominations, in a horizontal design, had the railway bridge at Holl-Holli. The stamps were engraved by C. Hourriez and typographed in two-colour combinations. New colours and values appeared between 1922 and 1933 and provisional surcharges between 1922 and 1927.

6. French Somali Coast, 5 centimes, 1943
After the Italians were defeated in East Africa, French Somali Coast withdrew its allegiance to the Vichy regime and threw in its lot with the Free French. The 1938–40 definitive series was over-printed 'France Libre' in 1943 pending the supply of a distinctive series designed by Edmund Dulac and printed in photogravure by Harrison and Sons. The stamps featured a native hut and a dhow, symbolizing the interior and coastal districts of the territory, while the locomotive represented the Djibouti railway linking Addis Ababa in Ethiopia with the sea. It is interesting that the name of the capital received greater prominence on these stamps than that of the country itself.

7. French Somali Coast, 10 centimes, 1947
The postwar definitive series was designed by Magnan (ordinary postage) and Planson (airmails) and both were printed in two-colour photogravure by Vaugirard. The nine designs were of native types, landmarks and scenery.

8. French Somali Coast, 3 centimes, 1938
In common with the majority of other French colonies the French Somali Coast adopted recess-printed stamps in the late 1930s. J. Kerhor designed stamps showing the mosque at Djibouti for a series introduced in December 1938. A curious feature of this series was the reintroduction of the large pictorial design used by Djibouti in the 1890s, for the three higher denominations. The stamps were recess-printed by the Institut de Gravure in Paris.

9. French Somali Coast, 40 centimes, 1958
The standard of design and production in the stamps of this territory began to improve in the middle fifties when recess-printing was re-introduced and increasing use was made of colour combinations. Apart from the various French colonial omnibus issues French Somali Coast produced few distinctive commemoratives but these were fairly evenly balanced between local events (the centenary of Obock, 1962) and international ones (such as the Tokyo Olympic Games, 1964). A recess-printed definitive series was released between 1958 and 1962 with animals, birds and fishes as its theme. Subsequent thematic issues depicted fauna, flora, fishing boats and marine life.

10. French Territory of Afars and Issas, 10 francs, 1967
Agitation by neighbouring Somalia for the incorporation of the French colony into the independent republic gathered momentum in the 1960s and led to the referendum of 1966. The population voted to remain under French rule and the name of the territory was consequently changed to minimize the Somali connection. The Afars and Issas are the principal tribes of this area. Animals and birds were featured on the definitive series introduced in August–September 1967. Subsequently sets show-

ing sports, outposts and public buildings in Obock and Djibouti have been released.

11. French Territory of the Afars and Issas, 85 francs, 1968
A new definitive series was introduced in 1968 with the theme of buildings and monuments of the territory. The stamps ranged from 1f. (the broadcasting station) to 200f. (Sayed Hassan Mosque) and were recess-printed in multicolour by the French Government Printing Works in Paris.

12. Benadir, 10 centesimi, 1907
Distinctive stamps were adopted in Italian Somaliland in October 1903. The first series was inscribed 'Benadir', the Arab word for a seaport. The 1 and 2 besa denominations showed an elephant, the anna values a lion. The stamps were surcharged in Italian currency at various times from 1905 to 1916 and then in local currency (100 besa = 1 rupia) in 1922–23. Italian and Benadir stamps overprinted 'Somalia Italiana' were gradually adopted from 1916 onward.

13. Jubaland, 2 lire, 1926
In 1925 Britain ceded to Italy a tract of territory west of the Juba river, formerly part of Kenya. Italian stamps overprinted 'Oltre Giuba' (beyond the Juba) were issued in June 1925, pending the release of a distinctive series in April 1926. These, from 5c. to 2l., carried a map of the district. The Commissariat-General of Jubaland was incorporated in Italian Somaliland in 1926 and subsequently used the stamps of that colony.

14. Italian Somaliland, 25 + 2 lire, 1934
Before 1930 Italian Somaliland used Italian stamps overprinted or inscribed 'Somalia Italiana'. The first distinctive issue was a commemorative series of 1930 marking the 25th anniversary of the Italian Colonial Agricultural Institute and two years later a pictorial definitive series was released. The visit of King Victor Emmanuel III to the capital, Mogadishu, in 1934 was celebrated by a lengthy series of ordinary and airmail stamps bearing different portraits of the king. The 25l. stamp in carmine instead of green and overprinted 'Servizio di Stato' was provided for official correspondence. The stamps of Italian Somaliland were superseded by the general series of Italian East Africa (see plate 87) in 1936.

15. British Somaliland, ½ anna, 1903
Stamps in denominations from ½ to 8a. of the King Edward VII series of India were overprinted 'British Somaliland' and released in 1903. At the same time the obsolescent stamps portraying Queen Victoria were similarly overprinted. Many of these stamps are known with the second 'i' in 'British' omitted. They were superseded by distinctive series the following year.

16. British Somaliland, 12 annas, 1904
Indian stamps were used in British Somaliland before 1903, but in that year the contemporary Indian series portraying Queen Victoria or King Edward VII was overprinted 'British Somaliland'. The following year a series typographed by De La Rue was released in denominations from ½a. to 5r.

17. British Somaliland, 3 rupees, 1919
Similar stamps, but portraying King George V, were released in December 1912. In 1919 the 2a. was issued in new colours and 2, 3 and 5a. denominations added to the series. The watermark of this series was changed from Crown CA to Script CA in 1921.

18. British Somaliland, 3 rupees, 1938
H. W. Claxton produced three designs for the

PLATE 88 SOMALILAND

George VI definitive series recess-printed by Waterlow and Sons in 1938. The anna values depicted Berbera sheep or a Greater Kudu antelope, while a map of the protectorate appeared on the rupee values. British Somaliland was invaded by Italian troops in August 1940 but the country was liberated the following year. The stamps were reissued with a full-face portrait, instead of a three-quarter profile, since the original series had been looted by Italian troops. The new version was introduced in April 1942.

19. British Somaliland, 20 cents, 1957
The East African shilling of 100 cents was adopted in 1951 and the 1942 definitives surcharged in new values. The Elizabethan series was recess-printed by Bradbury Wilkinson and issued in September 1953, seven designs being used for the twelve values, from 5c. to 10s. The 20c. and 1s. stamps were overprinted in May 1957 to mark the opening of the Legislative Council. The 20c. and 1.30s. values were overprinted in April 1960 to mark the Legislative Council Unofficial (i.e. elected) Majority, which paved the way for the withdrawal of British colonial rule and the unification of British and Italian Somaliland to form the republic of Somalia.

20. East African Forces, 5 pence, 1943
British stamps overprinted E.A.F. were issued in January 1943 for the use of East African Forces occupying Italian Somaliland. They were in denominations from 1d. to 1s., but a 2s.6d. value was added in 1946. They were superseded by the stamps of the British Military Administration.

21. British Administration of Somalia, 25 cents, 1948
British stamps, from ½d. to 5s., were overprinted 'B.M.A. Somalia' and surcharged in East African cents and shillings for use in Italian Somaliland in May 1948. Similar stamps overprinted 'B.A.' were adopted in January 1950 after the administration was handed over to the civil authorities. Somalia reverted to Italian administration in April 1950, as a United Nations Trust Territory.

22. Somalia, 10 cents, 1955
Somalia, formerly Italian Somaliland, was under Italian administration from April 1950 till June 1960. During that decade stamps designed and produced in Italy were issued, though a few were printed by Courvoisier in Switzerland. The definitive series of 1950 repeated designs previously used in 1932–36, with the words 'Poste Italiane' omitted. A floral definitive series in multicolour photogravure was released between February 1955 and June 1959. The corresponding airmail series featured antelopes and gazelles.

23. Somalia, 2 centesimi, 1950
Somalia used contemporary postage due stamps of Italy with a suitable overprint from 1906 until World War II. Following the return of the territory to Italian control in 1950 a series from 1 centesimo to 1 somalo was designed by E. Pizzi and printed in photogravure at the Italian Government Printing Works in Rome.

24. Somalia, 50 centesimi, 1960
In June 1960 Somalia gained independence and at the same time the former British Protectorate joined the independent republic. Three stamps of the former Italian Somaliland were overprinted 'Somaliland Independence 26 June 1960'. These stamps overprinted in English were only issued in the former British Protectorate.

25. Somalia, 1 somalo, 1963
Since independence Somalian stamps have continued in the tradition laid down during the period of the Italian mandate. The majority of stamps up to 1966 were produced in photogravure at the Italian Government Printing Works in Rome, but since then a number of issues have been lithographed by De La Rue or Poligrafica Ercolano of Naples. The union of the British and Italian territories, however, is reflected in the use of English and Italian as well as Arabic in the inscriptions and the dual system of shillings and somalos in the expression of values. This stamp was one of a pair issued in June 1963 to mark the Freedom from Hunger campaign. Both were designed by C. Mancioli, who produced the majority of designs for Somalia between 1958 and 1968.

AMERICA

PLATE 89

Canada

1. 12½ cents, 1859

Canada adopted adhesive postage stamps in April 1851, following the separation of the Canadian postal administration from the General Post Office in London. The stamps were recess-printed by the New York firm of Rawdon, Wright, Hatch and Edson (later the American Bank Note Co.). Sir Sandford Fleming designed the 3d. stamp, featuring the beaver, Canada's national emblem. Prince Albert the Prince Consort appeared on the 6d. and the Chalon portrait of Queen Victoria graced the top value. The inscription 'Twelve pence' was used rather than 'one shilling' since that coin had a different value in various parts of British North America. The celebrated 'Twelve pence Black' is now Canada's rarest stamp.

2. 15 cents, 1868

On 1 July 1867 Canada (Ontario and Quebec) joined with Nova Scotia and New Brunswick to form the Confederation of Canada. The other British colonies in North America joined the Confederation at various times between 1871 and 1948 and continued to issue their own stamps (see plate 90). The British American Bank Note Co. of Ottawa and Montreal recess-printed a series portraying Queen Victoria. These stamps are known to collectors as the 'Large Cents' on account of their size. The shades and quality of paper varied considerably in this series. Decimal currency was adopted by Canada in July 1859 and the designs of the previous series were redrawn with values in cents instead of pence. The fluctuation in the value of Canada's pence was reflected in the stamp of 1857 intended for packet postage to Britain. It was inscribed with two values – 6 pence in sterling and 7½ pence in local currency. The sterling equivalent continued to appear on the modified design in 1859 but the local currency was changed to 12½ cents. These stamps were superseded by the 'Large Cents' in 1868.

3. 3 cents, 1870

Between 1870 and 1888 the British American Bank Note Co. recess-printed a new definitive series from 1 to 10c., in a smaller format than before, hence its nickname 'Small Cents'. On account of its long life this series was subject to an even greater variety of shades, paper and perforation than its predecessor.

4. 50 cents, 1897

L. Pereira and F. Brownell designed the series issued in June 1897 to celebrate the Diamond Jubilee of Queen Victoria. The high face value of the sixteen denominations, ranging from ½c. to $5, provoked an enormous outcry from philatelists at the time, since when Canada has never issued a stamp with a face value of more than a dollar. The design featured the Chalon and Von Angeli portraits of the Queen, representing the 60 years of her reign. The 1c. stamp has been recorded bisected on cover and used as a ½c. stamp.

5. 10 cents, 1898

Canada introduced a special delivery service in the leading cities in 1898. On the payment of a 10c. fee, letters could be expedited from the post office to the addressee outside normal postal deliveries. This stamp was recess-printed by the American Bank Note Co. and remained current till 1922, when the fee was doubled. During that long period, the colour of the stamps varied from blue-green to yellow-green. Subsequent stamps, inscribed SPECIAL DELIVERY – EXPRÈS, were issued up to 1947 but since then ordinary stamps have been used.

6. 2 cents, 1898

To celebrate the introduction of Imperial Penny Postage (2 cents rate) Canada issued this stamp on 7 December 1898. It was designed by the postmaster general Sir William Mulock and shows the British Empire shaded red – somewhat prematurely since all of southern Africa is in red, though the Boer republics of the Transvaal and Orange Free State were still independent at that time. The quotation at the foot of the design is taken from A Song of Empire composed by Sir Lewis Morris in honour of Queen Victoria's Golden Jubilee in 1887. The new imperial letter rate came into effect on Christmas Day, hence the inscription. This has often been regarded as the world's first Christmas stamp, though it was not until 1964 that Canada adopted special issues for Christmas greetings.

7. 10 cents, 1908

The tercentenary of Quebec was celebrated in July 1908 by a set of eight stamps, from ½ to 20c., designed by Machado and recess-printed by the American Bank Note Co. Four stamps bore double portraits – Cartier and Champlain, Montcalm and Wolfe, the King and Queen and the Prince and Princess of Wales. The remaining values depicted incidents in the early history of Quebec. Most denominations may be found on either white or toned paper and all eight values are recorded imperforate.

8. 20 cents, 1912

A profile of King George V in admiral's full-dress uniform was engraved by Robert Savage for the definitive series of 1912–18, popularly known to collectors as the 'Admirals'. The series ranged from 1 to 50c., but among the new colours and values introduced between 1922 and 1931 was a $1 stamp. The stamps may be found in several different gauges of perforation, sometimes partially imperforate, from coils used in slot machines. The design was modified in 1915–16 for the War Tax stamps of that period.

9. 12 cents, 1927

The Diamond Jubilee of the Confederation was celebrated in June 1927 by a set of eight stamps. Three small stamps portrayed Sir John Macdonald, Sir Wilfrid Laurier and Darcy McGee, the architects of the Confederation. Two double-sized stamps portrayed two men on each – Laurier and Macdonald (12c.) and Robert Baldwin and L. H. Fontaine (20c.). The 2c. reproduced the painting entitled The Fathers of Confederation, by Robert Harris, painted at the time of the Quebec Conference in 1864. This design had been used for a 3c. stamp issued in 1917 to mark the 50th anniversary. The 3c. depicted the Parliament buildings in Ottawa and another 12c. stamp showed a map of Canada, indicating the growth of the Confederation between 1867 and 1927.

10. 13 cents, 1935

To mark the Silver Jubilee of King George V, Canada issued a set of six stamps in May 1935, undoubtedly the most interesting and novel of all the many issues produced for that event. King George V and Queen Mary were portrayed on the 3c. value, while three small-format stamps portrayed Princess Elizabeth (1c.), her father the Duke of York (later King George VI) and the Prince of Wales (later King Edward VIII and Duke of Windsor) on the 2c. and 5c. stamps respectively. A fine view of Windsor Castle, from the Eton bank of the Thames, and the Royal Yacht Britannia were featured on the 10c. and 13c. stamps.

11. 1 dollar, 1938

Canadian definitive sets from 1938 onwards have used small-format stamps for the lower denomina-

PLATE 89 CANADA · PLATE 90 CANADIAN PROVINCES

tions (portraits of the monarch), and double-sized stamps for the higher values (scenery and occupations). Sets of this type appeared in 1928–29, 1930–31, 1935 and 1937–38. In the last of these a portrait of King George VI in civilian clothes was used for the stamps from 1 to 8c., while landmarks and scenery appeared on the higher values. The Château de Ramezay in Montreal was on this dollar stamp. This blend of royal portraiture and scenic stamps has continued to the present day.

12. 8 cents, 1946
The return to peace was marked by a new definitive series issued in September 1946 on which peacetime occupations and postwar Canadian development projects appeared, in contrast with the martial flavour of the series of 1942–43 which publicized Canadian contributions to the war effort. Low value stamps, portraying King George VI in civilian clothes, were not released till 1949.

13. 5 cents, 1954
Following the precedent of the 1927 Confederation commemoratives, Canada instituted a regular series of stamps in 1951 portraying past prime ministers. The inaugural pair showed Sir Robert Borden and William Lyon Mackenzie King, the prime ministers during the two World Wars. Three subsequent pairs of stamps with this theme appeared between 1952 and 1955. This stamp, from the series of November 1954, portrays Sir Mackenzie Bowell, prime minister 1894–96.

14. 10 cents, 1942
Like South Africa (see plate 67) Canada issued a definitive series aimed at furthering the war effort. The low values portrayed King George VI in naval, military and air force uniforms, the higher values various aspects of the war, with vignettes of tanks, corvettes, artillery, an air training camp and a a destroyer. The home front was not neglected, the 4 and 8c. stamps showing a grain elevator and a farm scene respectively. The 10c. depicted the Parliament buildings in Ottawa with the Union Jack and Maple Leaf emblem of Canada symbolizing the solidarity of the British Commonwealth.

15. 1 dollar, 1953
The pictorial high values used in the early years of Queen Elizabeth's reign were issued piecemeal and not as a single set. The dollar denomination, featuring a Pacific Coast Indian house and totem pole, was issued in February 1953. It was the work of Emmanuel Hahn, who has designed numerous Canadian stamps in recent years.

16. 5 cents, 1959
Canada has been most punctilious in recording royal visits by means of stamps. The first series, a set of three, appeared in 1939 to mark the prewar tour of Canada and the United States by King George VI and Queen Elizabeth. A 4c. stamp appearing in 1951 portrayed the then Duke and Duchess of Edinburgh on the first of their postwar visits. Subsequently stamps appeared in 1957, 1959, 1964 and 1967 to mark Queen Elizabeth's visits to Canada. This stamp marked the visit of June 1959, when the Queen inaugurated the St Lawrence Seaway. It was the first stamp to reproduce the Annigoni portrait full-length.

17. 6 cents, 1969
The eightieth anniversary of the birth of Vincent Massey, the first Canadian-born Governor General, was belatedly commemorated by this stamp, issued in February 1969. Massey, the elder brother of the film actor Raymond Massey, was born in 1887 and served as Governor-General from 1952 till 1959. The stamp was designed by Professor Imre von Mosdossy and printed in combined lithography

and recess by the Canadian Bank Note Co. Canada has used recess-printing for the vast majority of her stamps up to the present time, but in recent years has combined it with offset lithography to achieve multicolour effects.

18. United Nations Post Office in Montreal, 5 cents, 1967
A set of five stamps was produced for use at the UN Pavilion at the Montreal World Fair in 1967. They were inscribed in Canadian currency and were valid for postage only from the Fair although they were also on sale to collectors at the UN Headquarters in New York, its Geneva office and at UN sales agencies throughout the world. Four of them were designed by Ole Hamann and reproduced door panel bas reliefs by E. Cormier in the UN General Assembly building. A fifth (8 cents) showed the façade of the UN Pavilion at the Fair. The bas relief stamps were produced by the British American Bank Note Company with lithographed frames and recess-printed vignettes.

19. 20 cents, 1956
Before 1949 Canadian stamps used on correspondence by government departments were perforated with the initials OHMS (On His Majesty's Service). Between 1949 and 1950 contemporary definitive stamps were issued with O.H.M.S. overprinted. From 1950 till 1963 various definitive stamps were overprinted with a letter 'G' (Government). The use of such stamps was discontinued at the end of December 1963.

20. 5 cents, 1959
The opening of the St Lawrence Seaway was celebrated in June 1959 by a 5c. stamp with the maple leaf of Canada and the American eagle superimposed on a map of the seaway. A similar stamp was issued simultaneously in the United States. A. L. Pollock and G. Trottier of Canada and W. H. Buckley, A. J. Copeland and E. Metzel of the United States collaborated in the design. The Canadian version has been recorded with the centre inverted.

21. 6 cents, 1968
A definitive series appeared in Centennial Year (1967), the five lower denominations bearing a portrait of the Queen by Anthony Buckley, with scenery in the background. The higher denominations, from 8c. to $1, reproduced scenic paintings by various Canadian artists. An increase in the inland letter rate from 5 to 6c. in 1968 led to the introduction of a new design symbolizing the different methods of transport. The stamp changed from red to black in 1970 and was subsequently re-engraved to strengthen the detail of the background design. These stamps may be found with different perforations (from coils or sheets) and with phosphor bands used in electronic sorting experiments in the Winnipeg area.

22. 6 cents, 1970
The centenaries of Manitoba and the Northwest Territories were marked by two 6c. stamps issued on 27 January 1970. Both adopted designs which were highly criticized at the time. The Manitoba stamp, designed by K. C. Lochhead, had symbolic crossroads, but the stark simplicity of this design was not appreciated by the general public. The Kenojouak Indian drawing of the Enchanted Owl was adapted for a stamp by N. E. Hallendy and Miss S. van Raalte. Both stamps were printed by the Canadian Bank Note Co., the Manitoba stamp being lithographed, the Northwest Territories issue recess-printed.

23. 5 cents, 1968
Professor von Mosdossy designed this stamp,

printed in multicolour lithography and issued in October 1968 to mark the 50th anniversary of the death of John McCrae the soldier and poet. It reproduces the opening lines of McCrae's immortal poem *In Flanders Fields*, and shows the poppies growing among the crosses of a war cemetery. Lieutenant-Colonel John McCrae was killed in action shortly before the Armistice.

24. 15 cents, 1969
The 50th anniversary of the first non-stop Trans-Atlantic flight was celebrated on 13 June 1969, by a 15c. stamp designed by Robert Bradford. It showed the Vickers Vimy bomber crewed by Sir John Alcock and Sir Arthur Whitten-Brown above a map of the Atlantic. A stamp honouring this event was also issued by Great Britain.

25. 15 cents, 1970
The Christmas stamps issued by Canada since 1964 have never resorted to the Old Masters expedient adopted by most other countries, though G. Holloway's adaptation of Dürer's *Praying Hands* (1966) came close to it. Instead the stamps have drawn on Canadian themes for inspiration, reproducing Eskimo art (1968) and symbolic compositions of typical Canadian Christmas scenes. In 1970 an ambitious series of twelve stamps was produced – five 5c, five 6c, one 10c and one 15c. The stamps were adapted from prize-winning paintings by schoolchildren. The 15c stamp reproduces T. Dojcak's version of *Trees and Sledge*. The stamps were lithographed in multicolour by the Canadian Bank Note Co.

PLATE 90
Canadian Provinces

1. British Columbia and Vancouver's Island, 2½ pence, 1860
Note the curious spelling of 'Vancouver's Island'. Adhesive stamps were introduced in Canada's far western provinces in 1860, a solitary 2½d. denomination being sufficient. The stamps were typographed by De La Rue and were issued either imperforate or perforated 14. From 20 June 1864 to 1 November 1865, this stamp was sold for 3d. after an increase in the letter rate. Separate stamps for Vancouver Island and British Columbia were issued in 1865.

2. Vancouver Island, 10 cents, 1865
Decimal currency was adopted by the island in 1865 but not by the mainland territory of British Columbia, so separate issues of stamps became necessary. De La Rue typographed 5 and 10c. stamps for the island, using a profile of Queen Victoria as the motif. They were issued either imperforate or perforated 14. On 19 November 1866, the two territories were united to form British Columbia and stamps thus inscribed were used in both areas from then onward.

3. British Columbia, 3 pence, 1865
De La Rue typographed a 3d. stamp issued in British Columbia in November 1865, with the crowned monogram and heraldic flowers of the United Kingdom. After the adoption of decimal currency the stamp was reprinted in various colours and surcharged with values from 2c. to $1. The stamps of this province were withdrawn on 20 July 1871, when it joined the Confederation of Canada.

4. Prince Edward Island, 9 pence, 1862
Adhesive stamps were introduced in Prince Edward Island in January 1861. The series consisted of 2d., 3d. and 6d. stamps but 1d. and 9d. values were

PLATE 90 CANADIAN PROVINCES

added the following year. Bearing a profile of Queen Victoria, the stamps were typographed by Charles Whiting of Beaufort House, London, from electrotyped stereos. A curious feature was their inscription in two currencies, reflecting the fluctuating value of money in different parts of British North America at that time. The legend at the foot is self-explanatory – 'Nine Pence Currency equal to Six Pence Stg' (sterling). The stamps were printed on yellowish toned paper (1861–68) or coarse-wove bluish white paper (1867–68) in several different gauges of perforation.

5. Prince Edward Island, 3 pence, 1870
The Chalon portrait of Queen Victoria was used for a 3d. stamp recess-printed by the British-American Bank Note Co. of Montreal and Ottawa and issued in June 1870. The dual system of currency indicates the value of the stamp as 3d. sterling or 4½d. in local currency.

6. Prince Edward Island, 2 cents, 1872
Decimal currency was adopted by the island in January 1872 and a new series, from 1 to 12c., was typographed by Charles Whiting in designs somewhat similar to the 1861 series. The stamps were withdrawn in July 1873 when Prince Edward Island joined the Canadian Confederation.

7. Nova Scotia, 3 pence, 1851
Adhesive stamps were introduced in Nova Scotia in September 1851 in denominations of 3d., 6d. and 1s. They were recess-printed by Perkins Bacon in a diamond-format featuring the heraldic flowers of the United Kingdom and the mayflower of Nova Scotia, with the imperial crown in the centre. They were often bisected or quartered to make up fractional amounts of postage. Examples of these bisects on cover are highly prized. A 1d. stamp, in a square format portraying Queen Victoria, was added to the series in 1853.

8. Nova Scotia, 1 cent, 1860
Decimal currency was adopted in 1860 and the contract to print the decimal stamps went to the American Bank Note Company, New York, whose stamps were recess-printed in various denominations from 1 to 12½c. A profile of the queen was used for the 1, 2 and 5c. denominations.

9. Nova Scotia, 8½ cents, 1860
Full-face portraits of Queen Victoria were used for the 8½, 10 and 12½c. denominations. The rather odd values resulted from the conversion of existing rates in local pence currency to the new Canadian decimal system. The stamps were printed on yellowish or white paper and remained in use till 1867, when Nova Scotia became a founder member of the Canadian Confederation.

10. New Brunswick, 1 cent, 1860
The first stamps of New Brunswick were recess-printed by Perkins Bacon in designs similar to those of Nova Scotia. Following the introduction of decimal currency in 1860 a series of stamps was produced by the American Bank Note Co. in denominations from 1 to 17c. The original 5c. value bore the portrait of the Postmaster General, Charles Connell, whose vanity led to his enforced resignation. A stamp bearing the Chalon portrait of Queen Victoria was substituted shortly afterward.

11. New Brunswick, 17 cents, 1860
The series of 1860 was one of the earliest attempts at pictorialism, with vignettes of a wood-burning locomotive (1c.) and a trans-Atlantic steamer (12½c.). The Prince of Wales (later King Edward VII) was portrayed in Highland costume on the 17c. stamp, thereby setting a precedent for the royal portraiture favoured later by Newfoundland.

12. Newfoundland, 6 pence, 1857
Perkins Bacon recess-printed a series of stamps for Newfoundland when that colony adopted stamps in January 1857. They consisted of six denominations from 1d. to 1s., and came in different shapes and sizes. A square format was used for the 1d. and a triangular design for the 3d.; the remaining values were upright rectangles. The stamps were printed between 1857 and 1861 on different kinds of paper and in various shades from brown-purple to orange-vermilion.

13. Newfoundland, 2 cents, 1866
Decimal currency was introduced into Newfoundland in 1866 and a new series in values from 2 to 24c. was produced accordingly. The stamps were recess-printed by the American Bank Note Co. of New York, whose imprint may sometimes be found in the margin of stamps from the edge of the sheet. A codfish (2c.), seal on an ice-floe (5c.) and a fishing schooner (13c.) alluded to Newfoundland's sealing and codfish industry. Queen Victoria was portrayed on the 12 and 24c. stamps, her late husband the Prince Consort (d. 1861) on the 10c.

14. Newfoundland, 1 cent, 1871
A 1c. stamp was added to the series in 1868, with the same portrait of the Prince of Wales as had appeared on the 17c. of New Brunswick eight years earlier. Two versions exist of this stamp. In the first printing the white oval at the top of the portrait was cut by the ribbon bearing the value. In a re-engraved version, issued in 1871, the oval was not cut by the ribbon.

15. Newfoundland, 6 cents, 1870
The first 3c. denomination, also recess-printed by the American Bank Note Co., was issued in 1870. Not only was Newfoundland always ready to portray members of the royal family other than the reigning monarch, it was also up-to-date with the queen's portrait. Whereas Britain and many British colonies clung to the same youthful profile of the Queen until her death, Newfoundland showed her as she was at various stages of her long life.

16. Newfoundland, ½ cent, 1894
The British-American Bank Note Co. of Montreal recess-printed a new pictorial series for Newfoundland in 1887 and introduced a ½c. denomination, produced in a small square format and depicting a Newfoundland dog. The stamp was reissued seven years later in black instead of the original red, but the colour was changed to orange-vermilion in 1896.

17. Newfoundland, 1 cent, 1897
Newfoundland's first commemorative series appeared in June 1897 and set the pattern for many of the issues in the early twentieth century. Ostensibly the series, from 1 to 60c., commemorated the quatercentenary of the discovery of the island, but the 1c. stamp, portraying Queen Victoria, also bore a reference to her Diamond Jubilee. Nine of the fourteen stamps showed the scenery and industry of Newfoundland – relevant neither to the quatercentenary nor the jubilee, but designed, like many later sets, to publicize the island and its potential.

18. Newfoundland, 6 cents, 1910
A set of eleven stamps, from 1 to 15c., was issued in August 1910 to mark the tercentenary of the settlement founded by the London and Bristol Company. The stamps were lithographed by Whitehead, Morris & Co. and combined portraits of King James I, John Guy and Sir Francis Bacon with the familiar mixture of scenery and industrial subjects. King Edward VII was portrayed on the 12c. stamp and King George V on the 15c. – the earliest

stamp from any part of the British Commonwealth to portray the new king. The 6c. stamp perpetrated what was strictly an inaccuracy, referring to Sir Francis Bacon as 'Lord Bacon'. When he was ennobled he became Lord Verulam. In the first version of the stamp the 'z' of 'Colonization' was printed back to front, but this was later corrected. The stamps from 6 to 15c. were reissued the following year, recess-printed by A. Alexander & Sons.

19. Newfoundland, 15 cents, 1933
An airmail series was issued in denominations from 15c. to $1 in 1931. The 15c. showed a modern biplane and a dog-team – the old and new methods of mail transportation. It was overprinted in February 1933 'L. & S. Post.' to denote that it could be used for Land and Sea Post as well as airmail. The series was recess-printed by Perkins Bacon, but overprinted by Messrs D. R. Thistle of St Johns. Various errors and varieties have been noted in the overprint.

20. Newfoundland, 3 cents, 1911
Newfoundland was the only Commonwealth country to issue stamps to mark the coronation of 1911, though Britain's ½ and 1d. 'Mackennals', released on Coronation Day, are often regarded as quasi-commemorative. The Newfoundland series pulled out all the stops, going through the entire royal family for portrait subjects. The king and queen appeared on the 2 and 1c. stamps, their children, from the Prince of Wales (Edward VIII) on the 3c. to Prince John on the 9c., the dowager Queen Alexandra on the 10c. and the aged Duke of Connaught (uncle of King George V) on the 12c. The stamps were recess-printed by De La Rue.

21. Newfoundland, 5 cents, 1928
Between 1923 and 1947 Newfoundland issued definitive sets designed quite frankly to publicize the island, its tourist attractions, its modern facilities and its industry and agriculture. The series of 1928 was originally printed by De La Rue, but was reissued the following year in new printings by Perkins Bacon. The two versions differed in minor details. Whereas the series of 1923 had concentrated on beauty spots of the island the series of 1928–29 emphasized modern buildings and communications. The 5c. showed a locomotive, the 2c. the steamship Caribou, the 15c. the Vickers Vimy piloted by Alcock and Brown on their Atlantic flight.

22. Newfoundland, 6 cents, 1932
Perkins Bacon recess-printed a definitive series issued in January 1932. The wildlife of Newfoundland and Labrador was represented by Caribou (5c.), dog (14c.) and seal (15c.), while codfish and salmon were also depicted. The series continued the tradition of royal portraiture with not only the king and queen but the Prince of Wales and the infant Princess Elizabeth, who made her philatelic début on the 6c. stamp, flanked by roses and thistles. A 7c. stamp, issued later the same year, portrayed the Duchess of York (now Queen Elizabeth, the Queen Mother).

23. Newfoundland, 24 cents, 1933
Perkins Bacon recess-printed a series issued in August 1933 to mark the 350th anniversary of the formal annexation of Newfoundland by Sir Humphrey Gilbert, and again the opportunity was taken to produce designs of prime interest to English collectors. The lower denominations traced Gilbert's career and even showed Compton Castle in Devon (his birthplace) and Eton College (where he was educated). Two stamps continued the royal portrait theme – the 7c. which showed Queen Elizabeth I granting the commission to Gilbert, and the 24c. with her portrait. Gilbert's statue at Truro in Cornwall (32c.) rounded off the series.

PLATE 90 CANADIAN PROVINCES · PLATE 91 UNITED STATES OF AMERICA

24. Newfoundland, 48 cents, 1937

As a crown colony Newfoundland participated in the colonial omnibus issues marking the coronation of King George VI in May 1937, but as a self-governing colony asserted its independence by issuing a second coronation series on the same day. This set was printed by Perkins Bacon and followed the age-old practice of promoting the island's image in a manner irrelevant to the subject commemorated. The existing definitive series was adapted with a very poor likeness of the king inset. Two versions exist of the perforations in each denomination, either line 14 or 13½ or comb 13.

25. Newfoundland, 30 cents, 1943

The inauguration of the Memorial University College was celebrated by this stamp, issued in January 1943. It was recess-printed by the Canadian Bank Note Co. and was reissued in March 1946 surcharged for use as a 2c. stamp. Newfoundland ceased issuing its own stamps in 1947 when it joined the Canadian Confederation. Its last issues, marking the 21st birthday of Princess Elizabeth and the 450th anniversary of Cabot's discovery of the island, were true to form.

PLATE 91
United States of America

1. Providence, Postmaster's issue, 5 cents, 1846

Adhesive postage stamps for use throughout the United States did not appear until 1847; before that local services were organized by private companies, many of whom issued their own stamps from 1842 onward. Uniform rates of postage were introduced in the United States in 1845, but two years elapsed before authority was given to the Postmaster General to issue stamps. In the interim the postmasters of certain cities produced their own, the first being a 5c. stamp issued by New York in 1845. Subsequently stamps were issued in Alexandria (Virginia), Annapolis (Maryland), Baltimore (Maryland), Boscawen (New Hampshire), Brattleboro (Vermont), Lockport (New York), Millbury (Massachusetts), New Haven (Connecticut), Providence (Rhode Island) and St Louis (Missouri).

2. U.S.P.O. Dispatch, 1 cent, 1851

Special stamps were used to defray the postage from a post office to the addressee (within the district served by the post office), both before and after the introduction of the general series in 1847. Many of the private companies held government contracts as carriers and thus their stamps are regarded as semi-official in status. The United States Post Office, however, also issued 1c. stamps either portraying Benjamin Franklin or depicting the American Eagle. These stamps were withdrawn in 1863.

3. 3 cents, 1851

The first general stamps of the United States portrayed Benjamin Franklin (5c.) and George Washington (10c.), the first Postmaster General and the first President respectively. This tradition has been continued with every definitive series up to the present time. The internal letter rate was reduced from 5 to 3c. in 1851 and a stamp portraying Washington was then introduced.

4. 10 cents, 1861

All previous issues were demonetized following the outbreak of the Civil War in 1861 and an entirely new series was introduced in the states adhering to the Union. Portraits of prominent personalities were used, George Washington appearing on five out of the eight stamps.

5. 2 cents, 1863

Local delivery of letters was introduced in 1863 and a 2c. rate levied for this purpose. The first stamp of this denomination is known popularly as the Black Jack or the Big Head, since it bore the Dodge portrait of General Andrew Jackson. The full-face portrait occupied far too much space and the inscriptions convey the impression of having been crammed in as an afterthought.

6. 15 cents, 1866

This stamp, printed in black, appeared within months of Lincoln's assassination and is thus regarded as the world's first mourning stamp. No living American may be portrayed on United States stamps, but memorial stamps have appeared shortly after the death of each president since Lincoln. This was also the first portrait stamp to be based on a photograph.

7. 2 cents, 1869

The National Bank Note Co. recess-printed a new definitive series which was released between March and September 1869. The low values included the obligatory portraits of Franklin (1c.) and Washington (6c.) and publicized methods of mail transportation then in use, including the celebrated Pony Express (2c.). The higher denominations were produced in two colours and showed paintings of historic subjects such as the Landing of Columbus (15c.) and the signing of the Declaration of Independence (24c.).

8. 5 dollars, 1893

The United States was one of the first countries to issue commemorative stamps. Stamped envelopes, but not adhesive stamps, were issued in 1876 in connection with the Centennial Exposition at Philadelphia, but the first adhesive commemorative appeared in 1893 to mark the Columbian Exposition at Chicago. The series of sixteen stamps, from 1c. to $5, reproduced paintings of scenes from the life and exploits of Columbus.

9. 2 cents, 1901

Most of the early commemorative issues of the United States were devoted to expositions and fairs. Several lengthy sets were produced between 1893 and 1915 for this purpose – a practice which met with loud protests from philatelists at the time. This stamp was one of a set of six released in May 1901 to mark the Pan-American Exposition at Buffalo. A few are known with the centre inverted.

10. 24 cents, 1918

The United States was the first country to issue a stamp showing an aircraft, but the 20c. stamp of 1912 was intended for parcel postage and not airmail. The inauguration of the internal airmail service in 1918 necessitated a set of stamps showing the famous Curtiss Jenny used by the airmail pilots. One sheet of the 24c. has been recorded with the centre inverted.

11. 5 cents, 1920

The tercentenary of the landing of the Pilgrim Fathers at Provincetown and Plymouth, Massachusetts, was marked by three stamps issued in December 1920. The 1c. featured the sailing vessel *Mayflower*; in the vertical panels were hawthorn blossoms and trailing arbutus – the British and American mayflowers. The other stamps depicted the landing (2c.) and the signing of the Compact with the Indians (5c.).

12. 20 cents, 1923

A definitive series portraying prominent Americans was released in 1922–23. The denominations from 15c. to $2, however, featured famous landmarks

including the Statue of Liberty (15c.) and the Golden Gate, San Francisco (20c.), while the $5 stamp showed a female figure symbolizing America.

13. 10 cents, 1927

The epic solo flight of Colonel Charles Lindbergh, non-stop across the Atlantic in 1927 was celebrated by a 10c. airmail stamp, issued in June 1927. For the first time the rule about living Americans not being commemorated on stamps of the United States was broken, insofar as this stamp bore Lindbergh's name and depicted his Ryan monoplane *Spirit of St Louis*. More recently stamps have depicted astronauts walking in space or landing on the Moon, and in both instances the individuals can be identified, though not actually named.

14. 16 cents, 1936

The late President Franklin D. Roosevelt was well-known as a stamp collector, but it is often forgotten that he also laid claim to be a stamp designer. The 16c. Airmail Special Delivery stamp of 1936 is said to have been produced from a design drafted by the President, incorporating the Great Seal of the United States. The first printing, made in 1934, was in blue, but a later printing (1936) was produced in red and blue.

15. 1½ cents, 1938

The definitive series of 1938 portrayed every American president (other than living persons) from George Washington (1c.) to Calvin Coolidge ($5). A novel feature of this set was that each of the first 22 presidents was portrayed on the denomination corresponding to their number. Thus John Tyler, tenth president, appeared on the 10c. stamp. Half-cent denominations were reserved for Franklin (½c.), Martha Washington (1½c.) and the White House (4½c.).

16. 10 cents, 1940

As a belated tribute to prominent Americans in various professions a series of 35 stamps was released at intervals between January and October 1940. There were seven groups of five stamps, ranging in value from 1 to 10c., and the groups portrayed respectively authors, poets, educationists, scientists, composers, artists and inventors. The large format adopted for this series was subsequently retained for many of the single stamps commemorating famous Americans.

17. 3 cents, 1946

This stamp, issued in June 1946 to mark the 150th anniversary of Tennessee statehood, is typical of the numerous stamps celebrating anniversaries of the admission of the various states to the Union. It depicts the State Capitol, flanked by portraits of President Andrew Jackson and Governor John Sevier.

18. 1¼ cents, 1960

The Liberty definitive series (so-called because the Statue of Liberty is shown on the 3 and 8c. stamps) appeared between 1954 and 1961 and depicted former presidents, historic personalities and famous landmarks. The series included a 1¼c. stamp, for use on printed matter – the only stamp of this unusual denomination issued in the United States.

19. 4 cents, 1962

Instances of American stamps with inverted centres are rare and none had, in fact, been recorded since 1918. In October 1962, however, a 4c. stamp portraying the late Dag Hammarskjold was released and one sheet was discovered to have the yellow background inverted. Before the lucky finder could sell his sheet at a huge profit the United States Post Office announced that it would deliberately print stamps with the background inverted, in order that every philatelist would have the chance to own such a curiosity. Consequently the Hammarskjold inverts are as plentiful as the normal variety. The finder attempted to sue the U.S. Post Office but failed to win redress.

20. 4 cents, 1962
Despite the government regulation that no stamps must display political or religious bias, the United States has issued Christmas stamps since 1962. In the early years non-controversial designs (wreath, tree, holly, etc.) were used, but in more recent years Old Master paintings of the Nativity have been used.

21. 3 cents, 1937
A set of four 3c. stamps appeared in 1937 in honour of the four territories of the United States. The stamps featured the statue of King Kamehameha I (Hawaii), Mount McKinley (Alaska), La Fortaleza (Puerto Rico) and a view of Charlotte Amalie (Virgin Islands).

22. 7 cents, 1959
In 1859 John Wise made a flight from La Fayette Indiana to Crawfordsville and carried, in the balloon *Jupiter*, a bag of mail entrusted to him by the postmaster of La Fayette. A century later the United States issued a 7c. airmail stamp to mark the centenary of the world's first official airmail service.

23. 8 cents, 1960
A large 8c. stamp was issued in 1957 in memory of Ramon Magsaysay, president of the Philippines. A medallion motif was used, with the caption 'Champion of Liberty'. A similar, though smaller, device was used for subsequent pairs of stamps honouring their Champions of Liberty: Simon Bolivar, Lajos Kossuth, San Martin, Ernst Reuter, Thomas Masaryk, Jan Paderewski, Gustav Mannerheim, Garibaldi and Gandhi.

24. 5 cents, 1965
Postage stamps are often used in the United States to educate the population and publicize federal campaigns in the social, welfare and medical fields. This stamp was issued in April 1965 to promote the government crusade against cancer and features a microscope and stethoscope with the slogan 'Early diagnosis saves lives.'

25. 5 cents, 1965
Many American stamps in recent years have paid tribute to famous personalities of other countries, reflecting the diverse ethnic origins of the American population. Stamps have honoured Shakespeare, Dante, Winston Churchill and Leif Eriksson as well as the 'Champions of Liberty' (see No. 23). Other stamps have celebrated the anniversaries of Polish and Finnish independence.

26. 5 cents, 1963
The United States has issued relatively few stamps in honour of international events and organizations. This stamp, ostensibly marking the centenary of the International Red Cross, was given a subtle political twist by displaying the Red Cross flag over the S.S. *Morning Light*, which repatriated survivors of the ill-fated Bay of Pigs invasion of Cuba in 1961.

27. 5 cents, 1964
Since 1962 the United States has issued stamps at regular intervals reproducing works by famous American artists. As a rule these stamps have illustrated established works of art but this example, dedicated 'to the fine arts', was specially commissioned. The abstract lithograph by S. Davis, reproduced on this stamp, had a very mixed reception.

28. 5 cents, 1967
As part of the policy of educating a diverse population in the history and traditions of the country the United States has begun to issue stamps highlighting aspects of American folklore. In recent years stamps have portrayed Johnny Appleseed, Davy Crockett and Daniel Boone, folk heroes from the pioneering days of the American West.

29. 8 cents, 1971
A jumbo-sized 6c. stamp was released in October 1969 following the death of Dwight Eisenhower, Supreme Allied Commander in World War II and President of the United States. The internal letter rate has increased from 6 to 8c. in 1971 and this stamp also portrayed Eisenhower.

PLATE 92
Confederate States and United Nations

Apart from the United States itself two postal administrations have functioned within the boundaries of the continental United States and received international recognition. Stamps were issued by the Confederate States of America from 1861 to 1865 and the United Nations Organization headquarters in New York have issued distinctive stamps since 1951.

1. Confederate Postmaster's Stamps (Memphis), 2 cents, 1861
After the secession of the southern states and the beginning of the American Civil War in 1861 the postmasters of various cities and towns in the seceded states were authorized to produce their own stamps pending the introduction of the general series. About 40 different towns issued their own stamps in 1861. A number of others produced postal stationery and numerous postmasters used handstruck provisional stamps. Among the more ambitiously designed were the stamps issued by the postmaster of Memphis, Tennessee, which bore his name (M. C. Callaway) and were typographed from a woodcut. Other stamps varied considerably from the crude handstruck 5 and manuscript initials used at Jetersville to the elaborate lithographed design used for the stamps of Mobile, Alabama.

2. Confederate States, 5 cents, 1861
The first stamps intended for use in the southern states consisted of 5c. and 10c. stamps portraying Jefferson Davis and Thomas Jefferson respectively. They were lithographed by Hoyer and Ludwig of Richmond and were issued imperforate. The shades of these stamps varied considerably.

3. Confederate States, 5 cents, 1862
The 5c. portraying President Jefferson Davis, issued in 1862 enjoys the distinction of being the only stamp of America to be printed outside that country. The earliest printings of the stamp were typographed by De La Rue – the first foreign contract held by that company.

4. Confederate States, 1 cent, 1862
At the same time De La Rue typographed a 1c. stamp portraying John C. Calhoun. The minimum postal rates were increased before this stamp could be released and the majority of them were seized by Federal warships which intercepted a Confederate blockade-runner. The Calhoun stamp thus has the status of prepared for use but never issued.

5. Confederate States, 10 cents, 1863
A Mr Halpin engraved the 10c. stamp of 1863

bearing a profile of Jefferson Davis. The first version of this design, engraved by M. Archer, had the value expressed as 'ten cents' whereas Halpin's version used the numerals. There were two dies of the Halpin version differing in the shading of the corner ornaments. Rough impressions of this stamp were made by Keatinge and Ball of Columbia, South Carolina, in 1864.

6. Confederate States, 20 cents, 1863
The top value issued by the Confederacy portrayed George Washington – the only instance of the same person being portrayed on the stamps of opposing sides in time of war. As with the other stamps of this series the colour and thickness of paper varied considerably.

7. United Nations, 15 cents, 1951
Distinctive stamps for use on mail from the headquarters of the United Nations in New York were adopted on 24 October – United Nations Day – 1951. The six designs of the ordinary series and the two designs of the airmail stamps were produced by artists of international repute and the stamps were recess-printed by De La Rue or Enschedé. The artists were faced with two major problems, the accommodation of the principal languages of the world in the inscriptions and the avoidance of anything controversial in the subject matter. As a result the designs are, for the most part, symbolic and derived from motifs which are easily recognizable the world over. Olaf Mathiesen produced this swallows in flight motif for the 15 and 25c. airmail stamps.

8. United Nations, 5 cents, 1952
The first commemorative issue consisted of this 5c. stamp issued in October 1952 to mark the seventh anniversary of the signing of the UN Charter. It was designed by J. van Noten of Belgium, recess-printed by the American Bank Note Co., and features the Veterans' War Memorial Building in San Francisco where the Charter was signed.

9. United Nations, 8 cents, 1958
Two stamps designed by Mathiesen and recess-printed by the American Bank Note Co. appeared in April 1958 to pay tribute to the first General Assembly of the United Nations. The 3 and 8c. stamps depicted the Methodist Central Hall in Westminster, London – of particular interest to philatelists as the home, for many years, of Britain's National Stamp Exhibition (STAMPEX). The caption on the 3c. was given in English while that on the 8c. was in French. It is customary for the captions on different stamps of a set to be given in the various languages of the UN.

10. United Nations, 5 cents, 1959
A 4c. airmail stamp, prepaying the American inland airmail rate, was issued in May 1957. The stamp, symbolizing Flight, was designed by Willy Wind and recess-printed by De La Rue. When the rate was increased to 5c. in 1959 a stamp of this denomination was released and the opportunity was taken to increase the size of the inscriptions in order to make them clearer.

11. United Nations, 8 cents, 1958
L. C. Mitchell of New Zealand designed the 4 and 8c. stamps recess-printed by the American Bank Note Co. and issued in December 1958 to mark the tenth anniversary of the declaration of Human Rights. Hands of different colours holding the globe formed the effective motif for conveying this message and an oval arrangement of the captions enabled all five major languages to be inscribed.

12. United Nations, 8 cents, 1959
The Scandinavian artists L. Helguer and Ole

PLATE 92 CONFEDERATE STATES, UNITED NATIONS · PLATE 93 MEXICO

Hamann designed the 4c. and 8c. stamps, recess-printed by the Canadian Bank Note Co. in honour of the UN Trusteeship Council. Reproducing Rodin's sculpture *The Age of Bronze*, they were issued in October 1959.

13. United Nations, 7 cents, 1959
Olaf Mathiesen designed this airmail stamp, recess-printed by Waterlow and Sons and released in February 1959. The prosaic design, showing the UN flag and an airliner, reflects the more predictable, less imaginative trend in United Nations stamp design in the late fifties.

14. United Nations, 8 cents, 1960
The Austrian artist, H. Woyty-Wimmer, designed 4 and 8c. stamps recess-printed by De La Rue in February 1960, showing the Palais de Chaillot in Paris, third venue of the General Assembly before it acquired its permanent home. Stamps of March 1959 illustrated the New York City Building at Flushing Meadows while a similar pair of 1963 featured the permanent headquarters in New York. The use of two-colour recess marked a more colourful approach to stamp design from 1960 onwards.

15. United Nations, 4 cents, 1960
The 4 and 8c. stamps of December 1960 were the first multicoloured stamps issued by the United Nations. A. M. Medina produced the design, featuring a double block and hook, and the stamps were printed in photogravure by the Government Printing Bureau in Tokyo to publicize the work of the International Bank for Reconstruction and Development (the 'World Bank').

16. United Nations, 4 cents, 1960
Stamps have been issued at five-yearly intervals to mark prominent anniversaries of the United Nations Organization. The 4 and 8c. stamps of October 1960, showing the UN headquarters and emblem, were designed by R. Perrot and recess-printed by the British-American Bank Note Co. of Ottawa. The captions were in English and French respectively.

17. United Nations, 4 cents, 1961
Kurt Plowitz designed 4 and 8c. stamps showing the scales of justice and the UN emblem in honour of the International Court of Justice in The Hague. The stamps, printed in three-colour photogravure by the Japanese Government Printing Bureau, were issued in February 1961.

18. United Nations, 11 cents, 1962
Increases in American postal rates led to the release of new designs and denominations in the definitive series in May 1962. Mathiesen designed the 11c. showing the UN emblem stretched across the globe and the stamp was printed in photogravure by Harrison and Sons, who also produced the new 1 and 3c. stamps. Flags, globes and emblems of peace formed the motifs of the other stamps. The 5c. was originally recess-printed in carmine by the Canadian Bank Note Co. but was reissued in a multicolour photogravure version, by Courvoisier, in 1967.

19. United Nations, 11 cents, 1965
Kurt Plowitz of the United States designed the 5 and 11c. stamps printed in multicolour photogravure by Courvoisier and issued in May 1965 to mark the centenary of the International Telecommunications Union. The design symbolizes the progress from semaphore to satellite in a hundred years.

20. United Nations, 75 cents, 1968
In 1967 the United Nations began issuing an annual series devoted to art of the UN. The first issue featured Marc Chagall's stained-glass window *The Kiss of Peace*. Two stamps were issued in March 1968 reproducing Henrik Starcke's statue in the Trusteeship Council Chamber. The 6c. was regarded as a commemorative issue whereas the 75c. was retained for definitive purposes.

21. United Nations, 21 cents, 1971
The United Nations International Schools in New York and Geneva were commemorated by three stamps issued in October 1971, two in English, with American currency, and one in French, with Swiss currency. Bearing the portrait by Pablo Picasso of his daughter Maria, they were designed by Ole Hamann and printed in multicolour photogravure by Courvoisier. Apart from the Peace Dove appearing on the stamps of certain Communist countries, and a reproduction of his mural *Guernica* on a Czech stamp of 1966, these stamps were the only others to reproduce works by Picasso.

22. United Nations, 60 cents, 1971
To meet the increased American rate for special delivery mail a 60c. definitive stamp was issued in October 1971. Designed by the French artist Robert Perrot, it had a patchwork motif representing the colours of national flags.

PLATE 93
Mexico

1. 2 reales, 1864
Adhesive stamps were adopted by Mexico in August 1856 when a series of five, from ½ to 8r., was issued. All stamps of the Mexican republic up to 1879 portrayed Don Miguel Hidalgo y Costilla, leader of the revolt against Spain in the early nineteenth century. The earliest issue was lithographed in Mexico, but in 1864 the design was modified for a set of four recess-printed by the American Bank Note Co. These were overprinted 'Saltillo' or 'Monterrey' before issue to the public. Stamps without these overprints came from remainder of stocks.

2. 25 centavos, 1866
An empire, under French auspices, was proclaimed in April 1864 and the Austrian Archduke Maximilian was made emperor. The first stamps of the empire bore the eagle and serpent emblem but in 1866–67 a series portraying Maximilian was issued. The earliest printings (August–December 1866) were lithographed but a recess-printed version was released between October 1866 and April 1867. These stamps were usually issued with a district name and consignment number overprinted.

3. 12 centavos, 1868
After the withdrawal of the French the republicans overthrew the erstwhile empire. Stamps of the first republican series were reintroduced overprinted 'Mexico' in Gothic script. A new Hidalgo series, lithographed in Mexico City, was issued in September 1868. The stamps may be found with thin or thick figures of value and both versions exist imperforate or perforated.

4. 25 centavos, 1874
Different designs were used for each of a series of five stamps, recess-printed by the American Bank Note Co. and released in 1874. A 4c. denomination was added in 1880. With this series the district overprints become more complex, usually including a district name and number, sub-consignment numbers and the date. Sometimes two sets of district names and numbers were overprinted and various colours were used.

5. 25 centavos, 1879
Señor de la Pena designed a series portraying Benito Juarez, leader of the republican movement against Maximilian, which was recess-printed at the Government Printing Works in Mexico City and issued between 1879 and 1883. Stamps of this series may be found with the usual medley of district overprints or with a second set of overprints. Such stamps, known to collectors as 'Habilitados', were returned to a central pool and overprinted a second time for distribution to offices which had run out of certain denominations.

6. 50 centavos, 1884
A profile of Hidalgo was used for the series of 1884 recess-printed in Mexico in denominations from 1c. to 10p. The centavo denominations were all printed in green and the peso values in blue. Although the overprinting of district names officially ceased with the previous series, stamps of this set may be found with these overprints. Different colours for each value were adopted in 1885 and then the design was altered, in 1886, the numeral of value being substituted for Hidalgo's profile.

7. 2 centavos, 1899
Bradbury Wilkinson recess-printed a series for Mexico issued in 1899. The low values had the eagle and serpent emblem in different frames, the three top values the Juanacatlan Falls. Popocatápetl and Mexico Cathedral. New colours and a 4c. value were introduced in 1903.

8. 2 centavos, 1914
A set of five stamps, from 1 to 10c., was lithographed at El Paso, Texas, in July 1914. The stamps, portraying President Madero, were never released on account of the fall of the Madero government and the murder of the president. Stamps overprinted or inscribed 'Gobierno Constitucionalista' (constitutional government) were issued in those areas controlled by the Constitutionalists (rebels) in the series of civil wars which swept Mexico between 1913 and 1915. For district provisional issues see below.

9. 2 centavos, 1915
Venustiano Carranza recaptured Mexico City in January 1915 and ousted his rivals by August; the following month a general series of stamps for use throughout the country was reintroduced. They were designed by T. A. Rico, with the coat of arms (1c.) and portraits of historic personalities, and lithographed by the American Book and Printing Co. of Mexico City. Cuauhtemoc, last of the Aztec rulers, was shown on the 2c. stamp.

10. 40 centavos, 1915
In November 1915 two double-sized stamps designed by F. Fernandez were recess-printed at the Government Printing Works. The 40c. showed a map of the country to emphasize its reunification, while the 1 peso stamp showed the lighthouse at Vera Cruz. A 5p. stamp featuring the Post Office in Mexico City was added the following year. The two peso stamps were printed in two colours and both are known with centres inverted. All three denominations have been recorded imperforate.

11. 2 centavos, 1937
A lengthy series of ordinary and airmail stamps was released in December 1934 to celebrate the inauguration of President Cardenas. Although primarily commemorative this series was retained for definitive use. In 1937 the imprint was changed at the foot of the design, from 'Oficina Impresora de Hacienda-Mexico' to 'Talleres de Imp(resion) de Est(ampillas) y Valores Mexico'. Though still recess-printed the stamps were considerably reduced in size. The 2c. stamp featured a Zapotec Indian woman.

251

PLATE 93 MEXICO · PLATE 94 CENTRAL AMERICA

12. 30 centavos, 1944

The Cardenas series of 1934 underwent several transformations in the ensuing decade. The perforations and watermark were changed and photogravure was adopted in 1944 for the lower values. The higher values continued to be recess-printed but new colours were used. The 30c., with the Heroic Children monument in Mexico City, was changed from scarlet to blue. Further changes of watermark took place between 1947 and 1950.

13. 20 centavos, 1938

A set of three ordinary and three airmail stamps was released in March 1938 to mark the 25th anniversary of the revolution. It featured workers, peasants and soldiers in different motifs. Appropriately one of the airmail stamps depicted an aircraft of the revolutionary period, the civil war being one of the earliest occasions in which aircraft were used militarily.

14. 15 centavos, 1947

The centenary of the first United States stamps was marked by a set of five, printed in photogravure and issued in May 1947. The earliest Mexican and American stamps were reproduced and three stamps also portrayed the late President Roosevelt, a well-known philatelist. It is interesting that Mexico was one of the countries which issued stamps to celebrate the centenary of Britain's Penny Black of 1840.

15. 80 centavos, 1962

Mexico has the distinction of being the first country to portray John F. Kennedy on a stamp. This 80c. stamp was released in June 1962 to mark the official visit of Kennedy to Mexico. Kennedy was also portrayed, with President A. Lopez Mateos, on a stamp of 1964 marking the ratification of the Chamizal Treaty by which a strip of territory on the Rio Grande was ceded by the United States to Mexico after a lengthy boundary dispute.

16. 20 centavos, 1965

The 50th anniversary of the Convention of Aguascalientes, which brought the civil war to an end, was belatedly celebrated by this stamp, issued in January 1965. The stamp, in two-colour photogravure, shows the Morelos Theatre, where the delegates met in 1914. Anniversaries of the civil war have provided Mexico with a constant source of material for stamps since 1934.

17. 40 centavos, 1965

Although inscribed '1964' this stamp was not released until April 1965, when it tardily commemorated the 150th anniversary of the Constitution. It reproduced in two-colour photogravure, the title page of the Constitutional Decree for the Liberty of Mexican America, drawn up at Apatzingan in 1814, and the statue of J. Morelos who drafted the document.

18. Porte de Mar, 100 centavos, 1875

Stamps inscribed 'Porte de Mar' (carried by sea) were adopted by Mexico in 1875 to prepay the separate postal fees on mail carried by French or British ships. These stamps may be found with or without the district name and with small or large numerals of value. A similar series in smaller format and in different colours for each denomination was prepared in 1879 but never issued since Mexico joined the Universal Postal Union that year and Porte de Mar stamps were no longer required.

19. 6 centavos, 1882

Señor de la Peña designed a numeral series for Mexico which was released in July 1882 in denominations from 2 to 100c. These stamps may be found with or without district overprints. Nine years later

the Australian state of New South Wales used this design as the basis for its series of postage due stamps and the same design was subsequently modified by the Australian Commonwealth for the postage due series issued between 1902 and 1909. Virtually the only difference between the Australian and Mexican designs was the omission of tiny numerals in the corners in the former version. This curious example of plagarism has never been explained.

20. Chihuahua, 1 peso, 1914

Stamps inscribed 'Correos Transitorio' (provisional postage) were lithographed by Maverick-Clarke of San Antonio, Texas, and issued in the state of Chihuahua in January 1914. The series ranged from 1c. to 1p. and was rouletted. Subsequently the 5c. was redrawn and perforated by W. M. Linn of Columbus, Ohio, the well-known American stamp dealer. The stamps were later overprinted 'Gobierno Constitucionalista', the overprint extending over three or more stamps.

21. Hermosillo, 1 centavo, 1914

Stamps commemorating the centenary of Mexican independence were issued in 1910 and later were overprinted by the Constitutionalists and other factions in various parts of the country under their control. They were overprinted in May 1914 for use in the state of Hermosillo with the monogram GCM (Constitutionalist Government of Mexico).

22. Monterey, 3 centavos, 1914

The 1910 series was overprinted 'Gobierno Constitucionalista' at Mazatlan, Monterey and various other places. A circular overprint thus inscribed was used on stamps issued at Aguascalientes, San Pedro and Torreon, with the initials of these towns in the centre. The Monterey series, overprinted in violet, was released in June 1914. All values are known with the error 'Consitucionalista'. Postage due stamps were similarly overprinted.

23. Pancho Villa, 4 centavos, 1914

Pancho Villa broke with Carranza in September 1914, became dictator of the northern states and captured Mexico City in November 1914. The 1910 series of stamps, seized in the capital, was overprinted GCM and released in December.

24. Carranza, 2 centavos, 1916

Venustiano Carranza retook Mexico City from the Villistas on 27 January 1915, and overprinted the 1910 series with his monogram in the following month. In March 1916 these stamps were issued with a second overprint 'GP de M' (Gobierno Provisorio de Mexico). As a result of the depreciation of the ordinary paper currency this overprint was applied to stamps to raise their value to par with the new 'infalsificable' paper money.

25. Mazatlan, 1 centavo, 1914

The commemorative series of 1910 was overprinted by the Constitutionalists in 1914 with a two-line overprint. Several stamps of the Chihuahua series were similarly treated. Mazatlan also produced stamps with a typewritten overprint – one of the rare examples in which typewriting has been used for philatelic purposes.

26. Sonora, 2 centavos, 1913

The state of Sonora took the opportunity of the civil war to declare its independence. Mexican stamps overprinted ES (Estado Sonora) appeared July 1914, but distinctive stamps designed and printed in Sonora were issued between May 1913 and October 1914. This stamp was one of a series of seven issued in July 1913. The lower label was supposed to be removed before the stamps were sold to the public but on rare occasions these stamps may be found postally used with the label attached.

The inscription signifies Constitutionalist Army of Mexico. Local issues continued to appear in certain districts of Mexico as late as July 1915 (Oaxaca) and a similar issue was made at Yucatán in the rebellion of 1924.

PLATE 94
Central America

1. Costa Rica, 2 reales, 1863

Costa Rica adopted adhesive stamps in 1863, issuing $\frac{1}{2}$ and 2r. stamps showing a sailing ship off the coast of Central America. They were recess-printed by the American Bank Note Co. of New York. Higher values, of 4r. and 1p., were issued the following year. These four stamps were sufficient until 1881–82 when decimal currency was introduced and the stamps surcharged in centavos.

2. Costa Rica, 20 centavos, 1889

Stamps portraying President Soto were recess-printed in 1887 and were followed two years later by a similar series by Waterlow and Sons, with different frames for each denomination. This series is notorious for the numerous errors in perforation, not to mention the different gauges in which the perforation may be found. The two London firms, Waterlow and Sons and Waterlow Brothers and Layton (no connection) vied with each other for the Costa Rican contracts between 1889 and 1912.

3. Costa Rica, 10 centimos, 1936

In 1935 Costa Rica laid claim to the remote Pacific Coco Island and the following year issued two sets of stamps to reinforce the claim. Perkins Bacon recess-printed a series of eight stamps, in values from 4c. to 5 colones, and in December 5 and 10c. stamps were produced by the American Bank Note Co. The latter showed the fleet of Christopher Columbus – an irrelevant detail since Columbus never explored that region.

4. Costa Rica, 3 centimos, 1938

A national exhibition was held at San José in December 1937 and two sets of stamps were produced to mark the event. The American Bank Note Co. recess-printed a series of three ordinary and four airmail stamps, while the following year Waterlow and Sons produced two ordinary and four airmail stamps. Both sets included unusual shapes, both triangular and diamond, as well as more orthodox formats. Waterlows' airmail series showed the National Bank but other designs had orchids, tunny fish and cocoa beans.

5. Costa Rica, 2 centimos, 1950

A series of fourteen stamps was issued in July 1950 to mark the National Agricultural, Cattle and Industries Fair. They featured cattle, fish, and agricultural products and were produced by Waterlow and Sons using photogravure vignettes and recess-printed frames.

6. Costa Rica, 25 centimos, 1960

Since World War II Costa Rica has issued comparatively few stamps and often falls back on obsolete issues overprinted to serve other purposes and commemorate other events. A wide variety of the world's security printers have been employed. This stamp was one of a series, from 10 centimos to 5 colones, recess-printed by Enschedé of Holland, issued in October 1960 to mark the tercentenary of the death of St Vincent de Paul.

7. Costa Rica, 5 centimos, 1960

In 1958 Costa Rica overprinted two obsolete

PLATE 94 CENTRAL AMERICA · PLATE 95 SALVADOR, NICARAGUA

stamps 'Sello de Navidad (Christmas stamp) and added a 5c. surcharge to raise money for a delinquent children's camp to be organized on the same lines as Boys Town, Nebraska. Appropriately Father Flanagan, founder of Boys Town, was portrayed on the Christmas stamps issued the following year, while Father Peralta, founder of the Costa Rican scheme, was shown on a stamp of 1960. These stamps were compulsory on correspondence posted during the Christmas season, and have been a regular feature of Costa Rican philately ever since.

8. Costa Rica, 45 centimos, 1965

A set of four stamps and a miniature sheet appeared in December 1965 in memory of John F. Kennedy. The designs, by C. Alonso, contrived to incorporate various other themes, in order to capture the attention of as wide a market as possible. Thus the 45c. stamp included a space capsule encircling the globe, to appeal to the Space thematic collectors. The stamps were lithographed in multicolour by De La Rue of Bogota, Colombia.

9. Guanacaste, 1 centimo, 1885

Separate issues were made for the province of Guanacaste between 1885 and 1889, contemporary stamps of Costa Rica being overprinted for this purpose. The first time consisted of the 1883 definitives portraying General Fernandez, overprinted in upper and lower case lettering in black or red. Subsequent issues were overprinted in capitals, either horizontally or vertically and several different types of lettering were used. Numerous misspellings and errors have been noted in these overprints.

10. Honduras, 2 reales, 1877

Honduras tentatively introduced adhesive stamps in 1866. In January of that year 2r. stamps, printed in black on green or rose-coloured paper, were issued but used copies are unknown and it seems that their release was somewhat premature, for the postal service was not developed until 1877. In that year the stamps were reintroduced, but overprinted with the value in cursive script. Stamps intended for use in Comayagua had the overprint enclosed in an oblong frame, whereas those issued in Tegucigalpa were unframed.

11. Honduras, 5 pesos, 1891

Honduras came under the Seebeck spell in 1890 and from then until 1895 was treated to a new definitive series each year, recess-printed by the Hamilton Bank Note Co. of New York. The series of 1890 bore a masonic symbol, but portraits of President Bogran were used on the series of 1891. The stamps from 1 centavo to 1 peso were in a small format and were printed in monochrome, whereas the 2, 5 and 10p. values were produced in a large design with the portrait in black. All three denominations are known with the portrait upside down.

12. Honduras, 30 centavos, 1893

Columbus in sight of land was the subject for the series of 1892, while the portrait of General Cabanas was used on the series of 1893. The last of the 'Seebeck' issues, with a female allegory of the republic, was released in January 1895. Mercifully these sets did not go beyond a 1p. denomination.

13. Honduras, 2 centavos, 1903

The American Bank Note Co. recess-printed the definitive series of 1903 portraying General Santos Guardiola. The stamps of this series may be found with an overprint 'Permitase' which served as a control mark to check on stocks. Note the inclusion of the initials UPU, a feature of stamps from many Latin American countries in the early twentieth century, merely to signify their adherence to the Universal Postal Union.

14. Honduras, 1 centavo, 1957

The vast majority of Honduranean stamps up to 1950 were recess-printed by the American Bank Note Co. and fall into the stereotyped designs and treatment accorded to the stamps of other Latin American countries in the same period. During the 1950s, however, the contracts passed to Waterlow and Sons, who produced definitive or commemorative stamps in recess or lithography. This stamp, showing the national flag, was one of a series of airmail stamps issued in 1957 to mark the revolution of October 1956. In July 1958, following the looting of stocks from the main post office, they were re-validated by overprinting with facsimile signatures. No fewer than eighteen different signatures are known to have been used.

15. Honduras, 15 centavos, 1964

Since 1890 various definitive and commemorative stamps have been overprinted for official use. At the same time Honduras had recourse to the time-honoured expedient of overprinting obsolete stamps to commemorate other events. Thus the series of 1959 marking the 150th anniversary of the birth of Abraham Lincoln was subsequently overprinted for official correspondence and then, in 1964, further overprinted as a tribute to John F. Kennedy. The same device was used to commemorate Sir Winston Churchill (1965), the visit of Pope Paul to the United Nations (1966) and other events.

16. Guatemala, ½ real, 1878

Guatemala began issuing stamps in 1871, a series with the national coat of arms being designed by Anatole Hulot and typographed at the French Government Printing Works. Seven years later E. Mouchon designed a series featuring a Guatemalan Indian and this set was typographed by A. Chaix et Cie at the Imprimerie Centrale des Chemins de Fer (Railway Central Printing Works). They were printed on paper lithographed with a ground of a colour paler than that used for the design itself.

17. Guatemala, 2 centavos, 1881

Stamps featuring the quetzal, Guatemala's national bird, first appeared in December 1879. The American Bank Note Co. recess-printed stamps in denominations of ½ and 1r. Similar stamps in denominations from 1 to 20c. were produced in 1881. The design, in modified form, was reintroduced for the definitive series of 1954–63.

18. Guatemala, 1 centavo, 1897

The Central American Exhibition held in Guatemala in 1897 was commemorated by a set of fourteen stamps ranging from 1 to 500c. M. M. Giron produced the design showing a steamship, the national coat of arms, the portrait of President J. M. Reyna Barrios and a locomotive in the centre, with the arms of Salvador, Honduras, Nicaragua and Costa Rica in the corners.

19. Guatemala, 6 centavos, 1902

The British security printers dominated Guatemalan philately in the early twentieth century. In 1902 Waterlow and Sons produced a fine pictorial series in two-colour combinations. Technically the 6c. denomination, with the Temple of Minerva, is one of Waterlows' greatest masterpieces. Across the façade of the building are engraved the words 'Don Manuel Estrada Cabrera, Presidente de la Republica, a la Juventud estudiosa' – though one would require a high-powered magnifier to read them. The stamps were re-engraved by Perkins Bacon in 1924, by Waterlows again in 1926, and then by De La Rue in 1929 – and each version contrived to reproduce this inscription.

20. Guatemala, 1 centavo de quetzal, 1927

Guatemala reformed its currency in 1927, abandon-ing the peso in favour of the quetzal on par with the United States dollar. This stamp, the first to appear in the new currency, was typographed by De La Rue and issued in October 1927 for compulsory use on correspondence in order to raise money for the new General Post Office.

21. Guatemala, 5 centavos de quetzal, 1929

The definitive series of January 1929, recess-printed by De La Rue, included portraits of presidents past and present, the coat of arms of Guatemala City and several of the previous designs re-engraved. This series remained in use into the 1940s, various denominations being overprinted for commemorative purposes, while the 2c. value was bisected and each half surcharged for use as a 1c. stamp in April 1941.

22. Guatemala, 5 centavos, 1966

Since 1943 the majority of Guatemalan stamps have been produced at the National Printing Works in Guatemala City, mainly by recess-printing. The imprint on this stamp, 'Grabados en acero', signifies 'engraved on steel'. Four denominations (2, 3, 4 and 5c.) were used for a set in memory of Mario M. Montenegro the revolutionary leader. The 5c. denomination was issued in four different colours, issued at various times between December 1966 and May 1967.

23. Guatemala, 5 centavos, 1967

The quetzal continues to provide the principal motif for definitive issues. This stamp prepaying the internal airmail rate, first appeared in orange, in November 1966, but was subsequently issued in green, grey, violet or blue. This practice, of changing the colour of certain stamps at frequent intervals, has been prevalent in Guatemala in recent years though there seems to be no adequate explanation for it.

24. Guatemala, 25 centavos, 1917

Waterlow & Sons recess-printed this stamp issued in March 1917 to celebrate the re-election of Don Manuel Estrada Cabrera for another term as President of the Republic. Cabrera, who was dictator of Guatemala for more than 20 years, was one of the earliest politicians to appreciate the value of postage stamps in furthering the cult of the personality, and this self-glorification can be seen at its most blatant in the design of this stamp.

PLATE 95

Salvador and Nicaragua

1. Salvador, ½ real, 1867

Adhesive stamps were introduced in 1867 and were recess-printed by the American Bank Note Co. in denominations of ½, 1, 2 and 4r. The design showed a volcano surmounted by eleven stars symbolizing the departments composing the republic. The stamps were overprinted in 1874 with a small circular control device inscribed 'Contra Sello', with the national coat of arms in the centre. A quantity of stamps having been stolen, the authorities adopted this device to render the stolen stock invalid.

2. Salvador, 1 centavo, 1894

From 1890 to 1898 the stamps were recess-printed by the Hamilton Bank Note Co. to the order of Nicholas Seebeck, contractor to the Salvadorean government. Seebeck supplied an annual definitive series on the same terms as he did for Honduras (see plate 94). Each series bore the date of issue in the design. The Seebeck sets of 1892–94 exploited

253

PLATE 95 SALVADOR, NICARAGUA

the craze for stamps commemorating Christopher Columbus. The series of 1892 depicted his landing in the Western Hemisphere, the series of 1893 showed scenes from his life and the set of 1894 reproduced paintings with the same theme. The lower denominations of the 1894 series, however, were in a small upright format showing the female allegory of Liberty, with the mountains of Central America in the background.

3. Salvador, 3 centavos, 1896
Though Columbus was still portrayed on the 100c. top value the 1896 series chose a medley of pictorial subjects. On the lower denominations scenery and landmarks vied with steamships and a wood-burning locomotive. This series was subsequently reprinted in different shades and on paper which was much thicker than the original. The series was then re-issued in new colours, but with the same date, in 1897. Shortly afterward the Salvadorean authorities revoked Seebeck's contract.

4. Salvador, 5 pesos, 1893
A small design portraying the president, General Ezeta, was used for the centavo denominations of the 1893 series, but larger designs were used for the 2, 5 and 10p. values showing respectively the founding of the city of Isabella, the statue of Columbus at Genoa and his departure from Palos. The three top values are not recorded in postally used condition, there being no demand for stamps of such high denomination.

5. Salvador, 13 centavos, 1907
A series depicting the presidential palace was designed and engraved by Thomas Macdonald and recess-printed by C. Parraga of Salvador in denominations from 1 to 100c. In the original printings the background was composed of fine brown dots, but these were omitted from reissues made in 1909. Both sets were overprinted with the national coat of arms in a sunburst. Most values are known with the shield omitted or inverted.

6. Salvador, 1 centavo, 1924
Salvador was the first country in America to adopt the photogravure process, which was used by Waterlow & Sons for the pictorial definitive series of 1924–25. The nine stamps featured landmarks and housing scenes. Curiously enough the 35c. denomination of the series portraying Senora Morazan was recess-printed.

7. Salvador, 15 centavos, 1948
What Columbus did for the 1890s Roosevelt did for the 1940s. The third anniversary of his death was marked by a set of twelve stamps and two miniature sheets issued in April 1948. The stamps were recess-printed by Waterlow and Sons and depicted scenes from Roosevelt's career. The 15c. denomination (ordinary postage) and 1 colon (airmail) showed him with Churchill and Mackenzie King at the Quebec Conference. The 12c. and 2co. stamps bore a large portrait of Roosevelt captioned in Spanish 'President Franklin Delano Roosevelt, World Paladin of democracy and the policy of good neighbourliness in the Americas'.

8. Salvador, 1 centavo, 1954
A series of 36 ordinary and airmail definitive stamps was introduced in June 1954. Printed in photogravure by Courvoisier, it featured scenery and landmarks with the emphasis on modern development in Salvador.

9. Salvador, 50 centavos, 1964
Inevitably John F. Kennedy was commemorated by a series of stamps from Salvador, though less generously than Roosevelt. Three ordinary and three airmail stamps, plus two miniature sheets, all in a uniform design, were issued in November 1964, on the first anniversary of the assassination. Salvador has produced few distinctive stamps in recent years and often revalidates obsolete issues by surcharging them with new values or overprinting them to commemorate other events.

10. Nicaragua, 10 centavos, 1869
The first stamps used in Nicaragua were the Victorian British series, distinguished by the numeral obliterator C 57. Much of the external mail from Nicaragua continued to pass through the British post office at Greytown till 1882, when Nicaragua joined the Universal Postal Union and assumed responsibility for its own external mails. Nicaragua's first stamps appeared in 1862 and consisted of 2 and 5c. values with the five mountains emblem of Central America. Seven years later 10 and 25c. denominations in similar designs were added to the series and a 1c. followed in 1871. The stamps were recess-printed by the American Bank Note Co. The series continued in use up to 1882 and underwent changes in perforation, roulette and types of paper.

11. Nicaragua, 2 pesos, 1892
Seebeck held the contract to print the stamps for Nicaragua from 1890 to 1899 inclusive and made the most of that period with the usual welter of annual sets which were subsequently reprinted for sale to collectors. Unlike Salvador, however, Nicaragua used Columbus for only one of these sets, that of 1892, from 1c. to 10p., with Columbus sighting the New World. The series was also printed in different colours and overprinted to denote telegraphic use. Stamps with the 'Telegrafos' overprint omitted are regarded as errors of colour, though this is not strictly the case.

12. Nicaragua, 15 centavos, 1900
The American Bank Note Co. took over the contracts previously held by the Hamilton Bank Note Co. and recess-printed a series from 1c. to 5p. in 1900. The uniform design showed the smoking volcano of Momotombo. The appearance of this series altered the course of history in a curious manner. In 1900 projects for a canal across the Central American isthmus were being lobbied in the American Congress. At one point it seemed as though the Nicaraguan faction would succeed, but then the Panama supporters got hold of the Nicaraguan stamps of 1900 and circulated them to every Congressman. The idea that Nicaragua was an area of volcanic activity was sufficient to destroy the scheme for a canal across that country.

13. Nicaragua, 1 centavo, 1922
A notorious feature of Nicaraguan philately from 1901 to 1939 was the prevalence of provisional overprints and surcharges by which obsolete stamps were revalidated and new denominations created. Hundreds of such overprints appeared in a period of almost forty years, and bristle with errors and varieties. Occasionally fiscal stamps were similarly treated and converted to postal duty. This stamp was lithographed locally in a purely ornamental design, with neither inscription nor value. These were subsequently supplied by overprinting in 1922–23.

14. Nicaragua, 10 centavos, 1937
For many years Nicaragua and Honduras were involved in a dispute over their common boundaries. Occasionally this erupted into full-scale war, but usually the campaign was waged by other means. In July 1937 Nicaragua issued a set of seven airmail stamps for use on external mail and used a map of Central America to state the Nicaraguan case, the disputed area being labelled 'Territorio en litigio' (territory in dispute).

15. Nicaragua, 1 centavo, 1939
In 1931 the American humorist Will Rogers paid a goodwill visit to Nicaragua, to entertain the American troops then garrisoning the country. After his death Nicaragua issued a set of five stamps in his memory. Recess-printed by the American Bank Note Co., they depicted scenes from his visit and bore his portrait.

16. Nicaragua, 32 centavos, 1946
Nicaragua was one of the first countries outside the United States to issue stamps in memory of President Roosevelt. A series of eleven appeared in June 1946, with scenes from the president's life and various portraits, including one of Roosevelt with his stamp albums. The famous wartime conferences were recalled on several stamps, showing Roosevelt with French, British and Russian leaders at Teheran and Casablanca. The vignettes were printed in photogravure and the frames in recess by the Wright Bank Note Co. of Philadelphia.

17. Nicaragua, 40 centavos, 1964
A set of 8 stamps was issued in October 1964 to publicize the Alliance for Progress (see also plate 98, No. 9). The stamps showed various aspects of social, economic and cultural welfare and were lithographed in multicolour by the Toppan Printing Company of Japan, the first occasion on which a Japanese firm had printed stamps for an American country.

18. Nicaragua, 2 cordobas, 1965
The stamps of Nicaragua since World War II have been colourful and interesting, and printed in different parts of the world. This stamp, commemorating the centenary of the death of Andres Bello, the poet, was one of a series lithographed in two-colour combinations by Litografia Nacional at Oporto in Portugal.

19. Nicaragua, 5 cordobas, 1967
The birth centenary of Nicaragua's national poet, Reuben Dario, was celebrated in January 1967 by a set of eight stamps and two miniature sheets. Each stamp bore Dario's portrait with a different scene in the background. The stamps were designed and lithographed at Oporto. The top value shows 'Faith opposing Death', symbolizing the eternal quality of Dario's poetry.

20. Nicaragua, 35 centavos, 1968
For the Olympic Games in Tokyo in 1964 Nicaragua issued a set of sports stamps, appropriately printed by the Dai Nippon Co. of Tokyo. In 1968 the Mexico Olympics were celebrated by a series designed by C. Carneiro and lithographed in multicolour in Oporto. Sporting themes were used for many of the stamps issued by Nicaragua in recent years.

21. Nicaragua, 5 cordobas, 1970
Following the success of its various Olympic sets, Nicaragua issued a set of twelve large stamps in 1970 illustrating the football 'Hall of Fame'. The stamps depicted a famous contemporary footballer from various countries except one stamp which featured the national flags of the sixteen finalists in the 1970 World Cup. An interesting feature of these stamps was the descriptive caption on the back, printed in English and thereby indicating clearly their potential market.

22. Nicaragua, 15 centavos, 1970
Nicaragua was one of the many countries which issued stamps in memory of the late President Franklin D. Roosevelt in the years immediately following his death. Relatively few countries, however, remembered the 25th anniversary, but from Nicaragua came a set of eight stamps bearing various

PLATE 95 SALVADOR, NICARAGUA · PLATE 96 BRITISH HONDURAS, PANAMA

portraits of the late President. The 15c. and 1 cordoba denominations depicted President Roosevelt with his famous stamp collection.

23. Nicaragua, 60 centavos, 1965
Since 1962 Nicaragua has released a number of sets with common themes including civic coats of arms, sporting events, butterflies, flowers and fruits. A series of 11 stamps appeared in March 1965 with the subject of Nicaraguan antiquities. The series was lithographed by De La Rue from designs prepared by Miss Jennifer Toombs. This prolific young designer made her début with this series.

24. Nicaragua, 50 centavos, 1964
The inauguration of the Central American Common Market was celebrated in November 1964 by a set of four stamps lithographed by De La Rue. A map of the member countries appeared as a background to various industrial and agricultural motifs.

25. Bluefields, 50 centavos, 1911
The currency used in the Bluefields district of the province of Zelaya was silver worth 50 centavos to the peso, whereas elsewhere paper money worth less than 25 centavos to the peso was in circulation. Consequently the stamps of Nicaragua were issued between 1904 and 1912 with a distinguishing overprint – B (for Bluefields) and DPTO. ZELAYO (Departmento Zelayo).

26. Cabo Gracias á Dios, 5 centavos, 1904
Similar stamps were overprinted 'Costa Atlantica' or 'Cabo' in the same period, for the same reasons, for use on the Atlantic coast or at Cabo Gracias á Dios where silver currency also circulated. Ordinary Nicaraguan stamps have been used since 1912.

PLATE 96
British Honduras and Panama

---

1. British Honduras, 6 cents, 1891
This design was typographed by De La Rue in denominations of 1d., 6d. and 1s. and issued in January 1866 on unwatermarked paper. Different watermarks were employed in 1872–79 and 1882–87 and it was in the latter series that the 4d. stamp was introduced. In 1888 stamps were surcharged in decimal currency. The 10c. on 4d. stamp was further surcharged in 1891 to create a 6c. denomination. The confusing array of provisional surcharges was swept away by the keyplate designs adopted in 1891–98.

2. British Honduras, 5 cents, 1915
A series of stamps, from 1c. to $5, was typographed by De La Rue between 1913 and 1921. A consignment of 1, 2 and 5c. stamps shipped out to Central America during World War I was overprinted with a *moiré* pattern as a security precaution. Had these stamps been captured by the enemy they could be distinguished and thus rendered invalid.

3. British Honduras, 2 cents, 1938
Bradbury Wilkinson recess-printed a pictorial series issued between January 1938 and 1947 in denominations from 1c. to 5. With the exception of the 1c. (Maya figures), 15c. (Sergeant's Cay) and the $5 (coat of arms) the stamps alluded to the timber, fruit and chicle industries.

4. British Honduras, 1 dollar, 1953
Waterlow and Sons recess-printed a pictorial series with a profile of Queen Elizabeth inset. The vignettes illustrated the industry of the country as before but also included examples of the wildlife, native types and flowers. The 25c. featured a butterfly, the first Commonwealth stamp with this subject. The perforations of the 2, 3 and 5c. values were changed in 1957. De La Rue printed later consignments of this series, from 1961 to 1968.

5. British Honduras, 15 cents, 1960
The centenary of the establishment of the first post office was celebrated in July 1960 by three stamps recess-printed by Bradbury Wilkinson. None of them alluded directly to the postal centenary, but showed a view of Belize in 1842 (2c.), the public seals of 1860 and 1960 (10c.) and the ancient tamarind tree at Newton Barracks (15c.). The same irrelevant approach was adopted in 1966, when four scenic stamps marked the centenary of the first adhesive stamps. From 1860 to 1865 ordinary British stamps were used in British Honduras, identifiable by the numeral obliterator A 06.

6. British Honduras, 5 dollars, 1962
The American ornithologist Don R. Eckleberry designed the series of twelve denominations, from 1c. to $5, printed in multicolour photogravure by Harrison and Sons in 1962. The original printings were on paper with an upright watermark but a sideways watermark was adopted for the values from 1 to 50c. in 1967. Five denominations were overprinted in 1964 to mark the grant of internal self-government and the same five denominations were released in July 1966 with an overprint recording the dedication of the new capital site.

7. British Honduras, 50 cents, 1971
The gradual development of the new capital city is well charted in stamps. Apart from the overprints of 1965 the move to Belmopan was mentioned in the 50c. stamp of 1968, ostensibly recording Human Rights Year but, with true Belizean irrelevance, depicting the monument on the new site, dedicated by Arthur Greenwood, the then Colonial Secretary. The actual move to Belmopan was celebrated by a set of six stamps, issued in January 1971, depicting important landmarks and public buildings. The stamps were designed by Gordon Drummond and lithographed by Enschedé.

8. British Honduras, 5 dollars, 1968
For the definitive series issued in October 1968 two themes were chosen – fishes and animals. The stamps were designed by staff artists of John Waddington Ltd, but the actual printing was entrusted to De La Rue who used multicolour lithography. A ½c. denomination, with a crana fish, was added to the series in September 1969. The $5 stamp was originally printed on unwatermarked paper but a supply issued in 1970 was printed on the standard colonial watermarked paper.

9. British Honduras, 22 cents, 1969
Since 1968 British Honduras has issued numerous short thematic sets featuring either orchids or indigenous hardwoods. The series of September 1969, designed by Victor Whiteley and lithographed by De La Rue, was printed on paper with a background simulating the grain of the different types of timber. A similar device was used for 'timber' stamps issued by the New Hebrides in 1969, also designed by this artist.

10. British Honduras, 15 cents, 1970
The first set of four stamps with orchids appeared in April 1968 ostensibly to commemorate the 20th anniversary of the Economic Commission for Latin America (ECLA). The stamps were designed by Sylvia Goaman and printed by Harrison and Sons. A year later a similar series, by the same artist and printer, was issued for no purpose other than as a thematic set. In April 1970 a second thematic series devoted to the orchids of Belize was issued. This time the stamps were designed by Gordon Drummond and lithographed by Format.

11. Panama, 1 centavo, 1904
In November 1903 Panama, with the connivance of the United States, seceded from Colombia and became an independent republic. Stamps issued by the former department of Panama under Colombian administration (see plate 100) were overprinted in 1903–04 'Panama' with the original name blotted out. The basic stamps were recess-printed by the American Bank Note Co. in 1892–96 with a map of the isthmus.

12. Panama, 5 centavos, 1904
Like Colombia, Panama issued stamps for the prepayment of the fee for acknowledgment of receipt. The American Bank Note Co. recess-printed this stamp, issued in August 1904, the first stamp of the new republic designed specifically for it. The date beneath the name of the country is that on which it declared its independence. Acknowledgment of Receipt stamps were last issued in 1916.

13. Panama, 1 centesimo, 1915
The inauguration of the Panama Canal was celebrated in March 1915 by a series of stamps from ½ to 20c., depicting scenery and landmarks along the route of the canal. The 2c. depicted Vasco Nunez de Balboa reaching the Pacific, while the 1c. had a map of the canal itself. The currency was changed from the peso of 100 centavos to the balboa of 100 centesimos in 1906.

14. Panama, 2 centesimos, 1928
In 1928 Colonel Charles Lindbergh made his trailblazing goodwill flight to Latin America and the Caribbean, pioneering the air routes later used by Pan-Am and Panagra. The tour is remembered in the two stamps produced as a spontaneous gesture by Panama. The 2c. showed the *Spirit of St Louis* and the old tower of Panama City, while the 5c. showed the Ryan monoplane over the isthmus of Panama. The stamps were typographed by the Panama Canal Press, at Mount Hope in the Canal Zone, from zinc plates etched by the *Star and Herald* newspaper of Panama City. Until 1955 these were the only stamps to be printed locally, all the others being produced in Europe or the United States. The 2c. was additionally overprinted to signify 'Homage to Lindbergh'.

15. Panama, ½ centesimo, 1906
The first distinctive series of the republic was recess-printed by the Hamilton Bank Note Co. of New York. In true American tradition the series portrayed leading political figures of Panama, though the Spanish explorers Cordoba and Balboa were included on the lower denominations. The national coat of arms was displayed on the 2½c. denomination. From the technical standpoint, however, the ½c. denomination was the most ambitious, being printed in four-colour recess – almost sixty years before the United States succeeded in producing multicolour recess by the Giori presses.

16. Panama, 1 balboa, 1958
Since 1955 many Panamanian stamps have been lithographed by Estrella de Panama, the printing corporation which grew out of the modest efforts at producing the Lindbergh stamps of 1928. This stamp is one of a series of seven and a miniature sheet issued in September 1958 to mark the Brussels World Fair. The designs showed the pavilions of Argentina, Brazil, Great Britain, the Vatican, the United States and the host country – no doubt with an eye to sales of the stamps to collectors in these countries.

255

PLATE 96 BRITISH HONDURAS, PANAMA · PLATE 97 ARGENTINA

17. Panama, 3 centesimos, 1962

The rival company of Editora Panama began printing stamps in 1961 and since then has vied with Estrella de Panama in producing stamps by photogravure or lithography. This stamp, marking the inauguration of the Social Security Hospital, Panama City, is typical of the designs favoured by Editora Panama, with a thin, coloured frame and a white background to the vignette.

18. Panama, 0.05 balboas, 1967

The worldwide popularity of paintings on stamps induced the philatelic agency controlling the stamps of Panama to produce a considerable number of stamps with this theme. Between 1966 and 1968 alone Panama issued 11 such sets. In many cases the sets consisted of single themes – paintings of ships, music, religion, hunting and horses.

19. Panama, $\frac{1}{2}$ centavo, 1968

Many countries issued stamps for the Winter Olympic Games held at Grenoble in 1968 and although it can hardly be supposed that its sportsmen played an active part in these events Panama issued a set of six stamps with the games emblem in honour of the event. The world-wide popularity of stamps with a sporting theme, particularly those connected with the Olympic Games, ensured a ready market for these stamps.

20. Panama, 0.01 balboas, 1964

A set of six stamps appeared in 1964 with the theme of aquatic sports. They were designed by Professor Mosdossy and lithographed in multicolour by De La Rue of Bogotá.

21. Canal Zone, 2 centesimos, 1909

In recognition of American support in the secession from Colombia the republic of Panama leased a strip of territory across the isthmus to the United States. Between 1904 and 1928 various stamps of the United States or Panama were overprinted 'Canal Zone' for use in this territory. The stamp illustrated here comes from the series of 1906–08 and exhibits the error with the portrait of Cordoba upside down. This must have confused the printer responsible for the overprint since normally it should read upwards and not downwards!

22. Canal Zone, 3 cents, 1934

Since the release of a distinctive series in 1928 all stamps of the Canal Zone have been recess-printed at the Bureau of Engraving and Printing in Washington. The definitive series of 1928–40 portrayed prominent Americans concerned with the administration of the zone and the construction of the canal. The first commemorative stamp appeared in August 1934 to mark the 20th anniversary of the opening of the canal and portrayed General Goethals who was in charge of the project.

23. Canal Zone, 4 cents, 1958

This stamp was issued in November 1958 to mark the centenary of the birth of Theodore Roosevelt. This event was overlooked in the United States itself but was appropriate to the Canal Zone since it was he who promoted the Panama Canal project and backed the cause of Panamanian independence. The stamp depicts obverse and reverse of the Roosevelt Medal, awarded to those engaged on the project, with a map of the Canal Zone in the background.

24. Canal Zone, 6 cents, 1965

Since 1962 the majority of stamps issued by the Canal Zone have been designated for airmail purposes. A series from 6 to 80c. was released between July 1965 and March 1968 showing the great seal of the Canal Zone and a modern airliner. It was printed in various colours with the inscriptions and motifs in black.

25. Canal Zone, 8 cents, 1971

In recent years the Canal Zone has been one of the most conservative countries anywhere in the world with regard to new issues of stamps. No stamp for ordinary postage appeared between 1962 and 1968 but in the later year a small-format 6c. stamp featuring the Goethals' Memorial in Balboa was released for ordinary postage. A similar stamp appeared in 1971 when the letter rate was increased to 8c. This stamp depicted Fort San Lorenzo and was recess-printed in multicolour on the Giori presses with which the United States Bureau of Engraving and Printing is now equipped.

PLATE 97
Argentina

---

1. Argentine Confederation, 5 centavos, 1858

Carlos Riviere of Rosario lithographed a set of three stamps, in denominations of 5, 10 and 15c., for use by the districts under the control of the Argentine federal government. Separate issues were prepared for use in Cordoba but never used, while Buenos Aires issued its own stamps from 1858 to 1862, and Corrientes from 1856 till 1880 (see below).

2. Argentina Republic, 5 centavos, 1862

Argentina was united in 1862 when the separatist regime in Buenos Aires was suppressed by the federalists. Henceforward the stamps used throughout the country were inscribed 'Republica Argentina'. R. Lange of Buenos Aires lithographed 5, 10 and 15c. stamps with the emblem of the republic. They were issued in January 1862. Considerable variation occurs, both in shade and the degree of wear shown in the plates. They were also extensively reprinted and forged for sale to collectors.

3. 5 centavos, 1864

Like most Latin American countries Argentina preferred portraits of national heroes as the predominant motif of its stamps. Bernardino Rivadavia was portrayed on 5, 10, and 15c. stamps issued in April 1864. Different designs were used for each value, the plates being engraved on copper in London and shipped out to Buenos Aires, where the stamps were printed at the Casa de Correos. Various printings, both imperforate and perforated, were made between 1864 and 1872.

4. 1 centavo, 1873

The National Bank Note Co. of New York recess-printed a series for Argentina in March–October 1873 portraying national heroes – Balcarce (1c.), Moreno (4c.), Alvear (30c.), Posadas (60c.) and Saavedra (90c.) – augmenting the 5, 10 and 15c. stamps of 1867 (Rivadavia, Belgrano and San Martin) which were produced by the American Bank Note Co. These two companies competed for the Argentinian contracts throughout much of the nineteenth century.

5. $\frac{1}{4}$ centavo, 1890

The South American Bank Note Co. of Buenos Aires engraved and printed a series of twelve stamps, each with a different portrait, released between 1888 and December 1890. The stamps were inscribed 'Correos y Telegrafos' to denote dual purpose but this inscription was dropped from 1892 onward.

6. $\frac{1}{2}$ centavo, 1911

The practice of relying on a wide range of printers, both at home and overseas, ceased in 1911 when a new definitive series was typographed at the Mint, Buenos Aires. Henceforward the vast majority of

Argentinian stamps have been produced there. The early printings of these stamps had a sunburst watermark but in 1912 Germany supplied paper with a lozenge watermark. Shortage of this paper caused by the outbreak of World War I led to subsequent printings being made on paper of Italian or French manufacture.

7. $\frac{1}{2}$ centavo, 1910

Like many other Latin American countries Argentina celebrated the centenary of independence in 1910 by issuing a lengthy series of stamps. The South American Bank Note Company of Buenos Aires engraved and recess-printed a series from $\frac{1}{2}c.$ to 20p. depicting monuments and buildings connected with the history of the republic and portraying leaders of the struggle for independence against Spain. The stamps were printed in two colours and several denominations have been recorded with inverted centres.

8. 12 centavos, 1923

General José de San Martin was featured on the top values of various definitive sets from 1892 to 1897 and then appeared exclusively on definitive issues in 1908–09, 1916, 1917 and 1918–22. Following this precedent the series of 1923 likewise bore his portrait, using a solid background and a frame in a second colour on the peso values. The earliest printings of this series were lithographed but between 1924 and 1933 the series was typographed. The two versions differ in shade, impression, minor details and perforations.

9. $\frac{1}{2}$ centavo, 1935

For the definitive series of 1935–36 different portraits were used for each denomination ranging from General Belgrano ($\frac{1}{2}c.$) to M. Güemes (20c.). The first version of the 20c. showed his name incorrectly rendered as 'Juan Martin Güemes' but subsequently the 'Juan' was omitted. New portraits and values were added from time to time between 1939 and 1951, and between 1945 and 1947 the series was reprinted on unwatermarked paper.

10. 5 centavos, 1938

A set of four stamps was lithographed and released in September 1938 to mark the fiftieth anniversary of the death of President Sarmiento whose statesmanship unified and developed Argentina after a period of civil war and internal dissension. Like the definitives, the commemorative stamps of the period up to World War II were invariably lithographed.

11. 15 centavos, 1946

The first anniversary of the revolution which brought Juan Perón to power was celebrated in October 1946 by a set of five stamps with a design symbolizing Argentina and the populace. These stamps followed the example set in December 1930 when a previous revolution was marked by a long set symbolizing the spirit of the republic and the people in arms. Anniversaries of the October Revolution, the accession of Perón and the death of Eva Perón were suitably commemorated. The overthrow of the Peronists was, in turn, the subject of a stamp symbolizing liberation, issued in October 1955.

12. 15 centavos, 1947

This stamp was released in September 1947 to publicize the Week of the Wing, an aeronautics exhibition. The design, showing the legendary fall of Icarus, is curiously reminiscent of *fin de siècle* book illustration, rather than the modernistic designs favoured for aeronautic themes in the 1940s.

13. 5 centavos, 1951

The completion of the first Five Year Plan of the

PLATE 97 ARGENTINA · PLATE 98 BOLIVIA, BRAZIL

Perón regime was celebrated by a set of three ordinary and one airmail stamps, designed by Garrasi and produced in photogravure. Each stamp had a different motif, combining realism and symbolism as in this case with its vignette of Pegasus and a locomotive. Photogravure, used occasionally from 1941 onwards, became increasingly popular after 1950 though the traditional recess and lithographic processes continued to be used.

14. 1.45 pesos, 1954
Under the Peronist regime Argentina began taking a more active interest in the Antarctic and sub-Antarctic regions, laying claim to certain territories and entering a prolonged dispute with Chile and Britain. Postage stamps played an important part in this campaign from 1947 onward. This stamp, designed by A. Dell'Acqua and engraved by V. Cerichelli, was issued in January 1954 to mark the 50th anniversary of the Argentine post office in the South Orkneys. It alludes to the handing over of the scientific station established by Dr Bruce in the South Orkneys to an Argentine party by the Scottish National Expedition of 1903–04. Argentina has maintained a station there sporadically ever since.

15. 2 pesos, 1956
The 75th anniversary of the national mint was commemorated by this stamp in July 1956. It shows a coin and coin die for the coinage series of 1881, the first to be minted there. Stamp production began there thirty years later and has continued to this day.

16. 2 pesos, 1961
This stamp marked the tenth anniversary of the San Martin Antarctic Base established by Argentina on Tierra San Martin (Graham Land). Note the map of the Argentine sector inset – since World War II a common feature of many Argentine stamps, not necessarily connected with the Antarctic theme. Argentina maintains a number of post offices in Antarctica using pictorial handstamps as part of her propaganda campaign.

17. 4 pesos, 1964
Since 1956 Argentina has portrayed a number of foreign personages on her stamps and the emphasis has been on Americans from Benjamin Franklin (1956) and Abraham Lincoln (1960) to John F. Kennedy (1964). Other portraits have included William Harvey, the English surgeon (1959), Kemal Ataturk (1963) and Pope John XXIII (1964). Dr Sun Yat-sen of China appeared on a stamp of 1966, but since then Argentina has concentrated on Argentinians.

18. 8 pesos, 1965
During the period in which it was fashionable to pay tribute to non-Argentinos this stamp was issued to mark the 700th anniversary of the birth of the Italian poet, Dante Alighieri. Designed by H. Guimarans, it reproduces the statue of Dante in the Sante Croce Church in Florence. It was intended as a tribute to the Argentinian population of Italian descent.

19. 10 centavos, 1959
The definitive series issued by Argentina between 1959 and 1968 and still current is one of the most interesting issues of recent years. Four different processes were used – lithography, typography, photogravure and recess – and in many cases stamps were printed in more than one process at various times. The 2p. denomination, for example, was originally typographed, subsequently redrawn in a slightly smaller size, and then lithographed in the original dimensions.

20. 4 pesos, 1964
Antarctic subjects continue to be a fruitful source of stamp designs. In 1964 Argentina issued a series of three stamps showing the Argentine flag planted on the Falkland Islands as well as the territories claimed by Britain in the Antarctic. Though something of the heat has gone out of the dispute over these territories Argentina continues to give philatelic publicity to developments in the far south.

21. 2 centavos official stamp, 1901
A series of six stamps portraying the goddess of Liberty was recess-printed by the South American Bank Note Co. and issued in December 1901 for use on official correspondence. Since 1884 various definitive stamps had been overprinted 'Oficial' for this purpose. Definitive stamps overprinted 'Servicio Oficial' were reintroduced in 1938 and are used to this day.

22. Ministry of Agriculture, 1 centavo, 1936
In 1913 Argentina adopted definitive stamps overprinted with the initials of eight different departments, in place of the single series previously in use. Stamps were overprinted for the ministries of Agriculture (M.A), War (M.G.), Finance (M.H.), Interior (M.I.), Justice and Instruction (M.J.I.), Marine (M.M.), Public Works (M.O.P.) and Foreign Affairs and Religion (M.R.C.). These departmental overprints were discontinued in 1938.

23. Buenos Aires, 1 peso, 1859
The province of Buenos Aires had its own government until 1862. Adhesive stamps were introduced in May 1858 and are known to collectors as 'Barquitos', the Spanish for little ships, from the steamboat motif on them. In denominations of 2, 3, 4 and 5p., they were designed by Pablo Cataldi and typographed by the Banca y Casa de Moneda in Buenos Aires. A 4 reales stamp was created in October 1858 by cunningly altering the inscriptions on the plate of the 4 pesos, and the same practice was adopted to convert the 5p. to 1p. stamps. The erasures were only partially successful and gave rise to a number of errors and varieties in the inscriptions. A new design, featuring Liberty, was used for 1 and 2p. and 4r. stamps issued between 1859 and 1862.

24. Cordoba, 10 centavos, 1858
Larsch of Buenos Aires lithographed 5 and 10c. stamps for the province of Cordoba in October 1858 but they were never issued. They varied considerably in colour and the type and quality of paper on which they were printed. Similar stamps, in values from 15c. to 1p., are thought to be bogus.

25. Corrientes, 3 centavos, 1875
Corrientes adopted adhesive stamps in August 1856 and perpetrated an early example of philatelic plagiarism. The stamps, designed and engraved by Matthew Pipet, were closely modelled on the contemporary Ceres stamps of the French republic. Originally a stamp of 1 real was issued but subsequently other denominations were created by erasing the value tablet and printing the stamps in various colours according to the value desired. The stamps of Corrientes were suppressed by the federal authorities in September 1880.

PLATE 98
Bolivia and Brazil

1. Bolivia, 5 centavos, 1866
The Bolivian government gave the contract for its mail service to Justiniano Garcia in 1863, and he produced a series of stamps with the national coat of arms. The contract was revoked, however, before these stamps could be issued and it was not until 1866 that Bolivia again attempted to introduce a postal service. Estruch La Paz designed, engraved and printed at Cochabamba a 5c. stamp featuring a condor. Apart from the wide range of shades, this stamp was re-engraved four times, and extensively retouched six times, making innumerable combinations for the delectation of the specialist collector.

2. Bolivia, 1 centavo, 1887
The American Bank Note Co. recess-printed a series featuring the national coat of arms introduced in April 1868. In the first version nine stars were shown, but three years later the design was redrawn to include eleven. In the original version of this series the numerals were slanting, but between 1887 and 1890 they were upright. A lithographed version of the nine-star design was made by Litografia Boliviana in 1893.

3. Bolivia, 10 centavos, 1904
Around the turn of the century Bolivia placed contracts with a number of firms, including Bradbury Wilkinson and the South American Bank Note Co. of Buenos Aires. Between 1901 and 1904, however, the American Bank Note Co. recess-printed a series portraying prominent personalities. The 10c. had General Ballivian, hero of the battle of Ingavi in 1843. Portraits and coats of arms continued to provide the bulk of the thematic material for Bolivian definitive sets up to 1940.

4. Bolivia, 2 centavos, 1935
The dispute with Paraguay over the Chaco district found philatelic expression on both sides (see plate 102). Bolivian stamps with a map of the country incorporating the Chaco first appeared in 1928 in retaliation for the Paraguayan stamps of 1924–27. As the propaganda campaign intensified on both sides stamps played an increasingly important part, culminating in the Bolivian definitive series of 1935 which broke with tradition by using a common subject for all denominations. The stamps were recess-printed by the American Bank Note Co. and issued at the height of the disastrous Chaco War (1932–35), which decimated the populations of both countries.

5. Bolivia, 5 centavos, 1939
The second National Eucharistic Congress was commemorated by a lengthy series in August 1939. Ten stamps, from 5c. to 10 bolivianos, were lithographed by Lito-Unidas of La Paz. Churches and religious paintings formed the subjects of nine stamps; a symbolic chalice, in a triangular format, was used for the 5c. value.

6. Bolivia, 15 centavos, 1946.
Since World War II the majority of Bolivian stamps have been lithographed by local firms. Tallares Offset of La Paz lithographed a set of six stamps and two miniature sheets issued in September 1946 to mark the centenary of the National Anthem. They portrayed the composers Vincenti and Sanjines with the opening bars of the music.

7. Bolivia, 30 centavos, 1951
Bolivia has continued to issue lengthy commemorative sets, often including airmail as well as ordinary postage denominations. Since 1951, moreover,

257

PLATE 98 BOLIVIA, BRAZIL · PLATE 99 CHILE, ECUADOR

long sets with a single theme have also been produced. This stamp was one of a set of seven ordinary and seven airmail stamps (with attendant miniature sheets) issued in July 1951 with the theme of sport. They were recess-printed by the Security Banknote Co.

8. Bolivia, 1,000 bolivianos, 1962
Since 1955 most Bolivian stamps have been lithographed in multicolour by Papelera S.A. of La Paz. Two stamps were issued in March 1962 in honour of the fourth National Eucharistic Congress. The 1000b. showed a group of people symbolizing union in Christ, the 1400b. the Virgin of Cotoca. At the end of 1962 the currency, hit by inflation, was reformed, 1,000 old bolivianos being equal to one new boliviano or peso or escudo of 100 cents.

9. Bolivia, 1.20 pesos, 1963
This airmail stamp appeared in November 1963 to mark the Alliance for Progress inaugurated by President Kennedy. Most countries in Latin America as well as the United States issued stamps for this occasion.

10. Brazil, 30 reis, 1850
Brazil was the first country in the Western Hemisphere to adopt adhesive postage stamps on an official basis, 30, 60 and 90r. stamps being released in August 1843 in the large circular design known to collectors as the 'Bull's Eyes'. Smaller numeral stamps in the same denominations (the 'Inclinados', on account of the sloping figures) appeared in 1844–46 and then the design known as the 'Goat's Eyes' appeared in 1850. This series was recess-printed at the Mint, Rio de Janeiro in denominations from 10 to 600 reis. Perforations were added to the series in 1866.

11. Brazil, 100 reis, 1866
More than twenty years elapsed before any inscription appeared on Brazilian stamps. The American Bank Note Co. recess-printed a series in 1866 with various portraits of the Emperor Pedro II. The earliest printings were perforated, but those made in 1876–7 were rouletted. A similar series, with older portraits of the Emperor, was issued in 1878–79. The shades of these stamps vary enormously.

12. Brazil, 500 reis, 1895
Brazil ceased to be an empire in November 1889 and became the United States of Brazil with republican status. In the ensuing decade stamps appeared with the Southern Cross constellation, the Sugar-Loaf Mountain at Rio, and portraits of Mercury and Liberty. The Sugar-Loaf, Mercury and Liberty series remained in use until 1906 and during the twelve years when it was current it underwent numerous changes in perforation, paper, colour and die variations.

13. Brazil, 50 reis, 1913
The American Bank Note Co. recess-printed definitive and official stamps for Brazil between 1906 and 1918, portraying historic personages. Whereas different portraits were used for each denomination of the definitive issues of 1906 and 1913 the corresponding official sets used one portrait apiece. President Affonso Penna was shown on the series of November 1906, President Hermes de Fonseca on the stamps of 1913.

14. Brazil, 50 reis, 1929
Although one of the designs in the 1920 definitive series was captioned 'Aviacao' and showed an aircraft, no stamps were designed specifically for airmail until 1929, when a set of five was issued. Dr G. Barroso produced three designs for this series, two of which portrayed Santos Dumont and

his airship *Paz* (peace) at Paris in 1901. The third design depicted the monument to Bartholomeu de Gusmao, a Jesuit priest who invented a hot-air balloon which he demonstrated before the King of Portugal in August 1709. Gusmao is now regarded as the forerunner of lighter-than-air flight.

15. Brazil, 400 reis, 1932
A series of eleven stamps was issued at São Paulo in September 1932 on behalf of the revolutionary government, whose headquarters were in that city. The stamps, lithographed locally, bore the slogan 'Pro Constitucao' (for the Constitution) with soldiers, maps, flags and symbols of justice, law and order.

16. Brazil, 300 reis, 1936
B. Laucetta produced the design and M. d'Oglio engraved the die of this stamp, issued in March 1936 to mark the first Numismatic Congress in São Paulo. Many of the stamps produced in the 1930s were designed and engraved by these artists and recess-printed at the Mint, Rio de Janeiro. Laucetta experimented with unusual forms of lettering in the Art Deco tradition and native art forms provided inspiration for the framework decoration.

17. Brazil, 1 milreis, 1941
This stamp was recess-printed and issued in August 1941 to commemorate the quatercentenary of the Order of Jesuits. It portrays Father José de Anchieta, founder of São Paulo, and is based on Anchieta's profile on contemporary Brazilian coins.

18. Brazil, 2 centavos, 1949
The definitive series of 1941–46 followed the precedents of 1920–40 by using designs symbolizing various aspects of industry and agriculture. Four different watermarks were used. Although a new currency was adopted in 1942 stamps continued to be inscribed in reis until 1947. Between 1947 and 1949 the same designs were used for a series in value from 2c. to 50 cruzeiros (1 cruzeiro being equal to 1000 old reis).

19. Brazil, 2 centavos, 1954
Nineteenth century celebrities formed the subject of the definitive series released between July 1954 and April 1960. The stamps were rather crudely printed in photogravure at the Mint in Rio. A sheet watermark inscribed BRASIL CORREIO was used for earlier printings, but stamps issued after August 1961 were on paper with a recurring watermark inscribed CASA DA MOEDA DO BRASIL.

20. Brazil, 3.30 cruzeiros, 1957
The majority of Brazilian stamps since 1950 have consisted of singles, usually prepaying the internal postal rates. This stamp appeared in August 1957 to mark the centenary of the birth of Lord Baden-Powell, founder of the Boy Scout movement. A high proportion of Brazilian stamps have portrayed non-Brazilians. Among the other stamps issued in 1957, for example, were commemoratives portraying the American Allen Kardec (founder of Spiritualism) and the French philosopher Auguste Comte.

21. Brazil, 2.50 cruzeiros, 1958
This stamp marking the Brussels World Fair was recess-printed and released in April 1958. The design, with the Brazilian pavilion and the fair emblems, was bold in concept but the execution was poor. Since World War II Brazilian stamps have been produced in photogravure or recess, but the standard of production is consistently low.

22. Brazil, 100 cruzeiros, 1962
To mark the centenary of the adoption of the metric

system Brazil issued this stamp in June 1962. The motif was simple but most effective – the reproduction of a metric scale. Unfortunately, the 40mm. reproduced on the stamp measure barely 39 millimetres, and this inattention to technical detail mars an interesting design.

23. Brazil, 8 cruzeiros, 1963
The centenary of the birth of the scientist Dr Alvaro Alvim was celebrated in December 1963 by this stamp. The quality of the photogravure is poor, though one suspects that the original artwork was coarse to begin with. But in this case shoddy production has been combined with deplorable lettering which, in many examples, is almost indecipherable. This marked the nadir of Brazilian stamp design, but there has been some improvement in both design and printing in recent years.

PLATE 99
Chile and Ecuador

---

1. Chile, 10 centavos, 1853
Adhesive stamps were adopted by Chile in July 1853, the first series consisting of 5 and 10c. stamps recess-printed by Perkins Bacon of London. The plates were shipped out to Chile where Narciso Desmadryl printed stamps in 1854–55. Subsequently the plates were used by H. C. Gillett and then by the Post Office at Santiago. Each of these printings varies from the Perkins Bacon version in shade and quality of paper. Desmadryl also lithographed stamps in 1855 from transfers taken from the recess plates. Perkins Bacon made new printings in 1861–62 and these in turn were followed up by the Santiago Post Office in 1866. The stamps portrayed Christopher Columbus (Colon, in Spanish) and Perkins Bacon used the background which they afterwards employed for the first stamps of New Zealand (see plate 116).

2. Chile, 1 centavo, 1900
A curious feature of Chilean stamps is that they all portrayed Columbus up to 1903. During that period of half a century numerous variations on his portrait were produced. The American Bank Note Co. produced them from 1867 to 1901. This stamp is from the series recess-printed by Waterlow and Sons. Two versions of this series exist, with or without shading in the background above the portrait.

3. Chile, 3 centavos, 1904
A temporary shortage of low-value postage stamps in 1904 was met by surcharging and overprinting telegraph stamps. The basic stamps were recess-printed by Bradbury Wilkinson and displayed the national coat of arms. Similar telegraph stamps by Waterlows or the American Bank Note Co. were overprinted in this way.

4. Chile, 50 centavos, 1911
The American Bank Note Co. produced an attractive series for Chile in 1911, portraying famous explorers, patriots and statesmen in denominations from 1c. to 10 pesos. In 1912–13 several new values were added to the series and the colour and detail of some existing denominations were changed. Up to 1915 the stamps were entirely recess-printed but in that year 1 and 2c. stamps were typographed in similar designs. Between 1916 and 1925 versions of the series were produced at the Chilean Mint in Santiago, in which the whole stamp was typographed, the head offset and the frame typographed, or the head recess-printed and the frame lithographed. Various denominations were subse-

PLATE 99 CHILE, ECUADOR

quently overprinted between 1928 and 1933 for airmail duty.

5. Chile, 25 centavos, 1930
The centenary of the first export of nitrate from Chile was marked by a set of six stamps issued in July 1930. Lithographed at the mint, they showed agricultural scenes, alluding to the use of nitrates as fertilizers. The slogan 'Salitre significa Prosperidad' (Nitrate means prosperity) indicates the importance of this industry to the Chilean economy.

6. Chile, 20 centavos, 1938
Industries and landscapes were chosen as the themes of the definitive series issued between 1938 and 1946. The centavo denominations were lithographed in a small upright format while the peso denominations were recess-printed in a large horizontal format. The stamps were issued on paper with a multiple star and shield watermark, but later printings, from 1942 onward, were on unwatermarked paper. The stamps illustrated aspects of agriculture, nitrates, petroleum, mineral spas and coastal fishing.

7. Chile, 15 centavos, 1910
Chile's first commemorative series, recording the centenary of the war of independence, was recess-printed in 1910 by the American Bank Note Co. The stamps were produced with black vignettes and coloured frames, and depicted scenes and personalities from the war. This stamp reproduces a bas-relief of the first sortie by the liberating forces.

8. Chile, 60 centavos, 1950
Stamps for use on mail carried by the national airlines were introduced by Chile in 1931 and bore the name of the airline across the foot. A new series, designed by E. Matthey and lithographed at the Santiago Mint, was introduced between 1941 and 1950. Similar stamps, with a new imprint, appeared between 1950 and 1955 in various designs. The original series was on watermarked paper, as were also the first printings of the 1950–55 series, but between 1951 and 1955 unwatermarked paper was used for several denominations.

9. Chile, 3 pesos, 1949
Two stamps were issued in March 1949 to commemorate the Chilean stateman Vicuna Mackenna, the 60c. for ordinary postage and the 3p. for airmail. Proceeds from philatelic sales of these stamps went towards the establishment of a museum in honour of Mackenna. The majority of Chilean commemorative issues from this time onward have consisted of one or two denominations, for ordinary or airmail postage.

10. Chile, 20 pesos, 1958
The centenary of the German school in Valdivia was marked by two stamps – a 40p. for ordinary postage with a view of the city and a 20p. airmail stamp portraying C. Anwandter, the founder of the school. The 40p. stamp also marked the philatelic exhibition held in Valdivia at that time.

11. Chile, 20 centesimos, 1964
The 150th anniversary of Chilean independence was celebrated in 1960 by two sets of stamps. The first consisted of two stamps issued in June–August 1960 showing the national coat of arms. The second series consisting of both ordinary and airmail stamps portraying Chilean patriots was released gradually between 1960 and 1965. The 20c., released in 1964, portrayed J. A. Eyzaguirre and J. M. Infante.

12. Chile, 40 pesos, 1959
The 50th anniversary of the death of the historian Don Diego Barros Arana was marked in August

1959 by 40 and 100p. stamps. In accordance with normal Chilean practice one stamp was designated for ordinary postage, the other for airmail.

13. Juan Fernandez, 5 centavos, 1910
Juan Fernandez and Easter Island in the South Pacific form part of Chile and stamps overprinted for use in the former island were issued in 1910. The 12c. and 1p. denominations of the Chilean definitive series of 1905 were overprinted 'Islas de Juan Fernandez' and surcharged for use as 5, 10 or 20c. values. Subsequently the overprinted stamps were authorized for use throughout Chile and ordinary Chilean stamps have been used in Juan Fernandez ever since. The island was the scene of the enforced residence of Alexander Selkirk, on whom Defoe based his character Robinson Crusoe. Chile issued a 30c. stamp in 1965 with Crusoe on Juan Fernandez.

14. Tierra del Fuego, 10 centavos, 1891
A mining company run by Julius Popper organized a mail service from Tierra del Fuego to Chile and Argentina and issued this 10c. stamp in 1891 to defray the cost of postage. The stamp, with the crossed hammer and pick emblem of the Popper company, was designed by R. Soucup and lithographed by Kidd & Co. of Buenos Aires.

15. Ecuador, ½ real, 1872
Adhesive stamps were adopted by Ecuador in 1865; they were designed and typographed by Emilio Rivadeneira of Quito with the national coat of arms set in a frame reminiscent of the contemporary French issues. A lithographed version of this design was used for a series issued in 1872, in denominations from ½r. to 1p. Two versions of the ½r. denomination are recorded, with or without a full stop after 'Medio'.

16. Ecuador, 5 centavos, 1881
A new currency based on the sucre of 100 centavos, was adopted in 1881, necessitating a new definitive series. The stamps were recess-printed by the American Bank Note Co. in denominations from 1 to 50c., each stamp with the national coat of arms in a different frame. Variations of this theme continued to appear up to 1892, when the contracts passed to the Hamilton Bank Note Co.

17. Ecuador, 5 sucres, 1894
Ecuador was more fortunate than many other Latin American countries in that the notorious Seebeck issues were current only there between 1892 and 1897 and had to compete with stamps produced elsewhere in the same period. The series of 1892 portrayed the president General Flores, while those dated 1894 and 1895 portrayed his successor, President Rocafuerte, in values from 1c. to 5s. In 1896 a series lithographed in Hamburg was issued to mark the success of the Liberal Party at the recent general elections. The Seebeck period came to an end in 1897, when the authorities cancelled the contract held by Henry N. Etheridge acting on behalf of Seebeck and the Hamilton Bank Note Co.

18. Ecuador, 1 sucre, 1908
The opening of the railway from Guayaquil to Quito was celebrated in June 1908 by a series recess-printed by Waterlow and Sons. The lower denominations, in triangular designs, portrayed the men who backed the project, while the rectangular 1s. top value depicted Mount Chimborazo.

19. Ecuador, 10 centavos, 1911
Waterlow and Sons also recess-printed the definitive series introduced between 1911 and 1913, portraying various presidents of the republic. New designs, colours and denominations were released in 1915–

16, while the colours were again changed between 1925 and 1928. This series continued in use until 1934. Various provisional surcharges and commemorative overprints were issued in that relatively long period.

20. Ecuador, 10 centavos, 1938
Ecuador was one of the many countries to issue stamps in 1937 to mark the 150th anniversary of the United States constitution, reflecting the zenith of American prestige in the continent at that time. The stamps were recess-printed by the American Bank Note Co., with variously coloured frames and the flags shown in yellow, blue and red. Two designs were used for the ordinary and airmail series respectively and included the figure of Liberty, and a portrait of George Washington with the American eagle.

21. Ecuador, 2 centavos, 1939
The popularity of the large-sized Constitution commemoratives of 1937 undoubtedly inspired Ecuador to repeat the formula two years later. In 1939 two sets, each of six ordinary and seven airmail stamps, were issued to mark the San Francisco International Exhibition and the New York World's Fair. The postage series of the first set showed the Dolores Mission in San Francisco, while the comparable issues in the second series depicted the trylon and perisphere emblem of the New York Fair. Both sets of airmail stamps featured the snow-clad summit of Mount Chimborazo, with the Golden Gate Bridge and the Empire State Building in the respective foregrounds. Both sets were recess-printed by De La Rue.

22. Ecuador, 90 centavos, 1955
De La Rue recess-printed two stamps to mark the 50th anniversary of the Rotary movement. They showed the Rotunda at Guayaquil and the Espejo Hospital at Quito, flanked by flags representing the worldwide nature of the movement. The great majority of Ecuadorean stamps issued in recent years have been produced by De La Rue of London, or their subsidiary company in Bogotá, Colombia.

23. Ecuador, 2 sucres, 1958
Richard Nixon, then vice-president of the United States under Dwight Eisenhower, made a goodwill tour of Latin America in 1958. The occasion is remembered in the 2s. stamp issued by Ecuador in May that year. It was lithographed in multicolour by the Austrian State Printing works and portrayed Nixon and the flags of Ecuador and the United States. No living American may appear on the stamps of the United States. This stamp was Nixon's philatelic début but since then he has appeared on relatively few stamps, when compared with his predecessors in the White House.

24. Ecuador, 2 sucres, 1962
Ecuador, like Brazil, has been only too ready to portray on stamps visiting heads of state or their representatives. In 1962 the Duke of Edinburgh visited Latin America and stamps bearing his portrait were subsequently released by Ecuador and Paraguay. The two stamps of Ecuador showed him with President Arosemena and the national coats of arms of Ecuador and the United Kingdom. They were designed by Professor von Mosdossy and lithographed in multicolour by De La Rue of Bogotá.

25. Galapagos Islands, 2 sucres, 1959
The Galapagos archipelago in the South Pacific is administered by Ecuador and uses ordinary Ecuadorean stamps. In 1957, however, a distinctive pictorial series was introduced with views of the islands and their wildlife. The stamps, in denominations of 20c. to 4.20s., were printed in photogravure

PLATE 99 CHILE, ECUADOR · PLATE 100 COLOMBIA

by the Austrian state printing works. Subsequently several commemorative issues of Ecuador were produced with a suitable inscription, but the only one actually issued was the United Nations triangular stamp of 1959. The Galapagos have now reverted to the use of ordinary Ecuadorean stamps.

PLATE 100
Colombia

1. Granada Confederation, 2½ centavos, 1859
The turbulent political state of Colombia in the mid-nineteenth century is reflected in the frequency with which the country changed its name and status. The first adhesive stamps were introduced in August 1859 and bore the inscription 'Confed(eracion) Granadina' (Granada Confederation). The stamps, in denominations from 2½c. to 1p., were lithographed by Ayalo and Medrano of Bogotá. A similar series, but inscribed 'Estados Unidos de Nueva Granada' (United States of New Granada), appeared in 1861.

2. United States of Colombia, 2½ centavos, 1865
The country changed its name for the third time in two years and stamps appeared in 1862 with the inscription 'E.U. de Colombia' (United States of Colombia). This form was retained for a comparatively long time, until 1886. A new series which appeared in 1865 and included one of the world's earliest triangular stamps, the 2½c., with its triple coat of arms motif, so that no matter which way up the stamp was viewed one of the arms would be more or less correct. Colombia's penchant for unusual shapes resulted in a 2½c. stamp of 1869 shaped like a scalene triangle – each of the three sides being of different lengths – whereas the stamp of 1865 was an isosceles triangle, with sides of the same length.

3. United States of Colombia, 2 centavos, 1870
With the exception of a few stamps issued in 1876–81 showing the head of Liberty, all of the stamps issued by the United States of Colombia bore the federal coat of arms. Indeed this preoccupation with the coat of arms continued up to the 1920s, though other motifs made a fleeting appearance. The monotony could only be relieved by varying the style of the lettering and framework, or resorting to gimmickry such as this 2c. stamp, in which the numeral of value assumes the dominant role and the coat of arms is relegated to a subsidiary position.

4. Republic of Colombia, 1 centavo, 1892
Colombia changed its name yet again in 1886, when a centralist constitution was adopted. Hitherto the component states had enjoyed wide powers of autonomy, but they were then demoted to the status of departments. From 1896 until 1926 the vast majority of stamps were inscribed 'Republica de Colombia', but a shorter form has been used in more recent years. Variously tinted papers were used for all the definitive stamps of the republic between 1886 and 1900.

5. Colombia, 5 centavos, 1902
Colombia was noted for the large number of stamps performing different duties. Three stamps were issued in 1865 inscribed 'Sobreporte' and designed for the prepayment of additional external postage. Subsequently stamps inscribed A(notacion) or R(ejistro) were provided for registered mail (AR = acknowledgment of receipt), or 'Retardo' (too late) for use on mail posted after the normal time of collection. These stamps prepaid the special fee which enabled late mail to catch up with the next normal delivery. Stamps for this purpose were issued between 1886 and 1914.

6. Colombia, 4 centavos, 1926
Perkins Bacon recess-printed a definitive series in 1917, with portraits of famous people on the low values, scenery and landmarks on the middle values and the national coat of arms on the top value. Between 1923 and 1926 new denominations and colours were introduced but in most cases the dies were also redrawn and differed in many respects from those of the 1917 series. These stamps were originally perforated 13½ but the 5 and 10p. denominations changed to gauge 11 in 1929.

7. Colombia, 20 centavos, 1948
To raise money for the reconstruction of the head post office in Bogotá a series of stamps was produced in 1939 for compulsory use on correspondence at certain times of year. It was lithographed at the National Printing Works in Bogotá and bore an artist's impression of the proposed building. Similar stamps were recess-printed by De La Rue in 1940 and from then until 1952 stamps in ever-decreasing dimensions appeared at regular intervals for this purpose. On several occasions these tax stamps have been authorized for ordinary postage, during shortages of postage stamps. Such a shortage arose in 1948, causing the release of these stamps overprinted 'Correos' (posts). Savings bank stamps were also overprinted in a similar fashion about the same time.

8. Colombia, 50 centavos, 1954
De La Rue recess-printed a lengthy airmail series featuring scenery and landmarks in denominations from 5c. to 10p. It was issued in January 1954, but 25c. stamps illustrating the Sanctuary of the Rocks at Narino were added to the series in 1958.

9. Colombia, 5 centavos, 1954
Stamps overprinted or inscribed 'Extra-Rapido' were used to prepay the additional cost of inland mail carried by the Avianca airline between 1953 and 1964. The use of such stamps for this purpose ceased in 1964 but after that date these stamps could be used for ordinary postal fees. Stamps depicting the Virgin of Chiquinquirá and St Andrew were released in December 1954. They were produced by De La Rue using a recess frame and a vignette lithographed in multicolour.

10. Colombia, 15 centavos, 1954
The tercentenary of the Senior College of Our Lady of the Rosary, Bogotá, was belatedly marked by four ordinary, four airmail stamps and two miniature sheets a year after the anniversary had passed. Recess-printed by De La Rue the stamps had views of the College and a portrait of Friar Cristobal de Torres, its founder. The 5c. (ordinary) and 15c. (airmail) reproduced the tapestry presented to the College by Queen Margaret of Austria.

11. Colombia, 1 centavo, 1957
The centenary of the foundation of the Colombian Order of St Vincent de Paul was commemorated in October 1957 by 1c. (ordinary) and 5c. (airmail) stamps showing the Saint and a group of children. They were printed in photogravure by the Austrian State Printing Works in Vienna, whose imprint appears in Spanish. Professor Imre von Mosdossy, who designed the stamps, has been responsible for the majority of Colombian stamp designs from 1956 to the present day.

12. Colombia, 5 centavos, 1960
Three ordinary and nine airmail stamps were issued in July 1960 to celebrate the 150th anniversary of independence. Note the imprint of the Austrian State Printing Works, rendered in German. Coins, statuary, symbolism and portraits of early nineteenth century patriots formed the subjects of this series. A miniature sheet was also produced, comprising four stamps inscribed 'Extra Rapido', similar to ordinary or airmail stamps but printed in new colours.

13. Colombia, 80 centavos, 1867
Two stamps were issued in September 1967 to mark the sixth Colombian Surgeons Congress and the centenary of the National University. The 80c. (ordinary postage) bore the university's coat of arms while the 80c. (airmail) reproduced Grau's painting 'Caesarian Operation, 1844'. Both stamps were lithographed in multicolour by De La Rue, whose subsidiary company in Bogotá has produced the stamps for Colombia and many other Latin American countries since 1961.

14. Colombia, 2 pesos, 1970
The majority of commemorative stamps released by Colombia in recent years have consisted of single stamps, many of which have had a strong religious flavour. This 2p. stamp was issued in 1970 to celebrate the elevation of St Teresa to Doctor of the Church. In multicolour photogravure by De La Rue of Bogotá it reproduced the painting by B. de Figueroa of St Teresa, the shepherdess, St Joseph and the child Jesus.

15. Colombia, 1.20 pesos, 1971
The twentieth anniversary of Colombia's participation in the Korean War was celebrated by this stamp, lithographed in multicolour by De La Rue. It shows the frigate *Almirante Padilla* and a Colombian infantryman. Although this seems a curious event to commemorate philatelically it is interesting to note that similar stamps have also been produced by countries as far apart as Brazil and Ethiopia, though none of the major belligerents (other than Korea itself) has issued stamps for this purpose.

16. Antioquia, 20 centavos, 1899
Adhesive stamps were adopted by Antioquia in 1868 and thenceforward the majority of issues bore the head of Liberty or the national coat of arms. General Cordova appeared on all the stamps of a series lithographed in 1899, from ½c. to 2p. Various portraits were also shown on the issues of 1902–04. Antioquia ceased to issue its own stamps in 1904, since when only Colombian stamps have been used.

17. Antioquia, 2½ centavos, 1899
Like Colombia itself, Antioquia had a predilection for distinctive stamps for specific duties. Registration stamps were issued between 1896 and 1902, a space being provided for the manuscript insertion of the serial number of the registered letter.

18. Antioquia, 1 centavo, 1901
Typeset stamps were issued by Antioquia on two occasions. In 1888 2½ and 5v. stamps were produced at Medellin during a shortage of the lithographed series then current. A shortage of 1c. stamps in 1901–02 resulted in a similar expedient. The stamps were typeset in blocks of four, each stamp in the blcok differing in some detail from its neighbours. The stamps may be found in carmine, stone, blue, or red.

19. Bolivar, 20 centavos, 1880
The state of Bolivar issued its own stamps between 1863 and 1904, the first issue having the distinction of being the smallest stamps ever issued. Like the other states Bolivar chose the national coat of arms, but loyalty to the statesman whose name it bore resulted in the introduction of a series portraying him. From 1880 till 1904 the majority of stamps showed various portraits of Simon Bolivar.

PLATE 100 COLOMBIA · PLATE 101 THE GUIANAS

Other national figures did not appear until 1903, when a series was lithographed by Francisco Valiente portraying Fernandez Madrid, Garcia de Toledo and other patriots.

20. Boyaca, 5 centavos, 1899
Boyaca did not introduce its own stamps until 1899, when a 5c. stamp portraying Mendoza Perez was issued. In 1903 a series lithographed by R. Ronderos of Bogotá appeared in a medley of designs bearing the coat of arms, portraits of national figures and the monument to the battle of Boyaca.

21. Cauca, 20 centavos, 1903
Apart from a solitary 5c. stamp handstruck in black in 1879 for use in the county of Choco, the department of Cauca did not issue stamps of its own until 1903, when typeset stamps on coloured paper did duty as 10 or 20c. values. These and a similar issue in the Tumaco district were suppressed at the end of the civil war of 1903. Typeset stamps alleged to have been issued in Barbacoas and Cali are now regarded as unauthorized local issues.

22. Cundinamarca, 10 centavos, 1885
The state of Cundinamarca issued its own stamps between 1870 and 1904, all, with the exception of typographed provisionals in 1883, had the national coat of arms. The majority of issues from 1877 to 1885 bore the inscription 'Estado Soberano' (sovereign state). Stamps of this series were replaced in 1904 by a series inscribed 'Departamento de Cundinamarca', reflecting the state's demotion and ordinary Colombian stamps superseded the distinctive series later that year.

23. Panama, 2 centavos, 1892
Stamps were issued by Panama under the authority of the Colombian government between 1878 and 1903, when it seceded and became an independent republic. The earliest stamps were inscribed 'Panama', with a view of the isthmus. Stamps issued from 1887 onward did not bear the state's name but a map of the isthmus. The American Bank Note Co. recess-printed the series of 1892–96, which, suitably overprinted, was used as the first series of the Panamanian Republic in 1903.

24. Santander, 1 centavo, 1890
Stamps were issued by Santander between 1884 and 1904. In that twenty-year period some thirty stamps were produced, all of them with the national coat of arms. This stamp was one of three lithographed locally and introduced in 1890. The 1c. has been recorded partially imperforate.

25. Tolima, 1 peso, 1886
Tolima issued its own stamps between 1870 and 1904 and, with the exception of the typeset series of 1870, all showed the national coat of arms. The series of 1886, in denominations from 5c. to 1p., exists in several versions. The first version of the design showed the condor with long wings, but a later version had the bird's wings clipped. The long-winged version may be divided into two sets, on white paper with clear impressions or on tinted paper with blurred impressions. Further variety is imparted by the presence or absence of perforation.

PLATE 101
The Guianas

1. British Guiana, 4 cents, 1860
British Guiana adopted stamps in 1850, the first issue being the crudely typeset 'cotton-reels' printed by the *Royal Gazette* in Georgetown. Stamps lithographed by Waterlow and Sons (the first produced by this company) appeared two years later, with the sailing ship emblem of the colony. A more substantial design was adopted by Waterlows in 1853 and this, with variations, remained in use till 1875. The date of each series was denoted by digits in the four corners of the frame. The ship emblem appeared on all definitive stamps of British Guiana up to 1934, though the designs from 1913 onward also incorporated a profile of King George V.

2. British Guiana, 10 cents, 1898
A set of five stamps dated 1897 appeared in 1898, belatedly commemorating the Diamond Jubilee of Queen Victoria. Apart from the date there was no indication in the designs that these stamps were intended to pay honour to the queen. On the other hand the use of two-colour recess by De La Rue to depict salient features in the scenery of British Guiana seems to indicate a desire to promote the country, along the same lines as North Borneo, New Zealand and Newfoundland, which all issued pictorial stamps around this time. The 5, 10 and 15c. values were surcharged for use as 2c. stamps the following year.

3. British Guiana, 1 dollar, 1931
The centenary of the union of Berbice, Essequibo and Demerara to form British Guiana was celebrated in July 1931 by a set of five stamps. Waterlow and Sons recess-printed the series, in denominations from 1c. to $1, featuring scenery and occupations, with a portrait of King George V inset. The same designs were later adapted for the pictorial definitive series of 1934, the commemorative dates being omitted. With the exception of the 1c. and 6c. denominations, which were inscribed with the names of the three counties, the stamps made no direct reference to the event they commemorated. The dies were engraved by J. A. C. Harrison.

4. British Guiana, 1 dollar, 1938
The pictorial series of 1938 repeated the designs of the 1934 issue, substituting the portrait of King George VI. Five designs of the 1934 series did not bear a royal portrait and were thus retained unaltered until 1954. The perforations of this series were changed on several occasions between 1944 and 1951.

5. British Guiana, 12 cents, 1954
The designs which, in one form or another, had served for commemorative or definitive purposes from 1931 onward, were superseded in December 1954 by a set of fifteen, from 1c. to $5, portraying Queen Elizabeth. This series was recess-printed by Waterlow and Sons until 1961, when De La Rue took over the contract. Unlike the majority of the other Waterlow/De La Rue printings of this period the Guianese stamps can be differentiated by their perforations. The Waterlow stamps have a single wide-toothed perforation on each side at the top, whereas in the De La Rue printings, the wide-toothed perforation is at the bottom. Between 1963 and 1965 many denominations were reissued on Block CA instead of the original Script CA paper.

6. British Guiana, 5 cents, 1961
British Guiana received self-governing status in October 1961 and to mark the event a set of three

stamps was issued, with the theme of solidarity among the four races of Guiana. Compare this design with that used in July of the same year by Singapore, another Commonwealth multi-national state. The Guianese set was printed by Harrison while the Singapore set was produced by Enschedé, though possibly both issues were the work of the same designer employed by the Crown Agents.

7. Guyana, 25 cents, 1967
British Guiana attained independence in May 1966 and assumed the new name of Guyana. The definitive series was accordingly overprinted to denote the change in status. One of the first commemorative issues of Guyana was a pair issued in February 1967. Designed by Victor Whiteley and lithographed by De La Rue, it reproduced a facsimile of the 'World's rarest stamp', the celebrated One Cent Black on Magenta issued in 1856. Actually this stamp is no rarer than any other unique item, of which there are numerous examples recorded in philately. But the mystery surrounding its issue, and the illustrious pedigree of millionaire owners have combined to invest this stamp with an aura of its own. It was purchased by Frederick Small in 1940 for about $40,000 and sold by him in 1970 for $280,000.

8. Guyana, 5 cents, 1969
Guyana began issuing Christmas stamps in 1967, with a set of four depicting Millie the bilingual parrot, whose swearing in French and English caused a furore at the Montreal Expo 67, where she was on display. Secular designs, showing modern telecommunications, were used for the Christmas stamps of 1968.

9. Guyana, 6 cents, 1969
Unissued stamps designed by Victor Whiteley or John Waddington were overprinted and released as Christmas stamps in November 1969. The reason for this makeshift has never been satisfactorily explained. Two of these stamps depicted the Mother Sally dance troupe, the other two the City Hall in Georgetown. The 25c. denomination has been recorded with the overprint omitted.

10. Guyana, 5 cents, 1970
Guyana became a Co-operative Republic in February 1970 and a set of four stamps was issued to mark the occasion. L. D. Curtis produced four designs with a map of the country and a portrait of the President, Forbes Burnham (5c.), rural self help (6c.), the University of Guyana (15c.) and Guyana House (25c.) They were lithographed by De La Rue in multicolour. The map of the country on the 5c. stamp is significant in view of the agitation by neighbouring Venezuela, which has laid claim to Guyanese territory since independence was attained in 1966.

11. French Guiana, 20 centimes, 1904
French Guiana used the French colonial general series until 1886 when local surcharges were introduced and the stamps overprinted 'Guy. Franc'. The 'Tablet' keyplate series, suitably inscribed, was issued in 1892 and twelve years later a distinctive pictorial series was adopted. The series was designed by Paul Merwart and engraved by J. Puyplat. Three designs were used; the lowest denominations featured an anteater, the middle values a goldwasher and the top values a coconut plantation. Provisional surcharges, new colours and denominations were issued between 1922 and 1928.

12. French Guiana, 40 centimes, 1945
French Guiana did not go over to the Gaullist Free French until the end of World War II, after the liberation of France, and thus continued to use its prewar definitive series until 1945. In that year,

PLATE 101 THE GUIANAS · PLATE 102 PARAGUAY, PERU

however, a series lithographed by De La Rue was released. The stamps, in denominations from 10*c*. to 20*f*., depicted the arms of French Guiana.

13. French Guiana, 10 centimes, 1947
The territory became a French overseas department in 1946 and ordinary French stamps were introduced two years later. In June 1947, however, French Guiana issued its last distinctive series. It was recess-printed in various pictorial designs with wildlife and native scenes.

14. Inini, 4 centimes, 1932
The Inini district of French Guiana was under a separate colonial administration from 1932 to 1946 when it joined the French overseas department of Guiana. During this period the 1929 definitive series of French Guiana was overprinted 'Territoire de l'Inini'. Between 1937 and 1939 Inini also issued several French colonial omnibus stamps suitably inscribed.

15. Surinam, 2½ cents, 1892
Surinam, or Dutch Guiana, began issuing stamps in 1873 and used the various Dutch colonial omnibus designs from then until the 1950s. The first distinctive stamp, however, appeared in August 1892 during a temporary shortage of 2½*c*. stamps. Several denominations of the definitive series were surcharged with this value, and then a locally designed stamp, typeset by H. B. Heijde of Paramaribo, was released. It was typographed in black on a background consisting of the word 'Frankeerzegel' (postage stamp) repeated continuously in yellow. Similar typeset stamps were issued in 1912.

16. Surinam, 1½ cents, 1936
The definitive series issued in March 1936 consisted of two designs. A. van der Vossen designed the low values from ½ to 7½*c*. depicting the ship *Johannes van Walbeeck*. The higher denominations bore a portrait of Queen Wilhelmina. The ship stamps were printed in offset lithography but in 1941, when further stocks were unobtainable from the Netherlands, 1 and 2*c*. denominations were slightly redrawn and typographed by Bradbury Wilkinson. Earlier in the same year 2½ and 7½*c* stamps were lithographed by G. Kolff and Company of Batavia. The Kolff versions may be recognized by their different gauge of perforation.

17. Surinam, 1 cent, 1945
After the Netherlands had been occupied by the Nazis in 1940 Surinam got its stamps from Kolff of Batavia. After the Japanese occupation of the Dutch East Indies the stamps were printed by Bradbury Wilkinson and the American Bank Note Co. This stamp was one of a series recess-printed by the latter company and issued in 1945. The stamps showed scenery and industries of Surinam, with a profile of Queen Wilhelmina inset. Vertical designs portraying the queen alone were used for the higher denominations. The Dutch keyplate designs were reintroduced in 1948.

18. Surinam, 20 cents, 1961
For a brief period in the early 1960s Surinam was advised by an American philatelic agency, but wisely cancelled the agreement and returned to the previous arrangement of having stamps produced and handled in the Netherlands. To the brief agency period belongs the pair of stamps publicizing space achievements. The 15*c*. stamp depicted Major Gagarin in a space capsule, the 20*c*. Commander Alan Shepard, the first American astronaut to make a sub-orbital flight. Issued in July, these stamps were among the earliest with this theme.

19. Surinam, 10 + 5 cents, 1969
Surinam began issuing special stamps for Easter

greetings in 1968, the first series consisting of five semi-postal stamps symbolizing Ash Wednesday, Palm Sunday, Maundy Thursday and other phases of the Easter celebration. This stamp was one of five, in a uniform design, used for Easter greetings in 1969. It shows the Western Hemisphere illuminated by a full moon.

20. Surinam, 25 + 12 cents, 1970
Since 1931 Surinam has issued semi-postal stamps each year in aid of Child Welfare. The earlier sets depicted children but in more recent years other themes have been explored. The series of five stamps issued in 1970 bore portraits of Beethoven at various stages of his career and coincided with the bicentenary of his birth.

21. Surinam, 30 cents, 1971
The tercentenary of the publication of the first map of Surinam was marked, in October 1971, by this stamp, designed and printed in offset-lithography by Enschedé. It reproduces the map published by Willem Mogge and demonstrates the capabilities of modern offset processes in reducing fine detail to the confines of a postage stamp. The use of brown on a plain yellow background, bled into the perforations, contrasts strangely with the multicolour effects usually found on Surinam's stamps.

22. Surinam, 30 cents, 1972
The 40th anniversary of the Surinam Waterworks Board was celebrated by two stamps issued in February 1972. Featuring a drop of water and a gushing tap, they were designed by Jules Chin Foeng of Paramaribo and printed in two-colour offset lithography by Enschedé.

23. Surinam, 65 cents, 1972
Since 1961 Surinam has issued lengthy sets with a common theme for definitive purposes. These sets have shown prominent buildings (1961), industrial installations (1965) and birds (1966). In 1972 a new airmail series appropriately featured butterflies of South America in multicolour.

PLATE 102

Paraguay and Peru

1. Paraguay, 2 reales, 1870
Paraguay adopted adhesive stamps in August 1870, when a set of three stamps, in denominations of 1, 2 and 3*r*., was released. They were lithographed by R. Lange of Buenos Aires, with the national emblem, a lion holding a pole and cap of liberty. A different frame was used for each denomination. All three stamps were surcharged for use as 5*c*. stamps in 1875, various numerals being overprinted locally. Genuine examples of these surcharges are very scarce, the majority now in circulation being reprints or forgeries.

2. Paraguay, 20 pesos, 1905
The South American Bank Note Co. of Buenos Aires recess-printed a series from 1*c*. to 20*p*. issued between 1905 and 1910. Each denomination is known in several colours, the top value being recorded with a black vignette and frames in olive-green, yellow or purple. The stamp illustrated here is something of a mystery. The vignette is identical with the series of 1905 but the frame is slightly different. Moreover the stamp is typographed instead of recess-printed and the colour is wrong. The inscription 'Gobierno Constitucional' (constitutional government) is a clue, indicating that it was one of a series prepared by the constitutionalist rebels during the civil war of 1904 but never issued.

3. Paraguay, 5 centavos, 1908
Like many other Latin American countries Paraguay resorted on many occasions to the time-honoured expedient of surcharging and revalidating obsolete stamps. This often happened when the print order far exceeded the actual postal demand and obsolete denominations were subsequently surcharged to produce values covering specific requirements. The basic stamp was one of a series issued in 1905, subsequently revalued as a 5*c*. denomination in July 1908.

4. Paraguay, 2 centavos, 1911
The years immediately before World War I witnessed a spate of handsome commemoratives throughout Latin America as the various countries celebrated the centenary of their rebellion against Spanish rule. Paraguay was content with a single design, depicting Liberty, for the series of seven stamps, recess-printed by the South American Bank Note Co. in 1911.

5. Paraguay, 1.50 pesos, 1927
The 1920s were dominated by the dispute between Bolivia and Paraguay over the ownership of the Chaco territory. Both countries resorted to a propaganda campaign, in which stamps promoted each side of the case. Three stamps of 1924 depicted a map of the country, leaving the precise boundaries vague, but in the definitive series of 1927 the outline claimed by Paraguay was clearly shaded. A detailed map of the Chaco Paraguayo appeared on stamps of 1932–36 with the slogan 'The northern Chaco has been, is and will be Paraguayan'. For the Bolivian version of this stamp war see plate 98. The 'c' overprint denotes 'Campaña' (country) for use on mail to addresses within Paraguay.

6. Paraguay, 10 centavos, 1933
Between 1931 and 1936 a series of airmail stamps was typographed at the Mint, Asunción. Five designs were used, with birds, aircraft or allegories of flight. The colours were changed at frequent intervals. The 10*c*. was originally printed in violet, changed to claret in February 1933, then to yellow-brown in July the same year and finally to ultramarine in 1935.

7. Paraguay, 2 pesos, 1939
The disastrous war between Bolivia and Paraguay, which decimated the latter's population, was brought to a close by the arbitration of the United States, Brazil, Argentina, Chile and Peru. As the peace conference resulted in a satisfactory solution for Paraguay the occasion was celebrated by a lengthy set of stamps with a map of the new frontiers and presidential portraits, flags and coats of arms of the adjudicating countries. This stamp portrays President Benavides of Peru, flanked by the flags of Peru and Paraguay. The stamps were printed in multicolour recess by the American Bank Note Co.

8. Paraguay, 3 pesos, 1940
A second series, printed in photogravure by Waterlow and Sons, was issued in January 1940 to mark the peace conference at Buenos Aires. The eight stamps of this series emphasized the return to peace and reconstruction and showed agricultural scenes. The 50*c*. stamp was surcharged 5*p*. and overprinted later that year in mourning for President Estigarribia who died on 7 September 1940.

9. Paraguay, 5 centimos, 1954
The currency of Paraguay suffered inflation in the 1940s and was reformed in 1943 when the guarani of 100 centimos (equal to 100 old pesos) was introduced. This stamp was one of a series issued in August 1954 to commemorate the three national heroes – Marshal Lopez, the great defender, Carlos

PLATE 102 PARAGUAY, PERU · PLATE 103 URUGUAY, VENEZUELA

Lopez, 'the constructor', and General Caballero, who organized the reconstruction of the economy after the Chaco war. The series was lithographed at the state mint in Asunción.

10. Paraguay, 25 centavos, 1968
Since 1962 the stamps of Paraguay have been handled by a foreign philatelic agency and new issues have proliferated for every conceivable event, generally with a strong thematic bias. Among the more popular themese those of religion and art have been highly favoured and in the case of this stamp, combined. Several sets of stamps from 1964 onward have commemorated the Eucharistic conferences, the series of 1968 reproducing religious paintings to mark the occasion. The vast majority of recent Paraguayan stamps have been boycotted by catalogues, dealers and collectors.

11. Peru, 1 dinero, 1858
British stamps were used at various seaports in Peru from 1857 to 1879 when Peru joined the Universal Postal Union. The first used for internal mail consisted of 1 and 2 real stamps of the Pacific Steam Navigation Company, which were sanctioned for postal use between 1 December 1857 and 28 February 1858. On 1 March 1858, stamps in denominations of 1 dinero and 1 peseta were introduced. They were lithographed by Emilio Prugue of Lima, with the national coat of arms. A $\frac{1}{2}$ peso stamp was subsequently issued in the same design.

12. Peru, 10 centavos, 1866
The currency of Peru (1 peso = 5 pesetas or 10 dineros) was changed to the decimal system of 100 centavos to the peso or sol in 1866. The American Bank Note Co. recess-printed stamps in denominations of 5, 10 and 20c. with llamas in various designs. New printings of this series were made in 1875–76 in slightly paler colours.

13. Peru, 2 centavos, 1873
In 1862 the Peruvian postal authorities acquired a Lecocq press from Paris and proceeded to print stamps in horizontal strips, with embossed designs. The oddest and crudest of these locally printed stamps was the 2c. of 1873, with the llama in colourless embossing against a blue background. This stamp was intended for use on local letters posted and delivered within Lima city limits, hence the name of that town in the inscription.

14. Peru, 1 sol, 1874
A definitive series was recess-printed by the National Bank Note Co. of New York between 1874 and 1879, and had various designs incorporating the national coat of arms. The top values, however, depicted the sun, a pun on the value (*sol* is Spanish for sun). The stamps were given an embossed grille as a security device, similar to that used on American stamps between 1867 and 1870. This was to make it difficult to wash off the postmark and use the stamp again.

15. Peru, 1 centavo, 1882
War broke out between Chile and Peru in 1879 and resulted in the defeat of the latter. Chilean stamps used in Peru in 1879–81, with identifiable postmarks of Peruvian towns, are of great interest to the specialist. Peruvian stamps were overprinted with the Chilean arms and issued in occupied territory in December 1881. A 'horseshoe' overprint was applied by hand to stamps issued in January 1882. Numerous local stamps appeared in various Peruvian towns between this date and 1884, when the Chileans withdrew and the country was reunited.

16. Peru, 5 centavos, 1884
Stamps issued by the postmaster general of Peru were gradually reintroduced from October 1883 onward, after the main Chilean forces had evacuated the country. This stamp was issued in April 1884 but was only valid in Callao, Lima and surrounding district. Various prewar stamps may also be found with a triangular overprint inscribed PERU to revalidate them after the Chilean occupation.

17. Peru, 2 centavos, 1894
Stamps of the 1874 definitive series were given a new lease of life when they appeared in October 1894 overprinted with a portrait of President R. M. Bermudez. The overprint was made with the old Lecocq machine of 1862–73, brought out of honourable retirement for this specific purpose. Stamps with the head double or inverted are thought to have been deliberately perpetrated by employees of the printers, but as they performed postal service they are generally listed in the stamp catalogues.

18. Peru, 5 centavos, 1897
Sanity was restored to Peruvian philately in 1896 when the American Bank Note Co. recess-printed a series portraying historic personages. The series appeared originally in February 1896 but was reissued in different colours between 1897 and 1900. Many stamps of this series were subsequently surcharged and revalidated in 1915–16, during a temporary shortage of 1 and 2c. denominations.

19. Peru, 2 centavos, 1909
The American Bank Note Co. returned to the portrait theme in 1909, but used smaller formats for the series from 1c. to 1s., portraying Columbus, Pizarro, San Martin, Bolivar, Manco Capac and other historic figures. A similar series, using new portraits, was recess-printed between 1924 and 1929 and similar designs used for a set of 1924 commemorating the centenary of the battle of Ayacucho. The latter series was recess-printed by De La Rue and Waterlows or printed in photogravure by Harrison and Sons.

20. Peru, 2 centavos, 1936
Waterlow and Sons printed a pictorial definitive series released in December 1936. The values from 2c. to 1s. were printed in photogravure, while the 2 to 10s. values were recess-printed. Sets were issued for both ordinary and airmail postage and depicted wildlife, scenery, native types, historic figures, landmarks and scenery. The entire lengthy series was reissued the following year in new colours.

21. Peru, 1.50 soles, 1938
Three ordinary and three airmail stamps were issued in December 1938 to mark the eighth Pan-American Congress, held in Lima. Five of them were printed in photogravure, but the sixth, a 15c. showing the seal of the city of Lima, was printed in combined recess (frame) and lithography (vignette). They were the work of Waterlow and Sons. The photogravure stamps featured landmarks in Lima and portraits of the presidents of the republics.

22. Peru, 5 centavos, 1957
The centenary of the first Peruvian stamps was celebrated in December 1957 with a set of ten stamps, recess-printed at the French Government Printing Works. The motif of the 5c. stamp was a selection of postmarks dating from the pre-adhesive period. Others reproduced the stamps of 1857–58 and portrayed the president and director of posts in 1857.

23. Peru, 1.60 soles, 1967
Peru has pursued a relatively conservative policy with regard to new issues of stamps in recent years and usually confines commemorative issues to pairs of single stamps. The 50th anniversary of Lions International was celebrated in December 1967 by this stamp featuring the emblem of the organization. Like many recent stamps of Peru it was lithographed in multicolour by the Austrian State Printing Works in Vienna.

PLATE 103
Uruguay and Venezuela

1. Uruguay, 120 centesimos, 1859
Uruguay adopted adhesive stamps in October 1856, when 60c., 80c. and 1 real stamps were lithographed by Mege and Willems of Montevideo. The first series were known from the inscription as the 'Diligencias', signifying the mode of transportation. The central motif was the rising sun, emblem of the so-called Eastern Republic, as Uruguay was then known. The stamps of 1857–62 bore the name of the capital city and are therefore known to collectors as the Montevideo Suns. Various denominations, from 60 to 240c., were produced in this design. The 1858 printing of 120 and 180c. include the excessively rare *tête-bêche* varieties and the error of colour in which a 180c. stamp was inserted by mistake in the plate of 240c. stamps.

2. Uruguay, 1 centesimo, 1866
A series of 1864, with the national coat of arms, was inscribed 'Republica Oriental' (eastern republic), but the first set to bear the name in full was the numeral series of 1866. The stamps were lithographed by Maclure, Macdonald & Co. of Glasgow and originally issued imperforate. Subsequently a consignment of stamps was perforated in London and latterly the lithographic stones were shipped out to Uruguay where Mege and Willems produced printings. In denominations of 1, 5, 10, 15 and 20c., they had a dominant numeral motif with the elements of the coat of arms woven into the background. Numeral designs continued to predominate in Uruguayan stamps up to the turn of the century.

3. Uruguay, 5 centesimos, 1889
The majority of Uruguayan stamps in the nineteenth century were either lithographed locally or recess-printed by the American Bank Note Co. In 1889, however, Waterlow and Sons secured the first of their many contracts to print stamps for this country. As before, the numerals of value were prominently depicted, with coats of arms and figures of Justice and Mercury. The colours of the stamps were changed in 1894, 1899 and 1901.

4. Uruguay, 5 milesimas, 1911
The basic series was recess-printed by Waterlows in 1900 in denominations from 1c. to 1p., with cattle, agricultural produce and allegorical portraiture. A poor travesty of this series was lithographed locally in 1904 at the Escuela de Artes y Oficios in Montevideo, supplies from London being unobtainable during the Civil War. A revision of postal rates in 1910–11 led to the provisional surcharge of certain stamps with new values.

5. Uruguay, 1 centesimo, 1923
Uruguay's national bird, the teru-teru, was the subject of a definitive series, lithographed by Barreiro and Ramos of Montevideo and issued in June 1923, in denominations from 5 milesimos to 2 pesos. The first printings had no imprint below the design, but in 1924 a new edition appeared with the imprint of Barreiro and Ramos. Subsequent versions of this series were lithographed at the National Printing Works and the marginal imprint was changed to 'Imp Nacional' in 1925–26. In 1927

263

PLATE 103 URUGUAY, VENEZUELA

the position of this imprint was altered, from the centre to the right-hand corner. Variations in perforation add to the complexity of the various teruteru printings.

6. Uruguay, 7 centesimos, 1933
Waterlow and Sons recaptured the Uruguayan stamp contracts in 1928 and from then onward produced some finely engraved portrait sets. The definitive series of July 1933 portrayed Lavalleja, General Rivera and J. Zorilla de San Martin. Note the exceptionally small format used by Uruguay for its definitive stamps since 1928. This series was superseded by a similar issue portraying Artigas, and this, with variations, has been in use from 1939 to the present day.

7. Uruguay, 1 centesimo, 1954
Waterlow and Sons recess-printed a pictorial series for Uruguay which was released in January 1954. The majority of the designs showed important landmarks in Montevideo, but the 1 and 14c. stamps had a gaucho breaking-in a horse. Four denominations, featuring flowers, were printed in multicolour photogravure.

8. Uruguay, 1.20 pesos, 1961
In April 1961 President Gronchi of Italy paid a state visit to Latin America and a set of three stamps bearing his portrait was released by Uruguay. These were the first stamps issued by this country in honour of a visiting head of state; subsequently, President de Gaulle, Archbishop Makarios and other rulers have been similarly portrayed.

9. Uruguay, 20 centesimos, 1965
Four stamps, two for ordinary postage, two for airmail were issued in December 1965 in memory of President Kennedy. They were designed by J. B. Gurewitsch and lithographed locally by Barreiro. The frames had various colours, but the vignettes were in black and the outer frame and wreath in gold metallic ink.

10. Uruguay, 40 centesimos, 1966
The death of Sir Winston Churchill was recorded by two stamps, designed by A. Medina and lithographed by the National Printing Works. The rectangular 40c. stamp showed Churchill's portrait against the Union Jack, while the 2p. airmail stamp bore a full-face portrait and a quotation (in Spanish) from Churchill's famous speech to Parliament on taking office as Prime Minister in 1940. The stamp also bore a facsimile signature of Churchill – the only one of the many Churchill commemoratives to do so.

11. Uruguay, 40 centavos, 1967
In recent years the majority of Uruguayan commemorative issues have been confined to single stamps. The 150th anniversary of the city of Carmelo was celebrated in August 1967 by this stamp with the civic coat of arms.

12. Venezuela, ½ real, 1865
Adhesive stamps were adopted by Venezuela in 1859, the first issue, with the coat of arms, being lithographed by an unidentified American printer. In 1863 F. Hernandez of Caracas lithographed a series for the Venezuelan Federation, with an eagle and the stars representing the states of the federation. The colour of the ½r. was changed from red to yellow in 1865 and, at the same time, the lettering of the inscription was greatly improved.

13. Venezuela, 1 real, 1866
The constitution of Venezuela was again changed, from a federation to the United States of Venezuela. This was reflected in the definitive series lithographed by Felix Rasco of Caracas and introduced between 1866 and 1870. Note the curious way in which the inscription is set out – EE. UU. (Estados Unidos = United States) DE VENEZ^A. All five denominations of this series were issued imperforate, but they may be found with various unofficial perforations.

14. Venezuela, 25 centimos, 1893
Various stamps inscribed 'Escuelas' (schools) or 'Instruccion' (education) were used for postal purposes between 1871 and 1899, though primarily intended for fiscal purposes, to denote a tax by which funds were raised for the state education system. From 1882 onward such stamps were, in fact, designated for use on inland mail, while a separate series inscribed 'Venezuela' was used on external correspondence. All of these fiscal and postage stamps, from 1871 to the end of the century, portrayed Simon Bolivar. This stamp was one of a series recess-printed by the American Bank Note Co. in 1893.

15. Venezuela, 10 centimos, 1896
Since the latter part of the nineteenth century Venezuela has laid claim to the neighbouring territory of British Guiana (now Guyana). Conflict between the British and Venezuelan authorities almost resulted in a war between the two countries in the 1890s and it was only resolved by international arbitration. In July 1896 Venezuela issued a set of five stamps to mark the 80th anniversary of the death of General Miranda and irrelevantly used this as an excuse to display a map of Venezuela showing the territory of Guyana to which claim was laid. The stamps were lithographed at Caracas. The 25 and 50c. denominations exist in tête-bêche pairs.

16. Venezuela, 1 bolivar, 1903
Civil war broke out in Venezuela in 1902. From November 1902 to January 1904 various local issues appeared in different parts of the country but principally in the state of Maturin and in the Carupano and Marino districts of Guyana. In March 1903 typeset issues picturing the rebel steamship Banrigh were released in the three main rebel-held areas. They were typographed in black on various coloured papers in denominations from 5c. to 1b. Provisional overprints on this series also appeared at Yrapa and Guiria.

17. Venezuela, 15 centimos, 1930
In connection with a government air service a series of airmail stamps was introduced in April 1930, in denominations from 5c. to 20b. They were lithographed by the Commercial Lithographic and Typographic Co. of Caracas, showing an aircraft over a map of the country. Note that the eastern part is vaguely inscribed 'Guayana' and includes, without distinction, both the Venezuelan state of that name and much of the British colony of Guiana, which Venezuela has claimed since the 1890s. The stamps were reissued in July 1932 in a recess-printed version by Waterlow and Sons. They were printed on paper covered with a greyish pattern inscribed 'Winchester Security Paper'. In 1938–39 the Waterlow series was reissued on plain white paper.

18. Venezuela, 10 centimos, 1948
The first anniversary of the Greater Colombian Mercantile Marine was celebrated in 1948 by a lengthy series of ordinary and airmail stamps with the motor-ship Republica de Venezuela and the shipping line emblem, a ship's wheel enclosing a map of Venezuela and Colombia. The stamps were recess-printed by the American Bank Note Co. and released over a period from 1948 to 1950 in denominations from 5c. to 5b.

19. Venezuela, 5 centimos, 1938
The American Bank Note Co. recess-printed a lengthy definitive series issued in February 1938. Three vertical designs were used for the ordinary series and showed a girl gathering coffee beans, Simon Bolivar and the GPO in Caracas. The airmail series used horizontal designs, with the port of La Guaira, the National Pantheon and oil-wells, each horizontal design also incorporating an aircraft. New values and changes of colour were introduced in May 1938 and several further changes were made in 1947.

20. Venezuela, 10 centimos, 1959
The quatercentenary of the city of Trujillo was celebrated in 1957 but a further two years elapsed before a series of stamps marked the event. A uniform design was used for both ordinary and airmail sets, with the arms of Trujillo and the Bolivar memorial. They were lithographed by the State Printing Works in Berlin, both sets ranging from 5c. to 1b. Venezuela was one of the few countries to perpetuate the Latin American practice of issuing long sets of ordinary and airmail stamps for commemorative purposes, though there has been a tendency in recent years to cut down the number of stamps in each series.

21. Venezuela, 5 cents, 1938
Venezuela took over the harbour installations of La Guaira in June 1937 and no doubt in celebration of this fact chose a view of La Guaira as one of the three designs used for the airmail definitive series issued in February 1938. The stamps were recess-printed by the American Bank Note Co. They were reissued in new colours in 1939 and again in 1947.

22. Venezuela, 10 centimos, 1963
The advent of multicolour lithography from the State Printing Works in Berlin coincided with Venezuela's policy of issuing frequent thematic sets from 1961 onwards. This stamp, issued in March 1963, comes from a series of twelve stamps featuring wildlife.

23. Venezuela, 10 centimos, 1964
With surprising economy Venezuela recorded both the National Industries Exhibition in Caracas and the centenary of the Ministry of Works by issuing a single series of stamps. Admittedly the set consisted of five ordinary and five airmail stamps. Though inscribed 1963, it did not appear until February 1964.

24. Venezuela, 80 centimos, 1965
Though the State Printing Works in Berlin has printed many modern stamps of this country it by no means enjoys a monopoly. This stamp is one of the set of four (two ordinary and two airmail) designed by Sandor Legrady and printed in photogravure by the State Printing Office in Budapest to publicize the Alliance for Progress campaign, which had been initiated by the late President Kennedy. Other printers who produced Venezuelan stamps at this time included De La Rue of Colombia and Rosenbaum Brothers of Vienna.

25. Venezuela, 20 centimos, 1966
A set of twelve stamps, lithographed in Berlin, was issued in April 1966 with the theme of Venezuelan country dances. Ranging from 5 to 90c., the stamps illustrated distinctive dances and costumes, with scenery from each district in the background.

PLATE 104 CUBA, HISPANIOLA

PLATE 104
Cuba and Hispaniola

1. Cuba and Puerto Rico, 2 reales, 1855
Adhesive stamps were introduced by the Spanish colonial administration in 1855. The earliest were similar to those issued in Spain, but inscribed in local currency, and were valid in both Cuba and Puerto Rico, the Spanish dominions in the Caribbean. They were typographed at the Government Printing Works, Madrid. The earliest printings were on bluish paper with a looped watermark. The following year the stamps were reprinted on yellowish paper with a watermark of crossed lines. In 1857 white unwatermarked paper was used. The annual changes of definitive stamps which were such a notorious feature of Spanish philately, did not extend to Cuba and Puerto Rico until 1866. The currency was inscribed in 'reales plata fuerte' – 'strong plate' meaning high-grade silver, to distinguish it from the almost worthless paper currency which was also in circulation.

2. Cuba and Puerto Rico, 10 centesimos, 1868
A decimal system, based on the peseta of 100c., was introduced in 1866. The series of 1868 was the first to give some indication in the inscription of the area in which the stamps were used. 'Ultramar' (overseas) served to distinguish them from the issues used in Spain itself. The series was reissued the following year with the date altered to 1869.

3. Cuba, 50 centesimos, 1878
Stamps inscribed 'Ultramar' continued to be issued until 1877, when similar designs portraying King Alfonso XII were issued with inscriptions signifying the different colonies. From 1873 to 1877, however, the stamps used in Puerto Rico could be distinguished from those current in Cuba by means of a paraph (squiggly line) overprint. The series of 1877 was reissued in 1878 and 1879 with the dates altered accordingly.

4. Cuba, 5 centavos, 1891
The 'Baby' keyplates of Alfonso XIII were adopted in 1890. Though undated they were reissued in successive years in new colours. Thus this stamp was first released in slate, but changed to blue-green in 1891 and then to indigo in 1896. The currency was changed to the peso of 100 centavos in 1881.

5. Cuba, 5 centimos, 1898
The last series issued under Spanish rule consisted of the 'Curly head' Alfonso XIII keyplates dated 1898–99. Stamps bearing these dates and the Spanish coat of arms were never issued for postal purposes. The island was occupied by United States troops during the Spanish–American War of 1898.

6. Cuba, 1 centavo de peso, 1899
Cuba was formally taken under United States protection on 1 January 1899. Various stamps of the Spanish series were surcharged with new values, under the authority of the U.S. Post Office in Puerto Principe. Subsequently contemporary United States stamps overprinted 'Cuba' and surcharged in centavos and pesos were issued in 1899. The 1 and 5c. stamps are recorded with the error CUPA instead of CUBA, while inverted or omitted overprints are also known on other values. The 2½c. stamp was unnecessary and was sold as a 2c. value.

7. Cuba, 10 centavos, 1905
Cuba remained under United States administration for three years, before receiving the status of an independent republic. The overprinted series was

superseded later in 1899 by a pictorial set, from 1 to 10c., recess-printed at the Bureau of Engraving and Printing in Washington. It illustrated the statue of Columbus, palm trees, the statue of Cuba, a liner and a farmer ploughing a tobacco field. The stamps were subsequently printed in 1905–07 by the American Bank Note Co. Minor details in the designs distinguish the American Bank Note from the Bureau printings. In the 10c., for example, there are small white dots at each end of the label containing the word CUBA; they are lacking in the Bureau version.

8. Cuba, 8 centavos, 1910
A series, from 1c. to 1p., was recess-printed by the American Bank Note Co. in 1910. It was printed in two-colour combinations and portrayed leaders of the recent war of independence. The 1, 2 and 10c. denominations have been recorded with the centres inverted. In 1911 the 1, 2, 5 and 8c. and 1p. values were reissued in new colours.

9. Cuba, 5 centavos, 1917
The definitive series, recess-printed by Rodriguez of Havana and issued in 1917, remained in use till after World War II. The early printings were on unwatermarked paper, perforated 12. In 1925 a star watermark was introduced and five years later the perforation gauge changed from 12 to 10. The shades of these stamps varied considerably over the period in which they were current. The 1, 2 and 3c. denominations exist in both flat plate and rotary press versions, differing in size and minor details. The 1, 2 and 5c. stamps exist imperforate.

10. Cuba, 1 centavo, 1943
The course of World War II was reflected in the stamps of Cuba in a curious way. Obligatory tax stamps, of ½c. value, with the V for Victory sign were issued at various times from July 1942 to 1944 to raise money for the Red Cross. In July 1943 a set of five stamps was issued as a form of propaganda against Fifth Column activities in the Caribbean. The stamps had symbolic designs with such slogans as 'Unmask Fifth Columnists', 'Be careful – the Fifth Column is spying on you' or 'Don't be afraid of the Fifth Column – attack it'. The *Quinta Columna* was the metaphor coined by General Franco during the Spanish Civil War to describe his allies working within the ranks of the Republicans defending Madrid, which he was then attacking with four columns of assault troops.

11. Cuba, 5 centavos, 1937
A definitive series, from 1c. to 1p., was released in 1954–56 portraying prominent Cubans as before. At the same time, however, a series of double-sized stamps, illustrating various aspects of the sugar industry, was issued for airmail purposes. They exhibit a curious device, used on Cuban stamps on several occasions, whereby the vignette is divided diagonally in order to depict two different (and often wholly unrelated) subjects. This idea was first adopted in 1937 for a set of three stamps marking the 400th anniversary of the sugar industry and was retained two years later for the 5c. stamp in a series picturing tobacco plants and a box of cigars. In the 1954 airmail series one half of the vignette contains an aircraft, the other half sugar processing and refining machinery.

12. Cuba, 13 centavos, 1963
The advent of the Castro regime in 1959 is reflected in the trend toward left-wing subjects in Cuban stamps. Since 1961 they have been issued annually to mark May Day. Two stamps were issued in 1963 with a five-pointed star encompassing revolutionaries (3c.) and workers *en fête* (13c.). From 1960 onward increasing use was made of multicolour lithography.

13. Cuba, 13 centavos, 1965
Another of the 'hardy annuals' from Cuba is the series of stamps in honour of Stamp Day (24 April). As a rule their theme has been historic developments in mail transportation and communications, portraits of postal reformers, reproductions of stamps and other aspects of Cuban philately. The 3c. stamp issued in 1965 featured a sailing packet and eighteenth century postmarks, commemorating the bicentenary of the maritime mail service between Cuba and Spain, while the 13c. showed a reproduction of the 1935 stamp of the International Air Train over the Capitol, Havana. The Air Train was the idea of two American aviators, O'Meara and Du Pont, who used a powered aircraft to tow a string of gliders (anticipating the use of gliders in World War II). Mail carried by the Air Train was franked with a special stamp bearing a 10c. premium.

14. Cuba, 7 centavos, 1966
The fifth anniversary of the first manned space flight was celebrated in April 1966 with a set of seven stamps portraying Tsiolkovsky, the Russian inventor credited with pioneering research in rocketry, and various Soviet cosmonauts. No reference was made to the comparable achievements of the United States, though other countries in the Soviet sphere of influence have been more generous in this respect. In recent years Cuba has been outspoken (philatelically at least) against American participation in the Vietnam War.

15. Cuba, 3 centavos, 1970
Although a high proportion of modern Cuban stamps have proclaimed a political message, other social problems continue to claim philatelic attention. Two stamps of 1970 marked Traffic Week aimed at improving road sense, especially among children, hence the whimsical nature of their designs. The 3c. showed a zebra on a pedestrian crossing, the 9c. the cartoon character Prudence Bear on point duty.

16. Dominican Republic, 80 centavos, 1891
The Dominican Republic adopted adhesive stamps in 1865, a series with the coat of arms being typographed locally. They were superseded in July 1879 by a pair of ½ and 1r. stamps, also bearing the coat of arms, and typographed by Nicholas F. Seebeck of New York. Seebeck later acted as a philatelic entrepreneur, securing contracts from many Latin American countries on behalf of the Hamilton Bank Note Co. with which he was subsequently associated. The Dominican Republic, however, was not involved in the Seebeck contracts of the 1890s (see plates 94–95) and at that time preferred to have its stamps printed in France or Spain. Stamps of 1879, surcharged in centavos, were issued in 1891 and are known as the Parisot series, after H. K. Parisot, a stamp dealer who first handled them.

17. Dominican Republic, 2 centavos, 1900
The Hamilton Bank Note Co. secured a contract to print Dominican stamps in 1900 and produced a lithographed series, from ½c. to 1 peso, showing a map of the island of Hispaniola (the east portion of which has been renamed Santo Domingo). The printers, for reasons best known to themselves, perpetrated a number of 'errors' in this series, transposing certain inscriptions. The 2c. is known with 'Haiti' on the right instead of the left, and the 50c. with the captions 'Atlantico' and 'Mar Caribe' transposed. The appearance of these stamps caused an international incident, Haiti being mightily displeased with the distortion of its national frontiers. Following an ultimatum from Haiti the Dominican authorities withdrew the offending stamps and they were replaced with a coat of arms series.

265

PLATE 104 CUBA, HISPANIOLA · PLATE 105 BRITISH WEST INDIES

18. Dominican Republic, ½ centavo, 1939

The Trujillo era (1930–61) was marked by flamboyance in stamp design, the accent being on gaudy lithography by Ferrua & Co. of Ciudad Trujillo (now renamed Santo Domingo) who printed all the stamps from 1927 to 1942, as well as many of the later issues. The stamps in this period served mainly to promote the image of General Trujillo or to raise funds for the ambitious Columbus Lighthouse project. Even the set of five stamps issued in 1939 to mark the New York World's Fair had to depict the Columbus Lighthouse as well as the Fair symbols.

19. Dominican Republic, 10 centavos, 1964

The first anniversary of the death of John F. Kennedy was marked by this stamp. It was lithographed in small sheets containing ten stamps with a commemorative inscription in the sheet margins. Since the end of the Trujillo regime the Dominican Republic has tended to issue fewer stamps and restrict commemorative issues to single stamps or short sets. Since 1952 Ferrua has printed the vast majority of Dominican stamps, by either lithography or photogravure.

20. Dominican Republic, 1 centavo, 1971

Obligatory tax stamps have been issued by the Dominican Republic on numerous occasions since 1940, when a ½ centavo stamp was issued for compulsory use on correspondence at certain times of the year in order to raise funds for a military hospital. Since then low-denomination stamps have been released at frequent intervals for anti-tuberculosis, cancer and child welfare funds. A 1c. stamp was issued in International Education Year (1970) to raise funds for new schools and a similar stamp appeared in 1971 for the same purpose.

21. Haiti, 1 centime, 1887

Haiti's first stamps, depicting the head of Liberty, were typographed from electrotypes made from a die engraved on wood. They were in use from 1881 to 1887, when they were replaced by a series recess-printed by Skipper and East of London, portraying President Salomon. The stamps were in denominations of 1, 2, 3 and 5c. The 3c. was subsequently surcharged for use as a 2c. stamp. Apart from inverted double, or double (one inverted) overprints, there are numerous minor varieties in the surcharge.

22. Haiti, 1 centime, 1893

A heraldic design was adopted for the stamps of Haiti in 1891. The first version, recess-printed in Paris, showed the palm-tree with its frond sticking up. Two years later Skipper and East produced a new design, with the frond drooping. In 1896 the French Government Printing Works made a similar version of this design, differing in minor details and printed in new colours.

23. Haiti, 20 centimes, 1904

The centenary of independence from French rule was celebrated in 1904 by a series of seven stamps, from 1 to 50c., recess-printed by M. E. Cote of Paris. The 1c. displayed the national arms, the other values portrayed prominent figures from the war of independence. The frames were in various colours and the portraits, in black, were positioned more or less in the central space. The series was first issued with a crude overprint 'Poste Paye' (postage paid) and the dates 1804 and 1904. Subsequently the set was released without this overprint. The portrait stamps have all been recorded with the heads inverted.

24. Haiti, 1.50 gourdes, 1954

By the time of the 150th anniversary of independence Haiti had become more sophisticated in matters of

stamp design and entrusted many of the more recent issues to international printers such as Courvoisier of Switzerland. A set of seven ordinary and eight airmail stamps appearing in January 1954 reproduced portraits of the leaders of the revolution, with President Magloire, ruler of Haiti in the era prior to 'Papa Doc' Duvalier.

25. Haiti, 25 + 25 centimes, 1959

Four stamps released in December 1958 in honour of the United Nations carried a map of Haiti surrounded by the initials of the various UN agencies. A fifth stamp displayed the flags of Haiti and the United Nations. Subsequently unsold stock of this, and other sets, were overprinted in April 1959 with premiums in aid of the Red Cross – a frequent practice in Haiti whereby the same stamps may be sold twice or thrice to the long-suffering philatelic public. During the early 1960s Haiti released very few entirely new stamps, but an enormous quantity of surcharges and overprints converting previous issues to new purposes were issued.

26. Haiti, 1.50 gourdes, 1958

To mark International Geophysical Year Haiti issued a set of seven stamps and a miniature sheet. None of the subjects had any relevance to Haiti and the inclusion of penguins on an ice-floe (20c. and 1.50g) on stamps of a tropical country seems to have been the ultimate in incongruity.

PLATE 105
British West Indies

Grouped together on this plate are the stamps of Jamaica, the Turks and Caicos Islands and the Cayman Islands, the latter groups having been dependent politically or philatelically on Jamaica at various times in their history.

1. Jamaica, 4 pence, 1860

Ordinary British stamps were used in Jamaica between 1858 and 1859 and can only be distinguished by the numeral obliterators A 01 or A 27 to A 78. An independent postal administration was established in 1859 and adopted distinctive adhesive stamps the following year. In the interim Jamaica reverted to the use of handstruck marks to indicate prepayment of postage. De La Rue typographed a series from 1 penny to 1 shilling on paper with a pineapple watermark. Subsequent printings were produced on paper with the standard colonial watermarks. Certain denominations of this series survived as late as 1900.

2. Jamaica, 1 penny, 1901

This stamp, first released in 1900, was an early attempt by Jamaica to brighten up the appearance of its stamps by using pictorial motifs. De La Rue departed from their normal typographic process to print this stamp in recess, using a single working plate in 1900, to print the stamp in red. Separate frame and vignette plates were employed the following year to print the bicoloured version. The stamp depicts the Llandovery Falls, from a photograph by Dr J. Johnson. The pictorial concept was not, however, developed till after World War I.

3. Jamaica, 6 pence, 1911

The pictorial penny was followed, in 1903–04, by a typographed series with the colonial coat of arms. One stamp in each sheet of certain denominations has the error SER.ET instead of SERVIET in the motto. The arms design was redrawn in 1905 and various values were issued between then and 1911.

4. Jamaica, 2 pence, 1921

In 1919 Jamaica issued a 1½d. stamp showing its war contingent embarking on the eve of World War I. This proved to be the first of a new definitive series, released over a period of two years, depicting scenery and landmarks of the island and alluding to outstanding events in its history, from the landing of Columbus (3d.) to the return of the war contingent in 1919 (2½d.). Two versions of the 2½d. exist. In the first printing the Union Jack in the left hand panel was inadvertently shown upside down – the distress signal – and this was subsequently corrected. A 6d. stamp showing the proclamation of the abolition of slavery was suppressed before issue, on account of labour unrest and racial tension in 1921.

5. Jamaica, 2½ pence, 1923

This stamp was one of a set of three issued in November 1923. Sold at a premium of ½d. in aid of the Child Welfare League it was on sale annually from 1 November to 31 January until 1927, when the remaining stocks were withdrawn and destroyed. The frames were designed by Frank Cundall, the historian, and the vignettes drawn by his sister, from photographs by Miss V. F. Taylor. The stamps were recess-printed by Bradbury Wilkinson.

6. Jamaica, 10 shillings, 1938

Entirely new designs were adopted for the definitive series of 1938 portraying King George VI. De La Rue recess-printed a small-format series for ½, 1 and 1½d. stamps and this 10s. denomination, with its allegorical design and quaint title 'George VI of Jamaica Supreme Lord'. The remaining denominations depicted scenery and agriculture of Jamaica and were recess-printed by Waterlow and Sons.

7. Jamaica, 5 shillings, 1945

At the end of World War II Jamaica was granted a new constitution permitting internal self-government and paving the way for complete independence 17 years later. The series, in denominations from 1½d. to 10s., was recess-printed by Waterlow and Sons. Three values depicted the Courthouse at Falmouth, the Institute of Jamaica and the House of Assembly, while the 2d. value portrayed King Charles II, in whose reign the first House of Assembly had been established. The 2s. and 5s. values used symbolic designs.

8. Jamaica, 6 pence, 1955

A set of four stamps was recess-printed by De La Rue and issued in May 1955 to celebrate the tercentenary of the capture of Jamaica from the Spaniards. Each denomination showed a historic scene or reproduced an old print of the island. The vignette in the 6d. value had what had been banned for political reasons 34 years earlier – the proclamation of the abolition of slavery in 1838.

9. Jamaica, 5 pence, 1962

The basic definitive series was recess-printed by De La Rue or Bradbury Wilkinson in 1956 but was overprinted six years later to celebrate the attainment of complete independence. The entire series, from ½d. to £1, was overprinted in this way. In 1963–64 several denominations of the Independence series were reissued on paper with the new St Edward's Crown watermark.

10. Jamaica, 3 shillings, 1968

A series of three stamps, designed by Jennifer Toombs, was prepared for release early in 1968 in honour of Human Rights Year. The local stamp advisory committee, however, raised strong objections to the designs and consequently an entirely new series had to be produced and issued late in December 1968. A few of the unadopted stamps were circulated to the philatelic press but were never actually issued for postal purposes. The three

PLATE 105 BRITISH WEST INDIES · PLATE 106 LEEWARD ISLANDS

unadopted designs featured bowls of grain (3d.), an abacus (1s.) and hands in prayer (3s.).

11. Jamaica, 30 cents, 1969
Jamaica abandoned sterling in favour of the dollar in September 1969. To publicize the change-over the entire definitive series was overprinted 'C-Day' and surcharged with new values from 1c. to $2. The basic series was printed in photogravure by Harrisons in 1964 with flowers, sea-shells, industries, tourism and scenery.

12. Jamaica, 10 cents, 1970
A set of three stamps was issued in October 1970 to mark the centenary of the Jamaican telegraph service. It was designed by Gordon Drummond and lithographed by John Waddington of Kirkstall, with the cable ship *Dacia*, Bright's cable gear and cross-sections of the cables, and a morse key and chart.

13. Turks Islands, 1 penny,
The Turks and Caicos Islands have had a varied political career. Colonized by Bermuda, governed by the Bahamas, they became a separate administration under Jamaican protection in 1848, then progressed to the status of an independent crown colony in 1866. A postal administration was established and the following year distinctive stamps, in denominations of 1d., 6d. and 1s. were introduced. The stamps, in a common design, were recess-printed by Perkins Bacon, one of the last colonial contracts held by this firm before they lost to De La Rue, who continued to recess-print these denominations from 1881 till 1900. This series was notorious for the numerous provisional surcharges of 1881, creating $\frac{1}{2}$, $2\frac{1}{2}$ and 4d. values; more than 40 different varieties of surcharge have been noted.

14. Turks and Caicos Islands, $\frac{1}{2}$ penny, 1900
The bulk of the population resides in the Caicos Islands but it was not until 1900 that stamps giving the full name of the group were issued. On account of economic depression the islands lost their crown colony status in 1873 and reverted to being a dependency of Jamaica. The definitive series recess-printed by De La Rue shows salt-raking, the islands' only industry. The dates mark the 52nd anniversary of the islands' separation from the Bahamas. Though quasi-commemorative this series remained in use till 1909.

15. Turks and Caicos Islands, 10 shillings, 1948
The centenary of the separation from the Bahamas was marked by a set of seven stamps, recess-printed by Waterlow and Sons, and issued in December 1948. This design, used for the three highest denominations, portrayed Queen Victoria and King George VI, separated by island plants and turtles, and flanked by the curious Turk's Head cacti which give the islands their name. Other stamps showed a map of the islands, their flag and their colonial emblem.

16. Turks and Caicos Islands, 35 cents, 1969
The islands were granted a new constitution in 1959, permitting internal self-government and crown colonial status. This, in turn, paved the way for yet another new constitution in 1969 which gave the islands Associated Statehood status with the United Kingdom. To mark the occasion two stamps depicting the new coat of arms were issued. They were designed by L. D. Curtis and lithographed in multicolour by Bradbury Wilkinson.

17. Turks and Caicos Islands, 1 cent, 1970
Comparatively few commemorative issues have been made by the Turks and Caicos Islands, other than the various colonial omnibus issues. A large-format set of four was issued in December 1970 to mark the tercentenary of the granting of letters patent by Charles II to George Monck, Duke of Albemarle, whose portrait and coat of arms appeared on two of the stamps. Victor Whiteley designed the stamps, which were lithographed by Enschedé en Zonen.

18. Cayman Islands, 1 farthing, 1908
The Cayman Islands used the stamps of Jamaica until 1901, when stamps were introduced portraying Queen Victoria ($\frac{1}{2}$ and 1d.) or Edward VII ($\frac{1}{2}$, 1, $2\frac{1}{2}$ and 6d., and 1s.) All the issues of the Cayman Islands up to 1921 were in the De La Rue keyplate designs then common throughout the British colonies. The sole distinctive design was this farthing stamp, prepaying the local printed matter rate, issued in 1908. A curious feature of it was that, although produced by De La Rue, it was lithographed – a process which that company very seldom used in stamp production.

19. Cayman Islands, 5 shillings, 1938
A pictorial definitive series, with the profile of King George V inset, was recess-printed by Waterlow in 1935. A new series, recess-printed by Waterlow or De La Rue, appeared in 1938 with the portrait of King George VI. The perforations on these stamps varied during and after World War II.

20. Cayman Islands, 5 shillings, 1962
The Cayman Islands were granted a new constitution in 1959 giving them the status of a crown colony fully independent of Jamaica. Bradbury Wilkinson recess-printed a definitive series, with the Annigoni portrait of the queen inset. The designs followed the pattern of previous pictorial sets, with an emphasis on tourism which was then beginning to develop as the islands' major industry.

21. Cayman Islands, 40 cents, 1969
The Caymen Islands, like a number of other countries, and unfortunately for collectors, issued a new definitive series only months before a currency change was scheduled. The basic series, designed by George Vasarhelyi and lithographed in multicolour by Format International, appeared on 5 June 1969, but was reissued on 8 September with decimal currency surcharges and overprinted 'C-DAY 8th September 1969'. Presumably the decimal overprints were in preparation at the time the sterling series was released. Needless to say, this series, in turn, was superseded by a similar one with values inscribed in cents and dollars (see below).

22. Cayman Islands, 2 shillings, 1968
A set of three stamps was released in October 1968 to mark the Olympic Games in Mexico. The stamps depicted long jumping (1s.), high jumping (1s.3d.), and pole vaulting (2s.). Richard Granger Barrett designed the stamps which were lithographed in multicolour by Perkins Bacon.

23. Cayman Islands, 2 dollars, 1970
On 8 September 1970 exactly one year after the decimal currency surcharge issue of the 1969 definitive stamps, the same designs were used for a series inscribed in decimal currency. Since the date of the changeover to decimal currency was known for a considerable length of time and provision was made for the changeover by commercial and business interests in the islands it seems somewhat remiss on the part of the postal authorities not to have planned their new definitive series accordingly.

PLATE 106
Leeward Islands

1. Leeward Islands, 6 pence, 1897
Using the colonial keyplate design, De La Rue typographed a series for general use throughout the colony of the Leeward Islands in 1890. This superseded the separate issues of Antigua, Dominica, Montserrat, Nevis, St Christopher and the Virgin Islands. Independent issues were resumed in 1903, but stamps inscribed 'Leeward Islands' continued to be used until 1956, when the colony was broken up into its component territories. The stamps of the Leeward Islands were used in Dominica until 1939, when that island transferred to the Windward group (see plate 108). The entire series was overprinted 'Sexagenary 1897' with the royal monogram in the centre, to celebrate the Diamond Jubilee of Queen Victoria. All eight denominations are known with double overprint, while the 1d. has been recorded with a triple overprint.

2. Leeward Islands, 1 pound, 1938
Throughout the 66 years of their existence as a philatelic entity (1890–1956) the Leeward Islands used the colonial keyplates typographed by De La Rue. This was the only colony to use these keyplates with the profile of Queen Elizabeth. A large format with an ornate frame was used for the higher denominations, this design having been introduced for the 10s. and £1 stamps of the George V series in 1928.

3. Antigua, 1 penny, 1863
British stamps, distinguished by the numeral obliterator A 02, were used in Antigua from 1858 till 1862, when a distinctive 6d. stamp was introduced. Designed by E. H. Corbould, it is believed to have been engraved by Charles Jeens. The stamps were recess-printed by Perkins Bacon until 1872, when the contract passed to De La Rue. The 1d. denomination, for local mail, was introduced in 1863.

4. Antigua, halfpenny, 1916
The basic design, with the great seal of Antigua, was adopted in 1903 for the low-value definitive stamps typographed by De La Rue. A similar format, with a portrait of Edward VII, was used for the 5s. denomination. During World War I Antigua levied a tax of $\frac{1}{2}d.$ on every article of correspondence and overprinted the $\frac{1}{2}d.$ definitive 'War Stamp' to denote this charge.

5. Antigua, 5 shillings, 1938
The way toward pictorialism was paved, in 1932, by a lengthy series commemorating the tercentenary of the colony. Waterlow and Sons later recess-printed a definitive series, with the profile of King George VI, following the pattern of the 1932 series, but in entirely new designs, showing English Harbour, St John's Harbour, Nelson's Dockyard and Fort James.

6. Antigua, 48 cents, 1953
The British Caribbean dollar was adopted in 1951, but the king died before a decimal definitive series could be prepared. The same designs were used for a series portraying Queen Elizabeth, issued in November 1953. A design showing a Martello tower was added to the range, for the 8 and 48c. denominations. The series was recess-printed by Waterlow and Sons until 1961, and by De La Rue from then until 1966. The earlier printings are indistinguishable, except by the marginal imprints, but stamps printed in 1963–65 were on the new Black CA watermarked paper. The 12c. was surcharged 15c. in 1965.

267

PLATE 106 LEEWARD ISLANDS · PLATE 107 ST CHRISTOPHER, NEVIS, ANGUILLA

7. Antigua, 35 cents, 1966

Antigua was one of the few British territories to retain recess-printing in the 1960s. This stamp was one of a series of sixteen definitive stamps produced by Bradbury Wilkinson in 1966, showing various buildings and landmarks in the colony, with the Annigoni portrait of the Queen inset. Note the use of engine-turning or *guilloche* as a background to the inscription.

8. Antigua, 35 cents, 1967

Antigua attained Associated Statehood status in February 1967 and marked the event with a set of four stamps designed by W. D. Cribbs and printed in multicolour photogravure by Harrison. It illustrated the state flag, map and premier's office, with the queen's portrait inset.

9. Barbuda, 6 pence, 1922

The island of Barbuda, a dependency of Antigua, agitated for its own stamps as a means of raising revenue and was granted a Leeward Islands over-printed series in July 1922. The stamps ranged in value from $\frac{1}{2}d$. to 5s. but after a short period they were withdrawn and Antiguan stamps reintroduced. Distinctive stamps were resumed in 1968 (see below).

10. Antigua, 50 cents, 1969

Antigua jumped on the West Indian Christmas bandwagon in 1969 with a series of four ultra-large stamps reproducing stained glass windows preserved in the Victoria and Albert Museum, London. The adaptations were made by Victor Whiteley and the set lithographed by Enschedé. Two stamps reproduced the *Adoration of the Magi* by Marcillat, the others an unknown fifteenth century German version of the Nativity.

11. Antigua, 35 cents, 1970

In the hunt for fresh themes to titillate the jaded palate of the stamp-collector, Antigua issued a set of four stamps and a miniature sheet in 1970 illustrating the uniforms of British regiments which had been stationed in the island at some time or other. This inaugural series featured uniforms of the Royal American and West India regiments and the 93rd Foot (the Sutherland Highlanders). It was designed by P. W. Kingsland and lithographed by Questa.

12. Barbuda, 20 cents, 1970

Barbuda resumed separate stamp issues in November 1968, with a series by Granger Barrett showing a map of the island. In February 1970 a change in postal rates led to this provisional 20c. surcharge on the $\frac{1}{2}c$. denomination. A 20 cent stamp in the same design was released in the following July. The stamps of Barbuda were also valid in Antigua and vice versa, and may be likened to the regional issues of the United Kingdom (see plate 18).

13. Barbuda, 35 cents, 1971

In February 1970 Barbuda issued a 35 cents stamp bearing a portrait of William the Conqueror (1066–87) and thus embarked on the most ambitious and spectacular series ever produced by a British territory. Other stamps of this denomination appeared at regular intervals over the ensuing two years, eventually completing a series of 42 stamps portraying every British monarch from the beginning of the Norman Dynasty to the present day. Each stamp bears a tiny serial number in the lower left-hand corner. They were designed by Richard Granger Barrett and lithographed in multicolour by Format International.

14. Montserrat, 2½ pence, 1908

From 1858 onward Montserrat used ordinary British stamps, which may be recognized by the numeral obliterator A 08. The first stamps of the independent postal administration consisted of the contemporary 1d. and 6d. stamps of Antigua overprinted 'Montserrat', released in 1876. Subsequently the colonial keyplate used in Nevis (see plate 107) was used with the appropriate inscription and separate issues were withdrawn in 1890. When distinctive stamps were resumed in 1903 Montserrat produced its first idiosyncratic design, a harpist embracing a cross. This emblem, used as the badge of the colony, alludes to the fact that Montserrat was colonized by Irish immigrants. The original version, typographed by De La Rue, appeared in two-colour combinations in 1903, but between 1908 and 1913 single working plates were adopted for the low values.

15. Montserrat, 1 shilling, 1938

Three pictorial designs were introduced in 1938 for the George VI definitive series, recess-printed by De La Rue, and showing Carr's Bay, the botanic station and the cultivation of sea island cotton. The colonial badge and the king's profile were incorporated in the frames. Wartime printings of this series exhibit the so-called Blitz perforations, when this part of the production was farmed out to other printers after the destruction of the De La Rue factory in a German air raid.

16. Montserrat, 5 cents, 1967

This is one of a set of four, designed and printed by Harrison and Sons, which Montserrat issued in December 1967 to mark International Tourist Year. They illustrated yachting, golfing, fishing, skin-diving and swimming, and the waterfall near Chance Mountain. Tourism is now Montserrat's most important source of revenue. A second tourism series appeared in 1970.

17. Montserrat, 1 dollar, 1970

Victor Whiteley designed a definitive series, printed by Harrisons, featuring birds of the Caribbean. Each of the thirteen designs, from 1c. to $5, had a different bird and gave its local and scientific names. The Crown Agents' persistence with the Latin language on stamps has not been altogether happy in recent years and several examples of misspelling have occurred on stamps of Samoa, St Kitts-Nevis and the Gambia. This stamp shows the misspelling *Orthorhyncus* instead of *Orthorhynchus*. This series was originally printed on chalk-surfaced paper, but was reprinted in January 1971 on glazed ordinary paper.

18. Virgin Islands, 1 penny, 1866

British stamps were used in the Virgin Islands from 1857 till 1866 and may be identified by the numeral obliterator A 13. Distinctive 1d. and 6d. stamps were lithographed by Waterlow and Sons in 1866, showing St Ursula, patron saint of the colony. The earliest printings were on unwatermarked paper, but between 1879 and 1889 De La Rue lithographed new versions of the 1d. stamp, in green or red, on paper with the colonial watermark. The separate issues of the Virgin Islands were superseded by the general series of the Leeward Islands in November 1890. Distinctive stamps were resumed in 1899 – four years before the other Leeward presidencies followed suit. The stamps issued up to 1956 were used contemporaneously with those of the Leewards.

19. Virgin Islands, 4.80 dollars, 1952

De La Rue recess-printed a definitive series for the Virgin Islands with values in British Caribbean currency. Different pictorial designs were used for each of the twelve denominations from 1c. to $4.80, with the Dorothy Wilding portrait of King George VI inset. Maps of the group and individual islands occupied five of the designs. The stamps were reissued in 1956 with the profile of Queen Elizabeth and in 1962 the series was surcharged with values in United States currency.

20. Virgin Islands, 25 cents, 1967

To mark the attainment of Associated Statehood a set of four stamps was issued in April 1967. The design, by George Vasarhelyi, showed a map and the national emblem. Note the abbreviation 'U.S. Cy.' (United States Currency) inscribed beside the figures of value – a feature peculiar to the stamps of this territory, reflecting its economic ties with the American Virgin Islands.

21. British Virgin Islands, 10 cents, 1969

The full name 'British Virgin Islands' was first used on stamps in 1968, to distinguish the islands from the larger and more important American group, formerly the Danish West Indies (see plate 111). Because of the associations of the islands with Robert Louis Stevenson – the Dead Man's Chest of the pirate song in *Treasure Island* is a reef in the Virgin group – a series of four stamps was issued in March 1969 to mark the 75th anniversary of the novelist's death. The stamps, designed by Jennifer Toombs and printed by Enschedé, depicted Long John Silver, Jim Hawkins and scenes from the adventure story.

22. British Virgin Islands, 25 cents, 1968

The Virgin Islands was one of the many countries which issued stamps in commemoration of Dr Martin Luther King. Victor Whiteley designed 4 and 25c. stamps with a portrait of Dr King and a Bible, sword and armoured gauntlet symbolizing his crusade for civil rights. The stamps were lithographed in multicolour by Format International.

23. British Virgin Islands, 10 cents, 1969

Tourism has developed in recent years as the main source of revenue for the islands and the amenities of the country were advertized by a set of four stamps issued in October 1969. John Cooter produced the designs showing yachts, sun bathing and tourists with fish and plant life of the islands. The stamps were lithographed in multicolour by Perkins Bacon, the world's premier stamp printers, who made a partial comeback in the late 1960s after having been out of the stamp business for more than 30 years.

24. British Virgin Islands, 1 dollar, 1968

A team of Royal Engineers visited the Virgin Islands in 1967–68 and reconstructed the airport at Beef Island, thus enabling international airlines to serve the islands. As a mark of gratitude to the soldiers, the Virgin Islands issued a set of four stamps depicting various aircraft and featuring the regimental badge of the Royal Engineers on the $1 stamp. They were designed by Richard Granger Barrett and lithographed by Format International.

PLATE 107

St Christopher, Nevis and Anguilla

Each of the three major islands in this group has issued its own stamps at some time or another, while two forms of the name have appeared on the corporate issues of this territory. The stamps of the Leeward Islands were used exclusively in St Christopher, Nevis and Anguilla between 1890 and 1900. From 1900 till 1956 the Leeward Islands stamps were used in addition to the distinctive stamps of these islands.

PLATE 107 ST CHRISTOPHER, NEVIS, ANGUILLA

1. Nevis, 1 penny, 1861
Ordinary British stamps were used in Nevis from 1856 till 1861 and can be identified by the numeral obliterator A 09. Distinctive stamps were introduced in 1861 and were at first recess-printed by Nissen and Parker of London. A different design was used for each of the four denominations (1, 4 and 6d., and 1s.), featuring the emblem of the colony which refers to the medicinal springs on the island. The frames of the stamps were a blatant plagiarism of contemporary British stamps of corresponding value. The last printing of these stamps was lithographed by transfer from the engraved plates by Nissen and Parker in 1876.

2. Nevis, 6 pence, 1883
The contract for printing the stamps of Nevis passed to De La Rue in 1879 and typographed stamps in the first of De La Rue's famous colonial keyplate designs were gradually introduced from that date to 1890. Distinctive stamps of Nevis were replaced by the general series of the Leeward Islands in 1890.

3. St Christopher, 1 penny, 1870
Ordinary British stamps, distinguished by the numeral obliterator A 12, were used in St Christopher until April 1870, when a distinctive series of 1d. and 6d. stamps was introduced. The stamps were typographed by De La Rue in a design which was subsequently modified for Lagos (1874) and Tobago (1879) and thus foreshadowed the colonial keyplates which brought an element of the assembly-line to stamp production for the British Commonwealth from 1880 till the 1930s. Other denominations up to 1s. were issued between 1879 and 1890 and provisional ½ and 4d. surcharges appeared in 1885. St Christopher's stamps were superseded by the Leewards general issue in 1890.

4. St Kitts-Nevis, 2 pence, 1903
Following complaints from the presidencies of the Leeward Islands that they had suffered a drop in revenue as a result of giving up individual stamp issues, the right of issuing their own stamps was restored to them in 1903. Though they continued to be separate members of the Universal Postal Union St Christopher (or St Kitts as it is popularly known) and Nevis joined forces to issue a definitive series inscribed with both names.

5. St Kitts-Nevis, 1 penny, 1907
Two designs were utilized, one showing a group of ladies 'taking the waters' of Nevis, and the other Christopher Columbus. This stamp shows Columbus using a telescope, an instrument which Galileo did not invent for more than a century later. This curious inaccuracy was perpetuated on stamps of St Kitts-Nevis as late as 1952. The 1d. stamp originally appeared in two colours, but changed to single-working plates in 1907.

6. St Kitts-Nevis, 1½ pence, 1920
De La Rue combined the colonial emblems of St Christopher and Nevis with the king's profile in a definitive series released between 1920 and 1922, using a long horizontal format. The series, in denominations from ½d. to £1, was first printed on Multiple Crown CA paper, but was reprinted on the Script watermarked paper between 1921 and 1929.

7. St Kitts-Nevis, 1 penny, 1923
St Kitts-Nevis set the pattern for a number of colonies in the 1920s by releasing a lengthy commemorative series to celebrate the tercentenary of the colony. Thirteen denominations, ranging from ½d. to £1, were typographed by De La Rue with vignettes in black and frames in colour. The stamps depicted Sir Thomas Warner's ship in Old Road

Bay, with Mount Misery in the background. Such long and expensive commemorative sets were unpopular with collectors at the time and consequently are now elusive.

8. St Kitts-Nevis, 10 shillings, 1948
De La Rue typographed a definitive series for St Kitts-Nevis, in 1938, portraying King George VI. The horizontal designs of the George V series, with the new portrait substituted, were retained for the middle values, but small format stamps with the king's profile alone were used for the ½, 1 and 2½d. denominations. Higher values, of 10s. and £1, were not added to the series till September 1948. Both stamps featured a map of Anguilla, politically administered with St Christopher and Nevis but geographically isolated from the other two and generally neglected by them. The appearance of the map stamps was a belated attempt to redress the balance. The frames were typographed but the maps were lithographed.

9. St Kitts-Nevis, 1 shilling, 1950
Philatelic recognition of Anguilla was repeated two years later when six denominations of the definitive series were overprinted to mark the tercentenary of the British settlement of the island. The 1½d. denomination of the overprinted series is known with two strange errors in its watermark, the first with the crown missing and the second with the wrong crown substituted – a St Edward's crown instead of the Tudor one then generally used.

10. St Christopher-Nevis-Anguilla, 4.80 dollars, 1952
The Leeward Islands adopted decimal currency in 1951 and stamps inscribed in British Caribbean cents and dollars were introduced in the presidency in June 1952. The values ranged from 1c. to $4.80 (1 cent = halfpenny, so that $4.80 = £1). The series was recess-printed by Waterlow and Sons and depicted scenery in the islands, with an inset portrait of King George VI, after a photograph by Dorothy Wilding. The series appeared posthumously, since the king died in February 1952. Similar stamps, portraying Queen Elizabeth, were recess-printed by Waterlow in 1954–57 and then by De La Rue in 1961–63.

11. St Christopher-Nevis-Anguilla, 24 cents, 1957
Eva Wilkin, a local artist, designed this stamp to celebrated the bicentenary of the birth of Alexander Hamilton, the American patriot who was born in Nevis. The background reproduces an eighteenth century print of the island. The stamp was recess-printed by Waterlow and Sons.

12. St Christopher-Nevis-Anguilla, 12 cents, 1961
Curiously enough the constitutional developments in these islands were allowed to pass unrecorded by stamps. In 1952 the islands ceased to be a presidency of the Leeward Islands and became a crown colony in their own right, and nine years later a new constitution was granted which instituted ministerial government. A set of four stamps, however, was released in July 1961 to mark the centenary of the first stamps in the colony, the Nevis series of 1861. Each of the four denominations of the commemorative series reproduced the corresponding denominations of the Nevis series. The series was recess-printed by Waterlow and Sons, one of the last produced by this firm before it ceased to exist as a security printing company.

13. St Christopher-Nevis-Anguilla, 3 cents, 1966
In September 1964 the annual Arts Festival was celebrated by overprinting the 3 and 25c. denominations of the definitive series. The 5c. has been recorded with a double overprint. No stamps appeared in 1965 for this event but in 1966, 3 and

25c stamps with the festival emblem were printed in multicolour photogravure by Harrison & Sons. Three stamps marked this event in 1970.

14. St Christopher-Nevis-Anguilla, 10 cents, 1967
St Christopher-Nevis-Anguilla achieved associated statehood on 27 February 1967, and issued a set of three stamps the following July to mark the occasion. They were designed by Victor Whiteley and printed in multicolour photogravure by Harrisons, featuring Government House, Basseterre, the national flag and the coat of arms. In September 1967, however, Anguilla broke away from the union and has since issued its own stamps (see below), though those of St Christopher and Nevis continue to bear the name of Anguilla.

15. St Christopher-Nevis-Anguilla, 60 cents, 1963
Victor Whiteley designed the stamps printed in multicolour by Harrisons which were issued in November 1963 in denominations from ½c. to $5. The 60c. value reproduced the bust of Alexander Hamilton by Giuseppe Ceracchi (also featured on the 30c. stamp in the United States series of 1870). Hamilton was the only person, other than royalty, to be portrayed on the definitive stamps of two different countries simultaneously. His portrait graced the $5 denomination of the United States definitive series of 1954–65.

16. St Kitts-Nevis-Anguilla, 25 cents, 1967
Note the use of the older, and popular, form of the name on this stamp. During the 1960s the contraction 'St Kitts' was sometimes used, though 'Anguilla' has continued to appear on all the stamps of this territory. The government of St Christopher-Nevis did not recognize the breakaway regime in Anguilla until July 1969, yet the name continues to appear on the stamps of St Christopher-Nevis to this day. This stamp was one of a set of three designed by Jennifer Toombs and lithographed by De La Rue to mark the West Indies Methodist Conference in 1967.

17. St Kitts-Nevis-Anguilla, 50 cents, 1968
Like many of the West Indian countries St Kitts issued stamps in 1968 in memory of Dr Martin Luther King, the assassinated leader of the American negroes. Many of these stamps were linked to Human Rights Year. This stamp was designed by George Vasarhelyi and lithographed in multicolour by Enschedé.

18. St Christopher-Nevis-Anguilla, 40 cents, 1969
Christmas stamps, reproducing Old Masters, were adopted by St Christopher Nevis in 1968. This stamp was one of a series of four depicting two versions of the Adoration of the Kings, by Mostaert and Geertgen respectively. They were designed by staff artists of Enschedé, but the actual lithography was entrusted to Bradbury Wilkinson; they were issued in November 1969.

19. St Kitts-Nevis-Anguilla, 40 cents, 1970
Several countries, including the United Kingdom, issued stamps in 1970 to mark the centenary of the death of Charles Dickens. This stamp, reproducing a photograph of the novelist, was one of a set of four designed by Jennifer Toombs and lithographed by Bradbury Wilkinson. Two stamps featured scenes from *Great Expectations* while the other design showed Dickens's birthplace in Portsmouth.

20. Anguilla, 25 cents, 1969
The island of Anguilla seceded from the state of St Christopher-Nevis-Anguilla in September 1967 and has issued its own stamps since that date. All the stamps of Anguilla have been designed by John Lister Ltd, a well known stamp dealer, and the emphasis has been on frequent colourful sets in all 269

PLATE 107 ST CHRISTOPHER, NEVIS, ANGUILLA · PLATE 108 WINDWARD ISLANDS

the more popular themes. This stamp was one of a pair released in March 1969 to commemorate Easter; they reproduced paintings of the Crucifixion and the Last Supper.

21. Anguilla, 1 cent, 1970
Christmas stamps have been issued by Anguilla since 1968 and like the Easter stamps the emphasis has been laid on reproductions of Old Master paintings. A set of five stamps was released in December 1970 lithographed by Questa.

22. Anguilla, 5 cents, 1970
Anguilla's third definitive series in three years appeared in November 1970, featuring aspects of industry, agriculture and modern developments on the island such as the extension to the Cottage Hospital shown on this stamp. Note the unusually ornate frame of birds and marine life of Anguilla. The stamps were lithographed in multicolour by Format International.

23. Anguilla, 40 cents, 1967
Following independence the stamps of St Christopher-Nevis-Anguilla were overprinted 'Independent Anguilla' by the Island Press Inc. of St Thomas in the United States Virgin Islands. Two months later, in November 1967, a distinctive pictorial series featuring scenery and landmarks of the island was released.

24. Anguilla, 6 cents, 1969
The pictorial definitive series of 1967–68 was reissued on 9 January 1969 with a two-line overprint 'Independence January 1969'. This marked the reaffirmation of Anguilla's independence despite protests by St Christopher and Nevis. In July 1969, however, the independence of the Anguilla post office was officially recognized by the government of St Christopher and Nevis and normal postal communications which had been suspended for two years, were resumed with St Christopher.

25. Anguilla, 10 cents, 1968
Apart from the frequent definitive issues and such hardy annuals as the Easter and Christmas stamps, Anguilla has produced numerous short thematic sets and occasional commemorative issues. The 35th anniversary of the Anguillan Girl Guides was celebrated in October 1968 by a set of four stamps with guide badges and emblems.

PLATE 108
Windward Islands

1. Dominica, 2 shillings 6 pence, 1921
British stamps, with the numeral obliterator A 07, were used in Dominica from 1858 till 1874, when the island introduced its own stamps, the design being similar to that used in St Christopher and Tobago. These were superseded by the general series of the Leeward Islands in 1890 and distinctive stamps did not reappear till 1903. A large-format pictorial design, with a view of Roseau from the sea, was adopted for the stamps from ½d. to 2s.6d., while a portrait of King Edward VII was used for the 5s. denomination. The watermark of the series changed in 1907–08 and new colours were adopted in 1908–21. Finally the watermark was again changed in 1921. The stamps were typographed by De La Rue, demonstrating the sorry fact that this process might be suitable for portraiture but was seldom satisfactory for pictorialism.

2. Dominica, 5 shillings, 1938
Waterlow and Sons recess-printed a pictorial

definitive series issued between 1938 and 1947 with the profile of King George VI inset. The four designs featured Fresh Water Lake, Layou River, lime-picking and the Boiling Lake. A farthing stamp, with a full-face portrait of the king, was printed in photogravure by Harrisons in 1940. A similar stamp was used in Grenada (see below). These represent some of the earliest attempts at photogravure for British colonial stamps.

3. Dominica, 10 cents, 1963
The earliest Elizabethan series of Dominica merely repeated the designs of the last Georgian series, but an entirely new series, printed in multicolour photogravure, was released between 1963 and 1965. The seventeen featured scenery, occupations and wild-life of the island. This stamp depicts the crapaud, or edible frog. Two versions exist of the 14c. denomination showing a girl in traditional costume; in the first version she is shown looking straight ahead, while in the second (released in 1965) her eyes are looking to the right. The series was reissued on sideways watermarked paper in 1966–67 and overprinted in 1968 to mark the attainment of associated statehood.

4. Dominica, 60 cents, 1969
Like the other West Indian islands, Dominica since receiving full statehood, has produced numerous colourful stamps. This was one of a set of four released on 3 November 1969 to mark National Day. Cashing in on the stained glass craze, they were designed by George Vasarhelyi and lithographed in multicolour by the Israeli Government Printer, Jerusalem. They were printed in sheets of sixteen, containing twelve stamps and four labels in the top row. The labels each contained two lines of a patriotic poem by W. O. M. Pond.

5. Dominica, 3 cents, 1969
The definitive series printed in photogravure by De La Rue and issued in November 1969 adopted a novel device, using the initial letter D, in the form of an illuminated capital, as the frame for the stamp designs. A curious feature of this series was the use of the Singapore half check pattern watermark on the higher denominations (60c. to $4.80). The lower denominations were printed on unwatermarked paper. The stamps featured scenery and wildlife of the islands.

6. Grenada, 1 penny, 1861
Before introducing its own stamps in 1861 Grenada used British stamps, identifiable by the numeral obliterator A 15. Perkins Bacon recess-printed 1d. and 6d. stamps, using the famous Chalon portrait of Queen Victoria. They were very roughly perforated in a gauge which varied from 14 to 16 and was so ineffective that the stamps often had to be separated by scissors. These handsome stamps were superseded by a De La Rue typographed issue in 1883.

7. Grenada, 2½ pence, 1898
Grenada was one of the few West Indian islands to issue a stamp in the 1890s to commemorate the exploits of Christopher Columbus. A 2½d. stamp, recess-printed by De La Rue, was issued in August 1898 to mark the quatercentenary of the discovery of the island by Columbus. 'La Concepcion' was the original name for the island. The stamp was normally issued on white paper but a small quantity was printed on bluish paper.

8. Grenada, 5 shillings, 1934
Grenada made a partial concession to the fashion for pictorialism which swept colonial philately in the 1930s, by issuing a series in 1934–36 with three pictorial designs (Grand Anse beach, Grand Etang and St George's) and a design combining heraldry

with the king's profile. The flagship of Columbus was adopted as the emblem of Grenada, and has been featured on many of the islands definitive stamps from 1906 to the present day.

9. Grenada, farthing, 1937
This stamp was the first photogravure stamp in the reign of King George VI; after the Gold Coast and Great Britain, Grenada was only the third Commonwealth country to use this process. This stamp was printed by Harrison and Sons whereas the remaining stamps of the series were recess-printed by De La Rue or Waterlows. A similar design was used for the farthing stamps of Dominica and, with a portrait of Queen Elizabeth, was current until 1963.

10. Grenada, half cent, 1951
In the 1950s there was an attempt, through the recess printing of Bradbury Wilkinson, to recapture the classic beauty of the first stamps of the West Indies. Thus Grenada adopted a small-format design for the series from ½c. to 12c. released in 1951, using a frame reminiscent of the Perkins Bacon series of 1861. A comparison reveals how coarse and insensitive the engraving of both frame and portrait had become in a space of ninety years, and how far short of perfection the series of 1951 had fallen.

11. Grenada, 25 cents, 1966
After flirting with recess-printing for the Elizabethan series of 1953–59 Grenada finally succumbed to the lure of multicolour photogravure and issued a series of miniature tourist posters, designed by Victor Whiteley, in April 1966. The stamps featured views and natural products of the island, with a map, the coat of arms, and the Queen's full-length portrait on the three-dollar denominations. The series was subsequently overprinted for commemorative and definitive purposes, after associated statehood had been granted in 1967.

12. Grenada, 1 dollar, 1969
Grenada was one of the many countries which issued stamps in 1969 to mark the centenary of the birth of Mahatma Gandhi. The series of four large stamps was designed by A. Robledo and lithographed by Bradbury Wilkinson. Striking use was made of coloured rectangles on which the image was outlined in black. Note the use of gold foil embossing to show the royal portrait.

13. Grenada, 35 cents, 1969
Granada had the distinction of being the first country in the Western Hemisphere to have a woman head of state. Dame Hylda Bynoe, a general practitioner, became governor of Grenada in 1967 and thus follows in the footsteps of such stateswomen as Mesdames Senenayake, Gandhi and Meir of Ceylon, India and Israel. Dame Hylda appeared on two Grenadan sets of 1969, publicizing Carifta Expo 69 and Human Rights Year. This stamp was one of a set of four printed by Enschedé, two portraying the governor, one portraying Dr Martin Luther King and the other reproducing Rembrandt's painting 'Belshazzar's Feast'.

14. St Lucia, 1 penny, 1864
From 1858 till 1860 St Lucia used British stamps with the numeral obliterator A 11. Perkins Bacon adopted the expedient of printing undenominated stamps in different colours, so that colour alone would serve to indicate the value. The first penny stamps were issued in 1860 and were printed in red, while blue and green stamps served as 4d. and 6d. values respectively. The colour scheme was altered in 1864 to black (1d.), yellow (4d.) and violet (6d.), with an additional brown-orange (1s.) value. These 'economy' stamps remained in use, with various

PLATE 108 WINDWARD ISLANDS · PLATE 109 BARBADOS, TRINIDAD

changes in perforation and watermark, until the typographed series by De La Rue were issued in 1882.

15. St Lucia, 1 pound, 1946
St Lucia got by with no stamps above a shilling till 1891 and from then until after World War II the highest denomination was 10s. In 1946 a £1 stamp was added to the George VI series. The low values, from ½ to 3½d., were introduced in this design in 1938, while the higher denominations used pictorial designs showing Columbus Square and Government House in Castries, the Pitons and banana-loading. The small-format design was recess-printed by Waterlow and Sons while Bradbury Wilkinson and De La Rue produced the other designs. The small-format design was retained for a series inscribed in Caribbean cents and dollars, in 1949–50.

16. St Lucia, 1 dollar, 1953
The basic design of this stamp was first used in 1938 for a 10s. stamp in the George VI series with a background of GRI monograms. It was retained for the higher denominations of the Georgian decimal series and then, with the EIIR monogram, used for the Elizabethan series of 1953–54. Bradbury Wilkinson were responsible for this design in all its variations and permutations. The motto 'Statio Haud Malefida Carinis' (a place without an unreliable anchorage) is a somewhat backhanded reference to the deep-water harbour, one of the finest in the West Indies.

17. St Lucia, 25 cents,
A new constitution was granted to the Windward Islands in 1959 leading to the establishment of ministerial government in place of the former crown colonial system. St Lucia celebrated the event by issuing a set of three stamps in January 1960. The stamps, recess-printed by Waterlow and Sons, show the flagship of Columbus off the Pitons.

18. St Lucia, 35 cents, 1968
Since achieving associated statehood in March 1967 St Lucia has embarked on a policy of prolific and colourful stamp issues. Two stamps, reflecting the West Indian passion for cricket, appeared in March 1968 to honour the M.C.C.'s West Indies tour. Designed by Victor Whiteley and printed by Harrisons, they depicted a batsman, with an inset photograph of the governor, Sir Frederick Clarke.

19. St Vincent, 5 pence, 1893
Like the other West Indian islands St Vincent used ordinary British stamps from 1858 onward, distinguishable by the numeral obliterator A 10. Distinctive stamps, recess-printed by Perkins Bacon, were introduced in May 1861 and certain denominations, subsequently printed by De La Rue, remained in use until 1899. A change in postal rates in 1892 led to the surcharge of 4 and 6d. stamps to create a 5d. value. A few examples are known with the surcharge double. Distinctive 2½ and 5d. stamps in this design were recess-printed by De La Rue in 1897. A typographed series by De La Rue appeared in 1899.

20. St Vincent, 1 pound, 1938
The colonial emblem, showing female allegories of peace and justice, first appeared on the stamps of St Vincent in 1880 (5s.) and was subsequently used for low value stamps between 1907 and 1911. The emblem was resurrected for certain denominations of the George VI series recess-printed by Bradbury Wilkinson in 1938–47. Four pictorial designs, featuring Young's Island and Fort Duvernette, Kingstown and Fort Charlotte, the bathing beach at Villa and Victoria Park, Kingstown, were used for other values of this series. The same designs, with values in cents and dollars, were used for the series of 1949–52.

21. St Vincent, 10 cents, 1955
Like Grenada, St Vincent had a penchant for Victorian classicism. This design, redolent of the Perkins Bacon issues of the 1860s, was recess-printed by Waterlow and Sons until 1961 and then produced by De La Rue – both demonstrating their inability to match the subtlety of the Old Masters either in portraiture or background engraving. Apart from the wide variety of shades found in many values of this series the perforations and watermarks were subject to an inordinate number of changes in the early 1960s.

22. St Vincent, 50 cents, 1964
One of a set of four stamps designed by Victor Whitely to mark the golden jubilee of the St Vincent Boy Scouts Association. Featuring the scout emblem and proficiency badges, they were lithographed in two-colour combinations by Harrison and Sons, one of the earliest examples of this process from that firm.

23. St Vincent, 25 cents, 1970
Though Britain herself left the occasion unrecorded several Commonwealth countries, including the Channel Islands and several of the West Indies, issued stamps in 1970 to celebrate the centenary of the British Red Cross, to which their national associations are affiliated. St Vincent's set of four stamps, designed by Richard Granger Barrett and printed by Harrisons, featured a children's nursery, first aid, a voluntary aid detachment and a blood transfusion.

24. St Vincent, 2.50 dollars, 1970
For the definitive series released in January 1970 St Vincent chose birds of the West Indies. The designs were prepared by staff artists of John Waddington Ltd, but the actual production, in multicolour photogravure, was entrusted to Harrison & Sons.

25. St Vincent, 5 cents, 1969
Carnival is one of the highlights of the tourist year in St Vincent and this formed the subject of a set of 4 stamps released in February 1969. Depicting a male masquerader (1c.), a steel bandsman (5c.), carnival revellers (8c.) and the Queen of Bands (25c.), they were designed by Victor Whiteley and lithographed in multicolour by Format International.

26. St Vincent, 35 cents, 1969
The Methodist Conference held in St Vincent in May 1969 was celebrated by the overprint of four denominations of the 1965–67 definitive series. Comparatively few of these stamps were available to the philatelic trade through the normal Crown Agents channels and consequently the 35c. denomination ranks as one of the rarest stamps issued by St Vincent in recent years.

PLATE 109
Barbados and Trinidad

Philatelically the two countries dealt with on this plate have much in common. Both issued stamps long before any of the other British West Indian islands, and both used a common design, the celebrated 'Britannia' recess-printed by Perkins Bacon. They were the only colonies not to make use of British stamps before embarking on their own issues. Trinidad, in fact, may claim to have been the first place in the British Empire, outside the United Kingdom, to issue adhesive stamps, albeit only with local validity. Both exhibited an early awareness of the value of commemorative issues.

1. Barbados, 1 penny, 1860
Barbados began issuing stamps in April 1851, using the design showing Britannia seated on sacks of sugar, with a sailing ship in the background. The stamps were undenominated, Perkins Bacon denoting the value according to the colour. The earliest printings were imperforate but various forms and gauges of perforation were introduced in 1860. The Britannia series remained in use until 1882.

2. Barbados, 4 pence, 1885
De La Rue took over the Barbados contracts in 1875 but continued to recess-print stamps using the Perkins Bacon plates. Between 1882 and 1886 a typographed series, in denominations from ½d. to 5s., was released. Asserting its independent spirit Barbados never accepted the monotony of the keyplate designs, but always made use of distinctive designs.

3. Barbados, 1 penny, 1897
Barbados was one of the few colonies to issue stamps celebrating the Diamond Jubilee of Queen Victoria. The central motif showed the Queen in a chariot drawn by sea-horses – an adaptation of the design used for the definitive series of 1892. The borders contain the heraldic emblems of the United Kingdom and the dates of the queen's reign. Two versions of this series exist, on white or blued paper, the latter appearing in 1898.

4. Barbados, 1 penny on 2 pence, 1907
The 2d. value of the definitive series was overprinted in 1907 and surcharged 1d. in aid of victims of the Kingston, Jamaica, earthquake. The stamp was sold for 2d., but was only valid for 1d. postage, the other 1d. being credited to the relief fund. This issue was remarkable for its wealth of errors, including inverted surcharge, double surcharge, and double surcharge one inverted. The inverted surcharges are as common as the normal version.

5. Barbados, 1 penny, 1906
The tercentenary of the annexation of Barbados was celebrated by this stamp, released rather tardily in August 1906. The stamp was designed by Lady Carter, the wife of the Governor, and purported to show the Olive Blossom which brought the first colonists to the island in 1609 – not 1605 as was thought at the time of the tercentenary celebrations. The stamps was recess-printed by De La Rue in three colours, a tour de force of stamp production for that period.

6. Barbados, 8 pence, 1938
The definitive issues of Barbados from 1892 to 1950 had the reigning sovereign in the full panoply of monarchy, riding in a chariot drawn by sea-horses. For each definitive series it was only necessary to alter the features to those of the reigning king or queen. In fact, however, the inscription and frame of the George V and George VI stamps sets differed in several respects. This series, recess-printed by De La Rue, also exhibited the same range of perforation found on other issues of this firm during World War II.

7. Barbados, 1.20 dollars, 1962
Barbados was granted self-government in 1961, but did not issue stamps to mark the occasion. The first stamps to appear under the new regime were a set of three issued in March 1962 to celebrate the golden jubilee of the Barbados Boy Scouts. They were recess-printed by Bradbury Wilkinson with the Scout emblem superimposed on a map of the island.

271

PLATE 109 BARBADOS, TRINIDAD · PLATE 110 BAHAMAS, BERMUDA

8. Barbados, 2.50 dollars, 1965
Three years after the attainment of self-government in 1962 Barbados adopted a definitive series with the common theme of marine life. It was designed by Victor Whiteley from original drawings by Mrs J. Walker and the stamps were printed in multicolour photogravure by Harrison & Sons in denominations from 1c. to $2.50. They were originally issued with an upright watermark but between 1966 and 1969 they were reissued with a sideways watermark and a $5 value was added to the series. In the original version the seahorse (4c.) stamp was incorrectly inscribed 'hippocanpus' but this misspelling was corrected to 'hippocampus' when the watermark was changed in 1966.

9. Barbados, 50 cents, 1967
Barbados became an independent member of the Commonwealth in December 1966 and issued a set of four stamps in honour of the event and a subsequent series to celebrate the first anniversary. This stamp was one of four designed by Victor Whiteley and printed by Harrison in December 1967. The series portrayed Governor General Sir Winston Scott, the Independence Arch, Treasury and Parliament Building. After such a promising beginning, however, Barbados has not issued further anniversary sets.

10. Barbados, 10 cents, 1970
The definitive series issued in May 1970 exemplifies modern stamp planning in countries under the aegis of the Crown Agents. The designs were produced by staff artists of John Waddington, but the printing was entrusted to De La Rue. Just as Harrisons have now embarked on lithography, so also De La Rue have changed over to photogravure in many of their more recent issues. This series, in values from 1c. to $5, depicts outstanding landmarks on the island.

11. Barbados, 25 cents, 1969
Scouting has continued to be a popular theme in Barbados. John Cooter designed a set of four stamps and a miniature sheet issued in December 1969 to mark the independence of the Barbados Boy Scouts Association and the 50th anniversary of the Barbados Sea Scouts, the latter commemoration being alluded to in the 25c. denomination, which showed sea scouts rowing in Bridgetown Harbour. The stamps were lithographed in multicolour by Enschedé.

12. Barbados, 25 cents, 1970
Since 1969 Barbados has issued a number of short thematic sets, usually including a miniature sheet. Five stamps appeared in August 1970 featuring flowers of Barbados. They were designed and lithographed in multicolour by John Waddington Ltd.

13. Barbados, 50 cents, 1969
The first thematic set issued by Barbados appeared in March 1969 with the theme of horse-racing. John Cooter produced the designs showing various aspects of horse racing and the stamps were lithographed in multicolour by Format International.

14. Trinidad, 1 penny, 1883
Although a 5c. stamp was provided by David Bryce for the prepayment of mail carried by his steamship *Lady McLeod* plying between San Fernando and Port of Spain, as early as April 1847, a further four years elapsed before the colonial authorities adopted this measure. The first series consisted of undenominated Britannia designs, identical in all but the name of the colony with those issued by Barbados and Mauritius. Stamps showing the denomination were issued from 1859 onward and De La Rue took over production in 1862. A

series of typographed stamps with Queen Victoria's profile replaced the Britannias in 1883–84, but in 1896 Trinidad reverted to a Britannia motif which, in various guises, remained in use until 1935.

15. Trinidad, 2 pence, 1898
Like Grenada, Trinidad celebrated the quatercentenary of its discovery by Columbus with a large-format pictorial commemorative stamp in 1898, recess-printed by De La Rue. Trinidad was discovered by Christopher Columbus on his third voyage to the West Indies and named by him in honour of the Holy Trinity.

16. Tobago, 1 shilling, 1894
British stamps were used in Tobago far longer than in any of the other West Indian islands, the A 14 numeral obliterator serving to identify them. Distinctive adhesive stamps were not adopted until August 1879 when a series typographed by De La Rue was introduced. At first fiscal stamps, in denominations from 1d. to £1, were used pending the arrival of the postal series. Both designs are similar, differing only in the inclusion of the word POSTAGE in the lower part of the circle surrounding the queen's portrait. The postal series did not come into use until December 1880. Tobago's stamps were superseded by those of Trinidad in 1896, but in 1913 stamps bearing the names of both islands were adopted.

17. Trinidad and Tobago, 4 pence, 1922
The first series bearing the inscription 'Trinidad & Tobago' appeared in 1913 and followed the Britannia designs previously inscribed 'Trinidad' alone. The profile of the reigning sovereign was reintroduced when De La Rue typographed a definitive series in 1922 showing the Britannia motif and a profile of King George V. The series was distinguished for De La Rue's use of colour combinations on paper of various colours. In the case of this stamp black and red were used on pale yellow.

18. Trinidad and Tobago, 4.80 dollars, 1940
Bradbury Wilkinson recess-printed a pictorial definitive series for Trinidad and Tobago in 1935 in a small horizontal format. Similar designs were retained for a larger format in 1938, to allow the inclusion of the portrait of King George VI. In most cases the designs matched those of the previous series, value for value, but a 60c. denomination replaced the 72c. stamp in featuring Blue Basin. The same designs, with the profile of Queen Elizabeth substituted, were used for the definitive series of 1953–55. Small designs for the $1.20 and $4.80 values were adopted in 1940.

19. Trinidad and Tobago, 25 cents, 1961
Multicolour photogravure came to Trinidad in 1960 when Harrisons produced a new pictorial definitive series. A few months later two stamps were released to mark the Second Caribbean Scout Jamboree. Both showed a group of scouts on a map of the islands. The badge beneath the queen's portrait is the gold wolf, the highest scouting award.

20. Trinidad and Tobago, 25 cents, 1962
Trinidad and Tobago attained complete independence in August 1962 and celebrated the occasion by issuing five stamps with a curious mixture of designs. The 5c. value reproduced a mural by Carlisle Chang of an underwater scene. The middle values depicted the Piarco Air Terminal and the new Hilton Hotel at Port of Spain, the top values a bird of paradise and a scarlet ibis on maps of the country.

21. Trinidad and Tobago, 5 cents, 1966
While an omnibus design was used by most of

the Caribbean islands visited by Queen Elizabeth in 1966, Trinidad, as an independent country, chose a distinctive series of four stamps, each with a different design. The Redhouse, or parliament building was shown on the 5c. value, while the Royal Yacht *Britannia*, the map and flag, or a flag and panoramic view graced the other denominations. The inscription on these stamps was unusually verbose but was handled unobtrusively by using upper and lower case lettering on a white panel.

22. Trinidad and Tobago, 5 cents, 1963
A set of three stamps designed by Michael Goaman was released in June 1963 to mark the United Nations Freedom from Hunger campaign. The design, featuring protein foods, was similar to that used for the colonial omnibus series, but omitted the queen's portrait and was in a somewhat narrower format.

23. Trinidad and Tobago, 60 cents, 1967
Trinidad pursued a comparatively conservative policy on new stamp issues in the years immediately following independence. Rather disappointingly the fifth anniversary of independence was celebrated merely by overprinting four denominations of the 1960 definitive series. The stamp depicts anthurium lilies, the national flower of Trinidad and Tobago.

24. Trinidad and Tobago, 10 cents, 1969
Since 1968, when Trinidad entrusted its philatelic affairs to an American agency, the stamps have brightened up considerably and made a more frequent appearance. Formerly Harrison and Sons enjoyed a virtual monopoly of Trinidadian stamps but recently the contracts have been placed elsewhere. This stamp was one of four designed by staff artists of the Austrian State Printing Works, Vienna, which also printed them in multicolour photogravure. The series marked the first anniversary of CARIFTA, the Caribbean Free Trade Area. It depicts a cornucopia, a map of the Carifta countries, a Boeing 707 in flight and the flags of the United Kingdom and the member countries.

25. Trinidad and Tobago, 30 cents, 1970
A set of four stamps was designed by Lee and printed in Vienna to mark the 25th anniversary of the United Nations. The stamps featured symbols of culture, science, arts and technology (5c.), children of different races (10c.), Noah's Ark, the rainbow and the dove (20c.) and the new headquarters of the Universal Postal Union in Berne, Switzerland (30c.).

PLATE 110

Bahamas and Bermuda

---

1. Bahamas, 1 penny, 1859
Ordinary British stamps were used in the Bahamas from 1857 till 1862 and may be identified by the numeral obliterator A 05. Such stamps were used on mail going out of the islands; local letters were usually prepaid in cash. This stamp was introduced in June 1859 and was intended, as the inscription suggests, for 'interinsular postage'. The stamp was recess-printed by Perkins Bacon using the Chalon portrait of Queen Victoria. This stamp remained current till 1884 and during that quarter century underwent numerous changes of shade, perforation and watermark. De La Rue produced the stamps from 1862 onward.

2. Bahamas, 2½ pence, 1884
Typographed stamps, in denominations of 4d., 6d. and 1s., were produced by De La Rue for the

PLATE 110 BAHAMAS, BERMUDA

Bahamas from 1863 onwards, but lower values using this process did not appear till 1884. De La Rue had a monopoly of Bahamian stamps until 1930. The tiny ornaments in the lower corners of the design, perpetuating a tradition established in 1859, are a cactus and a conch shell, emblems of the Bahamas which continued to appear on the definitive issues up to 1952.

3. Bahamas, 1 penny, 1919
The basic stamp was introduced in 1901, as part of the campaign to break away from the stereotyped royal profiles of De La Rue colonial stamps. Following the example of Jamaica (see plate 105) the Bahamas adopted a large design with a local landmark, the Queen's Staircase in Nassau. Two years later this design was extended to 5d., 2s. and 3s. denominations, and though typographed portrait stamps were issued from 1902 onward the Queen's Staircase stamps continued to appear alongside the definitive series. Between 1917 and 1919 the 1d. stamp was overprinted to raise funds either for the Red Cross, as a wartime levy on correspondence, or for charity generally. This version was overprinted '3.6.18' to celebrate the bicentenary of the appointment of the first governor of the Bahamas, but was not actually on sale until January 1919. Examples are known with the overprint double.

4. Bahamas, 3 shillings, 1931
A set of five stamps in this design was issued in 1930 to mark the tercentenary of the British colony. The following year 2 and 3s. stamps in this design, without the commemorative dates across the top, were issued as definitives, remaining in use until 1948. The Latin motto signifies 'The pirates having been expelled, commerce was restored' – an allusion to the first governor, Woods Rogers, who drove out the pirates.

5. Bahamas, 8 pence, 1942
The entire definitive series, from ½d. to £1, was overprinted in 1942 to mark the 450th anniversary of the landing of Columbus in the Western Hemisphere. The overprint alludes to his landfall on Salvador or Watling Island in the Bahamas. The basic definitive series, with a profile of King George VI, followed the design of the previous issues typographed by De La Rue. An 8d. stamp, intended for airmail postage, was introduced in 1935 and illustrated flamingoes in flight. The same design, with the portrait of King George VI substituted, appeared in July 1938, along with two other pictorial designs recess-printed by Waterlow and Sons: the Sea Garden, Nassau (4d.) and Fort Charlotte (6d.).

6. Bahamas, 1 pound, 1948
The Bahamas was the only British colony to issue lengthy and expensive sets of stamps in the 1940s. Six years after the Columbus overprints a long set was recess-printed by the Canadian Bank Note Co. to celebrate the tercentenary of the settlement of the island of Eleuthera. It featured industries and occupations, tourism and landmarks of the islands in general. The vignette of this stamp, featuring the Parliament Buildings, refers to the establishment of representative government in 1729. This series was the only one produced by the Canadian printers for a territory outside Canada. The tiny, ill-proportioned portrait of the king was reminiscent of that on the Newfoundland coronation series of 1937 (see plate 90).

7. Bahamas, 5 shillings, 1954
The vignettes of the Eleuthera series were adapted by Bradbury Wilkinson for the first Elizabethan definitive series, issued in January 1954. Prominent shades exist of many values of this series. In true

Bahamian fashion stamps of this series were subsequently overprinted to commemorate the Bahamas Talks (1962) and the Olympic Games (1964), and the entire series was overprinted in 1964 to celebrate the new constitution which accompanied self-government.

8. Bahamas, 10 pence, 1959
The centenary of the first Bahamian stamps was celebrated in June 1959 by a set of four stamps, recess-printed by Waterlows and emulating the design of the inter-insular stamp of 1859. Like the attempts to imitate the fine engraving of the stamps of Grenada and St Vincent, the experiment with the Bahamas also failed. Neither Waterlows nor Bradbury Wilkinson were able to match the delicacy of the engraving exhibited in the original Perkins Bacon stamps.

9. Bahamas, 1 dollar, 1967
A multicolour definitive series was produced by Bradbury Wilkinson in January 1965. The Queen's portrait (by Anthony Buckley) and the lettering were recess-printed while the vignettes were lithographed. The series appeared with surcharges in decimal currency in May 1966 and was reissued with the values redrawn in cents and dollars in May 1967. The 5s. and $1 denominations depicted the Williamson undersea film project of 1914 and the undersea post office at Nassau, established in 1939. A distinctive postmark, 'Posted on the Sea Floor', was applied to mail.

10. Bahamas, 10 pence, 1962
One of two stamps released in January 1962 to mark the centenary of the city of Nassau. They depicted Christ Church Cathedral and the Nassau public library and were printed in photogravure by Enschedé – the first British colonial stamps to be produced by that firm.

11. Bahamas, 15 cents, 1969
The Bahamas began issuing special Christmas stamps in October 1969 and since then a series featuring Old Master reproductions has appeared each season. This was one of a series of four designed by Gordon Drummond and lithographed by De La Rue. Two denominations had versions of the *Adoration of the Shepherds*, by Louis le Nain and Poussin, while the other two reproduced the *Adoration of the Kings* by Gerard David and Vincenzo Foppa respectively.

12. Bahamas, 15 cents, 1967
The Bahamas was one of the few countries to issue stamps marking the diamond jubilee of the world scout movement. Two stamps, designed by Richard Granger Barrett and printed by Enschedé, featured the Queen and Lord Baden-Powell, the movement's founder.

13. Bahamas, 15 cents, 1969
Tourism is one of the most important industries in the Bahamas. The arrival of the one millionth visitor to the islands was celebrated in August 1969 by a set of four stamps and a miniature sheet designed by John Cooter and lithographed in multicolour by Format International. The stamps illustrated game fishing boats (3c.), Paradise Beach (11c.), sunfish sailing boats (12c.) and a parade at Rawson Square, Nassau (15c.).

14. Bermuda, 6 pence, 1865
Between 1848 and 1861 the postmaster of Hamilton and St George's issued handstruck stamps for the prepayment of local postage. These had local validity only and little was known about them until the 1890s, when a few examples of the Hamilton stamps came to light. The Bermuda postal administration did not adopt adhesive

stamps until September 1865, when 1d., 6d. and 1s. stamps, typographed by De La Rue, were issued. The series, with additional values and various changes in watermark and perforation, remained in use until 1902.

15. Bermuda, 4 pence, 1909
The trend toward pictorialism, evident in the stamps of such colonies as Tasmania, Jamaica and the Bahamas, found its expression in the small format series of Bermuda issued in 1902–03. Typographed by De La Rue, it featured sailing vessels approaching Hamilton Dock. The watermark was changed in 1906 and various denominations were added to the series between 1907 and 1910. Single working plates were introduced for the ½, 1 and 2½d. stamps in 1908–10.

16. Bermuda, farthing, 1920
The tercentenary of the island's House of Assembly was celebrated in 1920 and not one but two sets of stamps were produced for the occasion. The first series, appearing between November 1920 and January 1921, demonstrates what is possible when the governor of a colony is allowed a free hand with stamp design. The series was the handiwork of General Sir James Willcocks and De La Rue the unwilling collaborators on what must be one of the worst designs ever inflicted on a British colony. The inscription 'Bermuda Commemoration Stamp' was needlessly verbose, while the caption 'Tercentenary of Establishment of Representative Institutions' defies description. Dissatisfaction with this monstrous set led to its early withdrawal and the appearance of a second series.

17. Bermuda, 1 shilling, 1921
The second series was designed by H. J. Dale and turned out to be not much of an improvement, though the omission of 'Commemoration Stamp' and the neat circular arrangement of the lengthy caption were more satisfactory. The design was marred, however, by the fussy arrangement of the sailing ship and coat of arms in the upper corners and the sword and disembodied hand clutching a judge's gavel in the lower corners, while the floral ornament and the needless repetition of the value only served to clutter all available space. The second series was recess-printed whereas the first was typographed, both by De La Rue.

18. Bermuda, 1 shilling 6 pence, 1936
Bradbury Wilkinson recess-printed a pictorial definitive series released in April 1936. Only two of the six designs incorporated a full-face portrait of King George V and the remaining denominations were therefore retained during the reign of George VI. The ½d. and 1s.6d. denominations showed yachts at anchor in Hamilton Harbour. This stamp remained in use until 1953.

19. Bermuda, 1 pound, 1953
An entirely new definitive series replaced the mixture of George V and George VI types in November 1953. The set of eighteen, from ½d. to £1, was produced by Bradbury Wilkinson, with landmarks, maps, flowers, birds and coins of Bermuda. The series was recess-printed, but typography was used for the coat of arms on the £1 denomination.

20. Bermuda, 1.20 dollars, 1970
W. H. Harrington designed a series for Bermuda, printed in multicolour by Harrisons, with historic views and old buildings of the island. It was released in October 1962 and a 10d. denomination was added three years later. Bermuda abandoned sterling in February 1970 and the series was issued with surcharges in cents and dollars, pending the release of an entirely new series later that year, featuring flowers of the island.

273

PLATE 110 BAHAMAS, BERMUDA · PLATE 111 AMERICA ISLAND COLONIES

21. Bermuda, 2 shillings 6 pence, 1968

After the grant of a new constitution Bermuda became an independent Commonwealth country in July 1968. A set of four stamps designed by Granger Barrett and printed by Harrisons, marked the occasion. Two stamps featured a parliamentary mace and the Queen's profile while the others showed the House of Assembly in Bermuda with the Houses of Parliament at Westminster in the background.

22. Bermuda, 2 shillings 6 pence, 1969

Since independence Bermuda has issued a number of colourful, large-format stamps. This one belongs to a series issued in September 1969 to highlight the emerald-studded gold treasure salvaged from the sea bed. The designs by K. Giles were improved by Victor Whiteley and printed by Harrison.

23. Bermuda, 10 cents, 1970

Pictorial demands are such that, sooner or later, countries run out of fresh ideas. This has encouraged the systematic exploration of a single theme at a time, in place of the random selection of former years. Thus the multicolour definitive series adopted by Bermuda in July 1970 has concentrated on flowers of the Caribbean. Designed by W. Harrington and printed by De La Rue, it appeared exactly six months after the surcharged series – the minimum decent interval permitted by the Crown Agents nowadays.

24. Bermuda, 15 cents, 1970

The 350th anniversary of the Bermuda parliament was celebrated in October 1970 by four stamps and a miniature sheet designed by Gordon Drummond and lithographed by Questa in multicolour. The stamps were of the State House (4c.). the Sessions House (15c.). St Peter's Church (18c.) and the Town Hall in Hamilton (24c.). It is interesting to compare the designs and layout of these stamps with the two series of 1920–21 marking the tercentenary of the same event (see nos. 16, 17 on this plate).

PLATE 111
American Island Colonies

Denmark, France, the Netherlands and Spain as well as Britain have issued stamps at one time or another for their colonies in the offshore islands of North America and the Caribbean. The six postal administrations have now been whittled down, by political and postal changes, to two.

1. St Pierre and Miquelon, 15 centimes, 1885

Before 1885 the tiny North Atlantic islands of St Pierre and Miquelon (last remnant of the French empire in Canada) used the colonial general issues. The first stamps consisted of the colonial series surcharged with new values and the initials SPM. Overprinted stamps of this type were superseded by the keyplate designs in 1892.

2. St Pierre and Miquelon, 10 centimes, 1917

Various stamps overprinted 'Colis Postaux' (postal parcels) were issued by this colony between 1901 and 1925. This stamp, issued in 1917, belongs to the definitive series introduced in 1909. Three designs, by C. J. Housez, were used for stamps ranging from 1c. to 5f., showing a fisherman, a seagull and a fishing boat. They were typographed in two-colour combinations by the French Government Printing Works in Paris. Provisional surcharges, changes of colour and new values augmented this series up to 1932.

3. St Pierre and Miquelon, 5 centimes, 1942

The colony joined the Free French movement in 1941 and the following year a photogravure definitive series showing a fishing schooner was designed by Edmund Dulac and printed by Harrisons. Additional values were produced by surcharging in 1945. Stamps of the series of 1938–40 are known with an overprint 'France Libre F.N.F.L.' or with 'Noël 1941', following the coup of Christmas 1941, but they seem to have been used mainly as fund-raisers and were not postally valid.

4. St Pierre and Miquelon, 30 centimes, 1955

A definitive series ranging from 30c. to 500f. was released between 1955 and 1959. It illustrated scenery and occupations of the islands with the emphasis on the fishing industry. Several denominations including the 30c. showed a refrigeration plant, others cod fishing and fishing craft. The stamps were recess-printed at the French Government Printing Works in Paris.

5. St Pierre and Miquelon, 6 francs, 1963

Since 1959 St Pierre and Miquelon have not issued a definitive series as such, but have produced occasional short sets and single values of a thematic rather than commemorative nature. This stamp was one of a set of four illustrating birds of the islands. Designed by P. Lambert, they were recess-printed in three-colour combinations, with eider duck, ptarmigan, ringed plovers and blue-winged teal.

6. Martinique, 30 centimes, 1908

Martinique's first stamps consisted of provisional surcharges on the colonial general series, issued in 1886, followed by the 'Tablet' keyplates in 1892. The first pictorial series was introduced in December 1908, typographed in colour with purple-brown vignettes. Three designs, by L. Colmet Daage, were used, featuring a woman's head, a woman and sugar cane and a view of Fort de France. Numerous provisional surcharges appeared between 1924 and 1927, and colour changes and additional denominations appeared from 1922 to 1930.

7. Martinique, 5 centimes, 1912

A shortage of 5 and 10 centime stamps in 1912 was met by surcharging various denominations of the obsolete 'Tablet' series. The basic series was introduced in November 1892 and new colours and values were issued in 1899.

8. Martinique, 10 centimes, 1947

In common with the other colonies Martinique adopted recess-printing for a pictorial definitive series after World War II. Nine different designs were used ranging in value from 10c. to 200f. picturing scenery, natural products and native types of the island. Martinique, as an overseas *département* of France, now uses ordinary French stamps.

9. Martinique, 10 centimes, 1933

The lengthy definitive series of 1933–40 was printed in photogravure by Vaugirard of Paris. C. Hourriez designed the stamps showing Basse Pointe village, C. Rollet those showing Government House and Martinique women. Changes in postal rates during the 1930s necessitated the frequent appearance of new denominations or changes in the colour of existing values.

10. Guadeloupe, 1 centime, 1891

French colonial stamps overprinted G.P.E. and surcharged with new values were used in Guadeloupe from February 1894 until March 1904. Apart from these provisional surcharges the colonial general issues were released in August 1891 overprinted with the name of the island, and the following year

the 'Tablet' keyplate designs were introduced, inscribed with the name 'Guadeloupe et Dépendances'. Apart from double and inverted overprinted, the series of 1891 was notorious for the spelling errors (Gnadeloupe, Guadelouep, Guadelonpe or Guadbloupe) recorded on every denomination of the set.

11. Guadeloupe, 4 centimes, 1905

J. Puyplat designed and engraved the series introduced in July 1905. Three designs were used, showing Mount Houllemont, Basse Terre, La Soufrière and Point-à-Pitre, Grand Terre. The stamps were typographed in monochrome, though judicious use was made of tinted paper to add variety to the series. Fewer surcharges, new values and changes of colour were needed for this series between 1922 and 1927 than for the contemporary issues of other colonies.

12. Guadeloupe, 2 centimes, 1928

A new typographed definitive series was released between 1928 and 1940. As before, three designs were used, showing a sugar refinery, Saints Harbour and Point-à-Pitre Harbour. Two-colour combinations, in the usual garish tradition of the French colonies, were used for the 42 stamps in this series. Several provisional surcharges appeared in 1943–44, pending the introduction of the Free French issue lithographed by De La Rue.

13. Guadeloupe, 2 centimes, 1928

Guadeloupe, like many of the French colonies, has favoured attractive pictorial designs for the postage due stamps, which contrast markedly with the mundane, utilitarian approach of most other countries to these labels. It is interesting that Guadeloupe had its own distinctive postage due stamps long before postage stamps, the earliest labels being type-set locally in 1876–79. The postage due stamps of 1905–06 featured Gustavia Bay on the island of St Bartholomew, the 1928 series depicted the Allée Dumanoir at Capesterre. Like Martinique, Guadeloupe became a French overseas department in 1946 and ceased issuing its own stamps two years later.

14. Guadeloupe, 30 centimes, 1947

Continuing the tradition of pictorial postage due stamps a series from 10c. to 20f. was released in June 1947. The uniform design by R. Serres featured palms and houses and was recess-printed at the Government Printing Works in Paris.

15. Danish West Indies, 1 cent, 1873

The Danish West Indies, now the American Virgin Islands, began issuing their own stamps in 1855 and from then until 1917 used the same designs as contemporary Danish issues, with few exceptions. Stamps in denominations of 3 or 4c. sufficed from 1855 till 1873, when a full definitive series, ranging from 1 to 50c., was adopted. These were modifications of the Danish series introduced in 1870 and were typographed by H. H. Thiele of Copenhagen. Considerable variation occurred in the quality of the paper and in the shades and perforations. Like their Danish counterparts, several values have been recorded with inverted frame.

16. Danish West Indies, 1 cent, 1900

This design, with the Danish coat of arms, was adopted in the mother country in 1882, but was not adapted for use in the West Indies till eighteen years later. It was engraved by Christian Danielsen and typographed by Thiele in denominations of 1 and 5c.; 2 and 8c. values were added in 1903. Subsequent sets portrayed Christian IX (1905) and Frederick VIII (1907). The Danish West Indies was purchased by the United States in 1917 since when ordinary United States stamps have been used.

17. Puerto Rico, ½ milesima de peso, 1893
A joint issue of stamps, for use in Cuba and Puerto Rico, was made between 1855 and 1873 (see plate 104). British stamps were also used in the island from 1865 till 1877 and may be identified by the numeral obliterators C 61 (Puerto Rico), F 83 (Arroyo), F 84 (Aguadilla), F 85 (Mayaguez), F 88 (Ponce), 582 (Naguabo). Spanish colonial stamps inscribed 'Ultramar' (overseas) were used until 1877 when similar stamps inscribed 'PTO RICO' were introduced.

18. Puerto Rico, 3 centavos, 1898
The Spanish colonial keyplate design known as the 'Curly head' series was adopted in 1898. Various provisional overprints of June to October 1898 were produced during the Spanish-American War, which ended with the surrender of the island to the United States. Various stamps of this series were overprinted 'Habilitado 17 Octubre 1898' – the date of the cession – but are regarded as a privately produced issue without proper government authority.

19. Puerto Rico, 1 cent, 1899
United States stamps, in denominations of 1, 2, 5, 8 and 10c., were overprinted 'Porto Rico' and introduced in 1899 to replace the Spanish colonial series. The basic stamps belonged to the series of 1898 portraying famous Americans.

20. Puerto Rico, 2 cents, 1900
The spelling of the overprint on the 1898 issue was corrected in 1900 when the American 1 and 2c. denominations were overprinted 'Puerto Rico'. The 2c. value is known with the overprint inverted. This issue was superseded by ordinary American stamps without distinguishing overprint later in 1900.

21. Curaçao, 2 cents, 1889
The Netherlands West Indies began issuing stamps in 1873, using the same portraits as the contemporary Dutch issues, but with distinctive frames. They were typographed by Enschedé en Zonen. All stamps from 1873 till 1889 were released on ungummed paper on account of the climatic conditions in Curaçao. This stamp, one of a numeral definitive series issued in April 1889, was the first to be printed on gummed paper.

22. Curaçao, 30 cents, 1942
After the Netherlands had been overrun by the Nazis in 1940 Curaçao had to look elsewhere for supplies of stamps. Bradbury Wilkinson recess-printed a two-colour pictorial definitive series which shows the strong influence of contemporary British colonial design, though it was actually the work of a Dutch artist, P. A. de Blieck. An airmail series, with various views and incorporating a portrait of Queen Wilhelmina, was released in October 1942, followed by a similar series for ordinary postage in 1943.

23. Curaçao, 1½ cents, 1943
The birth of Princess Margriet was taken as the opportunity for issuing a patriotic series showing the Dutch Royal Family. Queen Wilhelmina is shown with her youngest grand-daughter, while Irene and Beatrix look on. Princess Juliana and Prince Bernhard are in the background. The stamps, in denominations of 1½, 2½, 5 and 10c., were recess-printed by Bradbury Wilkinson and released in November 1943.

24. Netherlands Antilles, 15 + 5 cents, 1957
The group of islands hitherto known as Curaçao (the largest island) was renamed the Netherlands Antilles in 1948 and stamps bearing the revised name were introduced in 1949. This stamp is one of a set of three issued in February 1957 to mark the 50th anniversary of the world scout movement. They were designed by P. Koch and printed in photogravure by Enschedé, the small premiums going to local scout funds.

25. Netherlands Antilles, 7½ cents, 1954
The ratification of the Statute for the Kingdom was marked by the release of stamps in the Netherlands and the overseas territories. Identical designs were used in each case, differing only in the denominations and the colours. The names of the countries concerned were grouped in a circle round the portrait of Queen Juliana, the name of the issuing country appearing immediately above the portrait.

26. Netherlands Antilles, 25 + 10 cents, 1970
A set of four stamps issued in 1970 with premiums in aid of cultural and social welfare funds took the theme of mass media as their subject. Abstract designs symbolizing the press, films, radio and television were used respectively for the stamps from 10 to 25c. in value.

27. Netherlands Antilles, 15 cents, 1970
The 5th anniversary of the Trans World Radio Station at Bonaire was marked by 10 and 15c. stamps printed in multicolour photogravure by Enschedé. The 10c. stampd depicted the TWR station, the 15c. a symbolic cross.

28. Netherlands Antilles, 40 cents, 1971
Multicolour photogravure has become the rule in the stamps of this territory since 1957. This stamp commemorated the 150th anniversary of the death of Pedro Luis Brion, commander of the rebel fleet under Simon Bolivar in the war of the Spanish colonies against their motherland. Brion, despite his name, was born in Curaçao, the son of a Dutch businessman from Amsterdam, and returned to his native island shortly before he died. The stamp was designed by Charles Corsen of Willemstad and printed by Enschedé.

PLATE 112
Falkland Island and Dependencies

1. Falkland Islands, 2½ pence, 1891
The prepayment of postage in the Falkland Islands was indicated by means of small handstruck 'franks', used between 1861 and 1877. Adhesive stamps, recess-printed by Bradbury Wilkinson, were introduced in June 1878 in denominations of 1, 4 and 6d., and 1s. The first printings were on unwatermarked paper but from 1883 onward the colonial watermark was adopted. Various other denominations were added to the series between 1891 and 1902. Larger designs, for 2s.6d. and 5s. stamps, were introduced in 1898.

2. Falkland Islands, 1 penny, 1912
The same basic designs, with portraits of Edward VII and George V, were used for the definitive issues of 1904–12 and 1912–20 respectively. The original version of this series was recess-printed by De La Rue on Multiple Crown CA paper, but between 1921 and 1929 it was reissued on the Multiple Script CA paper. The 2½d. stamp of this series was bisected and used as a penny stamp at South Georgia in 1923.

3. Falkland Islands, 6 pence, 1929
The first concession to pictorialism was the definitive series of 1929, recess-printed by Perkins Bacon, with the king's profile above a whale and a penguin.

Variations in shade and perforation were made in the printings of 1936.

4. Falkland Islands, 1 pound, 1933
The centenary of the British settlement was celebrated by a set of eighteen stamps, in values from ½d. to £1, recess-printed by Bradbury Wilkinson. Scenery, ships, landmarks, sheep, whales and penguins accounted for most of the subjects, but the coat of arms and the king's portrait graced the two top values. The 3d. stamp carried a map of the colony, and provoked philatelic reaction from Argentina (see plate 97), the outbreak of the war of map stamps which has gone on ever since.

5. Falkland Islands, 3 pence, 1941
Bradbury Wilkinson recess-printed a pictorial series for the Falkland Islands in 1938, with coloured frame and black vignettes depicting scenery, landmarks, ships, animals and birds of the islands. Increases in postal rates led to changes in colour for certain denominations and the introduction of a 3d. value in July 1941. Further changes took place between 1942 and 1949.

6. Falkland Islands, 2 pence, 1956
Waterlow and Sons recess-printed a definitive series in 1952, using the postwar Wilding portrait of King George VI in conjunction with the usual potpourri of scenic and faunal designs. Between 1955 and 1957 six of these designs were produced by Waterlow using the portrait of Queen Elizabeth.

7. Falkland Islands, 2 shillings, 1962
The fiftieth anniversary of radio communications was celebrated by a set of three stamps designed by Michael Goaman and printed in two-colour photogravure by Enschedé. They illustrated a morse key (6d.), a one-valve receiver (1s.) and a rotary spark transmitter (2s.). Note the use of letters of the Morse Code as part of the decorative motif.

8. Falkland Islands, 4 pence, 1960
The piecemeal pictorial series of 1955–57 was scrapped in 1960 and an entirely new series, from ½d. to £1, was recess-printed by Waterlows using a single theme, the birds of the Falklands. The frames were in colour and the vignettes in black. De La Rue printed these stamps from 1962 onwards, the only difference being in the imprint shown in the marginal paper of the sheet. This series established a precedent, since taken up by other Commonwealth territories, of issuing single-theme definitive sets.

9. Falkland Islands, 2 shillings, 1964
De La Rue designed and recess-printed a set of four stamps, released in December 1964 to celebrate the fiftieth anniversary of the Battle of the Falkland Islands. The three horizontal low denominations depicted the British warships Glasgow (2½d.), Kent (6d.) and Invincible (1s.), the vertical 2s. stamp the battle memorial. The vignettes were printed in black and the frames in various colours and this gave rise to a curious error – the 6d. stamp showing H.M.S. Glasgow instead of H.M.S. Kent. Very few examples of this error have turned up; they were distributed in packets of assorted stamps through a philatelic wholesaler who had not noticed the wrong ship on the stamps.

10. Falkland Islands, 6 pence, 1969
Victor Whiteley designed a set of four stamps issued in April 1969 to mark the 21st anniversary of the Government Air Service. The lower values showed a DHC-2 Beaver floatplane (2d.), a Norseman (6d.) and an Auster (1s.); the 2s. showed the coat of arms of the Falkland Islands – an uninspired choice which was repeated on the corresponding denomination of the Defence Force series of the following year.

275

PLATE 112 FALKLAND ISLAND AND DEPENDENCIES

11. Falkland Islands, 2 shillings, 1970
Since 1968 the Falkland Islands have stepped up their output of commemorative issues. This stamp celebrate the golden jubilee of the Defence Force. Designed by Granger Barrett and lithographed by Bradbury Wilkinson, they depicted a defence post, a mounted volunteer, a corporal in Number One dress uniform and the Defence Force insignia.

12. Falkland Islands, 1 pound, 1968
Modern colonial practice is to change the definitive series every six years on average. The Falkland Islands waited until October 1968 before changing theirs to a photogravure set featuring flowers of the islands, designed by Sylvia Goaman. The names of the flowers such as Pig Vine, Pale Maiden and Diddle Dee, were more flamboyant than their colours deserved, and the use of rather sickly background colours did little to improve the generally insipid appearance of the set. The denominations up to 5s. were surcharged with decimal equivalents in February 1971.

13. Graham Land, 1 penny, 1944
Eight stamps of the Falkland Islands were overprinted and issued in February 1944 in Graham Land, the Antarctic peninsula occupied only by scientific expeditions. Since there was no permanent human population here the need for stamps was more political than postal. This was intended to counter the claims of Argentina and Chile to sovereignty over the area.

14. South Orkneys, 2 pence, 1944
The same eight values, from $\frac{1}{2}d$. to 1s., were likewise overprinted for use in the sparsely populated South Orkney Islands.

15. South Shetlands, 3 pence, 1944
Similar overprints appeared in the South Shetland Islands. The colour of the 6d. stamp was slightly altered in later printings, made in 1945. The overprinted stamps were superseded by the general series of the Falkland Islands Dependencies in 1946. The stamps of British Antarctic Territory were adopted in these three areas in 1963.

16. Falkland Islands Dependencies, 3 pence, 1946
The separate overprinted issues were replaced by a unified series, from $\frac{1}{2}d$. to 1s., carrying a map of the territories claimed by Britain. The map was lithographed and the frame recess-printed by De La Rue. Two versions exist of this set. In the earlier printings the lines of the map were thick and coarse, in the later version thin and clear. Various minor varieties in the map were constant on certain sheet positions in each denomination.

17. Falkland Islands Dependencies, $\frac{1}{2}$ penny, 1954
A pictorial series replaced the map issue in February 1954. Recess-printed by Waterlows (and, from 1962, by De La Rue) it depicted ships connected with famous Antarctic expeditions, from the Belgian expedition of 1897 to the postwar activities of the Falkland Islands Dependencies Survey. Four stamps of this series were released in 1956 with an overprint to commemorate the Trans-Antarctic Expedition of 1955–58 led by Dr Vivian Fuchs and Sir Edmund Hillary. These stamps were withdrawn in July 1963 when separate issues of South Georgia and British Antarctic Territory were adopted.

18. Falkland Islands Dependencies, $2\frac{1}{2}$ pence, 1956
In connection with International Geophysical Year a Trans-Antarctic Expedition led by Sir Edmund Hillary and Sir Vivian Fuchs made the first crossing of the Antarctic continent. Four stamps of the Falkland Islands Dependencies definitive series were overprinted for the use of the expedition, and released in January 1956.

19. South Georgia, 2 shillings, 1963
Along with the other Falkland dependencies South Georgia had issued a set of eight overprinted stamps in 1944. After the establishment of British Antarctic Territory as a separate colony in 1963 the general series of the Falkland Islands Dependencies was replaced by separate issues. Stamps for use in South Georgia and the South Sandwich Islands were recess-printed by De La Rue and introduced in July 1963, in denominations from $\frac{1}{2}d$. to £1. Fourteen of the sixteen designs featured the fauna of the sub-Antarctic; the 1d. depicted a map of the area; and the 2s. showed the cross raised to the memory of Sir Ernest Shackleton, who died at South Georgia in 1921. The series was reissued with decimal currency surcharges in February 1971.

20. South Georgia, 20 pence, 1972
South Georgia's first commemorative set appeared in January 1972 to mark the 50th anniversary of the death of Sir Ernest Shackleton. The famous explorer headed the Shackleton-Rowett Expedition of 1921 but died of angina pectoris at South Georgia and the expedition was subsequently abandoned. The stamps featured the ships *Endurance*, *James Caird* and *Quest* connected with Shackleton's Antarctic expeditions, while his portrait appeared on the top value.

21. British Antarctic Territory, 1 pound, 1963
The former Falkland Islands Dependencies of South Orkneys, South Shetlands and Graham Land became a separate crown colony on 1 February 1963, and a distinctive pictorial series of stamps replaced the general Dependencies set on that date. The stamps were designed by Michael Goaman and recess-printed by Bradbury Wilkinson. They depicted various methods of transportation in Antarctica and incorporated the Annigoni portrait of the Queen. The series up to 10s. was reissued in 1971 with decimal currency surcharges. The map design, used for the top value, was replaced in 1969 by a stamp showing Shackleton's ship *Endurance*.

22. British Antarctic Territory, 2 shillings, 1966
Thirty-three British colonies and protectorates, including British Antarctic Territory (but not South Georgia) issued a set of four stamps in 1966 to commemorate Sir Winston Churchill. A common design, by Jennifer Toombs, was used for all 132 stamps, printed in photogravure by Harrison and Sons. The design features the dome of St Paul's Cathedral at the time of the London Blitz, with portraits of Sir Winston Churchill and Queen Elizabeth. The British Antarctic series was issued in denominations of $\frac{1}{2}$ and 1d., 1 and 2s.

23. British Antarctic Territory, 25 pence, 1971
The definitive series of 1963 was surcharged with values in decimal currency and released in February 1971, pending the supply of a new series with decimal denominations.

PLATE 113 AUSTRALIAN STATES

AUSTRALIA AND POLYNESIA

PLATE 113
Australian States

Although the Commonwealth of Australia came into being in 1901 the individual states continued to issue their own stamps until the end of 1912. In the vast majority of cases stamps portraying Queen Victoria were still in use eleven years after her death. With the exception of two high-value stamps from Victoria portraying King Edward VII, neither the son nor the grandson of Queen Victoria was portrayed on the stamps of these states. For the collector this ultra-conservatism in stamp design is more than compensated for by the bewildering complexities of perforation gauges in the so-called Commonwealth period of 1901–12.

1. New South Wales, 2 pence, 1851
New South Wales was the first Australian state – by two days – to introduce adhesive stamps, on 1 January 1850. Twelve years earlier, however, the colony had made philatelic history by issuing stamped letter sheets two years before the mother country issued the Mulready sheets. These Sydney sheets of 1838 were unpopular and are relatively scarce in used condition, though they remained on sale throughout the 1840s. The first adhesive stamps reproduced the great seal of the colony, showing convicts landing at Botany Bay. The transportation of convicted felons to Australia ceased in 1852. The 'Sydney Views' were superseded in 1851 by a series portraying Queen Victoria and known to collectors as the 'Laureateds'. The stamps were designed by A. W. Manning from a sketch by W. T. Levinge and engraved on steel by John Carmichael of Sydney. A new plate of the 2d. value was engraved by H. C. Jervis in 1853; the original plate was entirely re-engraved by him two years later. The 'Sydney Views' and the 'Laureateds' are among the most complex of Australian stamps

2. New South Wales, 6 pence, 1854
The various local makeshifts were superseded by a series designed by E. H. Corbould and recess-printed in Sydney from plates made by Perkins Bacon. The series remained in use till the 1870s and in that period underwent numerous changes of colour and perforation. An interesting feature of these early stamps was the use of a different numeral watermark for each denomination, and occasionally a wrong one would be used by mistake.

3. New South Wales, 5 shillings, 1861
The first high-value stamp was introduced in 1861, taking the form of a circular medallion designed and engraved by E. H. Corbould. This remarkable design was used for various printings up to 1888 and numerous shades and changes of perforation occurred in that period. The 5s. stamp was revived in 1897 and remained current into the Commonwealth period, undergoing three further changes of perforation.

4. New South Wales, 1 penny, 1888
New South Wales has the honour of having issued the world's first adhesive commemorative stamps for general use throughout the country. A private series appeared in Germany the previous year but had local validity only. The stamps, in denominations from 1d. to 20s., were inscribed 'One Hundred Years' and celebrated the centenary of the settlement at Botany Bay. They portrayed Captain Cook, who discovered New South Wales, Captain Phillip and Lord Carrington, the governors in 1788 and 1888, a lyre bird, emu and kangaroo, a map of Australia, Queen Victoria and a view of Sydney. Although primarily commemorative the series was retained as a definitive issue until 1899 and during that period numerous changes in shade and perforation were introduced.

5. New South Wales, 7½ pence, 1891
Increases in postal rates led to the introduction of 7½ and 12½d. values – setting an awkward precedent for the curious fractional denominations of the Australian Commonwealth in the 1950s (see plate 114). Stamps of the 1871–84 definitive series were surcharged with the new values in words. A ½d. surcharged stamp was produced at the same time.

6. New South Wales, 2½ pence, 1892
The basic stamp, with an allegorical female figure of Australia, appeared in 1890 and was overprinted os for official correspondence two years later. It was designed to stimulate the campaign for Australian unity, which culminated eleven years later in the establishment of the Commonwealth.

7. New South Wales, 1 penny, 1897
One of three new stamps (1d., 2d. and 2½d.) introduced in 1897, it bore the state coat of arms. The other denominations depicted the 'old head' profile of Queen Victoria. This stamp remained current until 1912 and in that fifteen-year period it appeared in a fantastic number of combinations of perforation, shade and paper. To complicate the matter further two different dies were used throughout the period, distinguished by minor details in the crown.

8. New South Wales, 2½ pence, 1897
Between 1897 and 1899 New South Wales introduced new 1, 2 and 2½d. stamps. The 2½d. denomination featured the veiled portrait of Queen Victoria adopted for the last series of coinage issued in her reign. The colour changed from purple to blue in 1899.

9. New South Wales, 9 pence, 1903
Though politically united the Australian states remained postally separate until 1913 and there is little apparent indication in their stamps to suggest political unity. Nevertheless there was a move towards the standardization of stamp production, evident in the adoption of the Crowned A watermark of Australia. In 1903 a 9d. stamp with the seated figure of Australia was issued in New South Wales, with the word 'Commonwealth' prominently inscribed across the top and the abbreviated names of the states at the side. Similar stamps were issued in Queensland at the same time. No other state took part in this 'omnibus' issue.

10. Victoria, 3 pence, 1850
The first stamps of Victoria, in values of 1, 2 and 3d., appeared on 3 January 1850. The dies were engraved by Thomas Ham, of Melbourne, with a half-length portrait of Queen Victoria. Due to wear the dies had to be extensively reworked at frequent intervals, giving rise to numerous variations in the designs. These locally produced stamps were partially supplanted by a series recess-printed by Perkins Bacon in 1856–58, showing the queen on the throne.

11. Victoria, 1 pound, 1884
Under the terms of the Postage Act of 1883 the stamps of the three sets then in use (postage, stamp duty and stamp statute) became interchangeable. All stamps printed from 1884 till 1896 bore the inscription 'Stamp Duty' in their design, denoting use for postal or fiscal purposes. This stamp was typographed in 1884. A similar design, produced by lithography, had been introduced in 1879 and is usually classed as a postal fiscal stamp (e.g. a revenue stamp subsequently authorized for postage).

12. Victoria, 1 penny, 1870
This stamp was one of a lengthy series inscribed

277

PLATE 113 AUSTRALIAN STATES · PLATE 114 AUSTRALIA

'Stamp Statute', introduced in 1870 mainly to record the payment of various court fees. These stamps became valid for postage on 1 January 1884. A curious feature of the designs of this series was their use of contemporary coin obverses and reverses to denote the stamps of corresponding denominations.

13. Victoria, 1 penny, 1896
A series of stamps inscribed 'Stamp Duty' was issued in 1890. Samuel Reading designed and engraved the die for the 1d. stamp while M. Tannenberg designed the 2½ and 5d. stamps. The initial printings of the 1d. were in brown but in 1896 the colour was changed to red.

14. Victoria, 4 pence, 1901
During the 'Commonwealth' period (1901–12) Victoria issued separate sets for postal and fiscal purposes. The designs of 1890 were redrawn with the word 'Postage' substituted for 'Stamp Duty'. The stamps of Victoria were superseded by the issues of the Australian Commonwealth in January 1913.

15. Victoria, ½ penny, 1890
Victoria was the first Commonwealth country to adopt distinctive postage due stamps, a year before New South Wales, and fifteen years before the United Kingdom. The colours of the series were changed in 1895 to red and green and from then until 1908 the shades, watermarks and perforations were changed with monotonous regularity. This design was adopted by the Commonwealth of Australia in 1909 for its postage due series and remained in use, with variations in detail, colour, shade, and perforation, until the stamps were withdrawn from service in 1963.

16. Queensland, 6 pence, 1860
The first adhesive stamps used in Queensland, from 26 January 1860 to 1 November 1860, were the contemporary series of New South Wales, and these can only be distinguished by their postmarks. A distinctive series, with the Chalon portrait of Queen Victoria, was introduced in November 1860, It was issued imperforate at first, but perforated stamps were released later the same month. The dies were engraved by William Humphrys and the plates made by Perkins Bacon who also printed and perforated the stamps, before shipping the equipment out to Brisbane. Later printings were made by the Queensland Government Printer, who also produced a locally lithographed version in 1866. The Chalon series remained in use until 1878.

17. Queensland, 2 shillings, 1871
Stamps in denominations from 1d. to 20s. were typographed in 1866–79 for fiscal use. In January 1880 they were authorized for postal purposes and various stamps inscribed 'Stamp Duty' from then until 1892 were also valid for postage, in line with the practice current in the other Australian states.

18. Queensland, 1 penny, 1897
Stamps of this type, with a shaded background, were typographed for Queensland between 1879 and 1894, but the appearance of the profile was improved by reprinting the stamps with an unshaded background. This version appeared in 1895–96 without figures of value in the corner, and was reissued between 1897 and 1907 with numerals added. The perforations of these stamps were altered in 1908 and 1911.

19. Van Diemen's Land, 1 penny, 1864
The first stamps of Van Diemen's Land, as Tasmania was originally called, were crudely recess-printed by H. and C. Best at the office of the *Courier* newspaper in Hobart. They were followed, in 1855, by this design, recess-printed by Perkins Bacon.

The stamps were sent out to Tasmania in imperforate condition and it was left to the local authorities and various stationers to perforate the stamps as best they could. The series remained in use until replaced by the De La Rue typographed series of 1870.

20. Tasmania, 2½ pence, 1892
The island changed its name to Tasmania in 1858 and stamps produced after that date bore the new name, though the earlier denominations continued to bear the obsolete name till 1870. De La Rue manufactured plates which were then shipped to Hobart, but in 1878 and 1892 they carried out the printing of Tasmanian stamps themselves. This stamp belongs to a series, echoing the standard colonial keyplate designs, issued between 1892 and 1899.

21. Tasmania, 6 pence, 1899
Tasmania followed the lead of New Zealand (1898) by introducing a handsome pictorial definitive series in December 1899. It was recess-printed by De La Rue and illustrated famous beauty spots in the colony.

22. Tasmania, 1 penny, 1912
The pictorial series of Tasmania was subsequently printed in Melbourne by other processes. In 1902–03 the series was printed lithographically, with transfers made from the recess plates. Subsequently a version of the stamps was typographed from electrotypes made at Melbourne. The recess-printed, lithographed and typographed stamps all differ considerably from each other, the local versions being much coarser in impression.

23. Tasmania, 2 shillings 6 pence, 1864
Alfred Bock of Hobart recess-printed a set of four fiscal stamps in 1863. These stamps were authorised for postal use in 1882. The earliest printing of these stamps was imperforate but from 1864 onward they were perforated in various gauges. All four denominations from 3d. to 10s. reproduced the St George and dragon motif used by Benedetto Pistrucci for the crown and sovereign coins of the United Kingdom.

24. South Australia, 6 pence, 1868
Stamps in this design were engraved by William Humphrys and recess-printed by Perkins Bacon in 1855. Subsequent printings from these plates were made in Adelaide and first rouletting, then perforation, was adopted in 1858 and 1868. Stamps of this series, with various gauges of perforation, remained in use until the 1880s.

25. South Australia, halfpenny, 1883
From 1868 to 1898 De La Rue manufactured plates for South Australia and shipped them out to Adelaide, where the stamps were typographed. Like Victoria and the United Kingdom, South Australia adopted the curious device of issuing a halfpenny stamp in a format half the size of the ordinary definitive designs. This diminutive stamp appeared in various shades of brown between 1883 and 1899.

26. South Australia, 4 pence, 1890
This stamp appeared in various shades, perforations and watermarks between 1890 and 1896. Note the inscription POSTAGE & REVENUE distinctive to the stamps of South Australia, denoting its unified purpose after 1884 when separate postal and fiscal issues were abolished.

27. South Australia, 2½ pence, 1894
South Australia's first attempt at pictorialism was the 2½d. stamp issued in March 1894. The stamp was designed by M. Tannenberg of Melbourne and

the plates manufactured by De La Rue of London. The stamps were typographed by Sands and McDougall of Adelaide. A 5d. denomination issued at the same time featured the colonial coat of arms.

28. South Australia, ½ penny, 1898
South Australia's next attempt at pictorialism was this stamp, produced in various forms between 1898 and 1906. It shows the General Post Office in Adelaide and was typographed by De La Rue – yet another example of the conspicuous lack of success which attended De La Rue's attempts at pictorialism using the typographic process.

29. Western Australia, 1 penny, 1865
This stamp originally appeared in August 1854, when Western Australia adopted adhesive stamps. The first version was imperforate and printed in black showing the black swan, the national emblem of the Swan River Colony. The colour was changed to rose in 1861 and then to yellow in 1865. Printings from 1860 onwards were made at Perth, from the original Perkins Bacon plates.

30. Western Australia, 5 pence, 1885
The vast majority of Western Australian stamps featured the black swan. Indeed Queen Victoria's portrait did not appear on the stamps of this colony until 1902, the year after her death. Western Australia was much closer to the mother country in many respects, and this is borne out by the stamps which were produced in London by De La Rue from 1864 onwards and bore the Crown CC and Crown CA colonial watermarks until 1899. Stamps in the 'Commonwealth' period were printed in Melbourne on paper bearing the watermark V and Crown of Victoria or the crowned A of Australia.

PLATE 114
Australia

1. 2½ pence, 1913
Considering the length of time which elapsed before the Commonwealth of Australia released its own first stamps it is surprising there was such muddled thinking about them. The kangaroo on the map was designed by B. Young, winner of a competition, and the stamps were typographed by J. B. Cooke, the Government Printer. Controversy surrounded the appearance of the 'Roos', as these stamps are popularly known. A Labour Government was then in power, and the opposition parties made much political capital out of Australia's apparent disrespect to the monarchy for omitting the king's portrait. The government fell in 1913 and the Conservatives implemented their election promises by scrapping the Roos and adopting a George V design instead.

2. 2 pence, 1931
The first of the George V stamps appeared in December 1913. They had all the marks of haste in their design and when Labour returned to power they were quietly dropped – only to be restored by the next Conservative government. The later version was typographed by J. B. Cooke or T. S. Harrison, the government printers, from dies made by Perkins Bacon. A philatelic truce was called, and both Roos and George V sets remained in use simultaneously for many years. The last of the Roos was the 2s. denomination issued in 1946–48.

3. 1½ pence, 1927
Australia's first commemorative stamp, appropriately enough, celebrated the opening of the first federal Parliament to be held in Canberra. It was

PLATE 114 AUSTRALIA

designed by R. A. Harrison, engraved by J. A. C. Harrison (no relation) and recess-printed by A. J. Mullett. A few examples have been recorded vertically imperforate. The stamp depicts the allegory of Australia and the Parliament House.

4. 3 pence, 1930
Two stamps portraying Captain Charles Sturt were issued in June 1930 to mark the centenary of the exploration of the River Murray. The stamps were designed by R. A. Harrison, engraved by F. D. Manley and recess-printed by John Ash. A few examples of the 1½d. value were surcharged '2d. paid PMLHI' by the postmaster at Lord Howe Island when the postal rate was increased from 1½d. to 2d. This manuscript surcharge was not authorised by the Australian Post Office.

5. 2 pence, 1937
Although the centenary of the foundation of New South Wales resulted in a lengthy series of what is regarded as the world's first commemorative stamps, the 150th anniversary of the same event was marked by a set of only three stamps released prematurely in October 1937. In denominations of 2, 3 and 9d., they were recess-printed by John Ash, depicted Governor Phillip at Sydney Cove in 1788.

6. 2 shillings, 1935
Australia was one of the many Commonwealth countries to issue stamps to celebrate the Silver Jubliee of King George V in 1935 and it shares the honours with India for producing the most interesting designs. The Australian series, recess-printed by John Ash, in denominations of 1 and 3d., and 2s., depicted the king mounted on his charger *Anzac*, [*A*ustralian and *N*ew *Z*ealand *A*rmy *C*orps (World War I)].

7. 10 shillings, 1938
The accession of King George VI was taken as the opportunity to introduce a new definitive series, replacing the medley of Roos and George V portraits hitherto in use. The series of 1937–38 was a mixture of royal portraiture on a lavish scale and pictures of Australian fauna: kangaroo, koala, merino ram, platypus, kookaburra and lyre bird. The 5 and 10s. denominations presented full-length portraits of the king and queen in their coronation robes, the £1 half-length portraits of them side by side. The perforations of this series varied considerably during the war years and thin, rough paper was used for the higher denominations in 1948.

8. 2 pence, 1944
One of a series of six low value definitives issued between 1942 and 1944, as a result of wartime increases in postal rates. With the exception of the 5½d. showing an emu they portrayed King George VI or Queen Elizabeth, but incorporated Australian fauna and flora in the frames. This example shows a gum tree on the left-hand side of the design.

9. 3½ pence, 1945
The arrival of the Duke of Gloucester as Governor-General in 1945 was celebrated by a set of three stamps portraying the duke in the uniform of a general and the duchess in the uniform of the WAAF. These stamps were the only ones to portray the duke and duchess, and indicate the high-water-mark of royalist fervour in Australia.

10. 3½ pence, 1947
The 150th anniversary of the city of Newcastle, New South Wales, was celebrated in September 1947 by three stamps. The 2½d. purported to show Lieutenant John Shortland of the Royal Navy, the founder of Newcastle, but a portrait of his father was used by mistake. The 3½ and 5½d. stamps depicted aspects

of the steel and coal industry for which the city is noted.

11. 2½ + 2½ pence, 1950
To celebrate the centenary of the first adhesive stamp Australia issued two stamps of 2½d. denomination, printed side by side in the same sheet and reproducing the first stamps of New South Wales and Victoria, the 'Sydney View' and 'Half-Length' of January 1850. This expedient was subsequently used for a number of small format commemorative stamps and led the way to the booklet panes of the present day, in which each stamp in the pane is in a different design.

12. 7 pence, 1957
The world-famous Flying Doctor service was the subject of this stamp, designed by J. E. Lyle and issued in August 1957. It features a map of Australia and a caduceus whose shadow takes the shape of an aircraft. It was intended for the internal airmail rate. Many Australian commemorative stamps of the 1950s were recess-printed with a rather solid background to the design.

13. 5½ + 5½ pence, 1958
Since 1950 Australia has issued stamps on several occasions where different designs of the same denominations were printed *se-tenant*. In February 1958 two 5½d. stamps were issued to publicize the Australian War Memorial in Canberra. The designs were identical in every respect except the figures in the side panels. One stamp showed a soldier and service woman, the other a sailor and airman. They were printed alternately in vertical columns throughout the sheet.

14. 4 pence, 1959
The 150th anniversary of the establishment of a postal service in Australia was marked by this stamp issued in April 1959. It depicts postmaster Isaac Nichols going aboard the brig *Experiment*, which brought the mails from England to New South Wales in the early 19th century.

15. 5 pence, 1960
The centenary of the exploration of the Northern Territory was marked by this stamp reproducing Sir Daryl Lindsay's painting The Overlanders. Two types of this stamp exist, distinguished by the horse's mane which is either rough or smooth. The latter version occurs on 94 stamps in the sheet of 480.

16. 3 shillings, 1959
Like the previous Australian sets, the new definitive series released between 1959 and 1962 fell into two parts. The lower values, from 1 to 5d., bore various portraits of Queen Elizabeth, while the higher denominations, from 6d. to 5s., had pictorial designs. Eileen Mayo designed the six values from 6d. to 1s.2d. featuring some of Australia's exotic wildlife, and Margaret Stones the stamps from 1s.6d. to 3s. illustrating Australian flowers. A double-sized horizontal design, by staff artists of the Printing Bureau, was used for the 5s. stamp depicting an aboriginal stockman. In 1960 responsibility for stamp production passed from the Commonwealth Bank of Australia to the newly formed Reserve Bank of Australia.

17. 4 dollars, 1966
A series of high-value stamps, portraying famous explorers and admirals, from 4s. to £2, had been issued in 1963–65. The same designs, inscribed in decimal currency, were used for the series of 1966. The stamps were designed by W. Jardine and recess-printed by the Reserve Bank. In five of the designs the relevant ship of the explorer appeared in the background, this denomination showing Admiral

King and the *Mermaid*. The exception was the 7s.6d. (later 75 cents) denominations, which reproduced the Nathaniel Dance portrait of Captain James Cook.

18. 25 cents, 1968
The 1964–65 and 1966 low-value definitive stamps featured birds of Australia, printed in multicolour photogravure. They were superseded in July 1968 by a set of six stamps, from 6 to 30 cents, with the state floral emblems of Australia. This example shows the Cooktown Orchid, emblem of Queensland. Note the inclusion of the designer's name, R. Warner, and the initials of the printers in the margin of the design.

19. 25 cents, 1968
Since 1966 Australia has made increasing use of multicolour photogravure in the production of commemorative stamps. Two stamps designed by H. Williamson paid tribute to the Mexico Olympics. A vertical 5c. stamp showed an athlete carrying the Olympic torch, the 25c. a sunstone symbol and the Mexican flag.

20. 25 cents, 1969
Australia was the first Commonwealth country to issue Christmas stamps. Special stamps for use on Christmas mail have been released each October or November since 1957. In 1969 George Hamori designed a 5c. stamp showing a stained glass window of the Nativity while J. Coburn produced the 25c. with a stylized tree of life, Christmas star and infant Christ in a crib.

21. 5 cents, 1969
The majority of Australian commemorative stamps in recent years have followed the American practice of single stamps prepaying the inland letter rate. This stamp, designed by J. Mason, was issued in February 1969 to mark the sixth Biennial Conference of the International Association of Ports and Harbours. It depicts shipping in Melbourne Harbour.

22. 5 cents, 1968
A curious exception to the multicolour photogravure favoured for most modern Australian commemoratives is the combined recess and lithography used for this stamp, issued in November 1968 to mark the 150th anniversary of the Macquarie Lighthouse. This combination of recess and lithography was also used for the first issue of thematic booklet panes with portraits of famous Australians, which also appeared that month.

23. 30 cents, 1970
The bicentenary of Captain Cook's discovery of the east coast of Australia was celebrated in April 1970 by a set of five 5c. stamps and a 30c. stamp in an unusually long format. The five low values were printed *se-tenant* in a continuous design and was the team effort of R. Ingpen, T. Keneally, A. Leydin and J. R. Smith. The stamps simulated a mural with a montage of subjects symbolizing Cook's discovery and exploration of Australia. The 30c. stamp portrays Cook and depicts H.M.S. *Endeavour*, a quadrant, aborigines and a kangaroo. A miniature sheet incorporating all six stamps was released at the same time. The miniature sheet was overprinted to commemorate ANPEX, the Australian National Philatelic Exhibition at Sydney in April 1970, and subsequently a number of private 'overprints' was produced by speculators. These were quite unauthorised and the Australian Post Office took legal action against the perpetrators.

24. Australian Antarctic Territory, 2 shillings, 1957
Stamps have been issued since 1957 for use in the Australian scientific bases in Antarctica. They are

PLATE 114 AUSTRALIA · PLATE 115 AUSTRALIAN PACIFIC DEPENDENCIES

also on sale for a limited period in Australia and are theoretically valid for postage there. The first stamp consisted of a 2s. denomination showing a map of Australian Antarctica and the expedition of 1954 at the Vestfold Hills.

25. Australian Antarctic Territory, 1 dollar, 1966
The introduction of decimal currency was followed by a new definitive series, in multicolour photogravure. The series of ten stamps was designed by J. Mason and featured various aspects of scientific work in the Antarctic. The $1 stamp depicts a parahelion, or mock sun. A 5c. denomination, showing scientists branding elephant seals, was added to the series in September 1968.

PLATE 115
Australian Pacific Dependencies

1. British New Guinea, ½ penny
The first stamps used in British New Guinea consisted of those of Queensland, but a distinctive series, recess-printed by De La Rue, was introduced in 1901. The common design featured a lakatoi, or native sailing-canoe, with the village of Hanubada in the background. Four different versions of this series may be encountered, on thick or thin paper, with vertical or horizontal watermark in each case. The series was overprinted 'Papua' in 1906–07.

2. Papua, 9 pence, 1932
British New Guinea was transferred to the Commonwealth of Australia in 1906 and was renamed Papua. Actually Papua is the native name for the entire island, New Guinea being the European name adopted by the Spaniards in the seventeenth century. The overprinted series was superseded in 1907 by similar designs inscribed 'Papua' and lithographed at Melbourne from transfers taken from the original recess plates. This series, with numerous changes of perforation, watermark and shade, remained in use until 1932. Stamps printed from 1911 onward were typographed. The series was overprinted OS for use on official service, in 1931–32.

3. German New Guinea, 3 pfennigs, 1901
German stamps, diagonally overprinted 'Deutsch-Neu-Guinea' were introduced in 1898 and three years later the Hohenzollern yacht designs were adopted. Stamps with the inscription emended to 'Deutsch Neuguinea' appeared in 1914 at the philatelic bureau in Berlin but it is doubtful if any were ever put on sale in the island, since the German colony surrendered to British Imperial troops shortly after the outbreak of war.

4. North West Pacific Islands, 6 pence, 1919
German colonial stamps were overprinted G.R.I. (the British royal monogram) and surcharged with new values in sterling currency, following the capture of the German territories in 1914. Subsequently Australian stamps overprinted 'N.W. Pacific Islands' were issued from 1915 to 1923, during which period different settings and types of lettering were used in combination with the various perforations and watermarks of Australian stamps.

5. New Guinea, 3½ pence, 1932
The former German possessions in New Guinea were administered by Australia under a mandate from the League of Nations and the name of 'Territory of New Guinea' formally adopted in 1924. To mark the tenth anniversary of Australian rule a series was introduced in 1931 featuring a Bird of

Paradise. The entire series, from ½d. to £1, was simultaneously released with an airmail overprint. The following year the stamps were redrawn, omitting the commemorative dates, and used as a definitive series. As before, the entire series was likewise overprinted for airmail use. All four sets were recess-printed by John Ash of Melbourne.

6. New Guinea, 2 pence, 1931
The basic stamps were recess-printed between 1925 and 1928 by the Note Printing Branch, Commonwealth Bank of Australia, Melbourne. In June 1931 the entire series was overprinted for airmail use. Airmail was used extensively in the 1930s for shipping small packets of gold from the interior of the island, but the incidence of so many lengthy and expensive air sets in a short time seems excessive.

7. New Guinea, 5 shillings, 1939
The last stamps of New Guinea as a separate entity consisted of the airmail series of March 1939. Two air stamps, in denominations of £2 and £5 were issued in May 1935 and showed an aircraft over the Bulolo Goldfields, indicating the main purpose for which the stamps were issued. Lower denominations, from ½d. to £1, were recess-printed by John Ash four years later. Following the Japanese invasion of New Guinea in 1942 distinctive stamps were withdrawn and ordinary Australian stamps substituted.

8. Papua, 5 shillings, 1932
The 'Lakatoi' series was replaced in November 1932 by a pictorial series ranging from ½d. to £1. F. E. Williams designed the 2s., £1 and the frames of the other values, E. Whitehouse designed the 2, 4 and 6d. values as well as the 1 and 10s. stamps; the vignettes for the remaining stamps were based on photographs by Messrs Williams and Gibson. W. C. G. McCracken recess-printed initial consignments of the ½, 1, 2 and 4d. stamps, but later printings, as well as all the other denominations, were recess-printed by John Ash. This stamp portrays Sergeant Major Simoi, a native policeman.

9. Papua, 5 pence, 1934
A set of four stamps, recess-printed by John Ash, was issued in November 1934 to celebrate the fiftieth anniversary of the declaration of a British protectorate. This stamp shows the officer and men of H.M.S. *Nelson* meeting the native chiefs. The other design used for this set portrayed the chief Boe Vagi, the British commander, and the ceremony of hoisting the Union Jack at Port Moresby in 1884. Britain repudiated the annexation and it was not until 1888 that this was reluctantly agreed to – thereby giving the Papuan postal administration the opportunity for another set of stamps, in 1938.

10. Papua and New Guinea, 6½ pence, 1952
Australian stamps were used in both Papua and New Guinea from 1942 to 1952. After World War II the administration of both territories was unified and joint issues of stamps were resumed in October 1952. The stamps, ranging in value from ½d. to £1, featured aspects of life in the territory. The series was recess-printed by the Note Printing Branch of the Commonwealth Bank, Melbourne.

11. Papua and New Guinea, 1 shilling 2 pence, 1964
Since 1964 Papua and New Guinea have issued short thematic sets, averaging two or three each year and usually highlighting some aspect of native culture, fauna and flora. One of the earliest of these sets, however, publicized the welfare services, with subjects such as school dentistry, medical training and public health centres. It was recess-printed by the Note Printing Branch of the Reserve Bank of Australia, Melbourne.

12. Papua and New Guinea, 10 cents, 1971
Continuing in the series devoted to native culture Graham Wade designed a set of four featuring distinctive types of dwellings from the Eastern Highlands, Milne Bay, Purari Delta and Sepik districts. It was printed in multicolour photogravure by Courvoisier, who have produced many of the stamps of this country since 1962.

13. Papua and New Guinea, 30 cents, 1972
A somewhat similar series was produced in 1972 depicting the agricultural occupations and trading methods of the islanders. As before, the series was designed by Graham Wade and printed in Switzerland.

14. Papua and New Guinea, 10 + 10 cents, 1969
An attempt was made to break away from the rather stereotyped presentation of the annual cultural series by issuing pairs of 5 and 10c. stamps in such a way that each stamp of the pair depicted half of the motif. The stamps reproduced native folklore motifs and were printed in vertical *se-tenant* pairs separated by a line of rouletting. This curious arrangement was not continued by further sets. They were designed by the Rev H. A. Brown and were lithographed by Enschedé.

15. Nauru, 1 penny, 1916
The German Pacific island of Nauru was occupied by Imperial troops in 1916. British stamps overprinted 'Nauru' were introduced in October of that year and remained in use until 1924. The 1½ and 2d. denominations were added to the series in 1923 and both Waterlow and Bradbury Wilkinson versions of the Seahorse high values were thus overprinted. There was a great deal of variety in the setting of the overprints. Most denominations have been recorded with a double overprint, one being albino, while the error NAUP.U, caused by a broken letter, is constant on sheets of the lower values up to 6d.

16. Nauru, 1 shilling, 1935
The administration of Nauru was transferred, by League of Nations mandate, to Australia in 1924 and a distinctive series of stamps released that year. The stamps, from ½d. to 10s., featured a trading vessel offshore. Two versions of the series exist, the first on rough-surfaced, greyish paper (1924–34), the second on shiny-surfaced, white paper (1937–47). This series remained in use until 1954. Four of its stamps were overprinted in July 1935 to celebrate the Silver Jubilee of King George V.

17. Nauru, 2½ pence, 1937
To mark the Coronation of King George VI in 1937 the three Australian territories of Nauru, New Guinea and Papua each issued a set of four stamps in an omnibus design bearing the king's profile. They were recess-printed by John Ash of Melbourne in denominations from 1½d. to 1s.

18. Nauru, 1 dollar, 1968
A pictorial definitive series, from ½d. to 5s., was introduced in February 1954. Recess-printed in Australia, it featured scenery, occupations of the islanders and wildlife. The top value had a map of the island. The series remained in use until 1966 when it was reissued with values inscribed in Australian decimal currency. Two years later the entire series, from 1c. to $1, was overprinted to mark the status of Nauru as an independent republic within the British Commonwealth.

19. Norfolk Island, 4 pence, 1947
Norfolk Island used the stamps of Tasmania until 1913 and from then until 1947 the stamps of the Australian Commonwealth. A common design, featuring Ball Bay, was used for all denominations from ½d. to 2s. The inscription 'Founded 1788'

PLATE 115 AUSTRALIAN PACIFIC DEPENDENCIES · PLATE 116 NEW ZEALAND

refers to the original use of the island as a penal settlement to where the worst convicts were transferred from Botany Bay. The stamps were recess-printed by the Note Printing Branch of the Reserve Bank of Australia, which produced all the stamps of Norfolk Island up to 1962.

20. Norfolk Island, 2 shillings, 1956
The first commemorative stamps issued by Norfolk Island consisted of 3d. and 2s. values issued in June 1956 to mark the centenary of the landing of the Pitcairn islanders. They featured the Seal of Norfolk Island, and Pitcairners landing. Alternate stamps of the 2s. denomination were printed from a different die distinguishable by a dot in the bottom right corner. The stamps were recess-printed by the Reserve Bank of Australia.

21. Norfolk Island, 7 pence, 1958
A set of six pictorial stamps with landmarks and scenery of the islands, was issued in June 1953. New denominations of 7 and 8d. were created in July 1958 by surcharging the obsolescent 7½ and 8½d. stamps with new values.

22. Norfolk Island, 1 dollar, 1968
Since 1962 all the stamps of Norfolk Island, with few exceptions, have been printed in multicolour photogravure by Harrison and Sons. The exceptions are those commemorative stamps in designs common to the other Australian dependencies or Australia itself. This stamp was the top value of a series, introduced between April 1967 and June 1968, depicting ships connected with the history of the island. They ranged from H.M.S. *Resolution*, in which Captain Cook discovered the island in 1774, to the S.S. *Morinda*, which maintained communications between Norfolk Island and Australia in the 1930s. The side panel, an anchor and a white tern, are shown against a distant view of the island.

23. Norfolk Island, 5 cents, 1968
Apart from Christmas issues between 1960 and 1965, and a stamp marking the 50th anniversary of the Gallipoli campaign, the only stamps issued by Norfolk Islands in recent years to be produced in Australia were three low values intended for use in slot machines. These stamps, in denominations of 3c., 4c. and 5c., were similar to the corresponding coil stamps of Australia, with the portrait of Queen Elizabeth by Anthony Buckley.

24. Norfolk Island, 10 cents, 1970
The close connection between Norfolk Island and Captain Cook has been demonstrated in several of the stamps issued in recent years. Apart from the 1c. denomination of the 1968 definitive series Norfolk Island issued a 10c. stamp in 1969 to mark the bicentenary of Cook's observation of the transit of Venus across the Sun at Tahiti, and followed this, in April 1970, with two stamps celebrating the bicentenary of Cook's discovery of the east coast of Australia. The 5c. portrayed Captain Cook and showed a relief map of Australia, while the 10c. featured H.M.S. *Endeavour* and an aborigine. Neither event was directly relevant to Norfolk Island, and it is assumed that the island's own bicentenary in 1974 will be the occasion for lavish philatelic commemoration.

25. Norfolk Island, 30 cents, 1969
The 125th anniversary of the annexation of Norfolk Island to Van Diemen's Land (Tasmania) was commemorated by 5 and 30c. stamps with maps of Tasmania and Norfolk Island. They were designed by Mrs A. Bathie and Mrs M. J. McCoy.

26. Norfolk Island, 3 cents, 1970
A definitive series featuring birds of Norfolk

Island was released between February 1970 and February 1971 in denominations from 1 to 50c. It was designed by G. Mathews and printed by Harrison & Sons in multicolour photogravure.

PLATE 116
New Zealand

1. 6 pence, 1864
Adhesive stamps were introduced in New Zealand in July 1855, the first issue consisting of 1 and 2d., and 1s. stamps recess-printed by Perkins Bacon of London. Against the engine-turned background used for the first stamps of Chile two years previously Perkins Bacon placed the Chalon portrait of Queen Victoria, engraved by William Humphrys. The plates were shipped to New Zealand and various printings, from November 1855 onwards, were produced locally. The 6d. value was introduced in 1859 and various gauges of perforation were adopted between 1862 and 1867. The 'Chalon Heads' remained in use until 1874.

2. 2½ pence, 1898
New Zealand followed the example of North Borneo (1894) and Tonga (1897) by introducing a pictorial definitive series in April 1898. Hundreds of designs were submitted as a result of a public competition. The stamps were recess-printed by Waterlow and Sons. Eight small designs and five double-sized designs were used for the series, ranging from ½d. to 5s. and featuring scenery and wildlife. The 2½d. stamp, with Lake Wakatipu and Mount Earnslaw, was incorrectly captioned 'Wakitipu' in the original version, but this spelling error was subsequently emended. Both versions are worth about the same.

3. 4 pence, 1882
The 'Chalon Heads' were replaced by a series typographed at the Government Printing Office in Wellington from dies engraved by De La Rue of London or Bock & Cousins of Wellington. A second 'Side Face' series, engraved by Bock & Cousins, was adopted between 1882 and 1897 in denominations from ½d. to 1s. Five different gauges of perforation were employed in that period. Stamps of this series, released in 1893, may be found with commercial advertisements printed on the backs.

4. 1½ pence, 1900
The necessity for a 1½d. stamp in 1900 was seized as the opportunity to demonstrate New Zealand's loyalty to the mother country during the Boer War of 1899–1902. The first printing of this stamp was made, appropriately, in khaki, but subsequently brown was found to be more satisfactory. The design, by J. Nairn, shows troops of the New Zealand contingent answering 'The Empire's Call'. This stamp was the forerunner of the patriotic issues which many countries issued in both world wars and other campaigns since then.

5. 1 penny, 1901
The overseas letter rate was reduced to 1d. on New Year's Day 1901 and the introduction of 'Universal Penny Postage' was celebrated by the release of this stamp. The allegorical figure of Zealandia, designed by Guido Bach, was adapted from a banknote vignette. The background shows the S.S. *Dunedin* and Mount Egmont. The first version of this stamp was recess-printed, by Waterlows and later by the Government Printing Office. A typographed version was adopted in 1907 and two years later the word Dominion. was added to the inscription to

take note of New Zealand's status. The numerous variations of paper, watermark and perforation make the 'Penny Universal' one of the most complex stamps ever issued

6. 8 pence, 1909
Stamps portraying King Edward VII were introduced in 1909. The ½d. stamp was typographed in New Zealand from plates engraved by Perkins Bacon, while the other denominations (2d. to 1s.) were recess-printed in Wellington, from plates manufactured by W. R. Royle of London. These stamps continued in use until 1916 and during that period underwent numerous changes of perforation. The ½, 3 and 6d. values were overprinted to commemorate the Auckland Exhibition in 1913, the commemoratives being limited to letters in New Zealand and to Australia.

7. halfpenny, 1920
Victory in World War I was celebrated by a set of six stamps issued in January 1920. They were typographed by De La Rue, from plates made by Perkins Bacon, Waterlows and De La Rue. Apart from the 1½d. (Maori warrior) and 1s. (portrait of King George V) they depicted details from statues in London. The ½d. shows the monument to Field-Marshal Lord Clyde, the 1 and 6d. details from the Victoria memorial outside Buckingham Palace, and the 3d. one of Landseer's lions in Trafalgar Square. The ½d. stamp was surcharged for use as a 2d. stamp in 1922.

8. 1 shilling, 1915
H. Linley Richardson designed the definitive series introduced in July 1915, showing a profile of King George V on an engine-turned background, with Maori decoration in the side panels. The plates were made by Perkins Bacon but the actual printing took place in Wellington. Recess-printed versions of this design, from 1½d. to 1s., appeared between 1915 and 1925, but typographed versions of the ½, 1½, 2 and 3d. stamps appeared in 1915–19, from plates made by Perkins Bacon or W. R. Bock of Wellington.

9. halfpenny, 1925
For the New Zealand and South Seas Exhibition, held at Dunedin in 1925–26, Linley Richardson designed a set of three stamps (½, 1 and 4d.) depicting the exhibition venue. Maori textile patterns and carved heads provided the border decoration, a practice initiated by Richardson and followed by many other designers in subsequent years. One stamp in each sheet of 4d. stamps has the error POSTAGF in the bottom right hand corner.

10. 1 penny, 1923
Because of the war the letter rate was raised to 1½d. in 1915 and it was not until 1923 that it could be restored to the prewar level. To mark the resumption of Universal Penny Postage this stamp was released in 1923. Designed and engraved by W. R. Bock it was typographed at Wellington on chalky paper with thick yellowish gum. 'Jones' paper with white gum was adopted the following year and thick, opaque 'Cowan' paper in 1925.

11. 4 pence, 1935
After a gap of almost forty years New Zealand returned to pictorialism in May 1935 with a series of fourteen stamps from ½d. to 3s. De La Rue, who had recess-printed a Health stamp for New Zealand in 1934, secured the contract to produce the series by this process, with the exception of the 9d. value, which was lithographed by Waterlow and Sons. Later printings of the 9d. were lithographed in Wellington. The watermark was changed from single to multiple NZ and star in 1936 and from then until 1943 the perforations on many

PLATE 116 NEW ZEALAND · PLATE 117 NEW ZEALAND DEPENDENCIES

denominations were changed on several occasions, notably after Waterlows took over the printing and perforation from De La Rue, when the latter's premises were destroyed in a German air raid.

12. 1 + 1 penny, 1936
The 21st anniversary of the Gallipoli landings was commemorated by two stamps, each carrying a premium in aid of war veteran funds. The stamps, designed by L. C. Mitchell, showed a soldier of the Australia and New Zealand Army Corps at Anzac Cove, Gallipoli. The stamps were recess-printed by John Ash, printer to the Australian government, in Melbourne.

13. 1 shilling, 1940
The centenary of the proclamation of British sovereignty was celebrated in January 1940 by a series of twelve stamps, from $\frac{1}{2}d.$ to 1s. L. C. Mitchell and James Berry designed the series, which was recess-printed by Bradbury Wilkinson. Only three stamps referred directly to the centenary and showed the Treaty of Waitangi ($2\frac{1}{2}d.$), the landing of immigrants (3d.) and H.M.S. Britomar at Akaroa (5d.). The other stamps illustrated historic events from the arrival of the Maori in 1350 ($\frac{1}{2}d.$) to the first shipment of frozen mutton to Britain in 1882 (6d.). The 7d. (Maori Council) was replaced by an 8d. in the same design later that year.

14. 2 + 1 pence, 1945
Since 1929 New Zealand has issued Health stamps each year, the premiums going to provide children's health camps and TB sanatoriums. The themes of the earlier issues showed aspects of children's sports and recreation; others portrayed the younger members of the Royal Family, while more recent issues have shown birds or children's games. The stamps of 1945 and 1947, however, reproduced statues in London. Peter Pan in Kensington Gardens was the subject of the 1945 pair, and Eros in Piccadilly Circus appeared on the 1947 pair, both sets being designed by James Berry.

15. 1 shilling, 1947
Between 1938 and 1947 the pictorial definitives were gradually ousted by a series portraying King George VI, designed by W. J. Cooch and recess-printed by Bradbury Wilkinson. The pence values were in monochrome, while the shilling values were printed in two-colour combinations in a larger format. Two versions of the 1s. stamp exist, differing in the clarity and strength of the diagonal lines of shading behind the portrait.

16. 2 shillings 6 pence, 1957
The practice of dividing the contracts for definitive sets between two or more printers was continued in 1953 when the first Elizabethan series was produced by De La Rue and Bradbury Wilkinson. L. C. Mitchell designed the low-value stamps and James Berry the vertical-format high values showing Queen Elizabeth in Guards uniform at the Trooping of the Colour. Stamps in denominations of 3, 5 and 10s. were issued in 1953 and the 2s.6d. value added in July 1957.

17. 2 pence, 1948
The centenaries of the various provinces have been commemorated philatelically in recent years. The first of these occasions arose in February 1948 when four stamps marked the centennial of Otago. The series, designed by Berry and recess-printed by Bradbury Wilkinson, featured Port Chalmers in 1848, a view of Cromwell, First Church in Dunedin and the University of Otago. Berry's skill at incorporating motifs into the frames of his designs is ably demonstrated in this series. Note the miners' shovels in the side of the frame, and the 'ghost' stage-coach in the sky.

18. 3 pence, 1956
Stamp design by the mid-1950s was becoming more simplified, with bolder lettering and uncluttered frames. Nevertheless L. C. Mitchell managed to work a couple of thistles (alluding to the Scottish pioneers) into the corners of this stamp, one of three released in January 1956 to mark the centenary of Southland province. E. R. Leeming designed the 2d. showing whalers in Foveaux Strait, while M. R. Smith's 8d. design showed the Notornis, a bird long thought to be extinct but recently rediscovered.

19. 6 pence, 1958
Australia and New Zealand combined to release a commemorative stamp in August 1958 to mark the 30th anniversary of the first air crossing of the Tasman Sea. J. E. Lyle designed 8d. (Australia) and 6d. (New Zealand) stamps, recess-printed by the Commonwealth Bank of Australia's Note Printing Branch. The design shows Sir Charles Kingsford-Smith, the Southern Cross constellation and the monoplane of the same name. In 1965 Australia and New Zealand issued Churchill stamps in identical designs.

20. 8 pence, 1962
Monochrome photogravure stamps, by Harrison and Sons, had been issued on a few occasions between 1949 and 1960 but it was with the definitive series released in the latter year that New Zealand finally adopted multicolour photogravure. The majority of commemorative issues and health stamps since that date have been produced in this medium. A. G. and L. C. Mitchell designed the two stamps issued in June 1962 to mark the centenary of the telegraph system. The 3d. showed a morse key, with a view of the Lyttelton Hills in the background, the 8d. a modern teleprinter system.

21. 2½ pence, 1964
New Zealand has issued stamps for Christmas greetings each year since 1960. The earlier issues reproduced Old Master paintings of the Nativity or the Adoration of the Magi while the more recent issues have depicted religious art and architecture in New Zealand. An exception was this 2½d. Christmas stamp, which also commemorated the 150th anniversary of the first Christmas service held in New Zealand. L. C. Mitchell's impression of the Rev. Samuel Marsden preaching the Christmas message at Rangihoua Bay was reproduced in multicolour photogravure by Harrison and Sons. The inland rate went up to 3d. shortly before this stamp was issued, but in a rare gesture of goodwill towards the public the post office allowed the 2½d. rate to be reintroduced for the Christmas period.

22. 10 cents, 1970
New Zealand adopted the dollar of 100 cents in 1967 and the definitive series was reissued inscribed in new values. Horse-trotting is one of New Zealand's national pastimes and it is hardly surprising that a stamp should be issued to honour 'Cardigan Bay', the champion trotter. After winning numerous prizes this horse was sent to stud in Australia. His honourable retirement and return to his native land were celebrated by this stamp in January 1970. It was designed by L. C. Mitchell and printed by Courvoisier.

23. 20 cents, 1969
New definitive stamps, from 7c. to $2, were issued between August 1967 and July 1969. In some cases previous designs appeared in new colours, but a series of six double-sized stamps featured New Zealand agriculture and fisheries. Each stamp had two scenes illustrating different aspects of each industry. The 20c., for example, showed cattle grazing and a consignment of frozen beef being loaded on to a cargo ship. These stamps were

designed by the Post Office Display Section. Bradbury Wilkinson (lithography), Harrisons and De La Rue (photogravure) shared the contract for this series.

24. 18 cents, 1970
The Japanese Government Printing Bureau in Tokyo printed two stamps for New Zealand in 1968 but this provoked such an outcry that the venture was not immediately repeated. Then, in 1970, when New Zealand decided to issue a set of three stamps to mark Expo 70 at Osaka, it again placed the contract in Tokyo. The stamps, featuring aspects of the Expo, were designed by Mark Cleverley and even included Japanese inscriptions. Significantly there was less of an outcry on this occasion, and several subsequent issues of New Zealand have been produced in multicolour photogravure in Tokyo.

25. 2½ cents, 1969
Distinctive stamps have been used by the New Zealand Government Life Insurance Department since 1891, though the use of official stamps by other government departments ceased in 1965. The stamps from 1891 to 1947 had a lighthouse motif symbolizing state security. In 1947 a pictorial series depicting lighthouses of Britain and New Zealand was adopted. It was recess-printed by Bradbury Wilkinson from designs by James Berry. A series inscribed in decimal currency was issued in 1969, again designed by Berry, but printed by offset lithography.

PLATE 117
New Zealand Dependencies

1. Cook Islands, 1½ pence, 1893
The Cook Islands began issuing stamps in May 1892, when a typeset series inscribed 'Cook Islands Federation' was released. A year later a pictorial series was introduced, typographed at the Government Printing Office in Wellington. The two designs, engraved by A. E. Cousins, portrayed Queen Makea Takau and a torea (or wry-bill) in flight. The series remained in use till 1919, with frequent changes of perforation and watermark. In 1901 the Cook Islands became a New Zealand territory and the following year separate postal administrations were established in Rarotonga, Aitutaki, Niue and Penrhyn. The stamps inscribed 'Cook Islands' continued to be used in Rarotonga till 1919.

2. Penrhyn Island, 2½ pence, 1902
Contemporary New Zealand ½, 1 and 2½d. stamps overprinted 'Penrhyn Island' and surcharged with the equivalent values in Polynesian were introduced in 1902 and superseded the stamps of the Cook Islands. From 1920 to 1932 pictorial stamps in the Cook Islands omnibus design but inscribed 'Penrhyn Island' were used. Ordinary Cook Islands stamps were resumed in March 1932.

3. Aitutaki, halfpenny, 1920
New Zealand stamps overprinted 'Aitutaki' were first issued in June 1903 and followed the pattern of those used in Penrhyn Island, up to August 1920, when a series of six pictorial stamps, recess-printed by Perkins Bacon, was issued for each of the four territories comprising the Cook Islands. Uniform designs, with the landing of Captain Cook, the Dance portrait of Cook and views of the islands, were used, but the frames were inscribed with the name of the appropriate territory. Aitutaki's stamps were withdrawn in March 1932 and replaced by the

PLATE 117 NEW ZEALAND DEPENDENCIES

ordinary Cook Islands issues. Aitutaki re-introduced its own stamps in 1972, using Cook Islands stamps with a distinctive overprint.

4. Rarotonga, 1 penny, 1919
Contemporary stamps of New Zealand were issued in Rarotonga in 1919 with surcharges in Polynesian. These stamps were superseded the following year by the pictorial series printed by Perkins Bacon.

5. Rarotonga, 2½ pence, 1927
A change in the overseas letter rate led to the introduction of this stamp in October 1927. Showing a native chief, it was issued in four versions, for use in each territory of the Cook Islands. Rarotonga continued to use the Queen Makea definitives until 1920, when the pictorial series was introduced. Stamps inscribed 'Cook Islands' replaced the separate issues of Aitutaki, Penrhyn and Rarotonga in March 1932.

6. Niue, 1 penny, 1902
In January 1902 the New Zealand 'Penny Universal' overprinted NIUE in large block lettering was issued, followed in April by similar stamps which also bore the Polynesian equivalent of the value. Niue followed the pattern of the other Cook Islands, with overprinted stamps up to 1920, when the pictorial series was adopted. Numerous errors and varieties exist in the early overprinted issues.

7. Niue, 6 pence, 1920
One of the series of six recess-printed by Perkins Bacon and issued in August 1920, it features the village of Arorangi. The stamps were originally printed on unwatermarked paper but reprints in 1927 were produced on the standard NZ watermarked paper.

8. Niue, 3 shillings, 1932
Niue was administered separately and to this day continues as a dependency under direct New Zealand control, though issuing its own stamps. This ambiguous position was reflected in the stamps of 1932, which bore the inscription 'Niue Cook Islands'. The designs were those used for the general series of the Cook Islands, with the frame suitably emended. This practice continued until 1950, but various New Zealand stamps overprinted 'Niue' were issued at various times in the interim.

9. Niue, 30 cents, 1967
Niue's first distinctive series appeared in July 1950. The ten denominations, from ½d. to 3s., were designed by James Berry and recess-printed by Bradbury Wilkinson. A map of the island appeared on the ½d., Captain Cook's *Resolution* on the 1d., scenery and native occupations on the other values. The series was surcharged in decimal currency in July 1967.

10. Niue, 20 cents, 1969
The surcharged series was superseded by a set in the same ten denominations (½c. to 30c.), designed by Mrs. K. W. Billings and lithographed in multicolour by Enschedé. Nine denominations featured flowers but the portrait of Queen Elizabeth by Anthony Buckley was used for the 20c. value.

11. Niue, 30 cents, 1970
In recent years Niue has slightly relaxed its previously conservative policy on stamp issues. This stamp is one of a set of three with the theme of indigenous edible crabs, issued in August 1970. Featuring kalahimu (3c.), kalavi (5c.) and unga (30c.), they were designed by G. F. Fuller and printed in multicolour photogravure by Enschedé.

12. Cook Islands, 2 pence, 1949
James Berry designed a series of ten denominations for the Cook Islands in August 1949. This was the first series distinctive to the islands and not similar to those used in Niue. Recess-printed by Waterlow and Sons, the stamps featured maps and scenery of the islands. Printings of these stamps from 1958 to 1963 were on a much whiter, more opaque paper than had previously been used.

13. Cook Islands, 22 cents, 1967
Internal self-government was granted to the Cook Islands in September 1965, since when a more liberal policy on stamp issues has been pursued. At the time of independence the Minister of Posts naively announced that it was hoped to finance the islands' social welfare programme from philatelic revenue. Six stamps and a miniature sheet were printed in multicolour photogravure by Heraclio Fournier of Vitoria, Spain, and issued in October 1967 with the theme of Polynesian paintings by Gauguin. Many recent Cook Islands stamps have cashed in on the craze for reproductions of paintings.

14. Cook Islands, 4 cents, 1970
Since 1966 the Cook Islands have issued lengthy sets of stamps at Christmas, reproducing Old Master paintings with religious themes. This idea was extended to cover special Easter greetings stamps in 1970, and this has since become an annual issue, reproducing Old Master paintings of the Crucifixion and the Resurrection of Christ. This stamp depicts Raphael's version of the Resurrection.

15. Cook Islands, 50 + 20 cents, 1971
In February 1971 the 30c. definitive stamp was issued with a 20c. premium to prepay a private delivery service fee in Great Britain during the postal strike. The mail was flown to a forwarding address in the Netherlands and thence dispatched by the private courier to addresses in Britain. On 8 March 1971 the 50c. stamp was likewise overprinted and surcharged to cover registration fees. The strike came to an end on 8 March and these special mail service stamps were withdrawn from sale on 12 March.

16. Western Samoa, 2½ pence, 1914
The island of Western Samoa under German control surrendered to a New Zealand expeditionary force on 29 August 1914. Stocks of the German colonial stamps seized by the invading troops were overprinted with the Royal monogram G.R.I. by the *Samoanische Zeitung* in Apia and surcharged with values in sterling currency from ½d. to 5s. Numerous errors and varieties exist in these overprints.

17. Western Samoa, 1 penny, 1920
New Zealand stamps overprinted 'Samoa' were introduced in Western Samoa in September 1914, following the capture of the islands from Germany. The Victory series of 1920 was similarly overprinted. The stamp reproduces a detail from the Victoria memorial outside Buckingham Palace in London.

18. Western Samoa, 1 penny, 1935
Bradbury Wilkinson engraved the plates for a series recess-printed at the Government Printing Office in Wellington. Featuring a native hut and the New Zealand flag, the stamps were introduced in December 1921. The 1, 2½ and 6d. values were overprinted in May 1935 to celebrate the Silver Jubilee of King George V.

19. Western Samoa, 1 shilling, 1935
De La Rue recess-printed a pictorial definitive series which was issued in August 1935. The name of the territory was rendered correctly 'Western Samoa' for the first time, in deference to the United States, which governed Eastern Samoa. The stamps featured the people and scenery of the islands, and alluded to the Scottish novelist, Robert Louis Stevenson, who lived and died in Samoa. His house 'Vailima' was shown on the 6d. and his tomb on the 1s. Stevenson himself was portrayed on a 7d. stamp issued in 1939 to mark the 25th anniversary of New Zealand control.

20. Western Samoa, 2 pence, 1952
After World War II Western Samoa became a United Nations Trust Territory, under New Zealand administration, and during the 1950s developed constitutionally towards complete independence. This was reflected in the definitive series of March 1952, recess-printed by Bradbury Wilkinson, which showed the Samoan flag on several denominations. This design was reissued in 1958, inscribed entirely in Samoan, to mark the inauguration of the Samoan parliament. For stamps issued since independence see plate 120.

21. Tokelau Islands, 2 pence, 1948
Until 1948 the Tokelau Islands had used the stamps of the Gilbert and Ellice Islands (up to 1925) or Western Samoa (1925–48). Distinctive stamps, in denominations of ½, 1 and 2d., were introduced in June 1948. They were designed by James Berry and recess-printed by Bradbury Wilkinson, depicting maps and views of the three principal islands in the group. A shilling denomination was added to the series in March 1956 by surcharging the ½d. stamp. The only other stamp was the New Zealand 3d. coronation stamp inscribed 'Tokelau Islands', in 1953. New Zealand 'Arms' stamps, overprinted for use in the islands, and surcharged 6d., 8d. or 2s., were issued in 1966.

22. Tokelau Islands, 2 shillings, 1966
For almost 20 years the Tokelau Islands got by with no more than five stamps but in 1966 6 and 8d., and 2s. denominations were introduced. These stamps consisted of the New Zealand arms design (normally used for fiscal purposes) overprinted 'Tokelau Islands' and surcharged with the values. Similar stamps were issued in 1967 with the values rendered in New Zealand decimal currency.

23. Tokelau Islands, 20 cents, 1969
Since 1967 the output of stamps from the Tokelau Islands has increased enormously, and now averages two new sets a year. Bradbury Wilkinson lithographed a set of four, issued in August 1969 to illustrate the history of the islands. Each stamp had a scroll inscribed with an event – British protectorate (1877), annexation to the Gilbert and Ellice Islands (1916), New Zealand administration (1925) and New Zealand territory (1948). This must be one of the least-inspired commemorative sets ever issued.

24. Tokelau Islands, 2 cents, 1970
Since 1969 the Tokelau Islands have issued a Christmas stamp in the same design as one of the contemporary New Zealand issues. The stamp issued in 1970 reproduced the *Adoration of the Child* by Correggio and was lithographed in multicolour by De La Rue.

25. King Edward VII Land, 1 penny, 1908
A consignment of New Zealand 'Penny Universal' stamps was overprinted 'King Edward VII Land' and given to Sir Ernest Shackleton for use by his expedition to the Antarctic in 1908. They were also sold to the general public at a huge premium, the money being used to subsidize the expedition. Stamps from both Royle and Waterlow printings were overprinted, the latter being the scarcer. One example of the Royle printing has been recorded with a double overprint.

283

26. Victoria Land, 1 penny, 1911

Following the example of the Shackleton Expedition of 1908, New Zealand issued ½ and 1d. stamps overprinted 'Victoria Land' for the use of the Antarctic expedition led by Captain Scott in 1911–12. A few of the 1d. denomination are recorded with the full stop after 'Land' omitted.

27. Ross Dependency, 4 pence, 1957

Stamps for use in permanent New Zealand bases in the Antarctic were introduced in January 1957, during International Geophysical Year. In denominations from 3d. to 1s.6d., they were recess-printed by De La Rue in various designs, with H.M.S. *Erebus*, a map of the dependency and a portrait of Queen Elizabeth. The 4d. portrayed Shackleton and Scott against a map of Antarctica. The series was reissued in July 1967 inscribed in decimal currency.

28. Ross Dependency, 18 cents, 1972

One of a series of six pictorial stamps issued in 1972, this stamp features an ice-floe. The other denominations depicted a skua (3c.), Williams Airfield (4c.), Shackleton's hut at Cape Royds (5c.), a support ship (8c.), and Scott Base (10c.). The stamps were designed by Mark Cleverley and lithographed by Bradbury Wilkinson.

PLATE 118
Western Pacific High Commission

---

1. Fiji, 1 penny, 1871

A local mail service was established at Levuka in November 1870 by the *Fiji Times Express*, which produced 1, 3 and 6d., and 1s. stamps, typeset together in the same sheet. In June 1871 Fiji was united to form one kingdom under Cakobau and a government postal service was established the following November. Stamps in denominations of 1, 3 and 6d. were engraved by A. L. Jackson and typographed at the Government Printing Office in Sydney. The monogram signifies Cakobau Rex.

2. Fiji, 6 pence, 1878

Cakobau ceded his kingdom to Great Britain in 1874 and the islands were reconstituted as a crown colony. At first the stamps of the Cakobau series were overprinted V.R. but a new series, with this monogram, was produced at Sydney in 1878. This series, with variations, remained in use until 1903.

3. Fiji, 1 penny, 1895

A pictorial design, showing a native canoe, was introduced for the 1 and 2d. denominations in 1891. Originally the penny stamp was printed in black but the colour was changed to rosy mauve in 1896. Nevertheless black penny stamps continued to appear, with various gauges of perforation, down to 1902. The stamps were printed in Sydney from electrotyped plates.

4. Fiji, 5 shillings, 1911

The colonial keyplate designs were adopted in 1903, when De La Rue typographed a series, from ½d. to £1, with the profile of King Edward VII. Similar designs, with the profile of King George V substituted, were in use from 1912 till 1938.

5. Fiji, 2 pence, 1938

A pictorial definitive series, with the portrait of King George VI inset, was recess-printed, partly by De La Rue and partly by Waterlow and Sons. In the first version of the 2 and 6d. map stamps the 180° line (running through the words FIJI ISLANDS) did not have numerals. An emended design, show-

ing the degree, was substituted in 1940. Similarly the original version of the 1½d. stamp showed an unmanned outrigger canoe. A new version of this design, showing a native at the helm, was introduced in 1940. Various denominations were added to the series up to 1955.

6. Fiji, 2 pence, 1954

A curious feature of Fijian philately in recent years has been the release of definitive stamps piecemeal over a period of years. Thus the first Elizabethan series repeated designs from the latter part of the previous reign and appeared at various times between February 1954 and October 1956, only to be replaced by yet another series three years later. This stamp depicts the Government offices in Suva and was originally used for a 2d. denomination, with portrait of George VI, issued in May 1942.

7. Fiji, 1½ pence, 1962

Fiji was the first British Commonwealth country to issue stamps reproducing the Annigoni portrait of Queen Elizabeth, 1, 1½ and 2½d. stamps in this design being released in 1954. The design was substantially redrawn in 1962, shell ornaments being added to the inscription tablet and the letters of 'Fiji' dotted. The 1d. was reissued with a new watermark in 1964.

8. Fiji, 1 shilling, 1964

A set of three stamps, designed by Victor Whiteley and printed in two-colour photogravure by Harrisons, was issued in October 1964 to mark the 25th anniversary of the first airmail service between Fiji and Tonga. They depicted the flying boat *Aotearoa* on the inaugural flight, and a modern Heron aircraft of Fiji Airways.

9. Fiji, 1 pound, 1968

A design competition, judged by Jennifer Toombs, resulted in the issue of a new series in July 1968. The prize-winning designs were adapted by Victor Whiteley and printed in multicolour photogravure by De La Rue. In January 1969 the series was re-issued with decimal currency values. It covered a wide variety of subjects, from moths and butterflies to sea-shells and flowers. The top value reproduced the Annigoni portrait and the Fiji coat of arms.

10. Fiji, 10 + 10 cents, 1970

A set of four stamps was issued in May 1970 to mark the closing of the Makogai Leprosy Hospital. Horizontal designs were used for the 2 and 30c. stamps, depicting the Chaulmugra tree at Makogai and the Hospital respectively, while two 10c. stamps, printed *se-tenant*, featured pictures by Semisi Maya. The stamps were designed by Gordon Drummond and printed in photogravure by Harrison and Sons.

11. British Solomon Islands Protectorate, ½ penny, 1907

The British Solomon Islands adopted adhesive stamps in February 1907. C. M. Woodford, the British Resident, designed a series featuring a native war canoe and arranged for the stamps to be lithographed by W. E. Smith & Co. of Sydney in denominations from ½d. to 1s. A similar design in a smaller format was used for a series recess-printed by De La Rue, issued between 1908 and 1911.

12. British Solomon Islands, 10 shillings, 1942

From 1913 the colonial keyplate designs were used until 1938, when a pictorial series of wildlife and native artifacts, recess-printed by De La Rue and Waterlow and Sons, was released. Originally the series ranged from ½d. to 5s., but a 10s. denomination was added in 1942. This stamp featured the coconut plantations, source of the protectorate's wealth.

13. British Solomon Islands, 8 cents, 1969

The fashion for special Christmas stamps spread to the Solomons in 1969. L. D. Curtis strove to imbue the stamps with the atmosphere of the South Seas, and get away from the Old Master image of other Christmas stamps. The 8c. showed a typical South Sea island with the Star of Bethlehem above, while the 35c. showed a stylized stained glass window depicting a frigate bird, emblem of the Solomon Islands. The stamps were printed in multicolour photogravure by Harrison and Sons.

14. British Solomon Islands, 18 cents, 1970

A new constitution, extending the system of internal self-government, was granted in June 1970 and to mark the occasion two stamps were released in June. They were designed by Victor Whiteley, with the coat of arms (18c.) and a map of the islands (35c.).

15. Gilbert and Ellice Islands, 2 pence, 1911

Stamps of Fiji were overprinted 'Gilbert & Ellice Protectorate' in 1911, pending the arrival of a distinctive series recess-printed by De La Rue. The stamps, in denominations of ½, 1, 2 and 2½d., featured a pandanus pine and were printed on the Multiple Crown CA paper. Between 1912 and 1924 they were reprinted on Script watermark paper and other values, up to £1, were introduced.

16. Gilbert and Ellice Islands, 5 shillings, 1939

The islands became a crown colony in 1918 and subsequently adopted the colonial keyplate designs typographed by De La Rue. A pictorial definitive series was introduced in 1939. Bradbury Wilkinson printed the ½, 2d. and 2s.6d., De La Rue the 1½, 2½, 3d. and 1s., while Waterlow and Sons recess-printed the remaining denominations up to 5s. Native houses, canoes, seascapes, fauna and flora were the subjects. Note the motto beneath the coat of arms on this stamp, inscribed in both Gilbertese and Ellice dialects. The same designs, with the profile of Queen Elizabeth, were retained for the series of 1956.

17. Gilbert and Ellice Islands, 3 shillings 7 pence, 1964

The inauguration of the first air service linking the islands to Fiji was heralded by three stamps in July 1964. They were designed by Mrs Margaret Barwick, wife of a local magistrate, and were lithographed by Enschedé. Two vertical designs featured a Fiji Airways Heron aircraft over the route map and Tarawa Lagoon respectively, while the horizontal 1s. stamp showed a heron (bird) in flight.

18. Gilbert and Ellice Islands, 8 cents, 1966

A new definitive series, designed by Mrs Barwick and lithographed by Bradbury Wilkinson, was released in August 1965 in denominations from ½d. to £1. The entire series was surcharged with Australian decimal values in February 1966 and then redrawn with new values in January 1968. The fifteen denominations in each case featured aspects of life, folklore, dances and native customs of the islands.

19. Pitcairn Islands, 1 shilling, 1940

Pitcairn Islands had a New Zealand postal agency from 1926 till 1940 and used ordinary New Zealand stamps identified by various distinctive postmarks. Previously that mail from the island had been accepted free in New Zealand, since no stamps were available at Pitcairn. Bradbury Wilkinson recess-printed the 1, 3, 4 and 8d., and 2s.6d. values, and Waterlow the remaining denominations. With the exception of the ½d. (oranges) and 3d. (location map) the original designs of this series all alluded to the settlement of the island by the mutineers of the *Bounty* in 1791. Lieutenant William Bligh was portrayed on the 2d., since he was indirectly the cause of the settlement of the island. The plural form 'Islands' in the inscription refers to the uninhabited islands of Ducie, Oeno and Henderson forming part of the colony. The *Bounty* Bible (4d.) and the school (8d.) were the subjects of stamps added to the series in September 1951.

20. Pitcairn Islands, 3 cents, 1969

Jennifer Toombs, who actually spent some months on Pitcairn in 1968, designed a definitive series for the island based on her sketches and subsequent research in the British Museum. The series was lithographed by De La Rue, with the designs bled off into the margins. Gold ink was used for the crown and the queen's profile combining to give a most unusual effect. This stamp depicts the anchor from the *Bounty*. The previous series was surcharged with Australian currency in 1967 and a device in the shape of this anchor was used to blot out the original denominations.

21. Pitcairn Islands, 2 shillings 6 pence, 1957

De La Rue recess-printed a series for Pitcairn in denominations from ½d. to 2s.6d. Various views of the island and aspects of the islander's occupations were depicted. In the original version of the 4d. stamp the picture was incorrectly captioned 'Pitcairn School'; it was reissued the following year with the emended caption 'Schoolteacher's House'. This set was followed by a multicolour photogravure series depicting ships and birds of the island, in 1964.

22. Pitcairn Islands, 5 cents, 1968

In recent years Pitcairn has issued a number of short thematic sets. No doubt with the tourists in mind a series of four stamps was issued in August 1968 publicizing handicrafts which the islanders produced for sale to the passengers of passing ships. The 5c. denomination depicted the flower and timber of the Miro wood which forms the raw material for the intricate wood carvings of the islanders. The stamps were designed by Jennifer Toombs and printed in photogravure by Harrison and Sons.

23. New Hebrides, 5 gold centimes, 1938

The definitive series issued by the New Hebrides Condominium in 1938 reflects the close Anglo-French co-operation which has produced the stamps for this territory. The series from 5c. to 10f. was designed by the French artist J. Kerhor and recess-printed by Bradbury Wilkinson of England. The vignette depicts Lopevi island and a copra canoe.

24. New Hebrides, 30 gold centimes, 1957

The Anglo-French condominium of the New Hebrides began issuing stamps in 1908 when contemporary issues of Fiji and New Caledonia were overprinted in English and French respectively for use in these islands. A distinctive series, inscribed in French and English, appeared in 1911. Ever since, the dual nature of the administration has been reflected in the duplication of every stamp issue, with versions in English as well as French, and the use of the appropriate national emblems of both countries. This series was designed by two French artists, Henri Cheffer and Pierre Gandon, but recess-printed by Waterlow and Sons.

25. New Hebrides, 3 gold francs, 1965

A definitive series was introduced gradually between November 1963 and January 1967. Most of the designs were produced as the result of competitions. Several denominations were printed in photogravure by Harrison and Sons, while the others were recess-printed by the French Government Printing Works. An interesting feature of these stamps is that in the English version the RF monogram appears on the left and the British royal cypher on the right. In the French version the position of these monograms is reversed. See plate 119.

PLATE 119
French Pacific Islands

1. Tahiti, 10 centimes, 1903

Between 1882 and 1893 various French colonial stamps were surcharged or overprinted specifically for use in Tahiti. Thereafter the stamps of French Oceania were employed but, on two occasions, stamps were again surcharged or overprinted specifically for Tahiti. A shortage of 10c. stamps in March–June 1903 was met by surcharging various denominations of the Oceania series with this value. In 1915 the 15c. stamp was overprinted 'Tahiti' and surcharged in aid of the Red Cross.

2. French Oceania, 5 centimes, 1913

The 'Tablet' keytypes were used in French Oceania from November 1892 till 1913, when a typographed pictorial series was introduced. J. de la Nezière designed the three vignettes, featuring a Vahine (native girl), Kanakas (Polynesian men) and a view of the valley of Fautaua. The stamps were engraved by H. Lemasson and typographed in two-colour combinations at the French Government Printing Works. Thereafter the usual provisional surcharges (1921–27), new colours and denominations (1922–30) followed the pattern of the other French colonies.

3. French Oceania, 5 centimes, 1942

A Polynesian travelling canoe was the subject chosen by Edmund Dulac for the Free French definitive series of 1942, printed in photogravure by Harrison and Sons. Previously the recess-printed series of 1934–39 was overprinted 'France Libre' after the islands had transferred their allegiance to General de Gaulle in 1941.

4. French Oceania, 10 centimes, 1948

Messrs Boullaire and Gandon produced the eleven designs for the pictorial definitive series issued between March 1948 and September 1955. Scenery in the islands of Moorea, Bora-Bora, Tahiti and Maupiti formed the subjects of this series. The stamps were engraved by a galaxy of postwar craftsmen and recess-printed at the Government Printing Works in denominations from 10c. to 20f.

5. French Polynesia, 10 centimes, 1958

The colony of French Oceania was renamed French Polynesia in 1958, when the French Community was established. Stamps bearing the new name were introduced gradually between November 1958 and December 1960. They were designed and engraved by the same team as before, but three-colour combinations were used for the recess-printing, reflecting the tendency toward more colourful stamp production in the late 1950s.

6. French Polynesia, 20 francs, 1964

Since 1962 increasing use of multicolour production has resulted in stamps being printed in photogravure. This has coincided with the policy of issuing short thematic sets to augment the definitive series. P. Lambert designed a set of six stamps issued in December 1964 with the theme of landscapes of the islands. They were printed in photogravure by So.Ge.Im. (Société Générale d'Imprimerie).

7. French Polynesia, 10 francs, 1966

Few specifically commemorative issues have been made in French Polynesia. A recurring subject, however, is the South Pacific Games, for which sets of stamps with sporting themes have been issued every three years since 1963. J. Combet designed and engraved the series of four stamps issued in December 1966 to mark the Second Games, held that year in Noumea, New Caledonia. Stamps have also been issued for this triennial event by the other countries of the South Pacific and it is now developing into a major theme.

8. New Caledonia, 1 centime, 1892

New Caledonia had the distinction of producing its own stamps as long ago as 1860. A 10c. stamp portraying the Emperor Napoleon III appeared in January 1860 and remained in use till September 1862, when it was superseded by the French colonial general series. The stamp was drawn by Sergeant Triquerat, using a pin on stone, and lithographed in grey-black. From 1881 to 1892 various stamps of the general series were overprinted NCE and surcharged with new values. The 'Tablet' series was introduced in November 1892.

9. New Caledonia, 2 centimes, 1928

Three designs were adopted for a pictorial series used between 1905 and 1928, the majority of the series being printed on toned paper of various colours. A new series, in two-colour typography, was introduced in April 1928. Messrs Hourriez and Delzers designed the three vignettes featuring Pointe des Palétuviers, a chief's hut and portraits of La Perouse and De Bougainville. The entire series was overprinted in 1933 in connection with the first anniversary of the Paris–Noumea Flight, and was released with a 'France Libre' overprint in 1941 following the adherence to De Gaulle.

10. New Caledonia, 40 centimes, 1942

A kagu humming bird was the subject of the series designed by Dulac and printed by Harrisons for New Caledonia under Free French control. Kagus were the principal motif in the definitive series of 1905–28 and the low values of the series of 1948.

11. New Caledonia, 37 francs, 1963

Since 1958 New Caledonia has been a member of the French Community and, as a colonial territory, has continued to issue stamps in the various omnibus designs. This stamp, issued in September 1963, marked the centenary of the Red Cross and was produced in a standard design employed in the other colonies – Comoro, Afars and Issas, French Polynesia, St Pierre and Miquelon, Southern and Antarctic Territories and Wallis, and Futuna Is.

12. New Caledonia, 10 francs, 1964

Sporting events provide the bulk of the commemorative issues produced by New Caledonia. The Tokyo Olympic Games were recorded by this stamp, designed and engraved by C. Haley and recess-printed in December 1964. The classical Greek motif seems incongruous in a Polynesian setting. The various issues for the South Pacific Games have been more relevant to the subject commemorated.

13. Wallis and Futuna Islands, 15 centimes, 1920

Until 1920 the stamps of New Caledonia were used in the Wallis and Futuna Islands but in that year an overprinted series was adopted, and this practice of overprinting continued until 1944.

14. Wallis and Futuna Islands, 2 centimes, 1922

A shortage of low value stamps was met in January 1922 by surcharging the 15c. denomination of the obsolete New Caledonia series of 1905 and adding the names of the islands as an overprint. The basic stamp, featuring a kagu, was designed by H. Vollet and engraved by J. Puyplat.

285

PLATE 119 FRENCH PACIFIC ISLANDS · PLATE 120 PACIFIC ISLANDS

15. Wallis and Futuna Islands, 25 centimes, 1944
No distinctive stamps appeared in the Wallis and Futuna Islands until 1944. Previously the only move toward individuality had been provided by the French colonial omnibus designs of 1931–39 with an appropriate inscription. In 1941 the colony adhered to the Free French and the New Caledonia series of 1930–40 was overprinted with the names of the islands and the legend 'France Libre'. A Gaullist series did not appear until 1944 – two years after the majority of other Free French territories. Dulac used a native ivory head as the chief motif of the series, lithographed by Bradbury Wilkinson.

16. Wallis and Futuna Islands, 1 franc, 1962
After World War II the islands reverted to overprinted stamps of New Caledonia and it was not until 1955 that a distinctive pictorial series was adopted. Stamps in various denominations from 3 to 33f. were issued between 1955 and 1965, featuring scenery and native occupations. This was augmented by a lengthy thematic series of marine fauna, issued in 1962–63 in denominations from 25 centimes to 100 francs.

17. New Hebrides, 15 gold centimes, 1965
The New Hebrides are administered jointly by Britain and France and ever since distinctive stamps were introduced in 1908 they have been inscribed concurrently in English and French. For the designs of earlier stamps see plate 118. A curious result of the condominium is the tendency for the New Hebrides to issue stamps in both British and French colonial omnibus designs (in cases where both countries produce distinctive designs) or in English and French versions (where only one colonial omnibus series is produced). Thus two stamps of May 1965 were released in the French design for the centenary of the International Telecommunications Union, while a pair, in English, conformed to the British colonial design for the same event.

18. New Hebrides, 60 gold centimes, 1967
The 25th anniversary of the South Pacific campaign in World War II was marked by two sets of four stamps, in English or French. Both sets were designed by Richard Granger Barrett and printed in multicolour photogravure by Enschedé and Sons. They featured coast-watchers (15c.), a map of the war zone (25c.), H.M.A.S. Canberra (60c.), and an American Flying Fortress (1f.).

19. New Hebrides, 1.10 gold francs, 1970
The 30th anniversary of the Free French movement was celebrated in July 1970 by sets of two stamps portraying General Charles de Gaulle. An interesting example of Anglo-French co-operation, the stamps were designed by the English artist, Victor Whiteley, and printed in multicolour photogravure at the French Government Printing Works in Paris. They were reissued the following January, overprinted with black borders and the date of De Gaulle's death (9-11-70).

20. New Hebrides, 65 gold centimes, 1971
This stamp, and a similar version in English, was released in September 1971 in honour of the Royal Society Expedition to the South Pacific. The stamps, featuring an Agathis tree and fruit, were designed by P. B. Powell and lithographed in multicolour by Harrison and Sons.

PLATE 120
Pacific Islands

1. Hawaii, 2 cents, 1862
The first stamps, known to collectors as the 'Hawaiian Missionaries' – the majority of recorded examples having been used on letters from missionaries to their friends and relatives in America – were typeset at Honolulu in denominations of 2, 5 and 13c. The 2c., used on local letters, is the scarcest of the series, though all of them are in the major rarity class. There are two varieties of setting in each type of these stamps. A subsequent version of the 13c. stamp was inscribed 'H.I. & U.S. Postage' to denote the 5c. local and 8c. American postage, on mail going from the islands to the United States. Stamps portraying Kamehameha III and Kamehameha IV were issued in 1853 and 1862 respectively.

2. Hawaii, 5 cents, 1866
The National Bank Note Company of New York recess-printed a series in 1864–66 portraying members of the Hawaiian Royal Family. Other portraits and denominations were introduced at various times up to 1890 and were printed by the American Bank Note Co., in some cases reusing the original National Bank Note plates. This stamp portrays King Kamehameha V.

3. Hawaii, 2 cents, 1893
The Hawaiian monarchy was overthrown in a bloodless coup in 1893 and a republican form of government was instituted, with American backing. The contemporary postage stamps were overprinted 'Provisional GOVT. 1893' at the offices of the Hawaiian Gazette in red or black. Apart from double or inverted overprints there were numerous varieties in the setting, or omission of various letters, numerals and full stops.

4. Hawaii, 5 cents, 1899
Under the republican regime Hawaii was torn by dissension between the various factions. In 1898 the government invited the United States to annex the country and this took place in August of that year. During the interim period the colours of the republican 1 and 2c. stamps were changed and the design of the 5c. stamp was redrawn to include the word 'Cents' at the foot. This stamp, depicting the statue of King Kamehameha I, who united the islands into one kingdom about 1800, appeared in the original version in 1894. The stamps were designed by E. W. Holdsworth of Honolulu and recess-printed by the American Bank Note Co. Hawaii was incorporated into the United States on 30 April 1900, and ordinary American stamps replaced the distinctive issues on 14 June 1900.

5. Guam, 2 cents, 1899
The island of Guam, formerly administered as part of the Spanish Philippine Islands, was occupied by American troops in 1899 during the Spanish–American War. United States stamps overprinted GUAM were introduced in 1899 and remained in use until 29 March 1901, when the island was annexed to the United States and ordinary American stamps were issued instead.

6. Caroline Islands, 3 pfennigs, 1901
The Caroline Islands were colonized by the Spaniards intermittently from the seventeenth century till 1899, when they were sold to Germany. Contemporary German stamps, overprinted KAROLINEN, were introduced in October 1899 to be superseded by the Hohenzollern yacht keytypes in 1901. In July 1905 there was a shortage of 5pf. stamps because a typhoon destroyed the post office

at Ponape. Accordingly 10pf. stamps were bisected and used at half their value. The official seal of the post office was used to cancel these bisects, known to collectors as the 'typhoon provisionals'. The islands were occupied by Japanese troops in 1914 and ordinary Japanese stamps were used there from 1914 till 1945. The islands are now administered by the United States under a United Nations mandate, and use ordinary American stamps.

7. Mariana Islands, 5 pfennigs, 1901
This group of islands, sometimes known as the Ladrones, was administered by Spain as part of the Philippine Islands. Following the American occupation in 1899 several Filipino stamps appeared with an overprint 'Marianas Españolas' (Spanish Marianas) but the authenticity of this overprint has been questioned. The United States ceded the group to Germany in November 1899 and the overprinted stamps, followed by Hohenzollern keytypes, were used there until 1914. Japanese stamps were used from then until 1944, when the islands were captured by American forces. The stamps of the United States have been used ever since.

8. Marshall Islands, 5 pfennigs, 1901
The Marshall Islands became a German colony in 1855 and a post office was established at Jaluit three years later. Between 1888 and 1897 ordinary German stamps were used and can only be distinguished by their postmark. Overprinted German stamps appeared in 1897 and were followed by the Hohenzollern keytypes in 1901. The islands were captured by New Zealand forces in 1914 and the stamps were overprinted G.R.I. and surcharged in sterling. Australian stamps overprinted N.W. Pacific Islands' were introduced in 1915 (see plate 115) but after the transfer of the territory to Japan at the end of World War I ordinary Japanese stamps were used. Since 1945 ordinary American stamps have been used.

9. Samoa, 2 pence, 1877
The first postal service in Samoa was established in Apia in 1877 under the authority of King Malietoa by W. E. Agar, manager of the Samoan Times. A series of stamps inscribed 'Samoa Express' was designed by H. H. Glover and lithographed by S. T. Leigh & Co. of Sydney. The service was a financial failure and closed in 1882. Four different states of the lithographic transfers are known, and, in addition, the stamps were extensively reprinted for sale to collectors.

10. Samoa, 2½ pence, 1897
A postal service was revived by John Davis in 1886 and a series of stamps, engraved by Bock & Cousins and typographed at the Government Printing Office in Wellington, was issued in February 1887. Three designs were used, featuring a palm tree, King Malietoa and the Samoan flag. The series was reissued with new perforations in 1893 and 1895.

11. Samoa, 2 shillings 6 pence, 1899
Various temporary surcharged appeared between 1893 and 1899 and in the latter year the entire series was overprinted PROVISIONAL GOVT. On the death of Malietoa in 1898 civil war broke out between rival factions and this forced the three powers, Britain, Germany and the United States, to intervene. The monarchy was abolished and the country partitioned between Germany and the United States.

12. Samoa, 5 pfennigs, 1901
After the partition of 1900 German colonial keytype stamps were introduced in the western part of the archipelago. Ordinary American stamps were issued in the eastern islands and have remained in use till this day. Western Samoa was occupied by

PLATE 120 PACIFIC ISLANDS

New Zealand troops in September 1914 and the German series overprinted G.R.I. and surcharged in sterling. For subsequent issues under New Zealand rule see plate 117.

13. Samoa, 8 pence, 1966
Western Samoa became an independent state, with joint heads of state, on 1 January 1962 and since then has issued stamps inscribed 'Samoa i Sisifo' (Samoan for Western Samoa). A pictorial definitive series, lithographed by Bradbury Wilkinson, was introduced in July 1962 in denominations from 1*d.* to 5*s.* It depicted modern buildings, traditional costume and the map, flag and seal of the country. The 8*d.* stamp was overprinted and surcharged in September 1966 in aid of hurricane relief funds.

14. Samoa, 8 pence, 1967
The last stamps inscribed in sterling currency were issued in May 1967 to celebrate the centenary of the Samoan parliament at Mulinu'u. Designed by Victor Whiteley and printed in multicolour photogravure by Harrison and Sons, they depicted native houses of 1890 and the modern *Fono* (parliament building).

15. Samoa, 20 sene, 1968
A decimal currency based on the tala (dollar) of 100 sene (cents) was adopted in 1967 and a definitive series featuring birds was issued in July 1967. The stamps were designed by Victor Whiteley and printed in photogravure by Harrisons. Higher denominations of 2 and 4*t.* were lithographed by Format International and issued in 1969. The 10*s.* stamp was surcharged for use as a 20*s.* stamp and overprinted in June 1968 to commemorate the fortieth anniversary of the first trans-Pacific flight by Sir Charles Kingsford Smith.

16. Samoa, 20 sene, 1968
A set of four stamps, printed in photogravure by Enschedé, was issued in February 1968 to publicize agricultural development. Designed by Jennifer Toombs, it depicted cocoa, breadfruit, copra and bananas. The repetitive motif at the top of each design was created, in the original artwork, by means of potato-cuts. This is the only example of this childish pastime having been adapted for stamp production!

17. Samoa, 22 sene, 1969
The Scottish novelist, Robert Louis Stevenson, spent the last years of his life in Samoa and his house is now the seat of the government. A set of four stamps, lithographed by De La Rue from designs by Jennifer Toombs, was issued in April 1969 to mark the 75th anniversary of his death. The open-book motif was used to depict scenes and characters from *Treasure Island, Kidnapped, Dr Jekyll and Mr Hyde* and *Weir of Hermiston*.

18. Samoa, 30 sene, 1970
Samoa cashed in on the celebrations marking the bicentenary of Captain Cook's Pacific voyages with a set of four stamps issued in September 1970. They were designed by James Berry, the veteran New Zealand artist, and were lithographed in multicolour by Questa. Vertical designs of orthodox format were used for the 1, 2 and 20*s.*, featuring Cook's chronometer and sextant, his statue at Whitby and a portrait of the explorer, but an unusually long format (83 mm. across) was adopted for the top value showing Cook's statue, his ship *Endeavour* and a view of Samoa.

19. Samoa, 20 sene, 1969
Samoa had more justification than many countries for issuing stamps commemorating the Apollo moon shots since the splash down area was near the Samoan islands. In July 1969, 7 and 20*s.* stamps

were issued to commemorate the first man on the moon. Designed by J. Mason and printed in photogravure by the Note Printing Branch of the Reserve Bank of Australia, they portrayed an American astronaut on the moon and the splash down near Samoa.

20. Samoa, 20 sene, 1970
Few events of historic significance have occurred in Samoa and it is therefore hardly surprising that the great hurricane of Apia which occurred in 1889 should be considered worthy of philatelic commemoration in 1970. British, American and German warships had converged on Samoa to protect the interests of their nationals during the ensuring chaos, which led to the downfall of the native monarchy. A hurricane struck Apia at the moment of confrontation resulting in the wreck of the German ship *Adler*, the American warship *Nipsic* and the British warship *Calliope*. The wrecks of these ships appeared on the three low values of this series and a view of the devastation in Apia after the hurricane was shown on the 20*s.* stamp. The stamps were designed by staff artists of John Waddington Ltd and lithographed by Questa.

21. Samoa, 8 sene, 1971
The 25th anniversary of the South Pacific Commission was marked by special issues of stamps by the various countries in that area. Samoa's contribution to the commemoration consisted of four stamps designed by Victor Whiteley and lithographed in multicolour by Questa, with maps and flags of the member countries and the headquarters buildings in Noumea.

22. Tonga, 2 shillings 6 pence,
The first stamps of Tonga, introduced in 1886, were typographed in Wellington and portrayed King George I. Stamps portraying King George II appeared in 1895–96 and were followed by a pictorial series recess-printed by De La Rue in denominations from ½*d.* to 5*s.* In the early printings a watermark of turtles was used, but between 1942 and 1949 the series was reprinted on paper bearing the usual colonial watermark. The colours of the low values up to 1*s.* were changed between 1920 and 1937. This series, with variations in colour and watermark, remained in use until 1954 – a world record for philatelic longevity. Note the Polynesian spelling of the country's name. The European spelling was used on the stamps from 1886 to 1897 and was reintroduced on stamps from 1950 onward.

23. Tonga, 2 pence, 1938
The twentieth anniversary of the accession of Queen Salote (Charlotte) was celebrated in October 1938 by three stamps, recess-printed by De La Rue. A common design was used, showing the queen in her ceremonial robes. The same design, with the inscription modified, was used for a series of five stamps issued in 1944 to mark her Silver Jubilee.

24. Tonga, 1 shilling, 1962
James Berry designed a series of fourteen denominations issued in 1953. The series was recess-printed by Bradbury Wilkinson, the vignette of the £1 (showing the coat of arms) was lithographed in multicolour. Eight denominations of this series were overprinted in 1962 'Tau'ataina Emancipation' to mark the centenary of the introduction of democratic government in Tonga. The 1*s.* is known with the overprint inverted. Various denominations of this series were also overprinted at the same time for use on official airmail correspondence.

25. Tonga, 1 penny, 1963
Tonga introduced a series of three gold coins in 1963 and issued a set of thirteen stamps to mark the occasion. The stamps were circular in shape

and embossed in gold foil reproducing the obverse and reverse designs of the coins. The stamps ranged in diameter from 1⅝ in. to 3¼ in., the latter feauring the 1 koula coin. The stamps were designed by Ida West and produced by the Walsall Lithographic Co. They were the first circular gold foil stamps ever issued and were promptly nicknamed by collectors the 'Tonga Beermats'. Tonga, like Sierra Leone (see plate 71) has issued many free-form embossed or die-stamped stamps in the past decade.

This table lists the currency systems used throughout the world by the various countries since the adoption of adhesive postage stamps. The first date in each section refers to the year in which stamps were introduced. For reasons of space it has not been deemed necessary to include every territory and postal administration, where it would be obvious from the text that such territories used the currency of the mother country. The French, Italian and Spanish colonies, for example, always used the currency of their mother countries. The rare exceptions to this are, of course, duly noted.

The spelling of currency, particularly of plural forms, is that used in the English language. Thus the plural of 'pfennig' is given as 'pfennigs', though in written German this would be rendered as 'pfennige'. In those cases where the singular and plural forms are different the differences are noted in parentheses.

Abu Dhabi
1964 100 naye paise = 1 rupee
1966 1,000 fils = 1 dinar
Aden
1937 16 annas = 1 rupee
1951 100 cents = 1 shilling
Aden Protectorate States
1937 16 annas = 1 rupee
1951 100 cents = 1 shilling
1966 1,000 fils = 1 dinar
Afghanistan
1870 2 shahi = 1 sanar; 2 sanar = 1 abasi; 3 abasi = 1 rupee
1909 60 paisa = 1 rupee
1920 100 pouls (or puls) = 1 afghani (= 66 paisas)
Ajman
1964 100 naye paise = 1 rupee
1967 100 dirhams = 1 riyal
Albania
1913 40 paras = 1 piastre (or grosch)
1913 100 qint or qindar = 1 franc
1917 100 centimes = 1 franc
1919 100 qint = 1 franc
1947 5 lek = 1 franc
1965 100 qint = 1 lek
Algeria
1924 100 centimes = 1 franc
1964 100 centimes = 1 dinar
Andorra
1928 (Spanish P.O.) 100 centimos = 1 peseta
1931 (French P.O.) 100 centimes = 1 franc
Angola
1870 1,000 reis = 1 milreis
1913 100 centavos = 1 escudo
1932 100 centavos = 1 angolar
1954 100 centavos = 1 escudo
Anguilla
1967 100 cents = 1 West Indian dollar
Antigua
1862 12 pence = 1 shilling; 20 shillings = 1 pound
1951 100 cents = 1 West Indian dollar
Argentine Republic
1858 100 centavos = 1 peso
1969 100 old pesos = 1 new peso
Ascension
1922 12 pence = 1 shilling; 20 shillings = 1 pound
1971 100 pence = 1 pound
Australia and Australian States
1850 12 pence = 1 shilling; 20 shillings = 1 Australian pound
1966 100 cents = 1 Australian dollar

Austria
1850 60 kreuzer = 1 gulden
1858 100 kreuzer = 1 gulden
1900 100 heller = 1 krone
1925 100 groschen = 1 schilling
1938 100 pfennigs = 1 German reichsmark
1945 100 groschen = 1 schilling
Baden
1851 60 kreuzer = 1 gulden
Bahamas
1859 12 pence = 1 shilling; 20 shillings = 1 pound
1966 100 cents = 1 West Indian dollar
Bahrain
1933 12 pies = 1 anna; 16 annas = 1 rupee
1966 1,000 fils = 1 dinar
Barbados
1852 4 farthings = 1 penny; 12 pence = 1 shilling; 20 shillings = 1 pound
1950 100 cents = 1 West Indian dollar
Basutoland (*see also* Lesotho)
1933 12 pence = 1 shilling; 20 shillings = 1 pound
1961 100 cents = 1 rand
Bavaria
1849 60 kreuzer = 1 gulden
1874 100 pfennigs = 1 mark
Bechuanaland (*see also* Botswana)
1885 12 pence = 1 shilling; 20 shillings = 1 pound
1961 100 cents = 1 rand
Belgium
1849 100 centimes = 1 franc
Bergedorf
1861 16 schillings = 1 Hamburg mark
Bermuda
1865 4 farthings = 1 penny; 12 pence = 1 shilling; 20 shillings = 1 pound
1970 100 cents = 1 United States dollar
Bhutan
1962 100 chentrum = 1 ngultrum (*or* rupee)
Biafra
1968 12 pence = 1 shilling; 20 shillings = 1 pound
Bohemia & Moravia
1939 100 haleru = 1 koruna (*plural:* korun *or* koruny)
Bolivia
1866 100 centavos = 1 boliviano
1963 100 cents = 1,000 (old) bolivianos = 1 (new) boliviano (*or* peso boliviano *or* 1 escudo)
Bosnia & Herzegovina
1879 100 kreuzer (*or* novics) = 1 gulden
1900 100 heller = 1 krone
Botswana (*see also* Bechuanaland)
1966 100 cents = 1 rand
Brazil
1843 1,000 reis = 1 milreis
1942 100 centavos = 1 cruzeiro = 1,000 reis
1967 100 centavos = 1,000 (old) cruzeiros = 1 (new) cruzeiro
Bremen
1855 22 grote = 10 silbergroschen
72 grote = 1 thaler
British Antarctic Territory
1965 12 pence = 1 shilling; 20 shillings = 1 pound
1971 100 pence = 1 pound
British East Africa
1890 16 annas = 1 rupee
British Guiana (*see also* Guyana)
1850 100 cents = 1 dollar
British Honduras
1866 12 pence = 1 shilling
1888 100 cents = 1 dollar
British Indian Ocean Territory
1968 100 cents = 1 rupee
British Solomon Islands
1907 12 pence = 1 shilling; 20 shillings = 1 pound
1966 100 cents = 1 Australian dollar
Brunei
1906 100 cents = 1 Straits dollar
Brunswick
1852 30 silbergroschen = 1 thaler
Buenos Aires
1858 8 reales = 1 peso
Bulgaria
1879 100 centimes = 1 franc
1881 100 stotinki = 1 lev (*plural:* leva)
1947 100 (old) leva = 1 (new) lev
Burma
1937 12 pies = 1 anna; 16 annas = 1 rupee
1953 100 pyas = 1 kyat (rupee)
Burundi
1962 100 centimes = 1 franc
Cambodia (*see also* Khmer)
1951 100 cents = 1 piastre
1955 100 cents = 1 riel
Cameroun
1897 100 pfennigs = 1 mark

1915 (British Occupation) 12 pence = 1 shilling; 20 shillings = 1 pound
1915 (French Occupation) 100 centimes = 1 franc
Canada
1851 12 pence = 1 shilling
1859 100 cents = 1 dollar
Canal Zone
1904 100 cents — 1 balboa or dollar
Cape of Good Hope
1853 12 pence = 1 shilling; 20 shillings = 1 pound
Cape Verde Islands
1877 1,000 reis = 1 milreis
1913 100 centavos = 1 escudo
Cayman Islands
1901 12 pence = 1 shilling; 20 shillings = 1 pound
1969 100 cents = 1 Jamaican dollar
Central African Republic
1959 100 centimes = 1 franc
Central Lithuania
1920 100 fenigow = 1 marka (*plural:* marek *or* marki)
Ceylon (*see also* Sri Lanka)
1857 12 pence = 1 shilling; 20 shillings = 1 pound
1872 100 cents = 1 rupee
Chile
1853 100 centavos = 1 peso
1960 10 milesimas = 1 centesimo; 100 centesimos = 1 escudo
China
1878 100 candarins = 1 tael
1897 100 cents = 1 yuan (*or* Chinese dollar)
1948 100 cents = 1 gold yuan
1949 100 cents = 1 silver yuan
1955 100 fen = 1 yuan
China (People's Republic)
1949 100 cents = 1 silver yuan
1955 100 fen = 1 yuan
China (Formosa)
1949 100 cents = 1 silver yuan (*or* 1 new Taiwan yuan)
Christmas Island
1958 100 cents = 1 Malayan dollar
1968 100 cents = 1 Australian dollar
Cochin
1892 6 puttans = 5 annas
Later currency as India
Cocos (Keeling) Islands
1963 12 pence = 1 shilling; 20 shillings = 1 Australian pound
1969 100 cents = 1 Australian dollar
Colombia
1859 100 centavos = 1 peso
Congo (*see also* Zaire)
1960 100 centimes = 1 Belgian franc
1967 100 sengi = 1 (li)kuta; 100 (ma)kuta = 1 zaire
Cook Islands
1892 12 pence = 1 shilling; 20 shillings = 1 pound
1967 100 cents = 1 New Zealand dollar
Costa Rica
1863 8 reales = 1 peso
1881 100 centavos = 1 peso
1900 100 centimos = 1 colon
Crete
1900 100 lepta = 1 drachma
Croatia
1941 100 paras = 1 dinar
100 banicas = 1 kuna
Cuba
1855 8 reales plata fuerte = 1 peso
1866 100 centimos = 1 peseta
1881 1,000 milesimas = 100 centavos = 1 peso
1899 100 centavos = 1 peso
Cyprus
1880 12 pence = 1 shilling; 20 shillings = 1 pound
1881 40 paras = 1 piastre; 180 piastres = 1 pound
1955 1,000 mils = 1 pound
Czechoslovakia
1918 100 haleru = 1 koruna (*plural:* korun *or* koruny)
Danish West Indies
1855 100 cents = 1 dollar
1905 100 bits = 1 franc
Danzig
1920 100 pfennigs = 1 mark
1923 100 pfennigs = 1 gulden
Denmark
1851 96 rigsbankskilling (R.B.S.) = 1 rigsdaler
1854 92 skilling = 1 rigsdaler
1875 100 øre = 1 krone (*plural:* kroner)
Dominica
1874 12 pence = 1 shilling; 20 shillings = 1 pound
1949 100 cents = 1 West Indian dollar
Dominican Republic
1865 8 reales = 1 peso
1880 100 centavos = 1 peso
1883 100 centimos = 1 francos = 1 peso
1885 100 centavos = 1 peso

Dubai
1963 100 naye paise = 1 rupee
1966 100 paisa = 1 rupee
1966 100 dirhams = 1 riyal
East Africa
1964 100 cents = 1 shilling
Ecuador
1865 8 reales = 1 peso
1881 100 centavos = 1 sucre
Egypt
1866 40 paras = 1 piastre
1889 10 milliemes = 1 piastre;
    100 piastres = 1 Egyptian pound
Equatorial Guinea
1968 100 centimos = 1 peseta
Eritrea
1893 100 centesimi = 1 lira
1948 100 cents = 1 shilling
Estonia
1918 100 kopeks = 1 rouble
1919 100 penni = 1 mark
1928 100 senti = 1 kroon
Ethiopia
1894 & 1907 16 guerche = 1 piastre or mehalek =
    1 Maria Theresa Taler (dollar)
1905 100 centimes = 1 franc
1928 16 mehaleks = 1 thaler
1936 100 centimes = 1 thaler
1936 100 centesimi = 1 lira
1945 100 cents = 1 Ethiopian dollar (talari)
Falkland Islands
1878 12 pence = 1 shilling; 20 shillings = 1 pound
1971 100 pence = 1 pound
Faridkot
1879 1 folus = 1 paisa = ¼ anna
1887 12 pies = 1 anna; 16 annas = 1 rupee
Federated Malay States
1900 100 cents = 1 Straits dollar
Fiji
1870 12 pence = 1 shilling; 20 shillings = 1 pound
1969 100 cents = 1 dollar
Finland
1856 100 kopeks = 1 rouble
1866 100 penni = 1 Finnish markka
1963 100 (old) markka or penni =
    1 (new) markka
Fiume
1918 100 filler = 1 krone
1919 100 centesimi = 1 corona (or lira)
Fiume and Kupa
1941 100 paras = 1 dinar
France
1849 100 centimes = 1 franc
1960 100 old francs =
    1 new franc = 100 centimes
French Colonies
1859 100 centimes = 1 franc
French Levant
1885 40 paras = 1 piastre
1902 100 centimes = 1 franc
French Morocco
1891 100 centimos = 1 peseta
1917 100 centimes = 1 franc
French Post Offices in China
1894 100 centimes = 1 franc
1907 100 cents = 1 piastre
French Post Offices in Zanzibar
1894 16 annas = 1 rupee
Fujeira
1964 100 naye paise = 1 rupee
1967 100 dirhams = 1 riyal
Gabon
1886 100 centimes = 1 franc
Gambia
1869 12 pence = 1 shilling; 20 shillings = 1 pound
1971 100 butts = 1 dalasi
German Post Offices in China
1898 100 pfennigs = 1 mark
1905 100 cents = 1 Chinese dollar
German Post Offices in Morocco
1889 100 centimos = 1 peseta
German Post Offices in Turkey
1884 40 paras = 1 piaster
1908 100 centimes = 1 franc
Germany
1872 Northern areas and Alsace & Lorraine:
    30 groschen = 1 thaler
    Southern areas: 60 kreuzer = 1 gulden
1875 100 pfennigs = 1 mark
1923 100 renten-pfennigs = 1 rentenmark (gold currency)
1928 100 pfennigs = 1 reichsmark
1948 (West Germany) 100 pfennigs =
    1 Deutsche Mark (DM)
1948 (East Germany) 100 pfennigs =
    1 Mark der Deutschen Notenbank (MDN)

Ghana (*see also* Gold Coast)
1957 12 pence = 1 shilling; 20 shillings = 1 pound
1965 100 pesewas = 1 cedi
1967 100 new pesewas = 1 new cedi
Gibraltar
1886 12 pence = 1 shilling
1889 100 centimos = 1 peseta
1898 12 pence = 1 shilling; 20 shillings = 1 pound
1971 100 pence = 1 pound
Gilbert & Ellice Islands
1911 12 pence = 1 shilling;
    20 shillings = 1 Australian pound
1966 100 cents = 1 Australian dollar
Gold Coast (*see also* Ghana)
1875 12 pence = 1 shilling; 20 shillings = 1 pound
Great Britain
1840 12 pence = 1 shilling; 20 shillings = 1 pound
1971 100 pence = 1 pound
Greece
1861 100 lepta = 1 drachma
Greenland
1938 100 øre = 1 krone (*plural*: kroner)
Grenada
1861 12 pence = 1 shilling; 20 shillings = 1 pound
1949 100 cents = 1 West Indian dollar
Guatemala
1871 100 centavos = 8 reales = 1 peso
1927 100 centavos de quetzal = 1 quetzal (gold)
Guinea
1959 100 centimes = 1 franc
Guyana (*see also* British Guiana)
1966 100 cents = 1 dollar
Haiti
1881 100 centimes de gourde = 1 gourde
Hamburg
1859 16 schillings = 1 mark
Hanover
1850 12 pfennigs = 1 gutegroschen;
    24 gutegroschen = 1 thaler
1858 10 (new) pfennigs = 1 (new) groschen;
    30 (new) groschen = 1 thaler
Hatay
1938 100 centièmes = 1 piastre
1939 100 santims = 40 paras = 1 kurus
Hawaii
1851 100 cents = 1 dollar
Heligoland
1867 16 schillings = 1 mark
1875 100 pfennigs = 1 mark
Hoi-Hao
1902 100 centimes = 1 franc
1919 100 cents = 1 piastre
Honduras
1866 100 centavos = 8 reales = 1 peso or lempira
Hong Kong
1862 100 cents = 1 Hong Kong dollar
Hungary
1871 100 krajczar = 1 forint
1900 100 filler (*or* heller) =
    1 korona (*or* krone)
1926 100 filler = 1 pengo
1946 100 filler = 1 forint
Iceland
1873 96 skillings = 1 rigsdaler
1876 100 aurar = 1 króna (*plural*: kronur)
India
1852 12 pies (*singular*: pice) = 1 anna;
    16 annas = 1 rupee
1957 100 naye paise = 1 rupee
1964 100 paisa = 1 rupee
Indo-China
1889 100 centimes = 1 franc
1919 100 cents = 1 piastre
Indonesia
1945 100 cents (*or* sen) = 1 gulden (*or* rupiah)
Ingermanland
1920 100 penni = 1 markka
Iraq
1918 16 annas = 1 rupee
1932 1,000 fils = 1 dinar
Ireland
1922 12 pence (pingin) = 1 shilling (sgillin);
    5 shillings = 1 crown (coroin);
    20 shillings = 1 pound
1971 100 pence = 1 pound
Israel
1948 1,000 pruta (*singular*: prutot) = 1 Israeli pound
1960 100 agora (*singular*: agorot) = 1 Israeli pound
Italy
1862 100 centesimi = 1 lira (*plural*: lire)
Ivory Coast
1892 100 centimes = 1 franc
Jamaica
1860 12 pence = 1 shilling; 20 shillings = 1 pound
1969 100 cents = 1 dollar

Japan
1871 10 mon = 1 rin
1872 10 rin = 1 sen; 100 sen = 1 yen
Jhalawar
1887 4 paisa = 1 anna
Jordan
1920 10 millièmes = 1 piastre
1927 1,000 millièmes = 1 Palestinian pound
1950 1,000 fils = 1 Jordan dinar
Katanga
1960 100 centimes = 1 franc
Kenya
1963 100 cents = 1 shilling
Kenya, Uganda & Tanganyika
1903–19 16 annas = 100 cents = 1 rupee
1922 100 cents = 1 shilling
Khmer (*see also* Cambodia)
1971 100 cents = 1 riel
Kiautschou
1900 100 pfennigs = 1 mark
1905 100 cents = 1 Chinese dollar
Korea
1884 10 mon = 1 poon
1899 1,000 re = 100 cheun = 1 won
Korea, North
1959 1 old won = 100 chon; 100 chon = 1 new won
Korea, South
1946 100 cheun = 1 won
1953 100 old won = 1 hwan
1962 10 old hwan = 1 won
Kouang Tcheou
1906 100 centimes = 1 franc
1919 100 cents = 1 piastre
Kuwait
1923 16 annas = 1 rupee
1961 1,000 fils = 1 dinar
Labuan
1879 100 cents = 1 Malayan dollar
Lagos
1874 12 pence = 1 shilling;
    20 shillings = 1 pound
Laos
1951 100 cents = 1 piastre
1955 100 cents = 1 kip
Latakia
1931 100 centimes = 1 piastre
Latvia
1918 100 kapeikas = 1 rublis
1923 100 santimi (centimes) = 1 lat
Lebanon
1924 100 centièmes = 1 piastre
Leeward Islands
1890 12 pence = 1 shilling;
    20 shillings = 1 pound
1951 100 cents = 1 West Indian dollar
Lesotho (*see also* Basutoland)
1966 100 cents = 1 rand
Liberia
1860 100 cents = 1 dollar
Libya
1912 100 centesimi = 1 lira
1952 1,000 mills = 1 Libyan pound
Liechtenstein
1912 100 heller = 1 Austrian krone
1921 100 rappen = 1 Swiss franc
Lithuania
1918 100 skatiku = 1 auksinas
1922 100 centu = 1 litas
Lombardy & Venetia
1850 100 centesimi = 1 lira
1858 100 soldi = 1 florin
    100 kreuzer = 1 gulden
Lübeck
1859 16 schillings = 1 mark
Luxembourg
1852 12½ centimes = 1 silver groschen
1859 100 centimes = 1 franc
1940 100 pfennigs = 1 reichsmark
1944 100 centimes = 1 Belgian franc
Macao
1884 1,000 reis = 1 milreis
1894 78 avos = 1 rupee
1913 100 avos = 1 pataca
Malagasy Republic
1958 100 centimes = 1 franc
Malawi (*see also* Nyasaland)
1964 12 pence = 1 shilling; 20 shillings = 1 pound
1970 100 tambalas = 1 kwacha
Malaysia (Malaya & Malay States)
1876 100 cents (*or* sen) = 1 Malayan dollar
Maldive Islands
1906 100 cents = 1 rupee
1951 100 larees = 1 rupee
Mali
1959 100 centimes = 1 franc

289

Malta
1860 12 pence = 1 shilling; 20 shillings = 1 pound
1972 100 pence = 1 pound
Mauritania
1906 100 centimes = 1 franc
Mauritius
1847 12 pence = 1 shilling; 20 shillings = 1 pound
1878 100 cents = 1 rupee
Mecklenburg-Schwerin
1856 48 schillings = 1 thaler
Mecklenburg-Strelitz
1864 30 silbergroschen = 1 thaler
Mexico
1856 8 reales = 100 centavos = 1 peso
Modena
1852 100 centesimi = 1 lira
Monaco
1865 100 centimes = 1 French franc
Mongolia
1924 100 cents = 1 Chinese dollar
1926 100 mung = 1 tugrik
Mong-Tseu
1903 100 centimes = 1 franc
1919 100 cents = 1 piastre
Montenegro
1874 100 novics = 1 florin
1902 100 heller = 1 krone
1907 100 paras = 1 krone
1910 100 paras = 1 perper
Montserrat
1876 12 pence = 1 shilling;
        20 shillings = 1 pound
1951 100 cents = 1 West Indian dollar
Morocco
1956 10 centimos = 1 peseta
1956 100 centimes = 1 franc
1959 100 Moroccan francs = 1 dirham
Mozambique
1876 1,000 reis = 1 milreis
1912 100 centavos = 1 escudo
Muscat
1944 12 pies = 1 anna; 16 annas = 1 rupee
1957 100 naye paise = 1 rupee
Muscat & Oman
1966 64 baizas = 1 rupee
1970 1,000 baizas = 1 rial saidi
Naples
1858 100 grana = 200 tornesi = 1 ducato
Natal
1857 12 pence = 1 shilling; 20 shillings = 1 pound
Nauru
1916 12 pence = 1 shilling; 20 shillings = 1 pound
1966 100 cents = 1 Australian dollar
Neapolitan Provinces
1861 100 grana = 200 tornesi = 1 ducato
Nepal
1881 4 pice = 1 anna; 64 pice = 1 rupee
1954 100 pice = 1 rupee
Netherlands
1852 100 cents = 1 gulden (or florin)
Nevis
1861 12 pence = 1 shilling; 20 shillings = 1 pound
New Brunswick
1851 12 pence = 1 shilling; 20 shillings = 1 pound
1860 100 cents = 1 dollar
Newfoundland
1857 12 pence = 1 shilling; 20 shillings = 1 pound
1866 100 cents = 1 Canadian dollar
New Guinea
1898 100 pfennigs = 1 mark
1914 12 pence = 1 shilling;
        20 shillings = 1 Australian pound
New Hebrides
1908 12 pence = 1 shilling; 20 shillings = 1 pound
1908 100 centimes = 1 franc
1938 100 gold centimes = 1 gold franc
New Zealand
1855 12 pence = 1 shilling; 20 shillings = 1 pound
1967 100 cents = 1 dollar
Nicaragua
1862 100 centavos = 1 peso
1913 100 centavos = 1 cordoba
Niger
1921 100 centimes = 1 franc
Niger Coast Protectorate
1892 12 pence = 1 shilling; 20 shillings = 1 pound
Nigeria
1914 12 pence = 1 shilling; 20 shillings = 1 pound
Niue
1902 12 pence = 1 shilling;
        20 shillings = 1 New Zealand pound
1967 100 cents = 1 New Zealand dollar
Norfolk Island
1947 12 pence = 1 shilling;
        20 shilling = 1 Australian pound

1966 100 cents = 1 Australian dollar
North Borneo
1883 100 cents = 1 Malayan dollar
North German Confederation
1868 30 groschen = 1 thaler; 60 kreuzer = 1 gulden
Northern Rhodesia (see also Zambia)
1924 12 pence = 1 shilling
Norway
1855 120 skilling = 1 speciedaler
1877 100 øre = 1 krone (plural: kroner)
Nyasaland (see also Malawi)
1891 12 pence = 1 shilling; 20 shillings = 1 pound
Oldenburg
1852 72 grote = 1 thaler
Oman
1971 1,000 baizas = 1 rial saidi
Pakistan
1947 12 pies = 1 anna; 16 annas = 1 rupee
1961 100 paisa = 1 rupee
Palestine
1918 10 millièmes = 1 piastre
1927 1,000 millièmes = 1 Palestinian pound
Panama
1878 100 centavos = 1 peso
1906 100 centesimos de balboa = 1 balboa
Papua
1901 12 pence = 1 shilling;
        20 shillings = 1 Australian pound
Papua & New Guinea
1952 12 pence = 1 shilling;
        20 shillings = 1 Australian pound
1966 100 cents = 1 Australian dollar
Paraguay
1870 8 reales = 100 centavos = 1 peso
1944 100 centimos = 1 guarani =
        100 old Paraguayan pesos
Persia
1868 20 shahis = 1 kran; 10 krans = 1 toman
1881 100 centimes = 1 franc
1885 20 shahis = 1 kran; 10 kran = 1 toman
1933 100 dinars = 1 rial
Peru
1858 10 dineros = 5 pesetas = 1 peso
1866 100 centavos = 1 peso = 1 sol
Philippine Islands
1854 8 cuartos = 1 real; 8 reales = 1 peso plata fuerte
1864 100 centimos = 1 peso plata fuerte
1871 100 centimos = 1 escudo (= ½ peso)
1872 100 centimos = 1 peseta (= ¼ peso)
1876 1,000 milesimas = 100 centavos or centimos =
        1 peso
1889 100 cents = 1 dollar
1906 100 centavos (or sen) = 1 peso
Pitcairn Islands
1940 12 pence = 1 shilling;
        20 shillings = 1 New Zealand pound
1967 100 cents = 1 New Zealand dollar
Poland
1860 100 kopeks = 1 rouble
1918 100 pfennigs = 1 mark; 100 halerze = 1 koruna
        (German: krone; plural: 2 korun, 3 or more
        korony); 100 fenigi = 1 mark
1924 100 groszy = 1 zloty
Polish Post Offices in Turkey
1919 100 fenigi = 1 mark
Port Said
1899 100 centimes = 1 franc
1921 1,000 millièmes = 1 Egyptian pound
Portugal
1853 1,000 reis = 1 milreis
1912 100 centavos = 1 escudo
Portuguese India
1871 1,000 reis = 1 milreis
1882 12 reis (singular: reis) = 1 tanga (anna);
        16 tangas = 1 rupia
1959 100 centavos = 1 escudo
Prussia
1850 12 pfennigs = 1 silbergroschen;
        30 silbergroschen = 1 thaler
1867 60 kreuzer = 1 gulden
Puerto Rico
1873 100 centimos = 1 peseta
1881 1,000 milesimas = 100 centavos = 1 peso
1898 100 cents = 1 dollar
Qatar
1957 100 naye paise = 1 rupee
1966 100 dirhams = 1 riyal
Ras Al Khaima
1964 100 naye paise = 1 rupee
1966 100 dirhams = 1 riyal
Rhodesia
1890 12 pence = 1 shilling; 20 shillings = 1 pound
1968 100 cents = 1 rand
Romagna
1859 100 bajocchi = 1 scudo

Roman States
1852 100 bajocchi = 1 scudo
1866 100 centesimi = 1 lira (plural: lire)
Rumania
1858 40 parales = 1 piastre
1868 100 bani = 1 leu (plural: lei)
Russia
1858 100 kopeks = 1 rouble
Russian Post Offices in China
1899 100 kopeks = 1 rouble
1917 100 cents = 1 Chinese dollar
Russian Post Offices in Turkey
1863 100 kopeks = 1 rouble
1900 40 paras = 1 piastre
Rwanda
1962 100 cents = 1 franc
Ryukyu Islands
1948 100 sen = 1 yen
1958 100 cents = 1 United States dollar
Saar
1920 100 pfennigs = 1 mark
1921 100 centimes = 1 franc
1947 100 pfennigs = 1 mark
1947 100 centimes = 1 franc
St Helena
1856 12 pence = 1 shilling; 20 shillings = 1 pound
1971 100 pence = 1 pound
St Kitts-Nevis
1903 12 pence = 1 shilling; 20 shillings = 1 pound
1951 100 cents = 1 West Indian dollar
St Lucia
1860 12 pence = 1 shilling; 20 shillings = 1 pound
1949 100 cents = 1 West Indian dollar
St Vincent
1861 12 pence = 1 shilling; 20 shillings = 1 pound
1949 100 cents = 1 West Indian dollar
Salvador
1867 8 reales = 100 centavos = 1 peso
1911 100 centavos = 1 colon
Samoa
1877 12 pence = 1 shilling; 20 shillings = 1 pound
1900 100 pfennigs = 1 mark
1914 12 pence = 1 shilling; 20 shillings = 1 pound
1967 100 sene (or cents) = 1 tala (or dollar)
San Marino
1877 100 centesimi = 1 lira
Sardinia
1851 100 centesimi = 1 lira
Saudi Arabia
1934 110 guerches = 1 sovereign (gold)
1934 (Later) 880 guerches = 1 sovereign (gold)
1960 800 piastres = 1 sovereign (gold)
Saxony
1850 10 pfennigs = 1 neugroschen;
        30 neugroschen = 1 thaler
Schleswig-Holstein
1850 16 schillings = 1 mark
Serbia
1866 100 paras = 1 dinar
Seychelles
1890 100 cents = 1 rupee
Shanghai
1865 11 cash = 1 candareen;
        100 candareens = 1 tael
1866 100 cents = 1 Chinese dollar
Sharjah & Dependencies
1963 100 naye paise = 1 rupee
1966 20 piastres = 1 rial
1966 100 dirhams = 1 riyal
Sicily
1859 100 grana = 1 ducato
Sierra Leone
1859 12 pence = 1 shilling; 20 shillings = 1 pound
1964 100 cents = 1 leone
Slovakia
1939 100 halierou = 1 koruna
Somalia
1903 4 besa = 1 anna; 16 annas = 1 rupee
1905 100 centesimi = 1 lira
1922 100 besa = 1 rupia
1925 100 centesimi = 1 lira
1943 (British Occupation) 12 pence = 1 shilling;
        20 shillings = 1 pound
1948 (British Occupation) 100 cents = 1 shilling
1950 100 centesimi = 1 somalo
1961 100 cents = 1 Somali shilling
Somaliland Protectorate
1903 16 annas = 1 rupee
1951 100 cents = 1 shilling
South Africa
1910 12 pence = 1 shilling; 20 shillings = 1 pound
1961 100 cents = 1 rand
South Arabian Federation
1963 100 cents = 1 shilling
1965 1,000 fils = 1 dinar

South Bulgaria
1885 40 paras = 1 piastre
South West Africa
1897 100 pfennigs = 1 mark
1923 12 pence = 1 shilling; 20 shillings = 1 pound
1961 100 cents = 1 rand
Southern Rhodesia
1924 12 pence = 1 shilling; 20 shillings = 1 pound
Southern Yemen
1968 1,000 fils = 1 dinar
Spain
1850 8⅓ (later 8) cuartos = 1 real
1866 80 cuartos = 100 centimos de escudo = 1 escudo
1867 1,000 milesimas = 100 centimos de escudo =
        80 cuartos = 1 escudo
1872 100 centimos = 1 peseta
Sri Lanka (*see also* Ceylon)
1972 100 cents = 1 rupee
Straits Settlements
1867 100 cents = 1 Straits dollar
Sudan
1897 10 milliemes = 1 piastre; 100 piastres =
        1 Sudanese pound
Swaziland
1889 12 pence = 1 shilling; 20 shillings = 1 pound
1961 100 cents = 1 rand
Sweden
1855 40 skilling banco = 1 riksdaler
1858 100 øre = 1 riksdaler
1875 100 øre = 1 krona (*plural:* kronor)
Switzerland
1850 100 rappen = 1 franken;
        100 centimes = 1 franc
Syria
1919 40 paras = 10 milliemes = 1 piastre
1920 100 centimes (*or* centièmes) = 1 piastre
1921 5 piastres = 1 French franc
Tanganyika (*formerly* German East Africa)
1893 64 pesa = 100 heller = 1 rupee
1905 100 heller = 1 rupee
1915 16 annas = 1 rupee
1917 100 cents = 1 rupee
1922 100 cents = 1 East African shilling
Tanzania
1965 100 cents = 1 shilling
Tchonking
1903 100 centimes = 1 franc
1919 100 cents = 1 piastre
Thailand
1883 32 solots = 16 atts = 8 sio = 4 siks = 1 salung
1885 64 atts = 1 tical
1909 100 satangs = 1 tical = (1912) 1 baht
Thessaly
1898 40 paras = 1 piastre
Thrace
1919 100 stotinki = 1 lev
1920 100 lepta = 1 drachma
Thurn & Taxis
1852 Northern District: 30 silbergroschen = 1 thaler
        Southern District: 60 kreuzer = 1 gulden
Tibet
1912 6⅔ trangka = 1 sang
Tierra del Fuego
1891 100 centavos = 1 Chilean peso
Timor
1886 1,000 reis = 1 milreis
1895 100 avos (cents) = 1 pataca (dollar)
1960 100 centavos = 1 escudo
Togo
1897 100 pfennigs = 1 mark
1914 (British Occupation) 12 pence = 1 shilling;
        20 shillings = 1 pound
1916 (French Occupation) 100 centimes = 1 franc
Tokelau Islands
1948 12 pence = 1 shilling;
        20 shillings = 1 New Zealand pound
1967 100 cents = 1 New Zealand dollar
Tonga
1886 12 pence = 1 shilling; 20 shillings = 1 pound
1967 100 seniti = 1 pa'anga
Travancore
1888 16 cash = 1 chuckram; 28 chuckrams = 1 rupee
Trinidad & Tobago
1913 12 pence = 1 shilling; 20 shillings = 1 pound
1935 100 cents = 1 West Indian dollar
Tristan da Cunha
1952 12 pence = 1 shilling; 20 shillings = 1 pound
1961 100 cents = 1 rand
1963 12 pence = 1 shilling; 20 shillings = 1 pound
1971 100 pence = 1 pound
Trucial States
1961 100 naye paise = 1 rupee
Tunisia
1888 100 centimes = 1 franc
1959 1,000 millièmes = 1 dinar

Turkey
1863 40 paras = 1 piastre
1942 100 paras = 1 kurus
1947 100 kurus = 1 lira
Turks & Caicos Islands
1900 12 pence = 1 shilling; 20 shillings = 1 pound
1969 100 cents = 1 Jamaican dollar
Tuscany
1851 60 quattrini = 20 soldi = 12 crazie = 1 Tuscan lira
1859 1 Tuscan lira = 1 Italian lira
Tuva
1926 100 kopeks = 1 rouble
1934 100 kopeks = 1 tugrik
1936 100 kopeks = 1 aksa
Uganda
1895 200 cowries = 1 rupee
1896 16 annas = 1 rupee
1962 100 cents = 1 shilling
Ukraine
1918 100 kopeks = 1 rouble;
        100 shagiv = 1 grivni (= ½ rouble)
Umm Al Qiwain
1964 100 naye paise = 1 rupee
1967 100 dirhams = 1 riyal

United Nations
1951 (New York) 100 cents = 1 dollar
        (Geneva) 100 centimes = 1 Swiss franc
United States of America
1847 100 cents = 1 dollar
United States Post Offices in Shanghai
1919 100 cents = 1 Chinese dollar
Uruguay
1856 100 centavos = 1 real
1858 1,000 milesimas = 100 centesimos = 1 peso
Venezuela
1859 100 centavos = 8 reales = 1 peso
1879 100 centimos = 1 venezolano = (1880) 1 bolivar
Vietnam
1945 100 cents = 1 piastre; 100 xu = 1 dong
1946 100 hao = 1 dong
Vietnam, North
1948 100 xu = 1 dong
1959 100 xu = 1 new dong
Vietnam, South
1951 100 cents = 1 piastre (*or* dong)
Virgin Islands
1866 12 pence = 1 shilling; 20 shillings = 1 pound
1951 100 cents = 1 West Indian dollar
1962 100 cents = 1 United States dollar
Wadhwan
1888 4 pice = 1 anna
Württemberg
1851 60 kreuzer = 1 gulden
1875 100 pfennigs = 1 mark
Yemen
1926 40 bogaches = 1 imadi = 1 ahmadi (1951) =
        1 rial (1964)
Yemen People's Democratic Republic
1971 1,000 fils = 1 dinar
Yugoslavia
1918 100 filler (*or* heller) = 1 krone
1920 100 paras = 1 dinar
Zaire (*see also* Congo)
1971 100 sengi = 1 (li)kuta; 100 (ma)kuta = 1 zaire
Zambia (*see also* Rhodesia)
1964 12 pence = 1 shilling; 20 shillings = 1 pound
1968 100 ngwee = 1 kwacha
Zanzibar
1895 16 annas = 1 rupee
1908 100 cents = 1 rupee
1936 100 cents = 1 shilling

A number of the larger countries have state printing works or bureaus that print their stamps and, in many cases, the stamps of other countries as well. The *Staatsdruckerei* in Vienna, the Israeli Government Printer and the Japanese Government Printing Bureau in Tokyo are among those organizations that have printed stamps for many different countries in recent years. State printing works are in operation in many other countries including Australia, Czechoslovakia, France, Ireland, Italy, Germany, India, Portugal, Russia, South Africa, Spain, Sweden, Switzerland and the United States. Many of these enterprises form part of the government security printing complex and include banknotes and bonds among their products. Others operate as a branch of the government survey department (Egypt) or the internal revenue department (Somerset House in England) or as a branch of the state bank (Australia and Finland).

The production of stamps is also in the hands of many private or semi-official companies and a list of the more important ones is given below. For space reasons it is impossible to list all the companies that ever printed stamps, but the full names of the lesser firms are given in the text where relevant, whereas the more important firms are generally referred to only in a shortened form.

American Bank Note Co., New York
Aspioto-Elka Graphic Arts Co., Athens
    (formerly Aspiotis Brothers, Corfu)
A. Bagel, München-Gladbach, Germany
Jacob Bagge Bank Note Co., Stockholm
Bradbury, Wilkinson & Co., New Malden, England
British American Bank Note Co., Ottawa and Montreal
Canadian Bank Note Co., Ottawa
    (till 1923 a branch of the American Bank Note Co.)
Courvoisier S.A., La Chaux-des-Fonds, Switzerland
De La Rue & Co., London and Bogotá, Colombia
Delrieu, Paris
Johaan Enschedé en Zonen, Harrlem, Netherlands
Format International, London
Heraclio Fournier S.A., Vitoria, Spain
Giesecke-Devrient, Leipzig, Germany
Guzel Sanatlar Matbaasi, Ankara, Turkey
Harrison and Sons, London
Institut de Gravure, Paris
Klisecilik ve Matbaacilik, Istanbul, Turkey
Chr. H. Knudsen, Christiania, Oslo
G. Kolff & Co., Batavia, Indonesia
Kultura, Budapest
Lewin-Epstein, Bat Yam, Israel
Litografia Nacional, Oporto, Portugal
Mardon, Salisbury, Rhodesia
Emil Moestue & Co., Oslo
Pakistan Security Printing Corporation, Karachi
Perkins Bacon & Petch (later Perkins, Bacon & Co.),
    London
Postal Authority Press, Cairo
Questa Colour Printers, London
Rawdon, Wright, Hatch & Edson, New York
    (later American Bank Note Co.)
So. Ge. Im (Société Générale d'Imprimerie), Paris
South American Bank Note Co., Buenos Aires
H. H. Thiele, Copenhagen
Toppan Printing Co., Tokyo
Vaugirard, Paris
John Waddington, Kirkstall, England
Walsall Security Printers, Walsall, England
Waterlow Brothers & Layton, London
Waterlow & Sons, London
E. A. Wright Bank Note Co., Philadelphia

CYRILLIC INSCRIPTIONS

The Cyrillic alphabet may be found on the stamps of Russia, Bulgaria, Yugoslavia, Serbia, Montenegro, Rumania, Mongolia and Tuva.

АВИОПОЧТА	Airmail (Russia)
АСОБНЫ АТРАД	White Russia
БАКУ	Baku
БАТУМ	Batum
БНМАУ ШУУДАН	Mongolia
БЪЛГАРИЯ	Bulgaria
БЪЛГАРСКА ПОЩА	Bulgarian Post
ВЕНДЕНСКАЯ	Wenden
ВОСТОЧНАЯ КОРРЕСПОНДЕНЦИЯ	Eastern Correspondence (Russian Levant)
ГОЛОДАЮЩИМ	Famine Relief (Russia)
ДЕМОКРАТСКА ФЕДЕРАТИВНА ЈУГОСЛАВИЈА	Democratic Federative Yugoslavia
ДОПЛАТНА БИЛЕТА	Postage due (Montenegro)
ДОПЛАЩАНИЕ	Postage due (Bulgaria)
ДРЖАВА СХС	Slovenia
ЕРМАКЪ	Ermak (Don Cossack Government)
ЗВАНИЧНА ПОШТА	Official stamp (Serbia)
ЈУГОСЛАВИЈА	Yugoslavia
КАРПАТСЬКА УКРАÏНА	Carpatho Ukraine (Czechoslovakia)
КРАЛЬЕВИНА	Kingdom (Yugoslavia)
К. СРБСКА ПОШТА	Royal Serb Post
КОП	Kopek (Russian currency)
КИТАИ	China (overprint on Russian stamps used in China)
ЛЕВЬ	Lev (Bulgarian currency)
МАРКА	Stamp (Russia)
МОСКВА	Moscow (Russia)
МОНГОЛ ШУУДАН	Mongolia
НАРОДНЯ РЕСПУБЛІКА	People's Republic (Ukraine)
НОВУ	Novi (Montenegrin currency)
Н.Р. БЪЛГАРИЯ	People's Republic of Bulgaria
ОСВОБ ВОЙНА	War of Liberation (Bulgaria 1913, 1921)
ОБЩИНСКА	Official stamp (Bulgaria)
ПАРА, ПАРЕ	Para (Serb currency)
ПОЧТОВАЯ	Postal (Russia)
ПОЧТОВАЯ МАРКА	Postage stamp (Russia)
ПОЧТА	Posts (Russia)
ПОШТА	Posts (Serbia)
ПОШТE	Posts (Montenegro)
ПОЩА	Posts (Bulgaria)
ПОРТО СКРИСОРИ	Letter Post (Moldavia)
ПОРТО МАРКА	Postage Due (Serbia)
РОССІЯ	Russia
РУБ, РУБЛЬ	Rouble (Russian currency)
Р.С.Ф.С.Р.	Russian Socialist Federated Soviet Republic
САНТИМ	Santim (Bulgarian currency=centime)
С.С.С.Р.	S.S.S.R. = U.S.S.R.
СРБИЈА	Serbia
СРБА ХРВАТА И СЛОВЕНАЦА	Serbs, Croats and Slovenes (Yugoslavia)
СТОТ, СТОТИНКИ	Stotinki (Bulgarian currency)
ТЬВА	Tuva
УКР, УКРАÏНСКА	Ukraine, Ukrainian
ФОНДЬ САНАТОРИУМЬ	Sanatorium Fund (Bulgaria)
ХЕЛЕР	Heller (Montenegrin currency)
ЦРНА ГОРЕ	Montenegro

INDEX

Italic figures refer to the Plates

The figures on this map refer to the
plates that illustrate the postage
stamps of the area so numbered